LPIC

Linux Profess~~ional~~ Certification

Study Guide

Fourth Edition

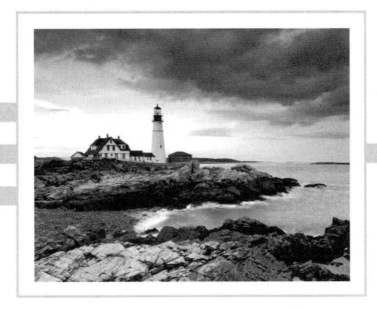

LPIC-1®:
Linux Professional Institute Certification Study Guide
Exams 101-400 and 102-400
Fourth Edition

Christine Bresnahan

Richard Blum

Senior Acquisitions Editor: Kenyon Brown
Development Editor: Gary Schwartz
Technical Editor: Kevin Ryan
Production Editor: Rebecca Anderson
Copy Editor: Judy Flynn
Editorial Manager: Mary Beth Wakefield
Production Manager: Kathleen Wisor
Associate Publisher: Jim Minatel
Media Supervising Producer: Richard Graves
Book Designers: Judy Fung and Bill Gibson
Proofreader: Word One, New York
Indexer: Johnna VanHoose
Project Coordinator, Cover: Brent Savage
Cover Designer: Wiley
Cover Image: © Getty Images Inc./Jeremy Woodhouse
Copyright © 2015 by John Wiley & Sons, Inc., Indianapolis, Indiana
Published simultaneously in Canada

ISBN: 978-1-119-02118-6
ISBN: 978-1-119-02120-9 (ebk.)
ISBN: 978-1-119-02119-3 (ebk.)

Library of Congress Control Number: 2015933955

Acknowledgments

First, all glory and praise go to God, who through His Son, Jesus Christ, makes all things possible, and gives us the gift of eternal life.

Many thanks go to the fantastic team of people at Sybex for their outstanding work on this project. Thanks to Kenyon Brown, the acquisitions editor, for offering us the opportunity to work on this book. Also thanks to Gary Schwartz, the development editor, for keeping things on track and making this book more presentable. Thanks, Gary, for all your hard work and diligence. The technical editor, Kevin E. Ryan, did a wonderful job of double-checking all of the work in the book in addition to making suggestions to improve the content. We would also like to thank Carole Jelen at Waterside Productions, Inc., for arranging this opportunity for us and for helping us out in our writing careers.

Christine would particularly like to thank her husband, Timothy, for his encouragement, patience, and willingness to listen, even when he has no idea what she is talking about.

About the Authors

Richard Blum, CompTIA Linux+, LPIC-1, has worked in the IT industry for more than 25 years as both a system and network administrator, and he has published numerous Linux and open-source books. Rich is an online instructor for Linux and Web programming courses that are used by colleges and universities across the United States. When he is not being a computer nerd, Rich enjoys spending time with his wife, Barbara, and two daughters, Katie Jane and Jessica.

    Christine Bresnahan, CompTIA Linux+, LPIC-1, started working with computers more than 25 years ago in the IT industry as a systems administrator. Christine is an Adjunct Professor at Ivy Tech Community College where she teaches Linux certification and Python programming classes. She also writes books and produces instructional resources for the classroom.

Contents at a Glance

Introduction   *xix*

Assessment Test   *xxxvii*

Answers to the Assessment Test   *xliv*

Part I   **Exam 101-400**   **1**

Chapter 1   Exploring Linux Command-Line Tools   3

Chapter 2   Managing Software   47

Chapter 3   Configuring Hardware   107

Chapter 4   Managing Files   177

Chapter 5   Booting Linux and Editing Files   233

Part II   **Exam 102-400**   **277**

Chapter 6   Configuring the X Window System, Localization,
                    and Printing   279

Chapter 7   Administering the System   343

Chapter 8   Configuring Basic Networking   407

Chapter 9   Writing Scripts, Configuring Email, and Using Databases   453

Chapter 10   Securing Your System   523

Appendix   **Answers**   **575**

Index   *613*

Contents

Introduction   *xix*

Assessment Test   *xxxvii*

Answers to the Assessment Test   *xliv*

Part I   **Exam 101-400**   **1**

Chapter   1   **Exploring Linux Command-Line Tools**   **3**

                     Understanding Command-Line Basics   4
                          Exploring Your Linux Shell Options   4
                          Using a Shell   5
                          Exploring Shell Configuration   13
                          Using Environment Variables   13
                          Getting Help   14
                     Using Streams, Redirection, and Pipes   16
                          Exploring File Descriptors   17
                          Redirecting Input and Output   17
                          Piping Data between Programs   19
                          Generating Command Lines   20
                     Processing Text Using Filters   22
                          File-Combining Commands   22
                          File-Transforming Commands   24
                          File-Formatting Commands   28
                          File-Viewing Commands   31
                          File-Summarizing Commands   33
                     Using Regular Expressions   35
                          Understanding Regular Expressions   35
                          Using *grep*   36
                          Using *sed*   38
                     Summary   41
                     Exam Essentials   41
                     Review Questions   42

Chapter   2   **Managing Software**   **47**

                     Package Concepts   48
                     Using RPM   50
                          RPM Distributions and Conventions   50
                          The *rpm* Command Set   52
                          Extracting Data from RPMs   56
                          Using Yum   57
                          RPM and Yum Configuration Files   61

RPM Compared to Other Package Formats 62
Using Debian Packages 63
Debian Distributions and Conventions 63
The *dpkg* Command Set 64
Using *apt-cache* 67
Using *apt-get* 68
Using *dselect*, *aptitude*, and Synaptic 72
Reconfiguring Packages 73
Debian Packages Compared to Other Package Formats 73
Configuring Debian Package Tools 74
Converting between Package Formats 75
Package Dependencies and Conflicts 77
Real and Imagined Package Dependency Problems 77
Workarounds for Package Dependency Problems 78
Startup Script Problems 80
Managing Shared Libraries 81
Library Principles 81
Locating Library Files 83
Library Management Commands 85
Managing Processes 87
Understanding the Kernel: The First Process 88
Examining Process Lists 88
Understanding Foreground and
Background Processes 95
Managing Process Priorities 96
Killing Processes 97
Summary 99
Exam Essentials 99
Review Questions 101

Chapter   3   **Configuring Hardware**   **107**

Configuring the Firmware and
Core Hardware 108
Understanding the Role of the Firmware 108
IRQs 112
I/O Addresses 115
DMA Addresses 116
Boot Disks and Geometry Settings 117
Coldplug and Hotplug Devices 119
Configuring Expansion Cards 120
Configuring PCI Cards 121
Learning about Kernel Modules 122
Loading Kernel Modules 124

Removing Kernel Modules   125
Configuring USB Devices   126
USB Basics   126
Linux USB Drivers   127
USB Manager Applications   128
Configuring Hard Disks   129
Configuring PATA Disks   129
Configuring SATA Disks   130
Configuring SCSI Disks   130
Configuring External Disks   132
Designing a Hard Disk Layout   132
Why Partition?   133
Understanding Partitioning Systems   133
An Alternative to Partitions: LVM   136
Mount Points   136
Common Partitions and Filesystem Layouts   137
Creating Partitions and Filesystems   139
Partitioning a Disk   140
Preparing a Partition for Use   145
Maintaining Filesystem Health   151
Tuning Filesystems   151
Maintaining a Journal   156
Checking Filesystems   157
Monitoring Disk Use   158
Mounting and Unmounting Filesystems   161
Temporarily Mounting or Unmounting Filesystems   162
Permanently Mounting Filesystems   167
Summary   169
Exam Essentials   170
Review Questions   172

Chapter   4   Managing Files   177

Using File Management Commands   178
Naming Files   178
Exploring Wildcard Expansion Rules   180
Understanding the File Commands   180
Archiving File Commands   187
Managing Links   195
Understanding the Directory Commands   198
Managing File Ownership   199
Assessing File Ownership   199
Changing a File's Owner   200
Changing a File's Group   200

Controlling Access to Files   200
    Understanding Permissions   201
    Changing a File's Mode   206
    Setting the Default Mode and Group   210
    Changing File Attributes   212
Managing Disk Quotas   213
    Enabling Quota Support   214
    Setting Quotas for Users   215
Locating Files   216
    Getting to Know the FHS   216
    Employing Tools to Locate Files   222
Summary   226
Exam Essentials   226
Review Questions   228

Chapter   5   Booting Linux and Editing Files   233

Installing Boot Loaders   234
    Boot Loader Principles   235
    Using GRUB Legacy as the Boot Loader   238
    Using GRUB 2 as the Boot Loader   243
    Using Alternative Boot Loaders   245
Understanding the Boot Process   247
    Extracting Information about the Boot Process   247
    Locating and Interpreting Boot Messages   248
    The Boot Process   248
The Initialization Process   249
Using the SysV Initialization Process   250
    Runlevel Functions   250
    Identifying the Services in a Runlevel   252
    Managing Runlevel Services   253
    Checking Your Runlevel   255
    Changing Runlevels on a Running System   255
Using the systemd Initialization Process   258
    Units and Targets   259
    Configuring Units   260
    Setting the Default Target   261
    The *systemctl* Program   262
Using the Upstart Initialization Process   263
    Using Upstart-Native Methods   264
    Using SysV Compatibility Methods   264
Editing Files with vi   265
    Understanding Vi Modes   265
    Exploring Basic Text-Editing Procedures   266
    Saving Changes   269

Summary	270
Exam Essentials	270
Review Questions	272

Part II   **Exam 102-400**   **277**

Chapter   6   **Configuring the X Window System, Localization, and Printing**   **279**

Configuring Basic X Features	280
X Server Options for Linux	280
Methods of Configuring X	282
X Configuration Options	285
Obtaining X Display Information	293
Configuring X Fonts	295
Font Technologies and Formats	296
Configuring X Core Fonts	296
Configuring a Font Server	299
Configuring Xft Fonts	300
Managing GUI Logins	301
The X GUI Login System	301
Running an XDMCP Server	302
Configuring an XDMCP Server	304
Using X for Remote Access	306
X Client-Server Principles	306
Using Remote X Clients	307
X Accessibility	310
Keyboard and Mouse Accessibility Issues	310
Screen Display Settings	312
Using Additional Assistive Technologies	314
Configuring Localization and Internationalization	315
Setting Your Time Zone	315
Querying and Setting Your Locale	318
Configuring Printing	321
Conceptualizing the Linux Printing Architecture	321
Understanding PostScript and Ghostscript	322
Running a Printing System	324
Configuring CUPS	324
Monitoring and Controlling the Print Queue	330
Summary	335
Exam Essentials	335
Review Questions	337

Chapter	**7**	**Administering the System**	**343**

Managing Users and Groups 344
Understanding Users and Groups 344
Configuring User Accounts 348
Configuring Groups 359
Viewing Individual Account Records 362
Tuning User and System Environments 364
Using Log and Journal Files 365
Understanding *syslogd* 366
Setting Logging Options 366
Manually Logging Data 369
Rotating Log Files 370
Reviewing Log File Contents 373
Exploring the *systemd* Journal System 374
Maintaining the System Time 379
Understanding Linux Time Concepts 379
Manually Setting the Time 380
Using Network Time Protocol 381
Running Jobs in the Future 389
Understanding the Role of *cron* 389
Creating System *cron* Jobs 390
Creating User *cron* Jobs 391
Using *anacron* 394
Using *at* 396
Summary 399
Exam Essentials 399
Review Questions 401

| **Chapter** | **8** | **Configuring Basic Networking** | **407** |

Understanding TCP/IP Networking 408
Knowing the Basic Functions of Network Hardware 408
Investigating Types of Network Hardware 409
Understanding Network Packets 411
Understanding Network Protocol Stacks 411
Knowing TCP/IP Protocol Types 413
Understanding Network Addressing 414
Using Network Addresses 414
Resolving Hostnames 421
Network Ports 424
Configuring Linux for a Local Network 427
Network Hardware Configuration 428
Configuring with DHCP 428

Configuring with a Static IP Address   429
Configuring Routing   432
Using GUI Configuration Tools   434
Using the *ifup* and *ifdown* Commands   434
Configuring Hostnames   435
Diagnosing Network Connections   438
Testing Basic Connectivity   438
Tracing a Route   439
Checking Network Status   441
Examining Raw Network Traffic   441
Using Additional Tools   443
Summary   445
Exam Essentials   445
Review Questions   447

**Chapter   9   Writing Scripts, Configuring Email, and
Using Databases   453**

Managing the Shell Environment   454
Reviewing Environment Variables   454
Understanding Common Environment Variables   455
Using Aliases   459
Modifying Shell Configuration Files   460
Writing Scripts   462
Beginning a Shell Script   463
Using Commands in Shell Scripts   463
Running a Shell Script   465
Using Variables in Shell Scripts   470
Using Conditional Expressions   478
Using Loops   485
Using Lists   493
Using Functions   495
Managing Email   497
Understanding Email   498
Choosing Email Software   498
Working with Email   500
Managing Data with SQL   504
Picking a SQL Package   505
Understanding SQL Basics   505
Using MySQL   506
Summary   515
Exam Essentials   515
Review Questions   517

Chapter	**10**	**Securing Your System**	**523**
		Administering Network Security	524
		Using Super Server Restrictions	525
		Disabling Unused Servers	530
		Administering Local Security	540
		Securing Passwords	540
		Limiting *root* Access	544
		Auditing User Access	547
		Setting Login, Process, and Memory Limits	551
		Locating SUID/SGID Files	553
		Configuring SSH	555
		Understanding SSH Basics	555
		Setting SSH Options	556
		Preventing SSH Security Problems	563
		Using GPG	563
		Generating Keys	564
		Importing Keys	565
		Revoking a Key	566
		Encrypting and Decrypting Data	566
		Signing Messages and Verifying Signatures	567
		Summary	567
		Exam Essentials	568
		Review Questions	570
Appendix		**Answers**	**575**
		Chapter 1: Exploring Linux Command-Line Tools	576
		Chapter 2: Managing Software	579
		Chapter 3: Configuring Hardware	583
		Chapter 4: Managing Files	586
		Chapter 5: Booting Linux and Editing Files	590
		Chapter 6: Configuring the X Window System, Localization, and Printing	593
		Chapter 7: Administering the System	597
		Chapter 8: Configuring Basic Networking	601
		Chapter 9: Writing Scripts, Configuring Email, and Using Databases	605
		Chapter 10: Securing Your System	609
		Index	*613*

Introduction

Why should you learn about Linux? It's a fast-growing operating system, and it is inexpensive and flexible. Linux is also a major player in the small and mid-size server field, and it's an increasingly viable platform for workstation and desktop use as well. By understanding Linux, you'll increase your standing in the job market. Even if you already know Windows or Mac OS and your employer uses these systems exclusively, understanding Linux will give you an edge when you're looking for a new job or you're looking for a promotion. For instance, this knowledge will help you make an informed decision about if and when you should deploy Linux.

The Linux Professional Institute (LPI) has developed its LPIC-1 certification as an introductory certification for people who want to enter careers involving Linux. The exam is meant to certify that an individual has the skills necessary to install, operate, and troubleshoot a Linux system and is familiar with Linux-specific concepts and basic hardware.

The purpose of this book is to help you pass the LPIC-1 exams (101-400 and 102-400), updated in 2015. Because these exams cover basic Linux installation, configuration, maintenance, applications, networking, and security, those are the topics that are emphasized in this book. You'll learn enough to get a Linux system up and running and to configure it for many common tasks. Even after you've taken and passed the LPIC-1 exams, this book should remain a useful reference.

What Is Linux?

Linux is a clone of the Unix operating system (OS) that has been popular in academia and many business environments for years. Formerly used exclusively on large mainframes, Unix and Linux can now run on small computers, which are actually far more powerful than the mainframes of just a few years ago. Because of its mainframe heritage, Unix (and hence also Linux) scales well to perform today's demanding scientific, engineering, and network server tasks.

Linux consists of a kernel, which is the core control software, and many libraries and utilities that rely on the kernel to provide features with which users interact. The OS is available in many different distributions, which are collections of a specific kernel with specific support programs.

Why Become Linux Certified?

Several good reasons to get your Linux certification exist. There are four major benefits:

Relevance   The exams were designed with the needs of Linux professionals in mind. Surveys of Linux administrators were performed to learn what they actually needed to know to do their jobs.

Quality   The exams have been extensively tested and validated using psychometric standards. The result is an ability to discriminate between competent administrators and those who must still learn more material.

Neutrality   LPI is an organization that doesn't itself market any Linux distribution. This fact removes the motivation to create an exam that's designed as a way to market a particular distribution.

Support   Major players in the Linux world support the exams.

How to Become Certified

The certification is available to anyone who passes the two required exams: 101-400 and 102-400 (often referred to as simply 101 and 102). You don't have to work for a particular company. It's not a secret society.

Pearson VUE administers the exam. The exam can be taken at any Pearson VUE testing center. If you pass, you will get a certificate in the mail saying that you have passed.

To register for the exam with Pearson VUE, call (877) 619-2096 or register online at www.vue.com. However you do it, you'll be asked for your name, mailing address, phone number, employer, when and where you want to take the test (that is, which testing center), and your credit card number (arrangement for payment must be made at the time of registration).

Who Should Buy This Book

Anybody who wants to pass the certification exams may benefit from this book. This book covers the material that someone new to Linux will need to learn the OS from the beginning, and it continues to provide the knowledge you need up to a proficiency level sufficient to pass the two exams. You can pick up this book and learn from it even if you've never used Linux before, although you'll find it an easier read if you've at least casually used Linux for a few days. If you're already familiar with Linux, this book can serve as a review and as a refresher course for information with which you might not be completely familiar. In either case, reading this book will help you pass the exams.

This book is written with the assumption that you know at least a little bit about Linux (what it is and possibly a few Linux commands). We also assume that you know some basics about computers in general, such as how to use a keyboard, how to insert a disc into an optical drive, and so on. Chances are that you have used computers in a substantial way in the past—perhaps even Linux, as an ordinary user, or maybe you have used Windows or Mac OS. We do not assume that you have extensive knowledge of Linux system administration, but if you've done some system administration, you can still use this book to fill in gaps in your knowledge.

As a practical matter, you'll need a Linux system with which to practice and learn in a hands-on way. Neither the exams nor this book covers actually installing Linux on a computer from scratch, although some of the prerequisites (such as disk partitioning) are covered. You may need to refer to your distribution's documentation to learn how to accomplish this task. Alternatively, several vendors sell computers with Linux preinstalled.

How This Book Is Organized

This book consists of 10 chapters plus supplementary information: an online glossary, this introduction, and the assessment test after the introduction. The chapters are organized as follows:

- Chapter 1, "Exploring Linux Command-Line Tools," covers the basic tools that you need to interact with Linux. These include shells, redirection, pipes, text filters, and regular expressions.

- Chapter 2, "Managing Software," describes the programs that you'll use to manage software. Much of this task is centered around the RPM and Debian package management systems. The chapter also covers handling shared libraries and managing processes (that is, running programs).

- Chapter 3, "Configuring Hardware," focuses on Linux's interactions with the hardware on which it runs. Specific hardware and procedures for using it include the BIOS, expansion cards, USB devices, hard disks, and the partitions and filesystems used on hard disks.

- Chapter 4, "Managing Files," covers the tools used to manage files. This includes commands to manage files, ownership, and permissions as well as Linux's standard directory tree and tools for archiving files.

- Chapter 5, "Booting Linux and Editing Files," explains how Linux boots up and how you can edit files in Linux. Specific topics include the GRUB Legacy and GRUB 2 boot loaders, boot diagnostics, runlevels, and the vi editor.

- Chapter 6, "Configuring the X Window System, Localization, and Printing," describes the Linux GUI and printing subsystems. Topics include X configuration, managing GUI logins, configuring location-specific features, enabling accessibility features, and setting up Linux to use a printer.

- Chapter 7, "Administering the System," describes miscellaneous administrative tasks. These include user and group management, tuning user environments, managing log files, setting the clock, and running jobs in the future.

- Chapter 8, "Configuring Basic Networking," focuses on basic network configuration. Topics include TCP/IP basics, setting up Linux on a TCP/IP network, and network diagnostics.

- Chapter 9, "Writing Scripts, Configuring Email, and Using Databases," covers these miscellaneous topics. Scripts are small programs that administrators often use to help automate common tasks. Email, of course, is an important topic for any computer user, particularly on Linux, which often runs an email server for local or remote use. Linux can run databases that help you store and retrieve information, and these tools can be very important ones on many Linux systems.

- Chapter 10, "Securing Your System," covers security. Specific subjects include network security, local security, and the use of encryption to improve security.

Chapters 1 through 5 cover the 101-400 exam, while Chapters 6 through 10 cover the 102-400 exam. These make up Part I and Part II of the book, respectively.

What's Included in the Book

We've included several study learning tools throughout the book:

Assessment Test   At the end of this introduction is an assessment test that you can use to check your readiness for the exam. Take this test before you start reading the book; it will help you determine the areas you might need to brush up on. The answers to the assessment test questions appear on a separate page after the last question of the test. Each answer includes an explanation and a note telling you the chapter in which the material appears.

Objective Map and Opening List of Objectives   An objective map shows you where each of the exam objectives is covered in this book. In addition, each chapter opens with a list of the exam objectives it covers. Use these to see exactly where each of the exam topics is covered.

Exam Essentials   Each chapter, just after the summary, includes a number of exam essentials. These are the key topics you should take from the chapter in terms of areas to focus on when preparing for the exam.

Chapter Review Questions   To test your knowledge as you progress through the book, there are review questions at the end of each chapter. As you finish each chapter, answer the review questions and then check your answers—the correct answers and explanations are in Appendix A. You can go back to reread the section that deals with each question you got wrong to ensure that you answer correctly the next time you're tested on the material.

> The review questions, assessment test, and other testing elements included in this book are *not* derived from the actual exam questions, so don't memorize the answers to these questions and assume that doing so will enable you to pass the exam. You should learn the underlying topic, as described in the text of the book. This will help you answer the questions provided with this book *and* pass the exam. Learning the underlying topic is also the approach that will serve you best in the workplace—the ultimate goal of a certification.

To get the most out of this book, you should read each chapter from start to finish and then check your memory and understanding with the end-of-chapter elements. Even if you're already familiar with a topic, you should skim the chapter; Linux is complex enough that there are often multiple ways to accomplish a task, so you may learn something even if you're already competent in an area.

Interactive Online Learning Environment and Test Bank

The interactive online learning environment that accompanies the book provides a test bank with study tools to help you prepare for the certification exam—and increase your chances of passing it the first time! The test bank includes the following:

Sample Tests   All of the questions in this book are provided, including the Assessment Test, which you'll find at the end of this introduction, and the Chapter Tests that include the Review Questions at the end of each chapter. In addition, there are two Practice Exams. Use these questions to test your knowledge of the study guide material. The online test bank runs on multiple devices.

Flashcards   Questions are provided in digital flashcard format (a question followed by a single correct answer). You can use the flashcards to reinforce your learning and provide last-minute test prep before the exam.

Other Study Tools   A glossary of key terms from this book and their definitions are available as a fully searchable PDF.

> Go to http://sybextestbanks.wiley.com to register and gain access to this interactive online learning environment and test bank with study tools.

Conventions Used in This Book

This book uses certain typographic styles in order to help you quickly identify important information and to avoid confusion over the meaning of words such as onscreen prompts. In particular, look for the following styles:

- *Italicized text* indicates key terms that are described at length for the first time in a chapter. (Italics are also used for emphasis.)

- A monospaced font indicates the contents of configuration files, messages displayed at a text-mode Linux shell prompt, filenames, text-mode command names, and Internet URLs.

- *Italicized monospaced text* indicates a variable—information that differs from one system or command run to another, such as the name of a client computer or a process ID number.

- **Bold monospaced text** is information that you're to type into the computer, usually at a Linux shell prompt. This text can also be italicized to indicate that you should substitute an appropriate value for your system. (When isolated on their own lines, commands are preceded by non-bold monospaced $ or # command prompts, denoting regular user or system administrator use, respectively.)

In addition to these text conventions, which can apply to individual words or entire paragraphs, a few conventions highlight segments of text:

> A note indicates information that's useful or interesting but that's somewhat peripheral to the main text. A note might be relevant to a small number of networks, for instance, or it may refer to an outdated feature.

A tip provides information that can save you time or frustration and that may not be entirely obvious. A tip might describe how to get around a limitation or how to use a feature to perform an unusual task.

 Warnings describe potential pitfalls or dangers. If you fail to heed a warning, you may end up spending a lot of time recovering from a bug, or you may even end up restoring your entire system from scratch.

Sidebar

A sidebar is like a note but longer. The information in a sidebar is useful, but it doesn't fit into the main flow of the text.

 Real World Scenario

Real World Scenario

A real-world scenario is a type of sidebar that describes a task or example that's particularly grounded in the real world. This may be a situation we or somebody we know has encountered, or it may be advice on how to work around problems that are common in real-world, working Linux environments.

EXERCISE

An exercise is a procedure that you should try on your own computer to help you learn about the material in the chapter. Don't limit yourself to the procedures described in the exercises though! Try other commands and procedures to truly learn about Linux.

The Exam Objectives

Behind every computer industry exam, you can be sure to find exam objectives—the broad topics in which exam developers want to ensure your competency. The official exam objectives are listed here. (They're also printed at the start of the chapters in which they're covered.)

Exam objectives are subject to change at any time without prior notice and at LPI's sole discretion. Please visit LPI's website (www.lpi.org) for the most current listing of exam objectives.

Exam 101-400 Objectives

Following are the areas in which you must be proficient in order to pass the 101-400 exam. This exam is broken into four topics (101–104), each of which has three to eight objectives. Each objective has an associated weight, which reflects its importance to the exam as a whole. The four main topics are as follows:

Subject Area

101 System Architecture

102 Linux Installation and Package Management

103 GNU and Unix Commands

104 Devices, Linux Filesystems, Filesystem Hierarchy Standard

101 System Architecture

101.1 Determine and configure hardware settings (Chapter 3)

- Enable and disable integrated peripherals
- Configure systems with or without external peripherals such as keyboards
- Differentiate between the various types of mass storage devices
- Know the differences between coldplug and hotplug devices
- Determine hardware resources for devices
- Tools and utilities to list various hardware information (e.g., lsusb, lspci, etc.)
- Tools and utilities to manipulate USB devices
- Conceptual understanding of sysfs, udev, hald, dbus
- The following is a partial list of the files, terms, and utilities covered in this objective: /sys, /proc, /dev, modprobe, lsmod, lspci, lsusb

101.2 Boot the system (Chapter 5)

- Provide common commands to the boot loader and options to the kernel at boot time
- Demonstrate knowledge of the boot sequence from BIOS to boot completion
- Understanding of SysVinit and systemd
- Awareness of Upstart
- Check boot events in the log file
- The following is a partial list of the files, terms and utilities covered in this objective: dmesg, BIOS, bootloader, kernel, init, initramfs, SysVinit, systemd

101.3 Change runlevels/boot targets and shutdown or reboot system (Chapter 5)

- Set the default runlevel or boot target
- Change between runlevels/boot targets, including single user mode
- Shutdown and reboot from the command line
- Alert users before switching runlevels/boot targets or other major system events
- Properly terminate processes
- The following is a partial list of the files, terms and utilities covered in this objective: /etc/inittab, shutdown, init, /etc/init.d, telinit, systemd, systemctl, /etc/systemd/, /usr/lib/systemd/, wall

102 Linux Installation and Package Management

102.1 Design hard disk layout (Chapter 3)

- Allocate filesystems and swap space to separate partitions or disks
- Tailor the design to the intended use of the system
- Ensure that the /boot partition conforms to the hardware architecture requirements for booting
- Knowledge of basic features of LVM
- The following is a partial list of the files, terms and utilities covered in this objective: / (root) filesystem, /var filesystem, /home filesystem, /boot filesystem, swap space, mount points, partitions

102.2 Install a boot manager (Chapter 5)

- Providing alternative boot locations and backup boot options
- Install and configure a boot loader such as GRUB Legacy

- Perform basic configuration changes for GRUB 2
- Interact with the boot loader
- The following is a partial list of the files, terms, and utilities covered in this objective: /boot/grub/menu.lst, grub.cfg and grub.conf, grub-install, grub-mkconfig, MBR

102.3 Manage shared libraries (Chapter 2)

- Identify shared libraries
- Identify the typical locations of system libraries
- Load shared libraries
- The following is a partial list of the files, terms and utilities covered in this objective: ldd, ldconfig, /etc/ld.so.conf, LD_LIBRARY_PATH

102.4 Use Debian package management (Chapter 2)

- Install, upgrade, and uninstall Debian binary packages
- Find packages containing specific files or libraries which may or may not be installed
- Obtain package information like version, content, dependencies, package integrity, and installation status (whether or not the package is installed)
- The following is a partial list of the files, terms and utilities covered in this objective: /etc/apt/sources.list, dpkg, dpkg-reconfigure, apt-get, apt-cache, aptitude

102.5 Use RPM and YUM package management (Chapter 2)

- Install, reinstall, upgrade. and remove packages using RPM and YUM
- Obtain information on RPM packages such as version, status, dependencies, integrity, and signatures
- Determine what files a package provides, as well as find which package a specific file comes from
- The following is a partial list of the files, terms and utilities covered in this objective: rpm, rpm2cpio, /etc/yum.conf, /etc/yum.repos.d/, yum, yumdownloader

103 GNU and Unix Commands

103.1 Work on the command line (Chapter 1)

- Use single shell commands and one-line command sequences to perform basic tasks on the command line
- Use and modify the shell environment. including defining, referencing, and exporting environment variables

- Use and edit command history
- Invoke commands inside and outside the defined path
- The following is a partial list of the files, terms, and utilities covered in this objective: bash, echo, env, exec, export, pwd, set, unset, man, uname, history, .bash_history

103.2 Process text streams using filters (Chapter 1)

- Send text files and output streams through text utility filters to modify the output using standard Unix commands
- The following is a partial list of the files, terms, and utilities covered in this objective: cat, cut, expand, fmt, head, od, join, less, nl, paste, pr, sed, sort, split, tail, tr, unexpand, uniq, wc

103.3 Perform basic file management (Chapter 4)

- Copy, move, and remove files and directories individually
- Copy multiple files and directories recursively
- Remove files and directories recursively
- Use simple and advanced wildcard specifications in commands
- Using find to locate and act on files based on type, size, or time
- Usage of tar, cpio, and dd
- The following is a partial list of the files, terms and utilities covered in this objective: cp, find, mkdir, mv, ls, rm, rmdir, touch, tar, cpio, dd, file, gzip, gunzip, bzip2, xz, file globbing

103.4 Use streams, pipes, and redirects (Chapter 1)

- Redirecting standard input, standard output, and standard error
- Pipe the output of one command to the input of another command
- Use the output of one command as arguments to another command
- Send output to both STDOUT and a file
- The following is a partial list of the files, terms and utilities covered in this objective: tee, xargs

103.5 Create, monitor, and kill processes (Chapter 2)

- Run jobs in the foreground and background
- Signal a program to continue running after logout
- Monitor active processes
- Select and sort processes for display

- Send signals to processes
- The following is a partial list of the files, terms and utilities covered in this objective: &, bg, fg, jobs, kill, nohup, ps, top, free, uptime, pgrep, pkill, killall, screen

103.6 Modify process execution priorities (Chapter 2)

- Know the default priority of a job that is created
- Run a program with higher or lower priority than the default
- Change the priority of a running process
- The following is a partial list of the files, terms, and utilities covered in this objective: nice, ps, renice, top

103.7 Search text files using regular expressions (Chapter 1)

- Create simple regular expressions containing several notational elements
- Use regular expression tools to perform searches through a filesystem or file content
- The following is a partial list of the files, terms and utilities covered in this objective: grep, egrep, fgrep, sed, regex(7)

103.8 Perform basic file editing operations using vi (Chapter 5)

- Navigate a document using vi
- Use basic vi modes
- Insert, edit, delete, copy, and find text
- The following is a partial list of the files, terms and utilities covered in this objective: vi, /, ?, h, j, k, l, i, o, a, c, d, p, y, dd, yy, ZZ, :w!, :q!, :e!

104 Devices, Linux Filesystems, Filesystem Hierarchy Standard

104.1 Create partitions and filesystems (Chapter 3)

- Manage MBR partition tables
- Use various mkfs commands to create various filesystems, such as ext2, ext3, ext4, xfs, vfat
- Awareness of ReiserFS and Btrfs
- Basic knowledge of gdisk and parted with GPT
- The following is a partial list of the files, terms, and utilities covered in this objective: fdisk, gdisk, parted, mkfs, mkswap

104.2 Maintain the integrity of filesystems (Chapter 3)

- Verify the integrity of filesystems
- Monitor free space and inodes
- Repair simple filesystem problems
- The following is a partial list of the files, terms, and utilities covered in this objective: du, df, fsck, e2fsck, mke2fs, debugfs, dumpe2fs, tune2fs, xfs tools (such as xfs_metadump and xfs_info)

104.3 Control mounting and unmounting of filesystems (Chapter 3)

- Manually mount and unmount filesystems
- Configure filesystem mounting on bootup
- Configure user mountable removeable filesystems
- The following is a partial list of the files, terms, and utilities covered in this objective: /etc/fstab, /media, mount, umount

104.4 Manage disk quotas (Chapter 4)

- Set up a disk quota for a filesystem
- Edit, check, and generate user quota reports
- The following is a partial list of the files, terms, and utilities covered in this objective: quota, edquota, repquota, quotaon

104.5 Manage file permissions and ownership (Chapter 4)

- Manage access permissions on regular and special files as well as directories
- Use access modes such as SUID, SGID, and the sticky bit to maintain security
- Know how to change the file creation mask
- Use the group field to grant file access to group members
- The following is a partial list of the files, terms, and utilities covered in this objective: chmod, umask, chown, chgrp

104.6 Create and change hard and symbolic links (Chapter 4)

- Create links
- Identify hard and/or soft links
- Copying versus linking files
- Use links to support system administration tasks
- This utility is covered in this objective: ln, ls

104.7 Find system files and place files in the correct location (Chapter 4)

- Understand the correct locations of files under the FHS
- Find files and commands on a Linux system
- Know the location and purpose of important files and directories as defined in the FHS
- The following is a partial list of the files, terms, and utilities covered in this objective: find, locate, updatedb, whereis, which, type, /etc/updatedb.conf

Exam 102-400 Objectives

The 102-400 exam comprises six topics (105–110), each of which contains three or four objectives. The six major topics are as follows:

Subject Area
105 Shells, Scripting, and Data Management
106 User Interfaces and Desktops
107 Administrative Tasks
108 Essential System Services
109 Networking Fundamentals
110 Security

105 Shells, Scripting, and Data Management

105.1 Customize and use the shell environment (Chapter 9)

- Set environment variables (e.g., PATH) at login or when spawning a new shell
- Write bash functions for frequently used sequences of commands
- Maintain skeleton directories for new user accounts
- Set command search path with the proper directory
- The following is a partial list of the files, terms, and utilities covered in this objective: source, /etc/bash.bashrc, /etc/profile, env, export, set, unset, ~/.bash_profile, ~/.bash_login, ~/.profile, ~/.bashrc, ~/.bash_logout, function, alias, lists

105.2 Customize or write simple scripts (Chapter 9)

- Use standard sh syntax (loops, tests)
- Use command substitution
- Test return values for success or failure or other information provided by a command
- Perform conditional mailing to the superuser
- Correctly select the script interpreter through the shebang (#!) line
- Manage the location, ownership, execution, and SUID rights of scripts
- The following is a partial list of the files, terms, and utilities covered in this objective: for, while, test, if, read, seq, exec

105.3 SQL data management (Chapter 9)

- Use of basic SQL commands
- Perform basic data manipulation
- The following is a partial list of the files, terms, and utilities covered in this objective: insert, update, select, delete, from, where, group by, order by, join

106 User Interfaces and Desktops

106.1 Install and configure X11 (Chapter 6)

- Verify that the video card and monitor are supported by an X server
- Awareness of the X font server
- Basic understanding and knowledge of the X Window configuration file
- The following is a partial list of the files, terms, and utilities covered in this objective: /etc/X11/xorg.conf, xhost, DISPLAY, xwininfo, xdpyinfo, X

106.2 Set up a display manager (Chapter 6)

- Basic configuration of LightDM
- Turn the display manager on or off
- Change the display manager greeting
- Awareness of XDM, KDM, and GDM
- The following is a partial list of the files, terms, and utilities covered in this objective: lightdm, /etc/lightdm

106.3 Accessibility (Chapter 6)

- Basic knowledge of keyboard accessibility settings (AccessX)
- Basic knowledge of visual settings and themes
- Basic knowledge of assistive technologies (ATs)
- The following is a partial list of the files, terms, and utilities covered in this objective: sticky/repeat keys, slow/bounce/toggle keys, mouse keys, high contrast/large Print Desktop themes, screen reader, Braille display, screen magnifier, onscreen keyboard, Gestures (used at login; for example, gdm), Orca, GOK, emacspeak

107 Administrative Tasks

107.1 Manage user and group accounts and related system files (Chapter 7)

- Add, modify, and remove users and groups
- Manage user/group info in password/group databases
- Create and manage special-purpose and limited accounts
- The following is a partial list of the files, terms, and utilities covered in this objective: /etc/passwd, /etc/shadow, /etc/group, /etc/skel, chage, getent, groupadd, groupdel, groupmod, passwd, useradd, userdel, usermod

107.2 Automate system administration tasks by scheduling jobs (Chapter 7)

- Manage cron and at jobs
- Configure user access to cron and at services
- Configure anacron
- The following is a partial list of the files, terms, and utilities covered in this objective: /etc/cron.{d,daily,hourly,monthly,weekly}, /etc/at.deny, /etc/at.allow, /etc /crontab, /etc/cron.allow, /etc/cron.deny, /var/spool/cron/*, crontab, at, atq, atrm, anacron, /etc/anacrontab

107.3 Localization and internationalization (Chapter 6)

- Configure locale settings and environment variables
- Configure time zone settings and environment variables
- The following is a partial list of the files, terms, and utilities covered in this objective: /etc/timezone, /etc/localtime, /usr/share/zoneinfo, environment variables (LC_*, LC_ALL, LANG, TZ), /usr/bin/locale, tzselect, tzconfig, date, iconv, UTF-8, ISO-8859, ASCII, Unicode

108 Essential System Services

108.1 Maintain system time (Chapter 7)

- Set the system date and time
- Set the hardware clock to the correct time in UTC
- Configure the correct time zone
- Basic NTP configuration
- Knowledge of using the pool.ntp.org service
- Awareness of the ntpq command
- The following is a partial list of the files, terms, and utilities covered in this objective: /usr/share/zoneinfo, /etc/timezone, /etc/localtime, /etc/ntp.conf, date, hwclock, ntpd, ntpdate, pool.ntp.org

108.2 System logging (Chapter 7)

- Configuration of the syslog daemon
- Understanding of standard facilities, priorities, and actions
- Configuration of logrotate
- Awareness of rsyslog and syslog-ng
- The following is a partial list of the files, terms, and utilities covered in this objective: syslog.conf, syslogd, klogd, /var/log, logger, logrotate, /etc/logrotate.conf, /etc/logrotate.d/, journalctl, /etc/system/journal.conf, /var/log/journal/

108.3 Mail Transfer Agent (MTA) basics (Chapter 9)

- Create email aliases
- Configure email forwarding
- Knowledge of commonly available MTA programs (postfix, sendmail, qmail, exim) (no configuration)
- The following is a partial list of the files, terms, and utilities covered in this objective: ~/.forward, sendmail emulation layer commands, newaliases, mail, mailq, postfix, sendmail, exim, qmail

108.4 Manage printers and printing (Chapter 6)

- Basic CUPS configuration (for local and remote printers)
- Manage user print queues
- Troubleshoot general printing problems
- Add and remove jobs from configured printer queues

- The following is a partial list of the files, terms, and utilities covered in this objective: CUPS configuration files, tools and utilities; `/etc/cups`; `lpd` legacy interface (`lpr`, `lprm`, `lpq`)

109 Networking Fundamentals

109.1 Fundamentals of Internet protocols (Chapter 8)

- Demonstrate an understanding of network masks and CIDR notation
- Knowledge of the differences between private and public "dotted quad" IP addresses
- Knowledge about common TCP and UDP ports (20, 21, 22, 23, 25, 53, 80, 110, 123, 139, 143, 161, 162, 389, 443, 465, 514, 636, 993, 995)
- Knowledge about the differences and major features of UDP, TCP, and ICMP
- Knowledge of the major differences between IPv4 and IPV6
- Knowledge of the basic features of IPv6
- The following is a partial list of the files, terms, and utilities covered in this objective: `/etc/services`, IPv4, IPv6, subnetting, TCP, UDP, ICMP

109.2 Basic network configuration (Chapter 8)

- Manually and automatically configure network interfaces
- Basic TCP/IP host configuration
- Setting a default route
- The following is a partial list of the files, terms, and utilities covered in this objective: `/etc/hostname`, `/etc/hosts`, `/etc/nsswitch.conf`, `ifconfig`, `ifup`, `ifdown`, `ip`, `route`, `ping`

109.3 Basic network troubleshooting (Chapter 8)

- Manually and automatically configure network interfaces and routing tables to include adding, starting, stopping, restarting, deleting, or reconfiguring network interfaces
- Change, view, or configure the routing table and correct an improperly set default route manually
- Debug problems associated with the network configuration
- The following is a partial list of the files, terms, and utilities covered in this objective: `ifconfig`, `ip`, `ifup`, `ifdown`, `route`, `host`, `hostname`, `dig`, `netstat`, `ping`, `ping6`, `traceroute`, `traceroute6`, `tracepath`, `tracepath6`, `netcat`

109.4 Configure client-side DNS (Chapter 8)

- Query remote DNS servers
- Configure local name resolution and use remote DNS servers

- Modify the order in which name resolution is done
- The following is a partial list of the files, terms, and utilities covered in this objective: /etc/hosts, /etc/resolv.conf, /etc/nsswitch.conf, host, dig, getent

110 Security

110.1 Perform security administration tasks (Chapter 10)

- Audit a system to find files with the SUID/SGID bit set
- Set or change user passwords and password aging information
- Be able to use nmap and netstat to discover open ports on a system
- Set up limits on user logins, processes, and memory usage
- Determine which users have logged in to the system or are currently logged in
- Basic sudo configuration and usage
- The following is a partial list of the files, terms, and utilities covered in this objective: find, passwd, lsof, nmap, chage, netstat, sudo, /etc/sudoers, su, usermod, ulimit, who, w, last

110.2 Set up host security (Chapter 10)

- Awareness of shadow passwords and how they work
- Turn off network services not in use
- Understand the role of TCP wrappers
- The following is a partial list of the files, terms, and utilities covered in this objective: /etc/nologin, /etc/passwd, /etc/shadow, /etc/xinetd.d/*, /etc/xinetd.conf, /etc/inetd.d/*, /etc/inetd.conf, /etc/inittab, /etc/init.d/*, /etc/hosts .allow, /etc/hosts.deny

110.3 Securing data with encryption (Chapter 10)

- Perform basic OpenSSH 2 client configuration and usage
- Understand the role of OpenSSH 2 server host keys
- Perform basic GnuPG configuration and usage
- Understand SSH port tunnels (including X11 tunnels)
- The following is a partial list of the files, terms, and utilities covered in this objective: ssh, ssh-keygen, ssh-agent, ssh-add, ~/.ssh/id_rsa and id_rsa.pub, ~/.ssh/id_dsa and id_dsa.pub, /etc/ssh/ssh_host_rsa_key and ssh_host_rsa_key.pub, /etc/ssh/ssh_host_dsa_key and ssh_host_dsa_key.pub, ~/.ssh/authorized_keys, /etc/ssh_known_hosts, gpg, ~/.gnupg/*

Assessment Test

1. Which section in the X server configuration file defines the combination of monitors and video cards that you're using on your Linux system?

   A. Monitor

   B. Screen

   C. Modeline

   D. Device

   E. Module

2. How can you tell whether your system is using inetd or xinetd as a super server? (Select two.)

   A. Type **ps ax | grep inetd**, and examine the output for signs of inetd or xinetd.

   B. Type **superserver** to see a report on which super server is running.

   C. Look for the /etc/inetd.conf file or /etc/xinetd.d subdirectory, which are signs of inetd or xinetd, respectively.

   D. Examine the /etc/inittab file to see which super server is launched by init, which is responsible for this task.

   E. Type **netstat -a | grep inet** and examine the output for signs of inetd or xinetd.

3. How does the lpc utility for CUPS differ from its counterpart in BSD LPD and LPRng?

   A. The lpc utility is unique to CUPS; it doesn't ship with BSD LPD or LPRng.

   B. CUPS doesn't ship with an lpc command, but BSD LPD and LPRng do.

   C. CUPS's lpc is much more complex than its counterpart in BSD LPD and LPRng.

   D. CUPS's lpc is much simpler than its counterpart in BSD LPD and LPRng.

   E. The lpc utility is identical in all three of these printing systems.

4. What file would you edit to restrict the number of simultaneous logins a user can employ?

   A. /etc/pam.d/login-limits

   B. /etc/bashrc

   C. /etc/security/limits.conf

   D. /etc/inittab

   E. /etc/passwd

5. Which of the following are required when configuring a computer to use a static IP address? (Select two.)

   A. The IP address of the DHCP server

   B. The hostname of the NBNS server

   C. The computer's IP address

   D. The network mask

   E. The IP address of the NTP server

6. What does the following command accomplish?

`$ wc report.txt | tee wc`

   A. It launches the wc editor on both the `report.txt` and `wc.txt` files; each file opens in its own window.

   B. It displays a count of the windows in which the `report.txt` file is displayed and shows that information in a new window called `wc`.

   C. It creates a count of newlines, words, and bytes in the `report.txt` file and then displays a count of these statistics about the report it just generated.

   D. It cleans up any memory leaks associated with the `tee` program's use of the `report.txt` file.

   E. It displays a count of newlines, words, and bytes in the `report.txt` file and copies that output to the `wc` file.

7. Which of the following characters defines the *end* of an OS or kernel definition in `/boot/grub/grub.cfg`?

   A. ;

   B.)

   C. }

   D. */

   E. None of the above; the definition ends with the `title` line beginning the next entry.

8. What does the number 703 represent in the following `/etc/passwd` entry?

`george:x:703:100:George Brown:/home/george:/bin/tcsh`

   A. The account's human ID (HID) number

   B. The account's process ID (PID) number

   C. The account's group ID (GID) number

   D. The account's globally unique ID (GUID) number

   E. The account's user ID (UID) number

9. What does the `grep` command accomplish?

   A. It creates a pipeline between two programs.

   B. It searches files' contents for a pattern.

   C. It concatenates two or more files.

   D. It displays the last several lines of a file.

   E. It locates files on the hard disk.

10. Which of the following are journaling filesystems for Linux? (Select three.)

   A. vfat

   B. ReiserFS

   C. Ext2fs

D. Ext3fs

E. XFS

11. You've configured your computer to use SMTP and IMAP via a tunneled SSH connection to your ISP's email server for improved security. Why might you still want to use GPG encryption for your emails on top of the encryption provided by SSH?

   A. The SSH tunnel reaches only as far as the first email server; GPG encrypts data on all of the computers all the way to or from your email correspondents.

   B. SSH encryption is notoriously poor for email, although it's perfectly adequate for login sessions; thus, adding GPG encryption improves security.

   C. SSH doesn't encrypt the headers of the email messages; GPG encrypts the headers to keep snoopers from learning your correspondents' identities.

   D. Using GPG guarantees that your email messages won't contain unwanted viruses or worms that might infect your correspondents' computers.

   E. Configured in this way, SSH will encrypt the email headers and bodies but not any attachments to your email.

12. Which of the following ports are commonly used to retrieve email from an email server computer? (Select two.)

   A. 110

   B. 119

   C. 139

   D. 143

   E. 443

13. You're experiencing sporadic problems with a Secure Shell (SSH) login server—sometimes users can log in and sometimes they can't. What might you try immediately after a failure to help diagnose this problem?

   A. On the server computer, type **http://localhost:631** into a web browser to access the SSH configuration page and check its error subpage for error messages.

   B. Type **diagnose sshd** to run a diagnostic on the SSH server daemon (sshd).

   C. Type **tail /var/log/messages** to look for error messages from the server.

   D. Examine the /dev/ssh device file to look for error messages from the server.

   E. On the server computer, type **sshd** to view SSH's diagnostic messages.

14. What is the function of the ~/.profile file?

   A. It's the user configuration file for the ProFTP server.

   B. It's one of a user's bash startup scripts.

   C. It's the user configuration file for the ProFile file manager.

   D. Its presence tells tcsh to ignore file modes.

   E. It holds the user's encrypted password.

15. You want your computer to remind you to get your car inspected in two years. What is the best way to do this among the specified options?

    A. Create a program that repeatedly checks the time and, when two years have passed, displays a message to get your car inspected.

    B. Type **cal *day month year***, where *day*, *month*, and *year* specify the date of the future inspection, to have Linux run a program that you then specify on that date.

    C. Create a `cron` job that runs hourly. This job should check the date and, when the correct date comes up, use `mail` to notify you of the need for a car inspection.

    D. Use the NTP GUI calendar program to create an alarm for the specified date. The program will then display the message you enter at the specified date and time.

    E. Type **at *date***, where *date* is a date specification. You can then specify a command, such as `mail` with appropriate options, to notify you of the need to get your car inspected.

16. How would you configure a computer to use the computer whose IP address is 172.24.21.1 as a gateway for all network traffic that's not otherwise configured?

    A. `gateway default 172.24.21.1`

    B. `gateway 172.24.21.1`

    C. `route gateway 172.24.21.1`

    D. `route add default gw 172.24.21.1`

    E. `gw 172.24.21.1`

17. What software can you use to drive a Braille display device? (Select two.)

    A. Emacspeak

    B. BRLTTY

    C. A 2.6.26 or later kernel

    D. GOK

    E. A framebuffer driver

18. Which is true of source RPM packages?

    A. They consist of three files: an original source tarball, a patch file of changes, and a PGP signature indicating the authenticity of the package.

    B. They require programming knowledge to rebuild.

    C. They can sometimes be used to work around dependency problems with a binary package.

    D. They are necessary to compile software for RPM-based distributions.

    E. They always contain software that's licensed under terms of the GPL.

19. Which utility should you use by itself to rename the file `pumpkin.txt` to `lantern.txt`?

    A. `dd`

    B. `rm`

   C. cp

   D. mv

   E. ln

20. You want to run a lengthy scientific simulation program, called simbigbang, which doesn't require any user interaction; the program operates solely on disk files. If you don't want to tie up the shell from which you run the program, what should you type to run simbigbang in the background?

   A. **start simbigbang**

   B. **simbigbang &**

   C. **bg simbigbang**

   D. **background simbigbang**

   E. **nice simbigbang**

21. Which of the following commands will install an RPM package file called theprogram-1.2.3-4.i386.rpm on a computer? (Select two.)

   A. **rpm -Uvh theprogram-1.2.3-4.i386.rpm**

   B. **rpm -i theprogram-1.2.3-4.i386.rpm**

   C. **rpm -U theprogram**

   D. **rpm -e theprogram-1.2.3-4.i386.rpm**

   E. **rpm -Vp theprogram-1.2.3-4.i386.rpm**

22. What tool can diagnose and fix many common Linux filesystem problems?

   A. mkfs

   B. fsck

   C. chkdsk

   D. scandisk

   E. fdisk

23. You've just installed MySQL, and you intend to use it to store information about the animals in a zoo, from the anteaters to the zebras. What command are you likely to use first, once you start MySQL?

   A. **CREATE DATABASE animals;**

   B. **USE animals;**

   C. **CREATE TABLE animals;**

   D. **INSERT INTO animals;**

   E. **UPDATE animals;**

24. Which of the following commands displays help on *topic*, when typed in a Linux shell? (Select two.)

   A. **manual *topic***

   B. **man *topic***

C. **?** *topic*

D. **info** *topic*

E. **hint** *topic*

25. A computer's hardware clock keeps track of the time while the computer is powered off. In what formats may this time be stored on an *x*86 Linux system? (Select two.)

   A. Coordinated Universal Time (UTC)

   B. Internet Time

   C. Local time

   D. 12-hour time

   E. Mars time

26. You want to know what kernel modules are currently loaded. What command would you type to learn this information?

   A. **insmod**

   B. **depmod**

   C. **modprobe**

   D. **lsmod**

   E. **modinfo**

27. You want to enable all members of the **music** group to read the **instruments.txt** file, which currently has 0640 (-rw-r-----) permissions, ownership by **root**, and group ownership by **root**. How might you accomplish this goal? (Select two.)

   A. Type **chown music instruments.txt** in the file's directory.

   B. Type **chgrp music instruments.txt** in the file's directory.

   C. Type **chgroup music instruments.txt** in the file's directory.

   D. Type **chmod 0600 instruments.txt** in the file's directory.

   E. Type **chown :music instruments.txt** in the file's directory.

28. You want to create a link to the **/usr/local/bin** directory in another location. Which of the following statements is true?

   A. You can do this only if **/usr/local/bin** is on a journaling filesystem.

   B. You must own **/usr/local/bin** to create the link.

   C. You can create the link only if the link's location is on the same filesystem as the original directory.

   D. Only the system administrator can do this.

   E. The link will probably have to be a symbolic link.

29. Which of the following, when typed in vi's command mode, saves a file and quits the program? (Select two.)

   A. **:rq**

   B. **:wq**

C. :re

D. :we

E. ZZ

30. A user's home directory includes a file called ~/.forward that consists of one line: |~/ junkme. What is the effect of this configuration?

A. The user's incoming mail is forwarded to the junkme user on the same system.

B. The user's incoming mail is stored in the ~/junkme file.

C. The user's incoming mail is sent through the ~/junkme program file.

D. The user's incoming mail is flagged as spam and deleted.

E. The user's incoming mail is forwarded to the same user on the junkme computer.

Answers to the Assessment Test

1. B. The Monitor section defines the monitor options and settings but doesn't combine it with the video card, so option A is incorrect. The Modeline line defines the available video modes in the Monitor section, but it doesn't define video cards, so option C is incorrect. Option D, the Device section, is also incorrect; it defines the video card but doesn't match it with a monitor on the system. Option E is incorrect because the Module section defines which X server modules (or drivers) are loaded but it doesn't match monitors and video cards. Option B, the Screen section, tells the X server about the combination of video cards and monitors that you're using, so it's the correct answer. For more information, see Chapter 6, "Configuring the X Window System, Localization, and Printing."

2. A, C. Examining a process listing (obtained from ps) for signs of the super server is the most reliable way to determine which one is actually running, so option A is correct. The presence of the super server's configuration file or files (as in option C) is also a good diagnostic, although some older systems that have been upgraded may have both sets of configuration files. There is no standard superserver utility to report on which one is used, so option B is incorrect. Most distributions launch the super server through a SysV startup script; the /etc/inittab file isn't directly involved in this process, so examining it would be pointless, and option D is incorrect. Although the output of **netstat -ap**, when typed as root, will include an indication of any instance of inetd or xinetd that's listening for connections, option E omits the critical -p option, which causes the program to display process names. Thus, option E is incorrect. For more information, see Chapter 10, "Securing Your System."

3. D. The lpc utility is used to start, stop, change the priority of, and otherwise control jobs in a print queue. CUPS ships with an lpc utility, but it's quite rudimentary compared to the lpc utilities of BSD LPD and LPRng. Instead, CUPS relies on its Web-based interface to provide the ability to control print jobs. Thus, option D is correct, and the remaining options must logically all be incorrect. For more information, see Chapter 6.

4. C. The /etc/security/limits.conf file defines various limits on user resources, including the number of simultaneous logins individual users are permitted. Thus, option C is correct. The /etc/pam.d/login-limits file (option A) is fictitious, although login limits do rely on the pam_limits module to the Pluggable Authentication System (PAM). The /etc/bashrc file (option B) is a global bash startup script file, but it's not normally used to impose login limits. The /etc/inittab file (option D) is a key Linux startup file, but it doesn't have any direct bearing on imposing login limits. The /etc/passwd file (option E) defines many key account features, but login limits are not among these. For more information, see Chapter 10.

5. C, D. The computer's IP address (option C) and network mask (aka subnet mask or netmask; option D) are the most critical components in TCIP/IP network configuration. (Additional information that you may need to provide on many networks includes the IP addresses of one to three DNS servers, the hostname or IP address of a router, and the computer's hostname.) You shouldn't need the IP address of a Dynamic Host

Configuration Protocol (DHCP) server (option A)—and if a DHCP server is present, chances are you should be using DHCP rather than static IP address assignment. A Net-BIOS Name Service (NBNS) server (option B) converts between names and IP addresses on NetBIOS networks. The hostname of such a computer isn't likely to be a critical configuration element, although you may need to provide this information to Samba for some operations to function correctly when sharing files. A Network Time Protocol (NTP) server (option E) helps you maintain system time on all of your computers, but this isn't required for basic network configuration. For more information, see Chapter 8, "Configuring Basic Networking."

6. E. The wc command displays a count of newlines, words, and bytes in the specified file (report.txt). Piping this data through tee causes a copy of the output to be stored in the new file (wc in this example—you shouldn't run this command in the same directory as the wc executable file!). Thus, option E is correct. Contrary to option A, wc is not an editor, and the remaining syntax wouldn't cause two files to open in separate windows even if wc were an editor. Contrary to option B, wc doesn't count windows or open a new window. Option C describes the effect of **wc report | wc**—that is, it overlooks the tee command. Contrary to option D, wc has nothing to do with cleaning up memory leaks, and tee doesn't directly use the report.txt file. For more information, see Chapter 1, "Exploring Linux Command-Line Tools."

7. C. The grub.cfg filename indicates a GRUB 2 configuration file. In such files, each OS or kernel stanza begins with a menuentry line and an open curly brace ({) and ends with a close curly brace (}). Thus, option C is correct. Some configuration files and programming languages use semicolons (;) at the end of most lines, but this isn't true of GRUB 2, so option A is incorrect. Although close parentheses ()) are used to terminate some types of options in some configuration files, including disk identifiers in GRUB 2's configuration file, they aren't used to terminate whole OS or kernel definitions in this file, so option B is incorrect. The string */ terminates comments in C program files but isn't commonly used in GRUB 2 configuration files, so option D is incorrect. Option E would be correct if the question had asked about a GRUB Legacy configuration file (menu.lst or grub.conf), but the question specifies a GRUB 2 configuration file (grub.cfg); the two boot loaders terminate their OS/kernel stanzas differently, so option E is incorrect. For more information, see Chapter 5, "Booting Linux and Editing Files."

8. E. The third field of /etc/passwd entries holds the UID number for the account, so option E is correct. Linux doesn't use any standard identifier called a human ID (HID; option A), although the acronym HID stands for human interface device, a class of USB devices. Accounts don't have PID numbers (option B); those belong to running processes. The account's GID number (option C) is stored in the fourth field of /etc/passwd—100 in this example. Linux accounts don't use globally unique ID (GUID) numbers, so option D is incorrect. For more information, see Chapter 7, "Administering the System."

9. B. The grep command scans files to find those that contain a specified string or pattern, as described by option B. In the case of text files, grep displays the matching line or lines; for binary files, it reports that the file matches the pattern. The method of creating a pipeline (option A) involves separating two commands with a vertical bar (|). The grep command can be used in a pipeline, but it doesn't create one. The command that concatenates files (option C) is cat, and the command that displays the last several lines of a file (option D) is tail. Several commands, such as find, locate, and whereis locate files (option E), but grep is not among them. For more information, see Chapter 1.

10. B, D, E. ReiserFS (option B) was written from scratch for Linux. The Third Extended Filesystem (ext3fs; option D) is a journaling filesystem based on the older non-journaling Second Extended Filesystem (ext2fs; option C). The Extents Filesystem (XFS; option E) is a journaling filesystem written by SGI for Irix and later ported to Linux. The Virtual File Allocation Table (vfat; option A) is a non-journaling filesystem designed by Microsoft for Windows. For more information, see Chapter 3, "Configuring Hardware."

11. A. Option A correctly describes the features of SSH and GPG in this context. Option B is incorrect because SSH should do a fine job of encrypting your email so that it can't be decoded between your system and your ISP's email server. Option C has it backward; email transferred via SSH will be completely encrypted, including both headers and body. GPG doesn't encrypt headers, just message bodies. Option D is incorrect because GPG isn't a virus scanner, just an encryption tool. Option E is incorrect because the SSH tunnel will encrypt everything in the SMTP transfer, including email attachments. For more information, see Chapter 10.

12. A, D. Port 110 (option A) is assigned to the Post Office Protocol (POP), and port 143 (option D) is assigned to the Internet Message Access Protocol (IMAP), both of which may be used to retrieve email messages from an email server system. Port 119 (option B) is assigned to the Network News Transfer Protocol (NNTP), port 139 (option C) is assigned to the Server Message Block/Common Internet File System (SMB/CIFS) protocol, and port 443 (option E) is assigned to the Hypertext Transfer Protocol with SSL encryption (HTTPS), none of which is commonly used for email retrieval. For more information, see Chapter 8.

13. C. Log files, such as /var/log/messages and sometimes others in /var/log, often contain useful information concerning server errors. The tail program displays the last few lines of a file, so using it to examine log files immediately after a problem occurs can be a useful diagnostic procedure. Option C correctly combines these features. The http:// localhost:631 URL of option A accesses the Common Unix Printing System (CUPS) configuration utility, which has nothing to do with SSH. There is no standard diagnose utility (option B) to help diagnose server problems, and there is no standard /dev/ssh file (option D). The **sshd** program is the SSH server itself, so option E will simply launch the server. For more information, see Chapter 5.

14. B. The ~./profile file is one of several bash startup scripts, as stated in option B. It has nothing to do with the ProFTP server (option A) or the tcsh shell (option D). The ProFile file manager mentioned in option C is fictitious. Users' encrypted passwords (option E) are usually stored in /etc/shadow. For more information, see Chapter 9, "Writing Scripts, Configuring Email, and Using Databases."

15. E. The at utility was created to run programs at one specified point in the future. Thus, option E will accomplish the stated goal. Options A and C might also work, but neither is the *best* way to accomplish this goal. Option A will tie up CPU time, and if the program

crashes or the system is shut down during the intervening two years, the message will never be displayed. Option C would be more reliable, but it adds unnecessary complexity to your hourly cron job schedule. The cal program displays a text-mode calendar, enabling you to identify the days of a week for a given month; it doesn't schedule future jobs, as option B suggests. A GUI calendar program, as specified in option D, might work, but NTP is the Network Time Protocol, a protocol and like-named program for synchronizing clocks across a network. Thus, NTP isn't the tool for the job, and option D is incorrect. For more information, see Chapter 7.

16. D. Option D provides the correct command to add 172.24.21.1 as the default gateway. Options A and B both use the fictitious gateway command, which doesn't exist and therefore won't work unless you create a script of this name. Option C uses the correct route command, but there is no gateway option to route; you must use add default gw, as in option D. There is no standard gw command, so option E is incorrect. For more information, see Chapter 8.

17. B, C. The BRLTTY package is an add-on daemon for handling a Braille display device, and some features for using these devices have been added to the 2.6.26 kernel, so options B and C are correct. Emacspeak (option A) is speech-synthesis software; it can be used to "speak" a text display to a user, but it doesn't interface with Braille displays. GOK (option D) is an onscreen keyboard, not a Braille display tool. Framebuffer drivers (option E) are kernel drivers for managing conventional video cards; they aren't used to drive Braille displays. For more information, see Chapter 6.

18. C. Some dependencies result from dynamically linking binaries to libraries at compile time, and so they can be overcome by recompiling the software from a source RPM, so option C is correct. Option A describes Debian source packages, not RPM packages. Recompiling a source RPM requires only issuing an appropriate command, although you must also have appropriate compilers and libraries installed. Thus, option B is overly pessimistic. Source tarballs can also be used to compile software for RPM systems, although this results in none of RPM's advantages. Thus, option D is overly restrictive. The RPM format doesn't impose any licensing requirements, contrary to option E. For more information, see Chapter 2.

19. D. The mv utility can be used to rename files as well as move them from one location to another, so option D is correct. The dd utility (option A) is used to copy files to backups, rm (option B) is used to remove (delete) files, cp (option C) copies files, and ln (option E) creates links. For more information, see Chapter 4.

20. B. Appending an ampersand (&) to a command causes that command to execute in the background. The program so launched still consumes CPU time, but it won't monopolize the shell you used to launch it. Thus, option B is correct. The start (option A) and background (option D) commands are fictitious. Although bg (option C) does place a job into the background, it doesn't launch a program that way; it places a process that has already been suspended (by pressing Ctrl+Z) into the background. The nice utility (option E) launches a program with modified priority, but a program so launched still monopolizes its shell unless you take additional steps. For more information, see Chapter 2.

21. A, B. The -Uvh parameter (option A) issues an upgrade command (which installs the program whether or not an earlier version is installed) and creates a series of hash marks to display the command's progress. The -i parameter (option B) installs the program if it's not already installed but causes no progress display. Option C uses a package name, not a complete filename, and so it will fail to install the package file. The -e option (option D) removes a package. Option E's -Vp option verifies the package file but doesn't install it. For more information, see Chapter 2.

22. B. Option B, fsck, is Linux's filesystem check utility. It's similar in purpose to the DOS and Windows CHKDSK and ScanDisk utilities (similar to options C and D), but these DOS and Windows utilities don't work on Linux filesystems like ext2fs or ReiserFS. Option A, mkfs, creates new filesystems; it doesn't diagnose or fix filesystem problems. Option E, fdisk, is a tool for creating or modifying disk partitions; it doesn't manage the filesystems they contain. For more information, see Chapter 3.

23. A. A freshly installed MySQL database is unlikely to have a ready-made database of animals, so your first task is to create that database with the CREATE DATABASE command, as shown in option A. (You could call the database something other than animals, of course.) The USE command in option B will be useful only once the database has been created. Once the database is created, you can use CREATE TABLE, as in option C, to create a table; however, you'll need an existing database first, and this command also requires information about the type of data to be stored, which option C doesn't provide. Option D's INSERT INTO command stores data into a table once it's been created, so it's far from the first command you'll use. It also requires additional specification of the data to be stored, so it's incomplete. Option E's UPDATE command modifies existing entries, so you'll use this command only after you've created the database and added at least one animal to it. (Option E is also an incomplete command even then.) For more information, see Chapter 9.

24. B, D. The correct answers, man and info (options B and D), are two common Linux help packages. Although ? (option C) is a common help command within certain interactive programs, it isn't a help command in bash or other common Linux shells. There is no common command called manual (option A), nor is hint (option E) a valid bash command or common program name. For more information, see Chapter 1.

25. A, C. Unix systems traditionally store time in UTC (aka Greenwich mean time), and Linux may do so as well. Thus, option A is correct. Most other $x86$ PC OSs traditionally store time as the local time, however, so Linux also supports this option and option C is also correct. Internet Time (option B) is an alternative to the 24-hour clock in which the day is broken into 1,000 "beats." Standard PC BIOSs don't support this time format. Likewise, a 12-hour clock isn't terribly useful to computers because it doesn't differentiate a.m. from p.m., making option D incorrect. Although the length of the Martian day is similar to that of Earth (24 hours and 37 minutes), those wanting to colonize Mars will have to wait for PC clocks to support setting time for the Red Planet; option E is incorrect. For more information, see Chapter 7.

26. D. Typing **lsmod** (option D) produces a list of the modules that are currently loaded. The insmod (option A) and modprobe (option C) programs both load modules—either a single module or a single module and all those on which it depends, respectively. The depmod command (option B) generates the modules.dep file that contains module dependency

information. The modinfo command (option E) displays information, such as its version number and author, on a single module. For more information, see Chapter 3.

27. B, E. The chgrp and chown commands can both change the group ownership of a file. The chgrp command takes a group name and a filename as parameters, as in option B. The chown command normally changes a file's owner; but if you provide a group name preceded by a dot (.) or a colon (:), as in option E, it changes the group of a file. The chown command as used in option A, will change the primary ownership of the file to the music user, if such a user exists on the system; it won't change the group ownership. There is no standard chgroup command, as in option C. Option D will change the permissions to 0600 (-rw-------), which will be a step backward with respect to the goal stated. For more information, see Chapter 4.

28. E. Hard links to directories are not permitted by most filesystems, so you'll probably have to create a symbolic link, as noted in option E. Links don't rely on a filesystem journal, so option A is incorrect. Contrary to option B, anybody may create a link, not just the original's owner. Option C describes a restriction of hard links, but because this link will probably have to be a symbolic link, this restriction is unimportant and option C is incorrect. Option D describes a more severe restriction than option B, but it's incorrect for the same reasons. For more information, see Chapter 4.

29. B, E. The colon (:) starts ex mode, from which you can enter commands. In ex mode, r includes a file in an existing one, w writes a file, e loads an entirely new file, and q quits the program. Thus the desired combination is :wq (option B). As a special case, ZZ does the same thing, so option E is also correct. For more information, see Chapter 5.

30. C. The ~/.forward file is a user email forwarding file. The vertical bar character (|) at the start of such a file is a code to send the email through the specified program file, so option C is correct. To do as option A describes, the file would need to read junkme or junkme@ *hostname*, where *hostname* is the computer's hostname. To do as option B describes, the leading vertical bar would have to be omitted. It's conceivable that the ~/junkme script does as option D describes, but there's no way of knowing this for certain. To do as option E describes, the file would have to read *user*@junkme, where *user* is the username. For more information, see Chapter 9.

LPIC-1®:

Linux Professional Institute Certification

Study Guide

Fourth Edition

Exam 101-400

Chapter

1

Exploring Linux Command-Line Tools

THE FOLLOWING EXAM OBJECTIVES ARE COVERED IN THIS CHAPTER:

✓ 103.1 Work on the command line

✓ 103.2 Process text streams using filters

✓ 103.4 Use streams, pipes, and redirects

✓ 103.7 Search text files using regular expressions

Linux borrows heavily from Unix, and Unix began as a text-based operating system (OS). Unix and Linux retain much of this heritage, which means to understand how to use and, especially administer Linux, you must understand at least the basics of its command-line tools. Using command-line tools requires the use of a shell. A *shell* is a program that accepts and interprets text-mode commands and provides an interface to the system.

This chapter begins with basic shell information, including the various shell programs available and the procedures for using them. From there, this chapter covers streams, pipes, and redirection, which you can use to move input and output between programs or between files and programs. These techniques are frequently combined with text processing using *filters*—commands you can use to manipulate text without the help of a conventional text editor. Sometimes you must manipulate text in an abstract way, using codes to represent several different types of text. This chapter, therefore, covers this topic as well.

Understanding Command-Line Basics

Before you do anything else with Linux, you should understand how to use a Linux shell. The shell allows you to enter commands as needed. Which commands can be entered depends on which shell program is running. Several of the available shell programs are briefly described.

In using shell commands, you should also understand shell *environment variables*, which are placeholders for data that may be useful to many programs. Finally, it is helpful to know how to get help with the shell commands you're trying to use.

Exploring Your Linux Shell Options

The shell to be used for entering commands is configured for each individual user, and Linux provides a range of available shells. A complete shell list would be quite long, but the following shells are among the more common choices:

bash   The GNU Bourne Again Shell (bash) is based on the earlier Bourne shell for Unix but extends it in several ways. In Linux, bash is the most common default shell for user accounts, and it's the one emphasized in this book and on the exam.

sh   The Bourne shell upon which bash is based goes by the name sh. It's not often used in Linux and the sh command is often a pointer to the bash shell or other shells.

tcsh   This shell is based on the earlier C shell (csh). It's a fairly popular shell in some circles, but no major Linux distributions make it the default shell. Although it's similar to bash in many respects, some operational details differ. For instance, you don't assign environment variables the same way in tcsh as in bash.

csh   The original C shell isn't used much on Linux, but if a user is familiar with csh, tcsh makes a good substitute.

ksh   The Korn shell (ksh) was designed to take the best features of the Bourne shell and the C shell and extend them. It has a small but dedicated following among Linux users.

zsh   The Z shell (zsh) takes shell evolution further than the Korn shell, incorporating features from earlier shells and adding still more.

In addition to these shells, dozens more obscure ones are available. In Linux, most users run bash because it is the most popular shell. Some other OSs use csh or tcsh as the default, so if your users have backgrounds on non-Linux Unix-like OSs, they may be more familiar with these other shells. You can change a user's default shell by editing their account, as described in Chapter 7, "Administering the System."

Be aware that there are two types of default shells. The *default interactive shell* is the shell program a user uses to enter commands, run programs from the command line, run shell scripts, and so on. The other default shell type is a default *system* shell. The *default system shell* is used by the Linux system to run system shell scripts, typically at startup.

The file /bin/sh is a pointer to the system's default system shell—normally /bin/bash for Linux. However, be aware that, on some distributions, the /bin/sh points to a different shell. For example, on Ubuntu, /bin/sh points to the dash shell, /bin/dash.

Using a Shell

Linux shell use is fairly straightforward for anybody who's used a text-mode OS before: You type a command, possibly including options to it, and the computer executes the command. For the most part, Linux commands are external—that is, they're programs that are separate from the shell.

A few commands are internal to the shell, though, and knowing the distinction can be important. You should also know some of the tricks that can make using the command shell easier—how to have the computer complete a long command or filename, retrieve a command you've recently run, or edit a command you've recently used (or haven't yet fully entered).

Starting a Shell

If you log into Linux using a text-mode login screen, you have logged into a virtual console terminal and, most likely, you'll be dropped directly into your default shell. The shell program is what presents the prompt and accepts subsequent commands.

If you log into Linux using a graphical user interface (GUI) login screen, you'll have to start a terminal emulator manually in order to reach your default shell. Some GUIs provide a menu option, such as xterm or terminal, to start a terminal emulator program. These programs enable you to run text-mode programs within Linux, and by default they come up running your shell. If you can't find such a menu option, look for a menu option that enables you to run an arbitrary command. Select it, and type **xterm** or **konsole** as the command name. This will launch a terminal emulator program that will run a shell.

Once you start a terminal or log into a virtual console terminal, the shell will provide you with a prompt for entering commands. Remember that the shell is a program providing you with an interface to the Linux system.

A good first command to try, uname, will show what operating system is being run:

```
$ uname
Linux
$
```

That's not too interesting. You can find out additional information by tacking on the -a option to the command. Be sure to include the necessary space between the command and the option:

```
$ uname -a
Linux server01.class.com 2.6.32-431.5.1.el6.x86_64 #1 SMP Wed Feb 12
00:41:43 UTC 2014 x86_64 x86_64 x86_64 GNU/Linux
$
```

The uname -a command provides a lot more information, including the current Linux kernel being used (2.6.32) as well as the system's hostname (server01.class.com). The uname command is an external command. The shell also provides internal commands. It's important to know the difference between the two command types, as explained in the next section.

Using Internal and External Commands

Internal commands are, as you might expect, built into the shell program. Thus they are also called *built-in commands*. Most shells offer a similar set of internal commands, but shell-to-shell differences do exist. Internal commands that you're likely to use enable you to perform some common tasks:

Change the Working Directory   Whenever you're running a shell, you're working in a specific directory. The cd command changes the current working directory. For instance, typing **cd /home/sally** changes the current working directory to the /home/sally directory.

You can use shortcut characters with the cd command as well. The tilde (~) character is a useful shortcut; it stands for your home directory. Thus typing **cd ~** will have the same effect as typing **cd /home/sally** if your home directory is /home/sally.

Display the Working Directory   The pwd command displays ("prints" to the screen) the current working directory. This command is helpful, especially after you have changed your working directory, to ensure you ended up in the right place.

Display a Line of Text   The echo command displays the text you enter. For instance, typing **echo Hello** causes the system to display the string Hello. This may seem pointless, but it's useful in scripts (described in Chapter 9, "Writing Scripts, Configuring Email, and Using Databases"), and it can also be a good way to review the contents of environment variables (described later in this chapter, in the section "Using Environment Variables").

Time an Operation   The time command times how long subsequent commands take to execute. For instance, typing **time pwd** tells you how long the system took to execute the pwd command. The time is displayed after the full command terminates. Three times are displayed: total execution time (aka real time), user CPU time, and system CPU time. The final two values tell you about CPU time consumed, which is likely to be much less than the total execution time.

Set Options   In its most basic form, the set command displays a wide variety of options relating to bash shell operation. These options are formatted much like environment variables, but they aren't the same things. You can pass various options to set to have it affect a wide range of shell operations.

Terminate the Shell   The exit and logout commands both terminate the shell. The exit command terminates any shell, but the logout command terminates only *login shells*. Login shells are shell programs that are launched automatically when you initiate a text-mode login as opposed to those that run in xterm windows or other terminal emulators.

 The preceding list isn't complete. Later sections of this chapter and later chapters describe some additional internal commands. Consult your shell's documentation for a complete list of its internal commands.

You can quickly determine if a command is a built-in command by using the type command. Just enter the command type before the name of the command you wish to check:

```
$ type pwd
pwd is a shell builtin
$
$ type cd
cd is a shell builtin
$
$ type bash
bash is /bin/bash
$
```

Some of these internal commands are duplicated by external commands that do the same thing. But those external commands aren't always installed on all systems. You can see if there are internal commands with installed duplicate external commands by using the -a option on the type command:

```
$ type -a cd
cd is a shell builtin
```

```
$
$ type -a pwd
pwd is a shell builtin
pwd is /bin/pwd
$
```

You can see that on this system, there is no external cd command installed. However, it does have an external pwd command installed.

Keep in mind that even when external commands are installed, the internal command takes precedence. To access the external command, you must provide the complete external command path, as in typing **/usr/bin/time** rather than **time**.

 Real World Scenario

Confusion over Internal and External Commands

When duplicate internal and external commands exist, they sometimes produce subtly different results or accept different options. These differences may occasionally cause problems if you are unaware of them. For example, the time built-in command returns slightly different results than the /usr/bin/time external command:

```
$ time pwd
/home/Christine

real    0m0.002s
user    0m0.002s
sys     0m0.001s
$
$ /usr/bin/time  pwd
/home/Christine
0.00user 0.00system 0:00.04elapsed 24%CPU
 (0avgtext+0avgdata 2336maxresident)k
56inputs+0outputs (1major+173minor)pagefaults 0swaps
$
```

As you can see, bash's internal time shows the time to execute the pwd command in a very nice format, while the external time command /usr/bin/time is not only a little sloppy in appearance, it also provides additional details. Be mindful of the potential behavior differences between internal and external commands.

When you type a command that's not recognized by the shell as one of its internal commands, the shell checks its path to find a program by that name to execute it. The *path* is a list of directories in which commands can be found. It's defined by the $PATH environment variable, as described shortly in "Using Environment Variables." A typical user account has about half a dozen or so directories in its path. You can add and remove directories to the shell's path by changing the $PATH environment variable in a shell configuration file, as described in "Exploring Shell Configuration" later in this chapter.

You can run programs that aren't on the path by providing a complete path name on the command line. For instance, typing **./myprog** runs the myprog program in the current directory. Typing **/home/arthur/thisprog** runs the thisprog program in the /home/arthur directory.

> **WARNING**   The root account should normally have a shorter path than ordinary user accounts. Typically, you'll omit directories that store GUI and other user-oriented programs from root's path in order to discourage use of the root account for routine operations. This minimizes the risk of security breaches related to buggy or compromised binaries being run by root. Most important, root's path should never include the current directory (./). Placing this directory in root's path makes it possible for a local troublemaker to trick root into running replacements for common programs. Omitting the current directory from ordinary user paths is also generally a good idea. If this directory must be part of the ordinary user path, it should appear at the end of the path so that the standard programs take precedence over any replacement programs in the current directory.

Whether you need to enter the path or not for a command, the program file must be marked as executable. This is done via the execute bit that's stored with the file. Standard programs are marked as executable when they're installed, but if you need to adjust a program's executable status, you can do so with the chmod command, as described in Chapter 4, "Managing Files."

Performing Some Shell Command Tricks

Many users find typing commands to be tedious and error-prone. This is particularly true of slow or sloppy typists. For this reason, Linux shells include various tools that can help speed up operations. The first of these is *command completion*: Type part of a command or a filename (as an option to the command), and then press the Tab key. The shell tries to fill in the rest of the command or the filename. If just one command or filename matches the characters you've typed so far, the shell fills the rest of the command (or filename) for you and adds a space after it.

If the characters you've typed don't uniquely identify a command (or filename), the shell fills in what it can and then stops. Depending on the shell and its configuration, it may beep. If you press the Tab key again, the system responds by displaying the possible completions. You can then type another character or two and, if you haven't completed the command (or filename), press the Tab key again to have the process repeat.

The most fundamental Linux commands have fairly short names—mv, ls, set, and so on. However, some other commands are much longer, such as traceroute or service --status-all. Filenames can also be quite lengthy—up to 255 characters on many filesystems. Thus command completion can save a lot of time when you're typing. It can also help you avoid typos.

> The most popular Linux shells, including bash and tcsh, support command and filename completion. Some older shells, though, don't support this helpful feature.

Another useful shell shortcut is *history*. The shell history keeps a record of every command you type. If you've typed a long command recently and want to use it again or use a minor variant of it, you can pull the command out of the history.

There are several rather easy methods to retrieve commands. It comes down to determining the method you like best:

Retrieve a Command   The simplest way to do this is to press the Up arrow key on your keyboard; this brings up the previous command. Pressing the Up arrow key repeatedly moves through multiple commands so you can find the one you want. If you overshoot, press the Down arrow key to move down the history. The Ctrl+P and Ctrl+N keystrokes double for the Up and Down arrow keys, respectively.

Search for a Command   Press Ctrl+R to begin a backward (reverse) search, and begin typing characters that should be unique to the command you want to find. The characters you type need not be the ones that begin the command; they can exist anywhere in the command. You can either keep typing until you find the correct command or, after you've typed a few characters, press Ctrl+R repeatedly until you find the one you want.

The Ctrl+S keystroke is used to search forward in the command history. You can press the Ctrl+S keystroke *while* using the backward search. This reverses the history search from backward to forward. If you used a backward search and have passed by what you need, then this keystroke is useful.

> If the Ctrl+S keystroke causes your terminal to hang, press Ctrl+Q to resume terminal operations. To keep your terminal from hanging when Ctrl+S is used, type **stty -ixon** at the command line.

In either event, if you can't find the command you want or if you change your mind and want to terminate the search, press Ctrl+G to do so.

Frequently, after finding a command in the history, you want to edit it. The bash shell, like many shells, provides editing features modeled after those of the Emacs editor:

Move within the Line   Press Ctrl+A or Ctrl+E to move the cursor to the start or end of the line, respectively. The Left and Right arrow keys move within the line a character at a time. Ctrl+B and Ctrl+F do the same, moving backward and forward within a line. Pressing Ctrl plus the Left or Right arrow key moves backward or forward a word at a time, as does pressing Esc and then B or F.

Delete Text Pressing Ctrl+D or the Delete key deletes the character under the cursor. Pressing the Backspace key deletes the character to the left of the cursor. Pressing Ctrl+K deletes all text from the cursor to the end of the line. Pressing Ctrl+X and then Backspace deletes all of the text from the cursor to the beginning of the line.

Transpose Text Pressing Ctrl+T transposes the character before the cursor with the character under the cursor. Pressing Esc and then T transposes the two words immediately before (or under) the cursor.

Change Case Pressing Esc and then U converts text from the cursor to the end of the word to uppercase. Pressing Esc and then L converts text from the cursor to the end of the word to lowercase. Pressing Esc and then C converts the letter under the cursor (or the first letter of the next word) to uppercase, leaving the rest of the word unaffected.

Invoke an Editor You can launch a full-fledged editor to edit a command by pressing Ctrl+X followed by Ctrl+E. The bash shell attempts to launch the editor defined by the $FCEDIT or $EDITOR environment variable, or it launches Emacs as a last resort.

These editing commands are just the most useful ones supported by bash. In practice, you're likely to make heavy use of command and filename completion, the command history, and perhaps a few editing features.

> If you prefer the vi editor to Emacs, you can use a vi-like mode in bash by typing **set -o vi**. (vi is described in Chapter 5, "Booting Linux and Editing Files.")

The history command provides an interface to view and manage the history. Typing **history** alone displays all of the commands in the history (typically the latest 500 commands).

To retrieve the last command in your shell history, type **!!** and press Enter. This will not only show you the command you recalled but execute it as well:

```
$ !!
type -a pwd
pwd is a shell builtin
pwd is /bin/pwd
$
```

You can execute a command by number via typing an exclamation mark followed by its number, as in **!210** to execute command 210. Typing **history -c** clears the history, which can be handy if you've recently typed commands you'd rather not have discovered by others, such as commands that include passwords.

The bash history is stored in the .bash_history file in your home directory. This is an ordinary plain-text file, so you can view it with a text editor or a command such as less (described later, in "Paging through Files with less").

WARNING   Because your bash history is stored in a file, it can be examined by anybody who can read that file. Some commands enable you to type passwords or other sensitive data on the same line as the commands themselves, which can therefore be risky. The ~/.bash_history file does *not* record what you type in response to other programs' prompts, just what you type at the bash prompt itself. Thus, if you have a choice, you should let commands that require passwords (or other sensitive data) prompt you to enter this data rather than enter such information as options to the command at the bash prompt.

In Exercise 1.1, you'll experiment with your shell's completion and command-editing tools.

EXERCISE 1.1

Editing Commands

To experiment with your shell's completion and command-editing tools, follow these steps:

1. Log in as an ordinary user.

2. Create a temporary directory by typing **mkdir test**. (Directory and file manipulation commands are described in more detail in Chapter 4.)

3. Change into the test directory by typing **cd test**.

4. Create a few temporary files by typing **touch one two three**. This command creates three empty files named one, two, and three.

5. Type **ls -l t** and, without pressing the Enter key, press the Tab key. The system may beep at you or display two three. If it doesn't display two three, press the Tab key again and it should do so. This reveals that either two or three is a valid completion to your command, because these are the two files in the test directory whose filenames begin with the letter t.

6. Type **h**, and again without pressing the Enter key, press the Tab key. The system should complete the command (ls -l three), at which point you can press the Enter key to execute it. (You'll see information on the file.)

7. Press the Up arrow key. You should see the ls -l three command appear on the command line.

8. Press Ctrl+A to move the cursor to the beginning of the line.

9. Press the Right arrow key once, and type **es** (without pressing the Enter key). The command line should now read less -l three.

10. Press the Right arrow key once, and press the Delete key three times. The command should now read less three. Press the Enter key to execute the command. (Note that you can do so even though the cursor isn't at the end of the line.) This invokes the less pager on the three file. (The less pager is described more fully later in

"Paging through Files with less.") Because this file is empty, you'll see a mostly empty screen.

11. Press the Q key to exit from the less pager.

Exploring Shell Configuration

Shells, like many Linux programs, are configured through files that hold configuration options in a plain-text format. The bash configuration files are actually bash shell scripts, which are described more fully in Chapter 9. A couple of examples of these configuration files are ~/.bashrc and /etc/profile.

Even without knowing much about shell scripting, you can make simple changes to these files. Edit them in your favorite text editor, and change whatever needs changing. For instance, you can add directories to the $PATH environment variable, which takes a colon-delimited list of directories.

 Be careful when changing your bash configuration files, particularly the global bash configuration files. Save a backup of the original file before making changes, and test your changes immediately by logging in using another virtual terminal. If you spot a problem, revert to your saved copy until you determine the problem's causes and create a working file.

Using Environment Variables

Environment variables are like variables in programming languages—they hold data to be referred to by the variable name. Environment variables differ from programs' internal variables in that they're part of the program's environment, and other programs, such as the shell, can modify this environment. Programs can rely on environment variables to set information that can apply to many different programs. For instance, many text-based programs need to know the capabilities of the terminal program you use. This information is conveyed in the $TERM environment variable, which is likely to hold a value such as xterm or linux. Programs that need to position the cursor, display color text, or perform other tasks that depend on terminal-specific capabilities can customize their output based on this information.

Chapter 9 describes environment variables and their manipulation in more detail. For the moment, you should know that you can set them in bash by using an assignment (=) operator followed by the export command. A fun environment variable to change is the $PS1 variable. It modifies your shell prompt:

```
$
$ PS1="My New Prompt: "
My New Prompt: export PS1
My New Prompt:
```

You can combine these two commands into a single form:

```
My New Prompt: export PS1="Prompt: "
Prompt:
Prompt:
```

Either method sets the $PS1 environment variable to a new setting. When setting an environment variable, you omit the dollar sign, but subsequent references include a dollar sign to identify the environment variable as such. Thereafter, programs that need this information can refer to the environment variable. In fact, you can do so from the shell yourself using the echo command:

```
$ Prompt: echo $PS1
Prompt:
```

An echo of the $PS1 variable value can be a little confusing because it just shows your current prompt setting. However, you can get a better feel for displaying an environment variable by viewing the $PATH variable using echo:

```
Prompt: echo $PATH
/usr/lib64/qt-3.3/bin:/usr/local/bin:/bin:/usr/bin:
/usr/local/sbin:/usr/sbin:/sbin:/home/Christine/bin
Prompt:
```

That's a little better. Remember, the $PATH environment variable provides the shell with a directory list to search when you're entering command or program names.

Some environment variables, including the $PATH environment variable, are set automatically when you log in via the shell configuration files. If a program uses environment variables, its documentation should say so.

You can also view the entire environment by typing **env**. The result is likely to be several dozen lines of environment variables and their values. Chapter 9 describes what many of these variables are in more detail.

To delete an environment variable, use the unset command. The command takes the name of an environment variable (without the leading $ symbol) as an option. For instance, **unset PS1** removes the $PS1 environment variable. But if you do this, you will have no shell prompt!

Getting Help

Linux provides a text-based help system known as man. This command's name is short for *manual*, and its entries (its man pages) provide succinct summaries of what a command, file, or other feature does. For instance, to learn about man itself, you can type **man man**. The result is a description of the man command.

To peruse the manual pages for a particular command or topic, you type **man** followed by the command or topic as an option. For example, to read about the export command, you would type **man export** at the prompt. If you wanted to learn more about the shell built-in (internal) commands, you would type **man builtin** at the prompt.

The man utility uses the less pager by default to display information. This program displays text a page at a time. Press the spacebar to move forward a page, Esc followed by V to move back a page, the arrow keys to move up or down a line at a time, the slash (/) key to search for text, and so on. (Type **man less** to learn all the details, or consult the upcoming section "Paging through Files with less.") When you're done, press Q to exit less and the man page it's displaying.

You aren't stuck using the less pager with the man utility. You can change the pager by using the -P option. For example, if you decided to use the more pager instead to look up information on the uname command, you would type **man -P /bin/more uname** at the shell prompt.

Occasionally, the problem arises where you can't remember the exact name of a command to look up. The man utility has an option to help you here. You can use the -k option along with a keyword or two to search through the man pages:

```
$ man -k "system information"
dumpe2fs  (8)  - dump ext2/ext3/ext4 filesystem information
[…]
uname     (1)  - print system information
$
```

The returned information (shown as a partial listing above) can give you some clues as to your desired command name. Be aware that poor keyword choices may not produce the results you seek.

> On some older Linux distributions, you may get no results from a man utility keyword search. This is most likely due to a missing whatis database. The *whatis database* contains a short description of each man page, and it is necessary for keyword searches. To create it or update it, type **makewhatis** at the prompt. You will need to do this as superuser, and it may take several minutes to run.

Linux man pages are organized into several sections, which are summarized in Table 1.1. Sometimes a single keyword has entries in multiple sections. For instance, passwd has entries under both section 1 and section 5. In most cases, man returns the entry in the lowest-numbered section, but you can force the issue by preceding the keyword by the section number. For instance, typing **man 5 passwd** returns information on the passwd file format rather than the passwd command.

TABLE 1.1 Manual sections

Section number	Description
1	Executable programs and shell commands
2	System calls provided by the kernel
3	Library calls provided by program libraries
4	Device files (usually stored in /dev)
5	File formats
6	Games
7	Miscellaneous (macro packages, conventions, and so on)
8	System administration commands (programs run mostly or exclusively by root)
9	Kernel routines

Some programs have moved away from man pages to info pages. The basic purpose of info pages is the same as that for man pages. However, info pages use a hypertext format so that you can move from section to section of the documentation for a program. Type **info info** to learn more about this system.

There are also pages specifically for the built-in (internal) commands called the help pages. To read the help pages for a particular built-in command, type **help command**. For instance, to get help on the pwd command, type **help pwd** at the shell prompt. To learn more about how to use the help pages, type **help help** at the shell prompt.

The man pages, info pages, and help pages are usually written in a terse style. They're intended as reference tools, not tutorials! They frequently assume basic familiarity with the command, or at least with Linux in general. For more tutorial information, you must look elsewhere, such in books or on the Web.

Using Streams, Redirection, and Pipes

Streams, redirection, and *pipes* are some of the more powerful command-line tools in Linux. Linux treats the input to and output from programs as a stream, which is a data entity that can be manipulated. Ordinarily, input comes from the keyboard and output goes to the screen. You can redirect these input and output streams to come from or go to other sources, such as files. Similarly, you can pipe the output of one program as input into another program. These facilities can be great tools to tie together multiple programs.

Part of the Unix philosophy to which Linux adheres is, whenever possible, to do complex things by combining multiple simple tools. Redirection and pipes help in this task by enabling simple programs to be combined together in chains, each link feeding off the output of the preceding link.

Exploring File Descriptors

To begin understanding redirection and pipes, you must first understand the different *file descriptors*. Linux handles all objects as files. This includes a program's input and output stream. To identify a particular file object, Linux uses file descriptors:

Standard Input   Programs accept keyboard input via *standard input*, abbreviated STDIN. Standard input's file descriptor is 0 (zero). In most cases, this is the data that comes into the computer from a keyboard.

Standard Output   Text-mode programs send most data to their users via *standard output*, abbreviated STDOUT. Standard output is normally displayed on the screen, either in a full-screen text-mode session or in a GUI terminal emulator, such as an xterm. Standard output's file descriptor is 1 (one).

Standard Error   Linux provides a second type of output stream, known as *standard error*, abbreviated STDERR. Standard error's file descriptor is 2 (two). This output stream is intended to carry high-priority information such as error messages. Ordinarily, standard error is sent to the same output device as standard output, so you can't easily tell them apart. You can redirect one independently of the other, though, which can be handy. For instance, you can redirect standard error to a file while leaving standard output going to the screen. This allows you to view the error messages at a later time.

Internally, programs treat STDIN, STDOUT, and STDERR just like data files—they open them, read from or write to the files, and close them when they're done. This is why the file descriptors are necessary and why they can be used in redirection.

Redirecting Input and Output

To redirect input or output, you use operators following the command, including any options it takes. For instance, to redirect the STDOUT of the echo command, you would type something like this:

```
$ echo $PATH 1> path.txt
$
$ cat path.txt
/usr/lib64/qt-3.3/bin:/usr/local/bin:/bin:/usr/bin:
/usr/local/sbin:/usr/sbin:/sbin:/home/Christine/bin
$
```

The result is that the file path.txt contains the output of the command (in this case, the value of the $PATH environment variable). The operator used to perform this redirection was > and the file descriptor used to redirect STDOUT was 1 (one).

The cat command allows you to display a file's contents to STDOUT. It is described further in the section "Processing Text Using Filters" later in this chapter.

A nice feature of redirecting STDOUT is that you do not have to use its file descriptor, only the operator. Here's an example of leaving out the 1 (one) file descriptor, when redirecting STDOUT:

```
$ echo $PATH > another_path.txt
$
$ cat another_path.txt
/usr/lib64/qt-3.3/bin:/usr/local/bin:/bin:/usr/bin:
/usr/local/sbin:/usr/sbin:/sbin:/home/Christine/bin
$
```

You can see that even without the STDOUT file descriptor, the output was redirected to a file. However, the redirection operator (>) was still needed.

You can also leave out the STDIN file descriptor when using the appropriate redirection operator. Redirection operators exist to achieve several effects, as summarized in Table 1.2.

TABLE 1.2 Common redirection operators

Redirection operator	Effect
>	Creates a new file containing standard output. If the specified file exists, it's overwritten. No file descriptor necessary.
>>	Appends standard output to the existing file. If the specified file doesn't exist, it's created. No file descriptor necessary.
2>	Creates a new file containing standard error. If the specified file exists, it's overwritten. File descriptor necessary.
2>>	Appends standard error to the existing file. If the specified file doesn't exist, it's created. File descriptor necessary.
&>	Creates a new file containing both standard output and standard error. If the specified file exists, it's overwritten. No file descriptors necessary.
<	Sends the contents of the specified file to be used as standard input. No file descriptor necessary.
<<	Accepts text on the following lines as standard input. No file descriptor necessary.
<>	Causes the specified file to be used for both standard input and standard output. No file descriptor necessary.

Most of these redirectors deal with output, both because there are two types of output (standard output and standard error) and because you must be concerned with what to do in case you specify a file that already exists. The most important input redirector is <, which takes the specified file's contents as standard input.

 A common trick is to redirect standard output or standard error to /dev/null. This file is a device that's connected to nothing; it's used when you want to get rid of data. For instance, if the whine program is generating too many unimportant error messages, you can type **whine 2> /dev/null** to run it and discard its error messages.

One redirection operator that requires elaboration is the << operator. This operator implements something called a *here document*. A *here document* takes text from subsequent lines as standard input. Chances are you won't use this redirector on the command line. Subsequent lines *are* standard input, so there's no need to redirect them. Rather, you might use this command in a script to pass data to an interactive program. Unlike with most redirection operators, the text immediately following the << code isn't a filename; instead, it's a word that's used to mark the end of input. For instance, typing **someprog << EOF** causes someprog to accept input until it sees a line that contains *only* the string EOF (without even a space following it).

 Some programs that take input from the command line expect you to terminate input by pressing Ctrl+D. This keystroke corresponds to an end-of-file marker using the American Standard Code for Information Interchange (ASCII).

Piping Data between Programs

Programs can frequently operate on other programs' outputs. For instance, you might use a text-filtering command (such as the ones described shortly in "Processing Text Using Filters") to manipulate text output by another program. You can do this with the help of redirection operators: send the first program's standard output to a file, and then redirect the second program's standard input to read from that file. This method is awkward, though, and it involves the creation of a file that you might easily overlook, leading to unnecessary clutter on your system.

The solution is to use data pipes (aka pipelines). A pipe redirects the first program's standard output to the second program's standard input, and it is denoted by a vertical bar (|):

```
$ first | second
```

For instance, suppose that *first* generates some system statistics, such as system uptime, CPU use, number of users logged in, and so on. This output might be lengthy, so you want to trim it a bit. You might therefore use *second*, which could be a script or command that echoes from its standard input only the information in which you're interested. (The grep command, described in "Using grep," is often used in this role.)

Pipes can be used in sequences of arbitrary length:

```
$ first | second | third | fourth | fifth | sixth [...]
```

Another redirection tool often used with pipes is the tee command. This command splits standard input so that it's displayed on standard output and in as many files as you specify. Typically, tee is used in conjunction with data pipes so that a program's output can be both stored and viewed immediately. For instance, to view and store the output of the echo $PATH command, you might type this:

```
$ echo $PATH | tee path.txt
/usr/lib64/qt-3.3/bin:/usr/local/bin:/bin:/usr/bin:
/usr/local/sbin:/usr/sbin:/sbin:/home/Christine/bin
$
$ cat path.txt
/usr/lib64/qt-3.3/bin:/usr/local/bin:/bin:/usr/bin:
/usr/local/sbin:/usr/sbin:/sbin:/home/Christine/bin
$
```

Notice that not only were the results of the command displayed to STDOUT, but they were also redirected to the path.txt file by the tee command. Ordinarily, tee overwrites any files whose names you specify. If you want to append data to these files, pass the -a option to tee.

Generating Command Lines

Sometimes you'll find yourself needing to conduct an unusual operation on your Linux server. For instance, suppose you want to remove every file in a directory tree that belongs to a certain user. With a large directory tree, this task can be daunting!

The usual file-deletion command, rm (described in more detail in Chapter 4), doesn't provide an option to search for and delete every file that matches a specific criterion. One command that can do the search portion is find (also described in more detail in Chapter 4). This command displays all of the files that match the criteria you provide. If you could combine the output of find to create a series of command lines using rm, the task would be solved. This is precisely the purpose of the xargs command.

The xargs command builds a command from its standard input. The basic syntax for this command is as follows:

```
xargs [options] [command [initial-arguments]]
```

The *command* is the command you want to execute, and *initial-arguments* is a list of arguments you want to pass to the command. The *options* are xargs options; they aren't passed to *command*. When you run xargs, it runs *command* once for every word passed to it on standard input, adding that word to the argument list for *command*. If you want to pass multiple options to the command, you can protect them by enclosing the group in quotation marks.

For instance, consider the task of deleting several files that belong to a particular user. You can do this by piping the output of find to xargs, which then calls rm:

```
# find / -user Christine | xargs -d "\n" rm
```

The first part of this command (find / -user Christine) finds all of the files in directory tree (/) and its subdirectories that belong to user Christine. (Since you are looking through the entire directory tree, you need superuser privileges for this to work properly.) This list is then piped to xargs, which adds each input value to its own rm command. Problems can arise if filenames contain spaces because by default xargs uses both spaces and newlines as item delimiters. The -d "\n" option tells xargs to use only newlines as delimiters, thus avoiding this problem in this context. (The find command separates each found filename with a newline.)

It is important to exercise caution when using the rm command with superuser privileges. This is especially true when piping the files to delete into the rm command. You could easily delete the wrong files unintentionally.

A tool that's similar to xargs in many ways is the backtick (`` ` ``), which is a character to the left of the 1 key on most keyboards. The backtick is *not* the same as the single quote character ('), which is located to the right of the semicolon (;) on most keyboards.

Text within backticks is treated as a separate command whose results are substituted on the command line. For instance, to delete those user files, you can type the following command:

```
# rm `find ./ -user Christine`
```

The backtick solution works fine in some cases, but it breaks down in more complex situations. The reason is that the output of the backtick-contained command is passed to the command it precedes as if it had been typed at the shell. By contrast, when you use xargs, it runs the command you specify (rm in these examples) once for each of the input items. What's more, you can't pass options such as -d "\n" to a backtick. Thus these two examples will work the same in many cases, but not in all of them.

Use of the backtick is falling out of favor because backticks are so often confused with single quotation marks. In several shells, you can use $() instead. For instance, the backtick example used in the preceding example would be changed to

```
# rm $(find ./ -user Christine)
```

This command works just as well, and it is much easier to read and understand.

Processing Text Using Filters

In keeping with Linux's philosophy of providing small tools that can be tied together via pipes and redirection to accomplish more complex tasks, many simple commands to manipulate text are available. These commands accomplish tasks of various types, such as combining files, transforming the data in files, formatting text, displaying text, and summarizing data.

 Many of the following descriptions include input-file specifications. In most cases, you can omit these input-file specifications, in which case the utility reads from standard input instead.

File-Combining Commands

The first text-filtering commands are those used to combine two or more files into one file. Three important commands in this category are cat, join, and paste, which join files end to end based on fields in the file or by merging on a line-by-line basis.

Combining Files with *cat*

The cat command's name is short for *concatenate*, and this tool does just that: It links together an arbitrary number of files end to end and sends the result to standard output. By combining cat with output redirection, you can quickly combine two files into one:

```
$ cat first.txt second.txt > combined.txt
$
$ cat first.txt
Data from first file.
$
$ cat second.txt
Data from second file.
$
$ cat combined.txt
Data from first file.
Data from second file.
$
```

Although cat is officially a tool for combining files, it's also commonly used to display the contents of a short file to STDOUT. If you type only one filename as an option, cat displays that file. This is a great way to review short files; but for long files, you're better off using a full-fledged pager command, such as more or less.

You can add options to have `cat` perform minor modifications to the files as it combines them:

Display Line Ends   If you want to see where lines end, add the `-E` or `--show-ends` option. The result is a dollar sign ($) at the end of each line.

Number Lines   The `-n` or `--number` option adds line numbers to the beginning of every line. The `-b` or `--number-nonblank` option is similar, but it numbers only lines that contain text.

Minimize Blank Lines   The `-s` or `--squeeze-blank` option compresses groups of blank lines down to a single blank line.

Display Special Characters   The `-T` or `--show-tabs` option displays tab characters as `^I`. The `-v` or `--show-nonprinting` option displays most control and other special characters using carat (`^`) and `M-` notations.

The `tac` command is similar to `cat`, but it reverses the order of lines in the output:

```
$ cat combined.txt
Data from first file.
Data from second file.
$
$ tac combined.txt
Data from second file.
Data from first file.
$
```

Joining Files by Field with *join*

The `join` command combines two files by matching the contents of specified fields within the files. Fields are typically space-separated entries on a line. However, you can specify another character as the field separator with the `-t` *char* option, where *char* is the character you want to use. You can cause `join` to ignore case when performing comparisons by using the `-i` option.

The effect of `join` may best be understood through a demonstration. Consider Listing 1.1 and Listing 1.2, which contain data on telephone numbers. Listing 1.1 shows the names associated with those numbers, and Listing 1.2 shows whether the numbers are listed or unlisted.

Listing 1.1: Demonstration file containing telephone numbers and names

```
555-2397 Beckett, Barry
555-5116 Carter, Gertrude
555-7929 Jones, Theresa
555-9871 Orwell, Samuel
```

Listing 1.2: Demonstration file containing telephone number listing status

```
555-2397 unlisted
555-5116 listed
555-7929 listed
555-9871 unlisted
```

You can display the contents of both files using join:

```
$ join listing1.1.txt listing1.2.txt
555-2397 Beckett, Barry unlisted
555-5116 Carter, Gertrude listed
555-7929 Jones, Theresa listed
555-9871 Orwell, Samuel unlisted
```

By default, join uses the first field as the one to match across files. Because Listing 1.1 and Listing 1.2 both place the phone number in this field, it's the key field in the output. You can specify another field by using the -1 or -2 option to indicate the join field for the first or second file, respectively. For example, type **join -1 3 -2 2 cameras.txt lenses.txt** to join using the third field in cameras.txt and the second field in lenses. txt. The -o *FORMAT* option enables more complex specifications for the output file's format. You can consult the man page for join for even more details.

The join command can be used at the core of a set of simple customized database-manipulation tools using Linux text-manipulation commands. It's very limited by itself, though. For instance, it requires its two files to have the same ordering of lines. (You can use the sort command to ensure this is so.)

Merging Lines with *paste*

The paste command merges files line by line, separating the lines from each file with tabs, as shown in the following example, using Listings 1.1 and 1.2 again:

```
$ paste listing1.1.txt listing1.2.txt
555-2397 Beckett, Barry     555-2397 unlisted
555-5116 Carter, Gertrude   555-5116 listed
555-7929 Jones, Theresa     555-7929 listed
555-9871 Orwell, Samuel     555-9871 unlisted
```

You can use paste to combine data from files that aren't keyed with fields suitable for use by join. Of course, to be meaningful, the files' line numbers must be exactly equivalent. Alternatively, you can use paste as a quick way to create a two-column output of textual data; however, the alignment of the second column may not be exact if the first column's line lengths aren't exactly even.

File-Transforming Commands

Many of Linux's text-manipulation commands are aimed at transforming the contents of files. These commands don't actually change files' contents but instead send the changed files' contents to standard output. You can then pipe this output to another command or redirect it into a new file.

> An important file-transforming command is sed. This command is very complex and is covered later in this chapter in "Using sed."

Converting Tabs to Spaces with *expand*

Sometimes text files contain tabs but programs that need to process the files don't cope well with tabs. In such a case, you may want to convert tabs to spaces. The expand command does this.

By default, expand assumes a tab stop every eight characters. You can change this spacing with the -t *num* or --tabs=*num* option, where *num* is the tab spacing value.

Displaying Files in Octal with *od*

Some files aren't easily displayed in ASCII. For example, most graphics files, audio files, and so on use non-ASCII characters that look like gibberish. Worse, these characters can do strange things to your display if you try to view such a file with cat or a similar tool. For instance, your font may change, or your console may begin beeping uncontrollably. Nonetheless, you may sometimes want to display such files, particularly if you want to investigate the structure of a data file.

In such a case, od (whose name stands for *octal dump*) can help. It displays a file in an unambiguous format—octal (base 8) numbers by default. For instance, consider Listing 1.2 as parsed by od:

```
$ od listing1.2.txt
0000000 032465 026465 031462 033471 072440 066156 071551 062564
0000020 005144 032465 026465 030465 033061 066040 071551 062564
0000040 005144 032465 026465 034467 034462 066040 071551 062564
0000060 005144 032465 026465 034071 030467 072440 066156 071551
0000100 062564 005144
0000104
```

The first field on each line is an index into the file in octal. For instance, the second line begins at octal 20 (16 in base 10) bytes into the file. The remaining numbers on each line represent the bytes in the file. This type of output can be difficult to interpret unless you're well versed in octal notation and perhaps in the ASCII code.

Although od is nominally a tool for generating octal output, it can generate many other output formats, such as hexadecimal (base 16), decimal (base 10), and even ASCII with escaped control characters. Consult the man page for od for details on creating these variants.

Sorting Files with *sort*

Sometimes you'll create an output file that you want sorted. To do so, you can use a command that's called, appropriately enough, sort. This command can sort in several ways, including the following:

Ignore Case   Ordinarily, sort sorts by ASCII value, which differentiates between upper-case and lowercase letters. The -f or --ignore-case option causes sort to ignore case.

Month Sort   The -M or --month-sort option causes the program to sort by three-letter month abbreviation (JAN through DEC).

Numeric Sort   You can sort by number by using the -n or --numeric-sort option.

Reverse Sort Order   The -r or --reverse option sorts in reverse order.

Sort Field   By default, sort uses the first field as its sort field. You can specify another field with the -k *field* or --key=*field* option. (The *field* can be two numbered fields separated by commas, to sort on multiple fields.)

As an example, suppose you wanted to sort Listing 1.1 by first name. You could do so like this:

```
$ sort -k 3 listing1.1.txt
555-2397 Beckett, Barry
555-5116 Carter, Gertrude
555-9871 Orwell, Samuel
555-7929 Jones, Theresa
```

The sort command supports a large number of additional options, many of them quite exotic. Consult sort's man page for details.

Breaking a File into Pieces with *split*

The split command can split a file into two or more files. Unlike most of the text-manipulation commands described in this chapter, this command requires you to enter an output filename or, more precisely, an output filename prefix, to which is added an alphabetic code. You must also normally specify how large you want the individual files to be:

Split by Bytes   The -b *size* or --bytes=*size* option breaks the input file into pieces of *size* bytes. This option can have the usually undesirable consequence of splitting the file mid-line.

Split by Bytes in Line-Sized Chunks   You can break a file into files of no more than a specified size without breaking lines across files by using the -C=*size* or --line-bytes=*size* option. (Lines will still be broken across files if the line length is greater than *size*.)

Split by Number of Lines   The -l *lines* or --lines=*lines* option splits the file into chunks with no more than the specified number of lines.

As an example, consider breaking Listing 1.1 into two parts by number of lines:

```
$ split -l 2 listing1.1.txt numbers
```

The result is two files, numbersaa and numbersab, which together hold the original contents of listing1.1.txt.

If you don't specify any defaults (as in **split listing1.1.txt**), the result is output files split into 1,000-line chunks, with names beginning with x (xaa, xab, and so on). If you don't specify an input filename, split uses standard input.

Translating Characters with *tr*

The tr command changes individual characters from standard input. Its syntax is as follows:

```
tr [options] SET1 [SET2]
```

You specify the characters you want replaced in a group (*SET1*) and the characters with which you want them to be replaced as a second group (*SET2*). Each character in *SET1* is replaced with the one at the equivalent position in *SET2*. Here's an example using Listing 1.1:

```
$ tr BCJ bc < listing1.1.txt
555-2397 beckett, barry
555-5116 carter, Gertrude
555-7929 cones, Theresa
555-9871 Orwell, Samuel
```

> The tr command relies on standard input, which is the reason for the input redirection (<) in this example. This is the only way to pass the command a file.

This example translates some, but not all, of the uppercase characters to lowercase. Note that *SET2* in this example was shorter than *SET1*. The result is that tr substitutes the last available letter from *SET2* for the missing letters. In this example, the J in Jones became a c. The -t or --truncate-set1 option causes tr to truncate *SET1* to the size of *SET2* instead.

Another tr option is -d, which causes the program to delete the characters from *SET1*. When using -d, you omit *SET2* entirely.

The tr command also accepts a number of shortcuts, such as [:alnum:] (all numbers and letters), [:upper:] (all uppercase letters), [:lower:] (all lowercase letters), and [:digit:] (all digits). You can specify a range of characters by separating them with dashes (-), as in A-M for characters between A and M, inclusive. Consult tr's man page for a complete list of these shortcuts.

Converting Spaces to Tabs with *unexpand*

The unexpand command is the logical opposite of expand; it converts multiple spaces to tabs. This can help compress the size of files that contain many spaces and can be helpful if a file is to be processed by a utility that expects tabs in certain locations.

Like expand, unexpand accepts the -t *num* or --tabs=*num* option, which sets the tab spacing to once every *num* characters. If you omit this option, unexpand assumes a tab stop every eight characters.

Deleting Duplicate Lines with *uniq*

The uniq command removes duplicate lines. It's most likely to be useful if you've sorted a file and don't want duplicate items. For instance, suppose you want to summarize Shakespeare's vocabulary. You might create a file with all of the Bard's works, one word per line. You can then sort this file using sort and pass it through uniq. Using a shorter example file containing the text to be or not to be, that is the question (one word per line), the result looks like this:

```
$ sort shakespeare.txt | uniq
be
is
not
or
question
that
the
to
```

Note that the words to and be, which appeared in the original file twice, appear only once in the uniq-processed version.

File-Formatting Commands

The next three commands—fmt, nl, and pr—reformat the text in a file. The first of these is designed to reformat text files, such as when a program's README documentation file uses lines that are too long for your display. The nl command numbers the lines of a file, which can be helpful in referring to lines in documentation or correspondence. Finally, pr is a print-processing tool; it formats a document in pages suitable for printing.

Reformatting Paragraphs with *fmt*

Sometimes text files arrive with outrageously long line lengths, irregular line lengths, or other problems. Depending on the difficulty, you may be able to cope simply by using an appropriate text editor or viewer to read the file. If you want to clean up the file a bit, though, you can do so with fmt. If called with no options (other than the input filename, if you're not having it work on standard input), the program attempts to clean up paragraphs, which it assumes are delimited by two or more blank lines or by changes in indentation. The new paragraph formatting defaults to paragraphs that are no more than 75 characters wide. You can change this with the -*width*, -w *width*, and --width=*width* options, which set the line length to *width* characters.

Numbering Lines with *nl*

As described earlier, in "Combining Files with cat," you can number the lines of a file with that command. The cat line-numbering options are limited, though, if you need to do complex line numbering. The nl command is the tool to use in this case. In its simplest form, you can use nl alone to accomplish much the same goal as cat -b achieves: numbering all the non-blank lines in a file. You can add many options to nl to achieve various special effects:

Body Numbering Style   You can set the numbering style for the bulk of the lines with the -b *style* or --body-numbering=*style* option, where *style* is a style format code, described shortly.

Header and Footer Numbering Style   If the text is formatted for printing and has headers or footers, you can set the style for these elements with the -h *style* or --header-numbering=*style* option for the header and -f *style* or --footer-numbering=*style* option for the footer.

Page Separator   Some numbering schemes reset the line numbers for each page. You can tell nl how to identify a new page with the -d=*code* or --section-delimiter=*code* option, where *code* is a code for the character that identifies the new page.

Line-Number Options for New Pages   Ordinarily, nl begins numbering each new page with line 1. If you pass the -p or --no-renumber option, though, it doesn't reset the line number with a new page.

Number Format   You can specify the numbering format with the -n *format* or --number-format=*format* option, where *format* is ln (left justified, no leading zeros), rn (right justified, no leading zeros), or rz (right justified with leading zeros).

The body, header, and footer options enable you to specify a numbering style for each of these page elements, as described in Table 1.3.

TABLE 1.3   Styles used by nl

Style code	Description
t	The default behavior is to number lines that aren't empty. You can make this default explicit by using a style code of t.
a	This style code causes all lines to be numbered, including empty lines.
n	This style code causes all line numbers to be omitted, which may be desirable for headers or footers.
p*REGEXP*	This option causes only lines that match the specified regular expression (*REGEXP*) to be numbered. Regular expressions are described later in "Using Regular Expressions."

As an example, suppose you've created a script, buggy, but you find that it's not working as you expect. When you run it, you get error messages that refer to line numbers, so you want to create a version of the script with lines that are numbered for easy reference. You can do so by calling nl with the option to number all lines, including blank lines (-b a):

```
$ nl -b a buggy > numbered-buggy.txt
```

 Because the input file doesn't have any explicit page delimiters, the output will be numbered in a single sequence. The nl command doesn't try to impose its own page-length limits.

The numbered-buggy.txt file created by this command isn't useful as a script because of the line numbers that begin each line. You can, however, load it into a text editor or display it with a pager such as less to view the text and see the line numbers along with the commands they contain.

Preparing a File for Printing with *pr*

If you want to print a plain-text file, you may want to prepare it with headers, footers, page breaks, and so on. The pr command was designed to do this. In its most basic form, you pass the command a file:

```
$ pr myfile.txt
```

The result is text formatted for printing on a line printer—that is, pr assumes an 80-character line length in a monospaced font. Of course, you can also use pr in a pipe, either to accept input piped from another program or to pipe its output to another program. (The recipient program might be lpr, which is used to print files, as described in Chapter 6, "Configuring the X Window System, Localization, and Printing.")

By default, pr creates output that includes the original text with headers, which lists the current date and time, the original filename, and the page number. You can tweak the output format in a variety of ways, including the following:

Generate Multicolumn Output   Passing the -*numcols* or --columns=*numcols* option creates output with *numcols* columns. For example, if you typed **pr -3 myfile.txt**, the output would be displayed in three columns. Note that pr doesn't reformat text; if lines are too long, they're truncated or run over into multiple columns.

Generate Double-Spaced Output   The -d or --double-space option causes double-spaced output from a single-spaced file.

Use Form Feeds   Ordinarily, pr separates pages by using a fixed number of blank lines. This works fine if your printer uses the same number of lines that pr expects. If you have problems with this issue, you can pass the -F, -f, or --form-feed option, which causes pr to output a form-feed character between pages. This works better with some printers.

Set Page Length   The -l *lines* or --length=*lines* option sets the length of the page in lines.

Set the Header Text   The `-h` *text* or `--header=`*text* option sets the text to be displayed in the header, replacing the filename. To specify a multi-word string, enclose it in quotes, as in `--header="My File"`. The `-t` or `--omit-header` option omits the header entirely.

Set Left Margin and Page Width   The `-o` *chars* or `--indent=`*chars* option sets the left margin to *chars* characters. This margin size is added to the page width, which defaults to 72 characters and can be explicitly set with the `-w` *chars* or `--width` *chars* option.

These options are just the beginning; pr supports many more options, which are described in its man page. As an example of pr in action, consider printing a double-spaced and numbered version of a configuration file (say, `/etc/profile`) for your reference. You can do this by piping together cat and its `-n` option to generate a numbered output, pr and its `-d` option to double-space the result, and lpr to print the file:

```
$ cat -n /etc/profile | pr -d | lpr
```

The result should be a printout that might be handy for taking notes on the configuration file. One caveat, though: If the file contains lines that approach or exceed 80 characters in length, the result can be single lines that spill across two lines. The result will be disrupted page boundaries. As a workaround, you can set a somewhat short page length with `-l` and use `-f` to ensure that the printer receives form feeds after each page:

```
$ cat -n /etc/profile | pr -dfl 50 | lpr
```

The pr command is built around assumptions about printer capabilities that were reasonable in the early 1980s. It's still useful today, but you might prefer to look into GNU Enscript (www.codento.com/people/mtr/genscript/). This program has many of the same features as pr, but it generates Post-Script output that can take better advantage of modern printer features.

File-Viewing Commands

Sometimes you just want to view a file or part of a file. A few commands can help you accomplish this goal without loading the file into a full-fledged editor.

As described earlier, the cat command is also handy for viewing short files.

Viewing the Starts of Files with *head*

Sometimes all you need to do is see the first few lines of a file. This may be enough to identify what a mystery file is, for instance; or you may want to see the first few entries of a log file to determine when that file was started. You can accomplish this goal with the head command, which echoes the first 10 lines of one or more files to standard output. (If you specify multiple filenames, each one's output is preceded by a header to identify it.) You can modify the amount of information displayed by head in two ways:

Specify the Number of Bytes   The -c *num* or --bytes=*num* option tells head to display *num* bytes from the file rather than the default 10 lines.

Specify the Number of Lines   You can change the number of lines displayed with the -n *num* or --lines=*num* option.

Viewing the Ends of Files with *tail*

The tail command works just like head, except that tail displays the *last* 10 lines of a file. (You can use the -c or --bytes, and -n or --lines options to change the amount of data displayed, just as with head.) This command is useful for examining recent activity in log files or other files to which data may be appended.

The tail command supports several options that aren't present in head and that enable the program to handle additional duties, including the following:

Track a File   The -f or --follow option tells tail to keep the file open and to display new lines as they're added. This feature is helpful for tracking log files because it enables you to see changes as they're made to the file.

Stop Tracking on Program Termination   The --pid=*pid* option tells tail to terminate tracking (as initiated by -f or --follow) once the process with a process ID (PID) of *pid* terminates. (PIDs are described in more detail in Chapter 2, "Managing Software.")

Some additional options provide more obscure capabilities. Consult tail's man page for details.

> You can combine head with tail to display or extract portions of a file. For instance, suppose you want to display lines 11 through 15 of a file, sample.txt. You can extract the first 15 lines of the file with head and then display the last five lines of that extraction with tail. The final command would be **head -n 15 sample.txt | tail -n 5**.

Paging through Files with *less*

The less command's name is a joke; it's a reference to the more command, which was an early file pager. The idea was to create a better version of more, so the developers called it less ("less is more").

The idea behind less (and more, for that matter) is to enable you to read a file a screen at a time. When you type **less *filename***, the program displays the first few lines of *filename*. You can then page back and forth through the file:

- Pressing the spacebar moves forward through the file a screen at a time.
- Pressing Esc followed by V moves backward through the file a screen at a time.

- The Up and Down arrow keys move up or down through the file a line at a time.

- You can search the file's contents by pressing the slash (/) key followed by the search term. For instance, typing **/portable** finds the first occurrence of the string portable after the current position. Typing a slash followed by the Enter key moves to the next occurrence of the search term. Typing **n** alone repeats the search forward, while typing **N** alone repeats the search backward.

- You can search backward in the file by using the question mark (?) key rather than the slash key.

- You can move to a specific line by typing **g** followed by the line number, as in **g50** to go to line 50.

- When you're done, type **q** to exit from the program.

Unlike most of the programs described here, less can't be readily used in a pipe, except as the final command in the pipe. In that role, though, less is very useful because it enables you to examine lengthy output conveniently.

> Although less is quite common on Linux systems and is typically configured as the default text pager, some Unix-like systems use more in this role. Many of less's features, such as the ability to page backward in a file, don't work in more.

One additional less feature can be handy: Typing **h** displays less's internal help system. This display summarizes the commands you may use, but it's long enough that you must use the usual less paging features to view it all! When you're done with the help screens, just type **q** as if you were exiting from viewing a help document with less. This action will return you to your original document.

File-Summarizing Commands

The final text-filtering commands described here are used to summarize text in one way or another. The cut command takes segments of an input file and sends them to standard output, while the wc command displays some basic statistics on the file.

Extracting Text with *cut*

The cut command extracts portions of input lines and displays them on standard output. You can specify what to cut from input lines in several ways:

By Byte   The -b *list* or --bytes=*list* option cuts the specified list of bytes from the input file. (The format of *list* is described shortly.)

By Character   The -c *list* or --characters=*list* option cuts the specified list of characters from the input file. In practice, this method and the by-byte method usually produce identical results. (If the input file uses a multibyte encoding system, though, the results won't be identical.)

By Field   The -f *list* or --fields=*list* option cuts the specified list of fields from the input file. By default, a field is a tab-delimited section of a line, but you can change the delimiting character with the -d *char*, --delim=*char*, or --delimiter=*char* option, where *char* is the character you want to use to delimit fields. Ordinarily, cut echoes lines that don't contain delimiters. Including the -s or --only-delimited option changes this behavior so that the program doesn't echo lines that don't contain the delimiter character.

Many of these options take a *list* option, which is a way to specify multiple bytes, characters, or fields. You make this specification by number. It can be a single number (such as 4), a closed range of numbers (such as 2-4), or an open range of numbers (such as -4 or 4-). In this final case, all bytes, characters, or fields from the beginning of the line to the specified number (or from the specified number to the end of the line) are included in the list.

The cut command is frequently used in scripts to extract data from some other command's output. For instance, suppose you're writing a script and the script needs to know the hardware address of your Ethernet adapter. This information can be obtained from the ifconfig command (described in more detail in Chapter 8, "Configuring Basic Networking"):

```
$ ifconfig eth0
eth0      Link encap:Ethernet  HWaddr 00:0C:76:96:A3:73
          inet addr:192.168.1.3  Bcast:192.168.1.255
Mask:255.255.255.0
          inet6 addr: fe80::20c:76ff:fe96:a373/64 Scope:Link
          UP BROADCAST NOTRAILERS RUNNING MULTICAST MTU:1500
Metric:1
          RX packets:7127424 errors:0 dropped:0 overruns:0 frame:0
          TX packets:5273519 errors:0 dropped:0 overruns:0 carrier:0
          collisions:0 txqueuelen:1000
          RX bytes:6272843708 (5982.2 Mb)  TX bytes:1082453585 (1032.3 Mb)
          Interrupt:10 Base address:0xde00
```

Unfortunately, most of this information is extraneous for the desired purpose. The hardware address is the 6-byte hexadecimal number following HWaddr. To extract that data, you can combine grep (described shortly in "Using grep") with cut in a pipe:

```
$ ifconfig eth0 | grep HWaddr | cut -d " " -f 11
00:0C:76:96:A3:73
```

Of course, in a script, you would probably assign this value to a variable or otherwise process it through additional pipes. (Chapter 9 describes scripts in more detail.)

Obtaining a Word Count with *wc*

The wc command produces a word count (that's where it gets its name), as well as line and byte counts, for a file:

```
$ wc file.txt
 308   2343   15534 file.txt
```

This file contains 308 lines (or more precisely, 308 newline characters), 2,343 words, and 15,534 bytes. You can limit the output to the newline count, the word count, the byte count, or a character count with the --lines (-l), --words (-w), --bytes (-c), or --chars (-m) option, respectively. You can also learn the maximum line length with the --max-line-length (-L) option.

 For an ordinary ASCII file, the character and byte counts will be identical. These values may diverge for files that use multibyte character encodings.

Using Regular Expressions

Many Linux programs employ *regular expressions*, which are tools for describing or matching patterns in text. Regular expressions are similar in principle to the wildcards that can be used to specify multiple filenames. At their simplest, regular expressions can be plain text without adornment. However, certain characters are used to denote patterns. Because of their importance, regular expressions are described in the following section.

Two programs that make heavy use of regular expressions, grep and sed, are also covered. These programs search for text within files and permit editing of files from the command line, respectively.

Understanding Regular Expressions

Two forms of regular expression are common: basic and extended. Which form you must use depends on the program. Some accept one form or the other, but others can use either type, depending on the options passed to the program. (Some programs use their own minor or major variants on either of these classes of regular expression.) The differences between basic and extended regular expressions are complex and subtle, but the fundamental principles of both are similar.

The simplest type of regular expression is an alphabetic string, such as Linux or HWaddr. These regular expressions match any string of the same size or longer that contains the regular expression. For instance, the HWaddr regular expression matches HWaddr, This is the HWaddr, and The HWaddr is unknown. The real strength of regular expressions comes in the use of nonalphabetic characters, which activate advanced matching rules:

Bracket Expressions Characters enclosed in square brackets ([]) constitute bracket expressions, which match any one character within the brackets. For instance, the regular expression b[aeiou]g matches the words bag, beg, big, bog, and bug.

Range Expressions A range expression is a variant of a bracket expression. Instead of listing every character that matches, range expressions list the start and end points separated by a dash (-), as in a[2-4]z. This regular expression matches a2z, a3z, and a4z.

Any Single Character   The dot (.) represents any single character except a newline. For instance, a.z matches a2z, abz, aQz, or any other three-character string that begins with a and ends with z.

Start and End of Line   The carat (^) represents the start of a line, and the dollar sign ($) denotes the end of a line.

Repetition Operators   A full or partial regular expression may be followed by a special symbol to denote how many times a matching item must exist. Specifically, an asterisk (*) denotes zero or more occurrences, a plus sign (+) matches one or more occurrences, and a question mark (?) specifies zero or one match. The asterisk is often combined with the dot (as in .*) to specify a match with any substring. For instance, A.*Lincoln matches any string that contains A and Lincoln, in that order—Abe Lincoln and Abraham Lincoln are just two possible matches.

Multiple Possible Strings   The vertical bar (|) separates two possible matches; for instance, car|truck matches either car or truck.

Parentheses   Ordinary parentheses (()) surround subexpressions. Parentheses are often used to specify how operators are to be applied; for example, you can put parentheses around a group of words that are concatenated with the vertical bar to ensure that the words are treated as a group, any one of which may match, without involving surrounding parts of the regular expression.

Escaping   If you want to match one of the special characters, such as a dot, you must *escape* it—that is, precede it with a backslash (\). For instance, to match a computer hostname (say, twain.example.com), you must escape the dots, as in twain\.example\.com.

The preceding descriptions apply to extended regular expressions. Some details are different for basic regular expressions. In particular, the ?, +, |, (, and) symbols lose their special meanings. To perform the tasks handled by these characters, some programs, such as grep, enable you to recover the functions of these characters by escaping them (say, using \| instead of |). Whether you use basic or extended regular expressions depends on which form the program supports. For programs such as grep, which support both, you can use either. Which form you choose is mostly a matter of personal preference.

You can get more help on regular expressions at the command-line by typing **man 7 regex**. The certification objectives list this particular man page as regex(7).

Regular expression rules can be confusing, particularly when you're first introduced to them. Some examples of their use, in the context of the programs that use them, will help. The next couple of sections provide such examples.

Using *grep*

The grep command is extremely useful. It searches for files that contain a specified string and returns the name of the file and (if it's a text file) a line of context for that string. The basic grep syntax is as follows:

```
grep [options] regexp [files]
```

The *regexp* is a regular expression, as just described. The grep command supports a large number of options. Some of the common options enable you to modify the way the program searches files:

Count Matching Lines   Instead of displaying context lines, grep displays the number of lines that match the specified pattern if you use the -c or --count option.

Specify a Pattern Input File   The -f *file* or --file=*file* option takes pattern input from the specified file rather than from the command line.

Ignore Case   You can perform a search that isn't case sensitive, rather than the default case-sensitive search, by using the -i or --ignore-case option.

Search Recursively   The -r or --recursive option searches in the specified directory and all subdirectories rather than simply the specified directory. You can use rgrep rather than specify this option.

Use a Fixed Strings Pattern   If you want to turn off the grep command's use of regular expressions and use basic pattern searching instead, you can use the -F or --fixed-strings option. Alternatively, you can use fgrep rather than grep. Either way, the characters in the basic pattern string are treated literally. For example, $ is treated literally as a $ and not as a regular expression.

Use an Extended Regular Expression   The grep command interprets *regexp* as a basic regular expression by default. To use an extended regular expression, you can pass the -E or --extended-regexp option. Alternatively, you can call egrep rather than grep. This variant command uses extended regular expressions by default.

A simple example of grep uses a regular expression with no special components:

```
$ grep -r eth0 /etc/*
```

This example finds all the files in /etc that contain the string eth0 (the identifier for the first wired Ethernet device on most Linux distributions). Because the example includes the -r option, it searches recursively, so files in subdirectories of /etc are examined in addition to those in /etc itself. For each matching text file, the line that contains the string is printed.

NOTE   Some files in /etc can't be read by ordinary users. Thus if you type this command as a non-root user, you'll see some error messages relating to grep's inability to open files.

Suppose you want to locate all the files in /etc that contain the string eth0 or eth1. You can enter the following command, which uses a bracket expression to specify both variant devices:

```
$ grep eth[01] /etc/*
```

A still more complex example searches all files in /etc that contain the hostname twain.example.com or bronto.pangaea.edu and, later on the same line, the number

127. This task requires using several of the regular expression features. Expressed using extended regular expression notation, the command looks like this:

```
$ grep -E "(twain\.example\.com|bronto\.pangaea\.edu).*127" /etc/*
```

This command illustrates another feature you may need to use: shell quoting. Because the shell uses certain characters, such as the vertical bar and the asterisk, for its own purposes, you must enclose certain regular expressions in quotes lest the shell attempt to parse the regular expression and pass a modified version of what you type to grep.

You can use grep in conjunction with commands that produce a lot of output in order to sift through that output for the material that's important to you. (Several examples throughout this book use this technique.) For example, suppose you want to find the process ID (PID) of a running xterm. You can use a pipe to send the result of a ps command (described in Chapter 2) through grep:

```
# ps ax | grep xterm
```

The result is a list of all running processes called xterm, along with their PIDs. You can even do this in series, using grep to restrict further the output on some other criterion, which can be useful if the initial pass still produces too much output.

Using *sed*

The sed command directly modifies a file's contents, sending the changed file to standard output. Its syntax can take one of two forms:

```
sed [options] -f script-file [input-file]
sed [options] script-text [input-file]
```

In either case, *input-file* is the name of the file you want to modify. (Modifications are temporary unless you save them in some way, as illustrated shortly.) The script (*script-text* or the contents of *script-file*) is the set of commands you want sed to perform. When you pass a script directly on the command line, the *script-text* is typically enclosed in single quote marks. Table 1.4 summarizes a few sed commands that you can use in its scripts.

TABLE 1.4 Common sed commands

Command	Addresses	Meaning
=	0 or 1	Display the current line number.
a*text*	0 or 1	Append *text* to the file.
i*text*	0 or 1	Insert *text* into the file.

Command	Addresses	Meaning
r *filename*	0 or 1	Append text from *filename* into the file.
c*text*	Range	Replace the selected range of lines with the provided *text*.
s/*regexp*/ *replacement*	Range	Replace text that matches the regular expression (*regexp*) with *replacement*.
w *filename*	Range	Write the current pattern space to the specified file.
q	0 or 1	Immediately quit the script, but print the current pattern space.
Q	0 or 1	Immediately quit the script.

Table 1.4 is incomplete; sed is quite complex, and this section merely introduces this tool.

The Addresses column of Table 1.4 requires elaboration: sed commands operate on addresses, which are line numbers. Commands may take no addresses, in which case they operate on the entire file. If one address is specified, they operate on the specified line. If two addresses (a range) are specified, the commands operate on that range of lines, inclusive.

In operation, sed looks something like this:

```
$ sed 's/2012/2013/' cal-2012.txt > cal-2013.txt
```

This command processes the input file, cal-2012.txt, using sed's s command to replace the first occurrence of 2012 on each line with 2013. (If a single line may have more than one instance of the search string, you must perform a global search by appending g to the command string, as in s/2012/2013/g.) By default, sed sends the modified file to standard output, so this example uses redirection to send the output to cal-2013.txt. The idea in this example is to convert a file created for the year 2012 quickly so that it can be used in 2013. If you don't specify an input filename, sed works from standard input, so it can accept the output of another command as its input.

Although it's conceptually simple, sed is a very complex tool; even a modest summary of its capabilities would fill a chapter. You can consult its man page for basic information, but to understand sed fully, you may want to consult a book that tackles this tough subject, such as our book *Linux Command Line and Shell Scripting Bible, 3rd Edition* (Wiley, 2015).

Certain sed commands, including the substitution command, are also used in vi, which is described more fully in Chapter 5.

Real World Scenario

Doing One Thing in Many Ways

As you become experienced with Linux and compare notes with other Linux administrators, you may find that the way you work is different from the way others work. This is because Linux often provides multiple methods to solve certain problems. For instance, ASCII text files use certain characters to encode the end of a line. Unix (and Linux) use a single line feed character (ASCII 0x0a, sometimes represented as \n), whereas DOS and Windows use the combination of a carriage return (ASCII 0x0d or \r) and a line feed. When moving ASCII files between computers, you may need to convert from one form to the other. How can you do this?

One solution is to use a special-purpose program, such as dos2unix or unix2dos. You could type **dos2unix file.txt** to convert file.txt from DOS-style to Unix-style ASCII, for instance. This is usually the simplest solution, but not all distributions have these utilities installed by default or even available to install.

Another approach is to use tr. For instance, to convert from DOS style to Unix style, you might type this:

$ **tr -d \\r < dosfile.txt > unixfile.txt**

This approach won't work when converting from Unix style to DOS style, though. For that, you can use sed:

sed s/$/"\r"/ unixfile.txt > dosfile.txt

Variants on both the tr and sed commands exist. For instance, sometimes the quotes around \r may be omitted from the sed command; whether they're required depends on your shell and its configuration.

Yet another approach is to load the file into a text editor and then save it using different file-type settings. (Not all editors support such changes, but some do.)

Many other examples exist of multiple solutions to a problem. Sometimes one solution stands out above others as being superior, but at other times the differences may be subtle, or each approach may have merit in particular situations. Thus it's best to be at least somewhat familiar with many of the alternatives, such as the options described throughout this book.

Summary

The command line is the key to Linux. Even if you prefer GUI tools to text-mode tools, understanding text-mode commands is necessary to fully manage a Linux system. This task begins with the shell, which accepts commands you type and displays the results of those commands. In addition, shells support linking programs together via pipes and redirecting programs' input and output. These features enable you to perform complex tasks using simple tools by having each program perform its own small part of the task. This technique is frequently used with Linux text filters, which manipulate text files in various ways—sorting text by fields, merging multiple files, and so on.

Exam Essentials

Summarize features that Linux shells offer to speed up command entry.   The command history often enables you to retrieve an earlier command that's similar or identical to the one you want to enter. Tab completion reduces typing effort by letting the shell finish long command names or filenames. Command-line editing lets you edit a retrieved command or change a typo before committing the command.

Describe the purpose of the man command.   The man command displays the manual page for the keyword (command, filename, system call, or other feature) that you type. This documentation provides succinct summary information that's useful as a reference to learn about exact command options or features.

Explain the purpose of environment variables.   Environment variables store small pieces of data—program options, information about the computer, and so on. This information can be read by programs and used to modify program behavior in a way that's appropriate for the current environment.

Describe the difference between standard output and standard error.   Standard output carries normal program output, whereas standard error carries high-priority output, such as error messages. The two can be redirected independently of one another.

Explain the purpose of pipes.   Pipes tie programs together by feeding the standard output from the first program into the second program's standard input. They can be used to link together a series of simple programs to perform more complex tasks than any one of the programs could manage.

Describe the filter commands.   The various simple filter commands allow the manipulation of text. These commands accomplish tasks of various types, such as combining files, transforming the data in files, formatting text, displaying text, and summarizing data.

Summarize the structure of regular expressions.   Regular expressions are strings that describe other strings. They can contain normal alphanumeric characters, which match the exact same characters in the string they are describing, as well as several special symbols and symbol sets that match multiple different characters. The combination is a powerful pattern-matching tool used by many Linux programs.

Review Questions

1. You type a command into bash and pass a long filename to it, but after you enter the command, you receive a File not found error message because of a typo in the filename. How might you proceed?

   A. Retype the command, and be sure you type the filename correctly, letter by letter.

   B. Retype the command, but press the Tab key after typing a few letters of the long filename to ensure that the filename is entered correctly.

   C. Press the Up arrow key, and use bash's editing features to correct the typo.

   D. Any of the above.

   E. None of the above.

2. Which of the following commands is implemented as an internal command in bash?

   A. cat

   B. less

   C. tee

   D. sed

   E. echo

3. You type **echo $PROC**, and the computer replies Go away. What does this mean?

   A. No currently running processes are associated with your shell, so you may log out without terminating them.

   B. The remote computer PROC isn't accepting connections; you should contact its administrator to correct the problem.

   C. Your computer is handling too many processes; you must kill some of them to regain control of the computer.

   D. Your central processing unit (CPU) is defective and must be replaced as soon as possible.

   E. You, one of your configuration files, or a program you've run has set the $PROC environment variable to Go away.

4. What does the pwd command accomplish?

   A. It prints the name of the working directory.

   B. It changes the current working directory.

   C. It prints wide displays on narrow paper.

   D. It parses web page URLs for display.

   E. It prints the terminal's width in characters.

5. What is the surest way to run a program (say, myprog) that's located in the current working directory?

   A. Type **./** followed by the program name: **./myprog**.

   B. Type the program name alone: **myprog**.

C. Type **run** followed by the program name: **run myprog**.

D. Type **/.** followed by the program name: **/.myprog**.

E. Type the program name followed by an ampersand (&): **myprog &**.

6. How does man display information by default on most Linux systems?

    A. Using a custom X-based application

    B. Using the Firefox web browser

    C. Using the `info` browser

    D. Using the vi editor

    E. Using the `less` pager

7. You want to store the standard output of the `ifconfig` command in a text file (`file.txt`) for future reference, and you want to wipe out any existing data in the file. You do *not* want to store standard error in this file. How can you accomplish these goals?

    A. `ifconfig < file.txt`

    B. `ifconfig >> file.txt`

    C. `ifconfig > file.txt`

    D. `ifconfig | file.txt`

    E. `ifconfig 2> file.txt`

8. What is the effect of the following command?

`$ myprog &> input.txt`

    A. Standard error to myprog is taken from `input.txt`.

    B. Standard input to myprog is taken from `input.txt`.

    C. Standard output and standard error from myprog are written to `input.txt`.

    D. All of the above.

    E. None of the above.

9. How many commands can you pipe together at once?

    A. 2

    B. 3

    C. 4

    D. 16

    E. >16

10. You want to run an interactive script, gabby, which produces a lot of output in response to the user's inputs. To facilitate future study of this script, you want to copy its output to a file. How might you do this?

    A. `gabby > gabby-out.txt`

    B. `gabby | tee gabby-out.txt`

    C. `gabby < gabby-out.txt`

    D. `gabby &> gabby-out.txt`

    E. `gabby `gabby-out.txt``

11. A text-mode program, verbose, prints a lot of bogus "error" messages to standard error. How might you get rid of those messages while still interacting with the program?

A. `verbose | quiet`

B. `verbose &> /dev/null`

C. `verbose 2> /dev/null`

D. `verbose > junk.txt`

E. `quiet-mode verbose`

12. How do the > and >> redirection operators differ?

A. The > operator creates a new file or overwrites an existing one; the >> operator creates a new file or appends to an existing one.

B. The > operator creates a new file or overwrites an existing one; the >> operator appends to an existing file or issues an error message if the specified file doesn't exist.

C. The > operator redirects standard output; the >> operator redirects standard error.

D. The > operator redirects standard output; the >> operator redirects standard input.

E. The > operator writes to an existing file but fails if the file doesn't exist; the >> operator writes to an existing file or creates a new one if it doesn't already exist.

13. What program would you use to display the end of a configuration file?

A. `uniq`

B. `cut`

C. `tail`

D. `wc`

E. `fmt`

14. What is the effect of the following command?

`$ pr report.txt | lpr`

A. The file `report.txt` is formatted for printing and sent to the `lpr` program.

B. The files `report.txt` and `lpr` are combined together into one file and sent to standard output.

C. Tabs are converted to spaces in `report.txt`, and the result is saved in `lpr`.

D. The file `report.txt` is printed, and any error messages are stored in the file `lpr`.

E. None of the above.

15. Which of the following commands will number the lines in `aleph.txt`? (Select three.)

A. `fmt aleph.txt`

B. `nl aleph.txt`

C. `cat -b aleph.txt`

D. `cat -n aleph.txt`

E. `od -nl aleph.txt`

16. You have a data file, data.txt, to be processed by a particular program. However, the program cannot handle data separated by tabs. The data.txt file's data is separated by a tab stop at every eight characters. What command should you use before processing the data file with the program?

   A. `od data.txt > data1.txt`

   B. `expand data.txt >> data.txt`

   C. `fmt --remove-tabs data.txt`

   D. `expand data.txt > data1.txt`

   E. `unexpand -t 8 data.txt`

17. Which of the following commands will change all occurrences of dog in the file animals.txt to mutt in the screen display?

   A. `sed -s "dog" "mutt" animals.txt`

   B. `grep -s "dog||mutt" animals.txt`

   C. `sed 's/dog/mutt/g' animals.txt`

   D. `cat animals.txt | grep -c "dog" "mutt"`

   E. `fmt animals.txt | cut 'dog' > 'mutt'`

18. You've received an ASCII text file (longlines.txt) that uses no carriage returns within paragraphs but two carriage returns between paragraphs. The result is that your preferred text editor displays each paragraph as a very long line. How can you reformat this file so that you can more easily edit it (or a copy)?

   A. `sed 's/Ctrl-M/NL/' longlines.txt`

   B. `fmt longlines.txt > longlines2.txt`

   C. `cat longlines.txt > longlines2.txt`

   D. `pr longlines.txt > longlines2.txt`

   E. `grep longlines.txt > longlines2.txt`

19. Which of the following commands will print lines from the file world.txt that contain matches to changes and changed?

   A. `grep change[ds] world.txt`

   B. `sed change[d-s] world.txt`

   C. `od "change'd|s'" world.txt`

   D. `cat world.txt changes changed`

   E. `find world.txt "change(d|s)"`

20. Which of the following regular expressions will match the strings dog, dug, and various other strings but not dig?

   A. `d.g`

   B. `d[ou]g`

   C. `d[o-u]g`

   D. `di*g`

   E. `d.ig`

Chapter

2

Managing Software

THE FOLLOWING EXAM OBJECTIVES ARE COVERED IN THIS CHAPTER:

✓ 102.3 Manage shared libraries

✓ 102.4 Use Debian package management

✓ 102.5 Use RPM and Yum package management

✓ 103.5 Create, monitor, and kill processes

✓ 103.6 Modify process execution priorities

A Linux system is defined largely by the collection of software it contains. The Linux kernel, the libraries used by many packages, the shells used to interpret commands, the X Window System GUI, the servers, and more all make up the system's software environment. Many of the chapters in this book are devoted to configuring specific software components, but they all have something in common: tools used to install, uninstall, upgrade, and otherwise manipulate the software.

Ironically, this commonality is a major source of differences between Linux systems. Two major Linux package management tools exist: RPM Package Manager (RPM) and Debian. (Several less-common package management systems also exist.) With few exceptions, each individual Linux computer uses precisely one package management system, so you'll need to know only one to administer a single system. To be truly fluent in all things Linux, though, you should at least be somewhat familiar with both of them. Thus this chapter describes both.

This chapter also covers *libraries*—software components that can be used by many different programs. Libraries help reduce the disk space and memory requirements of complex programs, but they also require some attention. If that attention isn't given to them, they can cause problems by their absence or because of incompatibilities between them and their dependent software's versions.

Package management, and in some sense library management, relates to programs as files on your hard disk. Once run, though, programs are dynamic entities. Linux provides tools to help you manage running programs (known as *processes*)—you can learn what processes are running, change their priorities, and terminate processes that you don't want running.

Package Concepts

Before proceeding, you should understand some of the principles that underlie Linux package management tools. Any computer's software is like a house of cards: One program may rely on multiple other programs or libraries, each of which relies on several more, and so on. The foundation upon which all of these programs rely is the Linux kernel. Any of these packages can theoretically be replaced by an equivalent one; however, doing so sometimes causes problems. Worse still, removing one card from the stack could cause the whole house of cards to come tumbling down.

Linux package management tools are intended to help build and modify this house of cards by tracking what software is installed. The information that the system maintains helps to avoid problems in several ways:

Packages   The most basic information that package systems maintain is information about software *packages*—that is, collections of files that are installed on the computer. Packages are usually distributed as single files that are similar to *tarballs* (archives created with the tar utility and usually compressed with gzip or bzip2) or zip files. Once installed, most packages consist of dozens or hundreds of files, and the package system tracks them all. Packages include additional information that aids in the subsequent duties of package management systems.

Installed File Database   Package systems maintain a database of installed files. The database includes information about every file installed via the package system, the name of the package to which each of those files belongs, and associated additional information.

Dependencies   One of the most important types of information maintained by the package system is *dependency information*—that is, the requirements of packages for one another. For instance, if SuperProg relies on UltraLib to do its work, the package database records this information. If you attempt to install SuperProg when UltraLib isn't installed, the package system won't let you do so. Similarly, if you try to uninstall UltraLib when SuperProg is installed, the package system won't let you. (You can override these prohibitions, as described later in "Forcing the Installation." Doing so is usually inadvisable, though.)

Checksums   The package system maintains checksums and assorted ancillary information about files. This information can be used to verify the validity of the installed software. This feature has its limits, though; it's intended to help you spot disk errors, accidental overwriting of files, or other non-sinister problems. It's of limited use in detecting intrusions because an intruder could use the package system to install altered system software.

Upgrades and Uninstallation   By tracking files and dependencies, package systems permit easy upgrades and uninstallation: Tell the package system to upgrade or remove a package, and it will replace or remove every file in the package. Of course, this assumes that the upgrade or uninstallation doesn't cause dependency problems; if it does, the package system will block the operation unless you override it.

Binary Package Creation   Both the RPM and Debian package systems provide tools to help create binary packages (those that are installed directly) from source code. This feature is particularly helpful if you're running Linux on a peculiar CPU: you can download source code and create a binary package, even if the developers didn't provide explicit support for your CPU. Creating a binary package from source has advantages over compiling software from source in more conventional ways, because you can then use the package management system to track dependencies, attend to individual files, and so on.

Both the RPM and Debian package systems provide all of these basic features, although the details of their operation differ. These two package systems are incompatible with one another in the sense that their package files and their installed file databases are different; that is, you can't directly install an RPM package on a Debian-based system or vice versa. (Tools to convert between formats do exist, and developers are working on ways to integrate the two package formats better.)

Most distributions install just one package system. It's possible to install more than one, though, and some programs (such as `alien`) require both for full functionality. Actually *using* both systems to install software is inadvisable because their databases are separate. If you install a library using a Debian package and then try to install an RPM package that relies on that library, RPM won't realize that the library is already installed and will return an error.

Using RPM

The most popular package manager in the Linux world is the *RPM Package Manager (RPM)*. RPM is also available on non-Linux platforms, although it sees less use outside the Linux world. The RPM system provides all of the basic tools described in the preceding section, "Package Concepts," such as a package database that allows for identifying conflicts and ownership of particular files.

RPM Distributions and Conventions

Red Hat developed RPM for its own distribution. Red Hat released the software under the General Public License (GPL), however, so that others are free to use it in their own distributions—and this is precisely what has happened. Some distributions, such as Mandriva (formerly Mandrake) and Yellow Dog, are based on Red Hat, so they use RPMs as well as many other parts of the Red Hat distribution. Others, such as SUSE, borrow less from the Red Hat template, but they do use RPMs. Of course, all Linux distributions share many common components, so even those that weren't originally based on Red Hat are very similar to it in many ways other than their use of RPM packages. On the other hand, distributions that were originally based on Red Hat have diverged from it over time. As a result, the group of RPM-using distributions shows substantial variability, but all of them are still Linux distributions that provide the same basic tools, such as the Linux kernel, common shells, an X server, and so on.

Red Hat has splintered into three distributions: Fedora is the downloadable version favored by home users, students, and businesses on a tight budget. The *Red Hat* name is now reserved for the for-pay version of the distribution, known more formally as Red Hat Enterprise Linux (RHEL). CentOS is a freely redistributable version intended for enterprise users.

RPM is a cross-platform tool. As noted earlier, some non-Linux Unix systems can use RPM, although most don't use it as their primary package-distribution system. RPM supports any CPU architecture. Red Hat Linux is or has been available for at least five

CPUs: *x*86, *x*86-64 (aka AMD64, EM64T, and *x*64), IA-64, Alpha, and SPARC. Among the distributions mentioned earlier, Pidora is an ARM processor distribution. (It runs on the popular Raspberry Pi device.) and SUSE is available on *x*86, *x*86-64, and PowerPC systems. For the most part, source RPMs are transportable across architectures—you can use the same source RPM to build packages for *x*86, AMD64, PowerPC, ARM, SPARC, or any other platform you like. Some programs are composed of architecture-independent scripts and so need no recompilation. There are also documentation and configuration packages that work on any CPU.

The convention for naming RPM packages is as follows:

`packagename-a.b.c-x.arch.rpm`

Each of the filename components has a specific meaning:

Package Name   The first component (`packagename`) is the name of the package, such as `samba` or `samba-server` for the Samba file and print server. Note that the same program may be given different package names by different distribution maintainers.

Version Number   The second component (`a.b.c`) is the package version number, such as 3.6.5. The version number doesn't have to be three numbers separated by periods, but that's the most common form. The program author assigns the version number.

Build Number   The number following the version number (`x`) is the *build number* (also known as the *release number*). This number represents minor changes made by the package maintainer, not by the program author. These changes may represent altered startup scripts or configuration files, changed file locations, added documentation, or patches appended to the original program to fix bugs or to make the program more compatible with the target Linux distribution. Many distribution maintainers add a letter code to the build number to distinguish their packages from those of others. Note that these numbers are *not* comparable across package maintainers—George's build number 5 of a package is *not* necessarily an improvement on Susan's build number 4 of the same package.

Architecture   The final component preceding the `.rpm` extension (`arch`) is a code for the package's architecture. The `i386` architecture code is common; it represents a file compiled for any *x*86 CPU from the 80386 onward. Some packages include optimizations for Pentiums or newer (`i586` or `i686`), and non-*x*86 binary packages use codes for their CPUs, such as `ppc` for PowerPC CPUs or `x86_64` for the *x*86-64 platform. Scripts, documentation, and other CPU-independent packages generally use the `noarch` architecture code. The main exception to this rule is source RPMs, which use the `src` architecture code.

As an example of RPM version numbering, the Fedora 20 distribution for *x*86-64 ships with a Samba package called `samba-4.1.9-4.fc20.x86_64.rpm`, indicating that this is build 4.fc20 of Samba 4.1.9, compiled with *x*86-64 optimizations. These naming conventions are just that, though—conventions. It's possible to rename a package however you like, and it will still install and work. The information in the filename is retained within the package. This fact can be useful if you're ever forced to transfer RPMs using a medium that doesn't allow for long filenames. In fact, early versions of SUSE eschewed long filenames, preferring short filenames such as `samba.rpm`.

In an ideal world, any RPM package will install and run on any RPM-based distribution that uses an appropriate CPU type. Unfortunately, compatibility issues can crop up from time to time, including the following:

- Distributions may use different versions of the RPM utilities. This problem can completely prevent an RPM from one distribution from being used on another.

- An RPM package designed for one distribution may have dependencies that are unmet in another distribution. A package may require a newer version of a library than is present on the distribution you're using, for instance. You can usually overcome this problem by installing or upgrading the package dependencies, but sometimes doing so causes problems because the upgrade may break other packages. By rebuilding the package you want to install from a source RPM, you can often work around these problems, but sometimes the underlying source code also needs the upgraded libraries.

- An RPM package may be built to depend on a package of a particular name, such as samba-client depending on samba-common, but if the distribution you're using has named the package differently, the rpm utility will object. You can override this objection by using the --nodeps switch, but sometimes the package won't work once installed. Rebuilding from a source RPM may or may not fix this problem.

- Even when a dependency appears to be met, different distributions may include slightly different files in their packages. For this reason, a package meant for one distribution may not run correctly when installed on another distribution. Sometimes installing an additional package will fix this problem.

- Some programs include distribution-specific scripts or configuration files. This problem is particularly acute for servers, which may include startup scripts that go in /etc/rc.d/init.d or elsewhere. Overcoming this problem usually requires that you remove the offending script after installing the RPM and either start the server in some other way or write a new startup script, perhaps modeled after one that came with some other server for your distribution.

In most cases, it's best to use the RPMs intended for your distribution. RPM meta-packagers, such as the Yellow Dog Updater, Modified (Yum), can simplify locating and installing packages designed for your distribution. If you're forced to go outside of your distribution's officially supported list of packages, mixing and matching RPMs from different distributions usually works reasonably well for most programs. This is particularly true if the distributions are closely related or you rebuild from a source RPM. If you have trouble with an RPM, though, you may do well to try to find an equivalent package that was built with your distribution in mind.

The *rpm* Command Set

The main RPM utility program is known as rpm. Use this program to install or upgrade a package at the shell prompt. The rpm command has the following syntax:

```
rpm [operation][options] [package-files|package-names]
```

Table 2.1 summarizes the most common rpm operations, and Table 2.2 summarizes the most important options. Be aware, however, that rpm is a complex tool, so this listing is necessarily incomplete. For information about operations and options more obscure than those listed in Table 2.1 and Table 2.2, see the man pages for rpm. Many of rpm's less-used features are devoted to the creation of RPM packages by software developers.

TABLE 2.1   Common rpm operations

Operation	Description
-i	Installs a package; system must *not* contain a package of the same name
-U	Installs a new package or upgrades an existing one
-F or --freshen	Upgrades a package only if an earlier version already exists
-q	Queries a package—finds whether a package is installed, what files it contains, and so on
-V or --verify	Verifies a package—checks that its files are present and unchanged since installation
-e	Uninstalls a package
-b	Builds a binary package, given source code and configuration files; moved to the rpmbuild program with RPM version 4.2
--rebuild	Builds a binary package, given a source RPM file; moved to the rpmbuild program with RPM version 4.2
--rebuilddb	Rebuilds the RPM database to fix errors

TABLE 2.2   Most important rpm options

Option	Used with operations	Description
--root dir	Any	Modifies the Linux system having a root directory located at dir. This option can be used to maintain one Linux installation discrete from another one (say, during OS installation or emergency maintenance).
--force	-i, -U, -F	Forces installation of a package even when it means overwriting existing files or packages.

TABLE 2.2   Most important rpm options *(continued)*

Option	Used with operations	Description
-h or --hash	-i, -U, -F	Displays a series of hash marks (#) to indicate the progress of the operation.
-v	-i, -U, -F	Used in conjunction with the -h option to produce a uniform number of hash marks for each package.
--nodeps	-i, -U, F, -e	Specifies that no dependency checks be performed. Installs or removes the package even if it relies on a package or file that's not present or is required by a package that's not being uninstalled.
--test	-i, -U, -F	Checks for dependencies, conflicts, and other problems without actually installing the package.
--prefix path	-i, -U, -F	Sets the installation directory to path (works only for some packages).
-a or --all	-q, -V	Queries or verifies all packages.
-f file or --file file	-q, -V	Queries or verifies the package that owns file.
-p package-file	-q	Queries the uninstalled RPM package-file.
-i	-q	Displays package information, including the package maintainer, a short description, and so on.
-R or --requires	-q	Displays the packages and files on which this one depends.
-l or --list	-q	Displays the files contained in the package.

To use rpm, you combine one operation with one or more options. In most cases, you include one or more package names or package filenames as well. (A package filename is a complete filename, but a package name is a shortened version. For instance, a package filename might be samba-4.1.9-4.fc20.x86_64.rpm, whereas the matching package name is samba.) You can issue the rpm command once for each package, or you can list multiple packages, separated by spaces, on the command line. The latter is often preferable when you're installing or removing several packages, some of which depend on others in the group. Issuing separate commands in this situation requires that you install the depended-on package first or remove it last, whereas issuing a single command allows you to list the packages on the command line in any order.

Some operations require that you give a package filename, and others require a package name. In particular, -i, -U, -F, and the rebuild operations require package filenames; -q, -V, and -e normally take a package name, although the -p option can modify a query (-q) operation to work on a package filename.

When you're installing or upgrading a package, the -U operation is generally the most useful because it enables you to install the package without manually uninstalling the old one. This one-step operation is particularly helpful when packages contain many dependencies; rpm detects these and can perform the operation should the new package fulfill the dependencies provided by the old one.

To use rpm to install or upgrade a package from an RPM file that you have already downloaded to your local system, issue a command similar to the following:

```
# rpm -Uvh samba-4.1.9-4.fc20.x86_64.rpm
```

You can also use rpm -ivh in place of rpm -Uvh if you don't already have a samba package installed.

WARNING   It's possible to distribute the same program under different names. In this situation, upgrading may fail or it may produce a duplicate installation, which can yield bizarre program-specific malfunctions. Red Hat has described a formal system for package naming to avoid such problems, but they still occur occasionally. Therefore, it's best to upgrade a package using a subsequent release provided by the same individual or organization that provided the original.

Verify that the package is installed with the rpm -qi command, which displays information such as when and on what computer the binary package was built. Listing 2.1 demonstrates this command. (rpm -qi also displays an extended plain-English summary of what the package is, which has been omitted from Listing 2.1.)

Listing 2.1: RPM query output

```
$ rpm -qi samba
Name        : samba
Epoch       : 2
Version     : 4.1.9
Release     : 4.fc20
Architecture: x86_64
Install Date: Tue 02 Sep 2014 01:02:33 AM EDT
Group       : System Environment/Daemons
Size        : 1699739
```

```
License     : GPLv3+ and LGPLv3+
Signature   : RSA/SHA256, Sat 02 Aug 2014 12:05:26 PM EDT, Key ID
 2eb161fa246110c1
Source RPM  : samba-4.1.9-4.fc20.src.rpm
Build Date  : Fri 01 Aug 2014 05:51:43 PM EDT
Build Host  : buildvm-10.phx2.fedoraproject.org
Relocations : (not relocatable)
Packager    : Fedora Project
Vendor      : Fedora Project
URL         : http://www.samba.org/
Summary     : Server and Client software to interoperate with
Windows machines
Description :
Samba is the standard Windows interoperability suite of programs for
Linux and Unix.
```

Extracting Data from RPMs

Occasionally you may want to extract data from RPMs without installing the package. For instance, this can be a good way to retrieve the original source code from a source RPM for compiling the software without the help of the RPM tools or to retrieve fonts or other non-program data for use on a non-RPM system.

RPM files are actually modified cpio archives. Thus, converting the files into cpio files is relatively straightforward, whereupon you can use cpio to retrieve the individual files. To do this job, you need to use the rpm2cpio program that ships with most Linux distributions. (You can even use this tool on distributions that don't use RPM.) This program takes a single argument—the name of the RPM file—and outputs the cpio archive on standard output. Thus, if you want to create a cpio archive file, you must redirect the output:

```
$ rpm2cpio samba-4.1.9-4.fc20.src.rpm > samba-4.1.9-4.fc20.src.cpio
```

The redirection operator (>) is described in more detail in Chapter 1, "Exploring Linux Command-Line Tools," as is the pipe operator (|), which is mentioned shortly. Chapter 4, "Managing Files," describes cpio in more detail.

You can then extract the data using cpio, which takes the -i option to extract an archive and --make-directories to create directories:

```
$ cpio -i --make-directories < samba-4.1.9-4.fc20.src.cpio
```

Alternatively, you can use a pipe to link these two commands together without creating an intermediary file:

```
$ rpm2cpio samba-4.1.9-4.fc20.src.rpm | cpio -i --make-directories
```

In either case, the result is an extraction of the files in the archive in the current directory. In the case of binary packages, this is likely to be a series of subdirectories that mimic the layout of the Linux root directory—that is, usr, lib, etc, and so on, although precisely which directories are included depends on the package. For a source package, the result of the extraction process is likely to be a source code tarball, a .spec file (which holds information that RPM uses to build the package), and perhaps some patch files.

When you're extracting data from an RPM file using rpm2cpio and cpio, create a holding subdirectory and then extract the data into this subdirectory. This practice will ensure that you can find all of the files. If you extract files in your home directory, some of them may get lost among your other files. If you extract files as root in the root (/) directory, they could conceivably overwrite files that you want to keep.

Another option for extracting data from RPMs is to use alien, which is described later in "Converting between Package Formats." This program can convert an RPM into a Debian package or a tarball.

Using Yum

Yum (http://yum.baseurl.org), mentioned earlier, is one of several meta-packagers—it enables you to install a package and all its dependencies easily using a single command line. When using Yum, you don't even need to locate and download the package files because Yum does this for you by searching in one or more repositories—Internet sites that host RPM files for a particular distribution.

Yum originated with the fairly obscure Yellow Dog Linux distribution, but it's since been adopted by Red Hat, CentOS, Fedora, and some other RPM-based distributions. Yum isn't used by all RPM-based distributions, though; SUSE and Mandriva, to name just two, each uses their own meta-packager. Debian-based distributions generally employ the Advanced Package Tools (APT), as described later in "Using apt-get." Nonetheless, because of the popularity of Red Hat, CentOS, and Fedora, knowing Yum can be valuable.

The most basic way to use Yum is with the yum command, which has the following syntax:

```
yum [options] [command] [package...]
```

Which options are available depend on the command you use. Table 2.3 describes common yum commands.

TABLE 2.3 Common yum commands

Command	Description
`install`	Installs one or more packages by package name. Also installs dependencies of the specified package or packages.
`update`	Updates the specified package or packages to the latest available version. If no packages are specified, `yum` updates every installed package.
`check-update`	Checks to see whether updates are available. If they are, `yum` displays their names, versions, and repository area (`updates` or `extras`, for instance).
`upgrade`	Works like `update` with the `--obsoletes` flag set, which handles obsolete packages in a way that's superior when performing a distribution version upgrade.
`remove or erase`	Deletes a package from the system; similar to `rpm -e`, but `yum` also removes depended-on packages.
`list`	Displays information about a package, such as the installed version and whether an update is available.
`provides or whatprovides`	Displays information about packages that provide a specified program or feature. For instance, typing `yum provides samba` lists all the Samba-related packages, including every available update. Note that the output can be copious.
`search`	Searches package names, summaries, packagers, and descriptions for a specified keyword. This is useful if you don't know a package's name but can think of a word that's likely to appear in one of these fields but not in these fields for other packages.
`info`	Displays information about a package, similar to the `rpm -qi` command.
`clean`	Cleans up the Yum cache directory. Running this command from time to time is advisable, lest downloaded packages chew up too much disk space.
`shell`	Enters the Yum shell mode, in which you can enter multiple Yum commands one after another.
`resolvedep`	Displays packages matching the specified dependency.
`localinstall`	Installs the specified local RPM files, using your Yum repositories to resolve dependencies.

Command	Description
localupdate	Updates the system using the specified local RPM files, using your Yum repositories to resolve dependencies. Packages other than those updated by local files and their dependencies are not updated.
deplist	Displays dependencies of the specified package.

In most cases, using Yum is easier than using RPM directly to manage packages because Yum finds the latest available package, downloads it, and installs any required dependencies. Yum has its limits, though; it's only as good as its repositories, so it can't install software that's not stored in those repositories.

> **WARNING** If you use Yum to upgrade all packages automatically on your system, you're effectively giving control of your system to the distribution maintainer. Although Red Hat or other distribution maintainers are unlikely to try to break into your computer in this way, an automatic update with minimal supervision on your part could easily break something on your system, particularly if you've obtained packages from unusual sources in the past.

If you don't want to install the package but merely want to obtain it, you can use yumdownloader. Type this command followed by the name of a package and the latest version of the package will be downloaded to the current directory. This can be handy if you need to update a system that's not connected to the Internet; you can use another computer that runs the same distribution to obtain the packages and then transfer them to the target system.

If you prefer to use GUI tools rather than command-line tools, you should be aware that GUI front-ends to yum exist. Examples include yumex and kyum. You can use the text-mode yum to install these front-ends, as in **yum install kyum.**

Exercise 2.1 runs you through the process of managing packages using the rpm utility.

EXERCISE 2.1

Managing Packages Using RPM

To manage packages using the rpm utility, follow these steps:

1. Log into the Linux system as a normal user.

2. Acquire a package to use for testing purposes. You can try using a package from your distribution that you know you haven't installed, but if you try a random package, you may find that it's already installed or has unmet dependencies. As an example, this lab uses the installation of zsh-5.0.6-1.fc20.x86_64.rpm, a shell that's not installed by default on most systems, from the Fedora 20 DVD onto a Fedora 20 system. You must adjust the commands as necessary if you use another RPM file in your tests.

3. Launch an xterm from the desktop environment's menu system if you used a GUI login.

4. Acquire root privileges. You can do this by typing **su** in an xterm, by selecting Session ≻ New Root Console from a Konsole window, or by using sudo (if it's configured) to run the commands in the following steps.

5. Type **rpm -q zsh** to verify that the package isn't currently installed. The system should respond with the message package zsh is not installed.

6. Type **rpm -qpi zsh-5.0.6-1.fc20.x86_64.rpm**. (You'll need to provide a complete path to the package file if it's not in your current directory.) The system should respond by displaying information about the package, such as the version number, the vendor, the hostname of the machine on which it was built, and a package description.

7. Type rpm **-ivh zsh-5.0.6-1.fc20.x86_64.rpm**. The system should install the package and display a series of hash marks (#) as it does so.

8. Type rpm **-q zsh**. The system should respond with the complete package name, including the version and build numbers. This response verifies that the package is installed.

9. Type **zsh**. This launches a Z shell, which functions much like the more common bash and tcsh shells. You're likely to see your command prompt change, but you can issue most of the same commands you can use with bash or tcsh.

10. Type **rpm -V zsh**. The system shouldn't produce any output—just a new command prompt. The verify (-V or --verify) command checks the package files against data stored in the database. Immediately after installation, most packages should show no deviations. (A handful of packages will be modified during installation, but zsh isn't one of them.)

11. Type **rpm -e zsh**. The system shouldn't produce any output—just a new command prompt. This command removes the package from the system. Note that you're removing the zsh package while running the zsh program. Linux continues to run the zsh program you're using, but you'll be unable to launch new instances of the program. Some programs may misbehave if you do this because files will be missing after you remove the package.

12. Type **exit** to exit zsh and return to your normal shell.

13. Type **rpm -q zsh**. The system should respond with a package zsh is not installed error because you've just uninstalled the package.

14. Type **yum install zsh**. The system should check your repositories, download zsh, and install it. It will ask for confirmation before beginning the download.

15. Type **rpm -q zsh**. The results should be similar to those in step 8, although the version number may differ.

16. Type **rpm -e zsh**. This step removes zsh from the system but produces no output, just as in step 11.

The final three steps will work only if your distribution uses Yum. If you're using a distribution that uses another tool, you may be able to locate and use its equivalent, such as zypper for SUSE.

RPM and Yum Configuration Files

Ordinarily, you needn't explicitly configure RPM or Yum; distributions that use RPM configure it in reasonable ways by default. Sometimes, though, you may want to tweak a few details, particularly if you routinely build source RPM packages and want to optimize the output for your computer. You may also want to add a Yum repository for some unusual software you run. To do so, you typically edit an RPM or Yum configuration file.

The main RPM configuration file is /usr/lib/rpm/rpmrc. This file sets a variety of options, mostly related to the CPU optimizations used when compiling source packages. You shouldn't edit this file, though; instead, you should create and edit /etc/rpmrc (to make global changes) or ~/.rpmrc (to make changes on a per-user basis). The main reason to create such a file is to implement architecture optimizations—for instance, to optimize your code for your CPU model by passing appropriate compiler options when you build a source RPM into a binary RPM. This is done with the optflags line:

```
optflags: athlon -O2 -g -march=i686
```

This line tells RPM to pass the -O2 -g -march-i686 options to the compiler whenever it's building for the athlon platform. Although RPM can determine your system's architecture, the optflags line by itself isn't likely to be enough to set the correct flags. Most default rpmrc files include a series of buildarchtranslate lines that cause rpmbuild (or rpm for older versions of RPM) to use one set of optimizations for a whole family of CPUs. For *x*86 systems, these lines typically look like this:

```
buildarchtranslate: athlon: i386
buildarchtranslate: i686: i386
buildarchtranslate: i586: i386
buildarchtranslate: i486: i386
buildarchtranslate: i386: i386
```

These lines tell RPM to translate the athlon, i686, i586, i486, and i386 CPU codes to use the i386 optimizations. This effectively defeats the purpose of any CPU-specific optimizations you create on the optflags line for your architecture, but it guarantees that the RPMs you build will be maximally portable. To change matters, you must alter the line for your CPU type, as returned when you type **uname -p**. For instance, on an Athlon-based system, you might enter the following line:

```
buildarchtranslate: athlon: athlon
```

Thereafter, when you rebuild a source RPM, the system will use the appropriate Athlon optimizations. The result can be a slight performance boost on your own system but reduced portability—depending on the precise optimizations you choose, such packages may not run on non-Athlon CPUs. (Indeed, you may not even be able to install them on non-Athlon CPUs!)

Yum is configured via the /etc/yum.conf file, with additional configuration files in the /etc/yum.repos.d/ directory. The yum.conf file holds basic options, such as the directory to which Yum downloads RPMs and where Yum logs its activities. Chances are that you won't need to modify this file. The /etc/yum.repos.d/ directory, on the other hand, potentially holds several files, each of which describes a Yum repository—that is, a site that holds RPMs that may be installed via Yum. You probably shouldn't directly edit these files; instead, if you want to add a repository, you should manually download the RPM that includes the repository configuration and install it using rpm. The next time you use Yum, it will access your new repository along with the old ones. Several Yum repositories exist, mostly for Red Hat, CentOS, and Fedora, such as the following:

Livna   This repository (http://rpm.livna.org/) hosts multimedia tools, such as additional codecs and video drivers.

KDE Red Hat   Red Hat, CentOS, and Fedora favor the GNU Network Object Model Environment (GNOME) desktop environment, although they ship with the K Desktop Environment (KDE) too. The repository at http://kde-redhat.sourceforge.net provides improved KDE RPMs for those who favor KDE.

Fresh RPMs   This repository (http://freshrpms.net) provides additional RPMs, mostly focusing on multimedia applications and drivers.

Many additional repositories exist. Try a Web search on terms such as *yum repository*, or check the web page of any site that hosts unusual software that you want to run to see whether it provides a Yum repository. If so, it should provide an RPM or other instructions on adding its site to your Yum repository list.

RPM Compared to Other Package Formats

RPM is a very flexible package management system. In most respects, it's comparable to Debian's package manager, and it offers many more features than tarballs. When compared to Debian packages, the greatest strength of RPMs is probably their ubiquity. Many software packages are available in RPM form from their developers and/or from distribution maintainers.

Distribution packagers frequently modify the original programs in order to make them integrate more smoothly into the distribution as a whole. For instance, distribution-specific startup scripts may be added, program binaries may be relocated from default /usr/local subdirectories, and program source code may be patched to fix bugs or add features. Although these changes can be useful, you may not want them, particularly if you're using a program on a distribution other than the one for which the package was intended.

The fact that there are so many RPM-based distributions can be a boon. You may be able to use an RPM intended for one distribution on another, although, as noted earlier, this isn't certain. In fact, this advantage can turn into a drawback if you try to mix and match too much—you can wind up with a mishmash of conflicting packages that can be difficult to disentangle.

> The RPMFind website, http://rpmfind.net, is an extremely useful resource when you want to find an RPM of a specific program. Another site with similar characteristics is Fresh RPMs, http://freshrpms.net. These sites include links to RPMs built by programs' authors, specific distributions' RPMs, and those built by third parties. Adding such sites as Yum repositories to your repository library can make it even easier to install new programs.

Compared to tarballs, RPMs offer much more sophisticated package management tools. This can be important when you're upgrading or removing packages and also for verifying the integrity of installed packages. On the other hand, although RPMs are common in the Linux world, they're less common on other platforms. Therefore, you're more likely to find tarballs of generic Unix source code, and tarballs are preferred if you've written a program that you intend to distribute for other platforms.

Using Debian Packages

In their overall features, Debian packages are similar to RPMs, but the details of operation for each differ, and Debian packages are used on different distributions than are RPMs. Because each system uses its own database format, RPMs and Debian packages aren't interchangeable without converting formats. Using Debian packages requires knowing how to use the dpkg, dselect, and apt-get commands. A few other commands can also be helpful.

Debian Distributions and Conventions

As the name implies, Debian packages originated with the Debian distribution. Since that time, the format has been adopted by several other distributions, including Ubuntu, Linux Mint, and Xandros. Such distributions are derived from the original Debian, which means that packages from the original Debian are likely to work well on other Debian-based systems. Although Debian doesn't emphasize flashy GUI configuration tools, its derivatives tend to be more GUI-centric, which makes these distributions more appealing to Linux novices. The original Debian favors a system that's as bug free as possible, and it tries to adhere strictly to open-source software principles rather than invest effort in GUI configuration tools. The original Debian is unusual in that it's maintained not by a company that is motivated by profit but rather by volunteers who are motivated by the desire to build a product they want to use.

Like RPM, the Debian package format is neutral with respect to both OS and CPU type. Debian packages are extremely rare outside Linux, although attempts to use various systems that used the Debian package system and software library atop non-Linux kernels have been made, and largely abandoned, with the exception of kFreeBSD (www.debian.org/ports/kfreebsd-gnu/).

The original Debian distribution has been ported to many different CPUs, including *x*86, *x*86-64, IA-64, ARM, PowerPC, Alpha, 680*x*0, MIPS, and SPARC. The original architecture was *x*86, and subsequent ports exist at varying levels of maturity. Derivative distributions generally work only on *x*86 or *x*86-64 systems, but this could change in the future.

Debian packages follow a naming convention similar to that for RPMs, but Debian packages sometimes omit codes in the filename to specify a package's architecture, particularly on *x*86 packages. When these codes are present, they may differ from RPM conventions. For instance, a filename ending in i386.deb indicates an *x*86 binary, powerpc.deb is a PowerPC binary, and all.deb indicates a CPU-independent package, such as documentation or scripts. As with RPM files, this file-naming convention is only that—a convention. You can rename a file as you see fit, either to include or omit the processor code. There is no code for Debian source packages because, as described in the upcoming section "Debian Packages Compared to Other Package Formats," Debian source packages consist of several separate files.

The *dpkg* Command Set

Debian packages are incompatible with RPM packages, but the basic principles of operation are the same across both package types. Like RPMs, Debian packages include dependency information, and the Debian package utilities maintain a database of installed packages, files, and so on. You use the dpkg command to install a Debian package. This command's syntax is similar to that of rpm:

dpkg [*options*][*action*] [*package-files*|*package-name*]

action is the action to be taken; common actions are summarized in Table 2.4. The options (Table 2.5) modify the behavior of the action, much like the options to rpm.

TABLE 2.4   dpkg primary actions

Action	Description
-i or --install	Installs a package
--configure	Reconfigures an installed package: runs the post-installation script to set site-specific options
-r or --remove	Removes a package but leaves configuration files intact
-P or --purge	Removes a package, including configuration files
--get-selections	Displays currently installed packages

Action	Description
`-p` or `--print-avail`	Displays information about an installed package
`-I` or `--info`	Displays information about an uninstalled package file
`-l pattern` or `--list pattern`	Lists all installed packages whose names match *pattern*
`-L` or `--listfiles`	Lists the installed files associated with a package
`-S pattern` or `--search pattern`	Locates the package(s) that own the file(s) specified by *pattern*
`-C` or `--audit`	Searches for partially installed packages and suggests what to do with them

TABLE 2.5   Options for fine-tuning dpkg actions

Option	Used with actions	Description
`--root=dir`	All	Modifies the Linux system using a root directory located at `dir`. Can be used to maintain one Linux installation discrete from another one, say during OS installation or emergency maintenance.
`-B` or `--auto-deconfigure`	`-r`	Disables packages that rely on one that is being removed.
`--force-things`	Assorted	Overrides defaults that would ordinarily cause dpkg to abort. Consult the dpkg man page for details of what (specified by `things`) this option does.
`--ignore-depends =package`	`-i`, `-r`	Ignores dependency information for the specified package.
`--no-act`	`-i`, `-r`	Checks for dependencies, conflicts, and other problems without actually installing or removing the package.
`--recursive`	`-i`	Installs all packages that match the package-name wildcard in the specified directory and all subdirectories.
`-G`	`-i`	Doesn't install the package if a newer version of the same package is already installed.
`-E` or `--skip-same-version`	`-i`	Doesn't install the package if the same version of the package is already installed.

As with rpm, dpkg expects a package name in some cases and a package filename in others. Specifically, --install (-i) and --info (-I) both require the package filename, but the other commands take the shorter package name.

As an example, consider the following command, which installs the samba_4.1.6+dfsg-1ubuntu2.1404.3_amd64.deb package:

```
# dpkg -i samba_4.1.6+dfsg-1ubuntu2.1404.3_amd64.deb
```

If you're upgrading a package, you may need to remove an old package before installing the new one. To do this, use the -r option to dpkg, as in the following:

```
# dpkg -r samba
```

To find information about an installed package, use the -p parameter to dpkg, as shown in Listing 2.2. This listing omits an extended English description of what the package does.

Listing 2.2: dpkg package information query output

```
$ dpkg -p samba
Package: samba
Priority: optional
Section: net
Installed-Size: 11157
Maintainer: Ubuntu Developers <ubuntu-devel-discuss@lists.ubuntu.com>
Architecture: amd64
Version: 2:4.1.6+dfsg-1ubuntu2.14.04.3
Replaces: libsamdb0 (<< 4.0.0~alpha17~), python-samba (<< 2:4.1.4+dfsg-3),
 samba-ad-dc, samba-common (<= 2.0.5a-2), samba-doc (<< 2:4.0.5~), samba-
libs (<< 2:4.1.4+dfsg-2), samba4
Depends: adduser, heimdal-hdb-api-8, libpam-modules, libpam-runtime (>=
 1.0.1-11), lsb-base (>= 4.1+Debian), procps, python (>= 2.7), python-
dnspython, python-ntdb, python-samba, samba-common (= 2:4.1.6+dfsg-
1ubuntu2.14.04.3), samba-common-bin (= 2:4.1.6+dfsg-1ubuntu2.14.04.3),
samba-dsdb-modules, tdb-tools, update-inetd, sysv-rc (>= 2.88dsf-24) |
file-rc (>= 0.8.16), python (<< 2.8), python2.7:any, libasn1-8-heimdal (>=
1.4.0+git20110226), libbsd0 (>= 0.5.0), libc6 (>= 2.14), libcomerr2 (>=
1.01), libhdb9-heimdal (>= 1.4.0+git20110226), libkdc2-heimdal (>=
1.4.0+git20110226), libkrb5-26-heimdal (>= 1.4.0+git20110226), libldb1
(>= 0.9.21), libpopt0 (>= 1.14), libpython2.7 (>= 2.7), libroken18-heimdal
 (>=
1.4.0+git20110226), libtalloc2 (>= 2.0.4~git20101213), libtdb1 (>=
1.2.7+git20101214), libtevent0 (>= 0.9.14), samba-libs (= 2:4.1.6+dfsg-
1ubuntu2.14.04.3)
Pre-Depends: dpkg (>= 1.15.6~), multiarch-support
```

```
Recommends: attr, logrotate, samba-vfs-modules
Suggests: bind9 (>= 1:9.5.1), bind9utils, ldb-tools, ntp, smbldap-tools,
winbind, ufw
Conflicts: libldb1 (<< 1:1.1.15), samba (<< 2:3.3.0~rc2-5), samba-ad-dc,
samba-doc (<< 2:4.0.5~), samba-tools, samba4 (<< 4.0.0~alpha6-2)
Enhances: bind9, ntp
Size: 838626
```

Debian-based systems often use a pair of somewhat higher-level utilities, apt-get and dselect, to handle package installation and removal. These utilities are described later in "Using apt-get" and "Using dselect, aptitude, and Synaptic." Their interfaces can be very useful when you want to install several packages, but dpkg is often more convenient when you're manipulating just one or two packages. Because dpkg can take package file-names as input, it's also the preferred method of installing a package that you download from an unusual source or create yourself.

Using *apt-cache*

The APT suite of tools includes a program, apt-cache, that's intended solely to provide information about the Debian package database (known in Debian terminology as the *package cache*). You may be interested in using several features of this tool:

Display Package Information   Using the showpkg subcommand, as in **apt-cache showpkg samba**, displays information about the package. The information displayed is different from that returned by dpkg's informational actions.

Display Package Statistics   You can learn how many packages you've installed, how many dependencies are recorded, and various other statistics about the package database by passing the stats subcommand, as in **apt-cache stats**.

Find Unmet Dependencies   If a program is reporting missing libraries or files, typing **apt-cache unmet** may help; this function of apt-cache returns information about unmet dependencies, which may help you track down the source of missing-file problems.

Display Dependencies   Using the depends subcommand, as in **apt-cache depends samba**, shows all of the specified package's dependencies. This information can be helpful in tracking down dependency-related problems. The rdepends subcommand finds reverse dependencies—packages that depend on the one you specify.

Locate All Packages   The pkgnames subcommand displays the names of all the packages installed on the system. If you include a second parameter, as in **apt-cache pkgnames sa**, the program returns only those packages that begin with the specified string.

Several more subcommands and options exist, but these are the ones you're most likely to use. Several apt-cache subcommands are intended for package maintainers and debugging serious package database problems rather than day-to-day system administration. Consult the man page for apt-cache for more information.

Using *apt-get*

APT, with its apt-get utility, is Debian's equivalent to Yum on certain RPM-based distributions. This meta-packaging tool lets you perform easy upgrades of packages, especially if you have a fast Internet connection. Debian-based systems include a file, /etc/apt/sources.list, that specifies locations from which important packages can be obtained. If you installed the OS from a CD-ROM drive, this file will initially list directories on the installation CD-ROM in which packages can be found. There are also likely to be a few lines near the top, commented out with hash marks (#), indicating directories on an FTP site or a website from which you can obtain updated packages. (These lines may be uncommented if you did a network install initially.)

> Don't add a site to /etc/apt/sources.list unless you're sure it can be trusted. The apt-get utility does automatic and semiautomatic upgrades, so if you add a network source to sources.list and that source contains unreliable programs or programs with security holes, your system will become vulnerable after upgrading via apt-get.

Although APT is most strongly associated with Debian systems, a port to RPM-based systems is also available. Check http://apt4rpm.sourceforge.net for information about this port.

The apt-get utility works by obtaining information about available packages from the sources listed in /etc/apt/sources.list and then using that information to upgrade or install packages. The syntax is similar to that of dpkg:

apt-get [*options*][*command*] [*package-names*]

Table 2.6 lists the apt-get commands, and Table 2.7 lists the most commonly used options. In most cases, you won't use *any* options with apt-get—just a single command and possibly one or more package names. One particularly common use of this utility is to keep your system up-to-date with any new packages. The following two commands will accomplish this goal if /etc/apt/sources.list includes pointers to up-to-date file archive sites:

```
# apt-get update
# apt-get dist-upgrade
```

TABLE 2.6   apt-get commands

Command	Description
update	Obtains updated information about packages available from the installation sources listed in /etc/apt/sources.list.
upgrade	Upgrades all installed packages to the newest versions available, based on locally stored information about available packages.

Command	Description
dselect-upgrade	Performs any changes in package status (installation, removal, and so on) left undone after running dselect.
dist-upgrade	Similar to upgrade, but performs "smart" conflict resolution to avoid upgrading a package if doing so would break a dependency.
install	Installs a package by package name (not by package filename), obtaining the package from the source that contains the most up-to-date version.
remove	Removes a specified package by package name.
source	Retrieves the newest available source package file by package filename using information about available packages and installation archives listed in /etc/apt/sources.list.
check	Checks the package database for consistency and broken package installations.
clean	Performs housekeeping to help clear out information about retrieved files from the Debian package database. If you don't use dselect for package management, run this from time to time in order to save disk space.
autoclean	Similar to clean, but removes information only about packages that can no longer be downloaded.

TABLE 2.7   Most-useful apt-get options

Option	Used with commands	Description
-d or --download-only	upgrade, dselect-upgrade, install, source	Downloads package files but doesn't install them.
-f or --fix-broken	install, remove	Attempts to fix a system on which dependencies are unsatisfied.
-m, --ignore-missing, or --fix-missing	upgrade, dselect-upgrade, install, remove, source	Ignores all package files that can't be retrieved (because of network errors, missing files, or the like).
-q or --quiet	All	Omits some progress indicator information. May be doubled (for instance, -qq) to produce still less progress information.

TABLE 2.7   Most-useful apt-get options *(continued)*

Option	Used with commands	Description
-s, --simulate, --just-print, --dry-run, --recon, or --no-act	All	Performs a simulation of the action without actually modifying, installing, or removing files.
-y, --yes, or --assume-yes	All	Produces a "yes" response to any yes/no prompt in installation scripts.
-b, --compile, or --build	source	Compiles a source package after retrieving it.
--no-upgrade	install	Causes apt-get to *not* upgrade a package if an older version is already installed.

WARNING   If you use APT to upgrade all packages on your system automatically, you're effectively giving control of your computer to the distribution maintainer. Although Debian or other distribution maintainers are unlikely to try to break into your computer in this way, an automatic update with minimal supervision on your part could easily break something on your system, particularly if you've obtained packages from unusual sources in the past.

In Exercise 2.2, you'll familiarize yourself with the Debian package system.

EXERCISE 2.2

Managing Debian Packages

To manage Debian packages, follow these steps:

1. Log into the Linux system as a normal user.

2. Acquire a package to use for testing purposes. You can try using a package from your distribution that you know you haven't installed; if you try a random package, however, you may find that it's already installed or has unmet dependencies. As an example, this lab uses the installation of zsh_5.0.2-3ubuntu6_amd64.deb, a shell that's not installed by default on most systems, obtained using the -d option to apt-get on an Ubuntu 14.04 system. You must adjust the commands as necessary if you use another package, distribution, or architecture in your tests.

3. Launch an xterm from the desktop environment's menu system if you used a GUI login.

4. Acquire root privileges. You can do this by typing su in an xterm, by selecting Session ⪢ New Root Console from a Konsole window, or by using sudo (if it's configured) to run the commands in the following steps.

5. Type dpkg **-L zsh** to verify that the package isn't currently installed. This command responds with a list of files associated with the package if it's installed or with an error that reads Package 'zsh' is not installed if it's not.

6. Type **dpkg –I zsh_5.0.2-3ubuntu6_amd64.deb**. (You'll need to add a complete path to the package file if it's not in your current directory.) The system should respond by displaying information about the package, such as the version number, dependencies, the name of the package maintainer, and a package description.

7. Type **dpkg -i zsh_5.0.2-3ubuntu6_amd64.deb**. The system should install the package and display a series of lines summarizing its actions as it does so.

8. Type **dpkg -p zsh**. The system should respond with information about the package similar to that displayed in step 6.

9. Type **zsh**. This launches a Z shell, which functions much like the more common bash and tcsh shells. You're likely to see your command prompt change slightly, but you can issue most of the same commands that you can use with bash or tcsh.

10. Type **dpkg -P zsh**. This command removes the package from the system, including configuration files. It may produce a series of warnings about non-empty directories that it couldn't remove. Note that you're removing the zsh package while running the zsh program. Linux continues to run the zsh program you're using, but you'll be unable to launch new instances of the program. Some programs may misbehave because files will be missing after you remove the package.

11. Type **exit** to exit from zsh and return to your normal shell.

12. Type **dpkg -L zsh**. The system should respond with a Package 'zsh' is not installed error, because you've just uninstalled it.

13. Type **apt-get install zsh** to install zsh using the APT system. Depending on your configuration, the system may download the package from an Internet site or ask you to insert a CD-ROM. If it asks for a CD-ROM, insert it and press the Enter key. The system should install the package.

14. Type **dpkg -p zsh**. The system should respond with information about the package similar to that displayed in step 6 or step 8.

15. Type **dpkg -P zsh**. This command removes the package from the system, as described in step 10.

Using *dselect, aptitude,* and Synaptic

The dselect program is a high-level package browser. Using it, you can select packages to install on your system from the APT archives defined in /etc/apt/sources.list, review the packages that are already installed on your system, uninstall packages, and upgrade packages. Overall, dselect is a powerful tool, but it can be intimidating to the uninitiated because it presents a lot of options that aren't obvious, using a text-mode interactive user interface. Because of that, most Linux distributions don't install it by default. Nonetheless, it's well worth taking the time to install it and getting to know how to use it.

Although dselect supports a few command-line options, they're mostly obscure or minor (such as options to set the color scheme). Consult dselect's man page for details. To use the program, type **dselect**. The result is the dselect main menu, as shown running in an Ubuntu desktop in Figure 2.1.

FIGURE 2.1   The dselect utility provides access to APT features using a menu system.

Another text-based Debian package manager is aptitude. In interactive mode, aptitude is similar to dselect in a rough way, but aptitude adds menus accessed by pressing Ctrl+T and rearranges some features. You can also pass various commands to aptitude on the command line, as in **aptitude search samba**, which searches for packages related to Samba. Features accessible from the command line (or the interactive interface) include the following:

Update Package Lists   You can update package lists from the APT repositories by typing **aptitude update**.

Install Software   The install command-line option installs a named package. This command has several variant names and syntaxes that modify its action. For instance, typing **aptitude install zsh** installs the zsh package, but typing **aptitude install zsh-** (with a trailing dash) and **aptitude remove zsh** both uninstall zsh.

Upgrade Software　The `full-upgrade` and `safe-upgrade` options both upgrade all installed packages. The `safe-upgrade` option is conservative about removing packages or installing new ones and so may fail; `full-upgrade` is less conservative about these actions, and so it is more likely to complete its tasks. However, it may break software in the process.

Search for Packages　The `search` option, noted earlier, searches the database for packages matching the specified name. The result is a list of packages, one per line, with summary codes for each package's install status, its name, and a brief description.

Clean Up the Database　The `autoclean` option removes already-downloaded packages that are no longer available, and `clean` removes all downloaded packages.

Obtain Help　Typing **aptitude help** results in a complete list of options.

　Broadly speaking, `aptitude` combines the interactive features of `dselect` with the command-line options of apt-get. All three programs provide similar functionality, so you can use whichever one you prefer.

　A tool that's similar to `dselect` and `aptitude` in some ways is Synaptic, but Synaptic is a GUI X-based program and, as such, is easier to use. Overall, `dselect`, `aptitude`, and Synaptic are useful tools, particularly if you need to locate software but don't know its exact name—the ability to browse and search the available packages can be a great boon. Unfortunately, the huge package list can be intimidating.

Reconfiguring Packages

Debian packages often provide more-extensive initial setup options than do their RPM counterparts. Frequently, the install script included in the package asks a handful of questions, such as querying for the name of an outgoing mail relay system for a mail server program. These questions help the package system set up a standardized configuration that has nonetheless been customized for your computer.

　In the course of your system administration, you may alter the configuration files for a package. If you do this and find that you've made a mess of things, you may want to revert to the initial standard configuration. To do so, you can use the `dpkg-reconfigure` program, which runs the initial configuration script for the package you specify:

```
# dpkg-reconfigure samba
```

　This command reconfigures the `samba` package, asking the package's initial installation questions and restarting the Samba daemons. Once this is done, the package should be in something closer to its initial state.

Debian Packages Compared to Other Package Formats

The overall functionality of Debian packages is similar to that of RPMs, although there are differences. Debian source packages aren't single files; they're groups of files—the original source tarball, a patch file that's used to modify the source code (including a file that controls the building of a Debian package), and a `.dsc` file that contains a digital "signature" to help verify the authenticity of the collection. The Debian package tools can combine these and compile the package to create a Debian binary package. This structure makes Debian source packages slightly less convenient to transport because you must move at least two files (the tarball and patch file; the .dsc file is optional) rather than just one. Debian source packages also support just one patch file, whereas RPM source packages may contain multiple patch files. Although you can certainly combine multiple patch files into one, doing so makes it less clear where a patch comes from, thus making it harder to back out of any given change.

These source package differences are mostly of interest to software developers. As a system administrator or end user, you need not normally be concerned with them unless you must recompile a package from a source form—and even then, the differences between the formats need not be overwhelming. The exact commands and features used by each system differ, but they accomplish similar overall goals.

Because all distributions that use Debian packages are derived from Debian, they tend to be more compatible with one another (in terms of their packages) than are RPM-based distributions. In particular, Debian has defined details of its system startup scripts and many other features to help Debian packages install and run on any Debian-based system. This helps Debian-based systems avoid the sorts of incompatibilities in startup scripts that can cause problems using one distribution's RPMs on another distribution. Of course, some future distribution could violate Debian's guidelines for these matters, so this advantage isn't guaranteed to hold over time.

As a practical matter, it can be harder to locate Debian packages than RPM packages for some exotic programs. Debian maintains a good collection at www.debian.org/distrib/packages, and some program authors make Debian packages available as well. If you can find an RPM but not a Debian package, you may be able to convert the RPM to Debian format using a program called alien, as described shortly in "Converting between Package Formats." If all else fails, you can use a tarball, but you'll lose the advantages of the Debian package database.

Configuring Debian Package Tools

With the exception of the APT sources list mentioned earlier, Debian package tools don't usually require configuration. Debian installs reasonable defaults (as do its derivative distributions). On rare occasions, though, you may want to adjust some of these defaults. Doing so requires that you know where to look for them.

The main configuration file for dpkg is /etc/dpkg/dpkg.cfg or ~/.dpkg.cfg. This file contains dpkg options, as summarized in Table 2.5, but without the leading dashes. For instance, to have dpkg always perform a test run rather than actually install a package, you'd create a dpkg.cfg file that contains one line:

```
no-act
```

For APT, the main configuration file you're likely to modify is /etc/apt/sources.list, which was described earlier in "Using apt-get." Beyond this file is /etc/apt/apt.conf, which controls APT and dselect options. As with dpkg.cfg, chances are you won't need to modify apt.conf. If you do need to make changes, the format is more complex and is modeled after those of the Internet Software Consortium's (ISC's) Dynamic Host Configuration Protocol (DHCP) and Berkeley Internet Name Domain (BIND) servers' configuration files. Options are grouped together by open and close curly braces ({}):

```
APT
{
  Get
  {
    Download-Only "true";
  };
};
```

These lines are equivalent to setting the --download-only option permanently, as described in Table 2.7. You can, of course, set many more options. For details, consult apt.conf's man page. You may also want to review the sample configuration file, /usr/share/doc/apt/examples/apt.conf. (The working /etc/apt/apt.conf file is typically extremely simple, or it may be missing entirely and therefore not be very helpful as an example.)

You should be aware that Debian's package tools rely on various files in the /var/lib/dpkg directory tree. These files maintain lists of available packages, lists of installed packages, and so on. In other words, this directory tree is effectively the Debian installed file database. As such, you should be sure to back up this directory when you perform system backups and be careful about modifying its contents.

Converting between Package Formats

Sometimes you're presented with a package file in one format, but you want to use another format. This is particularly common when you use a Debian-based distribution and can find only tarballs or RPM files of a package. When this happens, you can keep looking for a package file in the appropriate format, install the tools for the foreign format, create a package from a source tarball using the standard RPM or Debian tools, or convert between package formats with a utility like alien.

This section focuses on this last option. The alien program comes with Debian and a few other distributions, but it may not be installed by default. If it's not installed on your system, install it by typing **apt-get install alien** on a system that uses APT, or use the RPMFind or Debian package website to locate it. This program can convert between RPM packages, Debian packages, Stampede packages (used by Stampede Linux), and tarballs.

You need to be aware of some caveats. For one thing, alien requires that you have appropriate package manager software installed—for instance, both RPM and Debian—to convert between these formats. The `alien` utility doesn't always convert all dependency information completely and correctly. When converting from a tarball, `alien` copies the files directly as they had been in the tarball, so `alien` works only if the original tarball has files that should be installed off the root (/) directory of the system.

> Although `alien` requires both RPM and Debian package systems to be installed to convert between these formats, it doesn't use the database features of these packages unless you use the `--install` option. The presence of a foreign package manager isn't a problem as long as you don't use it to install software that might duplicate or conflict with software installed with your primary package manager.

The basic syntax of `alien` is as follows:

```
alien [options] file[...]
```

The most important options are `--to-deb`, `--to-rpm`, `--to-slp`, and `--to-tgz`, which convert to Debian, RPM, Stampede, and tarball format, respectively. (If you omit the destination format, `alien` assumes that you want a Debian package.) The `--install` option installs the converted package and removes the converted file. Consult the `alien` man page for additional options.

For instance, suppose you have a Debian package called `someprogram-1.2.3-4_i386.deb`, and you want to create an RPM from it. You can issue the following command to create an RPM called `someprogram-1.2.3-4.i386.rpm`:

```
# alien --to-rpm someprogram-1.2.3-4_i386.deb
```

If you use a Debian-based system and want to install a tarball but keep a record of the files it contains in your Debian package database, you can do so with the following command:

```
# alien --install binary-tarball.tar.gz
```

It's important to remember that converting a tarball converts the files in the directory structure of the original tarball using the system's root directory as the base. Therefore, you may need to unpack the tarball, juggle files around, and repack it to get the desired results *prior to* installing the tarball with `alien`. For instance, suppose you have a binary tarball that creates a directory called `program-files`, with `bin`, `man`, and `lib` directories under this. The intent may have been to unpack the tarball in `/usr` or `/usr/local` and create links for critical files. To convert this tarball to an RPM, you can issue the following commands:

```
# tar xvfz program.tar.gz
# mv program-files usr
# tar cvfz program.tgz usr
# rm -r usr
# alien --to-rpm program.tgz
```

By renaming the program-files directory to usr and creating a new tarball, you've created a tarball that, when converted to RPM format, will have files in the locations you want—/usr/bin, /usr/man, and /usr/lib. You might need to perform more extensive modifications, depending on the contents of the original tarball.

Package Dependencies and Conflicts

Although package installation often proceeds smoothly, sometimes it doesn't. The usual sources of problems relate to unsatisfied dependencies or conflicts between packages. The RPM and Debian package management systems are intended to help you locate and resolve such problems. However, on occasion (particularly when mixing packages from different vendors), they can actually cause problems. In either event, it pays to recognize these errors and know how to resolve them.

If you use a meta-packager, such as Yum or APT, for all of your package management, you're much less likely to run into problems with package dependencies and conflicts. These problems are most likely to arise when you install lone packages, especially those from unusual sources.

Real and Imagined Package Dependency Problems

Package dependencies and conflicts can arise for a variety of reasons, including the following:

Missing Libraries or Support Programs   One of the most common dependency problems is caused by a missing support package. For instance, all KDE programs rely on Qt, a widget set that provides assorted GUI tools. If Qt isn't installed, you won't be able to install any KDE packages using RPMs or Debian packages. Libraries—support code that can be used by many different programs as if it were part of the program itself—are particularly common sources of problems in this respect.

Incompatible Libraries or Support Programs   Even if a library or support program is installed on your system, it may be the wrong version. For instance, if a program requires Qt 4.8, the presence of Qt 3.3 won't do much good. Fortunately, Linux library-naming conventions enable you to install multiple versions of a library in case you have programs with competing requirements.

Duplicate Files or Features   Conflicts arise when one package includes files that are already installed and that belong to another package. Occasionally, broad features can conflict as well, as in two web server packages. Feature conflicts are usually accompanied by name conflicts. Conflicts are most common when mixing packages intended for different distributions, because distributions may split files across packages in different ways.

Mismatched Names   RPM and Debian package management systems give names to their packages. These names don't always match across distributions. For this reason, if one package checks for another package by name, the first package may not install on another distribution, even if the appropriate package is installed, because that target package has a different name.

Some of these problems are very real and serious. Missing libraries, for instance, must be installed. (Sometimes, though, a missing library isn't quite as missing as it seems, as described in the upcoming section "Forcing the Installation.") Others, like mismatched package names, are artifacts of the packaging system. Unfortunately, it's not always easy to tell into which category a conflict fits. When using a package management system, you may be able to use the error message returned by the package system, along with your own experience with and knowledge of specific packages, to make a judgment. For instance, if RPM reports that you're missing a slew of libraries with which you're unfamiliar, you'll probably have to track down at least one package—unless you know you've installed the libraries in some other way, in which case you may want to force the installation.

Workarounds for Package Dependency Problems

When you encounter an unmet package dependency or conflict, what can you do about it? There are several approaches to these problems. Some of these approaches work well in some situations but not others, so you should review the possibilities carefully. The options include forcing the installation, modifying your system to meet the dependency, rebuilding the problem package from source code, and finding another version of the problem package.

Forcing the Installation

One approach is to ignore the issue. Although this sounds risky, it's appropriate in some cases involving failed RPM or Debian dependencies. For instance, if the dependency is on a package that you installed by compiling the source code yourself, you can safely ignore the dependency. When using rpm, you can tell the program to ignore failed dependencies by using the --nodeps parameter:

```
# rpm -i apackage.rpm --nodeps
```

You can force installation over some other errors, such as conflicts with existing packages, by using the --force parameter:

```
# rpm -i apackage.rpm --force
```

WARNING   Do *not* use --nodeps or --force as a matter of course. Ignoring the dependency checks can lead you into trouble, so you should use these options only when you need to do so. In the case of conflicts, the error messages you get when you first try to install without --force will tell you which packages' files you'll be replacing, so be sure you back them up or that you are prepared to reinstall the packages in case of trouble.

If you're using dpkg, you can use the `--ignore-depends=`*package*, `--force-depends`, and `--force-conflicts` parameters to overcome dependency and conflict problems in Debian-based systems. Because there's less deviation in package names and requirements among Debian-based systems, these options are less often needed on such systems.

Upgrading or Replacing the Depended-on Package

Officially, the proper way to overcome a package dependency problem is to install, upgrade, or replace the depended-on package. If a program requires, say, Qt 4.8 or greater, you should upgrade an older version (such as 4.4) to 4.8. To perform such an upgrade, you'll need to track down and install the appropriate package. This usually isn't too difficult if the new package you want comes from a Linux distribution, especially if you use a meta-packager such as Yum or APT; the appropriate depended-on package should come with the same distribution.

One problem with this approach is that packages intended for different distributions sometimes have differing requirements. If you run Distribution A and install a package that was built for Distribution B, the package will express dependencies in terms of Distribution B's files and versions. The appropriate versions may not be available in a form intended for Distribution A, and by installing Distribution B's versions, you can sometimes cause conflicts with other Distribution A packages. Even if you install the upgraded package and it works, you may run into problems in the future when it comes time to install some other program or upgrade the distribution as a whole—the upgrade installer may not recognize Distribution B's package or may not be able to upgrade to its own newer version.

Rebuilding the Problem Package

Some dependencies result from the libraries and other support utilities installed on the computer that compiled the package, not from requirements in the underlying source code. If the software is recompiled on a system that has different packages, the dependencies will change. Therefore, rebuilding a package from source code can overcome at least some dependencies.

Most developer-oriented RPM-based systems, such as Fedora, include a command to rebuild an RPM package: You call `rpmbuild` (or `rpm` with old versions of RPM) with the name of the source package and use `--rebuild`, as follows:

```
# rpmbuild --rebuild packagename-version.src.rpm
```

Of course, to do this you must have the source RPM for the package. This can usually be obtained from the same location as the binary RPM. When you execute this command, `rpmbuild` extracts the source code and executes whatever commands are required to build a new package—or sometimes several new packages. (One source RPM can build multiple binary RPMs.) The compilation process can take anywhere from a few seconds to several hours, depending on the size of the package and the speed of your computer. The result should be one or more new binary RPMs in /usr/src/*distname*/RPMS/*arch*, where *distname* is a distribution-specific name (such as redhat on Red Hat or packages on SUSE) and *arch* is your CPU architecture (such as i386 or i586 for *x*86 or ppc for PowerPC). You can move these RPMs to any convenient location and install them just as you would any others.

Source packages are also available for Debian systems, but aside from sites devoted to Debian and related distributions, Debian source packages are rare. The sites that do have these packages provide them in forms that typically install easily on appropriate Debian or related systems. For this reason, it's less likely that you'll rebuild a Debian package from source.

Be aware that compiling a source package typically requires you to have appropriate development tools installed on your system, such as the GNU Compiler Collection (GCC) and assorted development libraries. *Development libraries* are the parts of a library that enable programs to be written for the library. Many Linux installations lack development libraries even when the matching binary libraries are installed. Thus, you may need to install quite a few packages to recompile a source package. The error messages you receive when you attempt but fail to build a source package can help you track down the necessary software, but you may need to read several lines of error messages and use your package system to search for appropriate tools and development libraries. (Development libraries often include the string dev or devel in their names.)

Locating Another Version of the Problem Package

Frequently, the simplest way to fix a dependency problem or package conflict is to use a different version of the package that you want to install. This could be a newer or older official version (4.2.3 rather than 4.4.7, say), or it might be the same official version but built for your distribution rather than for another distribution. Sites like RPMFind (www.rpmfind.net) and Debian's package listing (www.debian.org/distrib/packages) can be very useful in tracking down alternative versions of a package. Your own distribution's website or FTP site can also be a good place to locate packages.

If the package you're trying to install requires newer libraries than you have, and you don't want to upgrade those libraries, an older version of the package may work with your existing libraries. Before installing such a program, though, you should check to be sure that the newer version of the program doesn't fix security bugs. If it does, you should find another way to install the package.

The main problem with locating another version of the package is that sometimes you really need the version that's not installing correctly. It may have features that you need, or it may fix important bugs. On occasion, other versions may not be available, or you may be unable to locate another version of the package in your preferred package format.

Startup Script Problems

One particularly common problem when trying to install servers from one distribution in another is getting startup scripts to work. In the past, most major Linux distributions used SysV startup scripts, but these scripts weren't always transportable across distributions. Today, alternatives to SysV are common, such as the systemd startup method, which further complicates this problem. The result is that the server you installed may not start up. Possible workarounds include modifying the startup script that came with the server, building a new script based on another one from your distribution, and starting the server through a local startup script like /etc/rc.d/rc.local or /etc/rc.d/ boot.local. Chapter 5, "Booting Linux and Editing Files," describes startup scripts in more detail.

Startup script problems affect only servers and other programs that are started automatically when the computer boots; they don't affect typical user applications or libraries.

Managing Shared Libraries

Most Linux software relies heavily on *shared libraries*. The preceding sections have described some of the problems that can arise in managing shared library packages—for example, if a library isn't installed or is the wrong version, you may have problems installing a package. Library management goes beyond merely configuring them, though. To understand this, you must first understand a few library principles. You can then move on to setting the library path and using commands that manage libraries.

Library Principles

The idea behind a library is to simplify programmers' lives by providing commonly used program fragments. For instance, one of the most important libraries is the C *library* (libc), which provides many of the higher-level features associated with the C programming language. Another common type of library is associated with GUIs. These libraries are often called *widget sets* because they provide the onscreen *widgets* used by programs—buttons, scroll bars, menu bars, and so on. The GIMP Tool Kit (GTK+) and Qt are the most popular Linux widget sets, and both ship largely as libraries. Programmers choose libraries, not users; you usually can't substitute one library for another. (The main exceptions are minor version upgrades.)

Linux uses the *GNU C library (glibc)* version of the C library. Package-manager dependencies and other library references are to glibc specifically. As of glibc 2.15, for historical reasons the main glibc file is usually called /lib/libc.so.6 or /lib64/libc.so.6, but this file is sometimes a symbolic link to a file of another name, such as /lib/ libc-2.15.so.

In principle, the routines in a library can be linked into a program's main file, just like all of the object code files created by the compiler. This approach, however, has certain problems:

- The resulting program file is huge. This means it takes up a lot of disk space, and it consumes a lot of RAM when loaded.

- If multiple programs use the library, as is common, the program-size issue is multiplied several times; the library is effectively stored multiple times on disk and in RAM.

- The program can't take advantage of improvements in the library without being recompiled (or at least relinked).

For these reasons, most programs use their libraries as shared libraries (aka *dynamic libraries*). In this form, the main program executable omits most of the library routines. Instead, the executable includes references to shared library files, which can then be loaded along with the main program file. This approach helps keep program file size down, enables sharing of the memory consumed by libraries across programs, and enables programs to take advantage of improvements in libraries by upgrading the library.

Linux shared libraries are similar to the dynamic link libraries (DLLs) of Windows. Windows DLLs are usually identified by .dll filename extensions. In Linux, however, shared libraries usually have a .so or .so.*version* extension, where *version* is a version number. (.so stands for *shared object*.) Linux *static libraries* (used by linkers for inclusion in programs when dynamic libraries aren't to be used) have .a filename extensions.

On the downside, shared libraries can degrade program load time slightly if the library isn't already in use by another program, and they can create software management complications:

- Shared library changes can be incompatible with some or all programs that use the library. Linux uses library-numbering schemes to enable you to keep multiple versions of a library installed at once. Upgrades that shouldn't cause problems can overwrite older versions, whereas major upgrades get installed side by side with their older counterparts. This approach minimizes the chance of problems, but sometimes changes that *shouldn't* cause problems *do* cause them.

- Programs must be able to locate shared libraries. This task requires adjusting configuration files and environment variables. If it's done wrong, or if a program overrides the defaults and looks in the wrong place, the result is usually that the program won't run at all.

- The number of libraries for Linux has risen dramatically over time. When they're used in shared form, the result can be a tangled mess of package dependencies, particularly if you use programs that rely on many or obscure libraries. In most cases, this issue boils down to a package problem that can be handled by your package management tools.

- If an important shared library becomes inaccessible because it was accidentally over-written due to a disk error or for any other reason, the result can be severe system problems. In a worst-case scenario, the system might not even boot.

In most cases, these drawbacks are manageable and are much less important than the problems associated with using static libraries. Thus, dynamic libraries are very popular.

 Developers who create programs using particularly odd, outdated, or otherwise exotic libraries sometimes use static libraries. This enables them to distribute their binary packages without requiring users to obtain and install their oddball libraries. Likewise, static libraries are sometimes used on small emergency systems, which don't have enough programs installed to make the advantages of shared libraries worth pursuing.

Locating Library Files

The major administrative challenge of handling shared libraries involves enabling programs to locate those shared libraries. Binary program files can point to libraries either by name alone (as in libc.so.6) or by providing a complete path (as in /lib/libc.so.6). In the first case, you must configure a *library path*—a set of directories in which programs should search for libraries. This can be done both through a global configuration file and through an environment variable. If a static path to a library is wrong, you must find a way to correct the problem. In all of these cases, after making a change, you may need to use a special command to get the system to recognize the change, as described later in "Library Management Commands."

Setting the Path System Wide

The first way to set the library path is to edit the /etc/ld.so.conf file. This file consists of a series of lines, each of which lists one directory in which shared library files may be found. Typically, this file lists between half a dozen and a couple dozen directories. Some distributions have an additional type of line in this file. These lines begin with the include directive; they list files that are to be included as if they were part of the main file. For instance, Ubuntu 12.04's ld.so.conf begins with this line:

```
include /etc/ld.so.conf.d/*.conf
```

This line tells the system to load all of the files in /etc/ld.so.conf.d whose names end in .conf as if they were part of the main /etc/ld.so.conf file. This mechanism enables package maintainers to add their unique library directories to the search list by placing a .conf file in the appropriate directory.

Some distributions, such as Gentoo, use a mechanism with a similar goal but different details. With these distributions, the env-update utility reads files in /etc/env.d to create the final form of several /etc configuration files, including /etc/ld.so.conf.

In particular, the LDPATH variables in these files are read, and their values make up the lines in ld.so.conf. Thus, to change ld.so.conf in Gentoo or other distributions that use this mechanism, you should add or edit files in /etc/env.d and then type env-update to do the job.

Generally speaking, there's seldom a need to change the library path system wide. Library package files usually install themselves in directories that are already on the path or add their paths automatically. The main reason to make such changes would be if you installed a library package, or a program that creates its own libraries, in an unusual location via a mechanism other than your distribution's main package utility. For instance, you might compile a library from source code and then need to update your library path in this way.

After you change your library path, you must use ldconfig to have your programs use the new path, as described later in "Library Management Commands."

In addition to the directories specified in /etc/ld.so.conf, Linux refers to the trusted library directories, /lib and /usr/lib. These directories are always on the library path, even if they aren't listed in ld.so.conf.

Temporarily Changing the Path

Sometimes, changing the path permanently and globally is unnecessary and even inappropriate. For instance, you might want to test the effect of a new library before using it for all of your programs. To do so, you could install the shared libraries in an unusual location and then set the LD_LIBRARY_PATH environment variable. This environment variable specifies additional directories the system is to search for libraries.

Chapter 9, "Writing Scripts, Configuring Email, and Using Databases," describes environment variables in more detail.

To set the LD_LIBRARY_PATH environment variable using the bash shell, you can type a command like this:

```
$ export LD_LIBRARY_PATH=/usr/local/testlib:/opt/newlib
```

This line adds two directories, /usr/local/testlib and /opt/newlib, to the search path. You can specify as few or as many directories as you like, separated by colons. These directories are added to the *start* of the search path, which means they take precedence over other directories. This fact is handy when you're testing replacement libraries, but it can cause problems if users manage to set this environment variable inappropriately.

You can set this environment variable permanently in a user's shell startup script files, as described in Chapter 9. Doing so means the user will *always* use the specified library paths in addition to the normal system paths. In principle, you could set the LD_LIBRARY_PATH globally; however, using /etc/ld.so.conf is the preferred method of effecting global changes to the library path.

Unlike other library path changes, this one doesn't require that you run ldconfig for it to take effect.

Correcting Problems

Library path problems usually manifest as a program's inability to locate a library. If you launch the program from a shell, you'll see an error message like this:

```
$ gimp
gimp: error while loading shared libraries: libXinerama.so.1: cannot~CA
 open shared object file: No such file or directory
```

This message indicates that the system couldn't find the libXinerama.so.1 library file. The usual cause of such problems is that the library isn't installed, so you should look for it using commands such as find (described in Chapter 4, "Managing Files"). If the file isn't installed, try to track down the package to which it should belong (a Web search can work wonders for this task) and install it.

If, on the other hand, the library file is available, you may need to add its directory globally or to LD_LIBRARY_PATH. Sometimes, the library's path is hard-coded in the program's binary file. (You can discover this using ldd, as described shortly in "Library Management Commands.") When this happens, you may need to create a symbolic link from the location of the library on your system to the location the program expects. A similar problem can occur when the program expects a library to have one name but the library has another name on your system. For instance, the program may link to biglib.so.5, but your system has biglib.so.5.2 installed. Minor version-number changes like this are usually inconsequential, so creating a symbolic link will correct the problem:

```
# ln -s biglib.so.5.2 biglib.so.5
```

You must type this command as root in the directory in which the library resides. You must then run ldconfig, as described in the next section.

Library Management Commands

Linux provides a pair of commands that you're likely to use for library management. The ldd program displays a program's shared library dependencies—that is, the shared libraries that a program uses. The ldconfig program updates caches and links used by the system for locating libraries—that is, it reads /etc/ld.so.conf and implements any changes in that file or in the directories to which it refers. Both of these tools are invaluable in managing libraries.

Displaying Shared Library Dependencies

If you run into programs that won't launch because of missing libraries, the first step is to check which libraries the program file uses. You can do this with the ldd command:

```
$ ldd /bin/ls
    linux-vdso.so.1 =>  (0x00007fff77bfe000)
    libselinux.so.1=>/lib/x86_64/libselinux.so.1 (0x00007f878f48f000)
    libacl.so.1 => /lib/x86_64-linux-gnu/libacl.so.1 (0x00007f878f287000)
    libc.so.6 => /lib/x86_64-linux-gnu/libc.so.6 (0x00007f878eec0000)
    libpcre.so.3 => /lib/x86_64-linux-gnu/libpcre.so.3 (0x00007f878ec82000)
    libdl.so.2 => /lib/x86_64-linux-gnu/libdl.so.2 (0x00007f878ea7e000)
    /lib64/ld-linux-x86-64.so.2 (0x00007f878f6cb000)
    libattr.so.1 => /lib/x86_64-linux-gnu/libattr.so.1 (0x00007f878e878000)
$
```

Each line of output begins with a library name, such as librt.so.1 or libncurses.so.5. If the library name doesn't contain a complete path, ldd attempts to find the true library and displays the complete path following the => symbol, as in /lib/librt.so.1 or /lib/libncurses.so.5. You needn't be concerned about the long hexadecimal number following the complete path to the library file. The preceding example shows one library (/lib64/ld-linux-x86-64.so.2) that's referred to with a complete path in the executable file. It lacks the initial directory-less library name and => symbol.

The ldd command accepts a few options. The most notable of these is probably -v, which displays a long list of version information following the main entry. This information may be helpful in tracking down which version of a library a program is using, in case you have multiple versions installed.

Keep in mind that libraries can themselves depend on other libraries, thus you can use ldd to discover what libraries are used by a library. Because of this potential for a dependency chain, it's possible that a program will fail to run even though all of its libraries are present. When using ldd to track down problems, be sure to check the needs of all the libraries of the program, and all of the libraries used by the first tier of libraries, and so on, until you've exhausted the chain.

The ldd utility can be run by ordinary users as well as by root. You must run it as root if you can't read the program file as an ordinary user.

Rebuilding the Library Cache

Linux (or, more precisely, the ld.so and ld-linux.so programs, which manage the loading of libraries) doesn't read /etc/ld.so.conf every time a program runs. Instead, the system relies on a cached list of directories and the files they contain stored in binary format in /etc/ld.so.cache. This list is maintained in a format that's much more efficient than a plain-text list of files and directories. The drawback is that you must rebuild that cache every time you add or remove libraries. These additions and removals include both changing the contents of the library directories and adding or removing library directories.

The tool to do this job is called `ldconfig`. Ordinarily, it's called without any options:

```
# ldconfig
```

This program does, though, take options to modify its behavior:

Display Verbose Information   Ordinarily, `ldconfig` doesn't display any information as it works. The `-v` option causes the program to summarize the directories and files it's registering as it goes about its business.

Don't Rebuild the Cache   The `-N` option causes `ldconfig` *not* to perform its primary duty of updating the library cache. It will, though, update symbolic links to libraries, which is a secondary duty of this program.

Process Only Specified Directories   The `-n` option causes `ldconfig` to update the links contained in the directories specified on the command line. The system won't examine the directories specified in `/etc/ld.so.conf` or the trusted directories (`/lib` and `/usr/lib`).

Don't Update Links   The `-X` option is the opposite of `-N`; it causes `ldconfig` to update the cache but not manage links.

Use a New Configuration File   You can change the configuration file from `/etc/ld.so.conf` by using the `-f` *conffile* option, where *conffile* is the file you want to use.

Use a New Cache File   You can change the cache file that `ldconfig` creates by passing the `-C` *cachefile* option, where *cachefile* is the file you want to use.

Use a New Root   The `-r` *dir* option tells `ldconfig` to treat *dir* as if it were the root (`/`) directory. This option is helpful when you're recovering a badly corrupted system or installing a new OS.

Display Current Information   The `-p` option causes `ldconfig` to display the current cache—all of the library directories and the libraries they contain.

Both RPM and Debian library packages typically run `ldconfig` automatically after installing or removing the package. The same thing happens as part of the installation process for many packages compiled from source. Thus, you may well be running `ldconfig` more than you realize in the process of software management. You may need to run the program yourself if you manually modify your library configuration in any way.

Managing Processes

When you type a command name, that program is run and a *process* is created for it. Knowing how to manage these processes is critical to using Linux. Key details in this task include identifying processes, manipulating foreground and background processes, killing processes, and adjusting process priorities.

Understanding the Kernel: The First Process

The Linux kernel is at the heart of every Linux system. Although you can't manage the kernel process in quite the way you can manage other processes, short of rebooting the computer, you can learn about it. To do so, you can use the uname command, which takes several options to display information:

Node Name   The -n or --nodename option displays the system's node name; that is, its network hostname.

Kernel Name   The -s or --kernel-name option displays the kernel name, which is Linux on a Linux system.

Kernel Version   You can find the kernel version with the -v or --kernel-version option. Ordinarily, this holds the kernel build date and time, not an actual version number.

Kernel Release   The actual kernel version number can be found via the -r or --kernel-release option.

Machine   The -m or --machine option returns information about your machine. This is likely to be a CPU code, such as i686 or x86_64.

Processor   Using the -p or --processor option may return information about your CPU, such as the manufacturer, model, and clock speed; in practice, it returns unknown on many systems.

Hardware Platform   Hardware platform information is theoretically returned by the -i or --hardware-platform option, but this option often returns unknown.

OS Name   The -o or --operating-system option returns the OS name—normally GNU/Linux for a Linux system.

Print All Information   The -a or --all option returns all available information.

In practice, you're most likely to use uname -a at the command line to learn some of the basics about your kernel and system. The other options are most useful in multiplatform scripts, which can use these options to obtain critical information quickly in order to help them adjust their actions for the system on which they're running.

Examining Process Lists

One of the most important tools in process management is ps. This program displays processes' status (hence the name, ps). It sports many helpful options, and it's useful in monitoring what's happening on a system. This can be particularly critical when the computer isn't working as it should be—for instance, if it's unusually slow. The ps program supports an unusual number of options, but just a few of them will take you a long way. Likewise, interpreting ps output can be tricky because so many options modify the program's output. Some ps-like programs, most notably top, also deserve attention.

Using Useful *ps* Options

The official syntax for ps is fairly simple:

ps [*options*]

This simplicity of form hides considerable complexity because ps supports three different *types* of options as well as many options within each *type*. The three types of options are as follows:

Unix98 Options   These single-character options may be grouped together and are preceded by a single dash (-).

BSD Options   These single-character options may be grouped together and must *not* be preceded by a dash.

GNU Long Options   These multi-character options are never grouped together. They're preceded by two dashes (--).

Options that may be grouped together may be clustered without spaces between them. For instance, rather than typing **ps -a -f**, you can type **ps -af**. The reason for so much complexity is that the ps utility has historically varied a lot from one Unix OS to another. The version of ps that ships with major Linux distributions attempts to implement most features from all these different ps versions, so it supports many different personalities. In fact, you can change some of its default behaviors by setting the PS_PERSONALITY environment variable to posix, old, linux, bsd, sun, digital, or various others. The rest of this section describes the default ps behavior on most Linux systems.

Some of the more useful ps features include the following:

Display Help   The --help option summarizes some of the more common ps options.

Display All Processes   By default, ps displays only processes that were run from its own terminal (xterm, text-mode login, or remote login). The -A and -e options cause it to display all of the processes on the system, and x displays all processes owned by the user who gives the command. The x option also increases the amount of information that's displayed about each process.

Display One User's Processes   You can display processes owned by a given user with the -u *user*, U *user*, and --User options. The *user* variable may be a username or a user ID.

Display Extra Information   The -f, -l, j, l, u, and v options all expand the information provided in the ps output. Most ps output formats include one line per process, but ps can display enough information that it's impossible to fit it all on one 80-character line. Therefore, these options provide various mixes of information.

Display Process Hierarchy   The -H, -f, and --forest options group processes and use indentation to show the hierarchy of relationships between processes. These options are useful if you're trying to trace the parentage of a process.

Display Wide Output   The ps command output can be more than 80 columns wide. Normally, ps truncates its output so that it will fit on your screen or xterm. The -w and w options tell ps not to do this, which can be useful if you direct the output to a file, as in **ps w > ps.txt**. You can then examine the output file in a text editor that supports wide lines.

You can combine these ps options in many ways to produce the output you want. You'll probably need to experiment to learn which options produce the desired results because each option modifies the output in some way. Even those that would seem to influence just the selection of processes to list sometimes modify the information that's provided about each process.

Interpreting *ps* Output

Listing 2.3 and Listing 2.4 show a couple of examples of ps in action. Listing 2.3 shows **ps -u rodsmith --forest**, and Listing 2.4 shows **ps u rodsmith**.

Listing 2.3: Output of **ps -u rodsmith --forest**

```
$ ps -u rodsmith --forest
  PID TTY          TIME CMD
 2451 pts/3     00:00:00 bash
 2551 pts/3     00:00:00 ps
 2496 ?         00:00:00 kvt
 2498 pts/1     00:00:00 bash
 2505 pts/1     00:00:00  \_ nedit
 2506 ?         00:00:00        \_ csh
 2544 ?         00:00:00             \_ xeyes
19221 ?         00:00:01 dfm
```

Listing 2.4: Output of **ps u rodsmith**

```
$ ps u rodsmith
USER        PID %CPU %MEM   VSZ  RSS TTY      STAT START    TIME COMMAND
rodsmith 19221  0.0  1.5  4484 1984 ?        S    May07    0:01 dfm
rodsmith  2451  0.0  0.8  1856 1048 pts/3    S    16:13    0:00 -bash
rodsmith  2496  0.2  3.2  6232 4124 ?        S    16:17    0:00 /opt/kd
rodsmith  2498  0.0  0.8  1860 1044 pts/1    S    16:17    0:00 bash
rodsmith  2505  0.1  2.6  4784 3332 pts/1    S    16:17    0:00 nedit
rodsmith  2506  0.0  0.7  2124 1012 ?        S    16:17    0:00 /bin/cs
rodsmith  2544  0.0  1.0  2576 1360 ?        S    16:17    0:00 xeyes
rodsmith  2556  0.0  0.7  2588  916 pts/3    R    16:18    0:00 ps u
```

The output produced by ps normally begins with a heading line, which displays the meaning of each column. Important information that may be displayed (and labeled) includes the following:

Username   This is the name of the user who runs the programs. Listing 2.3 and Listing 2.4 restricted this output to one user to limit the length of the listings.

Process ID   The process ID (PID) is a number that's associated with the process. This item is particularly important because you need it to modify or kill the process, as described later in this chapter.

Parent Process ID   The parent process ID (PPID) identifies the process's parent. (Neither Listing 2.3 nor Listing 2.4 shows the PPID.)

TTY   The teletype (TTY) is a code used to identify a terminal. As illustrated by Listing 2.3 and Listing 2.4, not all processes have TTY numbers—X programs and daemons, for instance, don't. Text-mode programs do have these numbers, which point to a console, xterm, or remote login session.

CPU Time   The TIME and %CPU headings are two measures of CPU time used. The first indicates the total amount of CPU time consumed, and the second represents the percentage of CPU time the process is using when ps executes. Both can help you spot runaway processes—those that are consuming too much CPU time. Unfortunately, what constitutes "too much" varies from one program to another, so it's impossible to give a simple rule to help you spot a runaway process.

CPU Priority   As described shortly, in "Managing Process Priorities," it's possible to give different processes different priorities for CPU time. The NI column, if present (it's not in the preceding examples) lists these priority codes. The default value is 0. Positive values represent *reduced* priority, whereas negative values represent *increased* priority.

Memory Use   Various headings indicate memory use—for instance, RSS is resident set size (the memory used by the program and its data), and %MEM is the percentage of memory the program is using. Some output formats also include a SHARE column, which is memory that's shared with other processes (such as shared libraries). As with CPU-use measures, these columns can help point you to the sources of difficulties, but because legitimate memory needs of programs vary so much, it's impossible to give a simple criterion for when a problem exists.

Command   The final column in most listings is the command used to launch the process. This is truncated in Listing 2.4 because this format lists the complete command, but so much other information appears that the complete command won't usually fit on one line. (This is where the wide-column options can come in handy.)

As you can see, a lot of information can be gleaned from a ps listing—or perhaps that should be the plural *listings*, because no single format includes all of the available information. For the most part, the PID, username, and command are the most important pieces of information. In some cases, though, you may need other specific components. If your system's memory or CPU use has skyrocketed, for instance, you'll want to pay attention to the memory or CPU use column.

> It's often necessary to find specific processes. You might want to find the PID associated with a particular command in order to kill it, for instance. This information can be gleaned by piping the ps output through grep, as in **ps ax | grep bash** to find all of the instances of bash.

Although you may need a wide screen or xterm to view the output, you may find ps -A --forest to be a helpful command in learning about your system. Processes that aren't linked to others were either started directly by init or have had their parents killed, and so they have been "adopted" by init. (Chapter 5 describes init and the boot procedure in more detail.) Most of these processes are fairly important—they're servers, login tools, and so on. Processes that hang off several others in this tree view, such as xeyes and nedit in Listing 2.3, are mostly user programs launched from shells.

top: A Dynamic *ps* Variant

If you want to know how much CPU time various processes are consuming relative to one another, or if you want to discover quickly which processes are consuming the most CPU time, a tool called top is the one for the job. The top tool is a text-mode program, but of course it can be run in an xterm or similar window, as shown in Figure 2.2. There are also GUI variants, like kpm and gnome-system-monitor. By default, top sorts its entries by CPU use, and it updates its display every few seconds. This makes it a very good tool for spotting runaway processes on an otherwise lightly loaded system—those processes almost always appear in the first position or two, and they consume an inordinate amount of CPU time. Figure 2.2 shows a typical top output screen, displaying the different processes and their CPU utilization. You'll need to be familiar with the purposes and normal habits of programs running on *your* system in order to make such determinations; the legitimate needs of different programs vary so much that it's impossible to give a simple rule for judging when a process is consuming too much CPU time.

Like many Linux commands, top accepts several options. The most useful are listed here:

-d *delay* This option specifies the delay between updates, which is normally 5 seconds.

-p *pid* If you want to monitor specific processes, you can list them using this option. You'll need the PIDs, which you can obtain with ps, as described earlier. You can specify up to 20 PIDs by using this option multiple times, once for each PID.

-n *iter* You can tell top to display a certain number of updates (*iter*) and then quit. (Normally, top continues updating until you terminate the program.)

-b This option specifies batch mode, in which top doesn't use the normal screen-update commands. You might use this to log CPU use of targeted programs to a file, for instance.

FIGURE 2.2   The top command shows system summary information and information about the most CPU-intensive processes on a computer.

```
rich@rich-VirtualBox: ~
top - 00:33:31 up 20 min,  2 users,  load average: 0.47, 0.45, 0.35
Tasks: 165 total,   2 running, 163 sleeping,   0 stopped,   0 zombie
%Cpu(s): 19.5 us,  2.7 sy,  0.0 ni, 77.9 id,  0.0 wa,  0.0 hi,  0.0 si,  0.0 st
KiB Mem:   1773568 total,  1428692 used,   344876 free,    41996 buffers
KiB Swap:  1813500 total,        0 used,  1813500 free.   612756 cached Mem

  PID USER      PR  NI    VIRT    RES    SHR S %CPU %MEM     TIME+ COMMAND
 2200 rich      20   0 1319016 229808  39860 S 18.3 13.0   2:07.23 compiz
 1222 root      20   0  296656  71928  15492 S  4.0  4.1   0:25.85 Xorg
 4522 rich      20   0   29136   1644   1156 R  0.3  0.1   0:00.07 top
    1 root      20   0   33768   3068   1464 S  0.0  0.2   0:01.62 init
    2 root      20   0       0      0      0 S  0.0  0.0   0:00.00 kthreadd
    3 root      20   0       0      0      0 S  0.0  0.0   0:00.14 ksoftirqd/0
    4 root      20   0       0      0      0 S  0.0  0.0   0:00.00 kworker/0:0
    5 root       0 -20       0      0      0 S  0.0  0.0   0:00.00 kworker/0:0H
    6 root      20   0       0      0      0 S  0.0  0.0   0:00.37 kworker/u2:0
    7 root      20   0       0      0      0 S  0.0  0.0   0:00.81 rcu_sched
    8 root      20   0       0      0      0 R  0.0  0.0   0:01.46 rcuos/0
    9 root      20   0       0      0      0 S  0.0  0.0   0:00.00 rcu_bh
   10 root      20   0       0      0      0 S  0.0  0.0   0:00.00 rcuob/0
   11 root      rt   0       0      0      0 S  0.0  0.0   0:00.00 migration/0
   12 root      rt   0       0      0      0 S  0.0  0.0   0:00.04 watchdog/0
   13 root       0 -20       0      0      0 S  0.0  0.0   0:00.00 khelper
   14 root      20   0       0      0      0 S  0.0  0.0   0:00.00 kdevtmpfs
```

You can do more with top than watch it update its display. When it's running, you can enter any of several single-letter commands, some of which prompt you for additional information. These commands include the following:

h **and** ?   These keystrokes display help information.

k   You can kill a process with this command. The top program will ask for a PID number, and if it's able to kill the process, it will do so. (The upcoming section "Killing Processes" describes other ways to kill processes.)

q   This option quits from top.

r   You can change a process's priority with this command. You'll have to enter the PID number and a new priority value—a positive value will decrease its priority, and a negative value will increase its priority, assuming it has the default 0 priority to begin with. Only root may increase a process's priority. The renice command (described shortly, in "Managing Process Priorities") is another way to accomplish this task.

s   This command changes the display's update rate, which you'll be asked to enter (in seconds).

P   This command sets the display to sort by CPU usage, which is the default.

M   You can change the display to sort by memory usage with this command.

If you're just looking for the memory usage on the system, try using the free command. It provides a quick glance at how much physical and swap memory is in use, and how much is available.

More commands are available in top (both command-line options and interactive commands) than can be summarized here; consult top's man page for more information.

One of the pieces of information provided by top is the *load average*, which is a measure of the demand for CPU time by applications. In Figure 2.2, you can see three load-average estimates on the top line; these correspond to the current load average and two previous measures. A system on which no programs are demanding CPU time has a load average of 0.0. A system with one program running CPU-intensive tasks has a load average of 1.0. Higher load averages reflect programs competing for available CPU time. You can also find the current load average via the uptime command, which displays the load average along with information on how long the computer has been running. The load average can be useful in detecting runaway processes. For instance, if a system normally has a load average of 0.5 but suddenly gets stuck at a load average of 2.5, a couple of CPU-hogging processes may have hung—that is, become unresponsive. Hung processes sometimes needlessly consume a lot of CPU time. You can use top to locate these processes and, if necessary, kill them.

Most computers today include multiple CPUs or CPU cores. On such systems, the load average can equal the number of CPUs or cores before competition for CPU time begins. For instance, on a quad-core CPU, the load average can be as high as 4.0 without causing contention. Typically, one program can create a load of just 1.0; however, *multithreaded* programs can create higher load averages, particularly on multi-core systems.

jobs: Processes Associated with Your Session

The jobs command displays minimal information about the processes associated with the current session. In practice, jobs is usually of limited value, but it does have a few uses. One of these is to provide job ID numbers. These numbers are conceptually similar to PID numbers, but they're not the same. Jobs are numbered starting from 1 for each session and, in most cases, a single shell has only a few associated jobs. The job ID numbers are used by a handful of utilities in place of PIDs, so you may need this information.

A second use of jobs is to ensure that all of your programs have terminated prior to logging out. Under some circumstances, logging out of a remote login session can cause the client program to freeze up if you've left programs running. A quick check with jobs will inform you of any forgotten processes and enable you to shut them down.

pgrep: Finding Processes

The pgrep command was introduced in the Solaris operating system, but it has been ported to the open-source world and is becoming more popular in Linux. It allows you to perform simple searches within the process list; similar to piping the ps command output to the grep command.

The format of the pgrep command is as follows:

```
pgrep  [-flvx]  [-n  |  -o]  [-d delim]  [-P ppidlist] [-g pgrplist]
       [-s sidlist]  [-u euidlist]  [-U uidlist]  [-G gidlist]
```

```
[-J projidlist] [-t termlist] [-T taskidlist] [-c ctidlist]
[-z zoneidlist] [pattern]
```

You can search for processes based on the username, user ID, or group ID as well as any type of regular expression pattern:

```
$ pgrep -u root cron
812
$
```

This example searches for a process named cron, run by the root user account. Notice that the pgrep command only returns the process ID value of the processes that match the query.

Understanding Foreground and Background Processes

One of the most basic process-management tasks is to control whether a process is running in the foreground or the background; that is, whether it's monopolizing the use of the terminal from which it was launched. Normally, when you launch a program, it takes over the terminal, preventing you from doing other work in that terminal. (Some programs, though, release the terminal. This is most common for servers and some GUI programs.)

If a program is running but you decide you want to use that terminal for something else, pressing Ctrl+Z normally pauses the program and gives you control of the terminal. (An important point is that this procedure suspends the program, so if it's performing real work, that work stops!) This can be handy if, say, you're running a text editor in a text-mode login and you want to check a filename so that you can mention it in the file you're editing. You press Ctrl+Z and type **ls** to get the file listing. To get back to the text editor, you then type **fg**, which restores the text editor to the foreground of your terminal. If you've suspended several processes, you add a job number, as in **fg 2**, to restore job 2. You can obtain a list of jobs associated with a terminal by typing **jobs**, which displays the jobs and their job numbers.

A variant on fg is bg. Whereas fg restores a job to the foreground, bg restores a job to running status, but in the background. You can use this command if the process you're running is performing a CPU-intensive task that requires no human interaction but you want to use the terminal in the meantime. Another use of bg is in a GUI environment—after launching a GUI program from an xterm or similar window, that shell is tied up servicing the GUI program, which probably doesn't really need the shell. Pressing Ctrl+Z in the xterm window will enable you to type shell commands again, but the GUI program will be frozen. To unfreeze the GUI program, type **bg** in the shell, which enables the GUI program to run in the background while the shell continues to process your commands.

As an alternative to launching a program, using Ctrl+Z, and typing **bg** to run a program in the background, you can append an ampersand (&) to the command when launching the program. For instance, rather than editing a file with the NEdit GUI editor by typing **nedit myfile.txt**, you can type **nedit myfile.txt &**. This command launches the nedit program in the background from the start, leaving you able to control your xterm window for other tasks.

Managing Process Priorities

Sometimes, you may want to prioritize your programs' CPU use. For instance, you may be running a program that's very CPU intensive but that will take a long time to finish its work, and you don't want that program to interfere with others that are of a more interactive nature. Alternatively, on a heavily loaded computer, you may have a job that's more important than others that are running, so you may want to give it a priority boost. In either case, the usual method of accomplishing this goal is through the nice and renice commands. You can use nice to launch a program with a specified priority or use renice to alter the priority of a running program.

You can assign a priority to nice in any of three ways: by specifying the priority preceded by a dash (this works well for positive priorities but makes them look like negative priorities), by specifying the priority after the -n parameter, or by specifying the priority after the --adjustment= parameter. In all cases, these parameters are followed by the name of the program you want to run:

nice [*argument*] [*command* [*command-arguments*]]

For instance, the following three commands are all equivalent:

```
$ nice -12 number-crunch data.txt
$ nice -n 12 number-crunch data.txt
$ nice --adjustment=12 number-crunch data.txt
```

All three of these commands run the number-crunch program at priority 12 and pass it the data.txt file. If you omit the adjustment value, nice uses 10 as a default. The range of possible values is –20 to 19, with negative values having the highest priority. Only root may launch a program with increased priority (that is, give a negative priority value), but any user may use nice to launch a program with low priority. The default priority for a program run without nice is 0.

If you've found that a running process is consuming too much CPU time or it is being swamped by other programs and so should be given more CPU time, you can use the renice program to alter its priority without disrupting the program's operation. The syntax for renice is as follows:

renice *priority* [[-p] *pids*] [[-g] *pgrps*] [[-u] *users*]

You must specify *priority*, which takes the same values this variable takes with nice. In addition, you must specify one or more PIDs (*pids*), one or more group IDs (*pgrps*), or one or more usernames (*users*). In the latter two cases, renice changes the priority of all programs that match the specified criterion—but only root may use renice in this way. Also, only root may increase a process's priority. If you give a numeric value without a -p, -g, or -u option, renice assumes the value is a PID. You may mix and match these methods of specification. For instance, you might enter the following command:

```
# renice 7 16580 -u pdavison tbaker
```

This command sets the priority to 7 for PID 16580 and for all processes owned by pdavison and tbaker.

Killing Processes

Sometimes, reducing a process's priority isn't a strong enough action. A program may have become totally unresponsive, or you may want to terminate a process that shouldn't be running. In these cases, the kill command is the tool to use. This program sends a signal (a method that Linux uses to communicate with processes) to a process. The signal is usually sent by the kernel, the user, or the program itself to terminate the process. Linux supports many numbered signals, each of which is associated with a specific name. You can see them all by typing **kill -l**. If you don't use -l, the syntax for kill is as follows:

```
kill -s signal pid
```

Although Linux includes a kill program, many shells, including bash and csh, include built-in kill equivalents that work in much the same way as the external program. If you want to be sure you're using the external program, type its complete path, as in **/bin/kill.**

The -s *signal* parameter sends the specified signal to the process. You can specify the signal using either a number (such as 9) or a name (such as SIGKILL). The signals you're most likely to use are 1 (SIGHUP, which terminates interactive programs and causes many daemons to reread their configuration files), 9 (SIGKILL, which causes the process to exit without performing routine shutdown tasks), and 15 (SIGTERM, which causes the process to exit but allows it to close open files and so on). If you don't specify a signal, the default is 15 (SIGTERM). You can also use the shortened form -*signal*. If you do this and use a signal name, you should omit the SIG portion of the name—for instance, use KILL rather than SIGKILL. The *pid* option is, of course, the PID for the process that you want to kill. You can obtain this number from ps or top.

The kill program will kill only those processes owned by the user who runs kill. The exception is if that user is root; the superuser may kill any user's processes.

Real World Scenario

Running Programs Persistently

The kernel can pass signals to programs, even if you don't use the `kill` command. For instance, when you log out of a session, the programs you started from that session are sent the SIGHUP signal, which causes them to terminate. If you want to run a program that will continue running even when you log out, you can launch it with the nohup program:

$ **nohup** *program options*

This command causes the program to ignore the SIGHUP signal. It can be handy if you want to launch certain small servers that may legitimately be run as ordinary users.

A variant on `kill` is `killall`, which has the following form:

```
killall [options] [--] name [...]
```

This command kills a process based on its name rather than its PID number. For instance, **killall vi** kills all of the running processes called vi. You may specify a signal in the shortened form (-*signal*) or by preceding the signal number with -s or --signal. As with `kill`, the default is 15 (SIGTERM). One potentially important option to `killall` is -i, which causes it to ask for confirmation before sending the signal to each process. You might use it like this:

```
$ killall -i vi
Kill vi(13211) ? (y/n) y
Kill vi(13217) ? (y/n) n
```

In this example, two instances of the vi editor were running, but only one should have been killed. As a general rule, if you run `killall` as root, you should use the -i parameter; if you don't, it's all too likely that you'll kill processes that you shouldn't, particularly if many people are using the computer at once.

 Some versions of Unix provide a `killall` command that works very differently from Linux's `killall`. This alternate `killall` kills all of the processes started by the user who runs the command. This is a potentially much more destructive command, so if you ever find yourself on a non-Linux system, *do not* use `killall` until you've discovered what that system's `killall` does (say, by reading the `killall` man page).

Another variant on `kill` is the pkill command, which has the following format:

```
pkill  [-signal] [-fvx] [-n|-o] [-P ppidlist]
   [-g pgrplist] [-s sidlist] [-u euidlist] [-U uidlist]
```

```
[-G gidlist] [-J projidlist] [-t termlist] [-T taskidlist]
[-c ctidlist] [-z zoneidlist] [pattern]
```

The pkill command allows you to kill one or more processes based on usernames, user IDs, group IDs, and other features as well as using a matching regular expression. The pkill command was introduced in the Solaris operating system, but it has been ported to the Linux environment and is gaining in popularity.

WARNING   While the pkill command is extremely versatile, with that versatility comes danger. Be extremely careful if you're using regular expressions to match process names—it's very easy to match the wrong process names inadvertently!

Summary

Linux provides numerous tools to help you manage software. Most distributions are built around the RPM or Debian package systems, both of which enable installation, upgrade, and removal of software using a centralized package database to avoid conflicts and other problems that are common when no central package database exists. You can perform basic operations on individual files or, with the help of extra tools such as Yum and APT, keep your system synchronized with the outside world, automatically or semiautomatically updating all of your software to the latest versions.

No matter how you install your software, you may need to manage shared libraries. These software components are necessary building blocks of large modern programs, and, in the best of all possible worlds, they operate entirely transparently. Sometimes, though, shared libraries need to be upgraded or the system configuration changed so that programs can find the libraries. When this happens, knowing about critical configuration files and commands can help you work around any difficulties.

Beyond managing packages and libraries, Linux software management involves manipulating processes. Knowing how to manipulate foreground and background processes, adjust process priorities, and kill stray processes can help you keep your Linux system working well.

Exam Essentials

Identify critical features of RPM and Debian package formats.   RPM and Debian packages store all of the files for a given package in a single file that also includes information about what other packages the software depends on. These systems maintain a database of installed packages and their associated files and dependencies.

Describe the tools used for managing RPMs.   The rpm program is the main tool for installing, upgrading, and uninstalling RPMs. This program accepts operations and options that tell it precisely what to do. The Yum utility, and particularly its yum command, enables installation of a package and all its dependencies via the Internet rather than from local package files.

Describe the tools used for managing Debian packages.   The dpkg program installs or uninstalls a single package or a group of packages that you specify. The apt-get utility retrieves programs from installation media or from the Internet for installation, and it can automatically upgrade your entire system. The dselect program serves as a menu-driven interface to apt-get, enabling you to select programs that you want to install from a text-mode menu.

Summarize tools for extracting files and converting between package formats.   The rpm2cpio program can convert an RPM file to a cpio archive, enabling users of non-RPM systems to access files in an RPM. The alien utility can convert in any direction between Debian packages, RPMs, Stampede packages, and tarballs. This enables the use of packages intended for one system on another.

Summarize the reasons for using shared libraries.   Shared libraries keep disk space and memory requirements manageable by placing code that's needed by many programs in separate files from the programs that use it, enabling one copy to be used multiple times. More generally, libraries enable programmers to use basic "building blocks" that others have written without having to reinvent code constantly.

Describe methods available to change the library path.   The library path can be changed system wide by editing the /etc/ld.so.conf file and then typing ldconfig. For temporary or per-user changes, directories may be added to the path by placing them in the LD_LIBRARY_PATH environment variable.

Explain the difference between foreground and background processes.   Foreground processes have control of the current terminal or text-mode window (such as an xterm). Background processes don't have exclusive control of a terminal or text-mode window but are still running.

Describe how to limit the CPU time used by a process.   You can launch a program with nice or use renice to alter its priority in obtaining CPU time. If a process is truly out of control, you can terminate it with the kill command.

Review Questions

1. Which of the following is *not* an advantage of a source package over a binary package?

    A. A single source package can be used on multiple CPU architectures.

    B. By recompiling a source package, you can sometimes work around library incompatibilities.

    C. You can modify the code in a source package, thus altering the behavior of a program.

    D. Source packages can be installed more quickly than binary packages.

    E. You may be able to recompile source code for a non-Linux Unix program on Linux.

2. Which is true of using both RPM and Debian package management systems on one computer?

    A. It's generally inadvisable because the two systems don't share installed-file database information.

    B. It's impossible because their installed-file databases conflict with one another.

    C. It causes no problems if you install important libraries once in each format.

    D. It's a common practice on Red Hat and Debian systems.

    E. Using both systems simultaneously requires installing the `alien` program.

3. Which of the following statements is true about binary RPM packages that are built for a particular distribution?

    A. License requirements forbid using the package on any other distribution.

    B. They may be used in another RPM-based distribution only when you set the `--convert-distrib` parameter to `rpm`.

    C. They may be used in another RPM-based distribution only after you recompile the package's source RPM.

    D. They can be recompiled for an RPM-based distribution running on another type of CPU.

    E. They can often be used on another RPM-based distribution for the same CPU architecture, but this isn't guaranteed.

4. An administrator types the following command on an RPM-based Linux distribution:

    ```
    # rpm -ivh megaprog.rpm
    ```

    What is the effect of this command?

    A. If the `megaprog` package is installed on the computer, it is uninstalled.

    B. If the `megaprog.rpm` package exists, is valid, and isn't already installed on the computer, it is installed.

    C. The `megaprog.rpm` source RPM package is compiled into a binary RPM for the computer.

    D. Nothing; megaprog.rpm isn't a valid RPM filename, so rpm will refuse to operate on this file.

    E. The megaprog.rpm package replaces any earlier version of the package that's already installed on the computer.

5. Which of the following commands will extract the contents of the myfonts.rpm file into the current directory?

    A. `rpm2cpio myfonts.rpm | cpio -i --make-directories`

    B. `rpm2cpio myfonts.rpm > make-directories`

    C. `rpm -e myfonts.rpm`

    D. `alien --to-extract myfonts.rpm`

    E. `rpmbuild --rebuild myfonts.rpm`

6. To use dpkg to remove a package called theprogram, including its configuration files, which of the following commands would you issue?

    A. `dpkg -e theprogram`

    B. `dpkg -p theprogram`

    C. `dpkg -r theprogram`

    D. `dpkg -r theprogram-1.2.3-4.deb`

    E. `dpkg -P theprogram`

7. Which of the following describes a difference between apt-get and dpkg?

    A. apt-get provides a GUI interface to Debian package management; dpkg doesn't.

    B. apt-get can install tarballs in addition to Debian packages; dpkg can't.

    C. apt-get can automatically retrieve and update programs from Internet sites; dpkg can't.

    D. apt-get is provided only with the original Debian distribution, but dpkg comes with Debian and its derivatives.

    E. apt-get works only with Debian-based distributions, but dpkg can work with both RPMs and Debian packages.

8. What command would you type to obtain a list of all of the installed packages on a Debian system?

    A. `apt-get showall`

    B. `apt-cache showpkg`

    C. `dpkg -r allpkgs`

    D. `dpkg -i`

    E. `dpkg --get-selections`

9. As root, you type **apt-get update** on a Debian system. What should be the effect of this command?

    A. None: update is an invalid option to apt-get.

    B. The APT utilities deliver information about the latest updates you've made to the APT Internet repositories, enabling you to share your changes with others.

C. The APT utilities download all available upgrades for your installed programs and install them on your system.

D. The APT utilities retrieve information about the latest packages available so that you may install them with subsequent `apt-get` commands.

E. The APT utilities update themselves, ensuring that you're using the latest version of APT.

10. Which of the following commands would you type to update the `unzip` program on a Fedora system to the latest version? (Select all that apply.)

   A. `yum update unzip`

   B. `yum upgrade unzip`

   C. `yum -u unzip`

   D. `yum -U unzip`

   E. `yum check-update unzip`

11. How should you configure a system that uses Yum to access an additional Yum software repository?

   A. Edit the `/etc/apt/sources.list` file to include the repository site's URL, as detailed on the repository's website.

   B. Download a package from the repository site, and install it with RPM, or place a configuration file from the repository site in the `/etc/yum.repos.d` directory.

   C. Use the `add-repository` subcommand to yum or the Add Repository option in the File menu in yumex, passing it the URL of the repository.

   D. Edit the `/etc/yum.conf` file, locate the `[repos]` section, and add the URL to the repository after the existing repository URLs.

   E. Edit the `/etc/yum.conf` file, locate the `REPOSITORIES=` line, and add the new repository to the colon-delimited list on that line.

12. What is the preferred method of adding a directory to the library path for all users?

   A. Modify the `LD_LIBRARY_PATH` environment variable in a global shell script.

   B. Add the directory to the `/etc/ld.so.conf` file, and then type **ldconfig.**

   C. Type **ldconfig /new/dir**, where */new/dir* is the directory you want to add.

   D. Create a symbolic link from that directory to one that's already on the library path.

   E. Type **ldd /new/dir**, where */new/dir* is the directory you want to add.

13. You prefer the look of GTK+ widgets to Qt widgets, so you want to substitute the GTK+ libraries for the Qt libraries on your system. How would you do this?

   A. You must type **ldconfig --makesubs=qt,gtk**. This command substitutes the GTK+ libraries for the Qt libraries at load time.

   B. You must uninstall the Qt library packages and reinstall the GTK+ packages with the `--substitute=qt` option to rpm or the `--replace=qt` option to dpkg.

   C. You must note the filenames of the Qt libraries, uninstall the packages, and create symbolic links from the Qt libraries to the GTK+ libraries.

D. You can't easily do this; libraries can't be arbitrarily exchanged for one another. You would need to rewrite all of the Qt-using programs to use GTK+.

E. You must reboot the computer and pass the subst=qt,gtk option to the kernel. This causes the kernel to make the appropriate substitutions.

14. A user types **kill -9 11287** at a bash prompt. What is the probable intent, assuming the user typed the correct command?

   A. To cut off a network connection using TCP port 11287

   B. To display the number of processes that have been killed with signal 11287 in the last nine days

   C. To cause a server with process ID 11287 to reload its configuration file

   D. To terminate a misbehaving or hung program with process ID 11287

   E. To increase the priority of the program running with process ID 11287

15. What programs might you use to learn what your system's load average is? (Select two.)

   A. ld

   B. load

   C. top

   D. uptime

   E. la

16. Which of the following commands creates a display of processes, showing the parent-child relationships through links between their names?

   A. **ps --forest**

   B. **ps aux**

   C. **ps -e**

   D. **ps --tree**

   E. All of the above

17. You use top to examine the CPU time being consumed by various processes on your system. You discover that one process, dfcomp, is consuming more than 90 percent of your system's CPU time. What can you conclude?

   A. Very little: dfcomp could be legitimately consuming that much CPU time, or it could be an unauthorized or malfunctioning program.

   B. No program should consume 90 percent of available CPU time; dfcomp is clearly malfunctioning and should be terminated.

   C. This is normal; dfcomp is the kernel's main scheduling process, and it consumes any unused CPU time.

   D. This behavior is normal *if* your CPU is less powerful than a 2.5 GHz EM64T Pentium. However, on newer systems, no program should consume 90 percent of CPU time.

   E. This behavior is normal *if* your CPU has at least four cores, but on systems with fewer cores than this, no program should consume 90 percent of CPU time.

18. You type **jobs** at a bash command prompt and receive a new command prompt with no intervening output. What can you conclude?

    A. The total CPU time used by your processes is negligible (below 0.1).

    B. No processes are running under your username except the shell that you're using.

    C. The jobs shell is installed and working correctly on the system.

    D. The system has crashed; jobs normally returns a large number of running processes.

    E. No background processes are running that were launched from the shell that you're using.

19. Which of the following commands are equivalent to one another? (Select two.)

    A. `nice --value 10 crunch`

    B. `nice -n -10 crunch`

    C. `nice -10 crunch`

    D. `nice 10 crunch`

    E. `nice crunch`

20. Which of the following are restrictions on ordinary users' abilities to run `renice`? (Select two.)

    A. Users may not modify the priorities of processes that are already running.

    B. Users may not modify the priority of their programs launched from anything but their current shells.

    C. Users may not decrease the priority (that is, increase the priority value) of their own processes.

    D. Users may not modify the priorities of other users' processes.

    E. Users may not increase the priority (that is, decrease the priority value) of their own processes.

Chapter

3

Configuring Hardware

THE FOLLOWING EXAM OBJECTIVES ARE COVERED IN THIS CHAPTER:

- ✓ 101.1 Determine and configure hardware settings
- ✓ 102.1 Design hard disk layout
- ✓ 104.1 Create partitions and filesystems
- ✓ 104.2 Maintain the integrity of filesystems
- ✓ 104.3 Control mounting and unmounting of filesystems

All OSs run atop hardware, and this hardware influences how the OSs run. Obviously, hardware can be fast or slow, reliable or unreliable. A somewhat more subtle detail is that OSs provide various means of configuring and accessing the hardware—partitioning hard disks and reading data from *Universal Serial Bus (USB)* devices, for instance. You must understand at least the basics of how Linux interacts with its hardware environment in order to administer a Linux system effectively. This chapter presents that information.

This chapter begins with a look at *firmware*, which is the lowest-level software that runs on a computer. A computer's firmware begins the boot process and configures certain hardware devices. This chapter then moves on to expansion cards and USB devices.

The chapter concludes with an examination of disk hardware and the filesystems it contains—disk interface standards, disk partitioning, how to track disk usage, how to tune filesystems for optimal performance, how to check filesystems' internal consistency, and how to repair simple filesystem defects. Assuming that a filesystem is in good shape, you must be able to mount it to be able to use it, so that topic is also covered here. (One disk topic, boot managers, is covered in Chapter 5, "Booting Linux and Editing Files.")

Configuring the Firmware and Core Hardware

All computers ship with a set of core hardware—most obviously, a *central processing unit (CPU)*, which does the bulk of the computational work, and *random access memory (RAM)*, which holds data. Many additional basic features help glue everything together, and some of these can be configured both inside and outside of Linux. At the heart of much of this hardware is the firmware, which provides configuration tools and initiates the OS booting process. You can use the firmware's own user interface to enable and disable key hardware components. However, once Linux is booted, you may need to manage this hardware using Linux utilities. Key components managed by the firmware (and, once it's booted, Linux) include interrupts, I/O addresses, DMA addresses, the real-time clock, and Advanced Technology Attachment (ATA) hard disk interfaces.

Understanding the Role of the Firmware

Many hardware devices include firmware, so any given computer can have many types of firmware installed—for the motherboard, for a plug-in disk controller, for network interfaces, and so on. The most important firmware, though, is installed on the computer's motherboard. This firmware initializes the motherboard's hardware and controls the boot process. In the past, the vast majority of *x86*- and *x86-64*-based computers have used a type of firmware known as the *Basic Input/Output System (BIOS)*. Beginning in 2011, though, a new type of firmware, known as the *Extensible Firmware Interface (EFI)* or the *Unified EFI (UEFI)*, has become all but standard on new computers. Some older computers also use EFI. Despite the fact that technically EFI isn't a BIOS, most manufacturers refer to it by that name in their documentation. The exam objectives refer to the BIOS, but not to EFI. Nonetheless, in the real world, you're likely to encounter EFI on newer computers. The differences between BIOS and EFI are particularly important in booting the computer, as described in Chapter 5. For many of the setup tasks described in this chapter, the two types of firmware behave very similarly; although EFI implementations sometimes provide flashier graphical user interfaces, most BIOSs, and some EFIs, provide only text-mode user interfaces.

 In this book, we use the term *EFI* to refer both to the original EFI and to the newer UEFI, which is effectively EFI 2.*x*.

The motherboard's firmware resides in *electronically erasable programmable read-only memory (EEPROM)*, aka flash memory. When you turn on a computer, the firmware performs a *power-on self-test (POST)*, initializes hardware to a known operational state, loads the boot loader from the boot device (typically the first hard disk), and passes control to the boot loader, which in turn loads the OS.

Historically, an additional purpose of a BIOS was to provide fundamental input/output (I/O) services to the operating system and application programs, insulating them from hardware changes. Although the Linux kernel uses the BIOS to collect information about the hardware, once Linux is running, it doesn't use BIOS services for I/O. In theory, the OS can use some EFI services, but as of the 3.5.0 kernel, Linux takes advantage of few of these EFI features. Linux system administrators require a basic understanding of the BIOS or EFI because of the key role it plays in configuring hardware and in booting.

 Most *x86* and *x86-64* computers use a BIOS or an EFI; however, some computers use radically different software in place of these types of firmware. Older PowerPC-based Apple computers, for instance, use OpenFirmware. (Intel-based Macs use EFI.) Although OpenFirmware, EFI, and other firmware programs differ from the traditional (some now say "legacy") *x86* BIOS, these systems all perform similar tasks. If you must administer a computer with an unusual firmware, you should take some time to research the details of how its firmware operates; however, this won't greatly affect how Linux treats the hardware at the level of day-to-day system administration.

Although firmware implementations vary from manufacturer to manufacturer, most BIOSs and EFIs provide an interactive facility to configure them. Typically, you enter this setup tool by pressing the Delete key or a function key early in the boot sequence. (Consult your motherboard manual or look for onscreen prompts for details.) Figure 3.1 shows a typical BIOS setup main screen. You can use the arrow keys, the Enter key, and so on to move around the BIOS options and adjust them. Computers usually come delivered with reasonable BIOS defaults, but you may need to adjust them if you add new hardware or if a standard piece of hardware is causing problems.

FIGURE 3.1 A BIOS setup screen provides features related to low-level hardware configuration.

```
                        PhoenixBIOS Setup Utility
  Main   Advanced    Security   Power    Boot     Exit

                                              Item Specific Help
      System Time:      [22:18:26]
      System Date:      [03/21/2009]
                                             <Tab>, <Shift-Tab>, or
      Legacy Diskette A:  [1.44/1.25 MB  3½"]  <Enter> selects field.
      Legacy Diskette B:  [Disabled]

    ▶ Primary Master     [1048MB]
    ▶ Primary Slave      [None]
    ▶ Secondary Master   [CD-ROM]
    ▶ Secondary Slave    [None]

    ▶ Keyboard Features

      System Memory:     640 KB
      Extended Memory:   64512 KB
      Language:          [English  (US)]


  F1   Help    ↑↓  Select Item   -/+    Change Values    F9   Setup Defaults
  Esc  Exit    ←   Select Menu    Enter  Select ▶ Sub-Menu  F10  Save and Exit
```

PCs with EFIs may provide a setup utility similar to the one shown in Figure 3.1. As noted earlier, though, some EFIs feature flashier GUIs rather than a text-based user interface. Others are organized in a very different way, as shown in Figure 3.2. The variability makes it impossible to provide simple instructions on how to locate specific features; you may need to read your manual or explore the options your firmware provides.

One key ability of the firmware is to enable or disable onboard hardware. Modern motherboards provide a wide range of hardware devices, including video hardware, disk controllers, hard disk controllers, RS-232 serial ports, parallel ports, USB ports, Ethernet ports, and audio hardware. Usually, having this hardware available is beneficial, but sometimes it's not. The hardware may be inadequate, so you'll want to replace it with a more capable plug-in card, or you may not need it. In such cases, you can disable the device in the firmware. Doing so keeps the device from consuming the hardware resources that are described shortly, reducing the odds of an unused device interfering with the hardware you do use.

FIGURE 3.2   EFI firmware user interfaces vary greatly from one to another; you may need to spend some time exploring yours.

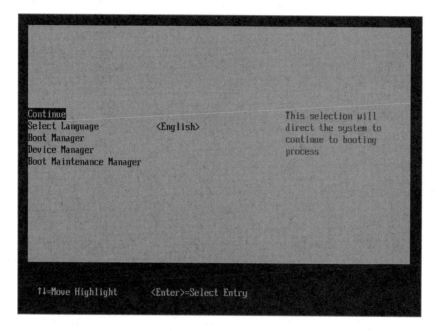

Precisely how to disable hardware in the firmware varies from one computer to another. You should peruse the available menus to find mention of the hardware you want to disable. Menus labeled Integrated Peripherals or Advanced are particularly likely to hold these features. Once you've spotted the options, follow the onscreen prompts for hints about how to proceed; for instance, Figure 3.1 shows an Item Specific Help area on the right side of the screen. Information about keys to press to perform various actions appears here. (Although not identified as a help area, the right side of the screen in Figure 3.2 provides similar hints.) Once you're finished, follow the onscreen menus and prompts to save your changes and exit. When you do so, the computer will reboot.

Once Linux boots, it uses its own drivers to access the computer's hardware. Understanding the hardware resources that Linux uses will help you determine when you may want to shut down, boot into the firmware, and disable particular hardware devices at such a low level.

Real World Scenario

Booting without a Keyboard

Most PCs have keyboards attached to them; however, many Linux computers function as servers, which don't require keyboards for day-to-day operation. In such cases, you may want to detach the keyboard to reduce clutter and eliminate the risk of accidental keystrokes causing problems.

Unfortunately, many computers complain and refuse to boot if you unplug the keyboard and attempt to boot the computer. To disable this warning, look for a firmware option called Halt On or something similar. This option tells the firmware under what circumstances it should refuse to boot. You should find an option that would stop the computer from checking for a keyboard. Once you select this option, you should be able to shut down, detach the keyboard, and boot normally. Of course, you'll need to be able to access the computer via a network connection or in some other way to administer it, so be sure this is configured before you remove the keyboard!

IRQs

An *interrupt request (IRQ),* or interrupt, is a signal sent to the CPU instructing it to suspend its current activity and to handle some external event such as keyboard input. On the *x86* platform, IRQs are numbered from 0 to 15. More modern computers, including *x86-64* systems, provide more than these 16 interrupts. Some interrupts are reserved for specific purposes, such as the keyboard and the real-time clock; others have common uses (and are sometimes overused) but may be reassigned; and some are left available for extra devices that may be added to the system. Table 3.1 lists the IRQs and their common purposes in the *x86* system. (On *x86-64* systems, IRQs are typically assigned as in Table 3.1, but additional hardware may be assigned to higher IRQs.)

TABLE 3.1   IRQs and their common uses

IRQ	Typical use	Notes
0	System timer	Reserved for internal use.
1	Keyboard	Reserved for keyboard use only.
2	Cascade for IRQs 8–15	The original *x86* IRQ-handling circuit can manage just 8 IRQs; 2 are tied together to handle 16 IRQs, but IRQ 2 must be used to handle IRQs 8–15.

IRQ	Typical use	Notes
3	Second RS-232 serial port (COM2: in Windows)	May also be shared by a fourth RS-232 serial port.
4	First RS-232 serial port (COM1: in Windows)	May also be shared by a third RS-232 serial port.
5	Sound card or second parallel port (LPT2: in Windows)	
6	Floppy disk controller	Reserved for the first floppy disk controller.
7	First parallel port (LPT1: in Windows)	
8	Real-time clock	Reserved for system clock use only.
9	ACPI system control interrupt	Used by Intel chipsets for the Advanced Configuration and Power Interface (ACPI) used for power management.
10	Open interrupt	
11	Open interrupt	
12	PS/2 mouse	
13	Math coprocessor	Reserved for internal use.
14	Primary ATA controller	The controller for ATA devices such as hard drives; traditionally /dev/hda and /dev/hdb under Linux.[1]
15	Secondary ATA controller	The controller for more ATA devices; traditionally /dev/hdc and /dev/hdd under Linux.[1]

[1]Most modern distributions treat Serial ATA disks as SCSI disks, which changes their device identifiers from /dev/hd*x* to /dev/sd*x*.

WARNING   IRQ 5 is a common source of interrupt conflicts on older computers because it's the default value for sound cards as well as for second parallel ports. Modern computers often use a higher IRQ for sound cards and also often lack parallel ports.

The original *Industry Standard Architecture (ISA)* bus design makes sharing an interrupt between two devices tricky. Ideally, every ISA device should have its own IRQ. The more recent *Peripheral Component Interconnect (PCI)* bus makes sharing interrupts a bit easier, so PCI devices frequently end up sharing an IRQ. The ISA bus has become rare on computers made since 2001 or so.

Once a Linux system is running, you can explore what IRQs are being used for various purposes by examining the contents of the /proc/interrupts file. A common way to do this is with the cat command:

```
$ cat /proc/interrupts
           CPU0
   0:          42   IO-APIC-edge      timer
   1:      444882   IO-APIC-edge      i8042
   4:          12   IO-APIC-edge
   6:          69   IO-APIC-edge      floppy
   8:           0   IO-APIC-edge      rtc
   9:           0   IO-APIC-fasteoi   acpi
  14:     3010291   IO-APIC-edge      ide0
  15:    11156960   IO-APIC-edge      ide1
  16:   125264892   IO-APIC-fasteoi   eth0
  17:           0   IO-APIC-fasteoi   cx88[0], cx88[0]
  20:     3598946   IO-APIC-fasteoi   sata_via
  21:     4566307   IO-APIC-fasteoi   uhci_hcd:usb1, uhci_hcd:usb2, ehci_hcd:usb3
  22:      430444   IO-APIC-fasteoi   VIA8237
 NMI:           0   Non-maskable interrupts
 LOC:   168759611   Local timer interrupts
 TRM:           0   Thermal event interrupts
 THR:           0   Threshold APIC interrupts
 SPU:           0   Spurious interrupts
 ERR:           0
```

The /proc filesystem is a *virtual filesystem*—it doesn't refer to actual files on a hard disk but to kernel data that's convenient to represent using a filesystem. The files in /proc provide information about the hardware, running processes, and so on. Many Linux utilities use /proc behind the scenes, or you can directly access these files using utilities like cat, which copies the data to the screen when given just one argument.

This output shows the names of the drivers that are using each IRQ. Some of these driver names are easy to interpret, such as eth0 for the Ethernet port. Others are more puzzling, such as cx88 (it's a driver for a video capture card). If the purpose of a driver isn't obvious, try doing a Web search on it; chances are you'll find a relevant hit fairly easily. Note that the preceding output shows interrupts numbered up to 22; this system supports more than the 16 base *x86* interrupts.

> **WARNING** The /proc/interrupts file lists IRQs that are in use by Linux, but Linux doesn't begin using an IRQ until the relevant driver is loaded. This may not happen until you try to use the hardware. Thus, the /proc/interrupts list may not show all of the interrupts that are configured on your system. For instance, the preceding example shows nothing for IRQ 7, which is reserved for the parallel port because the port hadn't been used prior to viewing the file. If the parallel port were used and /proc/interrupts viewed again, an entry for IRQ 7 and the parport0 driver would appear.

Although IRQ conflicts are rare on modern hardware, they still do occasionally crop up. When this happens, you must reconfigure one or more devices to use different IRQs. This topic is described shortly, in the section "Configuring Expansion Cards."

I/O Addresses

I/O addresses (also referred to as *I/O ports*) are unique locations in memory that are reserved for communications between the CPU and specific physical hardware devices. Like IRQs, I/O addresses are commonly associated with specific devices, and they should not ordinarily be shared. Table 3.2 lists some Linux device filenames along with the equivalent names in Windows, as well as the common IRQ and I/O address settings.

TABLE 3.2 Common Linux devices

Linux device	Windows name	Typical IRQ	I/O address
/dev/ttyS0	COM1	4	0x03f8
/dev/ttyS1	COM2	3	0x02f8
/dev/ttyS2	COM3	4	0x03e8
/dev/ttyS3	COM4	3	0x02e8
/dev/lp0	LPT1	7	0x0378-0x037f
/dev/lp1	LPT2	5	0x0278-0x027f
/dev/fd0	A:	6	0x03f0-0x03f7
/dev/fd1	B:	6	0x0370-0x0377

Although the use is deprecated, older systems sometimes use /dev/cuax (where *x* is a number 0 or greater) to indicate an RS-232 serial device. Thus, /dev/ttyS0 and /dev/cua0 refer to the same physical device.

Once a Linux system is running, you can explore what I/O addresses the computer is using by examining the contents of the /proc/ioports file. A common way to do this is with the cat command:

```
$ cat /proc/ioports
0000-001f : dma1
0020-0021 : pic1
0040-0043 : timer0
0050-0053 : timer1
0060-006f : keyboard
0070-0077 : rtc
0080-008f : dma page reg
00a0-00a1 : pic2
00c0-00df : dma2
00f0-00ff : fpu
```

This example truncates the output, which goes on for quite a while on the test system. As with IRQs, if your system suffers from I/O port conflicts, you must reconfigure one or more devices, as described in "Configuring Expansion Cards." In practice, such conflicts are more rare than IRQ conflicts.

DMA Addresses

Direct memory addressing (DMA) is an alternative method of communication to I/O ports. Rather than have the CPU mediate the transfer of data between a device and memory, DMA permits the device to transfer data directly, without the CPU's attention. The result can be lower CPU requirements for I/O activity, which can improve overall system performance.

To support DMA, the *x*86 architecture implements several DMA channels, each of which can be used by a particular device. To learn what DMA channels your system uses, examine the /proc/dma file:

```
$ cat /proc/dma
 4: cascade
```

This output indicates that DMA channel 4 is in use. As with IRQs and I/O ports, DMA addresses should not normally be shared. In practice, DMA address conflicts are more rare than IRQ conflicts, so chances are you won't run into problems. If you do, consult the upcoming section "Configuring Expansion Cards."

Boot Disks and Geometry Settings

Most firmware implementations let you choose the order in which devices are booted. This is an area in which BIOS and EFI differ, and there are substantial implementation-to-implementation differences too. Generally speaking, though, the rules are as follows:

BIOS   The BIOS boot process begins with the computer reading a *boot sector* (typically the first sector) from a disk and then executing that code. Thus, boot options for BIOS-based computers are limited; you can only select the order in which various boot devices (hard disks, optical disks, USB devices, network boot, and so on) are examined to find a boot sector.

EFI   Under EFI, the boot process involves the computer reading a boot loader file from a filesystem on a special partition, known as the *EFI System Partition (ESP)*. This file either can take a special default name or can be registered in the computer's NVRAM. Therefore, EFI computers often present an extended range of boot options, involving both default boot loader files from various devices (to enable granting precedence to a bootable USB flash drive, for example) and multiple boot loaders on the computer's hard disks. Some primitive EFI implementations, though, present simple BIOS-like boot options.

> Many EFI implementations support a BIOS compatibility mode, and so they can boot media intended for BIOS-based computers. This feature, intended to help in the transition from BIOS to EFI, can complicate firmware setup and OS installation because it creates extra boot options that users often don't understand.

Although boot sequences involving removable disks are common, they have their problems. For instance, if somebody accidentally leaves a CD or DVD in the drive, this can prevent the system from booting. Worse, some viruses are transmitted by BIOS boot sectors, so this method can result in viral infection. Using removable disks as the default boot media also opens the door to intruders who have physical access to the computer; they need only reboot with a bootable CD or DVD to gain complete control of your system. For these reasons, it's better to make the first hard disk (or a boot loader on a hard disk's ESP, in the case of EFI) the only boot device. (You must change this configuration when installing Linux or using an emergency boot disk for maintenance.) Most modern computers make temporary changes easier by providing a special key to allow a one-time change to the boot sequence. On older computers, to change the boot sequence, you must locate the appropriate firmware option, change it, and reboot the computer. It's usually located in an Advanced menu, so look there.

Another disk option is the one for detecting disk devices. Figure 3.1 shows three disk devices: the A: floppy disk (/dev/fd0 under Linux), a 1048 MB primary master hard disk, and a CD/DVD drive as the secondary master. In most cases, the firmware detects and configures hard disks and CD/DVD drives correctly. In rare circumstances, you must tell a BIOS-based computer about the hard disk's *cylinder/head/sector (CHS) geometry*.

The CHS geometry is a holdover from the early days of the $x86$ architecture. Figure 3.3 shows the traditional hard disk layout, which consists of a fixed number of read/write heads that can move across the disk surfaces (or platters). As the disk spins, each head marks out a circular track on its platter. These tracks collectively make up a cylinder. Each track is broken down into a series of sectors. Thus, any sector on a hard disk can be uniquely identified by three numbers: a cylinder number, a head number, and a sector number. The $x86$ BIOS was designed to use this three-number CHS identification code. One consequence of this configuration is that the BIOS must know how many cylinders, heads, and sectors the disk has. Modern hard disks relay this information to the BIOS automatically, but for compatibility with the earliest hard disks, BIOSs still enable you to set these values manually.

FIGURE 3.3 Hard disks are built from platters, each of which is broken into tracks, which are further broken into sectors.

 The BIOS will detect only certain types of disks. Of particular importance, SCSI disks and (on some older computers) serial ATA (SATA) disks won't appear in the main BIOS disk-detection screen. These disks are handled by supplementary firmware associated with the controllers for these devices. Some BIOSs do provide explicit options to add SCSI devices into the boot sequence, so you can give priority either to ATA or SCSI devices. For those without these options, SCSI disks generally take second seat to ATA disks.

CHS geometry, unfortunately, has its problems. For one thing, all but the earliest hard disks use variable numbers of sectors per cylinder—modern disks squeeze more sectors onto outer tracks than inner ones, fitting more data on each disk. Thus the CHS geometry presented to the BIOS by the hard disk is a convenient lie. Worse, because of limits on the numbers in the BIOS and in the ATA hard disk interface, plain CHS geometry tops out at 504 MiB, which is puny by today's standards. (Hard drive sizes use the more accurate mebibyte (MiB) size instead of the standard megabyte (MB). One mebibyte is 1,048,576 bytes.) Various patches, such as CHS geometry translation, can be used to expand the limit to about 8 GiB. Today though, the preference is to use *logical block addressing (LBA)* mode.

(Some sources use the expansion *linear block addressing* for this acronym.) In this mode, a single unique number is assigned to each sector on the disk, and the disk's firmware is smart enough to read from the correct head and cylinder when given this sector number. Modern BIOSs typically provide an option to use LBA mode, CHS translation mode, or possibly some other modes with large disks. EFI doesn't use CHS addressing at all, except in its BIOS compatibility mode; instead, EFI uses LBA mode exclusively. In most cases, LBA mode is the best choice. If you must retrieve data from very old disks, though, you may need to change this option.

 Because of variability in how different BIOSs handle CHS translation, moving disks between computers can result in problems because of mismatched CHS geometries claimed in disk structures and by the BIOS. Linux is usually smart enough to work around such problems, but you may see some odd error messages in disk utilities like fdisk. If you see messages about inconsistent CHS geometries, proceed with caution when using low-level disk utilities lest you create an inconsistent partition table that could cause problems, particularly in OSs that are less robust than Linux on this score.

Coldplug and Hotplug Devices

Whenever you deal with hardware, you should keep in mind a distinction between two device types: *coldplug* and *hotplug*. These device types differ depending on whether they can be physically attached and detached when the computer is turned on (that is, "hot"), versus only when it's turned off ("cold").

 Coldplug devices are designed to be connected physically and disconnected only when the computer is turned off. Attempting to attach or detach such devices when the computer is running can damage the device or the computer, so do not attempt to do so.

Traditionally, components that are internal to the computer, such as the CPU, memory, PCI cards, and hard disks, have been coldplug devices. A hotplug variant of PCI, however, has been developed and is used on some computers—mainly on servers and other systems that can't afford the downtime required to install or remove a device. Hot-plug SATA devices are also available.

Modern external devices, such as Ethernet, USB, and IEEE-1394 devices, are hotplug; you can attach and detach such devices as you see fit. These devices rely on specialized Linux software to detect the changes to the system as they're attached and detached. Several utilities help in managing hotplug devices:

Sysfs The *sysfs virtual filesystem*, mounted at /sys, exports information about devices so that user-space utilities can access the information.

A *user space* program is one that runs as an ordinary program, whether it runs as an ordinary user or as root. This contrasts with *kernel space* code, which runs as part of the kernel. Typically, only the kernel (and hence kernel-space code) can communicate directly with hardware. User-space programs are the ultimate users of hardware, though. Traditionally, the /dev filesystem has provided the main means of interface between user-space programs and hardware; however, the tools described here help expand on this access, particularly in ways that are useful for hotplug devices.

HAL Daemon   The *Hardware Abstraction Layer (HAL) Daemon*, or hald, is a user-space program that runs at all times (that is, as a daemon) and provides other user-space programs with information about available hardware.

D-Bus   The *Desktop Bus (D-Bus)* provides a further abstraction of hardware information access. Like hald, D-Bus runs as a daemon. D-Bus enables processes to communicate with each other as well as to register to be notified of events, both by other processes and by hardware (such as the availability of a new USB device).

udev   Traditionally, Linux has created device nodes as conventional files in the /dev directory tree. The existence of hotplug devices and various other issues, however, have motivated the creation of udev: a virtual filesystem, mounted at /dev, which creates dynamic device files as drivers are loaded and unloaded. You can configure udev through files in /etc/udev, but the standard configuration is usually sufficient for common hardware.

These tools all help programs work seamlessly in a world of hotplug devices by enabling the programs to learn about hardware, including receiving notification when the hardware configuration changes.

Older external devices, such as parallel and RS-232 ports, are officially coldplug in nature. In practice, many people treat these devices as if they were hotplug, and they can usually get away with it; but there is a risk of damage, so it's safest to power down a computer before connecting or disconnecting such a device. When RS-232 or parallel port devices are hotplugged, they typically aren't registered by tools such as udev and hald. The OS handles the ports to which these devices connect; it's up to user-space programs, such as terminal programs or the printing system, to know how to communicate with the external devices.

Configuring Expansion Cards

Many hardware devices require configuration—you must set the IRQ, I/O port, and DMA addresses used by the device. (Not all devices use all three resources.) Through the mid-1990s, this process involved tedious changes to jumpers on the hardware. Today, though, you can configure most options through software.

Even devices that are built into the motherboard are configured through the same means used to configure PCI cards.

Configuring PCI Cards

The PCI bus, which is the standard expansion bus for most internal devices, was designed with Plug-and-Play (PnP) style configuration in mind, thus automatic configuration of PCI devices is the rule rather than the exception. For the most part, PCI devices configure themselves automatically, and there's no need to make any changes. You can, however, tweak how PCI devices are detected in several ways:

- The Linux kernel has several options that affect how it detects PCI devices. You can find these in the kernel configuration screens under Bus Options. Most users can rely on the options in their distributions' default kernels to work properly; but if you recompile your kernel yourself and you are having problems with device detection, you may want to study these options.

- Most firmware implementations have PCI options that change the way PCI resources are allocated. Adjusting these options may help if you run into strange hardware problems with PCI devices.

- Some Linux drivers support options that cause them to configure the relevant hardware to use particular resources. You should consult the drivers' documentation files for the details of the options they support. You must then pass these options to the kernel using a boot loader (as described in Chapter 5) or as kernel module options.

- You can use the setpci utility to query and adjust PCI devices' configurations directly. This tool is most likely to be useful if you know enough about the hardware to fine-tune its low-level configuration; it's not often used to tweak the hardware's basic IRQ, I/O port, or DMA options.

In addition to the configuration options, you may want to check how PCI devices are currently configured. You can use the lspci command for this purpose; it displays all of the information about the PCI busses on your system and all of the devices connected to those busses. This command takes several options that fine-tune its behavior. Table 3.3 lists the most common of these options.

TABLE 3.3 Options for lspci

Option	Effect
-v	Increases verbosity of output. This option may be doubled (-vv) or tripled (-vvv) to produce yet more output.
-n	Displays information in numeric codes rather than translating the codes to manufacturer and device names.
-nn	Displays both the manufacturer and device names and their associated numeric codes.

TABLE 3.3   Options for `lspci` *(continued)*

Option	Effect
-x	Displays the PCI configuration space for each device as a hexadecimal dump. This is an extremely advanced option. Tripling (`-xxx`) or quadrupling (`-xxxx`) this option displays information about more devices.
-b	Shows IRQ numbers and other data as seen by devices rather than as seen by the kernel.
-t	Displays a tree view depicting the relationship between devices.
-s [[[[*domain*]:] *bus*]:][*slot*] [.[*func*]]	Displays only devices that match the listed specification. This can be used to trim the results of the output.
-d [*vendor*]:[*device*]	Shows data on the specified device.
-i *file*	Uses the specified file to map vendor and device IDs to names. (The default is `/usr/share/misc/pci.ids`.)
-m	Dumps data in a machine-readable form intended for use by scripts. A single `-m` uses a backward-compatible format, whereas doubling (`-mm`) uses a newer format.
-D	Displays PCI domain numbers. These numbers normally aren't displayed.
-M	Performs a scan in bus-mapping mode, which can reveal devices hidden behind a misconfigured PCI bridge. This is an advanced option that can be used only by root.
--version	Displays version information.

Learning about Kernel Modules

Kernel drivers, many of which come in the form of *kernel modules*, handle hardware in Linux. These are stand-alone driver files, typically stored in the `/lib/modules` directory tree, that can be loaded to provide access to hardware and unloaded to disable such access. Typically, Linux loads the modules it needs when it boots, but you may need to load additional modules yourself.

You can learn about the modules that are currently loaded on your system by using lsmod, which takes no options and produces output like this:

```
$ lsmod
Module            Size  Used by
isofs            35820  0
zlib_inflate     21888  1 isofs
bluetooth       433970  5 bnep
nls_iso8859_1     5568  1
nls_cp437         7296  1
vfat             15680  1
fat              49536  1 vfat
sr_mod           19236  0
ide_cd           42848  0
```

This output has been edited for brevity. Although outputs this short are possible with certain configurations, they're rare.

The most important column in this output is the first one, labeled Module. This column specifies the names of all of the modules that are currently loaded. You can learn more about these modules with modinfo, as described shortly, but sometimes their purpose is fairly obvious. For instance, the bluetooth module provides access to external wireless devices.

The Used by column of the lsmod output describes what's using the module. All of the entries have a number, which indicates the number of other modules or processes that are using the module. For instance, in the preceding example, the isofs module (used to access CD/DVD filesystems) isn't currently in use, as revealed by its 0 value, but the vfat module (used to read VFAT Windows hard disk and USB stick partitions) is being used, as shown by its value of 1. If one of the modules is being used by another module, the using module's name appears in the Used by column. For instance, the isofs module relies on the zlib_inflate module, so the latter module's Used by column includes the isofs module name. This information can be useful when you're managing modules. For instance, if your system produced the preceding output, you couldn't directly remove the zlib_inflate module because the isofs module is using it, but you could remove the isofs module, and after doing so, you could remove the zlib_inflate module. (Both modules would need to be added back to read most CD/DVDs, though.)

The lsmod command displays information only about kernel modules, not about drivers that are compiled directly into the Linux kernel. For this reason, a module may need to be loaded on one system but not on another to use the same hardware because the second system may compile the relevant driver directly into the kernel.

Loading Kernel Modules

Linux enables you to load kernel modules with two programs: insmod and modprobe. The insmod program inserts a single module into the kernel. This process requires you to have already loaded any modules on which the module you're loading relies. The modprobe program, by contrast, automatically loads any depended-on modules, and so it is generally the preferred way to do the job.

 In practice, you may not need to use insmod or modprobe to load modules because Linux can load them automatically. This ability relies on the kernel's module autoloader feature, which must be compiled into the kernel, and on various configuration files, which are also required for modprobe and some other tools. Using insmod and modprobe can be useful for testing new modules or for working around problems with the autoloader, though.

In practice, insmod is a fairly straightforward program to use; you type its name followed by the module filename:

```
# insmod /lib/modules/3.16.6/kernel/drivers/bluetooth/bluetooth.ko
```

This command loads the btusb.ko module, which you must specify by filename. Modules have module names too, which are usually the same as the filename but without the extension, as in bluetooth for the bluetooth.ko file. Unfortunately, insmod requires the full module name.

You can pass additional module options to the module by adding them to the command line. Module options are highly module specific, so you must consult the documentation for the module to learn what to pass. Examples include options to tell an RS-232 serial port driver what interrupt to use to access the hardware or to tell a video card framebuffer driver what screen resolution to use.

Some modules depend on other modules. In these cases, if you attempt to load a module that depends on others and those other modules aren't loaded, insmod will fail. When this happens, you must either track down and manually load the depended-on modules or use modprobe. In the simplest case, you can use modprobe much as you use insmod, by passing it a module name:

```
# modprobe bluetooth
```

As with insmod, you can add kernel options to the end of the command line. Unlike with insmod, you specify a module by its module name rather than its module filename when you use modprobe. Generally speaking, this helps make modprobe easier to use, as does the fact that modprobe automatically loads dependencies. This greater convenience means that modprobe relies on configuration files. It also means that you can use options (placed between the command name and the module name) to modify modprobe's behavior:

Be Verbose   The -v or --verbose option tells modprobe to display extra information about its operations. Typically, this includes a summary of every insmod operation it performs.

Change Configuration Files   The modprobe program uses a configuration file called /etc/modprobe.conf (or multiple files in /etc/modprobe.d). You can change the configuration file or directory by passing a new file with the -C *filename* option, as in **modprobe -C / etc/mymodprobe.conf bluetooth**.

Perform a Dry Run   The -n or --dry-run option causes modprobe to perform checks and all other operations *except* the actual module insertions. You might use this option in conjunction with -v to see what modprobe would do without loading the module. This may be helpful in debugging, particularly if inserting the module is having some detrimental effect, such as disabling disk access.

Remove Modules   The -r or --remove option reverses modprobe's usual effect; it causes the program to remove the specified module and any on which it depends. (Depended-on modules are *not* removed if they're in use.)

Force Loading   The -f or --force option tells modprobe to force the module loading even if the kernel version doesn't match what the module expects. This action is potentially dangerous, but it's occasionally required when using third-party binary-only modules.

Show Dependencies   The --show-depends option shows all of the modules on which the specified module depends. This option doesn't install any of the modules; it's purely informative in nature.

Show Available Modules   The -l or --list option displays a list of available options whose names match the wildcard you specify. For instance, typing **modprobe -l v*** displays all modules whose names begin with v. If you provide no wildcard, modprobe displays all available modules. Like --show-depends, this option doesn't cause any modules to be loaded.

> This list of options is incomplete. The others are relatively obscure, so you're not likely to need them often. Consult the modprobe man page for more information.

Removing Kernel Modules

In most cases, you can leave modules loaded indefinitely; the only harm that a module does when it's loaded but not used is to consume a small amount of memory. (The lsmod program shows how much memory each module consumes.) Sometimes, though, you may want to remove a loaded module. Reasons include reclaiming that tiny amount of memory, unloading an old module so that you can load an updated replacement module, and removing a module that you suspect is unreliable.

The work of unloading a kernel module is done by the rmmod command, which is basically the opposite of insmod. The rmmod command takes a module name as an option, though, rather than a module filename:

```
# rmmod bluetooth
```

This example command unloads the bluetooth module. You can modify the behavior of rmmod in various ways:

Be Verbose   Passing the -v or --verbose option causes rmmod to display some extra information about what it's doing. This may be helpful if you're troubleshooting a problem.

Force Removal   The -f or --force option forces module removal even if the module is marked as being in use. Naturally, this is a very dangerous option, but it's sometimes helpful if a module is misbehaving in some way that's even more dangerous. This option has no effect unless the CONFIG_MODULE_FORCE_UNLOAD kernel option is enabled.

Wait Until Unused   The -w or --wait option causes rmmod to wait for the module to become unused rather than return an error message if the module is in use. Once the module is no longer being used (say, after a bluetooth device is disconnected), rmmod unloads the module and returns. Until then, rmmod doesn't return, making it look like it's not doing anything.

A few more rmmod options exist; consult the rmmod man page for details.

Like insmod, rmmod operates on a single module. If you try to unload a module that's depended on by other modules or is in use, rmmod will return an error message. (The -w option modifies this behavior, as just described.) If other modules depend on the module, rmmod lists those modules so you can decide whether to unload them. If you want to unload an entire *module stack*—that is, a module and all those upon which it depends—you can use the modprobe command and its -r option, as described earlier in "Loading Kernel Modules."

Configuring USB Devices

USB is an extremely popular (perhaps the most popular) external interface form. This fact means that you must understand something about USB, including USB itself, Linux's USB drivers, and Linux's USB management tools.

USB Basics

USB is a protocol and hardware port for transferring data to and from devices. It allows for many more (and varied) devices per interface port than either ATA or SCSI, and it gives better speed than RS-232 serial and parallel ports. The USB 1.0 and 1.1 specifications allow for up to 127 devices and 12Mbps of data transfer. USB 2.0 allows for much higher transfer rates—480Mbps, to be precise. USB 3.0, introduced in 2010, supports a theoretical maximum speed of 4.8Gbps, although 3.2Gbps is a more likely top speed in practice. USB 3.0 devices require a different physical connector than 1.0, 1.1, and 2.0 connectors.

NOTE   Data transfer speeds may be expressed in bits per second (bps) or multiples thereof, such as megabits per second (Mbps) or gigabits per second (Gbps). Or they can be expressed in bytes per second (Bps) or multiples thereof, such as megabytes per second (MBps). In most cases, there are 8 bits per byte, so multiplying or dividing by 8 may be necessary if you're trying to compare speeds of devices that use different measures.

USB is the preferred interface method for many external devices, including printers, scanners, mice, digital cameras, flash drives, and music players. USB keyboards, Ethernet adapters, modems, speakers, hard drives, and other devices are also available, although USB has yet to dominate these areas as it has some others.

Most desktop computers ship with four to eight *USB ports* (though laptops tend to include just two or three USB ports). Each port can handle one device by itself, but you can use a *USB hub* to connect several devices to each port. Thus you can theoretically connect huge numbers of USB devices to a computer. In practice, you may run into speed problems, particularly if you're using USB 1.*x* for devices that tend to transfer a lot of data, such as scanners, printers, or hard drives.

If you have an older computer that lacks USB 3.0 support and you want to connect a high-speed USB 3.0 device, you can buy a separate USB 3.0 board. You can continue to use the computer's built-in USB ports for slower devices.

Linux USB Drivers

Several different USB controllers are available, with names such as UHCI, OHCI, EHCI, and R8A66597. Modern Linux distributions ship with the drivers for the common USB controllers enabled, so your USB port should be activated automatically when you boot the computer. The UHCI and OHCI controllers handle USB 1.*x* devices, but most other controllers can handle USB 2.0 devices. You need a 2.6.31 or newer kernel to use USB 3.0 hardware. Note that these basics merely provide a means to access the actual USB hardware and address the devices in a low-level manner. You'll need additional software—either drivers or specialized software packages—to make practical use of the devices.

You can learn a great deal about your devices by using the lsusb utility. A simple use of this program with no options reveals basic information about your USB devices:

```
$ lsusb
Bus 003 Device 008: ID 0686:400e Minolta Co., Ltd
Bus 003 Device 001: ID 0000:0000
Bus 002 Device 002: ID 046d:c401 Logitech, Inc. TrackMan Marble Wheel
Bus 002 Device 001: ID 0000:0000
Bus 001 Device 001: ID 0000:0000
```

In this example, three USB busses are detected (001, 002, and 003). The first bus has no devices attached, but the second and third each have one device—a Logitech TrackMan Marble Wheel trackball and a Minolta DiMAGE Scan Elite 5400 scanner, respectively. (The scanner's name isn't fully identified by this output, except insofar as the ID number encodes this information.) You can gather additional information by using various options to lsusb:

Be Verbose   The -v option produces extended information about each product.

Restrict Bus and Device Number   Using the -s [[*bus*]:][*devnum*] option restricts output to the specified bus and device number.

Restrict Vendor and Product   You can limit output to a particular vendor and product by using the -d [*vendor*]:[*product*] option. *vendor* and *product* are the codes just after ID on each line of the basic lsusb output.

Display Device by Filename   Using -D *filename* displays information about the device that's accessible via *filename*, which should be a file in the /proc/bus/usb directory tree. This directory provides a low-level interface to USB devices, as described shortly.

Tree View   The -t option displays the device list as a tree so that you can see what devices are connected to specific controllers more easily.

Version   The -V or --version option displays the version of the lsusb utility and exits.

Early Linux USB implementations required a separate driver for every USB device. Many of these drivers remain in the kernel, and some software relies on them. For instance, USB disk storage devices use USB storage drivers that interface with Linux's SCSI support, making USB hard disks, removable disks, and so on look like SCSI devices.

Linux provides a USB filesystem that in turn provides access to USB devices in a generic manner. This filesystem appears as part of the /proc virtual filesystem. In particular, USB device information is accessible from /proc/bus/usb. Subdirectories of /proc/bus/usb are given numbered names based on the USB controllers installed on the computer, as in /proc/bus/usb/001 for the first USB controller. Software can access files in these directories to control USB devices rather than use device files in /dev as with most hardware devices. Tools such as scanner software and the Linux printing system can automatically locate compatible USB devices and use these files.

USB Manager Applications

USB can be challenging for OSs because it was designed as a hot-pluggable technology. The Linux kernel wasn't originally designed with this sort of activity in mind, so the kernel relies on external utilities to help manage matters. Two tools in particular are used for managing USB devices: usbmgr and hotplug. While these tools are not commonly installed by default in Linux distributions, they can come in handy when working with USB devices.

The usbmgr package (located at http://freecode.com/projects/usbmgr) is a program that runs in the background to detect changes on the USB bus. When it detects changes, it loads or unloads the kernel modules that are required to handle the devices. For instance, if you plug in a USB Zip drive, usbmgr will load the necessary USB and SCSI disk modules. This package uses configuration files in /etc/usbmgr to handle specific devices and uses /etc/usbmgr/usbmgr.conf to control the overall configuration.

With the shift from in-kernel device-specific USB drivers to the USB device filesystem (/proc/bus/usb), usbmgr has been declining in importance. In fact, it may not be installed on your system. Instead, most distributions rely on the Hotplug package (http://linux-hotplug.sourceforge.net), which relies on kernel support added with the 2.4.*x* kernel series. This system uses files stored in /etc/hotplug to control the configuration of specific

USB devices. In particular, /etc/hotplug/usb.usermap contains a database of USB device IDs and pointers to scripts in /etc/hotplug/usb that are run when devices are plugged in or unplugged. These scripts might change permissions on USB device files so that ordinary users can access USB hardware, run commands to detect new USB disk devices, or otherwise prepare the system for a new (or newly removed) USB device.

Configuring Hard Disks

Hard disks are among the most important components in your system. Three different hard disk interfaces are common on modern computers: *Parallel Advanced Technology Attachment (PATA)*, aka ATA; *Serial Advanced Technology Attachment (SATA)*; and *Small Computer System Interface (SCSI)*. In addition, external USB and IEEE-1394 drives are available, as are external variants of SATA and SCSI drives. Each has its own method of low-level configuration.

Configuring PATA Disks

PATA disks once ruled the roost in the *x*86 PC world, but today SATA disks have largely supplanted them. Thus, you're most likely to encounter PATA disks on older computers—say, from 2005 or earlier. PATA disks are still readily available, though.

As the full name implies, PATA disks use a parallel interface, meaning that several bits of data are transferred over the cable at once. Therefore, PATA cables are wide, supporting a total of either 40 or 80 lines, depending on the variety of PATA. You can connect up to two devices to each PATA connector on a motherboard or plug-in PATA controller, meaning that PATA cables typically have three connectors—one for the motherboard and two for disks.

PATA disks must be configured as masters or as slaves. This can be done via jumpers on the disks themselves. Typically, the master device sits at the end of the cable, and the slave device resides on the middle connector. All modern PATA disks also support an option called *cable select*. When set to this option, the drive attempts to configure itself automatically based on its position on the PATA cable. Thus, your easiest configuration usually is to set all PATA devices to use the cable-select option; you can then attach them to whatever position is convenient, and the drives should configure themselves.

For best performance, disks should be placed on separate controllers rather than configured as master and slave on a single controller because each PATA controller has a limited throughput that may be exceeded by two drives. Until recently, most motherboards have included at least two controllers, so putting each drive on its own controller isn't a problem until you install more than two drives in a single computer.

All but the most ancient BIOSs auto-detect PATA devices and provide information about their capacities and model numbers in the BIOS setup utilities. In the past, most motherboards would boot PATA drives in preference to other drives, but modern firmware usually provides more options to control your boot preferences.

In Linux, PATA disks have traditionally been identified as /dev/hda, /dev/hdb, and so on, with /dev/hda being the master drive on the first controller, /dev/hdb being the slave drive on the first controller, and so on. This means that gaps can occur in the numbering scheme—if you have master disks on the first and second controllers but no slave disks, your system will contain /dev/hda and /dev/hdc but no /dev/hdb. Partitions are identified by numbers after the main device name, as in /dev/hda1, /dev/hda2, and so on.

The naming rules for disks also apply to optical media, except that these media typically aren't partitioned. Most Linux distributions also create a link to your optical drive under the name /dev/cdrom or /dev/dvd.

Most modern Linux distributions favor newer PATA drivers that treat PATA disks as if they were SCSI disks. Thus, you may find that your device filenames follow the SCSI rules rather than the PATA rules even if you have PATA disks.

Configuring SATA Disks

SATA is a newer interface than PATA, and SATA has largely displaced PATA as the interface of choice. New motherboards typically host four or more SATA interfaces and frequently lack PATA interfaces.

SATA disks connect to their motherboards or controllers on a one-to-one basis—unlike with PATA, you can't connect more than one disk to a single cable. This fact simplifies configuration; there typically aren't jumpers to set, and you needn't be concerned with the position of the disk on the cable.

As the word *serial* in the expansion of *SATA* implies, SATA is a serial bus—only one bit of data can be transferred at a time. SATA transfers more bits per unit of time on its data line, though, so SATA is faster than PATA (1.5–6.0Gbps for SATA vs. 128–1,064Mbps for PATA, but these are theoretical maximums that are unlikely to be achieved in real-world situations). Because of SATA's serial nature, SATA cables are much thinner than PATA cables.

Modern firmware detects SATA disks and provides information about them just as for PATA disks. The firmware may provide boot order options too. Older BIOSs are likely to be more limited. This is particularly true if your motherboard doesn't provide SATA support but you use a separate SATA controller card. You may be able to boot from a SATA disk in such cases if your controller card supports this option, or you may need to use a PATA boot disk.

Most Linux SATA drivers treat SATA disks as if they were SCSI disks, so you should read the next section, "Configuring SCSI Disks," for information about device naming. Some older drivers treat SATA disks like PATA disks, so you may need to use PATA names in some rare circumstances.

Configuring SCSI Disks

There are many types of SCSI definitions, which use a variety of different cables and operate at various speeds. SCSI is traditionally a parallel bus, like PATA, although the latest variant, Serial Attached SCSI (SAS), is a serial bus like SATA. SCSI has traditionally been considered a superior bus to PATA; however, the cost difference has risen dramatically over the past decade or two, so few people today use SCSI. You may find it on older systems or on very high-end systems.

SCSI supports up to 8 or 16 devices per bus, depending on the variety. One of these devices is the SCSI host adapter, which either is built into the motherboard or comes as a plug-in card. In practice, the number of devices that you can attach to a SCSI bus is more restricted because of cable-length limits, which vary from one SCSI variety to another. Each device has its own ID number, typically assigned via a jumper on the device. You must ensure that each device's ID is unique. Consult its documentation to learn how to set the ID.

If your motherboard lacks built-in SCSI ports, chances are it won't detect SCSI devices. You can still boot from a SCSI hard disk *if* your SCSI host adapter has its own firmware that supports booting. Most high-end SCSI host adapters have this support, but low-end SCSI host adapters don't have built-in firmware. If you use such a host adapter, you can still attach SCSI hard disks to the adapter and Linux can use them, but you'll need to boot from a PATA or SATA hard disk.

SCSI IDs aren't used to identify the corresponding device file on a Linux system. Hard drives follow the naming system /dev/sd*x* (where *x* is a letter from a up), SCSI tapes are named /dev/st*x* and /dev/nst*x* (where *x* is a number from 0 up), and SCSI CD-ROMs and DVD-ROMs are named /dev/scd*x* or /dev/sr*x* (where *x* is a number from 0 up).

SCSI device numbering (or lettering) is usually assigned in increasing order based on the SCSI ID. If you have one hard disk with a SCSI ID of 2 and another hard disk with a SCSI ID of 4, they will be assigned to /dev/sda and /dev/sdb, respectively. The real danger is if you add a third SCSI drive and give it an ID of 0, 1, or 3. This new disk will become /dev/sda (for an ID of 0 or 1) or /dev/sdb (for ID 3), bumping up one or both of the existing disks' Linux device identifiers. For this reason, it's usually best to give hard disks the lowest possible SCSI IDs so that you can add future disks using higher IDs.

 The mapping of Linux device identifiers to SCSI devices depends in part on the design of the SCSI host adapter. Some host adapters result in assignments starting from SCSI ID 7 and working down to 0 rather than the reverse, with Wide SCSI device numbering continuing on from there to IDs 14 through 8.

Another complication is when you have multiple SCSI host adapters. In this case, Linux assigns device filenames to all of the disks on the first adapter, followed by all of those on the second adapter. Depending on where the drivers for the SCSI host adapters are found (compiled directly into the kernel or loaded as modules) and how they're loaded (for modular drivers), you may not be able to control which adapter takes precedence.

 Remember that some non-SCSI devices, such as USB disk devices and SATA disks, are mapped onto the Linux SCSI subsystem. This can cause a true SCSI hard disk to be assigned a higher device ID than you'd expect if you use such "pseudo-SCSI" devices.

The SCSI bus is logically one-dimensional—that is, every device on the bus falls along a single line. This bus must not fork or branch in any way. Each end of the SCSI bus must be *terminated*. This refers to the presence of a special resistor pack that prevents signals from bouncing back and forth along the SCSI chain. Consult your SCSI host adapter and SCSI devices' manuals to learn how to terminate them. Remember that both ends of the SCSI chain must be terminated, but devices mid-chain must *not* be terminated. The SCSI host adapter qualifies as a device, so if it's at the end of the chain, it must be terminated. Termination is a true hardware requirement; it doesn't apply to SATA or USB disk devices, even though they use Linux SCSI drivers.

Incorrect termination often results in bizarre SCSI problems, such as an inability to detect SCSI devices, poor performance, or unreliable operation. Similar symptoms can result from the use of poor-quality SCSI cables or cables that are too long.

Configuring External Disks

External disks come in several varieties, the most common of which are USB, IEEE-1394, and SCSI. SCSI has long supported external disks directly, and many SCSI host adapters have both internal and external connectors. You configure external SCSI disks just like internal disks, although the physical details of setting the SCSI ID number and termination may differ; consult your devices' manuals for details.

Linux treats external USB and IEEE-1394 disks just like SCSI devices, from a software point of view. Typically, you can plug in the device, see a /dev/sd*x* device node appear, and use it as you would a SCSI disk. This is the case for both true external hard disks and media such as solid-state USB flash drives.

WARNING   External drives are easily removed, and this can be a great convenience; however, you should never unplug an external drive until you've unmounted the disk in Linux using the umount command, as described later in "Temporarily Mounting and Unmounting Filesystems." Failure to unmount a disk is likely to result in damage to the filesystem, including lost files. In addition, although USB and IEEE-1394 busses are hot pluggable, most SCSI busses aren't, so connecting or disconnecting a SCSI device while the computer is running is dangerous.

Designing a Hard Disk Layout

Whether your system uses PATA, SATA, or SCSI disks, you must design a disk layout for Linux. If you're using a system with Linux preinstalled, you may not need to deal with this task immediately; however, sooner or later you'll have to install Linux on a new computer or one with an existing OS or upgrade your hard disk. The next few pages describe the *x*86 partitioning schemes, Linux mount points, and common choices for a Linux partitioning scheme. The upcoming section "Creating Partitions and Filesystems" covers the mechanics of creating partitions.

Why Partition?

The first issue with partitioning is the question of why you should do it. The answer is that partitioning provides a variety of advantages, including the following:

Multiple-OS Support   *Partitioning* enables you to keep the data for different OSs separate. In fact, many OSs can't easily coexist on the same partition because they don't support each other's primary filesystems. This feature is obviously important mainly if you want the computer to boot multiple OSs. It can also be handy to help maintain an emergency system—you can install a single OS twice, using the second installation as an emergency maintenance tool for the first in case problems develop.

Filesystem Choice   By partitioning your disk, you can use different *filesystems*—data structures designed to hold all of the files on a partition—on each partition. Perhaps one filesystem is faster than another and so it is important for time-critical or frequently accessed files, but another may provide accounting or backup features you want to use for users' data files.

Disk Space Management   By partitioning your disk, you can lock certain sets of files into a fixed space. For instance, if you restrict users to storing files on one or two partitions, they can fill those partitions without causing problems on other partitions, such as system partitions. This feature can help keep your system from crashing if space runs out. On the other hand, if you get the partition sizes wrong, you can run out of disk space on just one partition much sooner than would be the case if you'd used fewer partitions.

Disk Error Protection   Disks sometimes develop problems. These problems can be the result of bad hardware or errors that creep into the filesystems. In either case, splitting a disk into partitions provides some protection against such problems. If data structures on one partition become corrupted, the errors affect only the files on that partition. This separation can therefore protect data on other partitions and simplify data recovery.

Security   You can use different security-related mount options on different partitions. For instance, you might mount a partition that holds critical system files in read-only mode, preventing users from writing to that partition. Linux's file security options should provide similar protection, but taking advantage of Linux filesystem mount options provides redundancy that can be helpful in case of an error in setting up file or directory permissions.

Backup   Some backup tools work best on whole partitions. By keeping partitions small, you may be able to back up more easily than you could if your partitions were large.

In practice, most Linux computers use several partitions, although precisely how the system is partitioned varies from one computer to another. (The upcoming section "Common Partitions and Filesystem Layouts" describes some possibilities.)

Understanding Partitioning Systems

Partitions are defined by data structures that are written to specified parts of the hard disk. Several competing systems for defining these partitions exist. On x86 and x86-64 hardware, the most common method up until 2010 had been the *Master Boot Record (MBR) partitioning system,* so called because it stores its data in the first sector of the disk, which is also known as the MBR. The MBR system, however, is limited to partitions and partition placement of 2 tebibytes (TiB; 1TiB is 2^{40} bytes), at least when using the nearly universal sector size of 512 bytes. The successor to MBR is the *GUID Partition Table (GPT) partitioning system,* which has much higher limits and certain other advantages. The tools and methods for manipulating MBR and GPT disks differ from each other, although there's substantial overlap.

> Still more partitioning systems exist, and you may run into them from time to time. For instance, Macintoshes that use PowerPC CPUs generally employ the Apple Partition Map (APM), and many Unix variants employ Berkeley Standard Distribution (BSD) disk labels. You're most likely to encounter MBR and GPT disks, so those are the partitioning systems covered in this book. Details for other systems differ, but the basic principles are the same.

MBR Partitions

The original *x*86 partitioning scheme allowed for only four partitions. As hard disks increased in size and the need for more partitions became apparent, the original scheme was extended in a way that retained backward compatibility. The new scheme uses three partition types:

- *Primary partitions,* which are the same as the original partition types
- *Extended partitions,* which are a special type of primary partition that serve as placeholders for the next type
- *Logical partitions,* which reside within an extended partition

Figure 3.4 illustrates how these partition types relate. Because logical partitions reside within a single extended partition, all logical partitions must be contiguous.

FIGURE 3.4 The MBR partitioning system uses up to four primary partitions, one of which can be a placeholder extended partition that contains logical partitions.

For any one disk, you're limited to four primary partitions, or three primary partitions and one extended partition. Many OSs, such as Windows, and FreeBSD, *must* boot from primary partitions, and because of this, most hard disks include at least one primary partition. Linux, however, is not so limited, so you could boot Linux from a disk that contains no primary partitions, although in practice few people do this.

The primary partitions have numbers in the range of 1–4, whereas logical partitions are numbered 5 and up. Gaps can appear in the numbering of MBR primary partitions; however, such gaps cannot exist in the numbering of logical partitions. That is, you can have a disk with partitions numbered 1, 3, 5, 6, and 7 but not 1, 3, 5, and 7—if partition 7 exists, there must be a 5 and a 6.

In addition to holding the partition table, the MBR data structure holds the primary BIOS boot loader—the first disk-loaded code that the CPU executes when a BIOS-based computer boots. Thus the MBR is extremely important and sensitive. Because the MBR exists only in the first sector of the disk, it's vulnerable to damage; accidental erasure will make your disk unusable unless you have a backup.

> You can back up your MBR partitions by typing **sfdisk -d /dev/sda >
> sda-backup.txt** (or similar commands to specify another disk device
> or backup file). You can then copy the backup file (sda-backup.txt in
> this example) to a removable disk or another computer for safekeeping.
> You can restore the backup by typing **sfdisk -f /dev/sda < sda-
> backup.txt**. Be sure that you're using the correct backup file, though; a
> mistake can generate incorrect or even impossible partition definitions!

MBR partitions have type codes, which are 1-byte (two-digit hexadecimal) numbers, to help identify their purpose. Common type codes you may run into include 0x0c (FAT), 0x05 (an old type of extended partition), 0x07 (NTFS), 0x0f (a newer type of extended partition), 0x82 (Linux swap), and 0x83 (Linux filesystem).

Although the MBR data structure has survived for three decades, its days are numbered because it's not easily extensible beyond 2TiB disks. Thus, a new system is needed.

GPT Partitions

GPT is part of Intel's EFI specification, but GPT can be used on computers that don't use EFI, and GPT is the preferred partitioning system for disks bigger than 2TiB. Most EFI-based computers use GPT even on disks smaller than 2TiB.

GPT employs a *protective MBR*, which is a legal MBR definition that makes GPT-unaware utilities think that the disk holds a single MBR partition that spans the entire disk. Additional data structures define the true GPT partitions. These data structures are duplicated, with one copy at the start of the disk and another at its end. This provides redundancy that can help in data recovery should an accident damage one of the two sets of data structures.

GPT does away with the primary/extended/logical distinction of MBR. You can define up to 128 partitions by default (and that limit may be raised, if necessary). Gaps can occur in partition numbering, so you can have a disk with three partitions numbered 3, 7, and 104, to name just one possibility. In practice, though, GPT partitions are usually numbered consecutively starting with 1.

GPT's main drawback is that support for it is relatively immature. The fdisk utility (described shortly in "Partitioning a Disk") doesn't work with GPT disks, although alternatives to fdisk are available. Some versions of the GRUB boot loader also don't support it.

The situation is worse in some OSs—particularly older ones. Nonetheless, you should be at least somewhat familiar with GPT because of MBR's inability to handle disks larger than 2TiB.

Like MBR, GPT supports partition type codes; however, GPT type codes are 16-byte GUID values. Disk partitioning tools typically translate these codes into short descriptions, such as "Linux swap." Confusingly, most Linux installations use the same type code for their filesystems that Windows uses for its filesystems, although a Linux-only code is available and is gaining in popularity among Linux distributions.

An Alternative to Partitions: LVM

An alternative to partitions for some functions is *logical volume management (LVM)*. To use LVM, you set aside one or more partitions and assign them MBR partition type codes of 0x8e (or an equivalent on GPT disks). You then use a series of utilities, such as pvcreate, vgcreate, lvcreate, and lvscan, to manage the partitions (known as *physical volumes* in this scheme), to merge them into volume groups, and to create and manage logical volumes within the volume groups. Ultimately, you then access the logical volumes using names you assigned to them in the /dev/mapper directory, such as /dev/mapper/myvol-home.

LVM sounds complicated, and it is. Why would you want to use it? The biggest advantage to LVM is that it enables you to resize your logical volumes easily without worrying about the positions or sizes of surrounding partitions. In a sense, the logical volumes are like files in a regular filesystem; the filesystem (or volume group, in the case of LVM) manages the allocation of space when you resize files (or logical volumes). This can be a great boon if you're not sure of the optimum starting sizes of your partitions. You can also easily add disk space, in the form of a new physical disk, to expand the size of an existing volume group.

On the downside, LVM adds complexity, and not all Linux distributions support it out of the box. LVM can complicate disaster recovery, and if your LVM configuration spans multiple disks, a failure of one disk will put all files in your volume group at risk. It's easiest to configure a system with at least one filesystem (dedicated to /boot, or perhaps the root filesystem containing /boot) in its own conventional partition, reserving LVM for /home, /usr, and other filesystems.

Despite these drawbacks, you might consider investigating LVM further in some situations. It's most likely to be useful if you want to create an installation with many specialized filesystems and you want to retain the option of resizing those filesystems in the future. A second situation where LVM is handy is if you need to create very large filesystems that are too large for a single physical disk to handle.

Mount Points

Once a disk is partitioned, an OS must have some way to access the data on the partitions. In Windows, assigning a drive letter, such as C: or D:, to each partition does this. (Windows uses partition type codes to decide which partitions get drive letters and which to ignore.) Linux, though, doesn't use drive letters; instead, Linux uses a unified directory tree. Each partition is *mounted* at a *mount point* in that tree. A *mount point* is a directory that's used as a way to access the filesystem on the partition, and mounting the filesystem is the process of linking the filesystem to the mount point.

For instance, suppose that a Linux system has three partitions: the root (/) partition, /home, and /usr. The root partition holds the basic system files, and all other partitions are accessed via directories on that filesystem. If /home contains users' home directories, such as sally and sam, those directories will be accessible as /home/sally and /home/sam once this partition is mounted at /home. If this partition were unmounted and remounted at /users, the same directories would become accessible as /users/sally and /users/sam.

Partitions can be mounted just about anywhere in the Linux directory tree, including in directories on the root partition as well as directories on mounted partitions. For instance, if /home is a separate partition, you can have a /home/morehomes directory that serves as a mount point for another partition.

The upcoming section "Mounting and Unmounting Filesystems" describes the commands and configuration files that are used for mounting partitions. For now, you should be concerned only with what constitutes a good filesystem layout (that is, what directories you should split off into their own partitions) and how to create these partitions.

Common Partitions and Filesystem Layouts

So, what directories are commonly split off into separate partitions? Table 3.4 summarizes some popular choices. Note that typical sizes for many of these partitions vary greatly depending on how the system is used. Therefore, it's impossible to make recommendations on partition size that will be universally acceptable.

TABLE 3.4   Common partitions and their uses

Partition (mount point)	Typical size	Use
Swap (not mounted)	One to two times the system RAM size	Serves as an adjunct to system RAM. It is slow but enables the computer to run more or larger programs.
/home	200MiB–3TiB (or more)	Holds users' data files. Isolating it on a separate partition preserves user data during a system upgrade. Size depends on the number of users and their data storage needs.
/boot	100–500MiB	Holds critical boot files. Creating it as a separate partition lets you circumvent limitations of older BIOSs and boot loaders, which often can't boot a kernel from a point above a value between 504MiB and 2TiB.

TABLE 3.4   Common partitions and their uses *(continued)*

Partition (mount point)	Typical size	Use
/usr	500MiB–25GiB	Holds most Linux program and data files; this is sometimes the largest partition, although /home is larger on systems with many users or if users store large data files. Changes implemented in 2012 are making it harder to create a separate /usr partition in many distributions.
/usr/local	100MiB–3GiB	Holds Linux program and data files that are unique to this installation, particularly those that you compile yourself.
/opt	100MiB–5GiB	Holds Linux program and data files that are associated with third-party packages, especially commercial ones.
/var	100MiB–3TiB (or more)	Holds miscellaneous files associated with the day-to-day functioning of a computer. These files are often transient in nature. Most often split off as a separate partition when the system functions as a server that uses the /var directory for server-related files like mail queues.
/tmp	100MiB–20GiB	Holds temporary files created by ordinary users.
/mnt	N/A	Not a separate partition; rather, it or its subdirectories are used as mount points for removable media like CDs and DVDs.
/media	N/A	Holds subdirectories that may be used as mount points for removable media, much like /mnt or its subdirectories.

Some directories—/etc, /bin, /sbin, /lib, and /dev—should *never* be placed on separate partitions. These directories host critical system configuration files or files without which a Linux system can't function. For instance, /etc contains /etc/fstab, the file that specifies what partitions correspond to what directories, and /bin contains the mount utility that's used to mount partitions on directories. Changes to system utilities are making it harder, but not impossible, to split off /usr as a separate partition.

The 2.4.*x* and newer kernels include support for a dedicated /dev filesystem, which obviates the need for files in a disk-based /dev directory; so, in some sense, /dev can reside on a separate filesystem, although not a separate partition. The udev utility controls the /dev filesystem in recent versions of Linux.

Creating Partitions and Filesystems

If you're installing Linux on a computer, chances are that it will present you with a tool to help guide you through the partitioning process. These installation tools will create the partitions that you tell them to create or create partitions sized as the distribution's maintainers believe appropriate. If you need to partition a new disk that you're adding, though, or if you want to create partitions using standard Linux tools rather than rely on your distribution's installation tools, you must know something about the Linux programs that accomplish this task. Partitioning involves two tasks: creating the partitions and preparing the partitions to be used. In Linux, these two tasks are usually accomplished using separate tools, although some tools can handle both tasks simultaneously.

 Real World Scenario

When to Create Multiple Partitions

One problem with splitting off lots of separate partitions, particularly for new administrators, is that it can be difficult to settle on appropriate partition sizes. As noted in Table 3.4, the appropriate size of various partitions can vary substantially from one system to another. For instance, a workstation is likely to need a fairly small /var partition (say, 100MiB), but a mail or news server may need a /var partition that's gigabytes in size. Guessing wrong isn't fatal, but it is annoying. You'll need to resize your partitions (which is tedious and dangerous) or set up symbolic links between partitions so that subdirectories on one partition can be stored on other partitions. LVM can simplify such after-the-fact changes, but as noted earlier, LVM adds its own complexity.

For this reason, we generally recommend that new Linux administrators try simple partition layouts first. The root (/) partition is required, and swap is a very good idea. Beyond this, /boot can be helpful on hard disks of more than 8GiB with older distributions or BIOSs, but it is seldom needed with computers or distributions sold since 2000. Aside from user data (in /home or elsewhere), most Linux installations require 5 to 25GiB, so setting root (/) to a value in this range makes sense. An appropriate size for /home is often relatively easy for new administrators to guess, or you can devote all of your disk space after creating root (/) and swap to /home. Beyond these partitions, we recommend that new administrators proceed with caution.

As you gain more experience with Linux, you may want to break off other directories into their own partitions on subsequent installations or when upgrading disk hardware. You can use the du command to learn how much space is used by files within any given directory.

Partitioning a Disk

The traditional Linux tool for MBR disk partitioning is called fdisk. This tool's name is short for *fixed disk,* and the name is the same as a Windows tool that accomplishes the same task. (When we mean to refer to the Windows tool, we capitalize its name, as in FDISK. The Linux tool's name is always entirely lowercase.) Both Window's FDISK and Linux's fdisk are text-mode tools used to accomplish similar goals, but the two are very different in operational details.

Although fdisk is the traditional tool, several others exist. One of these is GNU Parted, which can handle several different partition table types, not just the MBR that fdisk can handle. If you prefer fdisk to GNU Parted but must use GPT, you can use GPT fdisk (http://www.rodsbooks.com/gdisk/); this package's gdisk program works much like fdisk but on GPT disks.

Using *fdisk*

To use Linux's fdisk, type the command name followed by the name of the disk device that you want to partition. For example, type the command **fdisk /dev/hda** to partition the primary PATA disk. The result is an fdisk prompt:

```
# fdisk /dev/hda
Command (m for help):
```

At the Command (m for help): prompt, you can type commands to accomplish various goals:

Display the Current Partition Table   You may want to begin by displaying the current partition table. To do so, type **p.** If you *only* want to display the current partition table, you can type **fdisk -l /dev/hda** (or whatever the device identifier is) at a command prompt rather than enter fdisk's interactive mode. This command displays the partition table and then exits.

Create a Partition   To create a partition, type **n.** The result is a series of prompts asking for information about the partition—whether it should be a primary, extended, or logical partition; the partition's starting cylinder; the partition's ending cylinder or size; and so on. The details of what you're asked depend in part on what's already defined. For instance, fdisk won't ask you if you want to create an extended partition if one already exists. Older versions of fdisk measure partition start and end points in cylinders, not megabytes. This is a holdover from the CHS measurements used by the *x*86 partition table. Recent versions of fdisk use sectors as the default unit of measure, although you can specify a partition's size by using a plus sign, number, and suffix, as in **+20G** to create a 20GiB partition.

In the past, partitions were aligned on CHS cylinders. This was beneficial given the hardware of the 1980s, but today it's detrimental. Many modern disks require partition alignment on 8-sector or larger boundaries for optimum performance. Recent partitioning programs begin partitions on 1MiB (2048-sector) boundaries for this reason. Failure to align partitions properly can result in severe performance degradation. For more on this topic see

www.ibm.com/developerworks/library/l-linux-4kb-sector-disks/index.html

Delete a Partition   To delete a partition, type **d**. If more than one partition exists, the program will ask for the partition number, which you must enter.

Change a Partition's Type   When you create a partition, fdisk assigns it a type code of 0x83, which corresponds to a Linux filesystem. If you want to create a Linux swap partition or a partition for another OS, you can type **t** to change a partition type code. The program then prompts you for a partition number and a type code.

List Partition Types   Several dozen partition type codes exist, so it's easy to forget what they are. Type **l** (that's a lowercase *L*) at the main fdisk prompt to see a list of the most common ones. You can also get this list by typing **L** when you're prompted for the partition type when you change a partition's type code.

Mark a Partition Bootable   Some OSs, such as Windows, rely on their partitions having special bootable flags in order to boot. You can set this flag by typing **a**, whereupon fdisk asks for the partition number.

Get Help   Type **m** or **?** to see a summary of the main fdisk commands.

Exit   Linux's fdisk supports two exit modes. First, you can type **q** to exit the program without saving any changes; anything you do with the program is lost. This option is particularly helpful if you've made a mistake. Second, typing **w** writes your changes to the disk and exits the program.

As an example, consider deleting a primary, an extended, and a logical partition on a USB flash drive and creating a single new one in their place:

```
# fdisk /dev/sdc
Command (m for help): p
Disk /dev/sdc: 2038 MB, 2038431744 bytes
63 heads, 62 sectors/track, 1019 cylinders, total 3981312 sectors
Units = sectors of 1 * 512 = 512 bytes
Sector size (logical/physical): 512 bytes / 512 bytes
I/O size (minimum/optimal): 512 bytes / 512 bytes
Disk identifier: 0x88a46f2c
   Device Boot      Start         End      Blocks   Id  System
/dev/sdc1            2048     2099199     1048576   83  Linux
/dev/sdc2         2099200     3981311      941056    5  Extended
/dev/sdc5         2101248     3981311      940032   83  Linux
Command (m for help): d
Partition number (1-5): 5
Command (m for help): d
Partition number (1-5): 2
Command (m for help): d
Selected partition 1
Command (m for help): n
```

```
Partition type:
   p   primary (0 primary, 0 extended, 4 free)
   e   extended
Select (default p): p
Partition number (1-4, default 1): 1
First sector (2048-3981311, default 2048): 2048
Last sector, +sectors or +size{K,M,G} (2048-3981311, default 3981311):
Using default value 3981311
Command (m for help): w
The partition table has been altered!
Calling ioctl() to re-read partition table.
Syncing disks.
```

This process begins with a p command to verify that the program is operating on the correct disk. With this information in hand, the three existing partitions are deleted. Note that the first two deletions ask for a partition number, but the third doesn't because only one partition is left. Once this is done, n is used to create a new primary partition. Once the task is complete, the w command is used to write the changes to disk and exit the program. The result of this sequence is a disk with a single primary partition (/dev/sdc1) marked as holding a Linux filesystem.

Using *gdisk*

If you're working with a GPT-formatted hard drive, you'll need to use the gdisk utility. On the surface, it works exactly like the fdisk utility, including using the same command letters:

```
$ gdisk /dev/sda
GPT fdisk (gdisk) version 0.8.8

Partition table scan:
  MBR: protective
  BSD: not present
  APM: not present
  GPT: present

Found valid GPT with protective MBR; using GPT.

Command (? for help):
```

To display the existing partitions, just use the print command:

```
Command (? for help): print
Disk /dev/sda: 23311984 sectors, 11.1 GiB
Logical sector size: 512 bytes
Disk identifier (GUID): 69816054-1280-4B53-BA4B-6829B0D4FD6D
Partition table holds up to 128 entries
```

```
First usable sector is 34, last usable sector is 23311950
Partitions will be aligned on 2048-sector boundaries
Total free space is 3629 sectors (1.8 MiB)

Number  Start (sector)   End (sector) Size       Code  Name
   1         2048            382975   186.0 MiB   EF00  EFI System Partition
   2       382976           1406975   500.0 MiB   0700
   3      1406976           3737599   1.1 GiB     8200
   4      3737600          23310335   9.3 GiB     0700

Command (? for help):
```

Remember that the GPT format doesn't use primary, extended, or logical partitions—all of the partitions are the same. The Code column shows the 16-byte GUID value for the GPT partition, indicating the type of partition. However, this particular Linux distribution (Fedora 20) uses the proper 8200 code for the Linux swap area but uses the 0700 Windows partition code instead of the 8300 code commonly used for Linux partitions.

From the gdisk prompt, you can delete existing partitions, create new partitions, and write the changes to the hard drive, just as with the fdisk utility.

Using GNU Parted

GNU Parted (www.gnu.org/software/parted/) is a partitioning tool that works with MBR, GPT, APM, and BSD disk labels, and other disk types. It also supports more features than fdisk and is easier to use in some ways. On the other hand, GNU Parted uses its own way of referring to partitions, which can be confusing. It's also more finicky about minor disk partitioning quirks and errors than fdisk. Although GNU Parted isn't covered on the exam, knowing a bit about it can be handy.

You start GNU Parted much as you start fdisk; that is, by typing its name followed by the device you want to modify, as in **parted /dev/sda** to partition the /dev/sda hard drive:

```
$ parted /dev/sda
GNU Parted 3.1
Using /dev/sda
Welcome to GNU Parted! Type 'help' to view a list of commands.
(parted)
```

The result is some brief introductory text followed by a (parted) prompt at which you type commands. Type **?** to see a list of commands, which are multicharacter commands similar to Linux shell commands. For instance, print displays the current partition table:

```
(parted) print
Model: ATA VBOX HARDDISK (scsi)
Disk /dev/sda: 11.9GB
Sector size (logical/physical): 512B/512B
Partition Table: gpt
```

```
Disk Flags:

Number  Start   End     Size    File system  Name                  Flags
 1      1049kB  196MB   195MB   fat16        EFI System Partition  boot
 2      196MB   720MB   524MB   ext4
 3      720MB   1914MB  1193MB  linux-swap(v1)
 4      1914MB  11.9GB  10.0GB  ext4
```

(parted)

To use parted to create a GPT disk, use the `mklabel` command:

(parted) mklabel gpt

Then to create a new partition, use the `mkpart` command:

(parted) mkpart primary ext4 1024kb 2tb

Some still more advanced partitioning capabilities appear only in flashy GUI tools, such as the GNOME Partition Editor, aka GParted (http://gparted.sourceforge.net), which is shown in Figure 3.5. Aside from its novice-friendly user interface, GParted's main claim to fame is that it enables you to move or resize partitions easily. You may need to run the program from an emergency disk to use these features, though; you can't move or resize any partition that's currently in use. Such partitions are marked with a key icon, as shown next to all the paritions in Figure 3.5.

FIGURE 3.5   GParted enables point-and-click partition management, including partition moving and resizing.

Resizing or moving a filesystem can be dangerous. If the resizing code contains a bug, or if there's a power failure during the operation, data can be lost. We strongly recommend that you back up any important data before resizing or moving a partition. Also, resizing or moving your boot partition on a BIOS-based computer can render the system unbootable until you reinstall your boot loader.

Preparing a Partition for Use

Once a partition is created, you must prepare it for use. This process is often called "making a filesystem" or "formatting a partition." It involves writing low-level data structures to disk. Linux can then read and modify these data structures to access and store files in the partition. You should know something about the common Linux filesystems and know how to use filesystem creation tools to create them.

The word *formatting* is somewhat ambiguous. It can refer either to *low-level formatting*, which creates a structure of sectors and tracks on the disk media, or *high-level formatting*, which creates a filesystem. Hard disks are low-level formatted at the factory and should never need to be low-level formatted again.

Common Filesystem Types

Linux supports quite a few different filesystems, both Linux-native filesystems and those intended for other OSs. Some of the latter barely work under Linux, and even when they do work reliably, they usually don't support all of the features that Linux expects in its native filesystems. Thus when preparing a Linux system, you'll use one or more of its native filesystems for most or all partitions:

Ext2fs The *Second Extended File System (ext2fs or ext2)* is the traditional Linux-native filesystem. It was created for Linux and was the dominant Linux filesystem throughout the late 1990s. Ext2fs has a reputation as a reliable filesystem. It has since been eclipsed by other filesystems, but it still has its uses. In particular, ext2fs can be a good choice for a small /boot partition, if you choose to use one, and for small (sub-gigabyte) removable disks. On such small partitions, the size of the journal used by more advanced filesystems can be a real problem, so the non-journaling ext2fs is a better choice. (Journaling is described in more detail shortly.) The ext2 filesystem type code is ext2.

On an EFI-based computer, using ext2fs, ext3fs, or ReiserFS on a separate /boot partition enables the firmware to read this partition with the help of suitable drivers. This can expand your options for boot loader configuration.

Ext3fs   The *Third Extended File System (ext3fs or ext3)* is basically ext2fs with a journal added. The result is a filesystem that's as reliable as ext2fs but that recovers from power outages and system crashes much more quickly. The ext3 filesystem type code is `ext3`.

Ext4fs   The *Fourth Extended File System (ext4fs or ext4)* is the next-generation version of this filesystem family. It adds the ability to work with very large disks (those over 16TiB, the limit for ext2fs and ext3fs) or very large files (those over 2TiB) as well as extensions intended to improve performance. Its filesystem type code is `ext4`.

ReiserFS   This filesystem was designed from scratch as a journaling filesystem for Linux. It's particularly good at handling large numbers of small files (say, smaller than about 32KB) because ReiserFS uses various tricks to squeeze the ends of files into each other's unused spaces. These small savings can add up when files are small. You can use `reiserfs` as the type code for this filesystem.

As of Linux kernel version 3.6.0, ReiserFS version 3.*x* is current. A from-scratch rewrite of ReiserFS, known as Reiser4, is under development, although this development has slowed to the point that it's uncertain if Reiser4 will ever be included in the mainstream kernel.

JFS   IBM developed the *Journaled File System (JFS)* for its AIX OS on mainframe systems and later reimplemented it on its attempt at a workstation OS, called OS/2. After the demise of OS/2, the OS/2 version of JFS was subsequently donated to Linux. JFS is a technically sophisticated journaling filesystem that may be of particular interest if you're familiar with AIX or OS/2 or want an advanced filesystem to use on a dual-boot system with one of these OSs. As you might expect, this filesystem's type code is `jfs`.

XFS   Silicon Graphics (SGI) created its *Extents File System (XFS)* for its IRIX OS and, like IBM, later donated the code to Linux. Like JFS, XFS is a very technically sophisticated filesystem. XFS has gained a reputation for robustness, speed, and flexibility on IRIX, but some of the XFS features that make it so flexible on IRIX aren't supported well under Linux. Use `xfs` as the type code for this filesystem.

Btrfs   This filesystem (pronounced "butter eff ess" or "bee tree eff ess") is an advanced filesystem with features inspired by those of Sun's Zettabyte File System (ZFS). Like ext4fs, JFS, and XFS, Btrfs is a fast performer, and it is able to handle very large disks and files. As of the 3.6.0 kernel, Btrfs is considered experimental; however, its advanced features make it a likely successor to the current popular filesystems.

In practice, most administrators choose ext3fs, ext4fs, or ReiserFS as their primary filesystems; however, JFS and XFS also work well, and some administrators prefer them, particularly on large disks that store large files. (Ext4fs also handles large files.) Hard data on the merits and problems with each filesystem is difficult to come by, and even when it does exist, it's suspect because filesystem performance interacts with so many other factors. For instance, as just noted, ReiserFS can cram more small files into a small space than can other filesystems, but this advantage isn't very important if you'll be storing mostly larger files.

If you're using a non-*x*86 or non-*x*86-64 platform, be sure to check filesystem development on that platform. A filesystem may be speedy and reliable on one CPU but sluggish and unreliable on another.

In addition to these Linux-native filesystems, you may need to deal with some others from time to time, including the following:

FAT   The *File Allocation Table (FAT)* filesystem is old and primitive—but ubiquitous. It's the only hard disk filesystem supported by DOS and early versions of Windows (such as the Windows *9x* series and the short-lived Windows Me). For this reason, every major OS understands FAT, making it an excellent filesystem for exchanging data on removable disks. Two major orthogonal variants of FAT exist: they vary in the size of the FAT data structure, after which the filesystem is named (12-, 16-, or 32-bit pointers), and have variants that support long filenames. Linux automatically detects the FAT size, so you shouldn't need to worry about this. To use the original FAT filenames, which are limited to eight characters with an optional three-character extension (the so-called *8.3 filenames*), use the Linux filesystem type code of msdos. To use Windows-style long filenames, use the filesystem type code of vfat. A Linux-only long filename system, known as umsdos, supports additional Linux features—enough that you can install Linux on a FAT partition, although this practice isn't recommended except for certain types of emergency disks or to try Linux on a Windows system.

NTFS   The *New Technology File System (NTFS)* is the preferred filesystem for Windows NT and beyond. Unfortunately, Linux's NTFS support is rather rudimentary. As of the 2.6.*x* kernel series, Linux can reliably read NTFS and can overwrite existing files, but the Linux kernel can't write new files to an NTFS partition. There are separate drivers outside of the kernel that you can use in Linux to create new files on an NTFS filesystem. Of these, the NTFS-3G driver is the most popular, and it is included by default in most Linux distributions.

HFS and HFS+   Apple has long used the *Hierarchical File System (HFS)* with its Mac OS, and Linux provides full read/write HFS support. This support isn't as reliable as Linux's read/write FAT support, though, so you may want to use FAT when exchanging files with Mac users. Apple has extended HFS to better support large hard disks and many Unix-like features with its HFS+ (aka Extended HFS). Linux 2.6.*x* and newer provide limited HFS+ support, but write support works only with the HFS+ journal disabled.

ISO-9660   The standard filesystem for CD-ROMs has long been *ISO-9660*. This filesystem comes in several levels. Level 1 is similar to the original FAT in that it supports only 8.3 filenames. Levels 2 and 3 add support for longer 32-character filenames. Linux supports ISO-9660 using its iso9660 filesystem type code. Linux's ISO-9660 support also works with the *Rock Ridge extensions*, which are a series of extensions to ISO-9660 to enable it to support Unix-style long filenames, permissions, symbolic links, and so on. Similarly, *Joliet* provides support for long filenames as implemented for Windows. If a disc includes Rock Ridge or Joliet extensions, Linux will automatically detect and use them.

UDF   The *Universal Disc Format (UDF)* is the next-generation filesystem for optical discs. It's commonly used on DVD-ROMs and recordable optical discs. Linux supports it, but read/write UDF support is still in its infancy.

As a practical matter, if you're preparing a hard disk for use with Linux, you should probably use Linux filesystems only. If you're preparing a disk that will be used for a dual-boot configuration, you may want to set aside some partitions for other filesystem types. For removable disks, you'll have to be the judge of what's most appropriate. You might use ext2fs for a Linux-only removable disk, FAT for a cross-platform disk, or ISO-9660 (perhaps with Rock Ridge and Joliet) for a CD-R or recordable DVD.

 ISO-9660 and other optical disc filesystems are created with special tools intended for this purpose. Specifically, mkisofs creates an ISO-9660 filesystem (optionally with Rock Ridge, Joliet, HFS, and UDF components added), while cdrecord writes this image to a blank CD-R. The growisofs program combines both functions but works only on recordable DVD media.

Creating a Filesystem

Linux tools exist that can create most filesystems on a partition, including all Linux-native filesystems. Typically, these tools have filenames in the form of mkfs.*fstype*, where *fstype* is the filesystem type code. These tools can also be called from a front-end tool called mkfs; you pass the filesystem type code to mkfs using its -t option:

```
# mkfs -t ext3 /dev/sda6
```

 For ext2 and ext3 filesystems, the mke2fs program is often used instead of mkfs. The mke2fs program is just another name for mkfs.ext2.

This command creates an ext3 filesystem on /dev/sda6. Depending on the filesystem, the speed of the disk, and the size of the partition, this process can take anywhere from a fraction of a second to a few seconds. Most filesystem-build tools support additional options, some of which can greatly increase the time required to build a filesystem. In particular, the -c option is supported by several filesystems. This option causes the tool to perform a bad-block check—every sector in the partition is checked to be sure it can reliably hold data. If it can't, the sector is marked as bad and isn't used.

 If you perform a bad-block check and find that some sectors are bad, chances are the entire hard disk doesn't have long to live. Sometimes this sort of problem can result from other issues, though, such as bad cables or SCSI termination problems.

Of the common Linux filesystems, ext2fs, ext3fs, and ext4fs provide the most options in their mkfs tools. (In fact, these tools are one and the same; the program simply creates a filesystem with the appropriate features for the name that's used to call it.) You can type **man mkfs.ext2** to learn about these options, most of which deal with obscure and unimportant features. One obscure option that does deserve mention is -m *percent*, which sets the reserved-space percentage. The idea is that you don't want the disk to fill up completely with user files; if the disk starts getting close to full, Linux should report that the disk *is* full before it really is, at least for ordinary users. This gives the root user the ability to log in and create new files, if necessary, to help recover the system.

The ext2fs/ext3fs/ext4fs reserved-space percentage defaults to 5 percent, which translates to quite a lot of space on large disks. You may want to reduce this value (say, by passing -m 2 to reduce it to 2 percent) on your root (/) filesystem and perhaps even lower (1 percent or 0 percent) on some, such as /home. Setting -m 0 also makes sense on removable disks, which aren't likely to be critical for system recovery and may be a bit cramped to begin with.

In addition to providing filesystem creation tools for Linux-native filesystems, Linux distributions usually provide such tools for various non-Linux filesystems. The most important of these may be for FAT. The main tool for this task is called mkdosfs, but it's often linked to the mkfs.msdos and mkfs.vfat names as well. This program can automatically adjust the size of the FAT data structure to 12, 16, or 32 bits depending on the device size. You can override this option with the -F *fat-size* option, where *fat-size* is the FAT size in bits—12, 16, or 32. No special options are required to create a FAT filesystem that can handle Windows-style (VFAT) long filenames; the OS creates these.

In Exercise 3.1, you'll practice creating filesystems using mkfs and related utilities.

EXERCISE 3.1

Creating Filesystems

Try creating some filesystems on a spare partition or a removable disk. Even a floppy disk will do, although you won't be able to create journaling filesystems on a floppy disk. The following steps assume that you're using a USB flash drive, /dev/sdc1; change the device specification as necessary.

> *WARNING: Be sure to use an empty partition!* Accidentally entering the wrong device filename could wipe out your entire system!

This exercise uses a few commands that are described in more detail later in this chapter. To create some filesystems, follow these steps:

1. Log in as root.

2. Use fdisk to verify the partitions on your target disk by typing **fdisk -l /dev/ sdc**. You should see a list of partitions, including the one you'll use for your tests. (If fdisk reports a single partition with ee under the Id column, the disk is a GPT disk, and you should verify the disk's partitions with gdisk rather than fdisk.)

3. Verify that your test partition is *not* currently mounted. Type **df** to see the currently mounted partitions and verify that /dev/sdc1 is not among them.

4. Type **mkfs -t ext2 /dev/sdc1**. You should see several lines of status information appear.

5. Type **mount /dev/sdc1 /mnt** to mount the new filesystem to /mnt. (You may use another mount point if you like.)

6. Type **df /mnt** to see basic accounting information for the filesystem. On our test system with a /dev/sdc1 that's precisely 1000MiB in size, 1,007,896 blocks are present; 1,264 are used, and 955,432 blocks are available. Most of the difference between the present and available blocks is caused by the 5 percent reserved space.

7. Type **umount /mnt** to unmount the filesystem.

8. Type **mkfs -t ext2 -m 0 /dev/sdc1** to create a new ext2 filesystem on the device, but without any reserved space.

9. Repeat steps 5–7. Note that the available space has increased (to 1,006,632 blocks on our test disk). The available space plus the used space should now equal the total blocks.

10. Repeat steps 4–7, but use a filesystem type code of ext3 to create a journaling file-system. (This won't be possible if you use a floppy disk.) Note how much space is consumed by the journal.

11. Repeat steps 4–7, but use another filesystem, such as JFS or ReiserFS. Note how the filesystem creation tools differ in the information that they present and in their stated amounts of available space.

Be aware that, because of differences in how filesystems store files and allocate space, a greater amount of available space when a filesystem is created may not translate into a greater capacity to store files.

Creating Swap Space

Some partitions don't hold files. Most notably, Linux can use a *swap partition*, which is a partition that Linux treats as an extension of memory. (Linux can also use a *swap file*, which is a file that works in the same way. Both are examples of *swap space*.) Linux uses the MBR partition type code of 0x82 to identify swap space, but as with other partitions, this code is mostly a convenience to keep other OSs from trying to access Linux swap partitions; Linux uses /etc/fstab to define which partitions to use as swap space, as described in "Permanently Mounting Filesystems" later in this chapter.

WARNING

Solaris for *x86* also uses an MBR partition type code of 0x82. However, in Solaris, this code refers to a Solaris partition. If you dual-boot between Solaris and Linux, this double meaning of the 0x82 partition type code can cause confusion. This is particularly true when installing the OSs. You may need to use Linux's fdisk to change the partition type codes temporarily to keep Linux from trying to use a Solaris partition as swap space or to keep Solaris from trying to interpret Linux swap space as a data partition.

Although swap space doesn't hold a filesystem *per se*, and it isn't mounted in the way that filesystem partitions are mounted, swap space does require preparation similar to that for creation of a filesystem. This task is accomplished with the mkswap command, which you can generally use by passing it nothing but the device identifier:

```
# mkswap /dev/sda7
```

This example turns /dev/sda7 into swap space. To use the swap space, you must activate it with the swapon command:

```
# swapon /dev/sda7
```

To activate swap space permanently, you must create an entry for it in /etc/fstab, as described in "Permanently Mounting Filesystems," later in this chapter.

Maintaining Filesystem Health

Filesystems can become "sick" in a variety of ways. They can become overloaded with too much data, they can be tuned inappropriately for your system, or they can become corrupted because of buggy drivers, buggy utilities, or hardware errors. Fortunately, Linux provides a variety of utilities that can help you keep an eye on the status of your filesystems, tune their performance, and fix them.

WARNING   Many of Linux's filesystem maintenance tools should be run when the filesystem is not mounted. Changes made by maintenance utilities while the filesystem is mounted can confuse the kernel's filesystem drivers, resulting in data corruption. In the following pages, we mention when utilities can and can't be used with mounted filesystems.

Tuning Filesystems

Filesystems are basically just big data structures—they're a means of storing data on disk in an indexed method that makes it easy to locate the data at a later time. Like all data structures, filesystems include design compromises. For instance, a design feature may enable you to store more small files on disk, but it might chew up disk space, thus reducing the total capacity available for storage of larger files. In many cases, you have no choice concerning these compromises, but some filesystems include tools that enable you to set filesystem options that affect performance. This is particularly true of ext2fs and the related ext3fs and ext4fs. Three tools are particularly important for tuning these filesystems: dumpe2fs, tune2fs, and debugfs. The first of these tools provides information about the filesystem, and the other two enable you to change tuning options.

Obtaining Filesystem Information

You can learn a lot about your ext2 or ext3 filesystem with the dumpe2fs command. This command's syntax is fairly straightforward:

```
dumpe2fs [options] device
```

device is the filesystem device file, such as /dev/sdb7. This command accepts several options (signified by *options*), most of which are rather obscure. The most important option is probably -h, which causes the utility to omit information about group descriptors. (This information is helpful in very advanced filesystem debugging but not for basic filesystem tuning.) For information about additional options, consult the man page for dumpe2fs.

Unless you're a filesystem expert and need to debug a corrupted filesystem, you'll most likely to want to use dumpe2fs with the -h option. The result is about three-dozen lines of output, each specifying a particular filesystem option, like these:

```
Last mounted on:            <not available>
Filesystem features:        has_journal filetype sparse_super
Filesystem state:           clean
Inode count:                657312
Block count:                1313305
Last checked:               Wed Sep 03 14:23:23 2014
Check interval:             15552000 (6 months)
```

Some of these options' meanings are fairly self-explanatory; for instance, the filesystem was last checked (with fsck, described in "Checking Filesystems" later in this chapter) on September 3, 2014. Other options aren't so obvious; for instance, the Inode count line may be puzzling. (It's a count of the number of *inodes* supported by the filesystem. Each inode contains information for one file, so the number of inodes effectively limits the number of files you can store.)

The next two sections describe some of the options that you may want to change. For now, you should know that you could retrieve information about how your filesystems are currently configured using dumpe2fs. You can then use this information when modifying the configuration; if your current settings seem reasonable, you can leave them alone, but if they seem ill adapted to your configuration, you can change them.

Unlike many low-level disk utilities, dumpe2fs can be safely run on a filesystem that's currently mounted. This can be handy when you're studying your configuration to decide what to modify.

Most other filesystems lack an equivalent to dumpe2fs, but XFS provides something with at least some surface similarities: xfs_info. To invoke it, pass the command the name of the partition that holds the filesystem that you want to check:

```
# xfs_info /dev/sda7
meta-data=/dev/sda7   isize=256    agcount=88, agsize=1032192 blks
          =            sectsz=512   attr=0
data      =            bsize=4096   blocks=89915392, imaxpct=25
```

```
            =            sunit=0      swidth=0 blks, unwritten=1
naming   =version 2   bsize=4096
log      =internal    bsize=4096    blocks=8064, version=1
            =            sectsz=512   sunit=0 blks
realtime =none         extsz=65536  blocks=0, rtextents=0
```

Instead of the partition name, you can pass the mount point, such as /home or /usr/local. Unlike most filesystem tools, xfs_info requires that the filesystem be mounted. The information returned by xfs_info is fairly technical, mostly related to block sizes, sector sizes, and so on.

Another XFS tool is xfs_metadump. This program copies the filesystem's metadata (filenames, file sizes, and so on) to a file. For instance, **xfs_metadump /dev/sda7 ~/dump-file** copies the metadata to ~/dump-file. This command doesn't copy actual file contents and so isn't useful as a backup tool. Instead, it's intended as a debugging tool; if the filesystem is behaving strangely, you can use this command and send the resulting file to XFS developers for study.

Adjusting Tunable Filesystem Parameters

The tune2fs program enables you to change many of the filesystem parameters that are reported by dumpe2fs. This program's syntax is fairly simple, but it hides a great deal of complexity:

```
tune2fs [options] device
```

The complexity arises because of the large number of options that the program accepts. Each feature that tune2fs enables you to adjust requires its own option:

Adjust the Maximum Mount Count   Ext2fs, ext3fs, and ext4fs require a periodic disk check with fsck. This check is designed to prevent errors from creeping onto the disk undetected. You can adjust the maximum number of times the disk may be mounted without a check with the -c *mounts* option, where *mounts* is the number of mounts. You can trick the system into thinking the filesystem has been mounted a certain number of times with the -C *mounts* option; this sets the mount counter to *mounts*.

Adjust the Time between Checks   Periodic disk checks are required based on time as well as the number of mounts. You can set the time between checks with the -i *interval* option, where *interval* is the maximum time between checks. Normally, *interval* is a number with the character d, w, or m appended, to specify days, weeks, or months, respectively.

Add a Journal   The -j option adds a journal to the filesystem, effectively converting an ext2 filesystem into an ext3 filesystem. Journal management is described in more detail in "Maintaining a Journal."

Set the Reserved Blocks   The -m *percent* option sets the percentage of disk space that's reserved for use by root. The default value is 5, but this is excessive on multi-gigabyte hard disks, so you may want to reduce it. You may want to set it to 0 on removable disks intended to store user files. You can also set the reserved space in blocks, rather than as a percentage of disk space, with the -r *blocks* option.

The options described here are the ones that are most likely to be useful. Several other options are available; consult tune2fs's man page for details.

As with most low-level disk utilities, you shouldn't use tune2fs to adjust a mounted filesystem. If you want to adjust a key mounted filesystem, such as your root (/) filesystem, you may need to boot up an emergency disk system, such as the CD-based Parted Magic (http://partedmagic.com). Many distributions' install discs can be used in this capacity as well.

In XFS, the xfs_admin command is the rough equivalent of tune2fs. Some options that you may want to adjust include the following:

Use Version 2 Journal Format   The -j option enables version 2 log (journal) format, which can improve performance in some situations.

Obtain the Filesystem Label and UUID   You can use the -l and -u options to obtain the filesystem's label (name) and *universally unique identifier (UUID)*, respectively. The name is seldom used in Linux but can be used in some cases. The UUID is a long code that is increasingly used by distributions to specify a filesystem to be mounted, as described in "Permanently Mounting Filesystems" later in this chapter.

The blkid command can display the label and UUID of any partition's filesystem, not just an XFS partition.

Set the Filesystem Label and UUID   You can change the filesystem's label or UUID by using the -L *label* or -U *uuid* option, respectively. The label is at most 12 characters in length. You'll normally use the -U option to set the UUID to a known value (such as the UUID the partition used prior to it being reformatted), or you can use generate as the *uuid* value to have xfs_admin create a new UUID. You should *not* set the UUID to a value that's in use on another partition!

In use, xfs_admin might look something like this:

```
# xfs_admin -L av_data /dev/sda7
writing all SBs
new label = "av_data"
```

This example sets the name of the filesystem on /dev/sda7 to av_data. As with tune2fs, xfs_admin should be used only on unmounted filesystems.

Interactively Debugging a Filesystem

In addition to reviewing and changing filesystem flags with dumpe2fs and tune2fs, you can interactively modify a filesystem's features using debugfs. This program provides the abilities of dumpe2fs, tune2fs, and many of Linux's normal file-manipulation tools all rolled into one. To use the program, type its name followed by the device filename corresponding to the filesystem that you want to manipulate. You'll then see the debugfs prompt:

```
# debugfs /dev/sda11
debugfs:
```

You can type commands at this prompt to achieve specific goals:

Display Filesystem Superblock Information   The show_super_stats or stats command produces superblock information, similar to what dumpe2fs displays.

Display Inode Information   You can display the inode data on a file or directory by typing **stat *filename***, where *filename* is the name of the file.

Undelete a File   You can use debugfs to undelete a file by typing **undelete *inode name***, where *inode* is the inode number of the deleted file and *name* is the filename you want to give to it. (You can use undel in place of undelete if you like.) This facility is of limited utility because you must know the inode number associated with the deleted file. You can obtain a list of deleted inodes by typing **lsdel** or **list_deleted_inodes,** but the list may not provide enough clues to let you zero in on the file you want to recover.

Extract a File   You can extract a file from the filesystem by typing **write *internal-file external-file***, where *internal-file* is the name of a file in the filesystem that you're manipulating and *external-file* is a filename on your main Linux system. This facility can be handy if a filesystem is badly damaged and you want to extract a critical file without mounting the filesystem.

Manipulate Files   Most of the commands described in Chapter 4 work within debugfs. You can change your directory with cd, create links with ln, remove a file with rm, and so on.

Obtain Help   Typing **list_requests, lr, help,** or **?** produces a summary of available commands.

Exit   Typing **quit** exits from the program.

This summary just scratches the surface of debugfs's capabilities. In the hands of an expert, this program can help rescue a badly damaged filesystem or at least extract critical data from it. To learn more, consult the program's man page.

WARNING   Although debugfs is a useful tool, it's potentially dangerous. Don't use it on a mounted filesystem, don't use it unless you have to, and be very careful when using it. If in doubt, leave the adjustments to the experts. Be aware that the exam does cover debugfs, though.

The closest XFS equivalent to debugfs is called xfs_db. Like debugfs, xfs_db provides an interactive tool to access and manipulate a filesystem, but xfs_db provides fewer tools that are amenable to novice or intermediate use. Instead, xfs_db is a tool for XFS experts.

Maintaining a Journal

Ext2fs is a traditional filesystem. Although it's a good performer, it suffers from a major limitation: after a power failure, a system crash, or another uncontrolled shutdown, the filesystem could be in an inconsistent state. The only way to mount the filesystem safely so that you're sure its data structures are valid is to perform a full disk check on it, as described in the next section, "Checking Filesystems." This task is usually handled automatically when the system boots, but it takes time—probably several minutes, or perhaps more than an hour on a large filesystem or if the computer has many smaller filesystems.

The solution to this problem is to change to a *journaling filesystem*. Such a filesystem maintains a *journal*, which is a data structure that describes pending operations. Prior to writing data to the disk's main data structures, Linux describes what it's about to do in the journal. When the operations are complete, their entries are removed from the journal. Thus, at any given moment, the journal should contain a list of disk structures that *might* be undergoing modification. The result is that, in the event of a crash or power failure, the system can examine the journal and check only those data structures described within it. If inconsistencies are found, the system can roll back or complete the changes, returning the disk to a consistent state without checking every data structure in the filesystem. This greatly speeds the disk-check process after power failures and system crashes. Today, journaling filesystems are the standard for most Linux disk partitions. Very small partitions (such as a separate /boot partition, if you use one) and small removable disks (such as USB sticks) often lack journals, though.

Five journaling filesystems are common on Linux: ext3fs, ext4fs, ReiserFS, XFS, and JFS. Of these, the last three require little in the way of journal configuration. Ext3fs is a bit different; it's basically just ext2fs with a journal added. This fact means you can add a journal to an ext2 filesystem, converting it into an ext3 filesystem. This is what the -j option to tune2fs does, as described earlier in "Adjusting Tunable Filesystem Parameters." Ext4fs is a further enhancement of this filesystem family.

Although using tune2fs on a mounted filesystem is generally inadvisable, it's safe to use its -j option on a mounted filesystem. The result is a file called .journal that holds the journal. If you add a journal to an unmounted filesystem, the journal file will be invisible.

Adding a journal alone won't do much good, though. To use a journal, you must mount the filesystem with the correct filesystem type code—ext3 rather than ext2 for ext3fs or ext4 for ext4fs. (The upcoming section "Mounting and Unmounting Filesystems" describes how to do this.)

The journal, like other filesystem features, has its own set of parameters. You can set these with the -J option to tune2fs. In particular, the size=*journal-size* and device=*external-journal* suboptions enable you to set the journal's size and the device on which it's stored. By default, the system creates a journal that's the right size for the filesystem and stores it on the filesystem itself.

Checking Filesystems

Tuning a filesystem is a task that you're likely to perform every once in a while—say, when making major changes to an installation. Another task is much more common: checking a filesystem for errors. Bugs, power failures, and mechanical problems can all cause the data structures on a filesystem to become corrupted. The results are sometimes subtle, but if left unchecked, they can cause severe data loss. For this reason, Linux includes tools for verifying a filesystem's integrity and for correcting any problems that may exist. The main tool that you'll use for this purpose is called fsck. This program is actually a front end to other tools, such as e2fsck (aka fsck.ext2, fsck.ext3, and fsck.ext4) or XFS's xfs_check and xfs_repair. The syntax for fsck is as follows:

```
fsck  [-sACVRTNP] [-t fstype] [--] [fsck-options]  filesystems
```

 The exam objectives include both e2fsck and fsck, but because fsck is the more general tool that's useful on more filesystems, it's the form described in more detail in this book.

The more common parameters to fsck enable you to perform useful actions:

Check All Files The -A option causes fsck to check all of the filesystems marked to be checked in /etc/fstab. This option is normally used in system startup scripts.

Indicate Progress The -C option displays a text-mode progress indicator of the check process. Most filesystem check programs don't support this feature, but e2fsck does.

Show Verbose Output The -V option produces verbose output of the check process.

No Action The -N option tells fsck to display what it would normally do without actually doing it.

Set the Filesystem Type Normally, fsck determines the filesystem type automatically. You can force the type with the -t fstype flag, though. Used in conjunction with -A, this causes the program to check only the specified filesystem types, even if others are marked to be checked. If fstype is prefixed with no, then all filesystems except the specified type are checked.

Filesystem-Specific Options Filesystem check programs for specific filesystems often have their own options. The fsck command passes options it doesn't understand, or those that follow a double dash (--), to the underlying check program. Common options include -a or -p (perform an automatic check), -r (perform an interactive check), and -f (force a full filesystem check even if the filesystem initially appears to be clean).

Filesystem List The final parameter is usually the name of the filesystem or filesystems being checked, such as /dev/sda6.

Normally, you run fsck with only the filesystem device name, as in **fsck /dev/sda6**. You can add options as needed, however. Check fsck's man page for less common options.

WARNING   Run fsck *only* on filesystems that are not currently mounted or that are mounted in read-only mode. Changes written to disk during normal read/write operations can confuse fsck and result in filesystem corruption.

Linux runs fsck automatically at startup on partitions that are marked for this in /etc/fstab, as described later in "Permanently Mounting Filesystems." The normal behavior of e2fsck causes it to perform just a quick cursory examination of a partition if it's been unmounted cleanly. The result is that the Linux boot process isn't delayed because of a filesystem check unless the system wasn't shut down properly. This rule has a couple of exceptions, though: e2fsck forces a check if the disk has gone longer than a certain amount of time without checks (normally six months) or if the filesystem has been mounted more than a certain number of times since the last check (normally 20). You can change these options using tune2fs, as described earlier in "Adjusting Tunable Filesystem Parameters." Therefore, you'll occasionally see automatic filesystem checks of ext2, ext3, and ext4 filesystems, even if the system was shut down correctly.

Journaling filesystems do away with full filesystem checks at system startup even if the system wasn't shut down correctly. Nonetheless, these filesystems still require check programs to correct problems introduced by undetected write failures, bugs, hardware problems, and the like. If you encounter odd behavior with a journaling filesystem, you might consider unmounting it and performing a filesystem check—but be sure to read the documentation first. Some Linux distributions do odd things with some journaling filesystem check programs. For instance, Mandriva uses a symbolic link from /sbin/fsck.reiserfs to /bin/true. This configuration speeds system boot times should ReiserFS partitions be marked for automatic checks, but it can be confusing if you need to check the filesystem manually. If this is the case, run /sbin/reiserfsck to do the job. Similarly, /sbin/fsck.xfs is usually nothing but a script that advises the user to run xfs_check or xfs_repair.

Monitoring Disk Use

One common problem with disks is that they can fill up. To avoid this problem, you need tools to tell you how much space your files are consuming. This is the task of the df and du programs, which summarize disk use on a partition-by-partition and directory-by-directory basis, respectively.

Monitoring Disk Use by Partition

The df command's syntax is as follows:

df [*options*] [*files*]

In the simplest case, you can type the command name to see a summary of disk space used on all of a system's partitions:

$ **df**

```
Filesystem      1K-blocks      Used Available Use% Mounted on
/dev/sdb10       5859784    4449900   1409884  76% /
/dev/sdb12       2086264     991468   1094796  48% /opt
/dev/hda13       2541468     320928   2220540  13% /usr/local
/dev/hda9       15361340   10174596   5186744  67% /home
/dev/hda10      22699288   13663408   7882820  64% /other/emu
/dev/hda6         101089      22613     74301  24% /boot
/dev/sdb5        1953216    1018752    934464  53% /other/shared
none              256528          0    256528   0% /dev/shm
speaker:/home    6297248    3845900   2451348  62% /speaker/home
//win/music     17156608    8100864   9055744  48% /win/mp3s
```

This output shows the device file associated with the filesystem, the total amount of space on the filesystem, the used space on the filesystem, the free space on the filesystem, the percentage of space that's used, and the mount point. Typically, when used space climbs above about 80 percent, you should consider cleaning up the partition. The appropriate ceiling varies from one computer and partition to another, though. The risk is greatest on partitions that hold files that change frequently—particularly if large files are likely to be created on a partition, even if only temporarily.

You can fine-tune the effects of df by passing it several options. Each option modifies the df output in a specific way:

Include All Filesystems   The -a or --all option includes pseudo-filesystems with a size of 0 in the output. These filesystems may include /proc, /sys, /proc/bus/usb, and others.

Use Scaled Units   The -h or --human-readable option causes df to scale and label its units; for instance, instead of reporting a partition as having 5859784 blocks, it reports the size as 5.6G (for 5.6GiB). The -H and --si options have a similar effect, but they use power of 10 (1,000, 1,000,000, and so on) units rather than power of 2 (1,024, 1,048,576, and so on) units. The -k (--kilobytes) and -m (--megabytes) options force output in their respective units.

Summarize Inodes   By default, df summarizes available and used disk space. You can instead receive a report on available and used inodes by passing the -i or --inodes option. This information can be helpful if a partition has very many small files, which can deplete available inodes sooner than they deplete available disk space.

 The -i option works well for ext2, ext3, ext4, XFS, and some other filesystems that create a fixed number of inodes when the filesystem is created. Other filesystems, such as ReiserFS and Btrfs, create inodes dynamically, rendering the -i option meaningless.

Local Filesystems Only   The -l or --local option causes df to omit network filesystems. This can speed up operation.

Display Filesystem Type   The -T or --print-type option adds the filesystem type to the information df displays.

Limit by Filesystem Type   The -t *fstype* or --type=*fstype* option displays only information about filesystems of the specified type. The -x *fstype* or --exclude-type=*fstype* option has the opposite effect; it excludes filesystems of the specified type from the report.

This list is incomplete. Consult df's man page for details about more options. In addition to these options, you can specify one or more files (using *files*) to df. When you do this, the program restricts its report to the filesystem on which the specified file or directory exists. For instance, to learn about the disk space used on the /home partition, you could type **df /home**. Alternatively, you can give a device filename, as in **df /dev/hda9**.

Monitoring Disk Use by Directory

The df command is helpful for finding out which partitions are in danger of becoming overloaded. Once you've obtained this information, however, you may need to fine-tune the diagnosis and track down the directories and files that are chewing up disk space. The tool for this task is du, which has a syntax similar to that of df:

du [*options*] [*directories*]

This command searches directories that you specify and reports how much disk space each is consuming. This search is recursive, so you can learn how much space the directory and all its subdirectories consume. The result can be a very long listing if you specify directories with many files, but several options can reduce the size of this output. Others can perform helpful tasks as well:

Summarize Files and Directories   Ordinarily, du reports on the space used by the files in directories but not the space used by individual files. Passing the -a or --all option causes du to report on individual files as well.

Compute a Grand Total   Adding the -c or --total option causes du to add a grand total to the end of its output.

Use Scaled Units   The -h or --human-readable option causes du to scale and label its units; for instance, instead of reporting the total disk space used as 5859784 blocks, it reports the size as 5.6G (for 5.6GiB). The -H and --si options have a similar effect, but they use power of 10 (1,000, 1,000,000, and so on) units rather than power of 2 (1,024, 1,048,576, and so on) units. The -k (--kilobytes) and -m (--megabytes) options force output in their respective units.

Count Hard Links   Ordinarily, du counts files that appear multiple times as hard links only once. This reflects true disk space used, but sometimes you may want to count each link independently—for instance, if you're creating a CD-R and the file will be stored once for each link. To do so, include the -l (that's a lowercase *L*) or --count-links option. (Links are described in more detail in Chapter 4.)

Limit Depth   The --max-depth=*n* option limits the report to *n* levels. (The subdirectories' contents are counted even if they aren't reported.)

Summarize   If you don't want a line of output for each subdirectory in the tree, pass the -s or --summarize option, which limits the report to those files and directories that you specify on the command line. This option is equivalent to --max=depth=0.

Limit to One Filesystem   The -x or --one-file-system option limits the report to the current filesystem. If another filesystem is mounted within the tree that you want summarized, its contents aren't included in the report.

This list is incomplete; you should consult du's man page for information about additional options.

As an example of du in action, consider using it to discover which of your users is consuming the most disk space in /home. Chances are you're not concerned with the details of which subdirectories within each home directory are using the space, so you'll pass the -s option to the program:

```
# du -s /home/*
12          /home/ellen
35304       /home/freddie
1760        /home/jennie
12078       /home/jjones
0           /home/lost+found
10110324    /home/mspiggy
```

In this example, the wildcard character (*) stands for all of the files and directories in /home, thus producing summaries for all of these subdirectories. (For more on this topic, consult Chapter 4.) Clearly, mspiggy (or whoever owns the /home/mspiggy directory) is the biggest disk space user—or at least that directory's contents are consuming the most space. You could investigate further, say by typing **du -s /home/mspiggy/*** to learn where the disk space is being used within the /home/mspiggy directory. In the case of user files, if this space consumption is a problem, you may want to contact this user instead of trying to clean it up yourself.

WARNING   Many types of files shouldn't simply be deleted. For instance, most program files should be removed via the system's package management system, if you decide to remove them. (This topic is covered in Chapter 2, "Managing Software.") If you're not sure what a file is or how it should be removed, don't delete it—try a Web search, type **man filename**, or otherwise research it to figure out what it is.

Mounting and Unmounting Filesystems

Maintaining filesystems is necessary, but the whole reason filesystems exist is to store files—in other words, to be useful. Under Linux, filesystems are most often used by being *mounted*—that is, associated with a directory. This task can be accomplished on a one-time basis by using tools such as mount (and then unmounted with umount) or persistently across reboots by editing the /etc/fstab file.

Temporarily Mounting or Unmounting Filesystems

Linux provides the mount command to mount a filesystem to a mount point. The umount command reverses this process. (Yes, umount is spelled correctly; it's missing the first n.) In practice, these commands usually aren't too difficult to use, but they support a large number of options.

Syntax and Parameters for *mount*

The syntax for mount is as follows:

```
mount [-alrsvw] [-t fstype] [-o options] [device]  [mountpoint]
```

Common parameters for mount support a number of features:

Mount All Filesystems   The -a parameter causes mount to mount all of the filesystems listed in the /etc/fstab file, which specifies the most-used partitions and devices. The upcoming section "Permanently Mounting Filesystems" describes this file's format.

Mount Read-Only   The -r parameter causes Linux to mount the filesystem read-only, even if it's normally a read/write filesystem.

Show Verbose Output   As with many commands, -v produces verbose output—the program provides comments on operations as they occur.

Mount Read/Write   The -w parameter causes Linux to attempt to mount the filesystem for both read and write operations. This is the default for most filesystems, but some experimental drivers default to read-only operation. The -o rw option has the same effect.

Specify the Filesystem Type   Use the -t *fstype* parameter to specify the filesystem type. Common filesystem types are ext2 (for ext2fs), ext3 (for ext3fs), ext4 (for ext4fs), reiserfs (for ReiserFS), jfs (for JFS), xfs (for XFS), vfat (for FAT with VFAT long filenames), msdos (for FAT using only short DOS filenames, the old 8.3 naming standard), iso9660 (for CD filesystems), udf (for DVD and some CD filesystems), nfs (for NFS network mounts), and cifs (for SMB/CIFS network shares). Linux supports many others. If this parameter is omitted, Linux will attempt to auto-detect the filesystem type.

Linux requires support in the kernel or as a kernel module to mount a filesystem of a given type. If this support is missing, Linux will refuse to mount the filesystem in question.

Mount by Label or UUID   Instead of the device name, you can use the -L *label* or -U *uuid* options to tell mount to mount the filesystem with the specified label or UUID, respectively.

Additional Options   You can add many options using the -o parameter. Many of these are filesystem specific.

Device   The *device* parameter is the device filename associated with the partition or disk device, such as /dev/hda4, /dev/fd0, or /dev/cdrom. This parameter is usually required, but it may be omitted under some circumstances, as described shortly.

Mount Point   The *mountpoint* parameter is the directory to which the device's contents should be attached. As with *device*, it's usually required, but it may be omitted under some circumstances.

The preceding list of mount parameters isn't comprehensive; consult the mount man page for some of the more obscure options. The most common applications of mount use few parameters because Linux generally does a good job of detecting the filesystem type, and the default parameters work reasonably well. For instance, consider this example:

```
# mount /dev/sdb7 /mnt/shared
```

This command mounts the contents of /dev/sdb7 on /mnt/shared, auto-detecting the filesystem type and using the default options. Ordinarily, only root may issue a mount command; however, if /etc/fstab specifies the user, users, or owner option, an ordinary user may mount a filesystem using a simplified syntax in which only the device *or* mount point is specified, but not both. For instance, a user may type **mount /mnt/cdrom** to mount a CD-ROM if /etc/fstab specifies /mnt/cdrom as its mount point and uses the user, users, or owner option.

> Most Linux distributions ship with auto-mounter support, which causes the OS to mount removable media automatically when they're inserted. In GUI environments, a file browser may also open on the inserted disk. To eject the disk, the user will need to unmount the filesystem by using umount, as described shortly, or by selecting an option in the desktop environment.

When Linux mounts a filesystem, it ordinarily records this fact in /etc/mtab. This file has a format similar to that of /etc/fstab and is stored in /etc, but it's not a configuration file that you should edit. You might examine this file to determine what filesystems are mounted, though. (The df command, described in more detail earlier in "Monitoring Disk Use by Partition," is another way to learn what filesystems are mounted.)

Options for *mount*

When you do need to use special parameters (via -o or in /etc/fstab), it's usually to add filesystem-specific options. Table 3.5 summarizes the most important filesystem options. Some of these are meaningful only in the /etc/fstab file.

TABLE 3.5   Important filesystem options for the mount command

Option	Supported filesystems	Description
defaults	All	Causes the default options for this filesystem to be used. It's used primarily in the /etc/fstab file to ensure that the file includes an options column.
loop	All	Causes the loopback device for this mount to be used. Allows you to mount a file as if it were a disk partition. For instance, **mount -t vfat -o loop image.img /mnt/image** mounts the file image.img as if it were a disk.
auto or noauto	All	Mounts or doesn't mount the filesystem at boot time or when root issues the **mount -a** command. The default is auto, but noauto is appropriate for removable media. Used in /etc/fstab.
user or nouser	All	Allows or disallows ordinary users to mount the filesystem. The default is nouser, but user is often appropriate for removable media. Used in /etc/fstab. When included in this file, user allows users to type **mount /mountpoint** (where /mountpoint is the assigned mount point) to mount a disk. Only the user who mounted the filesystem may unmount it.
users	All	Similar to user, except that any user may unmount a filesystem once it's been mounted.
owner	All	Similar to user, except that the user must own the device file. Some distributions, such as Red Hat, assign ownership of some device files (such as /dev/fd0 for the floppy disk) to the console user, so this can be a helpful option.
remount	All	Changes one or more mount options without explicitly unmounting a partition. To use this option, you issue a mount command on an already-mounted filesystem but with remount along with any options that you want to change. This feature can be used to enable or disable write access to a partition, for example.
ro	All	Specifies a read-only mount of the filesystem. This is the default for filesystems that include no write access and for some with particularly unreliable write support.
rw	All read/write filesystems	Specifies a read/write mount of the filesystem. This is the default for most read/write filesystems.

Option	Supported filesystems	Description
uid=*value*	Most filesystems that don't support Unix-style permissions, such as vfat, hpfs, ntfs, and hfs	Sets the owner of all files. For instance, uid=1000 sets the owner to whomever has Linux user ID 1000. (Check Linux user IDs in the /etc/passwd file.)
gid=*value*	Most filesystems that don't support Unix-style permissions, such as vfat, hpfs, ntfs, and hfs	Works like uid=*value*, but sets the group of all files on the filesystem. You can find group IDs in the /etc/group file.
umask=*value*	Most filesystems that don't support Unix-style permissions, such as vfat, hpfs, ntfs, and hfs	Sets the umask for the permissions on files. *value* is interpreted in binary as bits to be removed from permissions on files. For instance, umask=027 yields permissions of 750, or -rwxr-x---. Used in conjunction with uid=*value* and gid=*value*, this option lets you control who can access files on FAT, HPFS, and many other foreign filesystems.
dmask=*value*	Most filesystems that don't support Unix-style permissions, such as vfat, hpfs, ntfs, and hfs	Similar to umask, but sets the umask for directories only, not for files.
fmask=*value*	Most filesystems that don't support Unix-style permissions, such as vfat, hpfs, ntfs, and hfs	Similar to umask, but sets the umask for files only, not for directories.
conv=*code*	Most filesystems used on Microsoft and Apple OSs: msdos, umsdos, vfat, hpfs, and hfs	If *code* is b or binary, Linux doesn't modify the files' contents. If *code* is t or text, Linux auto-converts files between Linux-style and Windows- or Macintosh-style end-of-line characters. If *code* is a or auto, Linux applies the conversion unless the file is a known binary file format. It's usually best to leave this at its default value of binary because file conversions can cause serious problems for some applications and file types.
norock	iso9660	Disables Rock Ridge extensions for ISO-9660 CD-ROMs.
nojoliet	iso9660	Disables Joliet extensions for ISO-9660 CD-ROMs.

Some filesystems support additional options that aren't described here. The man page for mount covers some of these, but you may need to look at the filesystem's documentation for some options. This documentation may appear in /usr/src/linux/Documentation/file-systems or /usr/src/linux/fs/*fsname*, where *fsname* is the name of the filesystem.

Using *umount*

The umount command is simpler than mount. The basic umount syntax is as follows:

umount [-afnrv] [-t *fstype*] [*device* | *mountpoint*]

Most of these parameters have meanings similar to their meanings in mount, but some differences deserve mention:

Unmount All   Rather than unmount the partitions listed in /etc/fstab, the -a option causes the system to attempt to unmount all of the partitions listed in /etc/mtab, the file that holds information about mounted filesystems. On a system running normally, this operation is likely to succeed only partly because it won't be able to unmount some key filesystems, such as the root partition.

Force Unmount   You can use the -f option to tell Linux to force an unmount operation that might otherwise fail. This feature is sometimes helpful when unmounting NFS mounts shared by servers that have become unreachable.

Fall Back to Read-Only   The -r option tells umount that if it can't unmount a filesystem, it should attempt to remount it in read-only mode.

Unmount Partitions of a Specific Filesystem Type   The -t *fstype* option tells the system to unmount only partitions of the specified type. You can list multiple filesystem types by separating them with commas.

The Device and Mount Point   You need to specify only the device (with *device*) or only the mount point (with *mountpoint*), not both.

As with mount, normal users can't ordinarily use umount. The exception is if the partition or device is listed in /etc/fstab and specifies the user, users, or owner option, in which case normal users can unmount the device. (In the case of user, only the user who mounted the partition may unmount it; in the case of owner, the user issuing the command must also own the device file, as with mount.) These options are most useful for removable-media devices.

Be cautious when unplugging USB disk-like devices (USB flash drives or external hard disks). Linux caches accesses to most filesystems, which means that data may not be written to the disk until some time after a write command. Because of this, it's possible to corrupt a disk by ejecting or unplugging it, even when the drive isn't active. You must *always* issue a umount command before ejecting a mounted disk. (GUI unmount tools do this behind the scenes, so using a desktop's unmount or eject option is equivalent to using umount.) After issuing the umount command, wait for the command to return, and if the disk has activity indicators, wait for them to stop blinking to be sure that Linux has finished using the device. Another way to write the cache to disk is to use the sync command, but because this command does *not* fully unmount a filesystem, it's not a substitute for umount.

Permanently Mounting Filesystems

The /etc/fstab file controls how Linux provides access to disk partitions and removable media devices. Linux supports a unified directory structure in which every disk device (partition or removable disk) is mounted at a particular point in the directory tree. For instance, you might access a USB flash drive at /media/usb. The root of this tree is accessed from /. Directories off this root may be other partitions or disks, or they may be ordinary directories. For instance, /etc should be on the same partition as /, but many other directories, such as /home, may correspond to separate partitions. The /etc/fstab file describes how these filesystems are laid out. (The filename fstab is an abbreviation for *filesystem table*.)

The /etc/fstab file consists of a series of lines that contain six fields each; the fields are separated by one or more spaces or tabs. A line that begins with a hash mark (#) is a comment and is ignored. Listing 3.1 shows a sample /etc/fstab file.

Listing 3.1: Sample /etc/fstab file

```
#device        mount point   filesystem options        dump fsck
/dev/hda1      /             ext4       defaults         1 1
UUID=3631a288-673e-40f5-9e96-6539fec468e9 \
               /usr          reiserfs   defaults         0 0
LABEL=/home    /home         reiserfs   defaults         0 0
/dev/hdb5      /windows      vfat       uid=500,umask=0 0 0
/dev/hdc       /media/cdrom  iso9660    users,noauto     0 0
/dev/sda1      /media/usb    auto       users,noauto     0 0
server:/home   /other/home   nfs        users,exec       0 0
//winsrv/shr   /other/win    cifs       users,credentials=/etc/creds 0 0
/dev/hda4      swap          swap       defaults         0 0
```

The meaning of each field in this file is as follows:

Device   The first column specifies the mount device. These are usually device filenames that reference hard disks, USB drives, and so on. Most distributions now specify partitions by their labels or UUIDs, as in the LABEL=/home and UUID=3631a288-673e-40f5-9e96-6539fec468e9 entries in Listing 3.1. When Linux encounters such an entry, it tries to find the partition whose filesystem has the specified name or UUID and mount it. This practice can help reduce problems if partition numbers change, but some filesystems lack these labels. It's also possible to list a network drive, as in server:/home, which is the /home export on the computer called server, or //winsrv/shr, which is the shr share on the Windows or Samba server called winsrv.

Mount Point   The second column specifies the mount point. This is where the partition or disk will be mounted in the unified Linux filesystem. This should usually be an empty directory in another filesystem. The root (/) filesystem is an exception. So is swap space, which is indicated by an entry of swap.

Filesystem Type   The filesystem type code is the same as the type code used to mount a filesystem with the mount command. You can use any filesystem type code you can use directly with the mount command. A filesystem type code of auto lets the kernel auto-detect the filesystem type, which can be a convenient option for removable media devices. Auto-detection doesn't work with all filesystems, though.

Mount Options   Most filesystems support several mount options, which modify how the kernel treats the filesystem. You may specify multiple mount options, separated by commas. For instance, uid=500,umask=0 for /windows in Listing 3.1 sets the user ID (owner) of all files to 500 and sets the umask to 0. (User IDs and umasks are covered in more detail in Chapter 4.) Table 3.5 summarizes the most common mount options.

Backup Operation   The next-to-last field contains a 1 if the dump utility should back up a partition or a 0 if it shouldn't. If you never use the dump backup program, this option is essentially meaningless. (The dump program was once a common backup tool, but it is much less popular today.)

Filesystem Check Order   At boot time, Linux uses the fsck program to check filesystem integrity. The final column specifies the order in which this check occurs. A 0 means that fsck should *not* check a filesystem. Higher numbers represent the check order. The root partition should have a value of 1, and all others that should be checked should have a value of 2. Some filesystems, such as ReiserFS, shouldn't be automatically checked and so should have values of 0.

If you add a new hard disk or have to repartition the one you have, you'll probably need to modify /etc/fstab. You may also need to edit it to alter some of its options. For instance, setting the user ID or umask on Windows partitions mounted in Linux may be necessary to let ordinary users write to the partition.

 Real World Scenario

Managing User-Mountable Media

You may want to give ordinary users the ability to mount certain partitions or removable media, such as CDs, DVDs, and USB drives. To do so, create an ordinary /etc/fstab entry for the filesystem, but be sure to add the user, users, or owner option to the options column. Table 3.5 describes the differences between these three options. Listing 3.1 shows some examples of user-mountable media: /media/cdrom, /media/usb, /other/home, and /other/win. The first two of these are designed for removable media and include the noauto option, which prevents Linux from wasting time trying to mount them when the OS first boots. The second pair of mount points are network file shares that are mounted automatically at boot time; the users option on these lines enables ordinary users to unmount and then remount the filesystem, which might be handy if, say, ordinary users have the ability to shut down the server.

As with any filesystems that you want to mount, you must provide mount points—that is, create empty directories—for user-mountable media. Removable media are usually mounted in subdirectories of /mnt or /media.

Many modern distributions include auto-mount facilities that automatically mount removable media when they're inserted. These tools typically create mount points in /media and create icons on users' desktops to enable easy access to the media. This configuration produces effects that are familiar to users of Windows and Mac OS.

The credentials option for the /other/win mount point in Listing 3.1 deserves greater elaboration. Ordinarily, most SMB/CIFS shares require a username and password as a means of access control. Although you can use the username=*name* and password=*pass* options to smbfs or cifs, these options are undesirable, particularly in /etc/fstab, because they leave the password vulnerable to discovery—anybody who can read /etc/fstab can read the password. The credentials=*file* option provides an alternative—you can use it to point Linux at a file that holds the username and password. This file has labeled lines:

```
username=hschmidt
password=yiW7t9Td
```

Of course, the file you specify (/etc/creds in Listing 3.1) must be well protected—it must be readable only to root and perhaps to the user whose share it describes.

Summary

Most Linux tools and procedures provide a layer around the hardware, insulating you from the need to know too many details. Nonetheless, sometimes you have to dig in and configure hardware directly. Firmware settings can control onboard devices such as hard disk controllers and USB ports. USB and SCSI devices have their own quirks, and USB in particular is quickly evolving.

Hard disks are one class of hardware that's likely to require more attention than most. Specifically, you must know how to create partitions and prepare filesystems on those partitions. These tasks are necessary when you install Linux (although most distributions provide GUI tools to help guide you through this task during installation), when you add a hard disk, or when you reconfigure an existing system. You should also know something about boot managers. These programs help get Linux up and running when you turn on a computer's power, so they're unusually critical to Linux operation.

Filesystem management is basic to being able to administer or use a Linux system. The most basic of these basic tasks are filesystem tasks—the ability to mount filesystems, check their health, and repair ailing filesystems. Once a filesystem is mounted, you may want to check it periodically to see how full it is, lest you run out of disk space.

Exam Essentials

Summarize BIOS and EFI essentials.   The BIOS and EFI provide two important functions: First, they configure hardware—both hardware that's built into the motherboard and hardware on many types of plug-in cards. Second, they begin the computer's boot process, passing control on to the boot loader in the MBR or EFI partition in GPT-formatted disks. The BIOS is currently being retired in favor of EFI, which performs these tasks on modern computers.

Describe what files contain important hardware information.   There are many files under the /proc filesystem. Many of these files have been mentioned throughout this chapter. Familiarize yourself with these files, such as /proc/ioports, /proc/interrupts, /proc/dma, /proc/bus/usb, and others.

Explain Linux's model for managing USB hardware.   Linux uses drivers for USB controllers. These drivers in turn are used by some device-specific drivers (for USB disk devices, for instance) and by programs that access USB hardware via entries in the /proc/bus/usb directory tree.

Summarize how to obtain information about PCI and USB devices.   The lspci and lsusb programs return information about PCI and USB devices, respectively. You can learn manufacturers' names and various configuration options by using these commands.

Identify common disk types and their features.   PATA disks were the most common type on PCs until about 2005. Since then, SATA disks, which are more easily configured, have gained substantially in popularity. SCSI disks have long been considered the top-tier disks, but their high price has kept them out of inexpensive commodity PCs.

Describe the purpose of disk partitions.   Disk partitions break the disk into a handful of distinct parts. Each partition can be used by a different OS, can contain a different filesystem, and is isolated from other partitions. These features improve security and safety and can greatly simplify running a multi-OS system.

Summarize important Linux disk partitions.   The most important Linux disk partition is the root (/) partition, which is at the base of the Linux directory tree. Other possible partitions include a swap partition, /home for home directories, /usr for program files, /var for transient system files, /tmp for temporary user files, /boot for the kernel and other critical boot files, and more.

Describe commands that help you monitor disk use.   The df command provides a one-line summary of each mounted filesystem's size, available space, free space, and percentage of space used. The du command adds up the disk space used by all of the files in a specified directory tree and presents a summary by directory and subdirectory.

Summarize the tools that can help keep a filesystem healthy. The fsck program is a front end to filesystem-specific tools such as e2fsck and fsck.jfs. By whatever name, these programs examine a filesystem's major data structures for internal consistency and can correct minor errors.

Explain how filesystems are mounted in Linux. The mount command ties a filesystem to a Linux directory; once the filesystem is mounted, its files can be accessed as part of the mount directory. The /etc/fstab file describes permanent mappings of filesystems to mount points; when the system boots, it automatically mounts the described filesystems unless they use the noauto option (which is common for removable disks).

Review Questions

1. What are common IRQs for RS-232 serial ports? (Select two.)

   A. 1

   B. 3

   C. 4

   D. 8

   E. 16

2. What tool would you use to disable a motherboard's sound hardware if you don't want to use it?

   A. The firmware.

   B. The `alsactl` utility.

   C. The `lsmod` command.

   D. The `lspci` program.

   E. None of the above; onboard sound devices can't be disabled.

3. What is the purpose of udev?

   A. To aid in the development of software

   B. To unload Linux device drivers

   C. To load Linux device drivers

   D. To store devices' BIOS configurations in files

   E. To manage the `/dev` directory tree

4. You've just installed Linux on a new computer with a single SATA hard disk. What device identifier will refer to the disk?

   A. `/dev/sda`

   B. `/dev/mapper/disk1`

   C. `/dev/hda`

   D. `C:`

   E. `/dev/sda` or `/dev/hda`

5. Which files contain essential system information such as IRQs, direct-memory access channels, and I/O addresses? (Select three.)

   A. `/proc/ioports`

   B. `/proc/ioaddresses`

   C. `/proc/dma`

   D. `/proc/interrupts`

   E. `/proc/hardware`

6. Typing **fdisk -l /dev/sda** on a Linux computer with an MBR disk produces a listing of four partitions: /dev/sda1, /dev/sda2, /dev/sda5, and /dev/sda6. Which of the following is true?

    A. The disk contains two primary partitions and two extended partitions.

    B. Either /dev/sda1 or /dev/sda2 is an extended partition.

    C. The partition table is corrupted; there should be a /dev/sda3 and a /dev/sda4 before /dev/sda5.

    D. If you add a /dev/sda3 with fdisk, /dev/sda5 will become /dev/sda6, and /dev/sda6 will become /dev/sda7.

    E. Both /dev/sda1 and /dev/sda2 are logical partitions.

7. A new Linux administrator plans to create a system with separate /home, /usr/local, and /etc partitions, in addition to the root (/) partition. Which of the following best describes this configuration?

    A. The system won't boot because critical boot-time files reside in /home.

    B. The system will boot, but /usr/local won't be available because mounted partitions must be mounted directly off their parent partition, not in a subdirectory.

    C. The system will boot only if the /home partition is on a separate physical disk from the /usr/local partition.

    D. The system will boot and operate correctly, provided each partition is large enough for its intended use.

    E. The system won't boot because /etc contains configuration files necessary to mount non-root partitions.

8. Which of the following directories is *most likely* to be placed on its own hard disk partition?

    A. /bin

    B. /sbin

    C. /mnt

    D. /home

    E. /dev

9. You discover that an MBR hard disk has partitions with type codes of 0x0f, 0x82, and 0x83. Assuming these type codes are accurate, what can you conclude about the disk?

    A. The disk holds a partial or complete Linux system.

    B. The disk holds a Windows installation.

    C. The disk holds a FreeBSD installation.

    D. The disk is corrupt; those partition type codes are incompatible.

    E. The disk holds a Mac OS X installation.

10. You run Linux's fdisk and modify your partition layout. Before exiting the program, you realize that you've been working on the wrong disk. What can you do to correct this problem?

    A. Nothing; the damage is done, so you'll have to recover data from a backup.

    B. Type **w** to exit fdisk without saving changes to disk.

    C. Type **q** to exit fdisk without saving changes to disk.

    D. Type **u** repeatedly to undo the operations you've made in error.

    E. Type **t** to undo all of the changes and return to the original disk state.

11. What does the following command accomplish?

    ```
    # mkfs -t ext2 /dev/sda4
    ```

    A. It sets the partition table type code for /dev/sda4 to ext2.

    B. It converts a FAT partition into an ext2fs partition without damaging the partition's existing files.

    C. Nothing; the -t option isn't valid, and so it causes mkfs to abort its operation.

    D. It converts an ext2 filesystem to an ext4 filesystem.

    E. It creates a new ext2 filesystem on /dev/sda4, overwriting any existing filesystem and data.

12. Which of the following best summarizes the differences between Windows's FDISK and Linux's fdisk?

    A. Linux's fdisk is a simple clone of Windows's FDISK but written to work from Linux rather than from Windows.

    B. The two are completely independent programs that accomplish similar goals, although Linux's fdisk is more flexible.

    C. Windows's FDISK uses GUI controls, whereas Linux's fdisk uses a command-line interface, but they have similar functionality.

    D. Despite their similar names, they're completely different tools—the Windows FDISK command handles disk partitioning, whereas Linux's fdisk formats floppy disks.

    E. The Windows FDISK command manages GPT disks, whereas Linux's fdisk manages MBR disks.

13. What mount point should you associate with swap partitions?

    A. /

    B. /swap

    C. /boot

    D. /mem

    E. None of the above

14. Which of the following options is used with fsck to force it to use a particular filesystem type?

    A. -A

    B. -N

    C. -t

D. -C

E. -f

15. Which of the following pieces of information can df *not* report?

   A.   How long the filesystem has been mounted

   B.   The number of inodes used on an ext3fs partition

   C.   The filesystem type of a partition

   D.   The percentage of available disk space used on a partition

   E.   The mount point associated with a filesystem

16. What is an advantage of a journaling filesystem over a conventional (non-journaling) filesystem?

   A.   Journaling filesystems are older and better tested than non-journaling filesystems.

   B.   Journaling filesystems never need to be checked with fsck.

   C.   Journaling filesystems support Linux ownership and permissions; non-journaling filesystems don't.

   D.   Journaling filesystems require shorter disk checks after a power failure or system crash.

   E.   Journaling filesystems record all transactions, enabling them to be undone.

17. To access files on a USB flash drive, you type **mount /dev/sdc1 /media/flash** as root. Which types of filesystems will this command mount?

   A.   Ext2fs

   B.   FAT

   C.   HFS

   D.   ReiserFS

   E.   All of the above

18. Which of the following /etc/fstab entries will mount /dev/sdb2 as the /home directory at boot time?

   A.   /dev/sdb2 reiserfs /home defaults 0 0

   B.   /dev/sdb2 /home reiserfs defaults 0 0

   C.   /home reiserfs /dev/sdb2 noauto 0 0

   D.   /home /dev/sdb2 reiserfs noauto 0 0

   E.   reiserfs /dev/sdb2 /home noauto 0 0

19. What filesystem options might you specify in /etc/fstab to make a removable disk (such as a USB flash drive) mountable by an ordinary user with a UID of 1000? (Select three.)

   A.   user

   B.   users

   C.   owner

   D.   owners

   E.   uid=1000

20. What is the minimum safe procedure for removing a USB flash drive, mounted from /dev/sdb1 at /media/usb, from a Linux computer?

    A. Type **umount /media/usb**, wait for the command to return and disk-activity lights to stop, and then unplug the drive.

    B. Unplug the drive, and then type **umount /media/usb** to ensure that Linux registers the drive's removal from the system.

    C. Unplug the drive, and then type **sync /dev/sdb1** to flush the caches to ensure that problems don't develop.

    D. Type **usbdrive-remove**, and then quickly remove the disk before its activity light stops blinking.

    E. Type **fsck /dev/sdb1**, wait for the command to return and disk-activity lights to stop, and then unplug the drive.

Chapter

4

Managing Files

THE FOLLOWING EXAM OBJECTIVES ARE COVERED IN THIS CHAPTER:

- ✓ 103.3 Perform basic file management

- ✓ 104.4 Manage disk quotas

- ✓ 104.5 Manage file permissions and ownership

- ✓ 104.6 Create and change hard and symbolic links

- ✓ 104.7 Find system files and place files in the correct location

Ultimately, Linux is a collection of files stored on your hard disk. Thus, being able to manage the filesystems' files is an important skill for any Linux system administrator. Chapter 3, "Configuring Hardware," described creating disk partitions, preparing filesystems on them, maintaining those filesystems, and mounting them. This chapter continues that topic by looking more closely at file management.

Beginning with an examination of the commands used to access and manipulate files, this chapter moves through these important basic utilities. As a multiuser OS, Linux provides tools that enable you to restrict *who* may access your files. The chapter looks at the Linux ownership model and the commands that are built on this model to control file access. Furthermore, Linux provides a system that enables you to restrict how much disk space individual users may consume. Thus, this feature is described within this chapter. Finally, the chapter looks at locating files—we cover both the formal description of where certain file types should reside and the commands you can use to locate specific files.

Using File Management Commands

Basic file management is critical to the use of any computer. This is particularly true on Unix-like systems, like Linux, because these systems treat almost everything as a file, including most hardware devices and various specialized interfaces. Therefore, being able to create, delete, move, rename, archive, and otherwise manipulate files is a necessary skill for any Linux user or system administrator.

To begin, you should understand the rules that govern filenames as well as the shortcuts you can use to refer to files. With this information in hand, you can move on to learn how to manipulate files and directories, how to archive files, and how to manage links.

Naming Files

Linux filenames are similar to the filenames on any other OS. However, every OS, including Linux, has its filename quirks. These differences can be problematic to those who move between systems and to those who want to move files between systems.

Linux filenames can contain uppercase or lowercase letters, numbers, and even most punctuation and control characters. To avoid confusion, it is recommended that you restrict any non-alphanumeric symbols in your Linux filenames to the dot (.), the dash (-), and the underscore (_). However, some programs create backup files that end in the tilde (~) as well.

> Although Linux filenames can contain spaces, they must be escaped on the Linux command line. This is accomplished by preceding the space with a backslash (\) or by enclosing the entire filename in quotes ("). This requirement makes spaces a bit awkward in Linux, so most Linux users substitute dashes or underscores.

A few characters have special meaning and should never be used in filenames:

asterisk (*)

question mark (?)

forward slash (/)

backslash (\)

quotation mark (")

Although you *can* create files that contain all of the above characters except for the forward slash (which serves to separate directory elements) by escaping them, it's not a good idea. These characters are likely to cause confusion when used in a filename.

Linux filename length depends on the filesystem in use. On ext2fs, ext3fs, ext4fs, XFS, Btrfs, and many others, the limit is 255 characters. A character requires 1 byte of storage. Therefore, you will often see the limit listed in bytes instead of characters. Thus, the 255-character file limit is often stated as 255 bytes.

One- to four-character filename extensions are common in Linux. As with other OSs, the filename extension typically follows a single dot. However, Linux filenames can contain an arbitrary number of dots. In fact, filenames can *begin* with a dot. These so-called *dot files* are hidden from view by most utilities that display files, so they're popular for storing configuration files in your home directory.

> If you access a File Allocation Table (FAT) filesystem on a removable disk or partition used by DOS, you can do so using either of two filesystem type codes: msdos, which limits you to 8.3 filenames; or vfat, which supports Windows-style long filenames. In addition, the umsdos filesystem type code was a Linux-only extension that supported Linux-style long filenames. UMSDOS support was discontinued after the 2.6.11 kernel.

Two filenames are particularly special. A filename that consists of a single dot (.) refers to the current directory, whereas a filename that consists of a double dot (..) refers to the parent directory. For instance, if your current directory is /home/jerry, then . refers to /home/jerry and .. refers to /home.

Be aware the Linux filenames are case sensitive. For example, Filename.txt is different from filename.txt or FILENAME.TXT. All three files can exist in a single Linux directory, and they are treated as completely different files. Under Windows, all three filenames refer to the same file. This difference isn't a major problem for most people who migrate from Windows to Linux, but you should be aware of it.

Exploring Wildcard Expansion Rules

You can use *wildcards* with many commands. A wildcard is a symbol or set of symbols that stands in for other characters. Three classes of wildcards are common in Linux:

? A question mark (?) stands in for a single character. For instance, b??k matches book, balk, buck, or any other four-character filename that begins with a b and ends with a k.

* An asterisk (*) matches any character or set of characters, including no character. For instance, b*k matches book, balk, and buck as well as bk, bbk, and backtrack. Any character and any number of characters can be in the filename as long as it begins with a b and ends with a k.

Bracketed Values   Characters enclosed in square brackets ([]) normally match any character in the set. For instance, b[ae]ok matches baok and beok. Each bracket group is used for single character matches. As in the example above, the second character in the name could be either an a or an e. You can use multiple brackets in the same name. For example, b[ae]o[ks] searches for character sets in both the second and fourth character position. The names that would match this wildcard setting would include baok, beok, baos, and beos.

It's also possible to specify a range of values using brackets. For instance, b[a-z]ck matches back, buck, and other four-letter filenames of this form whose second character is a lower-case letter. This differs from b?ck—because Linux treats filenames in a case-sensitive way and because ? matches any character (not just any lowercase letter).

Wildcards are implemented in the shell and passed to the command you call. For instance, if you type **ls b??k** and that wildcard matches the three files balk, book, and buck, the result is precisely as if you'd typed **ls balk book buck**. This process of wildcard expansion is known as *file globbing* or *filename expansion* or simply *globbing*.

Understanding the File Commands

A few file-manipulation commands are extremely important to everyday file operations. These commands enable you to list, copy, move, rename, and delete files.

Using the *ls* Command

To manipulate files, it's helpful to know information about them. This is the job of the ls command, whose name is short for *list*. The ls command displays the names of files in a directory. Its syntax is simple:

```
ls [options] [files]
```

Both of the *options* list and the *files* list are optional. If you omit the *files* list, ls displays the contents of the current directory:

```
$ pwd
/home/Christine/my-work
$
```

```
$ ls
project_a354   project_c923   project_m1321   punch_list.txt
$
```

To display contents that are not in your current directory, the directory name must be included:

```
$ ls -F /home/Christine/
afile.txt        file.dat       my-work/       newfile.dat
bfile.txt        hlink_afile    NewDir/        script.sh*
bigprogram.sh*   important/     new_file.dat   slink_bfile@
$
```

This outputs the contents of the /home/Christine directory, including the various file types via the -F option. The upcoming list entry "Display File Type" describes what these symbols, such as @, indicate.

You may provide one or more file or directory names in the ls command. In addition, you can use file globbing:

```
$ ls  *.txt  /home/Christine/my-work/
afile.txt  bfile.txt

/home/Christine/my-work:
project_a354   project_c923   project_m1321   punch_list.txt
$
```

In this case, the ls command displays information about all of the files and directories specified. This output shows both the *.txt files in the current working directory and the contents of the /home/Christine/my-work/ directory.

By default, ls creates a listing that's sorted by filename, as shown in this example. In the past, uppercase letters appeared before lowercase letters. However, recent versions of the ls command sort in a case-insensitive manner.

One of the most common ls options is -l, which creates a long listing. This output includes the permission strings, ownership, file sizes, file creation dates, and so on, in addition to the filenames:

```
$ ls -l *.txt
-rw-rw-r--. 2 Christine Users 1679 Sep 25 15:39 afile.txt
-rw-rw-r--. 1 Christine Users 1691 Sep 26 16:39 bfile.txt
$
```

The command supports a huge number of options. For details, consult the ls command's man page. The following options are the most useful:

Display All Files   Normally, ls omits files whose names begin with a dot (.). These dot files are often configuration files that aren't usually of interest. Adding the -a or --all parameter displays dot files.

Long Listing   The ls command normally displays filenames only. The -l parameter (a lowercase L) produces a long listing that includes information such as the file's permission string (described in "Understanding Permissions"), owner, group, size, and creation date.

Display File Type   The -F or --classify option appends an indicator code to the end of the filename so that you know what type of file it is. The meanings are as follows:

/   Directory

*   Executable

| Named pipe

=   Socket

@   Symbolic link

Color Listing   The --color option produces a color-coded listing that differentiates directories, symbolic links, and so on by displaying them in different colors. This works at the Linux console, in some terminal emulator windows in the GUI, and from some types of remote logins. However, some remote-login programs don't support color displays. Several Linux distributions configure their shells to use this option by default.

WARNING   Depending on color-coded listings can get you in trouble because color-coded displays are not always available. Color codes are not standardized and differ between Linux distributions. It is a better idea to use the file type option (-F) and memorize the symbols that represent each type. The file type symbols will be consistent no matter how you log into your Linux system.

Display Directory Names   Normally, if you type a directory name as a *files* option, ls displays that directory's contents. The same thing happens if a directory name matches a wildcard. Adding the -d or --directory parameter changes this behavior to list only the directory name, which is sometimes preferable.

Recursive Listing   The -R or --recursive option causes ls to display directory contents recursively. That is, if the target directory contains subdirectories, ls displays both the target directory's files *and* all of its subdirectories' files. The result can be a huge listing if a directory has many subdirectories.

NOTE   You can combine multiple options by merging them with a single preceding dash, as in **ls -lF**, to get a long listing that also includes file type codes. This can save a bit of typing compared to the alternative of **ls -l -F**.

Using the *cp* Command

The cp command copies a file. Its basic syntax is as follows:

```
cp [options] source destination
```

The *source* option can be one or more files. It is the original file or files that you wish to copy. The *destination* option may be a single file when the source is a single file:

```
$ ls
file.dat
$
$ cp file.dat new_file.dat
$
$ ls
file.dat   new_file.dat
$
```

The *destination* option may be a directory when the source is one or more files. When copying to a directory, cp preserves the original filename. Otherwise, it gives the new file the filename indicated by *destination*:

```
$ ls -F
file.dat   new_file.dat   TempDir/
$
$ cp file.dat TempDir/
$
$ cp file.dat TempDir/file2.dat
$
$ ls TempDir/
file2.dat   file.dat
$
```

This example uses a trailing forward slash (/) on the destination directory. This practice can help avoid problems caused by typos. For example, if the destination directory were mistyped as TempDi (missing the final r), cp would copy file.dat to the filename TempDi instead of into the TempDir directory. Adding the trailing slash makes it explicit that you intend to copy the file into a subdirectory. If the directory doesn't exist, cp complains so that you're not left with mysterious misnamed files.

In addition, the *source* and *destination* options may be entire directories containing files:

```
$ ls -F
file.dat  new_file.dat  TempDir/
$
$ ls TempDir/
file2.dat  file.dat
$
$ cp -R TempDir NewDir
$
$ ls NewDir/
file2.dat  file.dat
$
```

Notice that an option was used on the cp command, -R, in order to copy the directory and its contents. The cp command supports a large number of options. Here are a few useful options that enable you to modify the command's operation:

Force Overwrite The -f or --force option forces the system to overwrite any existing files without prompting.

Use Interactive Mode The -i or --interactive option causes cp to ask you before overwriting any existing files.

Preserve Ownership and Permissions Normally, the user who issues the cp command owns the copied file and uses that account's default permissions. The -p or --preserve option preserves ownership and permissions, if possible.

Perform a Recursive Copy If you use the -R or --recursive option and specify a directory as the *source* option, the entire directory, including its subdirectories, is copied. Although -r also performs a recursive copy, its behavior with files other than ordinary files and directories is unspecified. Most cp implementations use -r as a synonym for -R, but this behavior isn't guaranteed.

Perform an Archive Copy The -a or --archive option is similar to -R, but it also preserves ownership and copies links as is. The -R option copies the files to which symbolic links point rather than the symbolic links themselves. (Links are described in more detail later in this chapter in "Managing Links.")

Perform an Update Copy The -u or --update option tells cp to copy the file only if the original is newer than the target or if the target doesn't exist.

This list of cp options is incomplete, but it covers the most useful options. Consult cp's man page for information about additional cp options.

As an example, the following command copies the /etc/fstab configuration file to a backup location in /root, but only if the original /etc/fstab is newer than the existing backup:

```
# cp -u /etc/fstab /root/fstab-backup
```

Using the *mv* Command

The mv command (short for move) is commonly used both to move files and directories from one location to another and to rename them. Linux doesn't distinguish between these two types of operations, although many users do. The syntax of mv is similar to that of cp:

```
mv [options] source destination
```

The command takes many of the same *options* values as cp does. From the earlier list, --preserve, --recursive, and --archive don't apply to mv, but the others do.

To move one or more files or directories, specify the files as the *source* option and specify a directory or (optionally, for a single-file move) a filename for the *destination* option:

```
$ ls document.odt
document.odt
$
$ mv document.odt important/purchases/
$
$ ls document.odt
ls: cannot access document.odt: No such file or directory
$
$ ls important/purchases
document.odt
$
```

The preceding command moves the document.odt file into the important/purchases subdirectory. You can see that, unlike with the cp command, the original file is moved to the new directory location and a copy is not left in the original directory.

 If the move occurs on one low-level filesystem, Linux does the job by rewriting directory entries; the file's data need not be read and rewritten. This makes mv fast. When the target directory is on another partition or disk, though, Linux must read the original file, rewrite it to the new location, and delete the original. This slows down mv.

Renaming a file with mv works much like moving a file, except that the source and destination filenames are in the same directory. This mv command renames document.odt to washer-order.odt in the same directory:

```
$ ls *.odt
document.odt
```

```
$
$ mv document.odt washer-order.odt
$
$ ls *.odt
washer-order.odt
$
```

You can combine the moving and renaming actions. This command simultaneously moves and renames a file:

```
$ mv document.odt important/purchases/washer-order.odt
$
$ ls important/purchases/washer-order.odt
important/purchases/washer-order.odt
$
```

You can move or rename entire directories using mv, too; just specify one or more directories as the *source* option in the command. For instance, consider the following commands:

```
$ mv important critical
$
$ mv critical /tmp/
```

The first command renames the important subdirectory as critical in the current directory. The second command moves the renamed subdirectory to the /tmp directory. (You could combine these two commands to **mv important /tmp/critical**.) The form of these commands is identical to the mv command form when used with files. Optionally, when renaming entire directories, you may add a trailing slash (/) to directory names.

Using the *rm* Command

To delete a file, use the rm command. The command name is short for *remove*, and its syntax is simple:

```
rm [options] files
```

The rm command accepts many of the same specfied *options* values as cp or mv. Of those described with cp, --preserve, --archive, and --update don't apply to rm, but all of the others do apply. With rm, -r is synonymous with -R.

By default, Linux doesn't provide any sort of "trash-can" functionality for its rm command at the command line. Once you've deleted a file with rm, it's gone. It cannot be recovered without retrieving the file from a backup or performing low-level disk maintenance (such as with debugfs). Therefore, you should be cautious when using rm, particularly when you're logged on as root. This is especially true when you're using the -R option, which can destroy a large part of your Linux installation!

Using the *touch* Command

Linux-native filesystems maintain three time stamps for every file:

- Last file-modification time
- Last inode change time
- Last access time

Various programs rely on these time stamps. For instance, the make utility (which helps compile a program from source code) uses the time stamps to determine which source-code files must be recompiled if an object file already exists. Thus, sometimes you may need to modify the time stamps. This is the job of the touch command, which has the following syntax:

```
touch [options] files
```

By default, touch sets the modification and access times to the current time. You might use this if, for instance, you wanted make to recompile a particular source code file even though a newer object file existed. If the files specified by *files* don't already exist, touch creates them as empty files. This can be handy if you want to create dummy files—say, to experiment with other file-manipulation commands.

You can pass various values specified by *options* to touch to have it change its behavior:

Change Only the Access Time   The -a or --time=*atime* option causes touch to change the access time alone, not the modification time.

Change Only the Modification Time   The -m or --time=*mtime* option causes touch to change the modification time alone, not the access time.

Do Not Create File   If you don't want touch to create any files that don't already exist, pass it the -c or --no-create option.

Set the Time as Specified   The -t *timestamp* option sets the time to the value specified by *timestamp*. This value is given in the form *MMDDhhmm*[[*CC*]*YY*][.*ss*], where *MM* is the month, *DD* is the day, *hh* is the hour (on a 24-hour clock), *mm* is the minute, [*CC*]*YY* is the year (such as 2012 or 12, which are equivalent), and *ss* is the second. Another way to set a particular time is with the -r *reffile* or --reference=*reffile* option, where *reffile* is a file whose time stamp you want to replicate.

Archiving File Commands

A file-archiving tool collects a group of files into a single package file, called an *archive*. An archive is more easily moved around than a group of files for applications such as transferring across a network or moving to backup media.

Linux supports several archiving commands, the most prominent being tar and cpio. The dd command, although not technically an archiving command, is similar in some ways because it can copy an entire partition or disk into a file and vice versa.

> The zip format, which is common on Windows, is supported by the Linux zip and unzip commands. Other archive formats, such as the Roshal Archive (RAR) and StuffIt, can also be manipulated using Linux utilities.

Using the *tar* Utility

The tar program's name stands for "tape archiver." Despite this fact, you can use tar to archive data to other media. In fact, *tarballs* are often used for transferring multiple files between computers in one step, such as when distributing source code. A tarball is an archive file created by tar and typically compressed with gzip, xz, or bzip2.

The tar program is a complex package with many options. However, most of what you'll do with this utility can be covered with a few common commands. Table 4.1 lists the primary tar commands, and Table 4.2 lists the qualifiers that modify what the commands do. Whenever you run tar, you use only one command with one or more qualifiers. Collectively, the commands and qualifiers are called *options*.

TABLE 4.1   tar commands

Command	Abbreviation	Description
--create	c	Creates an archive
--concatenate	A	Appends tar files to an archive
--append	r	Appends non-tar files to an archive
--update	u	Appends files that are newer than those in an archive
--diff or --compare	d	Compares an archive to files on disk
--list	t	Lists an archive's contents
--extract or --get	x	Extracts files from an archive

TABLE 4.2   tar qualifiers

Qualifier	Abbreviation	Description
--directory *dir*	C	Changes to directory *dir* before performing operations
--file [*host:*]*file*	f	Uses the file called *file* on the computer called *host* as the archive file

Qualifier	Abbreviation	Description
`--listed-incre-mental` *file*	g	Performs an incremental backup or restore, using *file* as a list of previously archived files
`--multi-volume`	M	Creates or extracts a multi-volume archive
`--preserve-per-missions`	p	Preserves all protection information
`--absolute-paths`	P	Retains the leading / on filenames
`--verbose`	v	Lists all files read or extracted; when used with `--list`, displays file sizes, ownership, and time stamps
`--verify`	W	Verifies the archive after writing it
`--gzip` or `--ungzip`	z	Compresses an archive with gzip
`--bzip2`	j (some older versions used I or y)	Compresses an archive with bzip2
`--xz`	J	Compresses an archive with xz

Of the commands listed in Table 4.1, the following are most commonly used abbreviated commands:

c   Create archive

x   Extract archive

t   List archive

The most useful qualifiers from Table 4.2 are as follows:

g   Perform incremental backup

p   Keep permissions

z   Use gzip compression

j   Use bzip2 compression

J   Use xz compression

v   Be verbose

If you fail to specify a filename with the `--file` qualifier, tar will attempt to use a default device, which is often (but not always) a tape device file. Thus, it is always best to specify a filename.

Three compression tools—gzip, bzip2, and xz—are often used with the tar command. They apply compression to the archive file as a whole rather than to the individual files.

This compression method reduces the tarball's size compared to compressing individual files and then adding them to the archive. However, this compression method makes the archive more susceptible to damage.

Of the three compression tools, gzip is the oldest and provides the least compression, bzip2 provides improved compression, and xz is the newest and provides the best compression. Typically, files compressed with these utilities have .gz, .bz2, or .xz filename extensions, respectively. Compressed archives sometimes use their own special extensions, such as .tgz for a gzip-compressed tarball or .tbz for one compressed with bzip2.

 The xz compression tool has gained so much popularity, the Linux kernel is now compressed with it.

The tar utility is easy to use but very powerful. The basic syntax for the tar command is as follows:

```
tar [options]  destination/tar_file_name  files-to-archive
```

For example, a compressed archive can be made up of a subdirectory within your home directory. In the same tar command, the archive can be sent to a USB flash drive mounted at /media/pen. Also, the tar command's abbreviated commands and qualifiers (options) can be grouped together for simplicity:

```
$ tar cvfz /media/pen/my-work.tgz ~/my-work
tar: Removing leading '/' from member names
/home/Christine/my-work/
/home/Christine/my-work/punch_list.txt
/home/Christine/my-work/project_a354
/home/Christine/my-work/project_m1321
/home/Christine/my-work/project_c923
$
$ ls -l /media/pen/my-work.tgz
-rw-rw-r--. 1 Christine Users 780 Sep 25 10:44 my-work.tgz
$
$ ls -l ~/my-work
total 24
-rw-rw-r--. 1 Christine Users 9972 Sep 25 10:30 project_a354
-rw-rw-r--. 1 Christine Users 3324 Sep 25 10:30 project_c923
-rw-rw-r--. 1 Christine Users 2216 Sep 25 10:30 project_m1321
-rw-rw-r--. 1 Christine Users  218 Sep 25 10:27 punch_list.txt
$
```

The tar command takes all of the ~/my-work files, packs them into the /media/pen/my-work.tgz archive file, and compresses the file with the gzip utility. Notice how small the tarball archive file my-work.tgz is compared to the original files' sizes—pretty powerful for such a small command!

NOTE Historically a dash (-) would be put in front of tar options. However, the dash is no longer needed and on some Linux distributions generates an error.

The flash drive with the tarball archive can be moved to another system. If it is mounted at /media/usb, the tar command to extract it is as follows:

```
$ tar xvfz /media/usb/my-work.tgz
home/Christine/my-work/
home/Christine/my-work/punch_list.txt
home/Christine/my-work/project_a354
home/Christine/my-work/project_m1321
home/Christine/my-work/project_c923
$
$ ls -l home/Christine/my-work
total 24
-rw-rw-r--. 1 Christine Users 9972 Sep 25 10:30 project_a354
-rw-rw-r--. 1 Christine Users 3324 Sep 25 10:30 project_c923
-rw-rw-r--. 1 Christine Users 2216 Sep 25 10:30 project_m1321
-rw-rw-r--. 1 Christine Users  218 Sep 25 10:27 punch_list.txt
$
```

The preceding command creates a subdirectory called home/Christine/my-work in the current working directory. This new subdirectory was created because the tarball files' original subdirectory was /home/Christine/my-work. The original subdirectory was preserved by tar without the leading forward slash. After the subdirectory is created, the tar command populates it with the files from the archive.

If you don't know what's in an archive, it's a good practice to examine it with the --list command before extracting its contents. Although tarball archives usually contain a single subdirectory, sometimes they contain many files without a "carrier" subdirectory. Extracting such tarballs drops these files in your current directory, which can make it difficult to determine which files come from the tarball and which were already present.

Using the *cpio* Utility

The cpio program is similar in principle to tar, but the details of its operation differ. As with tar, you can direct its output straight to a media device or to a regular archive file. Backing up to a media device can be a convenient way to back up the computer because it requires no intermediate storage. To restore data, you use cpio to read directly from the media device file or from a regular archive file.

The cpio utility has three operating modes:

Copy-Out Mode This mode, activated by use of the -o or --create option, creates an archive and copies files into it.

Copy-In Mode   You activate copy-in mode by using the -i or --extract option. This mode extracts data from an existing archive. If you provide a filename or a pattern to match, cpio extracts only those files whose names match the pattern you provide.

Copy-Pass Mode   This mode is activated by the -p or --pass-through option. It combines the copy-out and copy-in modes, enabling you to copy a directory tree from one location to another.

 The copy-out and copy-in modes are named confusingly. To help keep the modes clear, focus on the directory instead of the archive file. Think of them as copying "out of" or "in to" the computer's directory tree.

In addition to the options used to select the mode, cpio accepts many other options, the most important of which are summarized in Table 4.3. To create an archive, you combine the --create (or -o) option with one or more of the options in Table 4.3. To restore data, you do the same, but you use --extract (or -i). In either case, cpio acts on filenames that you type at the terminal. In practice, you'll probably use the redirection operator (<) to pass a filename list to the program.

TABLE 4.3   Options for use with cpio

Option	Abbreviation	Description
--reset-access-time	-a	Resets the access time after reading a file so that it doesn't appear to have been read.
--append	-A	Appends data to an existing archive.
--pattern-file=*filename*	-E *filename*	Uses the contents of *filename* as a list of files to be extracted in copy-in mode.
--file=*filename*	-F *filename*	Uses *filename* as the cpio archive file; if this parameter is omitted, cpio uses standard input or output.
--format=*format*	-H *format*	Uses a specified format for the archive file. Common values for *format* include bin (the default, an old binary format), crc (a newer binary format with a checksum), and tar (the format used by tar).
N/A	-I *filename*	Uses the filename specified by *filename* instead of standard input. (Unlike -F, this option does not redirect output data.)

Option	Abbreviation	Description
`--no-absolute-file-names`	N/A	In copy-in mode, extracts files relative to the current directory, even if filenames in the archive contain full directory paths.
N/A	`-O` *filename*	Uses the filename specified by *filename* instead of standard output. (Unlike `-F`, this option does not redirect input data.)
`--list`	`-t`	Displays a table of contents for the input.
`--unconditional`	`-u`	Replaces all files without first asking for verification.
`--verbose`	`-v`	Displays filenames as they're added to or extracted from the archive. When used with `-t`, displays additional listing information (similar to `ls -l`).

To use cpio to archive a directory, you must pass a list of files to the utility using standard input. You can do this by piping the STDOUT of the find utility (described in more detail later in "The find Command") into the cpio command:

```
$ find ./my-work
./my-work
./my-work/my-work.tgz
./my-work/punch_list.txt
./my-work/project_a354
./my-work/project_m1321
./my-work/project_c923
$
$ find ./my-work | cpio -o > /media/usb/my-work.cpio
33 blocks
$
$ ls -l /media/usb/my-work.cpio
-rw-rw-r--. 1 Christine Users 16896 Sep 25 14:36 my-work.cpio
$
```

The resulting archive file is uncompressed. To compress the data, you must include a compression utility, such as gzip, in the pipe:

```
$ find ./my-work | cpio -o | gzip > /media/usb/my-work.cpio.gz
```

Extracting data from a cpio archive (say, on another computer with the media mounted at /media/usb) entails using the `-i` option, but no pipe is required:

```
$ gunzip /media/usb/my-work.cpio.gz
$ cpio -i < /media/usb/my-work.cpio
33 blocks
$
```

You can uncompress your compressed cpio archive and extract the data in one step by using the -c option with gunzip and passing its output to cpio in a pipe:

```
$ gunzip -c /media/usb/my-work.cpio.gz | cpio -i
33 blocks
$
```

To uncompress an archive compressed with bzip2, you would use bunzip2 -c in the pipe rather than gunzip -c. If the archive is compressed with xz, you would use unxz -b in the pipe.

Using the *dd* Utility

Sometimes you want to archive a filesystem at a very low level. For instance, you may want to create a representation of a DVD that you can store on your hard disk or back up a filesystem that Linux can't understand. To do so, you can use the dd program.

The dd utility is a low-level copying program. When you give it a partition device file as input, it copies that partition's contents to the output file you specify. This output file can be another partition identifier, a media device, or a regular file, to name three possibilities. The input and output files are passed with the if=*file* and of=*file* options:

```
# dd if=/dev/sda3 of=/dev/dvd
```

This command backs up the /dev/sda3 disk partition to /dev/dvd (a DVD drive). The result is a very low-level backup of the partition that can be restored by swapping the if= and of= options:

```
# dd if=/dev/dvd of=/dev/sda3
```

The dd utility can be a way to create exact backups of entire partitions. However, as a general backup tool, it has serious problems. It backs up the *entire* partition, including any empty space. Restoring individual files is also impossible unless the backup device is a random access device that can be mounted. Finally, you can't easily restore data to a partition that's smaller than the original partition, and when restoring to a larger partition, you'll end up wasting some of the space available on that partition.

Despite these problems, dd can be handy in some situations. Computer forensics experts often use it to get an exact partition copy. It can be a good way to make a duplicate of a removable disk. You can use dd to copy a disk for which Linux lacks filesystem drivers. If you need to create multiple identical Linux installations, you can do so by using dd to copy a working installation to multiple computers, as long as they have hard disks of the same size.

You can also use dd in some other capacities. For instance, if you need an empty file of a particular size, you can copy from the /dev/zero device (a Linux device that returns nothing but zeroes) to a target file:

```
$ dd if=/dev/zero of=empty-file.img bs=1024 count=720
```

The bs=*size* and count=*length* options are needed to set the block size and length of the file. The example above creates an (1024 × 720 bytes) empty file.

 Real World Scenario

Backing Up Using Optical Media

Optical media requires special backup procedures. Normally, cdrecord accepts input from a program like mkisofs, which creates an ISO-9660 or UDF filesystem—the type of filesystem that's most often found on CD-ROMs and DVDs.

One option for backing up to optical discs is to use mkisofs and then cdrecord to copy files to the disc. If you copy files "raw" this way, though, you'll lose some information, such as write permission bits. You'll have better luck if you create a tar or cpio archive on a hard drive disk. You can then use mkisofs to place that archive in an ISO-9660 or UDF filesystem and then burn the image file to the optical disc. The result will be a disc that you can mount and that will contain an archive that you can read with tar or cpio.

A somewhat more direct option is to create an archive file and burn it directly to the optical disc using cdrecord, bypassing mkisofs. Such a disc won't be mountable in the usual way, but you can access the archive directly by using the CD-ROM device file.

Managing Links

In Linux, a *link* is a way to give a file multiple identities, similar to shortcuts in Windows and aliases in Mac OS. There are a few reasons Linux employs links:

- To help make files more accessible
- To give commands multiple names
- To enable programs that look for the same files in different locations to access the same files

Two types of links exist: *hard links* and *symbolic links* (aka *soft links*). *Hard links* are produced by creating two directory entries that point to the same file (more precisely, the same inode). Both filenames are equally valid and prominent; neither is a "truer" filename than the other, except that one was created first (when creating the file) and the other was created second. To delete the file, you must delete both hard links to the file. The underlying filesystem must support hard links. All Linux-native filesystems support this feature, but some non-Linux filesystems don't. Because of the way hard links are created, they must exist on a single low-level filesystem. For example, you can't create a hard link from your root (/) filesystem to a separate filesystem you've mounted on it.

Symbolic links, by contrast, are special file types. The symbolic link is a separate file whose contents point to the linked-to file. Linux knows to access the linked-to file whenever you try to access the symbolic link. Therefore, in most respects, accessing a symbolic link works just like accessing the original file. Because symbolic links are basically files that contain filenames, they can point across low-level filesystems—you can point from the root (/) filesystem to a separate filesystem that you've mounted on it, for instance.

In practice, symbolic links are more common than hard links. Their disadvantages are minor and the ability to link across filesystems and to directories can be important. Linux employs links in certain critical system administration tasks. For instance, System V (SysV) startup scripts use symbolic links in runlevel directories, as described in Chapter 5, "Booting Linux and Editing Files."

The lookup process for accessing the original file from the link consumes a tiny bit of time, so symbolic link access is slower than hard link access—but not by enough that you'd notice in any but very bizarre conditions or artificial tests.

The ln command creates these links. Its syntax is similar to that of the cp command:

```
ln [options] source link
```

The original file is source, and link is the name of the link you want to create. This command supports options that have several effects:

Remove Target Files   The -f or --force option causes ln to remove any existing links or files that have the target link name. The -i or --interactive option has a similar effect, but it queries you before replacing existing files and links.

Create Directory Hard Links   Ordinarily, you can't create hard links to directories. The root user can *attempt* to do so, though, by passing the -d, -F, or --directory option to ln. (Symbolic links to directories aren't a problem.) In practice, this feature is unlikely to work because most filesystems don't support it.

Create a Symbolic Link   The ln command creates hard links by default. To create a symbolic link, pass the -s or --symbolic option to the command.

A few other options exist to perform more obscure tasks. You can consult the ln command's man page for more details.

Without any options, the ln command creates a hard link. The source file must exist before a hard link is created. The link file must not exist before the hard link is created:

```
$ ls -l afile.txt
-rw-rw-r--. 1 Christine Users 1679 Sep 25 15:39 afile.txt
```

```
$
$ ls -l hlink_afile
ls: cannot access hlink_afile: No such file or directory
$
$ ln afile.txt hlink_afile
$
$ ls -l *afile*
-rw-rw-r--. 2 Christine Users 1679 Sep 25 15:39 afile.txt
-rw-rw-r--. 2 Christine Users 1679 Sep 25 15:39 hlink_afile
$
```

Once the hard link is created, the *link* file, hlink_afile, is created. A long directory listing's second column shows the link count. When a file is not hard-linked to another file, the link count is set to one (1). Once a file becomes hard-linked to another file, the link count increases. Therefore, the long directory listing shows that both afile.txt and hlink_afile have a link count of two (2), and they are therefore hard-linked to another file.

Using the -i option, the ls command can also be used to show files' inode numbers. Below the inode numbers for the two hard-linked files are displayed. Notice that the inode numbers are the exact same number, because the files are hard-linked:

```
$ ls -i *afile*
527201 afile.txt  527201 hlink_afile
$
```

With the -s option, the ln command creates a symbolic link. Similar to the creation of a hard link, the *source* file must exist before a symbolic link is created and the *link* file must not exist:

```
$ ls -l bfile.txt
-rw-rw-r--. 1 Christine Users 1679 Sep 25 16:03 bfile.txt
$
$ ls -l slink_bfile
ls: cannot access slink_bfile: No such file or directory
$
$ ln -s bfile.txt slink_bfile
$
$ ls -l *bfile*
-rw-rw-r--. 1 Christine Users 1679 Sep 25 16:03 bfile.txt
lrwxrwxrwx. 1 Christine Users    9 Sep 25 16:04 slink_bfile -> bfile.txt
$
```

Unlike a hard link, the symbolically linked files' link counts do not increase. Also, a long listing conveniently shows the symbolically linked files with an arrow (->).

Understanding the Directory Commands

Most of the commands that apply to files also apply to directories. In particular, ls, mv, touch, and ln all work with directories, with the limitations mentioned earlier. The cp command also works with directories, but only when you use a recursion option, such as -r. A couple of additional commands, mkdir and rmdir, enable you to create and delete directories, respectively.

Using the *mkdir* Command

The mkdir command creates a directory. This command's official syntax is as follows:

mkdir [*options*] *directory-name(s)*

In most cases, mkdir is used without *options*, but a few options are supported:

Set Mode   The -m *mode* or --mode=*mode* option causes the new directory to have the specified permission mode, expressed as an octal number. (The upcoming section "Understanding Permissions" describes permission modes.)

Create Parent Directories   Normally, if you specify the creation of a directory within a directory that doesn't exist, mkdir responds with a No such file or directory error and doesn't create the directory. If you include the -p or --parents option, though, mkdir creates the necessary parent directory.

Using the *rmdir* Command

The rmdir command is the opposite of mkdir; it destroys a directory. Its syntax is similar:

rmdir [*options*] *directory-name(s)*

Like mkdir, rmdir supports few options, the most important of which handle these tasks:

Ignore Failures on Non-empty Directories   Normally, if a directory contains files or other directories, rmdir doesn't delete it and returns an error message. With the --ignore-fail-on-non-empty option, rmdir still doesn't delete the directory, but it doesn't return an error message.

Delete Tree   The -p or --parents option causes rmdir to delete an entire directory tree. For instance, typing **rmdir -p one/two/three** causes rmdir to delete one/two/three, then one/two, and finally one, provided no other files or directories are present.

When you're deleting an entire directory tree filled with files, you should use rm -R or rm -r rather than rmdir. This is because the rmdir command can delete only an empty directory.

Managing File Ownership

Security is an important topic that cuts across many types of commands and Linux subsystems. In the case of files, security is built on file ownership and file permissions. These two topics are closely intertwined: ownership is meaningless without permissions that use it, and permissions rely on the existence of ownership.

Ownership is two tiered: Each file has an individual owner and a group with which it's associated (sometimes called the group owner or simply the file's group). Each group can contain an arbitrary number of users, as described in Chapter 7, "Administering the System." The two types of ownership enable you to provide three tiers of permissions to control access to files: by the file's owner, by the file's group, and to all other users. The commands to manage these two types of ownership are similar, but they aren't identical.

Assessing File Ownership

You can learn who owns a file with the ls command, which was described earlier. In particular, that command's -l option produces a long listing, which includes both ownership and permission information:

```
$ ls -l
total 28

-rw-rw-r--. 1 Christine Users  826 Sep 25 11:09 my-work.tgz
-rw-rw-r--. 1 Christine Users 9972 Sep 25 10:30 project_a354
-rw-rw-r--. 1 Christine Users 3324 Sep 25 10:30 project_c923
-rw-rw-r--. 1 Christine Users 2216 Sep 25 10:30 project_m1321
-rw-rw-r--. 1 Christine Users  218 Sep 25 10:27 punch_list.txt
```

This long listing includes the owner's username, Christine, in column three and the files' group name, Users, in column four. The permission string, -rw-rw-r--, in column one, is also important for file security, as described later in "Controlling Access to Files."

WARNING   If you delete an account, as described in Chapter 7, the account's files don't vanish, but the account name does. Internally, Linux uses numbers rather than names, so you'll see numbers in place of the username and group name in the ls output.

A new user account could be assigned those numbers. This would allow the new user account access to those deleted account's files! Depending on the files, you may want to archive them, reassign ownership to an existing user, or delete them.

In most cases, the usernames associated with files are the same as login usernames. Files can, however, be owned by accounts that aren't ordinary login accounts. For instance, some servers have accounts of their own, and server-specific files may be owned by these accounts.

Changing a File's Owner

Whenever a file is created, it's assigned an owner. The superuser can change a file's owner using the chown command. It can also be used to change the file's group. The chown command has the following syntax:

chown [*options*] [*newowner*][:*newgroup*] *filenames*

As you might expect, the *newowner* and *newgroup* variables are the new owner and group for the file. You can provide both or omit one, but you can't omit both. For instance, suppose you want to give ownership of a file to sally and the skyhook group:

 # chown sally:skyhook forward.odt

 Linux's chown command accepts a dot (.) in place of a colon (:) to delimit the owner and group, at least as of the core file utilities version 8.14. The use of a dot has been deprecated, though, meaning that the developers favor the colon and may eventually eliminate the use of a dot as a feature.

You can use several options with chown, most of which are fairly obscure. One that's most likely to be useful is -R or --recursive, which implements the ownership change on an entire directory tree. Consult the man page for chown for information about additional options.

Only root may use the chown command to change the ownership of files. If an ordinary user tries to use it, the result is an Operation not permitted error message. Ordinary users *may*, however, use chown to change the group of files that they own, provided that the users belong to the target group.

Changing a File's Group

Both root and ordinary users may run the chgrp command, which changes a file's group. (Ordinary users may only change a file's group to a group to which they belong.) This command's syntax is similar to, but simpler than, that of chown:

chgrp [*options*] *newgroup filenames*

The chgrp command accepts many of the same options as chown, including -R or --recursive. In practice, chgrp provides a subset of the chown functionality.

Controlling Access to Files

The bulk of the complexity in file ownership and permissions is on the permissions end of things. The Linux permissions scheme is moderately complex, so understanding how it works is critical to any permission manipulation. With the basic information in hand, you can tackle the commands used to change file permissions.

Understanding Permissions

At the core of Linux permissions are permission bits, which provide access control for files. In addition, a few special permission bits exist. These special bits provide some unusual features.

Digging into the Meanings of Permission Bits

Consider the following file access control string that's displayed with the -l option to ls:

```
$ ls -l test
-rwxr-xr-x. 1 Christine Users 843 Sep 27 09:10 test
$
```

This string (-rwxr-xr-x in this example) is 10 characters long. The first character has special meaning—it's the *file type code*. The type code determines how Linux will interpret the file—as ordinary data, a directory, or a special file type. Table 4.4 summarizes Linux type codes.

TABLE 4.4   Linux file type codes

Code	Meaning
-	Normal data file: This may be text, an executable program, graphics, compressed data, or just about any other type of data.
d	Directory: Disk directories are files just like any others, but they contain filenames and pointers to disk inodes.
l	Symbolic link: The file contains the name of another file or directory. When Linux accesses the symbolic link, it tries to read the linked-to file.
p	Named pipe: A pipe enables two running Linux programs to communicate with each other. One opens the pipe for reading, and the other opens it for writing, enabling data to be transferred between the programs.
s	Socket: A socket is similar to a named pipe, but it permits network and bidirectional links.
b	Block device: This is a file that corresponds to a hardware device to and from which data is transferred in blocks of more than 1 byte. Disk devices (hard disks, USB flash drives, CD-ROMs, and so on) are common block devices.
c	Character device: A file that corresponds to a hardware device to and from which data is transferred in units of 1 byte. Examples include parallel port, RS-232 serial port, and audio devices.

The remaining permission string's nine characters (rwxr-xr-x in the example) are broken up into three groups of three characters each, as illustrated in Figure 4.1. The first group controls the file owner's access to the file, the second controls the group's access to the file, and the third controls all other users' access to the file (often referred to as world permissions).

FIGURE 4.1   The main Linux permission options are encoded in 10 bits, the last 9 of which are grouped into three groups of 3 bits each.

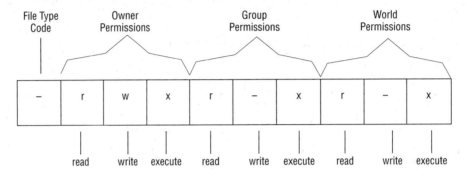

In each of these three cases, the permission string determines the presence or absence of the three access types: read, write, and execute. Read and write permissions are fairly self-explanatory, at least for ordinary files.

If the execute permission is present, it means that the file may be run as a program. Of course, this doesn't turn a non-program file into a program; it only means that a user may run a file if it is a program. Setting the execute bit on a non-program file will probably cause no real harm, but it could be confusing.

The absence of the permission is denoted by a dash (-) in the permission string. The presence of the permission is indicated by a letter—r for read, w for write, or x for execute.

Thus, the example permission string rwxr-xr-x means that the file's permissions are set as follows:

Owner: read, write, and execute permission

Group members: read and execute permission

Other users: read and execute permission

Individual permissions, such as execute access for the file's owner, are often referred to as *permission bits*. This is because Linux encodes this information in binary form. Because it's binary, the permission information can be expressed as a single 9-bit number. This number is usually expressed in octal (base 8) form because a base-8 number is 3 bits in length, which means that the base-8 representation of a permission string is three characters long; one character for each of the owner, group, and world permissions.

The result is that you can determine owner, group, or other permissions using this information. The read, write, and execute permissions correspond to these bits as follows:

1: execute permission

2: write permission

4: read permission

Permissions bits for a particular permission type are added together, thus permissions are expressed for each permission type (owner, group, other) as a single digit. To understand how this works, consider the following long listing:

```
$ ls -l script.sh
-rwxrw-r--. 1 Christine Users 821 Sep 25 17:49 script.sh
$
```

The owner permissions set on the script.sh file are read, write, and execute. To determine the owner permission digit, the corresponding permission bit numbers are added up — read (4) + write (2) + execute (1), which adds up to seven (7). Thus, the digit representing the owner permissions on this file is seven (7).

Each permission type is added up separately. For the script.sh file, the group permission digit would be read (4) + write (2), which equals six (6). Other permission had only the read permission bit set, and therefore its digit would be four (4).

The three permission digits are placed together to make a three-digit number (octal code) representing the file's permissions. The placement order is owner (7), group (6), and other (4). Therefore, the three digit octal code for the script.sh file is 764.

It helps to have additional permission examples to understand this concept. Table 4.5 shows some common permission examples and their meanings.

TABLE 4.5   Example permissions and their likely uses

Permission string	Octal code	Meaning
rwxrwxrwx	777	Read, write, and execute permissions for all users.
rwxr-xr-x	755	Read and execute permission for all users. The file's owner also has write permission.
rwx------	700	Read, write, and execute permissions for the file's owner only; all others have no access.
rw-rw-rw-	666	Read and write permissions for all users. No execute permissions for anybody.
rw-r--r--	644	Read and write permissions for the owner. Read-only permission for all others.
rw-r-----	640	Read and write permissions for the owner, and read-only permission for the group. No permission for others.
rw-------	600	Read and write permissions for the owner. No permission for anybody else.
r--------	400	Read permission for the owner. No permission for anybody else.

Execute permission makes sense for program files, but it's meaningless for most other file types, such as device files. Directories, though, use the execute bit another way. When a directory's execute bit is set, that means that the directory's contents may be searched. This is a highly desirable characteristic for directories, so you'll almost never find a directory on which the execute bit is *not* set in conjunction with the read bit.

Directories can be confusing with respect to the write permission. Recall that directories are files that are interpreted in a special way. As such, if a user can write to a directory, that user can create, delete, or rename files in the directory as well. This is true even if the user isn't the owner of those files and does not have permission to write to those files. You can use the *sticky bit* (described shortly, in "Understanding Special Permission Bits") to alter this behavior.

Symbolic links are unusual with respect to permissions. This file type always has 777 (rwxrwxrwx) permissions, thus granting all users full access to the file. This access applies only to the link file itself and not to the linked-to file. In other words, all users can read the contents of the link to discover the name of the file to which it points. The permissions on the linked-to file determine its file access. If you attempt to change the permissions on a symbolic link file, the linked-to file's permissions are changed instead.

Many of the permission rules don't apply to root. The superuser can read or write any file on the computer—even files that grant access to nobody (that is, those that have 000 permissions). The superuser still needs an execute bit to be set to run a program file, but the superuser has the power to change the permissions on any file, so this limitation isn't very substantial. Some files may be inaccessible to root, but only because of an underlying restriction. For instance, even root can't access a hard disk that's not installed in the computer.

Understanding Special Permission Bits

A few special permission options are also supported, and they may be indicated by changes to the permission string:

Set User ID (SUID)   The *set user ID (SUID)* option is used in conjunction with executable files. It tells Linux to run the program with the permissions of whoever owns the file rather than with the permissions of the user who runs the program. For instance, if a file is owned by root and has its SUID bit set, the program runs with root privileges and can therefore read any file on the computer. Some servers and other system programs run this way, which is often called SUID root. SUID programs are indicated by an s in the owner's execute bit position in the permission string, as in rwsr-xr-x.

If the SUID bit is set on a file without execution permission set, the permission string appears with a capital S, as in rwSr-xr-x. However, in this case, SUID will not function and the setting is called *benign*.

Set Group ID (SGID)   The *set group ID (SGID)* option is similar to the SUID option, but it sets the running program's group to the file's group. It's indicated by an s in the group execute bit position in the permission string, as in rwxr-sr-x.

Similar to SUID, if the SGID bit is set on a file without execution permission set, the permission string appears with a capital S, as in `rwsr-Sr-x`. Also in this case the setting is benign.

SGID is also useful on directories. When the SGID bit is set on a directory, new files or subdirectories created in the original directory will inherit the group ownership of the directory rather than be based on the user's current default group.

Sticky Bit   The *sticky bit* is used to protect files from being deleted by those who don't own the files. When this bit is present on a directory, the directory's files can be deleted only by their owners, the directory's owner, or `root`. The sticky bit is indicated by a `t` in the world execute bit position, as in `rwxr-xr-t`.

These special permission bits all have security implications. SUID and SGID programs (and particularly SUID `root` programs) are potential security risks. Although some programs must have their SUID bits set to function properly, most don't, and you shouldn't set these bits unless you're certain that doing so is necessary. The sticky bit isn't dangerous this way, but because it affects who may delete files in a directory, you should consider its effect—or the effect of not having it—on directories to which many users should have write access, such as `/tmp`. Typically, such directories have their sticky bits set.

 Real World Scenario

DAC, ACLs and SELinux

The permissions covered so far in this chapter have served Linux well since its creation. They fall under the umbrella of the *discretionary access control (DAC)* model, which is considered in the security world to be inefficient for properly securing a Linux system.

An improved permission system called an *access control list (ACL)* is a list of users or groups and the permissions they're given. Linux ACLs, like Linux owner, group, and world permissions, consist of three permission bits, one each for read, write, and execute permissions. To be set and viewed, ACLs require their own commands. The `setfacl` command sets an ACL, and the `getfacl` command displays the ACLs for a file. Consult these commands' man pages for more information.

An even better security approach is a model called mandatory access control (MAC) and its subcategory, *role-based access control (RBAC)*. These models are implemented by the SELinux utility available on many Linux distributions. SELinux is a very complex utility. It implements RBAC security using the Bell-LaPadula model and either type enforcement or multi-level security. SELinux is far too complex to learn about via the man pages. For more information, invest in a Linux security book and/or review SELinux information stored on the Web.

Changing a File's Mode

You can modify a file's permissions using the chmod command. This command may be issued in many different ways to achieve the same effect. Its basic syntax is as follows:

chmod [*options*] [*mode*[*,mode...*]] *filename*...

The chmod options are similar to those of chown and chgrp. In particular, --recursive (or -R) changes all of the files in a directory tree.

Most of the chmod command's complexity comes in the file's mode specification. You can specify the mode in two basic forms: as a three-digit octal number (covered earlier) or as a symbolic mode. A *symbolic mode* is a set of codes related to the string representation of the permissions.

The mode's octal representation is the same as that described earlier and summarized in Table 4.5. For instance, to view and change permissions on file.dat to rw-r--r--, you can issue the following commands:

```
$ ls -l file.dat
-rw-rw-r--. 1 Christine Users 199 Sep 15 14:36 file.dat
$
$ chmod 644 file.dat
$
$ ls -l file.dat
-rw-r--r--. 1 Christine Users 199 Sep 15 14:36 file.dat
$
```

In addition, you can precede the three octal mode digits for the owner, group, and other permissions with another digit that sets special permissions. The SUID, SGID, and sticky bit permissions correspond to these bits as follows:

1   Sticky bit permission

2   SGID permission

4   SUID permission

If you omit the first digit (as in the preceding example), Linux clears all three special permission bits. Thus, in the previous example, 644 is treated as 0644. Using four digits causes the first digit to be interpreted as the special permissions' code.

To set the special permissions using octal code, you add up the special permissions bits, just as you do for the other permission types. For instance, suppose you've acquired a script called bigprogram. You want to set the following:

- Both SUID and SGID special permission bits (6)
- Owner bits to make the program readable, writeable, and executable (7)
- Group bits to make the program readable and executable (5)
- Other bits to make the program completely inaccessible to all others (0)

Because SGID is a group permission, superuser privileges are required. The following commands illustrate how to do this; note the difference in the mode string before and after executing the chmod command:

```
# ls -l bigprogram.sh
-rw-r--r--. 1 Christine Users 8395 Sep 26 07:40 bigprogram.sh
#
# chmod 6750 bigprogram.sh
#
# ls -l bigprogram.sh
-rwsr-s---. 1 Christine Users 8395 Sep 26 07:40 bigprogram.sh
```

A mode's symbolic representation, by contrast, consists of three components:

- A code indicating the permission set to modify (the owner, the group, other, and so on)
- A symbol indicating whether you want to add, delete, or set the mode equal to a stated value
- A code specifying what the permission should be

Table 4.6 summarizes all of these codes. Note that these codes are all case-sensitive.

TABLE 4.6   Codes used in symbolic modes

Permission set code	Meaning	Change type code	Meaning	Permission to modify code	Meaning
u	Owner	+	Add	r	Read
g	Group	-	Remove	w	Write
o	Other	=	Set equal to	x	Execute
a	All			X	Execute only if the file is a directory or already has execute permission
				s	SUID or SGID
				t	Sticky bit
				u	Existing owner's permissions
				g	Existing group permissions
				o	Existing other permissions

To use symbolic permission settings, you combine one or more of the codes from the first column of Table 4.6 with one symbol from the third column and one or more codes from the fifth column. You can combine multiple settings by separating them with commas. Table 4.7 provides some examples of chmod using symbolic permission settings.

TABLE 4.7   Examples of symbolic permissions with chmod

Command	Initial permissions	End permissions
chmod a+x bigprogram	rw-r--r--	rwxr-xr-x
chmod ug=rw report.tex	r--------	rw-rw----
chmod o-rwx bigprogram	rwxrwxr-x	rwxrwx---
chmod g=u report.tex	rw-r--r--	rw-rw-r--
chmod g-w,o-rw report.tex	rw-rw-rw-	rw-r-----

As a general rule, symbolic permissions are most useful when you want to make a simple change (such as adding execute or write permissions to one or more classes of users) or when you want to make similar changes to many files without affecting their other permissions (for instance, adding write permissions without affecting execute permissions). Octal permissions are most useful when you want to set a specific absolute permission, such as rw-r--r-- (644). In any event, a system administrator should be familiar with both setting permission methods.

A file's owner and root are the only users who may adjust a file's permissions. Even if other users have write access to a directory in which a file resides and write access to the file itself, they may not change the file's permissions. However, they may modify or even delete the file. To understand why this is so, you need to know that the file permissions are stored as part of the file's inode, which isn't part of the directory entry. Read/write access to the directory entry, or even the file itself, doesn't give a user the right to change the inode structures (except indirectly—for instance, if a write changes the file's size or a file deletion eliminates the need for the inode).

In Exercise 4.1, you'll experiment with the effect of Linux ownership and permissions on file accessibility.

EXERCISE 4.1

Modifying Ownership and Permissions

During this exercise, you'll need to use three accounts: root and two user accounts, each in a different group. To study these effects, follow these steps:

1. Log in three times using three virtual terminals: once as root, once as user1, and once as user2. (Use usernames appropriate for your system, though. Be sure that user1 and user2 are in different groups.) If you prefer, instead of using virtual terminals, you can open three terminal emulator windows in an GUI session; use su user1 and su user2 to acquire their privileges and su - to acquire root's privileges.

2. As root, create a scratch directory—say, /tmp/scratch. Type **mkdir /tmp/ scratch**.

3. As root, give all users read and write access to the scratch directory by typing **chmod 0777 /tmp/scratch**.

4. In the user1 and user2 login sessions, change to the scratch directory by typing **cd /tmp/scratch**.

5. As user1, copy a short text file to the scratch directory using cp, as in **cp /etc/ fstab ./testfile**.

6. As user1, set 0644 (-rw-r--r--) permissions on the file by typing **chmod 0644 testfile**. Type **ls -l**, and verify that the permission string in the first column matches this value (-rw-r--r--).

7. As user2, try to access the file by typing **cat testfile**. The file should appear on the screen.

8. As user2, try to change the name of the file by typing **mv testfile changedfile**. The system won't produce any feedback, but if you type **ls**, you'll see that the file's name has changed. Note that user2 doesn't own the file but can rename it because user2 can write to the directory in which the file resides.

9. As user2, try to change the mode of the file by typing **chmod 0600 changedfile**. The system should respond with an Operation not permitted error because only the file's owner may change its permissions.

10. As user2, try to delete the file by typing **rm changedfile**. Depending on your configuration, the system may or may not ask for verification, but it should permit the deletion. This is true despite the fact that user2 doesn't own the file because user2 can write to the directory in which the file resides.

11. As user1, repeat step 5 to re-create the test file.

12. As user1, give the file more restrictive permissions by typing **chmod 0640**. Typing **ls -l** should reveal permissions of -rw-r-----, meaning that the file's owner can read and write the file, members of the file's group can read it, and other users are given no access.

13. As user2, repeat steps 7–10. The cat operation should fail with a Permission denied error, but steps 8–10 should produce the same results as they did the first time around. (If the cat operation succeeded, then either user2 belongs to the file's group or the file's mode is set incorrectly.)

14. Log out of the user1 and user2 accounts.

15. As root, type **rm -r /tmp/scratch** to delete the scratch directory and its contents.

If you like, you can perform tests with more file permission modes and other file-manipulation commands before step 14.

Setting the Default Mode and Group

When a user creates a file, that file has default ownership and permissions. The default owner is, understandably, the user who created the file. The default group is the user's primary group.

The default permissions are configurable. These are defined by the *user mask*, which is set by the umask command. This command takes as input an octal value that represents the bits to be removed from 777 permissions for directories, or from 666 permissions for files, when a new file or directory is created. Table 4.8 summarizes the effect of several possible umask values.

TABLE 4.8   Sample umask values and their effects

umask	Created files	Created directories
000	666 (rw-rw-rw-)	777 (rwxrwxrwx)
002	664 (rw-rw-r--)	775 (rwxrwxr-x)
022	644 (rw-r--r--)	755 (rwxr-xr-x)
027	640 (rw-r-----)	750 (rwxr-x---)
077	600 (rw-------)	700 (rwx------)
277	400 (r--------)	500 (r-x------)

Note that the umask isn't a simple subtraction from the values of 777 or 666; it's a bit-wise removal. Any bit that's set in the umask is removed from the final permission for new files, but if a bit isn't set (as in the execute bit in ordinary files), its specification in the umask doesn't do any harm.

Another way to view and understand umask is not in octal code and bit-wise removal but in symbolic representation. Ignoring umask for a moment, a file is created using the default 666 (octal code), which corresponds to rw-rw-rw- (symbolic representation). In Table 4.8, the umask value 022 (octal code) corresponds to ----w--w- (symbolic representation). Using this umask setting as an example, the write permission is subtracted from the file's group permission setting. Also, the write permission is subtracted from the file's other permission setting. Thus, when this umask value is applied, the created file permission ends up being 644 (octal code) or rw-r--r-- (symbolic representation). The group and other write permissions were subtracted by the umask setting.

Ordinary users can enter the umask command to change the permissions on new files they create. The superuser can also modify the default setting for all users by modifying a system configuration file. Typically, /etc/profile contains one or more umask commands. Setting the umask in /etc/profile may or may not have an effect because it can be overridden at other points, such as a user's own configuration files. Nonetheless, setting the umask in /etc/profile or other system files can be a useful procedure if you want to change the default system policy. Most Linux distributions use a default umask of 002 or 022.

To find out the current umask setting, type **umask** alone without any parameters. When umask is displayed, the number is shown in four digits. The first digit represents the octal code for SUID, SGID, and the sticky bit. A umask setting example follows:

```
$ umask
0022
$
```

To change umask, use the four-digit octal code. Remember to verify that these are the permissions you want removed from the default file and directory settings. The umask command is entered followed by the desired code on the same line:

```
$ umask 0002
$
$ umask
0002
$
```

Typing **umask -S** produces the umask expressed symbolically rather than in octal form. However, the special permissions are not included in the display because the octal code is currently set to zero (0):

```
$ umask -S
u=rwx,g=rwx,o=rx
$
```

You may also specify a umask in this way when you want to change it. However, in this case, you specify the bits that you *do* want set. For instance, for changing umask, typing **umask u=rwx,g=rx,o=rx** is equivalent to typing **umask 022**. However, if a permission bit is not set in the default file or directory permissions, the specified permission will *not* be set. For example, the preceding umask configuration will not set group and other execute privileges for a file.

When umask is changed, the effect is immediate. Any newly created files or directories will show the modification:

```
$ umask
0022
$
$ touch newfile.dat
$
$ ls -l newfile.dat
-rw-r--r--. 1 Christine Users 0 Sep 26 08:24 newfile.dat
$
$ umask 0002
$
$ umask
0002
$
$ touch secondfile.dat
$
$ ls -l *file.dat
-rw-r--r--. 1 Christine Users  0 Sep 26 08:24 newfile.dat
-rw-rw-r--. 1 Christine Users  0 Sep 26 08:24 secondfile.dat
$
```

In addition to setting the default mask with umask, users can change their default group with newgrp, as in **newgrp skyhook** to create new files with the group set to the skyhook group. To use this command, the user must be a member of the specified group. The newgrp command also accepts the -l parameter, as in **newgrp -l skyhook**, which reinitializes the environment as if the user had just logged in.

Changing File Attributes

Some filesystems support additional attributes (other than those described in the preceding sections). In particular, some Linux-native filesystems support several attributes that you can adjust with the chattr command:

No Access Time Updates If you set the A attribute, Linux won't update the access time stamp when you access a file. This can reduce disk input/output, which is particularly helpful for saving battery life on laptops.

Append Only   The a attribute sets append mode, which disables write access to the file except for appending data. This can be a security feature to prevent accidental or malicious changes to files that record data, such as log files.

Compressed   The c attribute causes the kernel to compress data written to the file automatically and uncompress it when it's read back.

Immutable   The i flag makes a file immutable, which goes a step beyond simply disabling write access to the file. The file can't be deleted, links to it can't be created, and the file can't be renamed.

Data Journaling   The j flag tells the kernel to journal all data written to the file. This improves recoverability of data written to the file after a system crash but can slow performance. This flag has no effect on ext2 filesystems.

Secure Deletion   Ordinarily, when you delete a file, its directory entry is removed and its inode is marked as being available for recycling. The data blocks that make up the bulk of the file aren't erased. Setting the s flag changes this behavior; when the file is deleted, the kernel zeros its data blocks, which may be desirable for files that contain sensitive data.

No Tail-Merging   *Tail-merging* is a process in which small data pieces at a file's end that don't fill a complete block are merged with similar pieces of data from other files. The result is reduced disk space consumption, particularly when you store many small files rather than a few big ones. Setting the t flag disables this behavior, which is desirable if certain non-kernel drivers will read the filesystem, such as those that are part of the Grand Unified Boot Loader (GRUB).

This list of attributes is incomplete, but it includes the most useful options. You can consult the chattr command's man page to read about more flags.

You set the options that you want using the minus (-), plus (+), or equal (=) symbol to remove an option from an existing set, add an option to an existing set, or set a precise set of options (overwriting any that already exist), respectively. For instance, to add the immutable flag to the important.txt file, you enter the following command:

```
# chattr +i important.txt
```

The result is that you'll be unable to delete the file, even as root. To delete the file, you must first remove the immutable flag:

```
# chattr -i important.txt
```

Managing Disk Quotas

Just one user of a multiuser system can cause serious problems by consuming too much disk space. If a single user creates huge files (say, multimedia recordings), those files can use enough disk space to prevent other users from creating their own files. To help manage this situation, Linux supports *disk quotas*; that is, limits enforced by the OS on how many files or how much disk space a single user may consume. The Linux quota system supports quotas both for individual users and for Linux groups.

Enabling Quota Support

Quotas require support in both the kernel for the filesystem being used and various user-space utilities. The ext2fs, ext3fs, ext4fs, ReiserFS, JFS, and XFS filesystems support quotas, but this support is missing for some filesystems in early 2.6.*x* kernels. Try using the latest kernel if you have problems with your preferred filesystem. You must explicitly enable support via the Quota Support kernel option in the filesystem area when recompiling your kernel. Most distributions ship with this support enabled, so recompiling your kernel may not be necessary, but you should be aware of this option if you recompile your kernel.

Two general quota support systems are available for Linux. The first was used through the 2.4.*x* kernels and is referred to as the *quota v1 support* system. The second was added with the 2.6.*x* kernel series and is referred to as the *quota v2 support* system. This description applies to the latter system, but the former works in a similar way.

Outside of the kernel, you need support tools to use quotas. For the quota v2 system, this package is usually called quota and it installs a number of utilities, configuration files, system startup scripts, and so on.

You must modify your /etc/fstab entries for any partitions on which you want to use quota support. In particular, you must add the usrquota filesystem mount option to employ user quotas and the grpquota option to use group quotas. Entries that are so configured resemble the following:

```
/dev/sdc5  /home ext4  usrquota,grpquota  1  1
```

This line activates both user and group quota support for the /dev/sdc5 partition, which is mounted at /home. Of course, you can add other options if you like.

Depending on your distribution, you may need to configure the quota package's system startup scripts to run when the system boots. Chapter 5 describes startup script management in detail. Typically, you'll type a command such as **chkconfig quota on**, but you should check on the SysV scripts installed by your distribution's quota package. Some distributions require the use of commands other than chkconfig to do this task, as described in Chapter 5. Whatever its details, this startup script runs the quotaon command, which activates quota support.

The superuser can turn quotas on at any time by using the quotaon command. Likewise, the superuser can turn quotas off at any time by using the quotaoff command. See the various options for these commands in their man pages.

After making the necessary configuration file changes, you must activate the configurations. The simplest way to do this is to reboot the computer. However, you should be able to get by with less disruptive measures, such as running the startup script for the quota tools and remounting the filesystems on which you intend to use quotas.

Once the system is booted and the filesystems needing quotas are mounted, then the quotacheck command should be executed. The quotacheck command surveys the filesystem needing quotas and builds current disk usage data records.

There are two files the quotacheck command builds that are needed to enable quotas: aquota.user and aquota.group. To create these files (c) and check both user (u) and group (g) quotas, the quotacheck options -cug are used.

> The quotacheck command can also verify and update quota information on quota-enabled partitions. This command is normally run as part of the quota package's startup script, but you may want to run it periodically as a cron job. (Chapter 7 describes cron jobs.) Although theoretically not necessary if everything works correctly, quotacheck ensures that quota accounting doesn't become inaccurate.

For example, if quotas were only set for users in the /home directory, the following command would be needed. This would perform the necessary checks and create the needed quota file in the /home directory:

```
# quotacheck  -cu  /home
```

At this point, quota support should be fully active on your computer. However, the quotas themselves are not yet set.

Setting Quotas for Users

You can set the quotas by using the edquota command. This command uses a text editor, such as the vi editor. However, the editor of your choice is selected by setting or changing the EDITOR environment variable.

The editor opens a temporary configuration file, /etc/quotatab, which controls the specified user's quotas. When you exit the utility, edquota uses the temporary configuration file to write the quota information to low-level disk data structures. These structures control the kernel's quota mechanisms.

For instance, you might type **edquota sally** to edit sally's quotas. The contents of the editor show the current quota information:

```
Disk quotas for user sally (uid 21810):
Filesystem      blocks        soft         hard   inodes   soft    hard
/dev/sdc4       97104     1048576     1048576     1242      0       0
```

The temporary configuration file provides information about both the number of disk blocks in use and the number of inodes in use. Each file or symbolic link consumes a single inode, so the inode limits are effectively limits on the number of files a user may own. Disk blocks vary in size depending on the filesystem and filesystem creation options.

Changing the use information located under the blocks and inodes columns has no effect. These columns report only how many blocks or inodes the user is actually consuming.

You can alter the soft and hard limits for both blocks and inodes. The *hard limit* is the maximum number of blocks or inodes that the user may consume. The kernel won't permit a user to surpass hard limits.

Soft limits are somewhat less stringent. Users may temporarily exceed soft limit values, but when they do so, the system issues warnings. Soft limits also interact with a grace period. If the soft quota limit is exceeded for longer than the grace period, the kernel begins treating it like a hard limit and refuses to allow the user to create more files.

You can set the soft limit grace period by using edquota with its -t option, as in **edquota -t**. Grace periods are set on a per-filesystem basis rather than a per-user basis. Setting a limit to 0 (as in the inode limits in the preceding example) eliminates the use of quotas for that value. This allows users to consume as much disk space or create as many files as they like, up to the available space on the filesystem.

When using edquota, you can adjust quotas independently for every filesystem for which quotas are enabled and separately for every user or group. To edit quotas for a group, use the -g option, as in **edquota -g users** to adjust quotas for the users group.

A useful auxiliary quota command is repquota, which summarizes the quota information about the filesystem you specify or on all filesystems if you pass it the -a option. This tool can be very helpful in keeping track of disk usage.

The quota command has a similar effect. The quota tool takes a number of options to have them modify their outputs. For instance, -g displays group quotas, -l omits NFS mounts, and -q limits output to filesystems on which usage is over the limit. Consult the quota command's man page for still more obscure options.

Locating Files

Maintaining your filesystems in perfect health, setting permissions, and so on is pointless if you can't find your files. For this reason, Linux provides several tools to help you locate the files that you need to use.

The first of these tools is actually a standard for where files are located; with the right knowledge, you may be able to find files without the use of any specialized programs. The second class of tools includes specialized programs, which search a directory tree or a database for files that meet whatever criteria you specify.

Getting to Know the FHS

Linux's placement of files is derived from more than 40 years of Unix history. Given that fact, the structure is remarkably simple and coherent, but it's easy for a new administrator to become confused. Some directories seem, on the surface, to fulfill similar or even identical roles, but in fact there are subtle but important differences. The following sections describe the Linux directory layout standards and presents an overview of what goes where.

Comparing FSSTND and FHS

Although Linux draws heavily on Unix, Unix's long history has led to numerous splits and variants, starting with the *Berkeley Standard Distribution (BSD)*. BSD was initially a set of patches and extensions to AT&T's original Unix code. As a result of these schisms within the Unix community, early Linux distributions didn't always follow identical patterns. The result was a great deal of confusion. This problem was quite severe early in Linux's history, and it threatened to split the Linux community into factions. Various measures were taken to combat this problem, one of which was the development of the *Filesystem Standard (FSSTND)*, which was first released in early 1994. The FSSTND standardized several specific features, such as the following:

- Standardized the programs that reside in /bin and /usr/bin. Differences on this score caused problems when scripts referred to files in one location or the other.

- Specified that executable files shouldn't reside in /etc, as had previously been common.

- Removed changeable files from the /usr directory tree, enabling it to be mounted read-only (a useful security measure).

There have been three major versions of FSSTND: 1.0, 1.1, and 1.2. FSSTND began to rein in some of the chaos in the Linux world in 1994. By 1995, however, FSSTND's limitations were becoming apparent; thus a new standard was developed: the *Filesystem Hierarchy Standard (FHS)*. This new standard is based on FSSTND but extends it substantially. The FHS is more than a Linux standard; it may be used to define the layout of files on other Unix-like OSs.

The FHS comes in numbered versions, such as v2.3. Though it's not updated often, it is wise to check for FHS modifications. The URL for FHS's official web page is www.pathname.com/fhs/. You can find FHS modification workgroups at the Linux Foundation URL, www.linuxfoundation.org/.

One important distinction made by the FHS is that between *shareable files* and *unshareable files*. Shareable files may be reasonably shared between computers, such as user data files and program binary files. (Of course, you don't *need* to share such files, but you *may* do so.) If files are shared, they're normally shared through an NFS server. Unshareable files contain system-specific information, such as configuration files. For instance, you're not likely to want to share a server's configuration file between computers.

A second important distinction used in the FHS is that between *static files* and *variable files*. The former don't normally change except through direct intervention by the system administrator. Most program executables are examples of static files. Users, automated scripts, servers, or the like may change variable files. For instance, users' home directories and mail queues are composed of variable files. The FHS tries to isolate each directory into one cell of this 2 × 2 (shareable/unshareable × static/variable) matrix. Figure 4.2 illustrates these relationships. Some directories are mixed, but in these cases, the FHS tries to specify the status of particular subdirectories. For instance, /var is variable and it contains some shareable and some unshareable subdirectories, as shown in Figure 4.2.

FIGURE 4.2   The FHS attempts to fit each important directory in one cell of a 2 × 2 matrix.

	Shareable	Unshareable
Static	/usr /opt	/etc /boot
Variable	/home /var/mail	/var/run /var/lock

Studying Important Directories and Their Contents

The FHS defines some directories very precisely, but details for others are left unresolved. For instance, users' files normally go in the /home directory, but you may have reason to call this directory something else or to use two or more separate directories for users' files. Overall, the most common directories defined by the FHS or used by convention are the following:

/   Every Linux filesystem traces its roots to a single directory, known as / (pronounced, and often referred to, as the *root filesystem* or *root directory*). All other directories branch off this one. Linux doesn't use drive letters. Instead, every filesystem is mounted at a mount point within another partition (/ or something else). Certain critical subdirectories, such as /etc and /sbin, must reside on the root partition, but others can optionally be on separate partitions. Don't confuse the root directory with the /root directory, described shortly.

/boot   The /boot directory contains static and unshareable files related to the computer's initial booting. Higher-level startup and configuration files reside in another directory, /etc. In this directory, you will find GRUB or LILO configuration files along with the other files necessary for the initial boot. Typically, it is recommended that you store /boot on its own partition.

/etc   The /etc directory contains unshareable and static system configuration files. These higher-level startup and configuration files control the various programs and services offered on a system. For example, if the Linux distribution uses systemd system initialization, some systemd configuration files are stored in /etc/systemd directories. If the Linux distribution uses SysV system initialization, its configuration files are stored in /etc directories.

/bin This directory contains certain critical executable files, such as ls, cp, and mount. These commands are accessible to all users and constitute the most important commands that ordinary users might issue. You won't normally find commands for big application programs in /bin. The /bin directory contains static files. The directory is almost never shared—any potential clients must have their own local /bin directories.

/sbin This directory is similar to /bin, but it contains programs that are normally run only by the system administrator—tools like fdisk and e2fsck. It's static and theoretically shareable, but in practice it makes no sense to share it.

/lib This directory is similar to /bin and /sbin, but it contains program libraries. Program libraries consist of code that's shared across many programs and stored in separate files to save disk space and RAM. The /lib/modules subdirectory contains kernel modules—drivers that can be loaded and unloaded as required. Like /bin and /sbin, /lib is static and theoretically shareable, although it's not shared in practice.

/usr This directory hosts the bulk of a Linux computer's programs. Its contents are shareable and static, so it can be mounted read-only and may be shared with other Linux systems. For these reasons, many administrators split /usr off into a separate partition, although doing so isn't required. Some subdirectories of /usr are similar to their name-sakes in the root directory (such as /usr/bin and /usr/lib), but they contain programs and libraries that aren't absolutely critical to the computer's basic functioning.

/usr/local This directory contains subdirectories that mirror the organization of /usr, such as /usr/local/bin and /usr/local/lib. The /usr/local directory hosts files that a system administrator installs locally—for instance, packages that are compiled on the target computer. The idea is to have an area that's safe from automatic software upgrades when the OS as a whole is upgraded. Immediately after Linux is installed, /usr/local should be empty except for some stub subdirectories. Some system administrators split this off into its own partition to protect it from OS reinstallation procedures that might erase the parent partition.

/usr/share/man This directory stores the manual pages used by the man command. Alternatively, any local manual pages are stored in the /usr/local/share/man directory. The various subdirectories store specific manual page sections. For example, /usr/share/man/man1 and /usr/local/share/man/man1 directories contain the user program (section 1) manual pages.

/usr/X11R6 This directory houses files related to the X Window System (X for short), Linux's GUI environment. Like /usr/local, this directory contains subdirectories similar to those in /usr, such as /usr/X11R6/bin and /usr/X11R6/lib. Although commonly used several years ago, most modern distributions have moved the contents of this directory to others, such as /usr/bin.

/opt This directory is similar to /usr/local in many ways, but it's intended for ready-made packages that don't ship with the OS, such as commercial word processors or games.

Typically, these programs reside in subdirectories in /opt named after themselves, such as /opt/applix. The /opt directory is static and shareable. Some system administrators break it into a separate partition or make it a symbolic link to a subdirectory of /usr/local and make that a separate partition.

/home This directory contains users' data, and it's shareable and variable. Although the /home directory is considered optional in FHS, in practice it's a matter of the *name* being optional. For instance, if you add a new disk to support additional users, you might leave the existing /home directory intact and create a new /home2 directory to house the new users. The /home directory often resides on its own partition.

/root This is the home directory for the root user. Because the root account is so critical and system specific, this variable directory isn't really shareable.

/var This directory contains transient files of various types—system log files, print spool files, mail and news files, and so on. Therefore, the directory's contents are variable. Some subdirectories are shareable, but others are not. Many system administrators put /var in its own partition, particularly on systems that see a lot of activity in /var, like major Usenet news or mail servers.

/tmp Many programs need to create temporary (hence variable) files, and the usual place to do so is in /tmp. Most distributions include routines that clean out this directory periodically and sometimes wipe the directory clean at bootup. The /tmp directory is seldom shared. Some administrators create a separate /tmp partition to prevent runaway processes from causing problems on the root filesystem when processes create too-large temporary files. A similar directory exists as part of the /var directory tree (/var/tmp).

/mnt Linux mounts removable-media devices within its normal directory structure, and /mnt is provided for this purpose. Some (mostly older) distributions create subdirectories within /mnt, such as /mnt/cdrom, to function as mount points. Others use /mnt directly or even use separate mount points off /, such as /cdrom. The FHS mentions only /mnt; it doesn't specify how it's to be used. Specific media mounted in /mnt may be either static or variable. As a general rule, these directories are shareable.

/media This directory is an optional part of the FHS. It's like /mnt, but it should contain subdirectories for specific media types, such as /media/dvd. Many modern distributions use /media subdirectories as the default mount points for common removable disk types, often creating subdirectories on the fly.

/dev Because Linux treats most hardware devices as if they were files, the OS must have a location in its filesystem where these device files reside. The /dev directory is that place. It contains a large number of files that function as hardware interfaces. If a user has sufficient privileges, that user may access the device hardware by reading from and writing to the associated device file. The Linux kernel supports a device filesystem that enables /dev to be an automatically created *virtual filesystem*—the kernel and support tools create /dev entries on the fly to accommodate the needs of specific drivers. Most distributions now use this facility.

/proc   This is an unusual directory because it doesn't correspond to a regular directory or partition. Instead, it's a virtual filesystem that's created dynamically by Linux to provide access to certain types of hardware information that aren't accessible via /dev. For instance, if you type **cat /proc/cpuinfo**, the system responds by displaying information about your CPU—its model name, speed, and so on.

Knowledge of these directories and their purposes is invaluable in properly administering a Linux system. For instance, understanding the purpose of directories like /bin, /sbin, /usr/bin, /usr/local/bin, and others will help you when it comes time to install a new program. Placing a program in the wrong location can cause problems at a later date. For example, if you put a binary file in /bin when it should go in /usr/local/bin, that program may later be overwritten or deleted during a system upgrade when leaving it intact would have been more appropriate.

It is also useful to know what directories should be on their own partition. The recommended list of directories is as follows:

    /boot

    /home

    /opt

    /tmp

    /usr

    /usr/local

    /var

In addition, it is vital to know what directories should *not* be on their own partitions. These directories could cause a system to hang, or worse, if kept on a partition separate from the root filesystem:

    /bin

    /dev

    /etc

    /lib

    /sbin

WARNING   Some Linux distributions deviate from the FHS. These deviations may be major or minor. For example, a distribution may place all of the binaries in /usr/bin and /usr/sbin and set the /bin directory to be a symbolic link to /usr/bin and /sbin to be a symbolic link to /usr/sbin.

Employing Tools to Locate Files

You use file-location commands to locate a file on your computer. Most frequently, these commands help you locate a file by name, but sometimes you can use other criteria, such as modification date. These commands can search a directory tree (including root, which scans the entire system) for a file matching the specified criteria in any subdirectory.

Using the *find* Command

The find utility implements a brute-force approach to finding files. This program finds files by searching through the specified directory tree, checking filenames, file creation dates, and so on to locate the files that match the specified criteria. Because of this method of operation, find tends to be slow; but it's very flexible and is very likely to succeed, assuming the file for which you're searching exists. The find syntax is as follows:

find [*path...*] [*expression...*]

You can specify one or more paths in which find should operate. The program will restrict its operations to these paths. The *expression* option is a way of specifying what you want to find. The man page for find includes a great deal of information about various expressions. Some expressions that enable you to search by assorted common criteria are listed here:

Search by Filename   You can search for a filename using the -name *pattern* expression. Doing so finds files that match the pattern specified by *pattern*. If *pattern* is an ordinary filename, find matches that name exactly. You can use wildcards if you enclose *pattern* in quotes, and find will locate files that match the wildcard filename.

Search by Permission Mode   If you need to find files that have certain permissions, you can do so by using the -perm *mode* expression. The *mode* option may be expressed either symbolically or in octal form. If you precede *mode* with a +, find locates files in which *any* of the specified permission bits are set. If you precede *mode* with a -, find locates files in which all of the specified permission bits are set.

Search by File Size   You can search for a file of a given size with the -size *n* expression. Normally, *n* is specified in 512-byte blocks, but you can modify this by trailing the value with a letter code, such as c for bytes or k for kilobytes.

Search by Group   The -gid *GID* expression searches for files whose group ID (GID) is set to *GID*. The -group *name* option locates files whose group name is *name*. The former can be handy if the GID has been orphaned and has no name, but the latter is generally easier to use.

Search by User ID   The -uid *UID* expression searches for files owned by the user whose user ID (UID) is *UID*. The -user *name* option searches for files owned by *name*. Searching by UID is useful if the UID has been orphaned and has no name, but searching by user-name is generally easier.

Restrict Search Depth   If you want to search a directory and, perhaps, some limited number of subdirectories, you can use the -maxdepth *levels* expression to limit the search.

There are many variants and additional options; find is a very powerful command. As an example of its use, consider the task of finding all C source code files, which normally have names that end in the .c filename extension. To search all of the system's directories (/), you might issue the following command:

```
# find / -name *.c
/usr/share/gettext/intl/finddomain.c
/usr/share/gettext/intl/log.c
/usr/share/gettext/intl/tsearch.c
/usr/share/gettext/intl/langprefs.c
[…]
/usr/share/doc/libpng-1.2.49/example.c
/usr/share/doc/obex-data-server-0.4.3/ods-dbus-test.c
/usr/share/doc/rtkit-0.5/rtkit.c
#
```

The result will be a listing of all the files that match the search criteria. So many files were found in this search that the listing had to be snipped!

> Ordinary users may use find, but it doesn't overcome Linux's file permission features. If you lack permission to list a directory's contents, find will return that directory name and the error message Permission denied.

Using the *locate* Command

The locate utility works much like find if you want to find a file by name, but it differs in two important ways:

- The locate tool is far less sophisticated in its search options. You normally use it to search only for filenames. The program returns all files that contain the specified string. For instance, when searching for rpm, locate will return other programs, like gnorpm and rpm2cpio.

- The locate program works from a database that it maintains. Most distributions include a cron job that calls utilities to update the locate database. This job runs periodically, such as once a night or once a week. For this reason, locate may not find recent files, or it may return the names of files that no longer exist. However, you can use the updatedb command, which is configured via the /etc/updatedb.conf file, to do this task at any time. Keep in mind, if the database-update utilities omit certain directories, files in those directories won't be returned by a locate query.

Because locate works from a database, it's typically much faster than find, particularly on system-wide searches. It's likely to return many false alarms, though, especially if you want to find a file with a short name. To use it, type **locate *search-string***, where *search-string* is the string that appears in the filename.

> Some Linux distributions use slocate rather than locate. The slocate program includes security features to prevent users from seeing the names of files in directories they shouldn't be able to access. On most systems that use slocate, the locate command is a link to slocate, so locate implements slocate's security features. A few distributions don't install either locate or slocate by default.

Using the *whereis* Command

The whereis program searches for files in a restricted set of locations, such as standard binary file directories, library directories, and man page directories. This tool does *not* search user directories or many other locations that are easily searched by find or locate. The whereis utility is a quick way to find program executables and related files like documentation or configuration files.

The whereis program returns filenames that begin with whatever you type as a search criterion, even if those filenames contain extensions. This feature often turns up configuration files in /etc, man pages, and similar files. To use the program, type the name of the program you want to locate. For instance, the following command locates ls files:

```
$ whereis ls
ls: /bin/ls /usr/share/man/man1p/ls.1p.gz /usr/share/man/man1/ls.1.gz
$
```

The result shows both the ls executable (/bin/ls) and ls's man pages. The whereis program accepts several parameters that modify its behavior in various ways. These are detailed in the program's man page.

Using the *which* Command

Considered a search command, which is very weak; it merely searches your path for the command that you type and lists the complete path to the *first* match it finds. It's useful if you need to know the complete path for some reason. For instance, you might want to know where the xterm program is located:

```
$ which xterm
/usr/bin/xterm
```

You can search for all matches by adding the -a option. The which command is typically used in scripts to ensure the correct complete path name of a called program.

Using the *type* Command

This command isn't really a search command; instead, it tells you how a command you enter will be interpreted—as a built-in command, an external command, an alias, and so on. For instance, you can use it to identify several common commands:

```
$ type type
type is a shell builtin
$
$ type cat
cat is /bin/cat
$
$ type ls
ls is aliased to 'ls --color'
```

This example identifies type itself as a built-in shell command, cat as a separate program stored in /bin, and ls as an alias for ls --color. You can add several options to modify the command's behavior. For instance, -t shortens the output to builtin, file, alias, or other short identifiers. The -a option provides a complete list; for instance, it provides both the alias expansion and the location of the ultimate executable when provided with an alias name.

In Exercise 4.2, you'll use several methods of locating files.

EXERCISE 4.2

Locating Files

This exercise demonstrates several methods of locating files. You'll locate the startx program. (If your system doesn't have X installed, you can try searching for another program or file, such as pwd or fstab. You may need to change the path passed to find in step 5.) To find a file, follow these steps:

1. Log into the Linux system as a normal user.

2. Launch an xterm from the desktop environment's menu system if you used a GUI login method.

3. Type **locate startx**. The system should display several filenames that include the string startx. This search should take very little time. (A few distributions lack the locate command, so this step won't work on some systems.)

4. Type **whereis startx**. The system responds with the names of a few files that contain the string startx. Note that this list may be slightly different from the list returned by step 3 but that the search proceeds quickly.

5. Type **find /usr -name startx**. This search takes longer and, when run as an ordinary user, most likely returns several Permission denied error messages. It should also return a single line listing the /usr/bin/startx or /usr/X11R6/bin/ startx program file. Note that this command searches only /usr. If you searched /usr/X11R6, the command would take less time; if you searched /, the command would take more time.

6. Type **which startx**. This search completes almost instantaneously, returning the complete filename of the first instance of startx the system finds on its path.

7. Type **type startx**. Again, the search completes very quickly. It should identify startx as an external command stored at /usr/bin/startx, /usr/X11R6/bin/ startx, or possibly some other location.

Summary

File management is basic to being able to administer or use a Linux system. Various commands are useful to both users and administrators for copying, moving, renaming, and otherwise manipulating files and directories. You may also want to set up access controls, both to limit the amount of disk space users may consume and to limit who may access specific files and directories. Finally, Linux provides standards and tools to help you locate files using various criteria.

Exam Essentials

Describe commands used to copy, move, and rename files in Linux.   The cp command copies files, as in **cp first second** to create a copy of first called second. The mv command does double duty as a file-moving and file-renaming command. It works much like cp, but mv moves or renames the file rather than copying it.

Summarize Linux's directory-manipulation commands.   The mkdir command creates a new directory, and rmdir deletes a directory. You can also use many file-manipulation commands, such as mv and rm (with its -r option), on directories.

Explain the difference between hard and symbolic links.   Hard links are duplicate directory entries that both point to the same inode and hence to the same file. Symbolic links are special files that point to another file or directory by name. Hard links must reside on a single filesystem, but symbolic links may point across filesystems.

Summarize the common Linux archiving programs.   The tar and cpio programs are both file-based archiving tools that create archives of files using ordinary file access commands. The dd program is a file-copy program; however, when it's fed a partition device file, it copies the entire partition on a very low-level basis, which is useful for creating low-level image backups of Linux or non-Linux filesystems.

Explain the differences between compression utilities.   The gzip, bzip2, and xz utilities are compression tools, which reduce a file's size via compression algorithms. They are often used in conjunction with the tar command. The gzip utility is the oldest compression tool and provides the least compression. The bzip2 utility provides slightly improved file compression. The xz utility is the newest tool, provides the best compression, and is very popular.

Describe Linux's file ownership system.   Every file has an owner and a group, identified by number. File permissions can be assigned independently to the file's owner, the file's group, and to all other users.

Explain Linux's file permissions system.   Linux provides independent read, write, and execute permissions for the file's owner, the file's group, and all other users, resulting in nine main permission bits. Special permission bits are also available, enabling you to launch program files with modified account features or alter the rules Linux uses to control who may delete files.

Summarize the commands Linux uses to modify permissions.   The chmod command is Linux's main tool for setting permissions. You can specify permissions using either an octal (base 8) mode or a symbolic notation. The chown and chgrp commands enable you to change the file's owner and group, respectively. (The chown command can do both but can be run only by root.)

Describe the prerequisites of using Linux's disk quota system.   Linux's disk quota system requires support in the Linux kernel for the filesystem on which quotas are to be used. You must also run the quotaon command, typically from a startup script, to enable this feature.

Explain how quotas are set.   You can edit quotas for an individual user via the edquota command, as in **edquota larry** to edit larry's quotas. This command opens an editor on a text file that describes the user's quotas. You can change this description, save the file, and exit from the editor to change the user's quotas.

Summarize how Linux's standard directories are structured.   Linux's directory tree begins with the root (/) directory, which holds mostly other directories. Specific directories may hold specific types of information, such as user files in /home and configuration files in /etc. Some of these directories and their subdirectories may be separate partitions, which helps isolate data in the event of filesystem corruption.

Describe the major file-location commands in Linux.   The find command locates files by brute force, searching through the directory tree for files that match the criteria you specify. The locate (or slocate) command searches a database of files in publicly accessible directories. The whereis command searches a handful of important directories, and which searches the path. The type command identifies another command as a built-in shell command, a shell alias, or an external command (including the path to that command).

Review Questions

1. Why might you type **touch** *filename?*

   A. To move *filename* to the current directory

   B. To ensure that *filename*'s time stamp holds the current time

   C. To convert filename from DOS-style to Unix-style end-of-line characters

   D. To test the validity of *filename*'s disk structures

   E. To write cached data relating to filename to the disk

2. What parameter can you pass to ln to create a soft link? (Select two.)

   A. -s

   B. --soft

   C. --slink

   D. --symbolic

   E. --sl

3. You want to discover the sizes of several dot files in a directory. Which of the following commands might you use to do this?

   A. **ls -la**

   B. **ls -p**

   C. **ls -R**

   D. **ls -d**

   E. **ls -F**

4. You want to move a file from your hard disk to a USB flash drive. Which of the following is true?

   A. You'll have to use the --preserve option to mv to keep ownership and permissions set correctly.

   B. The mv command will adjust filesystem pointers without physically rewriting data if the flash drive uses the same filesystem type as the hard disk partition.

   C. You must use the same filesystem type on both media to preserve ownership and permissions.

   D. The mv command will delete the file on the hard disk after copying it to the flash drive.

   E. You must use the FAT filesystem on the USB flash drive; Linux-native filesystems won't work on removable disks.

5. You type **mkdir one/two/three** and receive an error message that reads, in part, No such file or directory. What can you do to overcome this problem? (Select two.)

   A. Add the --parents parameter to the mkdir command.

   B. Issue three separate mkdir commands: **mkdir one**, then **mkdir one/two**, and then **mkdir one/two/three**.

    C. Type **touch /bin/mkdir** to be sure the mkdir program file exists.

    D. Type **rmdir one** to clear away the interfering base of the desired new directory tree.

    E. Type **mktree one/two/three** instead of **mkdir one/two/three**.

6. Which of the following commands are commonly used to create archive files? (Select two.)

    A. restore

    B. vi

    C. tape

    D. cpio

    E. tar

7. You've received a tar archive called data79.tar from a colleague, but you want to check the names of the files it contains before extracting them. Which of the following commands would you use to do this?

    A. **tar uvf data79.tar**

    B. **tar cvf data79.tar**

    C. **tar xvf data79.tar**

    D. **tar rvf data79.tar**

    E. **tar tvf data79.tar**

8. You want to create a link from your home directory on your hard disk to a directory on a DVD drive. Which of the following link types might you use?

    A. Only a symbolic link

    B. Only a hard link

    C. Either a symbolic or a hard link

    D. Only a hard link, and then only if both directories use the same low-level filesystem

    E. None of the above; such links aren't possible under Linux

9. What command would you type (as root) to change the ownership of somefile.txt from ralph to tony?

    A. **chown ralph:tony somefile.txt**

    B. **chmod somefile.txt tony**

    C. **chown somefile.txt tony**

    D. **chmod tony:ralph somefile.txt**

    E. **chown tony somefile.txt**

10. Typing **ls -ld wonderjaye** reveals a symbolic file mode of drwxr-xr-x. Which of the following are true? (Select two.)

    A. wonderjaye is a symbolic link.

    B. wonderjaye is an executable program.

    C. wonderjaye is a directory.

    D. wonderjaye has its SUID bit set.

    E. wonderjaye may be read by all users of the system.

11. When should programs be configured SUID root?

    A. At all times. This permission is required for executable programs.

    B. Whenever a program should be able to access a device file.

    C. Only when they require root privileges to do their job.

    D. Never. This permission is a severe security risk

    E. Whenever the program file is owned by the root user.

12. Which of the following commands would you type to enable world read access to the file myfile.txt? (Assume that you're the owner of myfile.txt.)

    A. `chmod 741 myfile.txt`

    B. `chmod 0640 myfile.txt`

    C. `chmod u+r myfile.txt`

    D. `chmod a-r myfile.txt`

    E. `chmod o+r myfile.txt`

13. Which of the following umask values will result in files with rw-r----- permissions?

    A. 640

    B. 210

    C. 022

    D. 027

    E. 138

14. You see the usrquota and grpquota options in the /etc/fstab entry for a filesystem. What is the consequence of these entries?

    A. Quota support will be available if it's compiled into the kernel; it will be automatically activated when you mount the filesystem.

    B. User quotas will be available, but the grpquota option is invalid and will be ignored.

    C. Quota support will be disabled on the filesystem in question.

    D. Nothing. These options are malformed and so will have no effect.

    E. Quota support will be available if it's compiled into your kernel, but you must activate it with the quotaon command.

15. Which of the following commands can be used to summarize the quota information about all filesystems?

    A. `repquota`

    B. `repquota -a`

    C. `quotacheck`

    D. `quotacheck -a`

    E. `edquota -a`

16. You've installed a commercial spreadsheet program called WonderCalc on a workstation. In which of the following directories are you *most* likely to find the program executable file?

   A. `/usr/sbin`

   B. `/etc/X11`

   C. `/boot`

   D. `/opt/wcalc/bin`

   E. `/sbin/wcalc`

17. Which of the following file-location commands is likely to take the *most* time to find a file that may be located anywhere on the computer (assuming the operation succeeds)?

   A. The `find` command.

   B. The `locate` command.

   C. The `whereis` command.

   D. The `type` command.

   E. They're all equal in speed.

18. What can the `type` command do that `whereis` can't?

   A. Identify the command as being for *x*86 or *x*86-64 CPUs

   B. Locate commands based on their intended purpose, not just by name

   C. Identify a command as an alias, internal command, or external command

   D. Assist in typing a command by finishing typing it for you

   E. Identify a command as being a binary or a script

19. You want to track down all of the files in `/home` that are owned by karen. Which of the following commands will do the job?

   A. `find /home -uid karen`

   B. `find /home -user karen`

   C. `locate /home -username karen`

   D. `locate /home Karen`

   E. `find /home -name Karen`

20. What can you conclude from the following interaction?

```
$ which man
/usr/bin/man
```

   A. The only file called man on the computer is in `/usr/bin`.

   B. The `/usr/bin/man` program was installed by system package tools.

   C. The `/usr/bin/man` program will be run by any user who types **man**.

   D. The first instance of the man program, in path search order, is in `/usr/bin`.

   E. The user man owns the `/usr/bin/man` program file.

Chapter

5

Booting Linux and Editing Files

THE FOLLOWING EXAM OBJECTIVES ARE COVERED IN THIS CHAPTER:

✓ **101.2: Boot the system.**

✓ **101.3: Change runlevels and shutdown or reboot system.**

✓ **102.2: Install a boot manager.**

✓ **103.8: Perform basic file editing operations using vi.**

So far, this book has dealt largely with a running Linux system, but from time to time you'll need to boot Linux. Ordinarily, this process is a painless one: you press the power button, wait a couple of minutes, and see a Linux login prompt. Sometimes, though, you'll have to intervene in this process in one way or another.

The Linux boot process can be configured to boot Linux with particular options and even to boot other operating systems, so knowing how to configure the boot process can help you accomplish your boot-related goals. Once the system is booted, you should know how to study log files related to the boot process. This can help you diagnose problems or verify that the system is operating the way that it should.

Finally, this chapter looks at editing files with vi. While vi isn't particularly boot related, knowing how to edit files is vital to many administrative tasks, including editing the boot loader configuration files.

Installing Boot Loaders

The computer's boot process begins with a program called a *boot loader*. This program runs before any OS has loaded, although you normally install and configure it from within Linux (or some other OS). Boot loaders work in particular ways that depend on both the firmware you use and the OS you're booting. Understanding your boot loader's principles is necessary in order to configure them properly, so before delving into the details of specific boot loaders, we describe these boot loader principles.

In Linux, the most-used boot loader is the Grand Unified Boot Loader (GRUB), which is available in two versions: GRUB Legacy (with version numbers up to 0.97) and GRUB 2 (with version numbers from 1.9x to 2.x, with 2.00 being the latest version as we write). There is also an older Linux boot loader, the Linux Loader (LILO), which you may run into in older Linux systems. An assortment of alternative boot loaders is also available, though, and in some cases you may need to use one of them, so we provide a brief rundown of these less common boot loaders.

This chapter describes boot loaders for *x86* and *x86-64* computers. Other platforms have their own boot loaders. Some of these are similar to certain *x86/x86-64* boot loaders, but they aren't quite identical. You should consult platform-specific documentation if you need to reconfigure a non-*x86* boot loader.

Boot Loader Principles

In one way or another, your computer's firmware reads the boot loader into memory from the hard disk and executes it. The boot loader, in turn, is responsible for loading the Linux kernel into memory and starting it. Therefore, configuring a hard disk (or at least your boot hard disk) isn't complete until the boot loader is configured. Although Linux distributions provide semiautomated methods of configuring a boot loader during system installation, you may need to know more, particularly if you recompile your kernel or need to set up an advanced configuration—say, one to select between several OSs.

Although the exam objectives mention only the Basic Input/Output System (BIOS) firmware, beginning in 2011, the Extensible Firmware Interface (EFI) and its Unified EFI (UEFI) variant have become increasingly important. Thus, we describe the principles upon which both BIOS and EFI computers' boot loaders are based.

BIOS Boot Loader Principles

The BIOS boot process can be a bit convoluted, in part because so many options are available. Figure 5.1 depicts a typical configuration, showing a couple of possible boot paths. In both cases, the boot process begins with the BIOS. As described in Chapter 3, "Configuring Hardware," you tell the BIOS which boot device to use—a hard disk, a USB stick, a CD/DVD drive, or something else. Assuming that you pick a hard disk as the primary boot device (or if higher-priority devices aren't bootable), the BIOS loads code from the Master Boot Record (MBR), which is the first sector on the hard disk. This code is the primary boot loader code. In theory, it could be just about anything, even a complete (if tiny) OS.

FIGURE 5.1   The x86 boot system provides several options for redirecting the boot process, but ultimately an OS kernel is loaded.

In practice, the primary boot loader does one of two things:

- It examines the partition table and locates the partition that's marked as bootable. The primary boot loader then loads the boot sector from that partition and executes it. This boot sector contains a secondary boot loader, which continues the process by locating an OS kernel, loading it, and executing it. This option is depicted by the A arrows in Figure 5.1.

- It locates an OS kernel, loads it, and executes it directly. This approach bypasses the secondary boot loader entirely, as depicted by the B arrow in Figure 5.1.

Traditionally, *x86* systems running DOS or Windows follow path A. Windows systems ship with very simple boot loaders that provide little in the way of options. Later versions of Windows ship with a boot loader that can provide limited redirection in the second stage of the A path.

Linux's most popular BIOS boot loaders, LILO and GRUB, are both much more flexible. They support installation in either the MBR or the boot sector of a boot partition. Thus, you can either keep a Windows-style primary boot loader and direct the system to boot a kernel from a boot sector installation (path A) or bypass this step and load the kernel straight from the MBR (path B). The first option has the advantage that another OS is unlikely to wipe out LILO or GRUB, because it's stored safely in a Linux partition. Windows has a tendency to write its standard MBR boot loader when it's installed, so if you need to reinstall Windows on a dual-boot system, this action will wipe out an MBR-based boot loader. If the boot loader is stored in a Linux partition's boot sector, it will remain intact, although Windows might configure the system to bypass it. To reactivate the Linux boot loader, you must use a tool such as the Windows FDISK to mark the Linux partition as the boot partition.

A drawback of placing LILO or GRUB in a partition's boot sector is that this partition must normally be a primary partition, at least with disks that use the MBR partitioning system. (An exception is if you're using some other boot loader in the MBR or in another partition. If this third-party boot loader can redirect the boot process to a logical partition, this restriction goes away.) For this reason, many people prefer to put LILO or GRUB in the hard disk's MBR.

In the end, both approaches work, and for a Linux-only installation, the advantages and disadvantages of both approaches are very minor. Some distributions don't give you an option at install time. For them, you should review your boot loader configuration and, when you must add a kernel or otherwise change the boot loader, modify the existing configuration rather than try to create a new one.

On disks that use the GUID Partition Table (GPT) partitioning system, GRUB stores part of itself in a special partition, known as the *BIOS boot partition*. On MBR disks, the equivalent code resides in the sectors immediately following the MBR, which are officially unallocated in the MBR scheme.

A Linux boot loader can be installed to a USB flash drive as well as to a hard disk. Even if you don't want to use a flash drive as part of your regular boot process, you may want to create an emergency disk with your regular boot loader. You can then use it to boot Linux if something goes wrong with your regular boot loader installation.

This description provides a somewhat simplified view of boot loaders. Most Linux boot loaders are much more complicated than this. They can redirect the boot process to non-Linux boot sectors and present menus that enable you to boot multiple OSs or multiple Linux kernels. You can chain several boot loaders, including third-party boot loaders such as System Commander or BootMagic. Chaining boot loaders in this way enables you to take advantage of unique features of multiple boot loaders, such as the ability of System Commander to boot several versions of DOS or Windows on a single partition.

Sometimes when discussing BIOS boot loaders you'll hear a reference to the superblock. The superblock isn't really a boot loader concept; rather it's part of the filesystem. The superblock describes basic filesystem features, such as the filesystem's size and status. On BIOS-based computers, the superblock can hold a portion of the boot loader, so damage to it can cause boot problems. The debugfs and dump2efs commands, described in Chapter 3, provide some basic superblock information.

EFI Boot Loader Principles

The BIOS boot process, as just described, was designed in the 1980s, when the space available for a BIOS in the computer's firmware was tiny by today's standards. Thus, the boot process had to be very simple, and a great deal of the complexity had to be pushed into software stored on the hard disk.

The newer EFI firmware is much more complex than the older BIOS, so its boot process can be more sophisticated. Instead of relying on code stored in boot sectors on the hard disk, EFI relies on boot loaders stored as files in a disk partition known as the EFI System Partition (ESP), which uses the File Allocation Table (FAT) filesystem. Under Linux, the ESP is typically mounted at /boot/efi. Boot loaders reside in files with .efi filename extensions stored in subdirectories named after the OS or boot loader name under the EFI subdirectory of the ESP. Thus you might have a boot loader called /boot/efi/EFI/ubuntu/grub.efi or /boot/efi/EFI/suse/elilo.efi.

This configuration lets you store a separate boot loader for each OS that you install on the computer. The EFI firmware includes its own program, a *boot manager*, to help you select which boot loader to launch. The resulting boot path resembles Figure 5.2. In this figure, two boot loaders (loader1.efi and loader2.efi) are available, each of which launches its own OS kernel, located on its own partition.

FIGURE 5.2   The EFI boot process begins the boot redirection from the firmware level and employs files in filesystems rather than boot code hidden in boot sectors.

The exam objectives use the terms *boot loader* and *boot manager* interchangeably, but this book doesn't. A boot loader loads a kernel into memory and transfers control to it, whereas a boot manager presents a menu of boot options. Many programs, including the popular GRUB, combine both functions, which is the reason for the lack of clarity in many sources.

In order to work, the EFI must know about the boot loaders installed on the hard disk's ESP. This is normally done by registering the boot loaders with the firmware, either using a utility built into the firmware's own user interface or using a tool such as Linux's efibootmgr program. Alternatively, most x86-64 EFI implementations will use a boot loader called EFI/boot/bootx64.efi on the ESP as a default if no others are registered. This is the way you boot most removable disks; you store your boot loader using this name on the removable disk's ESP.

The most popular EFI boot loaders for Linux are based on BIOS boot loaders, so they provide functionality not required by EFI boot loaders generally, such as their own boot manager features that provide the ability to chainload to another EFI boot loader. Therefore, the boot process on a multi-OS computer might run a single EFI boot loader, which then chainloads other EFI boot loaders. In fact, this is sometimes a practical necessity because many EFI implementations provide such primitive boot managers that selecting an OS must be done by a separate boot program.

Using GRUB Legacy as the Boot Loader

GRUB is the default boot loader for most Linux distributions; however, GRUB is really two boot loaders: GRUB Legacy and GRUB 2. Although these two boot loaders are similar in many ways, they differ in many important details. GRUB Legacy is, as you might expect, the older of the two boot loaders. It used to be the dominant boot loader for Linux, but it has been eclipsed by GRUB 2. Nonetheless, because the two boot loaders are so similar, we describe GRUB Legacy first and in more detail. The upcoming section "Using GRUB 2 as the Boot Loader" focuses on its differences from GRUB Legacy. In the following pages, we describe how to configure, install, and interact with GRUB Legacy.

Configuring GRUB Legacy

The usual location for GRUB Legacy's configuration file on a BIOS-based computer is /boot/grub/menu.lst. Some distributions (such as Fedora, Red Hat, and Gentoo) use the filename grub.conf rather than menu.lst. The GRUB configuration file is broken into global and per-image sections, each of which has its own options. Before getting into section details, though, you should understand a few GRUB quirks.

 GRUB Legacy officially supports BIOS but not EFI. A heavily patched version, maintained by Fedora, provides support for EFI. If you're using this version of GRUB, its configuration file goes in the same directory on the ESP that houses the GRUB Legacy binary, such as /boot/efi/EFI/redhat for a standard Fedora or Red Hat installation.

GRUB Nomenclature and Quirks

Listing 5.1 shows a sample GRUB configuration file. This file provides definitions to boot several OSs—Fedora on /dev/sda5, Debian on /dev/sda6, and Windows on /dev/sda2. Fedora and Debian share a /boot partition (/dev/sda1), on which the GRUB configuration resides.

Listing 5.1: A sample GRUB configuration file

```
# grub.conf/menu.lst
#
# Global Options:
#
default=0
timeout=15
splashimage=/grub/bootimage.xpm.gz
#
# Kernel Image Options:
#
title Fedora (3.4.1)
   root (hd0,0)
   kernel /vmlinuz-3.4.1 ro root=/dev/sda5 mem=4096M
   initrd /initrd-3.4.1
title Debian (3.4.2-experimental)
   root (hd0,0)
   kernel (hd0,0)/bzImage-3.4.2-experimental ro root=/dev/sda6
#
# Other operating systems
#
title Windows
   rootnoverify (hd0,1)
   chainloader +1
```

GRUB doesn't refer to disk drives by device filename the way that Linux does. GRUB numbers drives, so instead of /dev/hda or /dev/sda, GRUB uses (hd0). Similarly, /dev/hdb or /dev/sdb is likely to be (hd1). GRUB doesn't distinguish between PATA, SATA, SCSI, and USB drives, so on a SCSI-only system, the first SCSI drive is (hd0). On a mixed system, ATA drives normally receive the lower numbers, although this isn't always the case. GRUB Legacy's drive mappings can be found in the /boot/grub/device.map file.

Additionally, GRUB Legacy numbers partitions on a drive starting at 0 instead of the 1 that is used by Linux. GRUB Legacy separates partition numbers from drive numbers with a comma, as in (hd0,0) for the first partition on the first disk (normally Linux's /dev/hda1 or /dev/sda1) or (hd0,4) for the first logical partition on the first disk (normally Linux's /dev/hda5 or /dev/sda5). GRUB Legacy treats USB flash drives just like hard disks, although it relies on the firmware to access these drives, so GRUB Legacy won't boot from a USB flash drive if you're using an older computer that doesn't support this option.

GRUB Legacy defines its own root partition, which can be different from the Linux root partition. GRUB's root partition is the partition in which GRUB's configuration file (menu.lst or grub.conf) resides. Because this file is normally in Linux's /boot/grub/ directory, the GRUB root partition will be the same as Linux's root partition if you do *not* use a separate /boot or /boot/grub partition. If you split off /boot into its own partition, as is fairly common, GRUB's root partition will be the same as Linux's /boot partition. You must keep this difference in mind when referring to files in the GRUB configuration directory.

Essential Global GRUB Legacy Options

GRUB's global section precedes its per-image configurations. Typically, you'll find just a few options in this global section:

Default OS   The default= option tells GRUB which OS to boot. Listing 5.1's default=0 causes the first listed OS to be booted (remember, GRUB indexes from 0). If you want to boot the second listed operating system, use default=1, and so on, through all your OSs.

Timeout   The timeout= option defines how long, in seconds, to wait for user input before booting the default operating system.

Background Graphic   The splashimage= line points to a graphics file that's displayed as the background for the boot process. This line is optional, but most Linux distributions point to an image to spruce up the boot menu. The filename reference is relative to the GRUB root partition, so if /boot is on a separate partition, that portion of the path is omitted. Alternatively, the path may begin with a GRUB device specification, such as (hd0,5), to refer to a file on that partition.

Essential GRUB Legacy Per-Image Options

GRUB Legacy's per-image options are often indented after the first line, but this is a convention, not a requirement, of the file format. The options begin with an identification and continue with options that tell GRUB how to handle the image:

Title   The title line begins a per-image stanza, and it specifies the label to display when the boot loader runs. The GRUB Legacy title option can accept spaces, and it is conventionally moderately descriptive, as shown in Listing 5.1.

GRUB Root   The root option specifies the location of GRUB Legacy's root partition. This is the /boot partition if a separate one exists; otherwise, it's usually the Linux root (/) partition. GRUB *can* reside on a FAT partition, on a USB flash drive, or on certain other OSs' partitions, though, so GRUB's root could conceivably be somewhere more exotic.

Kernel Specification   The kernel setting describes the location of the Linux kernel as well as any kernel options that are to be passed to it. Paths are relative to GRUB Legacy's root partition. As an alternative, you can specify devices using GRUB's syntax, such as kernel (hd0,5)/vmlinuz ro root=/dev/sda5. Note that you pass most kernel options on this line. Some other boot loaders split off kernel options on separate lines, but in GRUB, you incorporate these options onto the kernel line. The ro option tells the kernel to mount its root filesystem read-only (it's later remounted read/write), and the root= option specifies the Linux root filesystem. Because these options are being passed to the kernel, they use Linux-style device identifiers, when necessary, unlike other options in the GRUB configuration file.

Initial RAM Disk   Use the `initrd` option to specify an initial RAM disk, which holds a minimal set of drivers, utilities, and configuration files that the kernel uses to mount its root filesystem before the kernel can fully access the hard disk. Most Linux distributions rely heavily on the initial RAM disk as a way to keep the main kernel file small and to provide tools to the kernel at a point in the boot process before they could be loaded from the hard disk.

Non-Linux Root   The `rootnoverify` option is similar to the `root` option except that GRUB Legacy won't try to access files on this partition. It's used to specify a boot partition for OSs for which GRUB Legacy can't directly load a kernel, such as Windows.

Chainloading   The `chainloader` option tells GRUB Legacy to pass control to another boot loader. Typically, it's passed a +1 option to load the first sector of the target OS's root partition (usually specified with `rootnoverify`) and to hand over execution to this secondary boot loader.

Chainloading as just described works on BIOS computers. If you're using an EFI-enabled version of GRUB Legacy, you can chainload, but you must tell GRUB Legacy to use the ESP (typically by specifying `root (hd0,0)`, although the device identification may differ) and then pass the name of an EFI boot loader file via the `chainloader` option, as in `chainloader /EFI/Microsoft/boot/bootmgfw.efi`.

To add a kernel to GRUB, follow these steps:

1. As root, load the `menu.lst` or `grub.conf` file into a text editor.
2. Copy a working configuration for a Linux kernel.
3. Modify the `title` line to give your new configuration a unique name.
4. Modify the `kernel` line to point to the new kernel. If you need to change any kernel options, do so.
5. If you're adding, deleting, or changing an `initramfs` RAM disk, make appropriate changes to the `initrd` line.
6. If desired, change the global `default` line to point to the new kernel.
7. Save your changes, and exit the text editor.

At this point, GRUB is configured to boot your new kernel. When you reboot, you should see it appear in your menu and you should be able to boot it. If you have problems, boot a working configuration to debug the issue.

Don't eliminate a working configuration for an old kernel until you've determined that your new kernel works correctly.

Installing GRUB Legacy

The command for installing GRUB Legacy on a BIOS-based computer is grub-install. You must specify the boot sector by device name when you install the boot loader. The basic command looks like:

```
# grub-install /dev/sda
```
   or
```
# grub-install '(hd0)'
```

Either command will install GRUB Legacy into the first sector (that is, the MBR) of your first hard drive. In the second example, you need single quotes around the device name. If you want to install GRUB Legacy in the boot sector of a partition rather than in the MBR, you include a partition identifier, as in /dev/sda1 or (hd0,0).

If you're installing Fedora's EFI-enabled version of GRUB Legacy, you should *not* use the grub-install command; instead, copy the grub.efi file to a suitable subdirectory on your ESP, such as /boot/efi/EFI/redhat, and copy grub.conf to the same location. If you install using Fedora's grub-efi RPM file, the grub.efi file should be placed in this location by default. After copying these files, you may need to use efibootmgr to add the boot loader to the EFI's list:

```
# efibootmgr -c -l \\EFI\\redhat\\grub.efi -L GRUB
```

This command adds GRUB Legacy, stored in the ESP's /EFI/redhat directory, to the EFI's boot loader list. You must use doubled-up backslashes (\\) rather than the Linux-style forward slashes (/) as directory separators. Consult the efibootmgr utility's man page for more information.

You do *not* need to reinstall GRUB after making changes to its configuration file. (Such a reinstallation is required for some older boot loaders, though.) You need to install GRUB this way only if you make certain changes to your disk configuration, such as resizing or moving the GRUB root partition, moving your entire installation to a new hard disk, or possibly reinstalling Windows (which tends to wipe out MBR-based boot loaders). In some of these cases, you may need to boot Linux via a backup boot loader, such as GRUB installed to a USB disk.

Interacting with GRUB Legacy

The first screen that the GRUB Legacy boot loader shows you is a list of all of the operating systems that you specified with the title option in your GRUB configuration file. You can wait for the timeout to expire for the default operating system to boot. To select an alternative, use your arrow keys to highlight the operating system that you want to boot. Once your choice is highlighted, press the Enter key to start booting.

Follow these steps when you want to change or pass additional options to your operating system:

1. Use your arrow keys to highlight the operating system that most closely matches what you want to boot.

2. Press the E key to edit this entry. You'll see a new screen listing all of the options for this entry.

3. Use your arrow keys to highlight the kernel option line.

4. Press the E key to edit the kernel options.

5. Edit the `kernel` line to add any options, such as 1 to boot to single-user mode. GRUB Legacy passes the extra option to the kernel.

6. Press the Enter key to complete the edits.

7. Press the B key to start booting.

You can make whatever changes you like in step 5, such as using a different `init` program. You do this by appending **init=/bin/bash** (or whatever program you want to use) to the end of the `kernel` line.

Using GRUB 2 as the Boot Loader

In principle, configuring GRUB 2 is much like configuring GRUB Legacy; however, some important details differ. First, the GRUB 2 configuration file is /boot/grub/grub.cfg. (Some distributions place this file in /boot/grub2, enabling simultaneous installations of GRUB Legacy and GRUB 2.) GRUB 2 adds a number of features, such as support for loadable modules for specific filesystems and modes of operation, which aren't present in GRUB Legacy. (The `insmod` command in the GRUB 2 configuration file loads modules.) GRUB 2 also supports conditional logic statements, enabling loading modules or displaying menu entries only if particular conditions are met.

If you merely want to add or change a single OS entry, you'll find the most important changes are to the per-image options. Listing 5.2 shows GRUB 2 equivalents to the image options shown in Listing 5.1.

Listing 5.2: GRUB 2 image configuration examples

```
#
# Kernel Image Options:
#
menuentry "Fedora (3.4.1)" {
    set root=(hd0,1)
    linux /vmlinuz-3.4.1 ro root=/dev/sda5 mem=4096M
    initrd /initrd-3.4.1
}
menuentry "Debian (3.4.2-experimental)" {
    set root=(hd0,1)
    linux (hd0,1)/bzImage-3.4.2-experimental ro root=/dev/sda6
}
#
# Other operating systems
#
menuentry "Windows" {
    set root=(hd0,2)
    chainloader +1
}
```

Important changes compared to GRUB Legacy include the following:

- The `title` keyword is replaced by `menuentry`.

- The menu title is enclosed in quotation marks.

- An opening curly brace ({) follows the menu title, and each entry ends with a closing curly brace (}).

- The `set` keyword precedes the `root` keyword, and an equal sign (=) separates the `root` keyword from the partition specification.

- The `rootnoverify` keyword has been eliminated; you use `root` instead.

- Partitions are numbered starting from 1 rather than from 0. A similar change in disk numbering is *not* implemented. This change can be very confusing if you're used to GRUB Legacy, but it makes partition-numbering mix-ups when "translating" from Linux-style partition numbering less likely. The most recent versions of GRUB 2 also support a more complex partition identification scheme to specify the partition table type, as in (`hd0,gpt2`) to specify that the second GPT partition should be used or (`hd1,mbr3`) to specify that the third MBR partition should be used.

GRUB 2 makes further changes in that it employs a set of scripts and other tools that help automatically maintain the `/boot/grub/grub.cfg` file. The intent is that system administrators need never explicitly edit this file. Instead, you would edit files in `/etc/grub.d`, and the `/etc/default/grub` file, to change your GRUB 2 configuration. After making such changes, you must explicitly rebuild the `grub.cfg` file, as described shortly.

Files in `/etc/grub.d` control particular GRUB OS probers. These scripts scan the system for particular OSs and kernels and add GRUB entries to `/boot/grub/grub.cfg` to support those OSs. You can add custom kernel entries, such as those shown in Listing 5.2, to the `40_custom` file to support your own locally compiled kernels or unusual OSs that GRUB doesn't automatically detect.

The `/etc/default/grub` file controls the defaults created by the GRUB 2 configuration scripts. For instance, if you want to adjust the timeout, you might change the following line:

```
GRUB_TIMEOUT=10
```

A distribution that's designed to use GRUB 2, such as Ubuntu, will automatically run the configuration scripts after certain actions, such as installing a new kernel with the distribution's package manager.

If you need to make changes to the GRUB 2 configuration file yourself, edit either the `/etc/default/grub` file or the files in the `/etc/grub.d` folder, and then use the `update-grub` or `grub-mkconfig` command (depending on your Linux distribution) to move the changes to the `/boot/grub/grub.cfg` file.

When you run the `update-grub` or `grub-mkconfig` command, it outputs the new `grub.cfg` file to the standard output. If you want to save the changes, you can type **update-grub** or **grub-mkconfig > /boot/grub/grub.cfg**. This command rereads these configuration files and writes a fresh /boot/grub/grub.cfg file. (Some installations use 2 after grub in command names, as in grub2-mkconfig rather than grub-mkconfig.)

WARNING   Don't forget to redirect the output of the update-grub or grub-mkconfig command to the grub.cfg file. By default, those commands send the configuration to the standard output, which won't change the GRUB configuration.

Unlike GRUB Legacy, GRUB 2 is designed to work with both BIOS- and EFI-based computers as well as with a few more-exotic firmware types. When you first install Linux, the installer should set up GRUB correctly, using grub-install in much the same way as described for GRUB Legacy. On EFI-based computers, GRUB 2's version of grub-install should install the GRUB 2 EFI binary file where it belongs, but if you have problems, you may need to use efibootmgr, as described earlier with reference to GRUB Legacy.

Using Alternative Boot Loaders

Although GRUB Legacy and GRUB 2 dominate the Linux boot loader arena today, and are the only boot loaders covered on the exam, there are several other loaders that you may encounter and that deserve mention:

Syslinux   The *Syslinux Project* (www.syslinux.org) is actually a family of BIOS-based boot loaders, each of which is much smaller and more specialized than GRUB Legacy or GRUB 2. The most notable member of this family is ISOLINUX, which is a boot loader for use on optical discs, which have unique boot requirements. The EXTLINUX boot loader is another member of this family; it can boot Linux from an ext2, ext3, or ext4 filesystem.

LILO   The Linux Loader was the most common Linux boot loader in the 1990s. It's primitive and limited by today's standards, and it works only on BIOS-based computers. You can tell if your Linux system uses LILO by the presence of the /etc/lilo.conf configuration file. For more information on LILO go to http://freshmeat.net/projects/lilo/.

The Linux Kernel   Since version 3.3.0, the Linux kernel has incorporated an EFI boot loader for *x*86 and *x*86-64 systems. On an EFI-based computer, this feature enables the kernel to serve as its own boot loader, eliminating the need for a separate tool such as GRUB 2 or ELILO.

rEFIt   This program, hosted at http://refit.sourceforge.net, is technically a boot manager, not a boot loader. It's popular on Intel-based Macs, but some builds of the program can be used on UEFI-based PCs too. It presents an attractive graphical interface, enabling users to select their boot OS using icons rather than a text-based interface. rEFIt appears to have been abandoned; as of this writing, the last update was in 2010.

rEFInd   This program is derived from rEFIt, so as to make it more useful on UEFI-based PCs and to extend its feature set. Like rEFIt, rEFInd is a boot manager, not a boot loader. It's intended to present a list of boot options to users. It's most useful on computers with EFI implementations that provide poor boot managers. It also provides features that are designed to work with the Linux kernel's built-in EFI boot loader in order to simplify the

passing of options required to get the kernel to boot. You can learn more at
www.rodsbooks.com/refind/.

gummiboot   This is an open-source EFI boot manager that's conceptually similar to rEFIt
or rEFInd, but it uses a text-mode interface and fewer options. You can learn more at
http://freedesktop.org/wiki/Software/gummiboot.

Although development of Linux boot loaders for BIOS-based computers has largely
stabilized, with GRUB 2 now dominating this field, EFI boot loader development is quite
dynamic. This is likely to continue to be the case because EFI-based computers are becoming common.

The fact that Microsoft is requiring use of a firmware feature known as *Secure Boot* is
having an impact on Linux boot loaders. With Secure Boot enabled, an EFI-based computer will launch a boot loader only if it's been cryptographically signed with a key whose
counterpart is stored in the computer's firmware. The goal is to make it harder for malware
authors to take over a computer by inserting their programs early in the boot process. The
problem from a Linux perspective is that use of Secure Boot requires the signing of a Linux
boot loader with Microsoft's key (since it's the only one that's guaranteed to be on most
computers), the addition of a distribution-specific or locally generated key to the computer's
firmware, or the disabling of Secure Boot. To date, both Fedora and Ubuntu can use Secure
Boot. You may need to disable Secure Boot or generate your own key to boot an arbitrary
Linux distribution or a custom-built kernel.

 Real World Scenario

Fixing a Damaged Boot Loader Installation

Linux systems sometimes become unbootable because the boot loader has been damaged. You can reinstall GRUB if you can manage to boot your system, but of course this
is a catch-22. Most Linux distributions provide a way to resolve this problem by enabling
you to boot the computer even if the on-disk boot loader isn't working. Try booting the
installation disc you used to install the OS, and look for an option to boot a kernel from
the hard disk. Once the system is booted, you can use grub-install to reinstall GRUB.
Alternatively, the installation disc may provide a recovery option that will help to restore
a broken system automatically or semiautomatically.

If your distribution's install disc isn't helpful, you can try Super GRUB Disk
(www.supergrubdisk.org), which is a bootable disc image with a variety of options to locate
and use the GRUB configuration file on your hard disk. If Super GRUB Disk can find your
GRUB configuration file, you can boot using it and then reinstall GRUB to your hard disk.

If all else fails, you may be able to use GRUB's interactive features to locate and boot a
kernel. Doing so, however, can be frustrating; a single typo can produce a failure to boot.

Understanding the Boot Process

Any time you modify the way that your computer boots, the possibility exists that you won't get the results that you would expect. In these cases, it's useful to know where you can turn for more information about what is happening during startup. The reports that you receive on a particular boot can better guide you, once you understand something about what's *supposed* to happen when a Linux system boots.

Extracting Information about the Boot Process

Certain Linux kernel and module log information is stored in what is called the *kernel ring buffer.* By default, Linux displays messages destined for the kernel ring buffer during the boot process—they're those messages that scroll past too quickly to read. (Some distributions hide most or all of these messages unless you select a special option during the boot process.) You can inspect this information with this command:

```
# dmesg
```

This command generates a lot of output, so you may want to pipe it through the `less` pager or redirect it to a file. Here are some examples of these commands:

```
# dmesg | less
# dmesg > boot.messages
```

Many Linux distributions store the kernel ring buffer to the /var/log/dmesg log file soon after the system boots. Because new information is logged to the kernel ring buffer as the system operates, and because the kernel ring buffer's size is finite, you may need to consult this log file to learn about the boot process once the system has been operating for a while. Also, because the kernel ring buffer is held in memory, its contents are cleared and generated anew with every boot of the computer. The dmesg log file will contain boot messages from several boot sessions.

Another source of logging information is the system logger (`syslogd`). The most useful `syslogd` file to examine is usually /var/log/messages, but /var/log/syslog and other log files in /var/log can also hold helpful information.

Some Linux distributions also log boot-time information to other files. Debian uses a daemon called bootlogd that, by default, logs any messages that go to /dev/console to the /var/log/boot file. Fedora and Red Hat use syslogd services to log information to /var/log/boot.log.

Locating and Interpreting Boot Messages

Boot messages in the kernel ring buffer or /var/log files can be cryptic to the uninitiated. Some tips can help you locate and interpret the information you find in these sources:

Use less and Its Search Functions   The less pager is a great tool for examining both the kernel ring buffer and log files. The search function (accessed by pressing the slash key, /) can help you look for particular strings.

Look for Hardware Type Names   Many boot messages, particularly in the kernel ring buffer, relate to hardware. Try searching for the name of the hardware type, such as SCSI or USB, if you're having problems with these subsystems. Remember that Linux treats many disk devices as SCSI disks too!

Look for Hardware Chipset Names   Linux drivers sometimes log messages along with their driver names, which are usually based on the chipset in question. If you know your hardware well enough to know the chipset name, search for it or for a subset of it. For instance, searching for 8169 may turn up messages related to a RealTek 8169 Ethernet interface. Similarly, you can search for higher-level kernel module names, such as reiserfs for messages from the ReiserFS filesystem driver.

Study the Output from a Working System   Familiarize yourself with the contents of the kernel ring buffer and log files on a working system. If you know what to expect when a system is functioning correctly, you'll find it easier to identify problems when they occur.

Sometimes a system won't boot at all. In this case, kernel boot messages (which ordinarily go into the kernel ring buffer) are displayed on the screen, which can help you identify the cause of a failure. Many modern Linux distributions hide these messages by default, but you can sometimes reveal them by pressing the Esc key during the boot process. Once the kernel boot process has completed, other systems take over, and the last few messages displayed on the screen can also provide clues. For example, if the last message displayed mentions starting a particular server, it's possible that the server is hanging and interrupting the boot process. You may be able to disable the server by using a single-user boot mode and therefore bypass the problem.

The Boot Process

The process of taking an x86 computer from its initial state when the power is turned on to having a working operating system running is complex because of the way modern personal computers have evolved. The steps a computer goes through in order to boot an operating system are as follows:

1.   The system is given power, and a special hardware circuit causes the CPU to look at a predetermined address and execute the code stored in that location. The firmware (BIOS or EFI) resides at this location, so the CPU runs the firmware.

2.   The firmware performs some tasks. These include checking for hardware, configuring hardware, and looking for a boot loader.

3. When the boot loader takes over from the firmware, it loads a kernel or chainloads to another boot loader, as described earlier in this chapter.

4. Once the Linux kernel takes over, it performs tasks such as initializing devices, mounting the root partition, and finally loading and executing the initial program for your system. By default, this is the program /sbin/init. It gets the *process ID* (PID) of 1, because it's the first program to run on the system.

The init program is the key to the Linux system. Just how it works is covered next, in the section "The Initialization Process."

The kernel step can get a bit complicated, especially if your system has advanced hardware. The kernel needs to load drivers to handle the hardware, but those drivers may not be accessible if the hard drive isn't mounted yet. To avoid this situation, most Linux distributions utilize an initramfs file, which contains the necessary modules to access the hardware. The boot loader mounts the initramfs file into memory as a virtual root filesystem during the boot step for the kernel to use. Once the kernel loads the necessary drivers, it unmounts the initramfs filesystem and mounts the real root filesystem from the hard drive.

If you would like more details about the Linux boot process, read:

www.linuxdevcenter.com/pub/a/linux/excerpts/linux_kernel
/how_computer_boots.html.

This page describes the process from the computer being powered up to the kernel being loaded and launching /sbin/init.

The Initialization Process

A Linux system comprises lots of programs running in the background to provide services for the system. It's the init program's job to start all of those programs when the Linux system starts up. This is called the *initialization process.*

You must configure the initialization process to start programs based on the desired features that you want running in your Linux system. For example, a Linux server doesn't necessarily need to start a graphical desktop environment, or a Linux desktop doesn't necessarily need to start the Apache web server service.

There are currently three popular initialization process methods used in Linux distributions:

- Unix System V (also called SysV)
- systemd
- Upstart

The original Linux init program was based on the Unix System V init program, and it became commonly called SysV. The SysV init program uses a series of shell scripts, divided into separate runlevels, to determine what programs run at what times. Each program uses a separate shell script to start and stop the program. The system administrator sets the runlevel in which the Linux system starts, which in turn determines which set of programs is running. The system administrator can also change the runlevel at any time while the system is running.

The SysV init program had served the Linux community well for many years, but as Linux systems became more complicated and required more services, the runlevel shell scripts became more complicated. This has caused Linux developers to look for other solutions.

The Upstart version of the init program was developed as part of the Ubuntu Linux distribution. Its main goal was to handle the dynamic environment that hotplug devices cause in Linux. The Upstart method uses separate configuration files for each service, and each service configuration file sets the runlevel in which the service should start. That way, you have just one service file that's used for multiple runlevels.

The systemd program was developed by the Red Hat Linux distribution to handle dynamic Linux environments as well. Similar to Upstart, it too uses separate configuration files to define program behavior.

The following sections take a closer look at each of these initialization process methods to help you get comfortable in any Linux environment.

Using the SysV Initialization Process

The key to the SysV initialization process is runlevels. The init program determines what services to start based on the runlevel of the system. Runlevels are numbered from 0 to 6, and each one is assigned a set of services that should be active for that runlevel. Upon booting, Linux enters a predetermined runlevel, which you can set. Knowing what these functions are, and how to manage runlevels, is important if you're to control the Linux boot process and ongoing operations. To this end, you must understand the purpose of runlevels, be able to identify the services that are active in a runlevel, be able to adjust those services, be able to check your default and current runlevels, and be able to change the default and current runlevels.

Runlevel Functions

Earlier in this chapter, we described single-user mode. To get to this mode when booting Linux, you use 1, S or s, or single as an option passed to the kernel by the boot loader. Single-user mode is simply an available runlevel for your system. The available runlevels on most systems are the numbers 0 through 6. The S and s are synonymous with runlevel 1 as far as many utilities are concerned.

Runlevels 0, 1, and 6 are reserved for special purposes; the remaining runlevels are available for whatever purposes you or your Linux distribution provider decide. Table 5.1 summarizes the conventional uses of the runlevels. Other assignments—and even runlevels outside the range of 0 to 6—are possible with some systems, but such configurations are rare. If you run into peculiar runlevel numbers, consult /etc/inittab—it defines them and often contains comments explaining the various runlevels.

TABLE 5.1   Runlevels and their purposes

Runlevel	Purpose
0	A transitional runlevel, meaning that it's used to shift the computer from one state to another. Specifically, it shuts down the system. On modern hardware, the computer should completely power down. If not, you're expected to either reboot the computer manually or power it off.
1, s, or S	Single-user mode. What services, if any, are started at this runlevel vary by distribution. It's typically used for low-level system maintenance that may be impaired by normal system operation, such as resizing partitions.
2	On Debian and its derivatives, a full multi-user mode with X running and a graphical login. Most other distributions leave this runlevel undefined.
3	On Fedora, Mandriva, Red Hat, and most other distributions, a full multi-user mode with a console (nongraphical) login screen.
4	Usually undefined by default and therefore available for customization.
5	On Fedora, Mandriva, Red Hat, and most other distributions, the same behavior as runlevel 3, with the addition of having X run with an XDM (graphical) login.
6	Used to reboot the system. This runlevel is also a transitional runlevel. Your system is completely shut down, and then the computer reboots automatically.

WARNING   Don't configure your default runlevel to 0 or 6. If you do, your system will immediately shut down or reboot once it finishes powering up. Runlevel 1 could conceivably be used as a default, but chances are you'll want to use 2, 3, or 5 as your default runlevel, depending on your distribution and use for the system.

As a general rule, distributions have been drifting toward Red Hat's runlevel set; however, there are some exceptions and holdouts, such as Debian. Distributions that use newer startup systems generally don't use runlevels natively, but they provide compatibility tools that make the computer appear to use runlevels for the benefit of scripts and programs that assume the use of runlevels.

Identifying the Services in a Runlevel

There are two main ways to affect what programs run when you enter a new SysV runlevel. The first is to add or delete entries in your /etc/inittab file. A typical /etc/inittab file contains many entries, and except for a couple of special cases, inspecting or changing the contents of this file is best left to experts. Once all of the entries in /etc/inittab for your runlevel are executed, your boot process is complete and you can log in.

Basics of the */etc/inittab* File

Entries in /etc/inittab follow a simple format. Each line consists of four colon-delimited fields:

```
id:runlevels:action:process
```

Each of these fields has a specific meaning:

Identification Code   The *id* field consists of a sequence of one to four characters that identifies its function.

Applicable Runlevels   The *runlevels* field consists of a list of runlevels for which this entry applies. For instance, 345 means the entry is applicable to runlevels 3, 4, and 5.

Action to Be Taken   Specific codes in the *action* field tell init how to treat the process. For instance, wait tells init to start the process once when entering a runlevel and to wait for the process's termination, and respawn tells init to restart the process whenever it terminates (which is great for login processes). Several other actions are available; consult the man page for inittab for details.

Process to Run   The *process* field is the process to run for this entry, including any options and arguments that are required.

The part of /etc/inittab that tells init how to handle each runlevel looks like this:

```
l0:0:wait:/etc/init.d/rc 0
l1:1:wait:/etc/init.d/rc 1
l2:2:wait:/etc/init.d/rc 2
l3:3:wait:/etc/init.d/rc 3
l4:4:wait:/etc/init.d/rc 4
l5:5:wait:/etc/init.d/rc 5
l6:6:wait:/etc/init.d/rc 6
```

These lines start with codes that begin with an l (a lowercase letter *L*, not a number 1) followed by the runlevel number—for instance, l0 for runlevel 0, l1 for runlevel 1, and so on. These lines specify scripts or programs that are to be run when the specified runlevel is entered. In the case of this example, all the scripts are the same (/etc/init.d/rc), but the script is passed the runlevel number as an argument. Some distributions call specific programs for certain runlevels, such as shutdown for runlevel 0.

> The upcoming section "Checking and Changing Your Default Runlevel" describes how to tell init what runlevel to enter when the system boots.

The SysV Startup Scripts

The /etc/init.d/rc or /etc/rc.d/rc script performs the crucial task of running all of the scripts associated with the runlevel. The runlevel-specific scripts are stored in /etc/rc.d /rc?.d, /etc/init.d/rc?.d, /etc/rc?.d, or a similar location. (The precise location varies between distributions.) In all of these cases, ? is the runlevel number. When entering a runlevel, rc passes the start parameter to all of the scripts with names that begin with a capital S, and it passes the stop parameter to all of the scripts with names that begin with a capital K. These SysV startup scripts start or stop services depending on the parameter they're passed, so the naming of the scripts controls whether they're started or stopped when a runlevel is entered. These scripts are also numbered, as in S10network and K35smb.

The rc program runs the scripts in numeric order. This feature enables distribution designers to control the order in which scripts run by giving them appropriate numbers. This control is important because some services depend on others. For instance, network servers must normally be started after the network is brought up.

In reality, the files in the SysV runlevel directories are symbolic links to the main scripts, which are typically stored in /etc/rc.d, /etc/init.d, or /etc/rc.d/init.d (again, the exact location depends on the distribution). These original SysV startup scripts have names that lack the leading S or K and number, as in smb instead of K35smb.

> You can also start services by hand. Run them with the start option, as in /etc/init.d/smb start to start the smb (Samba) server. Other useful options are stop, restart, and status. Most scripts support all of these options.

To determine which services are active in a runlevel, search the appropriate SysV startup script directory for scripts with filenames that begin with an S. Alternatively, you can use a runlevel management tool, as described next.

Managing Runlevel Services

The SysV startup scripts in the runlevel directories are symbolic links back to the original script. This is done so that you don't need to copy the same script into each runlevel directory. Instead, you can modify the original script without having to track down its copies in all of the SysV runlevel directories. You can also modify which programs are active in a runlevel by editing the link filenames. Numerous utility programs are available to help you manage these links, such as chkconfig, update-rc.d, and rc-update. We describe the first of these tools because it's supported on many distributions. If your distribution doesn't support these tools, you should check the specific distribution documentation. These tools may provide impaired functionality on systems that don't use SysV natively; you may need to locate Upstart- or systemd-specific tools instead.

To list the services and their applicable runlevels with chkconfig, use the --list option. The output looks something like this, but it is likely to be much longer:

```
# chkconfig --list
pcmcia          0:off   1:off   2:on    3:on    4:on    5:on    6:off
nfs-common      0:off   1:off   2:off   3:on    4:on    5:on    6:off
xprint          0:off   1:off   2:off   3:on    4:on    5:on    6:off
setserial       0:off   1:off   2:off   3:off   4:off   5:off   6:off
```

This output shows the status of the services in all seven runlevels. For instance, you can see that nfs-common is inactive in runlevels 0–2, active in runlevels 3–5, and inactive in runlevel 6.

If you're interested in a specific service, you can specify its name:

```
# chkconfig --list nfs-common
nfs-common      0:off   1:off   2:off   3:on    4:on    5:on    6:off
```

To modify the runlevels in which a service runs, use a command like this:

```
# chkconfig --level 23 nfs-common on
```

The previous example is for Debian-based systems. On Red Hat and similar systems, you would probably want to target runlevels 3, 4, and 5 with something like --level 345 rather than --level 23.

You can use on to activate the script, off to deactivate it, or reset to set it to its default value.

If you've added a startup script to the main SysV startup script directory, you can have chkconfig register it and add appropriate start and stop links in the runlevel directories. When you do this, chkconfig inspects the script for special comments to indicate default runlevels. If these comments are in the file and you're happy with the suggested levels, you can add it to these runlevels with a command like this:

```
# chkconfig --add nfs-common
```

This command adds the nfs-common script to those managed by chkconfig. You would, of course, change nfs-common to your script's name. This approach may not work if the script lacks the necessary comment lines with runlevel sequence numbers for chkconfig's benefit.

Checking Your Runlevel

Sometimes it's necessary to check your current runlevel. Typically, you'll do this prior to changing the runlevel or to check the status if something isn't working correctly. Two different runlevel checks are possible: checking your default runlevel and checking your current runlevel.

Checking and Changing Your Default Runlevel

On a SysV-based system, you can determine your default runlevel by inspecting the /etc /inittab file with the less command or opening it in an editor. Alternatively, you may use the grep command to look for the line specifying the initdefault action. On a Debian system, you'll see something like this:

```
# grep :initdefault: /etc/inittab
id:2:initdefault:
```

If grep returns nothing, chances are that you've either mistyped the command or your computer is using Upstart, systemd, or some other initialization tool. On some systems, the second colon-delimited field will contain a 3, 5, or some value other than the 2 shown here.

You may notice that the id line doesn't define a process to run. In the case of the initdefault action, the process field is ignored.

If you want to change the default runlevel for the next time you boot your system, edit the initdefault line in /etc/inittab and change the runlevel field to the value you want. If your system lacks an /etc/inittab file, create one that contains *only* an initdefault line that specifies the runlevel you want to enter by default.

Determining Your Current Runlevel

If your system is up and running, you can determine your runlevel information with the runlevel command:

```
# runlevel
N 2
```

The first character is the previous runlevel. When the character is N, this means the system hasn't switched runlevels since booting. It's possible to switch to different runlevels on a running system with the init and telinit programs, as described next. The second character in the runlevel output is your current runlevel.

Changing Runlevels on a Running System

Sometimes you may want to change runlevels on a running system. You might do this to get more services, such as going from a console to a graphical login runlevel, or to shut down or reboot your computer. This can be accomplished with the init (or telinit), shutdown, halt, reboot, and poweroff commands.

Changing Runlevels with *init* or *telinit*

The `init` process is the first process run by the Linux kernel, but you can also use it to have the system reread the `/etc/inittab` file and implement the changes it finds there or to change to a new runlevel. The simplest case is to have it change to the runlevel you specify. For instance, to change to runlevel 1 (the runlevel reserved for single-user or maintenance mode), you would type this command:

```
# init 1
```

To reboot the system, you can use `init` to change to runlevel 6 (the runlevel reserved for reboots) by entering:

```
# init 6
```

A variant of `init` is `telinit`. Just like `init`, this program can take a runlevel number to change to that runlevel, but it can also take the Q or q option to have the tool reread `/etc/inittab` and implement any changes it finds there. Thus, if you've made a change to the runlevel in `/etc/inittab`, you can immediately implement that change by typing **telinit q**.

 The man pages for these commands indicate slightly different syntaxes, but `telinit` is sometimes a symbolic link to `init` and, in practice, `init` responds just like `telinit` to the Q and q options.

Changing Runlevels with *shutdown*

Although you can shut down or reboot the computer with `init`, doing so has some problems. One issue is that it's simply an unintuitive command for this action. Another is that changing runlevels with `init` causes an immediate change to the new runlevel. This may cause other users on your system some aggravation because they'll be given no warning about the shutdown. It's therefore better to use the `shutdown` command in a multi-user environment when you want to reboot, shut down, or switch to single-user mode. This command supports extra options that make it friendlier in such environments.

The shutdown program sends a message to all users who are logged into your system and prevents other users from logging in during the process of changing runlevels. The `shutdown` command also lets you specify when to effect the runlevel change so that users have time to exit editors and safely stop other processes that they may have running.

When the time to change runlevels is reached, `shutdown` signals the `init` process for you. In the simplest form, `shutdown` is invoked with a time argument like this:

```
# shutdown now
```

This changes the system to runlevel 1, the single-user or maintenance mode. The now parameter causes the change to occur immediately. Other possible time formats include *hh:mm*, for a time in 24-hour clock format (such as 6:00 for 6:00 a.m. or 13:30 for 1:30 p.m.), and +*m* for a time *m* minutes in the future.

You can add extra parameters to specify that you want to reboot or halt (that is, power off) the computer. Specifically, -r reboots the system, -H halts it (terminates operation but doesn't power it off), and -P powers it off. The -h option may halt or power off the computer, but usually it powers it off. For instance, you can type **shutdown -r +10** to reboot the system in 10 minutes.

To give people some warning about the impending shutdown, you can add a message to the end of the command:

```
# shutdown -h +15 "system going down for maintenance"
```

If you schedule a shutdown but then change your mind, you can use the -c option to cancel it:

```
# shutdown -c "never mind"
```

Changing Runlevels with the *halt, reboot,* and *poweroff* Commands

Three additional shortcut commands are halt, reboot, and poweroff. (In reality, reboot and poweroff are usually symbolic links to halt. This command behaves differently depending on the name by which it's called.) As you might expect, these commands halt the system (shut it down without powering it off), reboot it, or shut it down and (on hardware that supports this feature) turn off the power, respectively. As with telinit and shutdown, these commands are available in SysV, Upstart, and systemd.

In Exercise 5.1, you'll experiment with some of the methods of changing the runlevels, as just described.

EXERCISE 5.1

Changing Runlevels

This exercise will demonstrate the effects of changing the runlevel in various ways on a working system. Be aware that some of the effects will be different from one system to another, depending on both the distribution and the system-specific configuration of the computer. Also, in the course of running this exercise, you'll reboot the computer, so you shouldn't do it on a system that anybody else is using. To manage your runlevels, follow these steps:

1. Log in as root, or acquire root privileges by using su or sudo with each of the following commands. Use a text-mode or remote login; some of the exercise activities will shut down X.

2. Type **runlevel** to learn your current runlevel. Recall that the first character returned refers to the previous runlevel (N denotes no previous runlevel; it hasn't been changed since the system booted). The second output character is the current runlevel. This is likely to be 2 on Debian or Debian-derived systems and 3 or 5 on Red Hat or Red Hat–derived systems.

3. If your system reports that it's in runlevel 5, type **telinit 3** to switch to runlevel 3. Chances are that your X server will stop working. (Pressing Alt+F7 from a text-mode console will show a blank text-mode screen rather than the X display this keystroke would normally reveal.)

4. If your system initially reported a runlevel of 3, type **telinit 5** to switch to runlevel 5. This will probably start X; however, if X is misconfigured, the screen is likely to blink two or three times and possibly display an error message. If X isn't installed, nothing much will happen, aside from a display about a few services being stopped and started. If X starts, you can get back to your text-mode console by pressing Ctrl+Alt+F1.

5. If your system reported that it was in runlevel 2, you can try other runlevels, such as 3, 4, or 5; however, this isn't likely to have much effect. You can temporarily start or stop X by typing **/etc/init.d/gdm start** or **/etc/init.d/gdm stop**. (You may need to change gdm to xdm, mdm, or kdm.)

6. Return to your original runlevel using telinit, as in **telinit 5**.

7. If your distribution uses /etc/inittab and sets the default runlevel to 5, edit that file and change the default runlevel by changing the number in the line that reads id:*n*:initdefault:. The number, *n*, is likely to be either 3 or 5; change it to the other value. (It's wise to make a backup of /etc/inittab before editing it!) If your distribution doesn't use /etc/inittab or sets a default runlevel of 2, don't make any changes to this file and skip ahead to step 11.

8. Reboot the computer by typing **reboot now** or **shutdown -r now**.

9. Log in as root again, and type **runlevel** to verify that you're running in the runlevel you specified in step 7.

10. Edit /etc/inittab to restore it to its original state, or restore it from its backup.

11. Type **telinit 6**. This enters runlevel 6, which reboots the system. The computer should now be running as it was before you began this exercise.

Using the systemd Initialization Process

The *systemd initialization process* method is quickly gaining in popularity in the Linux world. It's currently the default initialization process used in the Fedora, CentOS, and Red Hat Linux distributions.

The systemd initialization process introduced a major paradigm shift in how Linux systems handle services, which has also caused some controversy in the Linux world. Instead of lots of small initialization shell scripts, the systemd method uses one monolithic program that uses individual configuration files for each service. This is somewhat of a departure from earlier Linux philosophy.

The following sections walk through the basics of how the systemd initialization process works.

Units and Targets

Instead of using shell scripts and runlevels, the systemd method uses *units* and *targets*. A systemd unit defines a service or action on the system. It consists of a name, a type, and a configuration file. There are currently eight different types of systemd units:

- automount
- device
- mount
- path
- service
- snapshot
- socket
- target

The systemd program identifies units by their name and type using the format name .type. You use the systemctl command to list the units currently loaded in your Linux system:

```
# systemctl list-units
UNIT                     LOAD    ACTIVE SUB      DESCRIPTION
...
crond.service            loaded active running  Command Scheduler
cups.service             loaded active running  CUPS Printing Service
dbus.service             loaded active running  D-Bus System Message
...
multi-user.target        loaded active active   Multi-User System
network.target           loaded active active   Network
paths.target             loaded active active   Paths
remote-fs.target         loaded active active   Remote File Systems
slices.target            loaded active active   Slices
sockets.target           loaded active active   Sockets
...
#
```

Linux distributions can have hundreds of different units loaded and active; we just selected a few from the output to show you what they look like. The systemd method uses service-type units to manage the daemons on the Linux system. The target-type units are important in that they group multiple units together so that they can be started at the same time. For example, the network.target unit groups all of the units required to start the network interfaces for the system.

The systemd initialization process uses targets similarly to the way SysV uses runlevels. Each target represents a different group of services that should be running on the system. Instead of changing runlevels to alter what's running on the system, you just change targets.

To make the transition from SysV to systemd smoother, there are targets that mimic the standard 0 through 6 SysV runlevels, called runlevel0.target through runlevel6.target.

Configuring Units

Each unit requires a configuration file that defines what program it starts and how it should start the program. The systemd system stores unit configuration files in the /lib/systemd /system folder.

Here's an example of the sshd.service unit configuration file used in Fedora 20:

```
# cat sshd.service
[Unit]
Description=OpenSSH server daemon
After=syslog.target network.target auditd.service

[Service]
EnvironmentFile=/etc/sysconfig/sshd
ExecStartPre=/usr/sbin/sshd-keygen
ExecStart=/usr/sbin/sshd -D $OPTIONS
ExecReload=/bin/kill -HUP $MAINPID
KillMode=process
Restart=on-failure
RestartSec=42s

[Install]
WantedBy=multi-user.target
#
```

The sshd.service configuration file defines the program to start (/usr/sbin/sshd), along with some other features, such as what services should run before the sshd service starts (the After line), what target level the system should be in (the WantedBy line), and how to reload the program (the Restart line).

Target units also use configuration files. They don't define programs but instead define which service units to start. Here's an example of the graphical.target unit configuration file used in Fedora 20:

```
# cat graphical.target
#  This file is part of systemd.
#
# systemd is free software; you can redistribute it and/or modify it
# under the terms of the GNU Lesser General Public License as published by
#  the Free Software Foundation; either version 2.1 of the License, or
#  (at your option) any later version.
[Unit]
Description=Graphical Interface
Documentation=man:systemd.special(7)
Requires=multi-user.target
After=multi-user.target
Conflicts=rescue.target
Wants=display-manager.service
AllowIsolate=yes

[Install]
Alias=default.target
#
```

The target configuration defines what targets should be loaded first (the After line), what targets are required for this target to start (the Requires line), what targets conflict with this target (the Conflicts line), and what targets or services the target requires to be running (the Wants line).

Setting the Default Target

The default target used when the Linux system boots is defined in the /etc/systemd/system folder as the file default.target. This is the file the systemd program looks for when it starts up. This file is normally set as a link to a standard target file in the /lib/systemd /system folder:

```
# ls -al default.target
lrwxrwxrwx. 1 root root 36 Oct 1 09:14 default.target ->
 /lib/systemd/system/graphical.target
#
```

On this Fedora 20 system, the default target is set to the graphical.target unit.

The *systemctl* Program

In the systemd method, you use the systemctl program to control services and targets. The systemctl program uses options to define what action to take, as shown in Table 5.2.

TABLE 5.2   systemctl commands

systemctl Command Name	Explanation
list-units	Displays the current status of all configured units.
default	Changes to the default target unit.
isolate	Starts the named unit and stops all others.
start *name*	Starts the named unit.
stop *name*	Stops the named unit.
reload *name*	Causes the named unit to reload its configuration file.
restart *name*	Causes the named unit to shut down and restart.
status *name*	Displays the status of the named unit. (You can pass a PID value, rather than a name, if you like.)
enable *name*	Configures the unit to start when the computer next boots.
disable *name*	Configures the unit not to start when the computer next boots.

Instead of using shell scripts to start and stop services, you use the start and stop commands:

```
# systemctl stop sshd.service
# systemctl status sshd.service
sshd.service - OpenSSH server daemon
Loaded: loaded (/usr/lib/systemd/system/sshd.service; disabled)
Active: inactive (dead)
Oct 02 10:33:33 localhost.localdomain systemd[1]: Stopped OpenSSH server
  daemon.

# systemctl start sshd.service
# systemctl status sshd.service
```

```
sshd.service - OpenSSH server daemon
Loaded: loaded (/usr/lib/systemd/system/sshd.service; disabled)
Active: active (running) since Thu 2014-10-02 10:34:08 EDT; 4s ago
Process: 3882
ExecStartPre=/usr/sbin/sshd-keygen (code=exited, status=0/SUCCESS)
Main PID: 3889 (sshd)
CGroup: /system.slice/sshd.service
        3889 /usr/sbin/sshd -D
Oct 02 10:34:08 localhost.localdomain sshd-keygen[3882]: Generating
SSH2 RSA host key: [  OK  ]
Oct 02 10:34:08 localhost.localdomain systemd[1]: Started OpenSSH server daemon.
Oct 02 10:34:08 localhost.localdomain sshd[3889]: Server listening on
 0.0.0.0 port 22.
Oct 02 10:34:08 localhost.localdomain sshd[3889]: Server listening on ::
 port 22.
#
```

To change the target that is currently running, you must use the isolate command. For example, to enter single-user mode you'd use:

```
# systemctl isolate rescue.target
```

To go back to the default target for the system, you just use the default command.

> One of the more controversial features of the systemd initialization process is that it doesn't use the standard Linux syslogd log filesystem. Instead, it has its own log files, and those log files are not stored in text format. To view the systemd log files you need to use the journalctl program.

Using the Upstart Initialization Process

Several modern Linux distributions, including recent versions of Ubuntu, now use an init process called Upstart (http://upstart.ubuntu.com) rather than the venerable SysV startup system. Broadly speaking, Upstart does the same job as the SysV scripts, but Upstart is designed to better handle today's dynamically changing hotplug hardware, which can be connected to and disconnected from a computer while it's still running. Upstart provides SysV compatibility features, so you should be familiar with the SysV methods described earlier; however, it also has its own unique scripts and differs in some important ways. In particular, Upstart does away with /etc/inittab, instead providing an integrated set of startup scripts that can, in principle, completely replace the SysV-style /etc/inittab and runlevel-specific startup scripts. Upstart scripts also support starting or stopping services based on a wider variety of actions than SysV startup scripts; for instance, Upstart can launch a service whenever a particular hardware device is attached.

Using Upstart-Native Methods

A system that uses nothing but Upstart and its native scripts replaces both /etc/inittab and the runlevel-specific SysV startup script directories with scripts in the /etc/init directory. (This directory was called /etc/event.d on earlier versions of Upstart.) You may want to check the contents of this directory on your own Upstart-based system.

Upstart is under heavy development, and its configuration file format is subject to change. Thus, you may find differences from what is described in these pages.

To change the runlevels in which a particular service runs, you'll have to edit its configuration file in a text editor. Locate the script (typically /etc/init/*name*.conf, where *name* is the name of the service), and load it into a text editor. Look for lines that include the text start on and stop on, as in the following example:

```
start on (filesystem
          and started hal
          and tty-device-added KERNEL=tty7
          and (graphics-device-added or stopped udevtrigger))
stop on runlevel [016]
```

Locate any runlevel specification, and adjust it for your needs. For instance, you might change the preceding example's stop on runlevel specification to read stop on runlevel [0126] to include runlevel 2 in the list of runlevels on which the service is to be stopped.

After you make such a change, you can use the start or stop command to start or stop the service immediately, as in **stop gdm** to shut down the gdm server. Before changing your runlevel (as described earlier, in "Changing Runlevels on a Running System"), you should type **initctl reload** to have Upstart reread its configuration files.

If you upgrade the package that provides the Upstart configuration script, you may need to reconfigure it.

Using SysV Compatibility Methods

Because the SysV startup script system has been so common for so long, a large number of software packages include SysV startup scripts. To accommodate such packages, Upstart provides a compatibility mode: it runs SysV startup scripts in the usual locations (/etc /rc.d/rc?.d, /etc/init.d/rc?.d, /etc/rc?.d, or a similar location). Thus, if you install a package that doesn't yet include an Upstart configuration script, it should still launch in the usual way. Furthermore, if you've installed utilities such as chkconfig, you should be able to use them to manage your SysV-based services just as you would on a SysV-based system.

You may find, however, that chkconfig and other SysV-based tools no longer work for some services. As time goes on, this is likely to be true for more and more services because the developers of distributions that favor Upstart may convert their packages' startup scripts to use Upstart-native methods.

Editing Files with vi

vi was the first full-screen text editor written for Unix. It's designed to be small and simple, and it is often the only editor installed in emergency boot systems. For this reason alone, vi is worth learning; you may need to use it in an emergency recovery situation. Vi is, however, a bit strange, particularly if you're used to GUI text editors. To use vi, you should first understand the three modes in which it operates. Once you understand those modes, you can begin learning about the text-editing procedures vi implements. You'll also examine how to save files and exit vi.

Most Linux distributions ship with a variant of vi known as Vim, or "Vi IMproved." As the name implies, Vim supports more features than the original vi. The information presented here applies to both vi and Vim. Most distributions that ship with Vim support launching it by typing vi, as if it were the original vi.

Understanding vi Modes

At any given moment, vi is running in one of three modes:

Command Mode This mode accepts commands, which are usually entered as single letters. For instance, i and a both enter insert mode, although in somewhat different ways, as described shortly, and o opens a line below the current one.

Ex Mode To manipulate files (including saving your current file and running outside programs), you use ex mode. You enter ex mode from command mode by typing a colon (:), typically directly followed by the name of the ex-mode command you want to use. After you run the ex-mode command, vi returns automatically to command mode.

Insert Mode You enter text in insert mode. Most keystrokes result in text appearing on the screen. One important exception is the Esc key, which exits insert mode and returns to command mode.

If you're not sure what mode vi is in, press the Esc key. Doing so returns you to command mode, from which you can reenter insert mode, if necessary.

Unfortunately, terminology surrounding vi modes is inconsistent at best. For instance, command mode is sometimes referred to as normal mode, and insert mode is sometimes called edit mode or entry mode. Ex mode often isn't described as a mode at all but is referred to as *colon commands*.

Exploring Basic Text-Editing Procedures

As a method of learning vi, consider the task of editing /etc/fstab to add a new disk drive to the computer. Listing 5.3 shows the original fstab file used in this example. If you want to follow along, enter it using a text editor with which you're already familiar, and save it to a file on your disk. Alternatively, copy your own computer's /etc/fstab file to a temporary location, and make analogous changes to it.

Listing 5.3 Sample /etc/fstab file

```
/dev/sda2    /         ext4     defaults         1 1
/dev/sda1    /boot     ext4     defaults         1 2
/dev/sda4    /home     ext4     defaults         1 2
/dev/sda3    swap      swap     defaults         0 0
tmpfs        /dev/shm  tmpfs    defaults         0 0
devpts       /dev/pts  devpts   gid=5,mode=620   0 0
sysfs        /sys      sysfs    defaults         0 0
proc         /proc     proc     defaults         0 0
```

Don't try editing your *real* /etc/fstab file as a learning exercise; a mistake could render your system unbootable! You might put your test fstab file in your home directory for this exercise.

The first step to using vi is to launch it and have it load the file. In this example, type **vi fstab** while in the directory containing the file. The result should resemble Figure 5.3, which shows vi running in an Xfce Terminal window. The tildes (~) down the left side of the display indicate the end of the file. (This feature is absent on some systems, though.)

The bottom line shows the status of the last command—an implicit file-load command—because you specified a filename when launching the program.

FIGURE 5.3   The last line of a vi display is a status line that shows messages from the program.

```
Terminal - fstab (~) - VIM
File  Edit  View  Terminal  Go  Help
/dev/sda2  /          ext4    defaults          1 1
/dev/sda1  /boot      ext4    defaults          1 2
/dev/sda4  /home      ext4    defaults          1 2
/dev/sda3  swap       swap    defaults          0 0
tmpfs      /dev/shm   tmpfs   defaults          0 0
devpts     /dev/pts   devpts  gid=5,mode=620    0 0
sysfs      /sys       sysfs   defaults          0 0
proc       /proc      proc    defaults          0 0
~
~
~
~
~
~
~
~
~
~
~
"fstab" 8L, 392C                          1,1          All
```

You can add a new entry to fstab using vi either by typing it in its entirety or by duplicating an existing line and then modifying one copy. To do it the first way, follow these steps:

1. Move the cursor to the beginning of the /dev/sda3 line using the arrow keys.

2. Press the o (lowercase letter o, not number 0) key. This opens a new line immediately below the current line, moves the cursor to that line, and enters insert mode.

> Although vi's commands may seem arcane, many of them are mnemonic in their own way; that is, they're designed to be easily remembered, as in the letter o standing for open line.

3. Type a new entry, such as the following:

    /dev/sdb1 /home2   ext4   defaults   0 0

4. Press the Esc key to return to command mode.

    To practice making changes by modifying an existing entry, follow these steps:

1. Move the cursor to the beginning of the /dev/sdb1 line you just created by using the arrow keys, if necessary; you should see the cursor resting on the first / of /dev/sdb1.

> You can use the h, j, k, and l keys to move left, down, up, and right, respectively, if you prefer not to use the arrow keys.

2. You must now *yank* one line of text. This term is used much as *copy* is used in most text editors—you copy the text to a buffer from which you can later paste it back into the file. To yank text, you use the yy command preceded by the number of lines you want to yank. Thus type **1yy** (*do not* press the Enter key, though). The dd command works much like yy, but it deletes the lines as well as copying them to a buffer. Both yy and dd are special cases of the y and d commands, respectively, which yank or delete text in amounts specified by the next character, as in dw to delete the next word.

3. Move the cursor to the line *before* the one where you want the new line to appear.

4. Type **p** (again, without pressing the Enter key). Vi pastes the contents of the buffer starting on the line after the cursor. The file should now have two identical /dev/sdb1 lines. The cursor should be resting at the start of the second one. If you want to paste the text into the document starting on the line *before* the cursor, use an uppercase P command.

5. Move the cursor to the 1 in /dev/sdb1 on the line you've just pasted. You're about to begin customizing this line.

6. Until now, you've operated vi in command mode. You can use any of several commands to enter insert mode. At this point, the most appropriate is R, which enters insert mode so that it's configured for text replacement rather than insertion. If you prefer to insert text rather than overwrite it, you can use i or a (the latter advances the cursor one space, which is sometimes useful at the end of a line). For the purposes of these instructions, type **R** to enter insert mode. You should see -- REPLACE -- appear in the status line.

7. Type **2** to change /dev/sdb1 to /dev/sdb2.

8. Use the arrow keys to move the cursor to the 2 in /home2. You must modify this mount point name.

9. Type **3** to change /home2 to /home3.

> You can make more extensive changes to the fstab file, if you like, but be sure to work from a *copy* of the file!

10. Exit insert mode by pressing the Esc key.

11. Save the file and quit by typing **:wq**. This is an ex-mode command, as described shortly. (The ZZ command is equivalent to :wq.)

Many additional commands are available that you may want to use in some situations. Here are some of the highlights:

Change Case   Suppose you need to change the case of a word in a file. Instead of entering insert mode and retyping the word, you can use the tilde (~) key in command mode to change the case. Position the cursor on the first character you want to change, and press ~ repeatedly until the task is done.

Undo   To undo any change, type **u** in command mode.

Open Text   In command mode, typing **o** (a lowercase letter *o*) opens text—that is, it inserts a new line immediately below the current one and enters insert mode on that line.

Search   To search forward for text in a file, type **/** in command mode, followed immediately by the text you want to locate. Typing **?** searches backward rather than forward.

Change Text   The c command changes text from within command mode. You invoke it much like the d or y command, as in cw to change the next word or cc to change an entire line.

Go to a Line   The G key brings you to a line that you specify. The H key "homes" the cursor; that is, it moves the cursor to the top line of the screen. The L key brings the key to the bottom line of the screen.

Replace Globally   To replace all occurrences of one string with another, type **:%s/*original*/*replacement*/g**, where *original* is the original string and *replacement* is its replacement. Change % to a starting line number, comma, and ending line number to perform this change on a small range of lines.

Vi offers a great deal more depth than is presented here; the editor is quite capable, and some Linux users are very attached to it. Entire books have been written about vi. Consult one of these, or a vi web page like www.vim.org, for more information.

Saving Changes

To save changes to a file, type **:w** from command mode. This enters ex mode and runs the w ex-mode command, which writes the file using whatever filename you specified when you launched vi. Related commands enable other functions:

Edit a New File   The :e command edits a new file. For instance, entering **:e /etc/inittab** loads /etc/inittab for editing. Vi won't load a new file unless the existing one has been saved since its last change or unless you follow :e with an exclamation mark (!).

Include an Existing File   The :r command includes the contents of an old file in an existing one.

Execute an External Command   The ex-mode command :! executes the external command that you specify. For instance, typing **:!ls** runs ls, enabling you to see what files are present in the current directory.

Quit   Use the :q command to quit the program. As with :e, this command won't work unless changes have been saved or you append an exclamation mark to the command (as in :q!).

You can combine ex-mode commands such as these to perform multiple actions in sequence. For instance, typing **:wq** writes changes and then quits from vi. (ZZ is the equivalent of :wq.)

Summary

Although Linux distributions are designed to boot painlessly and reliably once installed, understanding the boot process will help you overcome problems and maintain your system. Most Linux systems employ a boot loader known as GRUB (either GRUB Legacy or GRUB 2). These programs both fit themselves into the standard BIOS boot system, enabling the computer to load the Linux kernel. GRUB 2, and some patched versions of GRUB Legacy, also work on EFI-based computers. The kernel then runs the init program, which in turn reads various configuration files to boot all of the services that make a running Linux system.

Modifying your GRUB configuration enables you to boot different Linux kernels or non-Linux OSs. You can also pass new boot options to Linux. Once the system is booted, you can use the dmesg command or log files to study the boot process in order to verify that it went correctly or to find clues as to why it didn't.

You can use the vi editor to edit your GRUB configuration file, your system initialization scripts and configuration files, or any other plain-text file on your computer. Although vi is old-fashioned in many ways, it's small and is used for emergency boot systems. Every administrator should be familiar with vi, even if it's not their editor of choice for day-to-day operations.

Exam Essentials

Describe how GRUB Legacy is configured and used.   GRUB Legacy uses the menu.lst or grub.conf configuration file in /boot/grub. This file contains global and per-image options. Use the grub-install program to install the boot loader. When GRUB boots, it presents a menu of OS options that you select using the keyboard arrow keys.

Describe how GRUB 2 is configured and used.   GRUB 2 uses the /boot/grub/grub.cfg configuration file; however, system administrators are discouraged from editing it directly. Instead, they should rely on automatic configuration scripts and set system-specific defaults in /etc/defaults/grub and the files in /etc/grub.d. As with GRUB Legacy, you can install GRUB 2 using the grub-install program.

Describe the boot process. The CPU runs the firmware, the firmware loads and runs a boot loader, the boot loader loads and runs secondary boot loaders (if needed) and the Linux kernel, the Linux kernel loads and runs the initial system program (init), and init starts the rest of the system services via startup scripts that are specific to the startup system (SysV, Upstart, systemd, or something more exotic). BIOS-based computers look for boot loaders in various boot sectors, including the MBR of a hard drive or the boot sector of a disk partition or USB flash drive. EFI-based computers look for boot loaders in files on the ESP.

Summarize where to look for boot-time log information. The dmesg command prints out logs from the kernel ring buffer, which holds boot-time and other kernel messages. Other useful log information can be found in /var/log/messages and other files in /var/log.

Summarize the role of /sbin/init. The init program is responsible for starting many programs and services on your Linux operating system.

Explain the SysV init system. The SysV init system uses a default runlevel specified with a line like id:2:initdefault: in the /etc/inittab file. Use commands such as chkconfig, update-rc.d, ntsysv, and systemctl to change which services are started when switching to specific runlevels. Runlevels 0, 1, and 6 are reserved for shutdown, single-user mode, and rebooting, respectively. Runlevels 3, 4, and 5 are the common user runlevels on Red Hat and most other distributions, and runlevel 2 is the usual user runlevel on Debian systems.

Describe how to change SysV init runlevels. The programs init and telinit can be used to change to other runlevels. The shutdown, halt, poweroff, and reboot programs are also useful when shutting down, rebooting, or switching to single-user mode.

Explain the systemd init system. The systemd init system uses units and targets to control services. The default target is specified by the file /etc/systemd/system/default.target and is a link to a target file in the /lib/systemd/system folder.

Describe how to change systemd init targets. You use the systemctl program to start and stop services as well as to change the target level of the system.

Describe vi's three editing modes. You enter text using insert mode, which supports text entry and deletion. The command and ex modes are used to perform more complex commands or to run outside programs to operate on the text entered or changed in insert mode.

Review Questions

1. Where might the BIOS find a boot loader?

   A. RAM

   B. /dev/boot

   C. MBR

   D. /dev/kmem

   E. The swap partition

2. You want to boot a Linux system into single-user mode. What option might you add to a Linux kernel's options list in a boot loader to accomplish this task?

   A. `one`

   B. `single-user`

   C. `1`

   D. `telinit 6`

   E. `telinit 1`

3. After the system boots, one of your hard disks doesn't respond. What might you do to find out what's gone wrong?

   A. Check the /var/log/diskerror log file to see what's wrong.

   B. Verify that the disk is listed in /mnt/disks.

   C. Check the contents of /etc/inittab to be sure it's mounting the disk.

   D. Type **dmesg | less**, and peruse the output for disk-related messages.

   E. Check the menu.lst, grub.conf, or grub.cfg configuration file.

4. What is the first program that the Linux kernel runs once it's booted in a normal boot process?

   A. dmesg

   B. init

   C. startup

   D. rc

   E. lilo

5. Which of the following is the GRUB 2 boot loader configuration file?

   A. /dev/grub

   B. The MBR

   C. /boot/grub/grub.conf

   D. /boot/grub/grub.cfg

   E. /boot/grub/menu.lst

6. How might you identify an initial RAM disk file in GRUB 2?

   A. initrd /boot/initrd-3.4.2

   B. initrd=/boot/initrd-3.4.2

   C. initramfs /boot/initrd-3.4.2

   D. initramfs=/boot/initrd-3.4.2

   E. ramdisk=/boot/initrd-3.4.2

7. Which command is used to install GRUB Legacy into the MBR of your first SATA hard drive?

   A. grub (hd0,1)

   B. grub-install /dev/sda1

   C. lilo /dev/sda

   D. grub-install /dev/sda

   E. grub-legacy /dev/sda1

8. The string root (hd1,5) appears in your /boot/grub/menu.lst file. What does this mean?

   A. GRUB Legacy tells the kernel that the kernel's root partition is the fifth partition of the first disk.

   B. GRUB Legacy looks for files on the sixth partition of the second disk.

   C. GRUB Legacy looks for files on the fifth partition of the first disk.

   D. GRUB Legacy installs itself in /dev/hd1,5.

   E. GRUB Legacy installs itself in /dev/sdb5.

9. What line in /etc/inittab would indicate that your default runlevel is 5?

   A. ca:12345:ctrlaltdel:/sbin/shutdown -t1 -a -r now

   B. id:5:initdefault:

   C. si:5:sysinit:/etc/init.d/rcS

   D. l5:5:wait:/etc/init.d/rc 5

   E. 1:2345:respawn:/sbin/getty 38400 tty1

10. Which SysV runlevels are reserved by init for reboot, shutdown, and single-user mode purposes? (Select three.)

    A. 0

    B. 1

    C. 2

    D. 5

    E. 6

11. You type the following command:

$ **runlevel**

5 3

What can you tell about your runlevel status? (Select two.)

A. The current runlevel is 5.

B. The current runlevel is 3.

C. The previous runlevel is 5.

D. The previous runlevel is 3.

E. The runlevel is in the process of changing.

12. A system administrator types the following command:

shutdown -c

What is the effect of this command?

A. A previously scheduled shutdown is cancelled.

B. The system shuts down and reboots immediately.

C. The system shuts down and halts immediately.

D. The system asks for confirmation and then shuts down.

E. The system closes all open windows in X without shutting down.

13. What program do you use to start or stop services when using the systemd initialization process?

A. journalctl

B. systemctl

C. init

D. service

E. systemd

14. You want to change to single-user mode on a running SysV system. What command might you use to do this?

A. runlevel 1

B. telinit 1

C. shutdown -1

D. single-user

E. halt to 1

15. What command would you use to change to single-user mode on a running systemd system?

A. systemctl isolate rescue.target

B. systemctl default

C. journalctl default

    D.   `systemd single`

    E.   `systemctl start sshd.service`

16. How would you remove two lines of text from a file using vi?

    A.   In command mode, position the cursor on the first line and type **2dd**.

    B.   In command mode, position the cursor on the last line and type **2yy**.

    C.   In insert mode, position the cursor at the start of the first line, hold down the Shift key while pressing the Down arrow key twice, and press the Delete key on the keyboard.

    D.   In insert mode, position the cursor at the start of the first line, and press Ctrl+K twice.

    E.   Using your mouse, select both lines and then press the Delete or Backspace key.

17. In vi's command mode, you type **:q!**. What is the effect?

    A.   Nothing. This isn't a valid vi command.

    B.   The text :q! is inserted into the file you're editing.

    C.   The program terminates and saves any existing files that are in memory.

    D.   The program terminates without saving your work.

    E.   An exclamation point (!) overwrites the character under the cursor in the text.

18. What is an advantage of vi over graphical text editors?

    A.   vi is X based, so it is easier to use than other graphical text editors.

    B.   vi encodes text in EBCDIC, which is more flexible than Emacs's ASCII.

    C.   vi's mode-based operations permit it to handle non-English languages.

    D.   vi includes a built-in web browser and email client; Emacs doesn't.

    E.   vi is smaller, so it can fit on compact emergency USB flash drive systems and embedded devices.

19. You want to enter insert mode from vi's command mode. How might you do this? (Select three.)

    A.   Type **R**.

    B.   Type **i**.

    C.   Type **a**.

    D.   Type **:**.

    E.   Press Esc.

20. How do you exit vi's insert mode to type command-mode commands?

    A.   Press the ~ key.

    B.   Press the Esc key.

    C.   Press Ctrl+X followed by Ctrl+C.

    D.   Press the F10 key.

    E.   Press the Shift+Insert key combination.

Exam 102-400

Chapter

6

Configuring the X Window System, Localization, and Printing

THE FOLLOWING EXAM OBJECTIVES ARE COVERED IN THIS CHAPTER:

✓ 106.1 Install and configure X11

✓ 106.2 Set up a display manager

✓ 106.3 Accessibility

✓ 107.3 Localization and internationalization

✓ 108.4 Manage printers and printing

Major modern desktop OSs all provide some form of *graphical user interface (GUI)* that provides the windows, menus, dialog boxes, flexible fonts, and so on with which you're familiar. In Linux, the main GUI is known as the *X Window System* (or *X* for short). X configuration is either very easy or moderately hard. Most distributions today provide auto-detection and easy configuration options during installation, and these usually work correctly. When they don't, or when you want to tweak the configuration, you must delve into the X configuration file or use a GUI X configuration tool. Doing either requires that you know how X treats the video hardware, among other things.

Beyond basic X configuration are a few extra topics. These include fonts, GUI login tools, user desktop environments, using X for remote access, and localization. Each of these topics is closely associated with basic X configuration, but they all go beyond it in one way or another, extending X's capabilities or providing more features for users, as described in this chapter.

The X display can be considered one form of output. Another is printing, and this chapter covers that topic as well. With a properly configured printer, you can obtain hard copies of the documents you create and edit using both X and text-based applications.

Configuring Basic X Features

Basic X configuration specifies features such as the mouse used, the keyboard layout, the screen resolution, the video refresh rate, the display color depth, and the video card you're using. Some of these options require telling X about what hardware you have installed, whereas others enable you to adjust settings on your hardware. In any event, before you proceed with actual configuration, you should know something about the X servers that are available for Linux, because your selection will determine what additional tools are available and what files you may need to adjust manually. GUI and text-mode configuration utilities can help you configure X, but sometimes you must delve into the configuration files, so knowing their format is important. This requires that you know what the major option groups do so that you can adjust them.

X Server Options for Linux

Although X is by far the dominant GUI for Linux, several implementations of X are available:

XFree86   The dominant X server in Linux until 2004 was XFree86 (www.xfree86.org). This open-source server supports a wide array of video cards and input devices, and most Linux software was originally designed with XFree86 in mind. As we write, the most recent version is 4.8.0. Significant changes occurred between version 3.3.6 and the 4.*x* series, and some older utilities work only with 3.3.6 and earlier versions of XFree86. Although a tiny number of elderly systems must run XFree86 3.3.6 or earlier for driver support reasons, most systems today run XFree86 4.*x* or X.org-X11. The latter is more common on distributions released since 2004.

X.org-X11   In 2004, most Linux distributions shifted from XFree86 to X.org-X11 because of licensing changes to XFree86. X.org-X11 6.7.0 was based on XFree86 4.3.99, but it has been developed independently up to the current version, 7.7. Because X.org-X11 is based on XFree86, the two are virtually identical in most important respects. One significant difference is the name of the configuration file and another is the default location for fonts. Subsequent sections of this chapter point out these differences. You can learn more at www.x.org/wiki/.

Accelerated-X   The commercial Accelerated-X server from Xi Graphics (www.xig.com) is an alternative to the open-source XFree86 and X.org-X11. In practice, running Accelerated-X is seldom necessary, but if you have problems getting your video card working, you may want to look into Accelerated-X; its driver base is independent of the more popular open-source choices, so it's possible that you'll have better luck with it. The Accelerated-X configuration tools and files are completely different from those described later in this chapter in "Methods of Configuring X" and "X Configuration Options," so you'll need to consult its documentation for help. The rest of this chapter's topics still apply to Accelerated-X.

In practice, it's usually easiest to stick with whatever X server your distribution provides. For modern distributions, this is most often X.org-X11.

 Real World Scenario

Using Manufacturer-Provided Video Drivers

One of X's functions is to provide drivers that control the video card. XFree86, X.org-X11, and Accelerated-X all ship with a wide variety of drivers that support most video cards. Some cards, though, have weak support in the stock packages. The standard drivers support other cards, but those drivers may not support all of a video device's features. XFree86 4.*x* and X.org-X11 both support a modular driver architecture, which means that you can drop in a driver module for your card and use it with minimal changes to your X configuration. Both AMD (formerly ATI) and nVidia provide Linux video card drivers designed to work with XFree86 and X.org-X11. (Both X servers can use the same drivers.) Thus, if you have problems with the standard X video drivers, you may want to check with your video card manufacturer and the video card chipset manufacturers for Linux drivers.

(continued)

Installing and using the manufacturer-provided video drivers is usually a matter of extracting files from a tarball and running an installation script. Consult the documentation that comes with the driver for details. Many of these drivers are particularly helpful for enabling the 3D acceleration features of modern cards. These features were first used by games; however, the desktop environments and other non-game software increasingly use them as well.

One problem with manufacturer-supplied drivers is that they're often proprietary. You might not have source code, which means that the drivers might not work on more exotic CPUs, and the drivers could cease working with a future upgrade to your X server. The AMD and nVidia drivers also both include Linux kernel drivers as a necessary component, so you'll need to reinstall the drivers if you upgrade your kernel.

Methods of Configuring X

Configuring X has traditionally been a difficult process because the X configuration file includes many arcane options. The task is made simpler if you can use a configuration utility, and most Linux distributions now run such a utility as part of the installation process. If the configuration utility doesn't do everything that you want it to do, though, you may need to delve into the X configuration file to set options manually. Thus, knowing something about its format will help a lot. You must also know how to go about restarting X in order to test your changes.

The upcoming section "X Configuration Options" describes the major X features and how to control them in more detail.

X Configuration Utilities

Several configuration tools for XFree86 4.*x* and X.org-X11 are available:

The X Server Itself   The X server itself includes the capacity to query the hardware and produce a configuration file. To do this, type **XFree86 -configure** (for XFree86) or **Xorg -configure** (for X.org-X11) as root when no X server is running. The result should be a file called /root/XF86Config.new (for XFree86) or /root/xorg.conf.new (for X.org-X11). This file may not produce optimal results, but it's at least a starting point for manual modifications.

Distribution-Specific Tools   Many modern distributions ship with their own custom X configuration tools. These include Red Hat's (and Fedora's) Display Settings tool (accessible from the default desktop menu or by typing **system-config-display** in an xterm) and SUSE's YaST and YaST2. These tools frequently resemble the distribution's install-time X configuration tools, which can vary substantially.

xf86cfg or xorgcfg   This utility is named differently for XFree86 vs. X.org-X11. It's deprecated, meaning that it's no longer supported; however, if it's present on your system, it can help you tweak settings once X is at least partially running.

All of these utilities gather the same type of information needed to configure X manually. Your best bet for understanding these tools and what they want is to understand the underlying X configuration file's format and contents.

> If you're using the old XFree86 3.3.6, the tools just described don't work. Instead, you'll need to use a tool such as xf86config, Xconfigurator, or XF86Setup, or you can configure X manually. Because so few systems today use anything as old as XFree86 3.3.6, we don't describe these tools in this book.

The X Configuration File Format

The X configuration file's name and location vary with the version of X being run:

X.org-X11   This server's configuration file is called xorg.conf, and it's usually stored in /etc/X11, although /etc and several other locations are also acceptable to the server.

> Many modern X.org-X11 configurations omit the X configuration file entirely, instead relying on runtime auto-detection of hardware. This often works fine, but if X doesn't work or if some of its features are set incorrectly, you may need to generate an xorg.conf file by typing Xorg -configure when X is *not* running and edit the file manually, as described in subsequent sections.

XFree86 4.*x*   The XFree86 4.*x* configuration file is called XF86Config-4 or XF86Config, and is found in /etc/X11 or sometimes in /etc. This file's format is the same as for the X.org-X11 configuration file.

XFree86 3.3.6 and earlier   The X configuration file's name is XF86Config, and the file is most commonly located in /etc/X11 or /etc. Although the filename can be the same as for XFree86 4.*x*, the file format is slightly different. This book, like the exam, covers the newer format used by X.org-X11 and XFree86 4.*x*.

All three of these classes of X server use configuration files that are broken down into multiline sections, one section for each major feature. These sections begin with a line consisting of the keyword Section and the section name in quotes and end with the keyword EndSection:

```
Section "InputDevice"
    Identifier  "Keyboard0"
    Driver      "kbd"
    Option      "XkbModel" "pc105"
    Option      "XkbLayout" "us"
    Option      "AutoRepeat" "500 200"
EndSection
```

This section tells X about the keyboard—its model, layout, and so on. Details for the sections you're most likely to need to adjust are described shortly in "X Configuration Options."

For the most part, the different X servers support the same sections and most of the same option names. A few exceptions to this rule do exist, however:

- The Option keyword isn't used in XFree86 3.3.6 and earlier. Instead, the option name (such as XkbLayout or AutoRepeat in the preceding example) appears without quotes as the first word on the line.

- XFree86 3.3.6 and earlier don't use the ServerLayout section, described later in "Putting It All Together."

- XFree86 3.3.6 and earlier lack the Identifier and Driver lines, which are common in the XFree86 4.x and X.org-X11 configuration files.

- Some section-specific features vary between versions. We describe the most important of these in the coming pages.

The X Configure-and-Test Cycle

If your X configuration isn't working correctly, you need to be able to modify that configuration and then test it. Many Linux distributions configure the system to start X automatically, but starting X automatically can make it difficult to test the X configuration. To a new Linux administrator, the only obvious way to test a new configuration is to reboot the computer.

A better solution is to kick the system into a mode in which X is *not* started automatically. On Red Hat, Fedora, and similar distributions, this goal can be achieved by typing **telinit 3**. This action sets the computer to use runlevel 3, in which X normally doesn't run. Chapter 5, "Booting Linux and Editing Files," covers runlevels in more detail.

Some distributions, such as Debian, Ubuntu, and Gentoo, don't use runlevels as a signal for whether to start X. With such distributions, you must shut down the GUI login server by typing **/etc/init.d/xdm stop**. (You may need to change xdm to gdm, kdm, mdm, or lightdm, depending on your configuration.)

Once the X session is shut down, you can log in using a text-mode login prompt and tweak your X settings manually, or you can use text-based X configuration programs. You can then type **startx** to start the X server again. If you get the desired results, quit from X (typically by selecting a "log out" option in your desktop environment) and type **telinit 5** (**/etc/init.d/xdm start** in Debian and other distributions that don't use runlevels to start the GUI login prompt) to restore the system to its normal X login screen. If after typing **startx** you don't get the results you want, you can end your X session and try modifying the system further.

If X is working minimally but you want to modify it using X-based configuration tools, you can do so after typing **startx** to get a normal X session running. Alternatively, you can reconfigure the system before taking it out of the X-enabled runlevel.

Another approach to restarting X is to leave the system in its X-enabled runlevel and then kill the X server. The Ctrl+Alt+Backspace keystroke does this on many systems, or you can do it manually with the `kill` command after finding the appropriate process ID with the ps command, as shown here:

```
# ps ax | grep X
1375 ?    S   6:32 /usr/bin/X -auth /var/gdm/:0.Xauth
# kill 1375
```

This approach works better on systems that don't map the running of X to specific runlevels, such as Debian and its derivatives.

X Configuration Options

When editing the X configuration file, the best approach is usually to identify the feature that's not working and zero in on the section that controls this feature. You can then edit that section, save your changes, and test the new configuration. In XFree86 4.*x* and X.org-X11, the major sections described here are called Module, InputDevice, Monitor, Device, Screen, and ServerLayout. You're likely to have two InputDevice sections, one for the keyboard and one for the mouse. (In XFree86 3.3.6 and earlier, a separate Pointer section handles the mouse.) The section order doesn't matter.

Fonts are a complex enough topic that they're described in more detail later in "Configuring X Fonts." Part of this configuration is handled in the Files section.

Loading Modules

The Module section controls the loading of X server modules—drivers for specific features or hardware. A typical example looks like this:

```
Section "Module"
    Load  "dbe"
    Load  "extmod"
    Load  "fbdevhw"
    Load  "glx"
    Load  "record"
    Load  "freetype"
```

```
    Load  "type1"
    Load  "dri"
EndSection
```

Each module is named (dbe, extmod, and so on), and it is loaded by name using the Load option. Most of these module names can be deciphered with a bit of knowledge about the features they control. For instance, freetype and type1 handle TrueType and Adobe Type 1 font rendering, respectively. If you're perusing your Module section and see modules that you don't understand, you shouldn't worry about it; generally speaking, modules that are configured automatically are necessary for normal operation, or at least they do no harm.

For the most part, if an X configuration works, you shouldn't try to adjust the Module section, even if you want to tweak the X configuration. Sometimes, though, you'll need to add lines to or remove lines from this section. This is particularly likely to be necessary if you're activating 3D acceleration support or some sort of exotic feature. In such cases, you should consult the documentation for the feature that you want to activate.

Many desktop environments and other user-level utilities provide tools to set the keyboard repeat rate. Thus, the options that you set in the X configuration file are used as defaults only and may be overridden by users' settings.

Setting the Keyboard

The keyboard is one of two common input devices configured via an InputDevice section:

```
Section "InputDevice"
    Identifier  "Keyboard0"
    Driver      "kbd"
    Option      "XkbModel" "pc105"
    Option      "XkbLayout" "us"
    Option      "AutoRepeat" "500 200"
EndSection
```

The Identifier line provides a label that's used by another section (ServerLayout, described in "Putting It All Together"). The string given on this line is arbitrary, but for a keyboard, a descriptive name such as this example's Keyboard0 will help you understand the file.

The Driver line tells X what driver to use to access the keyboard. This should be kbd, Keyboard, or evdev, depending on your X server. The kbd and Keyboard drivers are, as you might expect, keyboard-specific drivers. The evdev driver, by contrast, is a generic input device driver that works with many types of input devices. Unless your keyboard isn't working at all, you shouldn't adjust this line.

The Option lines set various options that adjust keyboard features, such as the model, the layout, and the repeat rate. For the most part, the defaults work well; however, you may want to change the AutoRepeat option or add it if it's not present. This option tells X when to begin repeating characters when you hold down a key and how often to repeat them. It takes two numbers as values, enclosed in quotes: the time until the first repeat and the time between subsequent repeats, both expressed in milliseconds (ms). In the preceding example, the system waits 500ms (half a second) for the first repeat and then 200ms for each subsequent repeat (that is, five repeats per second).

Setting the Mouse

A second InputDevice section controls how X treats the mouse:

```
Section "InputDevice"
    Identifier   "Mouse0"
    Driver       "mouse"
    Option       "Protocol" "IMPS/2"
    Option       "Device" "/dev/input/mice"
    Option       "Emulate3Buttons" "no"
    Option       "ZAxisMapping" "4 5"
EndSection
```

As with the keyboard, the Identifier line is used in the ServerLayout section to tell X which input device to use. The Driver line identifies the driver to use: mouse. (Many modern systems use evdev for the mouse.) The Option lines set mouse control options. The most important of these are Device and Protocol.

The Device line tells X what Linux device file to read to access the mouse. In this example, it's /dev/input/mice, but other possibilities include /dev/mouse (a pointer to the real mouse device, whatever its name), /dev/input/mouse1 (for a Bluetooth mouse device), /dev/usb/usbmouse (an old identifier for USB mice), /dev/ttyS0 (the first RS-232 serial port mouse), and /dev/ttyS1 (the second RS-232 serial port mouse). If your mouse is working at all (even if its motions are erratic), don't change this line. If your mouse isn't working, you may need to experiment.

The Protocol option tells X what signals to expect from the mouse for various movements and button presses. The Auto protocol causes X to try to guess the mouse's protocol, which usually works correctly. If it doesn't work, you can try more specific protocols, such as IMPS/2 and ExplorerPS/2, which are very similar in practice. (Note that PS/2 is both a hardware interface and a software protocol; many USB mice use the PS/2 mouse protocol even though they don't use the PS/2 mouse port.) If your mouse has a scroll wheel, chances are that you should use one of these protocols. If your mouse is older, you may need to try an older protocol, such as PS/2, Microsoft, or Logitech.

Additional options are usually less critical than the Device and Protocol options. The Emulate3Buttons option tells X whether to treat a *chord* (that is, a simultaneous press) of both buttons on a two-button mouse as if it were a middle-button press. This option is usually disabled on three-button mice and scroll mice (the scroll wheel does double duty as a middle mouse button). The ZAxisMapping option in the preceding example maps the scroll wheel actions to the fourth and fifth buttons, because X must treat scroll wheels as if they were buttons. When you scroll up or down, these "button" presses are generated. Software can detect this and take appropriate actions.

Setting the Monitor

Some of the trickiest aspects of X configuration relate to the monitor options. You set these in the Monitor section, which can sometimes be quite large. A modest Monitor section looks like this:

```
Section "Monitor"
    Identifier  "Monitor0"
    ModelName   "AOC e2343Fk"
    HorizSync   30.0 - 83.0
    VertRefresh 55.0 - 75.0
    # My custom 1920x1080 mode
    Modeline "1920x1080"  138.50  1920 1968 2000 2080  1080 1083 1088 1111
EndSection
```

As in the keyboard and mouse configurations, the Identifier option is a free-form string that contains information that's used to identify a monitor. The Identifier option can be just about anything you like. Likewise, the ModelName option can be anything you like; it's used mainly for your own edification when reviewing the configuration file.

As you continue down the section, you'll see the HorizSync and VertRefresh lines, which are extremely critical. They define the range of horizontal and vertical refresh rates that the monitor can accept, in kilohertz (kHz) and hertz (Hz), respectively. Together, these values determine the monitor's maximum resolution and refresh rate. Despite the name, the HorizSync item alone doesn't determine the maximum horizontal refresh rate. Rather, this value, the VertRefresh value, and the resolution determine the monitor's maximum refresh rate. X selects the maximum refresh rate that the monitor will support given the resolution you specify in other sections. Some X configuration utilities show a list of monitor models or resolution and refresh rate combinations (such as 1024 × 768 at 72Hz). You select an option, and the utility then computes the correct values based on that selection. This approach is often simpler to handle, but it's less precise than entering the exact horizontal and vertical sync values. You should enter these values from your monitor's manual.

WARNING   Don't set random horizontal and vertical refresh rates; on older hardware, setting these values too high can damage a monitor. (Modern monitors ignore signals presented at too high a refresh rate.)

To settle on a resolution, X looks through a series of *mode lines*, which are specified via the Modeline option. Computing mode lines is tricky, so we don't recommend that you try it unless you're skilled in such matters. The mode lines define combinations of horizontal and vertical timing that can produce a given resolution and refresh rate. For instance, a particular mode line might define a 1024 × 768 display at a 90Hz refresh rate, and another might represent 1024 × 768 at 72Hz.

Some mode lines represent video modes that are outside the horizontal or vertical sync ranges of a monitor. X can compute these cases and discard the video modes that a monitor can't support. If asked to produce a given resolution, X searches all of the mode lines that accomplish the job, discards those that the monitor can't handle, and uses the remaining mode line that creates the highest refresh rate at that resolution. (If no mode line supports the requested resolution, X drops down to another specified resolution, as described shortly, and tries again.)

Although you can include an arbitrary number of Modeline entries in your Monitor section, most such files lack these entries. The reason is that XFree86 4.*x* and X.org-X11 support a feature known as *Data Display Channel (DDC)*. This is a protocol that enables monitors to communicate their maximum horizontal and vertical refresh rates and appropriate mode lines to the computer. You may need to create a Modeline option if this feature fails, though. Try performing a Web search on the keywords *modeline* (or *mode line*) and your desired video resolution, or try the XFree86 Modeline Generator website (http://xtiming.sourceforge.net/cgi-bin/xtiming.pl), which can generate a Modeline option for any resolution and refresh rate you specify.

Setting the Video Card

Your monitor is usually the most important factor in determining your maximum refresh rate at any given resolution, but X sends data to the monitor only indirectly, through the video card. Because of this, it's important that you be able to configure this component correctly. An incorrect configuration of the video card is likely to result in an inability to start X.

In the past, video hardware was almost always implemented as a plug-in card. Most modern computers include video hardware on the motherboard, though. Despite this fact, it's common to refer to a *video card*, even if the computer lacks a separate plug-in card.

Choosing the Driver

Sometimes X, and particularly modern versions of X.org-X11, can pick the optimum video driver automatically. Other times, though, you must provide that information in the XF86Config or xorg.conf file. In particular, a line in the Device section, which resembles the following, sets the driver module:

```
Driver "nv"
```

This line sets the name of the driver. The drivers reside in the /usr/X11R6/lib/modules/drivers/ or /usr/lib/xorg/modules/drivers/ directory. (On some systems, lib becomes lib64.) Most of the drivers' filenames end in _drv.o, and if you remove this portion, you're left with the driver name. For instance, nv_drv.o corresponds to the nv driver.

 Some X configuration utilities provide a large list of chipsets and specific video card models, so you can select the chipset or board from this list to have the utility configure this detail.

   If you type **Xorg -configure** to create an initial configuration, the resulting file is likely to include multiple Device sections, each for a different driver. Some of these, such as fbdev and vesa, are generic drivers that work—but not optimally—on a wide variety of video cards. Today, you're most likely to use the nv or nouveau drivers (both of which work on nVidia cards), the radeon driver (which works on ATI/AMD cards), or the intel driver (which works on Intel cards). You'll need to know something about your video hardware to pick the best one. If you're in doubt, you can try using each one in turn by specifying each Device section in the Screen section, as described later, in "Setting the Resolution and Color Depth."

Setting Card-Specific Options

The Device section of the xorg.conf file sets various options related to specific X servers. A typical Device section resembles the following:

```
Section "Device"
     Identifier  "Videocard0"
     Driver      "nv"
     VendorName  "nVidia"
     BoardName   "GeForce 6100"
     VideoRam    131072
EndSection
```

   The Identifier line provides a name that's used in the subsequent Screen section to identify this particular Device section. The VendorName and BoardName lines provide information that's useful mainly to people reading the file.

   The VideoRam line is unnecessary with most boards because the driver can detect the amount of RAM installed in the card. With some devices, however, you may need to specify the amount of RAM installed in the card in kilobytes. For instance, the preceding example indicates a card with 128MB of RAM installed (the 131072 value is 128 times 1024).

   Many drivers support additional driver-specific options. They may enable support for features such as hardware cursors (special hardware that enables the card to handle mouse pointers more easily) or caches (using spare memory to speed up various operations). Consult the XF86Config or xorg.conf man page or other driver-specific documentation for details.

Setting the Resolution and Color Depth

The Screen section tells X about the combination of monitors and video cards that you're using. XFree86 4.*x* and X.org-X11 support multiple video cards and monitors on one system. This can be handy if you're testing a new monitor or video card driver. In any event, the Screen section looks something like this:

```
Section "Screen"
    Identifier "Screen0"
    Device      "Videocard0"
    Monitor     "Monitor0"
    DefaultDepth 24
    SubSection "Display"
        Depth    24
        Modes    "1920x1080" "1280x1024" "1024x768"
    EndSubSection
    SubSection "Display"
        Depth    8
        Modes    "1024x768" "800x600" "640x480"
    EndSubSection
EndSection
```

The Device and Monitor lines refer to the Identifier lines in your Device and Monitor sections, respectively. The Screen section includes one or more Display subsections, which define the video modes that X may use. This example creates two such displays. The first uses a color depth of 24 bits (Depth 24) and possible video mode settings of 1920×1080, 1280×1024, and 1024×768. (These video modes are actually names that refer to the mode lines defined in the Monitor section or to standard mode lines.) The second possible display uses an 8-bit color depth (Depth 8) and supports 1024×768, 800×600, and 640×480 video modes.

To choose between the Display subsections, you include a DefaultDepth line. In this example, X uses the 24-bit display if possible, unless it's overridden by other options when starting X.

Graphical video modes require a certain amount of RAM on the video card. (On some laptop computers and computers with video hardware integrated into the motherboard, a portion of system RAM is reserved for this use by the BIOS.) The total amount of RAM required is determined by an equation:

$$R = xres \times yres \times bpp \div 8{,}388{,}608$$

In this equation, R is the RAM in megabytes, $xres$ is the x resolution in pixels, $yres$ is the y resolution in pixels, and bpp is the bit depth. For instance, consider a 1280 × 1024 display at 24-bit color depth:

$$R = 1280 \times 1024 \times 24 \div 8{,}388{,}608 = 3.75MB$$

All modern video cards have at least 32MB of RAM—usually much more. This is more than enough to handle even very high resolutions at 32-bit color depth (the greatest depth possible). Thus, video RAM shouldn't be a limiting factor in terms of video mode selection—at least not with modern video hardware. Very old video cards can impose limits, so you should be aware of them.

Modern video cards ship with large amounts of RAM to support 3D acceleration features. X supports such features indirectly through special 3D acceleration packages, but 3D acceleration support is limited compared to basic video card support. If 3D acceleration is important to you, you should research the availability of this support.

Putting It All Together

XFree86 4.*x* and X.org-X11 require a section that's not present in the XFree86 3.3.6 configuration file: ServerLayout. This section links together all of the other components of the X configuration:

```
Section "ServerLayout"
    Identifier      "single head configuration"
    Screen          "Screen0" 0 0
    InputDevice     "Mouse0" "CorePointer"
    InputDevice     "Keyboard0" "CoreKeyboard"
EndSection
```

Typically, this section identifies one Screen section and two InputDevice sections (for the keyboard and the mouse). Other configurations are possible, though. For instance, XFree86 4.*x* and X.org-X11 support *multi-head displays*, in which multiple monitors are combined to form a larger desktop than either one alone would support. In these configurations, the ServerLayout section includes multiple Screen sections.

 Real World Scenario

If All Goes Well....

In practice, you may not need to edit the X configuration file. As already noted, most Linux distributions configure X automatically at installation. Indeed, most distributions now rely on launch-time auto-configuration of X along with user settings for features such as resolution, keyboard repeat rate, and so on.

Desktop environments typically provide a dialog box, such as the one shown in the following screen shot, which enables you to set the resolution, refresh rate, and sometimes other display options. Look for such options in the desktop environment's main settings tool, typically under a title such as Display or Monitor.

Obtaining X Display Information

Sometimes, it's helpful to know about the capabilities of your display as X manages it. The tool for this job is xdpyinfo. When you type **xdpyinfo**, it produces copious information about the current display, such as the X version number, the resolution and color depth of all the current displays, and so on. Much of this information is highly technical in nature, so you may not understand it all. That's OK. We recommend that you run this program and peruse the output to see what you can learn from it. If you should want to obtain similar information on another computer's display later, you'll know how to obtain it.

For still more technical information, you can use the -ext *extension* option to xpdyinfo. *extension* is the name of an X extension, which is a software module that provides extended capabilities to X. (The basic xpdyinfo command, without any options, lists all of the available extensions.)

You can obtain detailed technical information about a specific window with the xwininfo command. In basic use, you type **xwininfo**, move the mouse cursor over a window, and click. The result is a list of assorted data about the window you clicked, such as the following:

```
Absolute upper-left X:   1171
Absolute upper-left Y:   611
Relative upper-left X:   6
Relative upper-left Y:   25
Width: 657
Height: 414
Depth: 32
Visual Class: TrueColor
Border width: 0
```

```
Class: InputOutput
Colormap: 0x2800003 (not installed)
Bit Gravity State: NorthWestGravity
Window Gravity State: NorthWestGravity
Backing Store State: NotUseful
Save Under State: no
Map State: IsViewable
Override Redirect State: no
Corners:  +1171+611  -92+611  -92-55  +1171-55
-geometry 80x24-86-49
```

Some of this information, such as the window's position and size, is easy to interpret. Other information, such as the color map and gravity state, is highly technical, and we don't describe it further here. You can pass various options to xwininfo to modify the information that it displays or how you select a window, including the following:

Alternate Window Selection Methods   The -id and -name options enable you to identify a window by an ID number or by its name (normally displayed in the window's border), respectively. The -root option selects the root window—that is, the entire display.

Window Relationships   Like processes, windows can have parents and children. You can identify these relationships with the -children option. The -tree option works in a similar way, but it works recursively; that is, it displays information on the children of a window's children, and so on.

Basic Information   The -stats option is used by default. You can restrict the output by using the -bits option, which limits output to information on the window's bit states.

Additional Information   The -events option produces information on the events that the window processes; -size displays information on sizing hints; -wm displays window manager data; -shape is much like -stats, but it adds information on the window and border shapes; -frame modifies the display to include information on the window manager's frame; -metric adds measures in millimeters (mm) to the regular pixel-based measures; -english adds measures in feet and inches; and -all displays all available information.

Windows in X are created and managed by several programs. One of these, the *window manager*, handles the window's borders and enables you to drag the window around the screen and resize it. Some xwininfo statistics relate to the window *excluding* the window manager's elements, but others *include* these elements. Options such as -frame and -wm can modify this output or display information on the window manager's features specifically.

🌐 **Real World Scenario**

Wayland: The Future?

An entirely new method of managing displays, known as Wayland (http://wayland. freedesktop.org), has started gaining popularity. Wayland is intended to address many of the problems with X, which suffers from a design dating back to the 1980s, before many modern video features became available. Thus X is hobbled by legacy features such as a font model that's been largely replaced by add-on font libraries.

Wayland-native applications won't use X at all, which will theoretically result in simpler application design, better speed, and fewer video problems, particularly for certain graphics-intensive applications. Existing X applications will continue to work via an X server to be included with Wayland. Essentially, X will run as a process within Wayland, although ideally this will be a stopgap measure.

Both the KDE and GNOME desktop teams have indicated support for Wayland, and the developers of several major Linux distributions, including Fedora and Ubuntu, have expressed an intention to support Wayland, either as an option or as the default graphics system.

Configuring X Fonts

Fonts have long been a trouble spot for Linux (or more precisely, for X). X was created at a time when available font technologies were primitive by today's standards, and although X has been updated in various ways to take advantage of newer technologies, these updates have been lacking compared to the font subsystems in most competing OSs. X's core font system can be set up from the X configuration file. Alternatively, you can config-ure a *font server*—a program that delivers fonts to one or many computers using network protocols—to handle the fonts. The latest Linux font technology sets up fonts in a way that's more independent of X and that produces more pleasing results, at least to most people's eyes.

Some applications don't rely on either X or any other standard library to handle fonts; they manage their own fonts themselves. This practice is particularly common in word processors. If you configure your fonts as described here but find that an important program doesn't see the changes you've made, consult its documentation; you may need to tell the program where to look to use the fonts you've added.

Font Technologies and Formats

Font technologies can be classified as falling into one of two broad categories:

Bitmap Fonts The simplest type of font format is the *bitmap font*, which represents fonts much like bitmap graphics in which individual pixels in an array are either active or inactive. Bitmap fonts are fairly easy to manipulate and display from a programming perspective, which makes them good for low-powered computers. The problem is that each font must be optimized for display at a particular resolution. For instance, a font that's 20 pixels high will appear one size on the screen (typically 72 to 100 dots per inch, or dpi) but will be much smaller when printed (typically at 300 to 1200 dpi). Similarly, you need multiple files to display a single font at multiple sizes (such as 9 point versus 12 point). This means that a single font, such as Times, requires potentially dozens of individual files for display at different sizes and on different display devices. If you lack the correct font file, the result will be an ugly scaled display.

Outline Fonts Most modern fonts are distributed as *outline fonts* (aka *scalable fonts*). This type of format represents each character as a series of lines and curves in a high-resolution matrix. The computer can scale this representation to any font size or for any display resolution, enabling a single font file to handle every possible use of the font. The main problem with outline fonts is that this scaling operation is imperfect; scalable fonts often look slightly worse than bitmap fonts, particularly at small sizes. Scaling and displaying the fonts also takes more CPU time than displaying a bitmap font. This factor used to be important, but on modern CPUs it's not much of an issue.

Both bitmap and outline fonts come in several different formats. X ships with a number of basic bitmap and outline fonts, and you're unlikely to need to deal explicitly with bitmap fonts or their formats, so we don't describe them in any detail. Outline fonts are another matter, though. The two main formats are Adobe's *PostScript Type 1* (Type 1 for short) and the *TrueType* font standard, developed by both Apple and Microsoft. Fonts available on the Internet and on commercial font CDs come in one or both of these formats.

XFree86 3.3.6 and earlier supported Type 1 fonts but not TrueType fonts. XFree86 4.*x* and X.org-X11 support both Type 1 and TrueType fonts.

Configuring X Core Fonts

X core fonts are those that are handled directly by X. To configure these fonts, you must do two things: prepare a font directory that holds the fonts, and add the font directory to X's font path.

Preparing a Font Directory

The first step to installing fonts is to prepare a directory in which to store them. XFree86 has traditionally stored its fonts in subdirectories of /usr/X11R6/lib/X11/fonts/, but X.org-X11 changes this to /usr/share/fonts or /usr/share/X11/fonts. In either case, if you're adding fonts that you've downloaded from the Internet or obtained from a commercial font CD-ROM, you may want to store these additional fonts elsewhere, such as /opt/

fonts or /usr/local/fonts. (Chapter 4, "Managing Files," includes information about the logic behind Linux's directory system.) You may want to create separate subdirectories for fonts in different formats or from different sources.

When you're installing Type 1 fonts, Linux needs the font files with names that end in .pfa or .pfb; these files contain the actual font data. (The PFA and PFB files store the data in slightly different formats, but the two file types are equivalent.) Additional files distributed with Type 1 fonts aren't necessary for Linux. TrueType fonts come as TTF files, and that's all you need for Linux.

Linux uses fonts in the same format that Mac OS X, Windows, and most other OSs use. Earlier versions of the Mac OS used font files in special Macintosh-only "suitcases," which Linux can't use directly. If you want to use such fonts in Linux, you must convert them. The FontForge program (http://fontforge.sourceforge.net) can do this conversion, among other things.

Once you've copied fonts to a directory, you must prepare a summary file that describes the fonts. This file is called fonts.dir, and it begins with a line that specifies the number of fonts that are described. Subsequent lines provide a font filename and an *X logical font description (XLFD)*, which is a tedious-looking description of the font. A complete fonts.dir line can be rather intimidating:

courb.pfa -ibm-Courier-bold-r-normal--0-0-0-0-m-0-iso8859-1

Fortunately, you needn't create this file manually; programs exist to do so automatically. In XFree86 4.3 and later and in X.org-X11, the simplest way to do the job is to use mkfontscale and mkfontdir:

```
# mkfontscale
# mkfontdir
```

The mkfontscale program reads all of the fonts in the current directory and creates a fonts.scale file, which is just like a fonts.dir file but describes only outline fonts. The mkfontdir program combines the fonts.scale file with the fonts.dir file, creating it if it doesn't already exist.

Other programs designed to perform this task also exist. Most notably, ttmkfdir creates a fonts.dir file that describes TrueType fonts, and type1inst does the job for Type 1 fonts. The mkfontscale program is preferable because it handles both font types, but if you're using an older distribution that lacks this program, or if it's not doing a satisfactory job, you can try one of these alternative programs.

Adding Fonts to X's Font Path

Once you've set up fonts in a directory and created a fonts.dir file describing them, you must add the fonts to the X font path. You do this by editing the Files section of the XF86Config or xorg.conf file:

```
Section "Files"
    FontPath  "/usr/share/fonts/100dpi:unscaled"
    FontPath  "/usr/share/fonts/Type1"
    FontPath  "/usr/share/fonts/truetype"
    FontPath  "/usr/share/fonts/URW"
    FontPath  "/usr/share/fonts/Speedo"
    FontPath  "/usr/share/fonts/100dpi"
EndSection
```

If your `Files` section contains `FontPath` lines that refer to `unix:/7100` or `unix:/-1` but that don't list conventional directories, read the upcoming section "Configuring a Font Server"; your system is configured to rely on an X font server for its core fonts. In this case, you may want to modify your font server configuration rather than change the X core fonts directly, although you can add font directories to have X both use the font server and directly handle your new fonts. If your X server configuration lacks a `Files` section, it uses a hard-coded default font path. You can add your own complete `Files` section to add new font paths.

To add your new font directory to the font path, duplicate one of the existing `FontPath` lines and change the directory specification to point to your new directory. The order of these directories is significant; when matching font names, X tries each directory in turn, so if two directories hold fonts of the same name, the first one takes precedence. Thus, if you want your new fonts to override any existing fonts, place the new directory at the top of the list; if you want existing fonts to take precedence, add your directory to the end of the list.

The `:unscaled` string in the first entry in the preceding example tells X to use bitmap fonts from this directory only if they exactly match the requested font size. Without this string, X will attempt to scale bitmap fonts from a font directory (with poor results). Typically, bitmap directories are listed twice: once near the top of the font path with the `:unscaled` specification and again near the bottom of the list without it. This produces quick display of matching bitmapped fonts, followed by any matching scalable fonts, followed by scaled bitmap fonts.

Once you've added your font directory to X's font path, you should test the configuration. The most reliable way to do this is to shut down X and restart it. (If your system boots directly into X, consult "Running an XDMCP Server" for information on doing this.) A quicker approach, but one that presents some opportunity for error, is to add the font path to a running system by using the xset program:

```
$ xset fp+ /your/font/directory
$ xset fp rehash
```

The first of these commands adds */your/font/directory* to the end of the font path. (Substitute +fp for fp+ to add the directory to the start of the existing font path.) The second command tells X to reexamine all of the font directories to rebuild the list of available fonts. The result is that you should now be able to access the new fonts. (You'll need to restart any programs that should use the new fonts.) One program to test the matter quickly is xfontsel. This program enables you to select an X core font for display so that you can check to be sure that the fonts you've added are available and appear as you'd expect.

Configuring a Font Server

Prior to the release of XFree86 4.0, several Linux distributions began using TrueType-enabled font servers to provide TrueType font support. Most distributions have now abandoned this practice, but some haven't, and font servers can be useful in some environments.

A font server is a handy way to deliver fonts to many computers from a central location. This can be a great time-saver if you want to add fonts to many computers—set them up to use a font server and then tweak that server's font configuration. To use a font server, X must list that server in its font path:

```
Section "Files"
    FontPath   "unix:/7100"
    FontPath   "tcp/fount.pangaea.edu:7100"
EndSection
```

The first line in this example specifies a local font server. (Using unix:/-1 rather than unix:/7100 also works in some cases.) The second line specifies that the font server on the remote system fount.pangaea.edu is to be used. If your computer is already configured to use a font server, you needn't change the X configuration to add or delete fonts; instead, you can modify the font server's configuration. (You *can* still modify the X font configuration directly, but it may be cleaner to manage all of the local fonts from one configuration file.)

To add fonts to a font server, you should first install the fonts on the system, as described earlier in "Preparing a Font Directory." You should then modify the font server's configuration file, /etc/X11/fs/config. Rather than a series of FontPath lines, as in the main X configuration file, the font server's configuration lists the font path using the catalogue keyword as a comma-delimited list:

```
catalogue = /usr/share/fonts/100dpi:unscaled,
            /usr/share/fonts/Type1,
            /usr/share/fonts/truetype,
            /usr/share/fonts/URW,
            /usr/share/fonts/Speedo,
            /usr/share/fonts/100dpi
```

The catalogue list may span several lines or just one. In either event, all of the entries are separated by commas, but the final entry ends without a comma. You can add your new font directory anywhere in this list.

Once you've saved your changes, you must restart the font server. Typically, this is done via SysV startup scripts or the systemd `systemctl` command (described in more detail in Chapter 5):

```
# /etc/init.d/xfs restart
```

At this point, you should restart X or type **xset fp rehash** to have X reexamine its font path, including the fonts delivered via the font server.

Although X core fonts and font servers were once very important, most modern X applications now emphasize an entirely different font system: Xft. You can add the same fonts as both X core fonts and Xft fonts, but the Xft configuration requires doing things in a new way.

Configuring Xft Fonts

X core fonts (including fonts delivered via a font server) have several significant drawbacks:

- They aren't easy to integrate between the screen display and printed output. This makes them awkward from the point of view of word processing or other applications that produce printed output.

- They're server based. This means that applications may not be able to access the font files directly because the fonts may be stored on a different computer than the application. This can exacerbate the printing integration problem.

- They provide limited or no support for kerning and other advanced typographic features. Again, this is a problem for word processing programs and other programs that must generate printed output.

- They don't support *font smoothing* (aka *anti-aliasing*). This technology employs gray pixels (rather than black or white pixels) along curves to create the illusion of greater resolution than the display can produce.

These problems are deeply embedded in the X core font system, so developers have decided to bypass that system. The result is the Xft font system, which is based in part on the FreeType library (`www.freetype.org`), an open-source library for rendering TrueType and Type 1 fonts. Xft is a client-based system, meaning that applications access font files on the computer on which they're running. Xft also supports font smoothing and other advanced font features. Overall, the result is greatly improved font support. The cost, though, is that Linux now has *two* font systems: X core fonts and Xft fonts.

Fortunately, you can share the same font directories through both systems. If you've prepared a font directory as described earlier in "Preparing a Font Directory," you can add it to Xft. Load the /etc/fonts/local.conf file into a text editor. Look for any lines in this file that take the following form:

```
<dir>/font/directory</dir>
```

If such lines are present, duplicate one of them and change the duplicate to point to your new font directory. If such lines don't exist, create one just before the

</fontconfig> line. Be sure not to embed your new font directory specification within a comment block though. Comments begin with a line that reads <!-- and end with a line that reads -->.

 If you create a font directory that holds several subdirectories, you can add just the main directory to local.conf. For instance, if you created /opt/fonts/tt and /opt/fonts/type1, adding /opt/fonts to local.conf will be sufficient to access all of the fonts that you installed on the system.

Once you've made these changes, type **fc-cache** as root. This command causes Xft to run through its font directories and create index files. These files are similar to the fonts.dir file in principle, but the details differ. If you fail to take this step, you'll still be able to access these fonts, but each user's private Xft cache file will contain the lists of fonts. Generating these files can take some time, thus degrading performance.

To test your Xft fonts, use any Xft-enabled program. Most modern X-based Linux programs are so enabled, so loading a GUI text editor, word processor, web browser, or other tool that enables you to adjust fonts should do the trick.

Managing GUI Logins

Linux can boot into a purely text-based mode in which the console supports text-based logins and text-mode commands. This configuration is suitable for a system that runs as a server or for a desktop system for a user who dislikes GUIs. Most desktop users, though, expect their computers to boot into a friendly GUI. For such users, Linux supports a login system that starts X automatically and provides a GUI login screen. Configuring and managing this system requires you to understand a bit of how the system works, how to run it, and how to change the configuration.

The X GUI Login System

As described later in this chapter in "Using X for Remote Access," X is a network-enabled GUI. This fact has many important consequences, and one of these relates to Linux's GUI login system. This system employs a network login protocol, the *X Display Manager Control Protocol (XDMCP)*. To handle remote logins, an XDMCP server runs on a computer and listens for connections from remote computers' X servers. To handle local logins, an XDMCP server runs on a computer and starts the local computer's X server. The XDMCP server then manages the local X server's display—that is, it puts up a login prompt like the one shown in Figure 6.1.

FIGURE 6.1 An XDMCP server manages local GUI logins to a Linux system.

Five XDMCP servers are common on Linux: the X Display Manager (XDM), the KDE Display Manager (KDM), the GNOME Display Manager (GDM), the Light Display Manager (LightDM), and the MDM Display Manager (MDM; a recursive acronym). A few more exotic XDMCP servers are also available, but these five are the most important. Of these, the exam objectives explicitly cover the first four, so they're the ones described here.

As you may guess by their names, KDM and GDM are associated with the KDE and GNOME projects, respectively. MDM is a derivative of GDM. XDM is the oldest and least feature-heavy of these display managers. LightDM aims to be compact and compatible with multiple desktop environments, and it has become the default for the Ubuntu distribution. You can change which desktop manager your system uses if you don't like the default.

Although KDM and GDM are associated with KDE and GNOME, respectively, neither limits your choice of desktop environment. In fact, it's possible, and often necessary, to run programs associated with one desktop environment inside another one. This works fine, although it increases the memory load.

Running an XDMCP Server

Several methods exist to start an XDMCP server. The two most common are to launch it more or less directly from init via an entry in /etc/inittab or its ancillary configuration files or to launch it as part of a runlevel's startup script set via a system startup script.

Chapter 5 describes both init and system startup scripts in general, so consult it for information about these processes.

Whichever method is used, many distributions configure themselves to run their chosen XDMCP server when they start in runlevel 5 but not when they start in runlevel 3. This is the only difference between these two runlevels in most cases. Thus, changing from runlevel 3 to runlevel 5 starts X and the XDMCP server on many distributions, and switching back to runlevel 3 stops X and the XDMCP server. As described in more detail in Chapter 5, you can change runlevels as root with the telinit command:

```
# telinit 5
```

Permanently changing the runlevel on a SysV-based system requires editing the /etc/inittab file and, in particular, its id line:

```
id:5:initdefault:
```

Change the number (5 in this case) to the runlevel you want to use as the default. Most distributions that use Upstart or systemd start the XDMCP server via methods more akin to the methods traditionally used by Debian, as described next.

A few distributions—most notably Gentoo, Debian, and Debian's derivatives (including the popular Ubuntu)—attempt to start an XDMCP server in all runlevels (or don't do so at all). This is done through the use of a SysV startup script called xdm, kdm, or gdm. You can temporarily start or stop the XDMCP server by running this script and passing it the start or stop option. To enable or disable the XDMCP server permanently, you should adjust your SysV startup scripts, as described in Chapter 5.

In addition to the question of whether to run an XDMCP server is the question of *which* XDMCP server to run. Most distributions set a default XDMCP server in one way or another. Two common methods exist:

Selection via Configuration File   Some distributions hide the XDMCP server choice in a configuration file, often in the /etc/sysconfig directory. In Fedora, the /etc/sysconfig/desktop file sets the DISPLAYMANAGER variable to the path to the executable, as in DISPLAYMANAGER=/bin/xdm. In openSUSE, /etc/sysconfig/displaymanager sets the DISPLAYMANAGER variable to the display manager's name in lowercase letters, as in DISPLAYMANAGER="xdm".

Selection via Startup Script   In Debian and derivative distributions, such as Ubuntu, the display manager is set via a SysV, Upstart, or systemd startup script—use the gdm script to use GDM, kdm to use KDM, and so on. By default, only one XDMCP server (and associated startup script) is installed, so if you want to change your XDMCP server, you may need to install your desired server. Chapter 5 describes how to configure specific startup scripts to run automatically.

Unfortunately, distribution maintainers have had a habit of changing the details of how XDMCP servers are launched from time to time, and the settings are often buried in poorly documented configuration files. Therefore, you may need to go digging through the files in your /etc directory to find the correct setting. If you can't find the setting, try using grep to search for strings such as DISPLAYMANAGER or the name of the XDMCP server that's currently running.

Configuring an XDMCP Server

XDMCP servers, like most programs, can be configured. Unfortunately, this configuration varies from one server to another, although there are some commonalities. In the following pages, we provide some details for configuring XDM, KDM, and GDM.

Configuring XDM

XDM is the simplest of the major XDMCP servers. It accepts usernames and passwords, but it doesn't enable users to perform other actions, such as choosing which desktop environment to run. (This must be configured through user login files.)

XDM's main configuration file is /etc/X11/xdm/xdm-config. Most distributions ship with a basic xdm-config file that should work fine for a local workstation. If you want to enable the computer to respond to remote login requests from other X servers on the network, or if you want to verify that the system is *not* configured accordingly, you should pay attention to this line:

```
DisplayManager.requestPort: 0
```

This line tells XDM not to access a conventional server port. To activate XDM as a remote login server, you should change 0 to 177, the traditional XDMCP port. You must then restart XDM. When the file is so configured, users on other computers can initiate remote X-based logins to your computer via XDMCP. This can be handy on local networks, but it's also a security risk, which is why the default is not to enable such access.

The /etc/X11/xdm/Xaccess file is another important XDM configuration file. If XDM is configured to permit remote access, this file controls who may access the XDM server and in what ways. A wide-open system contains lines that use an asterisk (*) to denote that anybody may access the system:

```
*
* CHOOSER BROADCAST
```

The first line tells XDM that anybody may connect, and the second line tells XDM that anybody may request a *chooser*—a display of local systems that accept XDMCP connections. To limit the choices, you should list individual computers or groups of computers instead of using the asterisk wildcard:

```
*.pangaea.edu
tux.example.com
*.pangaea.edu CHOOSER BROADCAST
```

This example lets any computer in the pangaea.edu domain connect to or receive a chooser, and it also lets tux.example.com connect to but not receive a chooser.

Many additional options are set in the /etc/X11/xdm/Xresources file; it hosts X *resources*, which are similar to environment variables but apply only to X-based programs. For instance, you can change the text displayed by XDM by altering the xlogin*greeting resource in this file.

Configuring KDM

KDM is based partly on XDM, and so it shares many of its configuration options. Unfortunately, the location of the KDM configuration files is unpredictable; sometimes KDM uses the XDM configuration files, at other times they're stored in /etc/X11/kdm or /etc/kde/kdm, and occasionally they're stored in a truly strange location, such as /usr/lib/kde4/libexec/.

If you can't find the KDM configuration files, try using your package management tools, described in Chapter 2, "Managing Software." Try obtaining lists of files in the kdm or kdebase package or some other likely candidate, and look for the KDM configuration files.

KDM expands on XDM by enabling users to select a session type when they log in, to shut down the computer from the main KDM prompt, and so on. Most of these extra options are set in the kdmrc file, which appears in the same directory as the other KDM configuration files. Some of these options override the more common XDM configuration options for the same features. In particular, the [Xdmcp] section provides options relating to network operation. The Enable option in that section should be set to true if you want to support network logins.

Configuring GDM

GDM is more of a break from XDM than is KDM. GDM doesn't use the conventional XDM configuration files or similar files. Instead, it uses configuration files that are usually stored in /etc/X11/gdm or /etc/gdm. In the past, the most important of these files was gdm.conf, and it had a format similar to the kdmrc file. More recent versions of GDM, however, place this file elsewhere and give it a new format. With these versions, you can set local options in the custom.conf file in the GDM configuration directory. This file typically starts with no options, but the ones you set override the defaults. As with KDM, you should set the enable option to yes in the [xdmcp] section if you want to enable remote logins.

A GUI control tool for GDM exists on some systems, but it is missing from others. Type **gdmconfig** or **gdmsetup** as root to launch this program, which enables you to set GDM options using a point-and-click interface.

Like KDM, GDM provides extra options over those of XDM. These options include the ability to choose your login environment and shut down the computer. GDM is a bit unusual in that it prompts for the username and only then presents a prompt for the password. XDM and KDM both present fields for the username and password simultaneously.

Configuring LightDM

LightDM is intended to be a common XDMCP server that can be used in any desktop environment, independent of the graphical library used. Since the Ubuntu developers switched to the Unity desktop, they also decided to incorporate LightDM to provide the graphical login environment.

The system-generated LightDM configuration files are stored in the /usr/share/ lightdm/lightdm.conf.d folder:

```
$ ls -l
total 20
-rw-r--r-- 1 root root 72 Apr  8 00:30 50-greeter-wrapper.conf
-rw-r--r-- 1 root root 68 Apr  8 00:30 50-guest-wrapper.conf
-rw-r--r-- 1 root root 35 Mar 13  2014 50-ubuntu.conf
-rw-r--r-- 1 root root 45 Apr  8 00:36 50-unity-greeter.conf
-rw-r--r-- 1 root root 51 Apr  8 00:30 50-xserver-command.conf
$
```

You can override the system-generated defaults by either making changes in the /etc/ lightdm/lightdm.conf file or creating files in the /etc/lightdm/lightdm.conf.d folder.

For example, if you want to disable the Guest login feature in the Ubuntu login window, set by default in LightDM, you can change the /etc/lightdm/lightdm.conf file (or create it if it doesn't exist) to add the lines:

```
[SeatDefaults]
allow-guest=false
```

When you reboot your Ubuntu system, the option to log in as the Guest account will not be present in the login window.

Using X for Remote Access

As noted earlier, in "The X GUI Login System," X is a network-enabled GUI. This fact lets you run Linux programs remotely—you can set up a Linux system with X programs and run them from other Linux (or even non-Linux) computers. Similarly, you can use a Linux computer as an access terminal for X programs that run on a non-Linux Unix computer, such as one running Oracle Solaris. To do this, you should first understand something of X's network model, including where the client and server systems are located, how X controls access to itself, and so on. You can then proceed to perform the remote accesses.

X Client-Server Principles

Most people think of servers as powerful computers hidden away in machine rooms and of clients as the desktop systems that ordinary people use. Although this characteriza-tion is often correct, it's very wrong when it comes to X. X is a server, meaning that the X server runs on the computer at which the user sits. X clients are the programs that users run—xterm, xfontsel, KMail, LibreOffice, and so on. In most cases, the X server and its clients reside on the same computer, so this peculiar terminology doesn't matter, but when you use X for remote access, you must remember that the X server runs on the user's computer, while the X clients run on the remote system.

To make sense of this peculiarity, think of it from the program's point of view. For instance, consider a web browser such as Firefox. This program accesses web pages stored on a web server computer. The web server responds to requests from Firefox to load files. Firefox not only loads files, it also displays them on the screen and accepts input from its user. From the program's point of view, this activity is much like retrieving web pages, but an X server handles it rather than a web server. This relationship is illustrated in Figure 6.2.

FIGURE 6.2   From a program's point of view, the X server works much like a conventional network server such as a web server.

Ordinarily, Linux is configured in such a way that its X server responds only to local access requests as a security measure. Thus, if you want to run programs remotely, you must make some changes to have Linux lower its defenses—but not too far, lest you let anybody access the X server, which could result in security breaches.

Using Remote X Clients

Suppose your local network contains two machines. The computer called zeus is a powerful machine that hosts important programs like word processors and data analysis utilities. The computer called apollo is a much less powerful system, but it has an adequate monitor and keyboard. Therefore, you want to sit at apollo and run programs that are located on zeus. Both systems run Linux. To accomplish this task, follow these steps:

1. Log into apollo, and if it's not already running X, start it.

2. Open a terminal (such as an xterm) on apollo.

3. Type **xhost +zeus** in apollo's terminal. This command tells apollo to accept for display in its X server data that originates on zeus.

4. Log into zeus from apollo. You might use Telnet or Secure Shell (SSH), for instance. The result should be the ability to type commands in a shell on zeus.

5. On zeus, type **export DISPLAY=apollo:0.0**. (This assumes that you're using bash; if you're using tcsh, the command is **setenv DISPLAY apollo:0.0**.) This command tells zeus to use apollo for the display of X programs. (Chapter 9, "Writing Scripts, Configuring Email, and Using Databases," describes environment variables, such as DISPLAY, in greater detail.)

6. Type whatever you need to type to run programs at the zeus command prompt. For instance, you could type **loffice** to launch LibreOffice. You should see the programs open on apollo's display, but they're running on zeus—their computations use zeus's CPU, they can read files accessible on zeus, and so on.

7. After you're done, close the programs you've launched, log off zeus, and type **xhost -zeus** on apollo. This tightens security so that an intruder on zeus won't be able to modify your display on apollo.

Sometimes, you can skip some of these steps. For instance, depending on how it's configured, SSH can forward X connections, meaning that SSH intercepts attempts to display X information and passes those requests on to the system that initiated the connection. When this happens, you can skip steps 3 and 5, as well as the xhost command in step 7. (See the Real World Scenario sidebar "Encrypting X Connections with SSH.")

 Real World Scenario

Encrypting X Connections with SSH

The SSH protocol is a useful remote-access tool. Although it's often considered a text-mode protocol, SSH also has the ability to *tunnel* network connections—that is, to carry another protocol through its own encrypted connection. This feature is most useful for handling remote X access. You can perform the steps described in "Using Remote X Clients" but omit steps 3 and 5 and the xhost command in step 7. This greatly simplifies the login process and adds the benefits of SSH's encryption, which X doesn't provide. On the other hand, SSH's encryption is likely to slow down X access, although if you enable SSH's compression features, this problem may be reduced in severity. Overall, tunneling X through SSH is the preferred method of remote X access, particularly when any network in the process isn't totally secure.

SSH tunneling does require that certain options be set. In particular, you must either use the -X or -Y option to the ssh client program or set the ForwardX11 or ForwardX11Trusted option to yes in /etc/ssh_config on the client system. You must also set the X11Forwarding option to yes in the /etc/sshd_config file on the SSH server system. These options enable SSH's X forwarding feature; without these options, SSH's X forwarding won't work.

As an added security measure, many Linux distributions today configure X to ignore true network connections. If your distribution is thus configured, the preceding steps won't work;

when you try to launch an X program from the remote system, you'll get an error message. To work around this problem, you must make an additional change, depending on how X is launched:

GDM   On older versions of GDM, check the GDM configuration file (typically /etc/X11/gdm/gdm.conf), look for the line DisallowTCP=true, and change it to read DisallowTCP=false. On newer versions of GDM, edit /etc/gdm/custom.conf and add a line that reads DisallowTCP=false to the [security] section (adding the section if required).

KDM or XDM   These two XDMCP servers both rely on settings in the Xservers file (in /etc/X11/xdm for XDM, and in this location or some other highly variable location for KDM). Look for the line that begins with :0. This line contains the command that KDM or XDM uses to launch the X server. If this line contains the string -nolisten tcp, remove that string from the line. Doing so eliminates the option that causes X to ignore conventional network connections.

Special openSUSE Configuration   In openSUSE, you must edit /etc/sysconfig/display-manager and set the DISPLAYMANAGER_XSERVER_TCP_PORT_6000_OPEN option to yes.

X Launched from a Text-Mode Login   If you log in using text mode and type **startx** to launch X, you may need to modify the startx script itself, which is usually stored in /usr/bin. Search this script for the string -nolisten tcp. Chances are that this string will appear in a variable assignment (such as to defaultserverargs) or possibly in a direct call to the X server program. Remove the -nolisten tcp option from this variable assignment or program call.

Once you've made these changes, you'll need to restart X as described earlier in "Running an XDMCP Server." Thereafter, X should respond to remote access requests.

 WARNING   If X responds to remote network requests, the risk of an intruder using a bug or misconfiguration to trick users by displaying bogus messages on the screen is greatly increased. You should therefore disable this protection only if you're sure that doing so is necessary. You may be able to use an SSH link without disabling this protection.

Another option for running X programs remotely is to use the Virtual Network Computing (VNC) system (www.realvnc.com). VNC runs a special X server on the computer that is designed to be used from a distance, and a special VNC client runs on the computer at which you sit. You use the client to contact the server directly. This reversal of client and server roles over the normal state of affairs with conventional X remote access is beneficial in some situations, such as when you're trying to access a distant system from behind certain types of firewalls. VNC is also a cross-platform protocol; it's possible to control a Windows or Mac OS system from Linux using VNC, but this isn't possible with X. (X servers for Windows and Mac OS are available, enabling you to control a Linux system from these non-Linux OSs.)

X Accessibility

Historically, most computers have been designed for individuals with ordinary physical capabilities. As computers have become everyday tools, though, the need for people with various disabilities to be able to use computers has risen. Linux provides tools to help with this task.

Some basic X settings (controlled in xorg.conf or XF86Config) can help in this respect—for instance, you can adjust the keyboard repeat rate to prevent spurious key repeats for individuals who may keep keys pressed longer than average. Other settings are unusual and may require the use of unique accessibility tools to set. Some options must be set in specific desktop environments (KDE or GNOME, for example).

Keyboard and Mouse Accessibility Issues

You can set many keyboard and mouse options using ordinary desktop environment tools for personalizing keyboard and mouse responses. Other options are more exotic, such as onscreen keyboards.

Standard Keyboard and Mouse Options

Most Linux desktop environments include keyboard and mouse control panel options. For instance, in a standard Fedora 17 GNOME installation, you can find the keyboard options in the Keyboard item of the System Settings control panel, and you can find the mouse options in the Mouse and Touchpad item. The AccessX utility is an older program that works in any desktop environment to provide similar features. Figure 6.3 shows AccessX in operation. Because the locations of such options can be customized from one distribution to another, and can even change from one release to another, you may need to hunt for the options in your menus.

The exam objectives mention AccessX; however, this package is not available in most distributions and appears to be abandoned. Its functionality has been folded into desktop environment control panels. Thus, although we describe AccessX's features, chances are you'll need to look for equivalents in your desktop environment's control panel.

You can set the following keyboard and mouse accessibility features with AccessX or similar tools in desktop environments (sometimes under slightly different names):

Sticky Keys When enabled, this option causes keyboard modifier keys (Ctrl, Alt, and Shift) to "stick" when pressed, affecting the next regular key to be pressed even after release of the sticky key. This can be useful for users who have difficulty pressing multiple keys simultaneously. Some tools, including AccessX, provide additional options that affect the details of how sticky keys work.

FIGURE 6.3   AccessX and desktop environment control panels provide accessibility options.

Toggle Keys   When enabled plays a sound cue when the locking keys (Caps lock, Num lock, or Scroll lock) are pressed. A high-pitched sound plays when the features are activated, and a low-pitched sound plays when the features are deactivated.

Mouse Keys   This option enables you to use the cursor keypad on your keyboard to emulate a mouse.

Bounce (or Debounce) Keys   If a user tends to press a single key accidentally multiple times, the bounce keys option may be able to compensate for this tendency. (Aging keyboards also sometimes produce keybounce.)

Slow Keys   When activated, this option requires a key to be pressed for longer than a specified period of time before it registers as a keypress. This feature is useful for individuals who tend to press keys accidentally.

Keyboard Repeat Rate   The repeat delay and rate can be set using sliders. These settings override those set in the X configuration file, but if you use a bare window manager, you may need to set these options in the X configuration file. Disabling keyboard repeat or setting a very long delay may be necessary for some users.

Time Out   In AccessX, the TimeOut option sets a time after which its accessibility options will be disabled.

Mouse Tracking and Click Options   The ordinary mouse tracking and click options can be adjusted to unusual values for those who have special needs. (This and the next two options are not provided by AccessX but are provided by many desktop environments.)

Simulated Mouse Clicks   Some environments let you configure the mouse to simulate a click whenever the mouse pointer stops moving or to simulate a double click whenever the mouse button is pressed for an extended period.

Mouse Gestures   Gestures are similar to keyboard shortcuts but are designed for mice. They permit you to activate program options by moving your mouse in particular ways.

Using Onscreen Keyboards

If a user has difficulty using a regular keyboard but can use a mouse, that user can employ an onscreen keyboard. This is an application that displays an image of a keyboard. Using the mouse to press the keys on the keyboard image works much like using a real keyboard. Some other keyboards require the user to enter text into their own buffers and then cut and paste the text from the keyboard application into the target program.

Browse the menus for your desktop environment to locate the onscreen keyboards available on your system. If you can't find one, or if you don't like it, use your package manager to search for such programs—searching on *keyboard* should turn up some options.

The GNOME desktop development team created the *GNOME On-Screen Keyboard (GOK)*, which not only provides an onscreen keyboard, it also delivers tools that provide shortcuts for the various mouse, menu, and toolbar features of other programs as well as tools to help users navigate the GNOME desktop. Newer versions of the GNOME desktop have replaced GOK with *Caribou*, the successor to the GOK project. You can learn more at the main Caribou web page, `http://wiki.gnome.org/action/show/Projects/Caribou`.

Screen Display Settings

Users with poor eyesight can benefit from adjustments to screen settings and applications. These include font options, contrast settings, and screen magnification tools.

Adjusting Default Fonts

Most desktop environments provide options to set the default fonts used on the screen. Figure 6.4 shows the System Settings dialog box provided with KDE. You can access this by typing **systemsettings** in a terminal window or by selecting Configure Desktop from the main menu and then selecting Application Appearance from the options in the window that appears. A similar tool is available in Xfce, accessible from the Appearance item in its System Settings panel.

To adjust the fonts, click the Choose button to the right of the font for each of the main categories, such as General and Menu in Figure 6.4. The result is a font selection dialog box in which you can select the font family (Sans, Times, and so on), the font style (normal, bold, and so forth), and the font size in points. Adjust these options until you find a setting that works well. You'll have to adjust the font for each of the categories, or at least for those that are most important.

FIGURE 6.4 Linux desktop environments usually provide control panels with font options.

Dyslexic users often benefit from a special font that weights the bottoms of the characters more heavily than the tops. One such font is available from http://dyslexicfonts.com.

Unfortunately, although many applications take their cues on fonts from the desktop environment's settings, others don't. Thus, you may need to adjust options in at least some individual applications as well as in the desktop environment as a whole.

Adjusting Contrast

Desktop environments provide various themes—settings for colors, window manager decorations, and so on. Some themes are better than others in terms of legibility. For instance, some themes are very low in contrast, and others are high in contrast.

Monitors have their own contrast controls. You can adjust these for best legibility, of course, but the contrast adjustments afforded by desktop environment settings are independent of a monitor's contrast settings.

In KDE, you can set themes in the same System Settings preferences dialog box in which you set the fonts (see Figure 6.4); you click the Colors icon in the left pane and select the theme you want to use. The Workspace Appearance item (accessible by clicking Overview from the screen shown in Figure 6.4) provides additional options. Xfce provides similar options in its Appearance control panel.

Using Magnifier Tools

A screen magnifier application enlarges part of the screen—typically the area immediately surrounding the mouse. One common screen magnifier is KMag, which is part of the KDE suite. (You can use KMag even in GNOME, Xfce, or other desktop environments though.) To use it, type **kmag** or select it from your desktop menus. The result is the KMag window on the screen, which enlarges the area around the cursor by default.

Using Additional Assistive Technologies

In addition to keyboard, mouse, and conventional display tools, some programs can help those with special needs. Most notably, screen readers and Braille displays can help those who can't read conventional displays.

Configuring Linux to Speak

Computer speech synthesis has existed for decades. Today, several speech synthesis products are available for Linux, including these:

Orca   This program, which is based at http://live.gnome.org/Orca, is a screen reader that's been integrated into GNOME 2.16 and later.

Emacspeak   Similar to Orca in many respects, this program aims to enable those with visual impairments to use a Linux computer. You can learn more at http://emacspeak. sourceforge.net.

Using Braille Displays

A Braille display is a special type of computer monitor. Rather than display data visually, it creates a tactile display of textual information in Braille. As such, a Braille display is an efficient way for those with visual impairments to access text-mode information, such as that displayed at a Linux text-mode console. Many Linux text-mode programs can manage a Braille display with no changes.

To use a Braille display, special Linux software is required. The BRLTTY project (www.mielke.cc/brltty/) provides a Linux daemon that redirects text-mode console output to a Braille display. It includes features that support scrollback, multiple virtual terminals, and even speech synthesis.

Linux kernels since 2.6.26 include direct support for Braille displays. If you're familiar with Linux kernel compilation, you should check the Accessibility Support options in the Device Drivers area of the kernel configuration.

Configuring Localization and Internationalization

Linux is an international OS. Its developers and users reside in many countries around the world. Therefore, Linux supports a wide variety of character sets, keyboards, date/time display formats, and other features that can vary from one region to another. Many of these features are set up when you answer questions during installation, but knowing about them—and how to change them—can help you manage your system, particularly if you need to change these options for any reason.

Setting Your Time Zone

When you communicate with other computers (by sending email, transferring files, and so on), those computers may reside in the same city or on the other side of the world. For this reason, it's helpful for your computer to know something about its time zone. This can help keep files' time stamps set sensibly and avoid weird temporal problems when data is exchanged. For the most part, you need to be concerned with just one time zone setting for a Linux computer. but sometimes you may want to set the time zone one way for one account or login and another way for another account or login. Thus, we describe both methods of setting a time zone.

Setting a Linux Computer's Time Zone

Linux uses *Coordinated Universal Time (UTC)* internally. This is the time in Greenwich, England, uncorrected for daylight savings time. When you write a file to disk on a Linux-native filesystem, the time stamp is stored in UTC. When you use tools such as `cron` (described in Chapter 7, "Administering the System"), they "think" in UTC. Chances are, though, that you use local time. Thus a Linux computer must be able to translate between local time and UTC.

To perform this translation, Linux needs to know your time zone. Linux looks to the `/etc/localtime` file for information about its local time zone. This file is one of the rare configuration files that's *not* a plain-text file, so you shouldn't try editing it with a text editor. This file could be a file of its own, or it could be a symbolic or hard link to another file. If it's a symbolic link, you should be able to determine your time zone by performing a long file listing to see the name of the file to which `localtime` links:

```
$ ls -l /etc/localtime
lrwxrwxrwx  1 root root 36 May 14  2008 /etc/localtime -> ~CA
/usr/share/zoneinfo/America/New_York
```

If /etc/localtime is a regular file and not a symbolic link, or if you want further confirmation of your time zone, try using the date command by itself:

```
$ date
Mon Sep  3 12:50:58 EDT 2012
```

The result includes a standard three-letter time zone code (EDT in this example). Of course, you'll need to know these codes, or at least the code for your area. For a list of time zone abbreviations, consult

www.timeanddate.com/library/abbreviations/timezones/

Note that the time zone codes vary depending on whether daylight saving time is active, but the Linux time zone files don't change with this detail. Part of what these files do is to describe when to change the clock for daylight savings time. If you need to change your time zone, you should copy or link a sample file from a standard directory location to the /etc/localtime file:

1. Log in as root or acquire root privileges.

2. Change to the /etc directory.

3. View the contents of the /usr/share/zoneinfo directory. This directory contains files for certain time zones named after the zones or the regions to which they apply, such as GMT, Poland, and Japan. Most users will need to look in subdirectories, such as /usr/share/zoneinfo/US for the United States or /usr/share/zoneinfo/America for North and South America. These subdirectories contain zone files named after the regions or cities to which they apply, such as Eastern or Los_Angeles. (The US subdirectory contains files named after time zones or states, whereas the America subdirectory holds files named after cities.) Identify the file for your time zone. Note that you might use a zone file named after a city other than the one in which you reside but that's in the same time zone as you. For instance, the New_York file works fine if you're in Boston, Philadelphia, Cincinnati, or any other city in the same (Eastern) time zone as New York.

4. If a localtime file exists in /etc, delete it or rename it. (For instance, type **rm localtime**.)

5. Create a symbolic link from your chosen time zone file to the /etc/localtime file. For instance, you can type **ln -s /usr/share/zoneinfo/US/Eastern localtime** to set up a computer in the US Eastern time zone. Alternatively, you can copy a file (cp) rather than create a symbolic link (ln -s). If /etc and your target file are on the same filesystem, you can create a hard link rather than a symbolic link if you like.

At this point, your system should be configured to use the time zone you've selected. If you change time zones, you should be able to see the difference by typing **date**, as described earlier. The time zone code on your system should be different, compared to when you issued this command before you changed the /etc/localtime file or link. The time should also change by the number of hours between the time zones you've selected (give or take a bit for the time it took you to change the time zone files).

In addition to /etc/localtime, some distributions use a secondary file with text-mode time zone data. This file is called /etc/timezone on Debian and its derivatives. On Fedora and related distributions, it's /etc/sysconfig/clock. This file contains a line or two with the name of the time zone, sometimes in the form of a variable assignment. For instance, for the Eastern time zone in the US, the /etc/timezone file should look like this:

America/New_York

This file provides a quick way to check your time zone. It should also be updated when you change your time zone, lest higher-level configuration tools become confused.

Some distributions provide text-mode or GUI tools to help make time zone changes. Look for a program called tzsetup, tzselect, tzconfig, or something similar. Typically, these programs ask you for your location in several steps (starting with your continent, then your nation, and perhaps then your state or city) and create an appropriate symbolic link.

Setting an Individual Login's Time Zone

One final wrinkle on time zone issues is the TZ environment variable. (Chapter 9 covers environment variables in more detail.) This environment variable holds time zone information in any of three formats:

- The most common format on Linux is :*filename*, as in :/usr/share/zoneinfo/ Europe/London. This tells the system that the time zone is the one described in the specified file.

- A second format, common on non-Linux systems, is *std offset*, where *std* is a three-character or longer time zone name (such as EST) and *offset* is a time relative to UTC, with positive values representing offsets west of the prime meridian and negative values being east of it. For instance, EST+5 specifies US Eastern time. This format is used when daylight savings time is not in effect.

- If daylight savings time *is* in effect, a variant on the preceding method is possible: *std offset dst*[*offset*],*start*[/*time*],*end*[*time*]. This specification adds the daylight savings time code as well as encoded start and end dates (and optionally times). For instance, EST+5EDT,M3.10.0/2,M11.3.0/2 specifies US Eastern time with daylight savings time encoded with dates for 2013.

In the vast majority of cases, you won't need to use the TZ environment variable. It can be useful, though, in the event that you're using a computer remotely—say, if you're logging into a work computer that's physically located in San Francisco while you're traveling to London. Using TZ will enable programs that use this variable to display the correct local date and time in London, despite the fact that the computer's global time zone is (presumably) set for San Francisco.

In practice, the easiest way to use TZ for a single login is to issue a command such as the following:

```
$ export TZ=:/usr/share/zoneinfo/Europe/London
```

This example sets the time zone to London for a single session, but only from the shell at which you type this command. You can add this command to a user startup script if you want to use it regularly. You should *not* use this method if all of a computer's programs should use the target time zone; instead, set it by adjusting the /etc/localtime file, as described earlier in "Setting a Linux Computer's Time Zone."

Querying and Setting Your Locale

To localize your computer, you must first understand what a locale is in Linux parlance. Once you understand the basics, you can identify your current locale and other locales available to you. If necessary, you may need to install another locale's data. You can then set your computer to use that locale.

What Is a Locale?

In Linux, a *locale* is a way of specifying the computer's (or user's) language, country, and related information for the purpose of customizing displays. A single locale takes the following form:

[language[_territory][.codeset][@modifier]]

Each part of this string has a set of specific acceptable forms. For instance, language can be en (English), fr (French), ja (Japanese), and so on. These are two- or three-letter codes for languages.

The territory code can be US (United States), FR (France), JP (Japan), and so on. These are codes for specific regions—generally nations.

The codeset code can be ASCII, UTF-8, or other encoding names. The *American Standard Code for Information Interchange (ASCII)* is the oldest and most primitive encoding method; it supports 7-bit encodings (generally stored in 8-bit bytes) that can handle English, including common punctuation and symbols. ASCII can't handle characters used in many non-English languages, though, so it's awkward at best for international use. *ISO-8859* was an early attempt to extend ASCII; it employs an eighth bit to extend ASCII by 128 characters, giving room for the characters needed by a small number of non-Roman alphabets. ISO-8859 is broken down into many substandards, each of which handles one language or small group of languages. ISO-8859-1 covers Western European languages and ISO-8859-5 provides Cyrillic support, for instance.

The latest language codeset is the 8-bit *Unicode Transformation Format (UTF-8)*. Like ISO-8859, UTF-8 starts with ASCII, but it extends it by supporting variable-byte extensions so that a single character can take anywhere from 1 to 4 bytes to be encoded. This provides the ability to encode text in any language supported by *Unicode*, which is a character set designed to support as many languages as possible. The big advantage of UTF-8 over ISO-8859 is that there's no need to specify a substandard, such as ISO-8859-1 or ISO-8859-5; UTF-8 handles all of its writing systems automatically.

The *modifier* is a locale-specific code that modifies how it works. For instance, it may affect the sort order in a language-specific manner.

What Is Your Locale?

A locale code can be assigned to one or more of several environment variables. To learn how these are set on your system, issue the `locale` command without any arguments:

```
$ /usr/bin/locale
LANG=en_US.UTF-8
LC_CTYPE="en_US.UTF-8"
LC_NUMERIC="en_US.UTF-8"
LC_TIME="en_US.UTF-8"
LC_COLLATE="en_US.UTF-8"
LC_MONETARY="en_US.UTF-8"
LC_MESSAGES="en_US.UTF-8"
LC_PAPER="en_US.UTF-8"
LC_NAME="en_US.UTF-8"
LC_ADDRESS="en_US.UTF-8"
LC_TELEPHONE="en_US.UTF-8"
LC_MEASUREMENT="en_US.UTF-8"
LC_IDENTIFICATION="en_US.UTF-8"
LC_ALL=
```

As you can see, quite a few locale variables exist. When programs pay attention to these variables, they adjust themselves appropriately for your locale. For instance, a word processor may default to using common US paper sizes (such as 8.5 × 11 inches) when the *territory* code in LC_PAPER is set to US, but European paper sizes (such as A4, 210 × 297 mm) when *territory* is set to a code for a country where these paper sizes are more common.

Most of the locale variables set specific and obvious features, such as LC_PAPER (paper size), LC_MEASUREMENT (measurement units), and so on. The LC_ALL variable is a sort of master override—if it's set, it overrides all of the other LC_* variables.

A related environment variable is LANG. It takes the same type of locale specification as the LC_* variables. It sets the locale in case the LC_* variables aren't set.

While you're using the `locale` command, you should try it with the -a option, which identifies all of the locales that are available to you:

```
$ locale -a
C
en_US.utf8
POSIX
```

In this example (from an Ubuntu system), very few locales are installed. Some systems may have many more; one of our computers has hundreds of locales available, for example.

Changing Your Locale

If you want to change your locale, you should first verify that an appropriate one is available to you by using `locale -a`, as just described. If you don't see appropriate codes, you may need to install additional packages. Unfortunately, names for these packages aren't standardized. Your best bet is to use a GUI package manager such as yumex or Synaptic (described in Chapter 2) to search on package names and descriptions that include `locale` or `language`. In the case of an Ubuntu system that provides just a few locales, many more can be installed from packages called `language-support-??`, where *??* is a two-character language code.

To change your locale temporarily, the simplest method is to set the `LC_ALL` environment variable. For safety, you should also set `LANG`. For instance, to use the locale for Great Britain rather than the United States, you can type

```
$ export LANG=en_GB.UTF-8
$ export LC_ALL=en_GB.UTF-8
```

The result should be that all of the locale variables change for that session. There will also be changes in the output of programs that honor locales. Note that this change affects only the current shell and the programs launched from it; you won't see changes in programs that are already running or that you launch from another shell.

To change your locale permanently, you can adjust your bash startup script files, such as `~/.bashrc` or `/etc/profile`, as described in Chapter 1, "Exploring Linux Command-Line Tools." (Shell scripting is described in more detail in Chapter 9, but setting or adjusting the `LANG` and `LC_ALL` environment variables is fairly straightforward.)

X's configuration file (`xorg.conf` or `XF86Config`) includes an option called `XkbLayout` in the keyboard's `InputDevice` section. This option takes a partial or complete locale specification but converted to lowercase—for instance, `us` or `en_us.utf-8`. Adjusting this option can provide you with access to language- or country-specific keys. After changing this option, you'll have to restart X for the changes to take effect.

Some programs and sets of programs may require you to set the language independent of the overall system locale. Thus, you may need to adjust the language for certain specific programs. If a program doesn't seem to respond to the overall locale setting, check its documentation, or browse through its menus, to find a way to adjust its defaults.

One setting requires special mention: `LANG=C`. When you set `LANG` to `C`, programs that see this environment variable display output without passing it through locale translations. This can be helpful in some cases if a program's output is being corrupted by the locale—say by having conversions to UTF-8 change characters that need to be preserved as 8-bit entities. Thus, setting `LANG=C` can help avoid some types of problems, particularly in pipelines and scripts that pass one program's data to another program in binary form.

Localization support is, to some extent or another, the responsibility of each program's author. It's entirely possible to write a program that supports just one language or a small subset of languages. Thus, you won't be able to get every program to support your desired language, particularly if it's an uncommon one.

Modifying Text-File Locales

Sometimes it's necessary to access textual data that originated on a system that used one encoding but processed the data with a program that doesn't support that encoding. For instance, your preferred text editor might support UTF-8 but not ISO-8859. If you deal exclusively with English text files in ASCII, this isn't a problem; but if you receive an ISO-8859-1 text file with a few non-Roman characters, such as characters with umlauts, your editor might display those characters strangely.

To overcome this problem, the iconv utility converts between character sets. Its syntax is as follows:

```
iconv -f encoding [-t encoding] [inputfile]...
```

The -f and -t options specify the source and destination encodings. (You can obtain a list of encodings by typing **iconv --list**.) If you omit the target encoding, iconv uses your current locale for guidance. The program sends output to standard output, so if you want to store the data in a file, you must redirect it:

```
$ iconv -f iso-8859-1 -t UTF-8 umlautfile.txt > umlautfile-utf8.txt
```

Configuring Printing

Most Linux desktop users work with X, but many also work with another output medium: printed pages. Printing in Linux is a cooperative effort involving several tools. Applications submit print jobs as PostScript documents. Because most Linux systems aren't connected directly to true PostScript printers, a program called Ghostscript converts the print job into a form that the system's printer can actually handle. The print queue, which is managed by software known as the *Common Unix Printing System (CUPS)*, then sends the job to the printer. At various stages, administrators and users can examine the contents of a print queue and modify the queue. Understanding the tools used to create and manage print queues will help you to manage Linux printing.

Conceptualizing the Linux Printing Architecture

Linux printing is built around the concept of a *print queue*. This is a sort of holding area where files wait to be printed. A single computer can support many distinct print queues. These frequently correspond to different physical printers, but it's also possible to configure several queues to print in different ways to the same printer. For instance, you might use one queue to print single-sided and another queue for double-sided printing on a printer that supports duplexing.

Users submit print jobs by using a program called lpr. Users can call this program directly, or they may let another program call it. In either case, lpr sends the print job into a specified queue. This queue corresponds to a directory on the hard disk, typically in a subdirectory of the /var/spool/cups directory. The CUPS daemon runs in the background, watching for print jobs to be submitted. The printing system accepts print jobs from lpr or from remote computers, monitors print queues, and serves as a sort of "traffic cop," directing print jobs in an orderly fashion from print queues to printers.

 The exam emphasizes the CUPS printing system, which is the most common printing system on modern Linux systems. Older systems used the BSD Line Printer Daemon (LPD) or the similar LPRng printing system. Many of the CUPS tools are workalikes of the LPD tools. If you ever use a system that runs LPD or LPRng, you'll find that user commands such as lpr work in the way you would expect, but configuring the printer must be done in a very different way.

One important and unusual characteristic of Linux printing is that it's highly network oriented. As just noted, Linux printing tools can accept print jobs that originate from remote systems as well as from local ones. Even local print jobs are submitted via network protocols, although they don't normally use network hardware, so even a computer with no network connections can print. In addition to being a server for print jobs, CUPS can function as a client, passing print jobs to other computers that run the same protocols.

Applications can query CUPS about a printer's capabilities—its paper sizes, whether it supports color, and so on. The older LPD and LPRng printing systems didn't support such bidirectional communication. Thus, support for these features still isn't universal; some programs make assumptions about a printer's capabilities or must be told things that other programs can figure out by themselves.

Understanding PostScript and Ghostscript

If you've configured printers under Windows, Mac OS, or certain other OSs, you're probably familiar with the concept of a *printer driver*. In these OSs, the printer driver stands between the application and the printer queue. In Linux, the printer driver is part of Ghostscript (www.cs.wisc.edu/~ghost/), which exists as part of the printer queue, albeit a late part. This relationship can be confusing at times, particularly because not all applications or printers need Ghostscript. *Ghostscript* serves as a way to translate PostScript, a common printer language, into forms that can be understood by many different printers. Understanding Ghostscript's capabilities, and how it fits into a printer queue, can be important for configuring printers.

PostScript: The De Facto Linux Printer Language

PostScript printers became popular as accessories for Unix systems in the 1980s. Unix print queues weren't designed with Windows-style printer drivers in mind, so Unix programs that took advantage of laser printer features were typically written to produce PostScript output directly. As a result, *PostScript* developed into the de facto printing standard for Unix and, by inheritance, Linux. Where programs on Windows systems were built to interface with the Windows printer driver, similar programs on Linux generate PostScript and send the result to the Linux printer queue.

Some programs violate this standard. Most commonly, many programs can produce raw text output. Such output seldom poses a major problem for modern printers, although some PostScript-only models choke on raw text. Some other programs can produce either PostScript or *Printer Control Language (PCL)* output for Hewlett-Packard laser printers or their many imitators. A very few programs can generate output that's directly accepted by other types of printers.

The problem with PostScript as a standard is that it's uncommon on the low- and mid-priced printers with which Linux is often paired. Therefore, to print to such printers using traditional Unix programs that generate PostScript output, you need a translator and a way to fit that translator into the print queue. This is where Ghostscript fits into the picture.

Ghostscript: A PostScript Translator

When it uses a traditional PostScript printer, a computer sends a PostScript file directly to the printer. PostScript is a programming language, albeit one that's oriented toward the goal of producing a printed page as output. Ghostscript is a PostScript interpreter that runs on a computer. It takes PostScript input, parses it, and produces output in any of dozens of different bitmap formats, including formats that can be accepted by many non-PostScript printers. This makes Ghostscript a way to turn many inexpensive printers into Linux-compatible PostScript printers at very low cost.

One of Ghostscript's drawbacks is that it produces large output files. A PostScript file that produces a page filled with text may be just a few kilobytes in size. If this page is to be printed on a 600 dots per inch (dpi) printer using Ghostscript, the resulting output file could be as large as 4MB—assuming it's black and white. If the page includes color, the size could be much larger. In some sense, this is unimportant because these big files will be stored on your hard disk only briefly. They still do have to get from the computer to the printer, though, and this process can be slow. Also, some printers (particularly older laser printers) may require memory expansion to operate reliably under Linux.

For information about what printers are supported by Ghostscript, check the Ghostscript web page or the OpenPrinting database web page (www.openprinting.org/printers).

Squeezing Ghostscript into the Queue

Printing to a non-PostScript printer in Linux requires fitting Ghostscript into the print queue. This is generally done through the use of a *smart filter*. This is a program that's called as part of the printing process. The smart filter examines the file that's being printed, determines its type, and passes the file through one or more additional programs before the printing software sends it on to the printer. The smart filter can be configured to call Ghostscript with whatever parameters are appropriate to produce output for the queue's printer.

CUPS ships with its own set of smart filters, which it calls automatically when you tell the system what model printer you're using. CUPS provides a Web-based configuration tool, as described in the upcoming section "Using the Web-Based CUPS Utilities." This system, or distribution-specific GUI printer configuration tools, can make setting up a printer for CUPS fairly straightforward.

The end result of a typical Linux printer queue configuration is the ability to treat any supported printer as if it were a PostScript printer. Applications that produce PostScript output can print directly to the queue. The smart filter detects that the output is PostScript and runs it through Ghostscript. The smart filter can also detect other file types, such as plain-text and various graphics files, and it can send them through appropriate programs instead of or in addition to Ghostscript in order to create a reasonable printout.

If you have a printer that can process PostScript, the smart filter is usually still involved, but it doesn't pass PostScript through Ghostscript. In this case, the smart filter passes PostScript directly to the printer, but it still sends other file types through whatever processing is necessary to turn them into PostScript.

Running a Printing System

Because Linux printing systems run as daemons, they must be started before they're useful. This task is normally handled automatically via startup scripts in /etc/rc.d, /etc/init.d, or /etc/rc?.d (where ? is a runlevel number). Look for startup scripts that contain the string cups (or lpd or lprng for older systems) in their names to learn what your system is running. If you're unsure if a printing system is currently active, use the ps utility to search for running processes by these names, as in

```
$ ps ax | grep cups
 1896 ?         Ss     0:01 cupsd
```

This example shows that cupsd, the CUPS daemon, is running, so the system is using CUPS for printing. If you can't find any running printing system, consult your distribution's documentation to learn what is available and check that the appropriate package is installed. All major distributions include startup scripts that should start the appropriate printing daemon when the computer boots.

Configuring CUPS

CUPS uses various configuration files in the /etc/cups directory and its subdirectories to manage its operation. You can edit these files directly, and you may need to do so if you want to share printers or use printers shared by other CUPS systems. The simplest way to add printers to CUPS, though, is to use the tool's Web-based configuration utility.

Editing the CUPS Configuration Files

You can add or delete printers by editing the /etc/cups/printers.conf file, which consists of printer definitions. Each definition begins with the name of a printer, identified by the string DefaultPrinter (for the default printer) or Printer (for a nondefault printer) in angle brackets (<>), as in the following:

<DefaultPrinter okidata>

This line marks the beginning of a definition for a printer queue called okidata. The end of this definition is a line that reads </Printer>. Intervening lines set assorted printer options, such as identifying strings, the printer's location (its local hardware port or network location), its current status, and so on. Additional options are stored in a *PostScript Printer Definition (PPD)* file that's named after the queue and stored in the /etc/cups/ppd subdirectory. PPD files follow an industry-standard format. For PostScript printers, you can obtain a PPD file from the printer manufacturer, typically from a driver CD-ROM or from the manufacturer's website. CUPS and its add-on driver packs also ship with a large number of PPD files that are installed automatically when you use the Web-based configuration utilities.

As a general rule, you're better off using the CUPS Web-based configuration tools to add printers rather than adding printers by directly editing the configuration files. If you like, though, you can study the underlying files and tweak the configurations using a text editor to avoid having to go through the full Web-based tool to make a minor change.

One exception to this rule relates to configuring the CUPS Web-based interface tool itself and CUPS's ability to interface with other CUPS systems. One of the great advantages of CUPS is that it uses a new network printing protocol, known as the *Internet Printing Protocol (IPP)*, in addition to the older LPD protocol used by BSD LPD and LPRng. IPP supports a feature it calls *browsing*, which enables computers on a network to exchange printer lists automatically. This feature can greatly simplify configuring network printing. You may need to change some settings in the main CUPS configuration file, /etc/cups/cupsd.conf, to enable this support.

The /etc/cups/cupsd.conf file, which is structurally similar to the Apache web server configuration file, contains a number of configuration blocks that specify which other systems should be able to access it. Each block controls access to a particular location on the server. These blocks look like this:

```
<Location /printers>
Order Deny,Allow
Deny from All
BrowseAllow from 127.0.0.1
BrowseAllow from 192.168.1.0/24
BrowseAllow from @LOCAL
Allow from 127.0.0.1
Allow from 192.168.1.0/24
Allow from @LOCAL
</Location>
```

If you're configuring a workstation with a local printer that you don't want to share, or if you want to configure a workstation to use printers shared via LPD or some other non-IPP printing protocol, you shouldn't need to adjust /etc/cups/cupsd.conf. If you want to access remote IPP printers, however, you should at least activate browsing by setting the directive Browsing On, as described shortly. You shouldn't have to modify your location definitions unless you want to share your local printers.

The /printers location section of the configuration file controls access to the printers themselves. The following list includes features of this example:

Directive Order   The Order Deny,Allow line tells CUPS in which order it should apply allow and deny directives—in this case, allow directives modify deny directives.

Default Policy   The Deny from All line tells the system to refuse all connections except those that are explicitly permitted.

Browsing Control Lines   The BrowseAllow lines tell CUPS from which other systems it should accept browsing requests. In this case, it accepts connections from itself (127.0.0.1), from systems on the 192.168.1.0/24 network, and from systems connected to local subnets (@LOCAL).

Access Control Lines   The Allow lines give the specified systems non-browse access to printers—that is, those systems can print to local printers. In most cases, the Allow lines are the same as the BrowseAllow lines.

You can also create a definition that uses Allow from All and then creates BrowseDeny and Deny lines to limit access. As a general rule, though, the approach shown in this example is safer. Locations other than the /printers location can also be important. For instance, there's a root (/) location that specifies default access permissions to all other locations and an /admin location that controls access to CUPS administrative functions.

Before the location definitions in cupsd.conf are a few parameters that enable or disable browsing and other network operations. You should look for the following options specifically:

Enabling Browsing   The Browsing directive accepts On and Off values. The CUPS default is to enable browsing (Browsing On), but some Linux distributions disable it by default.

Browsing Access Control   The BrowseAddress directive specifies the broadcast address to which browsing information should be sent. For instance, to broadcast data on your printers to the 192.168.1.0/24 subnet, you'd specify BrowseAddress 192.168.1.255.

Once you've configured a CUPS server to give other systems access to its printers via appropriate location directions, and once you've configured the client systems to use browsing via Browsing On, all of the systems on the network should auto-detect all of the printers on the network. You don't need to configure the printer on any computer except the one to which it's directly connected. CUPS propagates all printer characteristics, including their network locations and PPD files, automatically. This feature is most important in configuring large networks with many printers or networks on which printers are frequently added and deleted.

Obtaining CUPS Printer Definitions

Most Linux distributions ship with CUPS smart filter support for a variety of printers. If you can't find support for your printer, you can look for additional printer definitions. These definitions may consist of PPD files, appropriate behind-the-scenes "glue" to tell CUPS how to use them, and possibly Ghostscript driver files. You can obtain these printer definitions from several sources:

Your Linux Distribution   Many distributions ship extra printer definitions under various names, so check your distribution for such a package. Many distributions include some of the driver packages described next.

Foomatic   The Linux Printing website hosts a set of utilities and printer definitions known collectively as Foomatic. These provide many additional printer definitions for CUPS (as well as for other printing systems). The Linux Printing website is at the following location:

www.linuxfoundation.org/en/OpenPrinting/Database/Foomatic

Gutenprint   The Gutenprint drivers, originally known as GIMP Print, after the GNU Image Manipulation Program (GIMP), support a wide variety of printers. Check http://gimp-print.sourceforge.net for more information.

CUPS DDK   The CUPS Driver Development Kit (DDK) is a set of tools designed to simplify CUPS driver development. It ships with a handful of drivers for Hewlett-Packard and Epson printers, and it is included with the CUPS source code.

Printer Manufacturers   Some printer manufacturers offer CUPS drivers for their printers. These may be nothing more than Foomatic, Gutenprint, or other open-source drivers, but a few provide proprietary drivers, some of which support advanced printer features that the open-source drivers don't support.

Chances are good that you'll find support for your printer in your standard installation, particularly if your distribution has installed the Foomatic or Gutenprint package. If you start configuring printers and can't find your model, though, you should look for an additional printer definition set from one of the preceding sources.

Using the Web-Based CUPS Utilities

The CUPS IPP printing system is closely related to the Hypertext Transfer Protocol (HTTP) used on the Web. The protocol is so similar, in fact, that you can access a CUPS daemon by using a web browser. You need only specify that you want to access the server on port 631—the normal printer port. To do so, enter **http://localhost:631** in a web browser on the computer running CUPS. (You may be able to substitute the hostname or access CUPS from another computer by using the server's hostname, depending on your cupsd.conf settings.) This action brings up a list of administrative tasks you can perform. Click Printers or Manage Printers to open the printer management page, shown in Figure 6.5.

FIGURE 6.5   CUPS provides its own Web-based configuration tool.

 If you're configuring a stand-alone computer or the only one on a network to use CUPS, the printer list may be empty, unlike the one shown in Figure 6.5. If other computers on your network use CUPS, you may see their printers in the printer list, depending on their security settings. Many modern distributions auto-configure USB printers when you plug them in or turn them on, so they may not need to be added either.

You can add, delete, or modify printer queues using the CUPS Web control system. To add a printer, follow these steps:

1. From the Administration tab, click Add Printer.

 CUPS is likely to ask for a username and password at this point. If you're using a system that utilizes the sudo command to gain root privileges (such as Ubuntu), you'll need to enter your user account and password. Otherwise, type **root** as the username and your root password as the password. The need to pass your root password unencrypted is one reason you should be cautious about configuring printers from a remote computer.

2. The system displays a page that shows options for printers to add in each of three categories: *local printers*, *discovered network printers*, and *other network printers*. One or more of these categories may be empty. If you're trying to add a local printer and the *local printers*

category is empty, either it was auto-detected or CUPS can't detect any likely printer interface hardware. Check your cables and drivers, and then restart CUPS and reload its web page. If you see an option for the printer you want to add, select it and click Continue.

3. If you entered a network printer, the result is a page in which you enter the complete path to the device. Type the path, such as **lpd://printserv/brother**, to print to the brother queue on the printserv computer. Click Continue when you're done.

4. CUPS displays a page in which you enter the printer's name, description, and location. You'll use the name to specify the printer in both command-line and GUI tools, so a short one-word name is best. The description and location fields are both descriptive expansions to help users positively identify the printer. You can also click the Share This Printer check box if you want to share the printer definition with other CUPS-using computers on the network.

5. You'll now see a list of manufacturers. Select one, and click Continue. Alternatively, you can point directly to a PPD file if you have one handy. If you do this, you'll skip the next step.

6. CUPS now displays a complete list of printer models in the class you selected in step 5. Select an appropriate model, and click Add Printer. Alternatively, you can provide a PPD file if you have one.

7. You should now see a page on which you can set default options, such as the paper size and print resolution. The details of what options are available depend on the printer model you selected. Change any options you like and click Set Default Options. Your printer is now defined.

If you click the Printers item at the top of the page, you should be returned to the printers list (Figure 6.5), but your new printer should be listed among the existing queues. You can print a test page by clicking the link to the printer and then selecting Print Test Page from the button selector that reads Maintenance by default. If all goes well, a test page will emerge from your printer. If it doesn't, go back and review your configuration by selecting Modify Printer from the button selector that reads Administration by default. This action takes you through the steps for adding a printer but with your previous selections already entered as the defaults. Try changing some settings until you get the printer to work.

Printing to Network Printers

If your network hosts many Windows computers, you may use the Server Message Block/Common Internet File System (SMB/CIFS) for file and printer sharing among Windows systems. Linux's Samba server also implements this protocol, and so it can be used for sharing printers from Linux.

On the flip side, you can print to an SMB/CIFS printer queue from a Linux system. To do so, you select an SMB/CIFS queue in the printer configuration tool. Under CUPS, it's called Windows Printer via SAMBA in step 2 in the preceding procedure. You must then provide your username, password, server name, and share name, but the format isn't obvious from the Web-based configuration tool:

smb://username:password@SERVER/SHARE

This is a URI for an SMB/CIFS share. You must substitute appropriate values for *username*, *password*, *SERVER*, and *SHARE*, of course. Once this is done and you've finished the configuration, you should be able to submit print jobs to the SMB/CIFS share.

 SMB/CIFS printers hosted by Windows systems are usually non-PostScript models, so you must select a local Linux smart filter and Ghostscript driver, just as you would for a local printer. Printers hosted by Linux systems running Samba, by contrast, are frequently configured to act like PostScript printers, so you should select a PostScript driver when connecting to them.

If you want to print to a Unix or Linux server that uses the old LPD protocol, the URI format is similar but omits a username and password:

```
lpd://hostname/queue
```

You can use the same format, but substitute `ipp://` for `lpd://`, to print to a CUPS server if browsing is disabled on your network.

In practice, you may be faced with a decision: Should you use LPD, IPP, or SMB/CIFS for submitting print jobs? To be sure, not all print servers support all three protocols, but a Linux server might support them all. As a general rule, IPP is the simplest to configure because it supports browsing, which means that CUPS clients shouldn't need explicit configuration to handle specific printers. This makes IPP the best choice for Linux-to-Linux printing, assuming both systems run CUPS. When CUPS isn't in use, LPD is generally easier to configure than SMB/CIFS, and it has the advantage of not requiring the use of a username or password to control access. Because SMB/CIFS security is password oriented, clients typically store passwords in an unencrypted form on the hard disk. This fact can become a security liability, particularly if you use the same account for printing as for other tasks. On the other hand, sometimes using a password on the server provides a security benefit that outweighs the risk of storing that password on the client. Generally speaking, if clients are few and well protected but the server is exposed to the Internet at large, using passwords can be beneficial. If clients are numerous and exposed to the Internet but the print server is well protected, a password-free security system that relies on IP addresses may be preferable.

Monitoring and Controlling the Print Queue

You can use several utilities to submit print jobs and to examine and manipulate a Linux print queue. These utilities are `lpr`, `lpq`, `lprm`, and `lpc`. All of these commands can take the `-P` parameter to specify that they operate on a specific print queue.

Printing Files with *lpr*

Once you've configured the system to print, you probably want to start printing. As mentioned earlier, Linux uses the `lpr` program to submit print jobs. This program accepts many options that you can use to modify the program's action:

Specify a Queue Name   The -Pqueuename option enables you to specify a print queue. This is useful if you have several printers, or if you've defined several queues for one printer. If you omit this option, the default printer is used.

 In the original BSD version of lpr, there should be no space between the -P and the *queuename* value. LPRng and CUPS are more flexible in this respect; you can insert a space or omit it as you see fit.

Delete the Original File   Normally, lpr sends a copy of the file you print into the queue, leaving the original unharmed. Specifying the -r option causes lpr to delete the original file after printing it.

Suppress the Banner   The -h option suppresses the banner for a single print job. Early versions of CUPS didn't support this option, but recent versions do.

Specify a Job Name   Print jobs have names to help identify them, both while they're in the queue and once they're printed (if the queue is configured to print banner pages). The name is normally the name of the first file in the print job, but you can change it by including the -J *jobname* option. The -C and -T options are synonymous with -J.

Notify a User by Email   The -m *username* option causes lpd to send email to *username* when the print job is complete. This option was unavailable in early versions of CUPS, but it is available in more recent versions.

Specify the Number of Copies   You can specify the number of copies of a print job by using the -# *number* option, as in -# 3, to print three copies of a job.

Suppose that you have a file called report.txt that you want to print to the printer attached to the lexmark queue. This queue is often busy, so you want the system to send an email to your account, ljones, when it's finished so that you know when to pick up the printout. You can use the following command to accomplish this task:

```
$ lpr -Plexmark -m ljones report.txt
```

The lpr command is accessible to ordinary users as well as to root, so anybody may print using this command. It's also called from many programs that need to print directly, such as graphics programs and word processors. These programs typically give you some way to adjust the print command so that you can enter parameters such as the printer name. For instance, Figure 6.6 shows Firefox's Print dialog box, which features a list of available print queues, Range options to enable you to print a subset of the document's pages, and a Copies field so that you can print multiple copies. Additional tabs enable you to set more options. Some programs provide a text entry field in which you type some or all of an lpr command instead of selecting from a list of available queues and options. Consult the program's documentation if you're not sure how it works.

FIGURE 6.6 Most Linux programs that can print do so by using lpr, but many hide the details of the lpr command behind a dialog box.

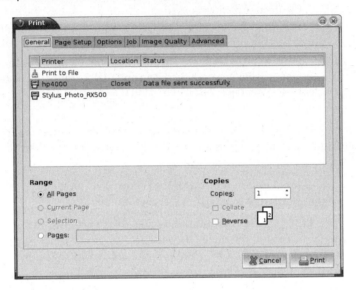

Sometimes you want to process a file in some way prior to sending it to the printer. Chapter 1 covers some commands that can do this, such as fmt and pr. Another handy program is mpage, which reads plain-text or PostScript files and reformats them so that each printed sheet contains several reduced-size pages from the original document. This can be a good way to save paper if you don't mind a reduction in the document's text or image size. In the simplest case, you can use mpage much as you'd use lpr:

```
$ mpage -Plexmark report.ps
```

This command prints the report.ps file reduced to fit four pages per sheet. You can change the number of source pages to fit on each printed page with the -1, -2, -4, and -8 options, which specify one, two, four, or eight input pages per output page, respectively. Additional mpage options exist to control features such as the paper size, the font to be used for plain-text input files, and the range of input file pages to be printed. Consult the man page for mpage for more details.

Displaying Print Queue Information with *lpq*

The lpq utility displays information about the print queue—how many files it contains, how large they are, who their owners are, and so on. By entering the user's name as an argument, you can also use this command to check on any print jobs owned by a particular user. To use lpq to examine a queue, you can issue a command such as the following:

```
$ lpq -Php4000
hp4000 is ready and printing
Rank     Owner    Job     File(s)                      Total Size
active   rodsmit  1630    file:///                     90112 bytes
```

Of particular interest is the job number—1630 in this example. You can use this number to delete a job from the queue or reorder it so that it prints before other jobs. Any user may use the lpq command.

Removing Print Jobs with *lprm*

The lprm command removes one or more jobs from the print queue. You can issue this command in a couple of ways:

- If lprm is used with a number, that number is understood to be the job ID (as shown in lpq's output) of the job that's to be deleted.
- If a user runs the BSD or CUPS lprm and passes a dash (-) to the program, it removes all of the jobs belonging to the user.

This program may be run by root or by an ordinary user, but as just noted, its capabilities vary depending on who runs it. Ordinary users may remove only their own jobs from the queue, but root may remove anybody's print jobs.

Controlling the Print Queue

In the original BSD LPD system, the lpc utility starts, stops, and reorders jobs within print queues. Although CUPS provides an lpc command, it has few features. Instead of using lpc, you should use the CUPS Web interface, which provides point-and-click print queue management:

- You can disable a queue by clicking the Stop Printer link for the printer on the CUPS Web interface. When you do so, this link changes to read Start Printer, which reverses the effect when clicked. The Jobs link also provides a way to cancel and otherwise manage specific jobs.
- You can use a series of commands, such as cupsenable, cupsdisable, and lpmove, to control the queue. These commands enable a queue, disable a queue, or move a job from one queue to another. Moving a job can be handy if you must shut down a queue for maintenance and want to redirect the queue's existing jobs to another printer.

 The CUPS Web interface also provides an easy way to troubleshoot general printing problems. You can easily stop the print queue and monitor jobs as applications submit them to the printer. Then you can release the print queue and watch if the printer attempts to process waiting jobs.

In Exercise 6.1, you'll practice using Linux's printing capabilities.

EXERCISE 6.1

Printing with Linux

To perform this exercise, you must have a printer connected to your Linux computer— either a local printer or a network model. To perform some of the steps, you must also have root access to your computer so that you can manage the queue. To begin, follow these steps:

EXERCISE 6.1 *(continued)*

1. Launch a web browser, enter **http://localhost:631** as the URI, and then click the Printers tab. This should produce a list of printers, as in Figure 6.5. If the list is empty, you'll need to define at least one printer queue, as described earlier, before proceeding. If printers are defined, take note of their names. For this exercise, assume that a queue named hp4000 exists; change this name as necessary in the following steps.

2. Type **lpr -Php4000 /etc/fstab** to obtain a printout of this system configuration file. Verify that it printed correctly.

3. Type **lpq -Php4000** to view the contents of the hp4000 queue. If you're using a single-user computer, chances are that the queue will be empty at this point.

4. Type **lpr -Php4000 /etc/fstab; lpq -Php4000**. This command prints another copy of /etc/fstab and immediately displays the contents of the print queue. It should not be empty this time because the job will have been submitted but won't have had time to clear the queue by the time lpq executes.

5. In another shell, type **su** to obtain root access.

6. In your root shell, type **cupsdisable hp4000**. This action disables the queue; it will still accept jobs, but they won't print.

7. Type **lpr -Php4000 /etc/fstab** to obtain yet another printout of /etc/fstab. Because the queue is disabled, it won't print.

8. Type **lpq -Php4000** to view the contents of the printer queue. Note that, instead of hp4000 is ready, lpq reports hp4000 is not ready; however, the job you submitted should appear in the queue. Suppose it has a job number of 497.

9. Type **lprm -Php4000 497** (changing the job number for your system).

10. Type **lpq -Php4000** again to verify that the job has been removed from the queue.

11. Type **cupsenable hp4000** in your root shell. This should reenable the queue.

12. Type **lpr -Php4000 /etc/fstab** to print another copy of this file and verify that the printer is actually working again.

Using cupsdisable and cupsenable in this exercise has two purposes: to give you experience using these commands and to give you a chance to delete a job from the queue. A short file such as /etc/fstab can be printed so quickly that you might not have time to remove it from the queue before it disappears because it's sitting in the printer's out tray!

Summary

X is Linux's GUI system. In part because of Linux's modular nature, X isn't a single program; you have your choice of X servers to run on Linux. Fortunately, most Linux distributions use the same X server as all others (X.org-X11). Both X.org-X11 and its main competitor, XFree86, are configured in much the same way, using the xorg.conf (for X.org-X11) or XF86Config configuration file. Whatever its name, this file consists of several sections, each of which controls one X subsystem, such as the mouse, the keyboard, or the video card. This file also controls X's core fonts system, but you can use a font server in addition to this system, and most modern programs are now emphasizing an entirely new font system, Xft, instead of X core fonts. For this reason, Linux font configuration can be complex.

X's GUI login system uses an XDMCP server, which starts X and manages the X display. Several XDMCP servers are in common use in Linux, the most important being XDM, KDM, GDM, and LightDM. They all perform the same basic tasks, but configuration details differ. (XDM is also less sophisticated than KDM and GDM.) X is a network-enabled GUI, which means that you can use an X server to access programs running on another computer. Doing so requires performing a few steps for each login session. You can also tunnel X accesses through SSH, which greatly improves the security of the connection.

An assortment of tools can help make Linux more accessible to users with visual or motor impairments. You can adjust font size, screen contrast, and other display features to improve legibility; use screen magnifiers to help users read part of a larger screen; or even bypass a visual display entirely and use a screen reader for auditory output or a Braille display for tactile output. On the input side, you can adjust keyboard repeat rates, use sticky keys, or modify the mouse tracking speed and click sensitivity to improve users' ability to input data accurately. You can even have a mouse stand in for a keyboard or vice versa by using the appropriate software.

The second main visual output tool on computers is a printer, and Linux provides sophisticated printer support. The CUPS package manages printers in Linux by accepting local or remote print jobs, passing them through a smart filter for processing, and queuing the jobs so that they print in a reasonable order. Most CUPS configuration is best handled via its own Web interface, but some options (particularly security features) can be set via text configuration files.

Exam Essentials

Name the major X servers for Linux. XFree86 has been the traditional standard Linux X server, but in 2004 X.org-X11 (which was based on XFree86) rapidly gained prominence as the new standard Linux X server. Accelerated-X is a commercial X server that sometimes supports video cards that aren't supported by XFree86 or X.org-X11.

Describe the X configuration file format. The XFree86 and X.org-X11 configuration file is broken into multiple sections, each of which begins with the keyword Section and ends with EndSection. Each section sets options related to a single X feature, such as loading modules, specifying the mouse type, or describing the screen resolution and color depth.

Summarize the differences between X core fonts, a font server, and Xft fonts. X core fonts are managed directly by X, and they lack modern font features such as font smoothing. Font servers integrate with the X core fonts but run as separate programs and may optionally deliver fonts to multiple computers on a network. Xft fonts bypass the X core font system to provide client-side fonts in a way that supports modern features such as font smoothing.

Explain the role of an XDMCP server. An XDMCP server, such as XDM, KDM, or GDM, launches X and controls access to X via a login prompt—that is, it serves as Linux's GUI login system. XDMCP servers are also network enabled, providing a way to log in remotely from another X server.

Describe X's client-server model. An X server runs on the user's computer to control the display and accept input from the keyboard and mouse. Client programs run on the same computer or on a remote computer to do the bulk of the computational work. These client programs treat the X server much as they treat other servers, requesting input from and sending output to them.

Explain the benefits of using SSH for remote X access. SSH can simplify remote X-based network access by reducing the number of steps required to run X programs from a remote computer. More important, SSH encrypts data, which keeps information sent between the X client and X server secure from prying eyes.

Summarize X accessibility features. You can adjust keyboard and mouse options to help those with motor impairments to use keyboards and mice or to substitute one device for the other. Font size, contrast, and magnification tools can help those with visual impairments. Finally, text readers and Braille displays can enable blind individuals to use a Linux system.

Describe how to set a time zone in Linux. Linux uses a binary file, /etc/localtime, to describe the features of the time zone. This file is copied or linked from a repository of such files at system installation, but you can replace the file at any time.

Explain the role of Ghostscript in Linux printing. PostScript is the standard Linux printing language, and Ghostscript converts PostScript into bitmap formats that are acceptable to non-PostScript printers. Thus, Ghostscript is a critical translation step in many Linux print queues, although it's not required for PostScript printers.

Summarize how print jobs are submitted and managed under Linux. You use lpr to submit a print job for printing, or an application program may call lpr itself or implement its functionality directly. The lpq utility summarizes jobs in a queue, and lprm can remove print jobs from a queue.

Review Questions

1. When you configure an X server, you need to make changes to configuration files and then start or restart the X server. Which of the following can help streamline this process?

   A. Shut down X by switching to a runlevel in which X doesn't run automatically, and then reconfigure it and use `startx` to test X startup.

   B. Shut down X by booting into single-user mode, and then reconfigure X and use `telinit` to start X running again.

   C. Reconfigure X, and then unplug the computer to avoid the lengthy shutdown process before restarting the system and X along with it.

   D. Use the `startx` utility to check the X configuration file for errors before restarting the X server.

   E. Connect the Linux computer's network port directly to the X server, without using any intervening routers, in order to reduce network latency.

2. Which of the following summarizes the organization of the X configuration file?

   A. The file contains multiple sections, one for each screen. Each section includes subsections for individual components (keyboard, video card, and so on).

   B. Configuration options are entered in any order desired. Options relating to specific components (keyboard, video card, and so on) may be interspersed.

   C. The file begins with a summary of individual screens. Configuration options are preceded by a code word indicating the screen to which they apply.

   D. The file is broken into sections, one or more for each component (keyboard, video card, and so on). The file also has one or more sections that define how to combine the main sections.

   E. The file is a rare binary configuration file that must be accessed using SQL database tools.

3. A monitor's manual lists its range of acceptable synchronization values as 27kHz–96kHz horizontal and 50Hz–160Hz vertical. What implications does this have for the resolutions and refresh rates the monitor can handle?

   A. The monitor can run at up to 160Hz vertical refresh rate in all resolutions.

   B. The monitor can handle up to 160Hz vertical refresh rate depending on the color depth.

   C. The monitor can handle up to 160Hz vertical refresh rate depending on the resolution.

   D. The monitor can handle vertical resolutions of up to 600 lines ($96{,}000 \div 160$), but no more.

   E. The monitor can handle horizontal resolutions of up to 600 columns ($96{,}000 \div 160$), but no more.

4. In what section of XF86Config or xorg.conf do you specify the resolution that you want to run?

   A. In the ServerLayout section, using the Screen option

   B. In the Monitor section, using the Modeline option

   C. In the Device section, using the Modeline option

   D. In the DefaultResolution section, using the Define option

   E. In the Screen section, subsection Display, using the Modes option

5. What is an advantage of a font server?

   A. It provides faster font displays than are otherwise possible.

   B. It can simplify font maintenance on a network with many X servers.

   C. It's the only means of providing TrueType support for XFree86 4.x.

   D. It enables the computer to turn a bitmapped display into an ASCII text file.

   E. It enables X to use font smoothing, which isn't possible with core fonts.

6. What methods do Linux distributions use to start X automatically when the system boots? (Select two.)

   A. Start an XDMCP server from the Start folder.

   B. Start an XDMCP server from an ~/.xinitrc script.

   C. Start an XDMCP server via a system startup script.

   D. Start an XDMCP server via a boot manager.

   E. Start an XDMCP server from init.

7. How would you change the text displayed by XDM as a greeting?

   A. Click Configure ➢ Greeting from the XDM main menu, and edit the text in the resulting dialog box.

   B. Pass greeting="text" as a kernel option in the boot loader, changing text to the new greeting.

   C. Edit the /etc/X11/xorg.conf file, and change the Greeting option in the xdm area.

   D. Run xdmconfig, and change the greeting on the Login tab.

   E. Edit the /etc/X11/xdm/Xresources file, and change the text in the xlogin*greeting line.

8. Which of the following features do KDM and GDM provide that XDM doesn't?

   A. An encrypted remote X-based access ability, improving network security

   B. The ability to accept logins from remote computers, once properly configured

   C. The ability to select the login environment from a menu on the main login screen

   D. A login screen that shows the username and password simultaneously rather than sequentially

   E. An option to log into text mode if X should fail to start

9. Which of the following commands tells the X server to accept connections from penguin. example.com?

   A. `xhost +penguin.example.com`

   B. `export DISPLAY=penguin.example.com:0`

   C. `telnet penguin.example.com`

   D. `xaccess penguin.example.com`

   E. `ssh penguin.example.com`

10. To assist an employee who has trouble with keyboard repeat features, you've disabled this function in /etc/X11/xorg.conf. Why might this step not be sufficient for the goal of disabling keyboard repeat?

    A. GNOME, KDE, or other desktop environment settings for keyboard repeat may override those set in xorg.conf.

    B. The xorg.conf file has been deprecated; you should instead adjust the /etc/X11/ XF86Config file.

    C. Keyboard settings in xorg.conf apply only to Bluetooth keyboards; you must use usbkbrate to adjust keyboard repeat for USB keyboards.

    D. You must also locate and reset the DIP switch on the keyboard to disable keyboard repeat.

    E. The keyboard repeat options in xorg.conf work only if the keyboard's nationality is set incorrectly, which is not often.

11. Which of the following programs may be used to provide computer-generated speech for users who have trouble reading computer displays? (Select two.)

    A. SoX

    B. Braille

    C. Orca

    D. talk

    E. Emacspeak

12. You manage a computer that's located in Los Angeles, California, but the time zone is misconfigured as being in Tokyo, Japan. What procedure can you follow to fix this problem? (Select two.)

    A. Run hwclock --systohc to update the clock to the correct time zone.

    B. Delete /etc/localtime, and replace it with an appropriate file from /usr/share/ zoneinfo.

    C. Edit the /etc/tzconfig file so that it specifies North_America/Los_Angeles as the time zone.

    D. Edit /etc/localtime, and change the three-letter time zone code on the TZ line.

    E. Use the tzselect program to select a new (Los Angeles) time zone.

13. You're configuring a Linux system that doesn't boot any other OS. What is the recommended time to which the computer's hardware clock should be set?

    A. Helsinki time

    B. Local time

    C. US Pacific time

    D. UTC

    E. Internet time

14. You've developed a script that uses several Linux commands and edits their output. You want to be sure that the script runs correctly on a computer in Great Britain, although you're located elsewhere, since the output includes features such as currency symbols and decimal numbers that are different from one nation to another. What might you do to test this?

    A. Enter the BIOS, locate and change the location code, reboot into Linux, and run the script.

    B. Edit /etc/locale.conf, change all the LC_* variables to en_GB.UTF-8, and then reboot and run the script.

    C. Type **export LC_ALL=en_GB.UTF-8**, and run the script from the same shell you used to type this command.

    D. Type **locale_set Great_Britain**, and run the script from the same shell you used to type this command.

    E. Type **export TZ=:/usr/share/zoneinfo/Europe/London**, and run the script from the same shell you used to type this command.

15. Which character set encoding is the preferred method on modern Linux systems?

    A. UTF-8

    B. ASCII

    C. ISO-8859-1

    D. ISO-8859-8

    E. ATASCII

16. Which of the following describes the function of a smart filter?

    A. It improves the legibility of a print job by adding font smoothing to the text.

    B. It detects information in print jobs that may be confidential as a measure against industrial espionage.

    C. It sends email to the person who submitted the print job, obviating the need to wait around the printer for a printout.

    D. It detects and deletes prank print jobs that are likely to have been created by troublemakers trying to waste your paper and ink.

    E. It detects the type of a file and passes it through programs to make it printable on a given model of printer.

17. What information about print jobs does the `lpq` command display? (Select two.)

   A. The name of the application that submitted the job

   B. A numerical job ID that can be used to manipulate the job

   C. The amount of ink or toner left in the printer

   D. The username of the person who submitted the job

   E. The estimated time to finish printing the job

18. You've submitted several print jobs, but you've just realized that you mistakenly submitted a huge document that you didn't want to print. Assuming that you can identify the specific job, that it's not yet printing, and that its job ID number is 749, what command would you type to delete it from the okidata print queue?

   A. The answer depends on whether you're using BSD, LPD, LPRng, or CUPS.

   B. Type **lpdel -Pokidata 749**.

   C. Type **lprm -Pokidata 749**.

   D. Type **cupsdisable -Pokidata 749**.

   E. None of the above; the task is impossible.

19. Which of the following is generally true of Linux programs that print?

   A. They send data directly to the printer port.

   B. They produce PostScript output for printing.

   C. They include extensive collections of printer drivers.

   D. They can print only with the help of add-on commercial programs.

   E. They specify use of the Verdana font.

20. What tool might you use to print a four-page PostScript file on a single sheet of paper?

   A. PAM

   B. mpage

   C. 4Front

   D. route

   E. 411toppm

Chapter

7

Administering the System

THE FOLLOWING EXAM OBJECTIVES ARE COVERED IN THIS CHAPTER:

✓ 107.1 Manage user and group accounts and related system files

✓ 107.2 Automate system administration tasks by scheduling jobs

✓ 108.1 Maintain system time

✓ 108.2 System logging

Much of Linux system administration deals with handling mundane day-to-day tasks. Many of these tasks relate to users and groups: adding them, deleting them, configuring their environments, and so on. On a small system, you might perform such tasks occasionally, but on a busy system you might adjust accounts frequently.

Another class of day-to-day tasks involves managing and reviewing *log files*. These are files that record the details of system operations, such as remote logins. Log files can be invaluable debugging resources, but even if you aren't experiencing a problem, you should review them periodically to be sure everything is working correctly.

Many Linux tasks relate to time, and so understanding how Linux treats time is important. So are the skills needed to set the time on a Linux server. You can also tell Linux to run particular jobs at specific times in the future. This can be handy to help automate repetitive tasks, such as synchronizing data with other systems on a regular basis.

Managing Users and Groups

Linux is a multiuser system that relies on *accounts*—data structures and procedures used to identify individual users of a computer. Managing these accounts is a basic but important system administration skill. Before delving into the details, you need to understand a few basic concepts about user and group administration, which are covered in the following sections. In addition, the tools and configuration files that you need to manage users and groups are covered.

Understanding Users and Groups

Chances are that you have a good basic understanding of accounts already. Fundamentally, Linux accounts are like accounts on Windows, Mac OS, and other OSs. Some websites use accounts too. Nonetheless, a few details deserve explanation. These include the various Linux users, the nature of Linux groups, and the way Linux maps the numbers it uses internally to the usernames and group names that people generally use.

Learning about Linux User Accounts

Typical Linux accounts are individual user accounts identified via the account's username. These accounts are for people who need access to the system.

Linux accounts can also be accounts for system services called daemons. A *daemon* is typically a program that provides a particular service, such as the CUPS daemon described in Chapter 6, "Configuring the X Window System, Localization, and Printing." This daemon program runs continuously in the background waiting for an event to trigger it to perform some service. While a daemon does not log into a Linux system, it still needs an account.

There can also be specialty accounts that are created for unique purposes. For example, you may want a user account to receive email but not be able to access the local system.

 Linux is fairly flexible about its usernames, although details vary from one distribution to another as well as from one utility to another. Some utilities are flexible while others impose rather restrictive rules. The traditional practice is to use entirely lowercase letters in Linux usernames, such as sally, sam, ellen, and george, with no symbols or numbers. However, the best practice is to create an account-naming standard after all of the various access and account management utilities' rules are reviewed.

Each account requires a *unique* username. If you can create accounts on your system with mixed-case usernames, Linux treats usernames in a case-sensitive way. Therefore, a single computer can support both ellen and Ellen as separate users. This practice can lead to a great deal of confusion, so it's best to avoid creating accounts whose usernames differ only in case.

Linking Users Together via Groups

Linux uses *groups* as a means of organizing users. In many ways, groups parallel users. In particular, they're defined in similar configuration files, have names similar to usernames, and are represented internally by numbers (as are accounts).

Groups are *not* accounts, however. Rather, groups help organize collections of accounts, largely as a security measure. Every file on a Linux system is associated with a specific user and a specific group. Various permissions can be assigned to members of a group. For instance, group members (such as faculty at a university) may be allowed to read a file, but others (such as students) may be disallowed such access. Because Linux provides access to most hardware devices (such as scanners) through files, you can also use this same mechanism to control access to hardware.

Every group has anywhere from no members to as many members as there are users on the computer. Group membership is controlled through the /etc/group file. This file contains a list of groups and the members belonging to each group. The details of this file's contents are described later in this chapter in the section "Configuring Groups."

In addition to membership defined in the /etc/group, each user has a default or *primary group*. The user's primary group is set in the user's configuration /etc/passwd record. The /etc/passwd file defines each system account via individual account configuration records. When users log onto a computer, their group membership is set to their primary group. When users create files or launch programs, those files and running programs are associated with a single group—the current group membership.

A user can access files belonging to other groups as long as the user belongs to that group and the group access permissions allow such access. To run programs or create files with a group other than the primary group, the user must run the newgrp command to switch current group membership. For instance, to change to the project2 group as your current group, you might type the following:

```
$ newgrp project2
```

If the user typing this command is listed as a project2 group member in the /etc/group file, the user's current group membership changes. Thereafter, files created by that user will be associated with the project2 group. Alternatively, users can change the group associated with an existing file by using the chgrp or chown command, as described in Chapter 4, "Managing Files."

This group structure enables you to design a security system that permits different collections of users to work on the same files effortlessly. Simultaneously, this structure keeps other users of the same computer from prying into files that they should not be able to access. In a simple case, you may create groups for different projects, with each user restricted to one of these groups. A user who needs access to multiple groups can be a member of each of these groups. For instance, a student who takes two classes can belong to the groups associated with each class, or a supervisor may belong to all of the supervised groups.

Mapping UIDs and GIDs to Users and Groups

As mentioned earlier, Linux defines users and groups by numbers, referred to as *user IDs (UIDs)* and *group IDs (GIDs)*, respectively. Internally, Linux tracks users and groups by these numbers, not by their name. For instance, the user sam may be tied to UID 536, and ellen may be UID 609. Similarly, the group project1 may be GID 512, and project2 may be GID 523.

For the most part, these details take care of themselves—you use names, and Linux uses /etc/passwd or /etc/group to locate the number associated with the name. You may occasionally need to know how Linux assigns numbers when you tell it to do something, though. This is particularly true when you're troubleshooting.

Linux distributions reserve at least the first 100 user and group IDs (0–99) for system use. The most important of these is 0, which corresponds to root (both the user and the group). Accounts and groups that are associated with specific Linux utilities and functions use succeeding low numbers. For instance, UID 2 and GID 2 may be the daemon account and group, respectively, which are used by various servers; and UID 8 and GID 12 might be the mail account and group, which can be used by mail-related servers and utilities. You can check your /etc/passwd and /etc/group files to determine which user and group IDs are so used.

Aside from UID 0 and GID 0, UID and GID numbers aren't fully standardized. Different distributions may use different UIDs for standard user accounts and different GIDs for standard groups. If you need to refer to a particular user or group, use the name rather than the number.

The first normal user account is usually assigned a UID of 500 or 1000. When you create additional accounts, the system typically locates the next-highest unused UID number. Therefore, the second user account you create is UID 1001, the third is 1002, and so on.

How many user accounts can be created on a Linux system? The limit is more than 4.2 billion with the 2.4.*x* and later kernels. However, the limit can be set lower in configuration files. Also, support program restrictions can lower the limit.

When you remove an account, that account's ID number may be reused. However, if subsequent numbers are in use, the automatic account-creation tools typically don't do so. This leaves a gap in the numbering sequence. This gap causes no harm unless you have so many user accounts that you run out of ID numbers. In fact, reusing an ID number can cause problems if you don't clear away the old user's files. In this case, the new user, with the reused ID number, will become the old user's files' owner, which can lead to confusion and security issues.

Account numbering limits are set in the /etc/login.defs file. In particular, UID_MIN and UID_MAX define the minimum and maximum UID values for ordinary user accounts. In current distributions, these values are generally 1000 and 60000, respectively.

On any but a very small system with few users, you'll probably want to create your own groups. Because different distributions have different default ways of assigning users to groups, it's best that you familiarize yourself with your distribution's way of doing this and plan your own group-creation policies. For instance, you may want to create your own groups within certain ranges of IDs to avoid conflicts with the distribution's default user- and group-creation processes.

It's possible to create multiple usernames that use the same UID or multiple group names that use the same GID. In some sense, these are different accounts or groups. They have different entries in /etc/passwd or /etc/group, so they can have different home directories, different passwords, and so on. Because these users or groups share IDs with other users or groups, though, they're treated identically in terms of file permissions. Unless you have a compelling reason to do so, you should avoid creating multiple users or groups that share an ID.

Intruders sometimes create accounts with UID 0 to give themselves root privileges on the systems they invade. *Any* account with a UID of 0 is effectively the root account, with all the power of a superuser. If you spot a suspicious account in your /etc/passwd file with a UID of 0, your system has probably been compromised.

Configuring User Accounts

How frequently you perform user maintenance depends on the nature of the system you administer. Some systems, such as small personal workstations, rarely require changes. Others, such as multiuser servers, may require daily maintenance. The latter situation would seem to require more knowledge of user account configuration tools. Yet, even in a seldom-changing system, it's useful to know how to add, modify, or delete accounts so that you can do so quickly and correctly when needed.

This chapter describes the traditional text-based tools for account creation and maintenance. Most modern Linux distributions ship with GUI tools that accomplish the same goals. These tools vary from one distribution or environment to another, so they're hard to summarize for Linux as a whole. The exam also emphasizes the text-based tools. Overall, the text-based tools provide the greatest flexibility and are most broadly applicable.

Adding Users

Adding users can be accomplished through the useradd utility. (This program is called adduser on some distributions.) Its basic syntax is as follows:

```
useradd [-c comment] [-d home-dir] [-e expire-date] [-f inactive-days] ↵
  [-g default-group] [-G group[,...]]  [-m [-k skeleton-dir] | -M] ↵
  [-p password] [-s shell]  [-u UID [-o]] [-r] [-N] username
```

 Some of these parameters modify settings that are valid only when the system stores its passwords in the shadow file, /etc/shadow. This is the standard configuration for most distributions today.

In its simplest form, you may type just **useradd username**, where *username* is the account name that you want to create. The rest of the parameters are used to modify the default values for the system, which are stored in the file /etc/login.defs.

The parameters for the useradd command modify the program's operation in various ways:

Comment   The -c *comment* parameter passes the comment field for the user. Some administrators store public information, such as a user's office or telephone number, in this field. Others store just the user's real name or no information at all.

Home Directory   You specify the account's home directory with the -d *home-dir* parameter. This defaults to /home/*username* on most systems.

Account Expiration Date   You set the date on which the account will be disabled, expressed in the form YYYY-MM-DD, with the -e *expire-date* option. (Many systems accept alternative forms, such as MM-DD-YYYY, as well.) By default, no expiration date is set.

Inactive Days   An account becomes completely disabled a certain number of days after a password expires. The -f *inactive-days* parameter sets the number of days. A value of -1 disables this feature, and it is the default.

Default Group   You set the name or GID of the user's default group with the -g *default-group* option. The default for this value varies from one distribution to another.

Additional Groups   The -G *group*[,...] parameter sets the names or GIDs of one or more groups to which the user belongs. These groups need not be the default group, and you can specify more than one by separating them with commas.

Home Directory Options   The /etc/login.defs file specifies whether or not to create a user's home directory when the account is created via the CREATE_HOME setting. If set to yes, the -m option has no effect. If set to no, the -m option toggles this specification and a user's home directory is created.

Normally, default configuration files (including subdirectories) are copied from the /etc/skel directory. You may specify another template directory with the -k *skeleton-dir* option.

No Home Directory Creation   The -M option forces the system *not* to create a home directory, even if /etc/login.defs specifies that this action is the default. You might use this option, often in conjunction with -u (described shortly) and -d (described earlier), if a new account is for a user who's taking over the home directory of an existing user—say, because a new employee is replacing one who is leaving.

Hashed Password Specification   The -p *password* parameter passes the *pre-hashed* password for the user to the system. The *password* value is added, *unchanged*, to the /etc/passwd or /etc/shadow file. This means that if you type an unhashed password, it won't work as you would probably expect. In practice, this parameter is most useful in scripts, which can hash a password (using crypt) and then send the hashed result through useradd. The default value disables the account, so you must run passwd to change the user's password.

The terms *encrypted* and *hashed* are often confused. A *hashed password* is created using a one-way mathematical (cryptographic) process. The original password's characters cannot be re-created from the hashed password. If a password were encrypted, you could decrypt it and obtain the original password characters. Passwords on Linux are hashed. However, often in Linux documentation you will see the word *encrypted* used mistakenly instead.

Default Shell   Set the name of the user's default login shell with the -s *shell* option. On most systems, this defaults to /bin/bash, but you can specify another shell or even a program that's not traditionally a shell.

UID   The -u *UID* parameter creates an account with the specified user ID value (*UID*). This value must be a positive integer, and it's normally greater than 1000 for user accounts. (Some distributions permit user account UIDs as low as 500, though.) System accounts typically have numbers less than 200, and often less than 100. The -o option allows the number to be reused so that two usernames are associated with a single UID.

System Account Creation   The -r parameter specifies the creation of a system account—an account with a value less than UID_MIN, as defined in /etc/login.defs. The useradd command doesn't create a home directory for system accounts.

No User Group   In some distributions, such as Red Hat, the system creates a group with the same name as the specified username. The -N parameter disables this behavior.

Suppose you've added a hard disk and mounted it as /home2. You want to create an account for a user named Sally in this directory and place her home directory on the new disk. You want to make the new user a member of the project1 and project4 groups, with default membership in project4. The following useradd command accomplishes this goal:

```
# useradd -m -d /home2/sally -g project4 -G project1,project4 sally
#
```

Modifying User Accounts

User accounts may be modified in many ways: You can directly edit critical files such as /etc/passwd (though not recommended), modify user-specific configuration files in the account's home directory, or use system utilities like those used to create accounts (the preferred method).

You usually modify an existing user's account at the user's request or to implement some new policy or system change, such as moving home directories to a new hard disk.

Setting a Password

Although useradd provides the -p parameter to set a password, this tool isn't very useful when directly adding a user because it requires a pre-hashed password. Therefore, it's usually easiest to create an account in disabled form (by not using -p with useradd) and set the password after creating the account. You can do this with the passwd command, which has the following syntax:

```
passwd [-k] [-l] [-u [-f]] [-d] [-S] [username]
```

Consider the previously created user account for Sally. In order for Sally to use her account, she must have the password set. It was not set using the useradd command. You can use the passwd command on her account as follows:

```
# passwd sally
Changing password for user sally
New UNIX password:
Retype new UNIX password:
passwd: all authentication tokens updated successfully
#
```

The parameters to the passwd command enable you to modify its behavior:

Update Expired Accounts   The -k parameter indicates that the system should update an expired account.

Lock Accounts   The -l parameter locks an account by prefixing the hashed password with an exclamation mark (!). The result is that the user can no longer log into the account but the files are still available. This lock is easily undone. The lock parameter is particularly handy if you want to suspend user access to an account temporarily, such as, for example, when you've spotted some suspicious activity involving the account.

Unlock Accounts   The -u parameter unlocks an account by removing a leading exclamation mark. Be aware that the useradd command creates accounts that are locked (disabled) and have no password, unless its -p parameter is specified. Therefore, using this passwd -u parameter on a fresh account, which is disabled, not only removes the lock but also results in an account with no password! Normally, passwd doesn't allow this—it returns an error if you attempt it. Adding -f forces passwd to turn the account into one with no password.

Remove an Account's Password   The -d parameter removes the password from an account, rendering it password-less. No warning messages are given.

Display Account Information   The -S option displays information about the password for an account. Information displayed includes whether it's set and what type of algorithm was used to hash the password.

Ordinary users may use passwd to change their passwords, but many passwd parameters may be used only by root. Specifically, -l, -u, -f, and -d are all off-limits to ordinary users. Similarly, only root may specify a username to passwd.

When ordinary users run the program, they should omit their usernames. The passwd utility will change the password for the user who ran the program. As a security measure, passwd asks for a user's old password before changing the password. This precaution is *not* taken when root runs the program so that the superuser may change a user's password without knowing the original password. This is necessary because the administrator normally doesn't know the user's password. It also provides a way for the system administrator to help a user who's forgotten a password. The administrator can type **passwd *username*** and then enter a new password for the user.

Linux passwords may consist of letters, numbers, and punctuation. Linux distinguishes between upper- and lowercase letters in passwords, which means that you can use mixed-case passwords, numbers, and punctuation to improve security. Chapter 10, "Securing Your System," provides information about selecting secure passwords.

Exercise 7.1 provides you with practice in creating accounts on a Linux system.

EXERCISE 7.1

Creating User Accounts

This exercise explores the process of creating user accounts. After performing this exercise, you should be familiar with the command-line Linux account-creation tools and be able to create new accounts, including preparing new users' home directories. To add and test a new account, follow these steps:

1. Log into the Linux system as a normal user.

2. Press Ctrl+Alt+F3 to go to a virtual text-mode login screen.

3. Acquire root privileges by logging in as root and entering the root password. Alternatively, you can log in as a regular user and use sudo (if it's configured) to run the commands in the following steps.

4. Type **useradd -m *username***, where *username* is the name you want to be associated with the account. This command creates an account. The -m parameter tells Linux to create a home directory for the user and fill it with default account configuration files.

5. Type **passwd *username***. You'll be asked to enter a password for the user and to type it a second time. Enter a random string or select a password as described in "Setting a Password."

6. Press Ctrl+Alt+F2 to go to a fresh text-mode login screen.

7. Try logging in as the new user to verify that the account works properly.

In practice, creating accounts on a production system may require variations on this procedure. You may need to use additional options in step 4, for instance; consult the section "Adding Users" or the useradd man page for details on these options.

Furthermore, setting the password may require changes. On a small system with few users, you may be able to create accounts in the presence of their future users, in which case the user can type the password in step 5. On other systems, you may need to generate passwords yourself and then give them to users in some way.

Using *usermod*

The usermod program closely parallels useradd in its features and parameters. This utility changes an existing account instead of creating a new one, though. The major differences between useradd and usermod are as follows:

- usermod allows the addition of an -m parameter when used with -d. The -d parameter alone changes the user's home directory, but it doesn't move any files. Adding -m causes usermod to move the user's files to the new location.

- usermod supports an -l parameter, which changes the user's login name to the specified value. For instance, typing **usermod -l sjones sally** changes the username from sally to sjones.

- You may lock and unlock a user's password with the -L and -U options, respectively. These options duplicate functionality provided by passwd if the /etc/shadow file is used to store the passwords.

The usermod program changes the contents of /etc/passwd or /etc/shadow, depending on the option used. If -m is used, usermod also moves the user's files, as already noted.

Changing an account's characteristics while the owner is logged in can have undesirable consequences. This is particularly true of the -d -m combination, which can cause the files on which a user is working to move. Most other changes, such as changes to the account's default shell, don't take effect until the user has logged out and back in again.

If you change the account's UID, this action does *not* change the UIDs associated with a user's *existing* files. Because of this, the user may lose access to these files. You can manually update the UIDs on all files by using the chown command (see Chapter 4).

When using the -G option to add a user to new groups, be aware that any groups *not* listed will be removed. Therefore, it's a good idea to use the -a option as well. Using the -a -G parameter options together allows you to add a user to a new group without having to list any old groups in the command. For instance, to add sally to the group Production, issue the following commands:

```
# groups sally
sally : sally users project1
#
# usermod -a -G Production sally
#
# groups sally
sally : sally users project1 Production
#
```

The preceding example uses the command groups to display the user (sally) account's current group memberships. (The groups command is covered shortly in the section "Configuring Groups"). The current groups are sally and users. To add an additional group membership, Production, to the sally account, the usermod command is used with both the -a and -G options. This allows the original group memberships to be preserved.

If you only use the usermod -G option *without* the -a option, you must list *all* of the user's current groups along with any additional new groups. Omitting any of the user's current groups will remove the user from those groups! It's best to use the -a option to avoid this hassle.

Using *chage*

The chage command allows you to modify account settings relating to account expiration. It's possible to configure Linux accounts so that they automatically expire if either of two conditions is true:

1.   The password hasn't been changed in a specified time period.

2.   The system date is past a predetermined time.

   These settings are controlled through the chage utility, which has the following syntax:

```
chage [-l] [-m mindays] [-M maxdays] [-d lastday]  [-I inactivedays] ⏎
 [-E expiredate] [-W warndays] username
```

   The program's parameters modify the command's actions:

Display Information   The -l option causes chage to display account expiration and password aging information for a particular user.

Setting Minimum Time between Password Changes   The -m *mindays* parameter sets the minimum number of days between password changes. 0 indicates that a user can change a password multiple times in a day, 1 means that a user can change a password once a day, 2 means that a user may change a password once every two days, and so on.

   It is best to set this field to at least 5 days. Leaving it at 0 will allow a user to change their password right back to the original password after a required password change.

Setting Maximum Time between Password Changes   The -M *maxdays* parameter sets the maximum number of days that may pass between password changes. For instance, 30 requires a password change approximately once a month.

Setting the Last Password Change Date   The -d *lastday* parameter sets the last day a password was changed. Linux normally maintains this value automatically, but you can use this parameter to alter the password change count artificially. *lastday* is expressed in the format *YYYY/MM/DD* or as the number of days since January 1, 1970.

Setting the Maximum Inactive Days   The -I *inactivedays* parameter sets the number of days between password expiration and account disablement. An expired account may not be used or may force the user to change the password immediately upon logging in, depending on the distribution. A disabled account is completely inoperative.

Setting the Expiration Date   You can set an absolute expiration date with the -E *expiredate* option. For instance, you might use -E 2016/05/21 to have an account expire on May 21, 2016. The date may also be expressed as the number of days since January 1, 1970. A value of -1 represents no expiration date.

Setting the Number of Warning Days   The -W *warndays* option sets the number of days before account expiration that the system will send impending expiration warnings to the user. It's generally a good idea to use this feature to alert users of their situation, particularly if you make heavy use of password-change expirations. Note that these warnings are usually shown only to text-mode login users. GUI login users, file-share users, and so on usually don't see these messages.

> If the user changes a password before the deadline, the counter is reset from the password-change date.

The chage command can normally be used only by root. The one exception to this rule is if the -l option is used. This feature allows ordinary users to check their account-expiration information.

Understanding Account Configuration Files

You can directly modify user configuration files. The /etc/passwd and /etc/shadow files control most aspects of an account's basic features.

> Manually editing the /etc/passwd and /etc/shadow files is a dangerous activity and not normally recommended. It is too easy to damage a file record, which in turn may block users from the system or worse. Use the provided utilities instead. If you absolutely must manually edit these files, then run the pwck utility to verify the files and make sure that they are in sync with each other.

Both files consist of a set of records, one line per account record. Each record begins with a username and continues with a set of fields, delimited by colons (:). Many of these items may be modified with usermod or passwd. A typical /etc/passwd record entry resembles the following:

```
sally:x:1029:503:Sally Jones:/home/sally:/bin/bash
```

Each record's field has a specific meaning, as follows:

Username The first field in each /etc/passwd line is the username (sally in this example).

Password The second field has traditionally been reserved for the password. Most Linux systems, however, use a shadow password system in which the password is stored in /etc/shadow. The x in the example's password field is an indication that shadow passwords are in use. In a system that doesn't use shadow passwords, a hashed password appears here instead.

UID Following the password is the account's user ID (1029 in this example).

Primary GID The default login group ID is next in the /etc/passwd line for an account. The example uses a primary GID of 503.

Comment The comment field may have different contents on different systems. In the preceding example, it's the user's full name. Some systems place additional information here, in a comma-separated list. Such information may include the user's telephone number, office number, title, and so on.

Home Directory   The user's home directory, /home/sally, is the next record data field.

Default Shell   The default shell is the final data item in each /etc/passwd record. This is normally /bin/bash, /bin/tcsh, or some other common command shell.

It's possible to use something unusual here. For instance, some systems include a shutdown account with /bin/shutdown as the default shell. If you log into this account, the computer immediately shuts down. You can create user accounts with a default shell of /bin/false, which prevents users from logging in as ordinary users but leaves other utilities intact. Users can still receive mail and retrieve it via a remote mail retrieval protocol like POP or IMAP, for instance. A variant on this scheme uses /bin/passwd as the default shell, so that users may change their passwords remotely but can't log in using a command shell.

A typical /etc/shadow record entry resembles the following:

```
sally:$6$EmoFkLZPkHkpczVN2XRcMdyj8/ZeeT5UnTQ:15505:0:-1:7:-1:-1:
```

Most fields correspond to options set with the chage utility, although some are set with passwd, useradd, or usermod. The meaning of each colon-delimited field in this record is as follows:

Username   Each line begins with the username. Note that the UID is *not* used in the /etc/shadow file. The username links entries in this file to those in /etc/passwd.

Password   The password is stored in hashed form, so it bears no obvious resemblance to the actual password. An asterisk (*) in the password field indicates an account that does not accept logins. However, the account will still be able to run cron and at jobs in most cases (see the section "Running Jobs in the Future" later in this chapter for more information on cron and at).

An exclamation mark (!) in front of the password hash denotes that the account is locked. When you lock a user account via the usermod -L command, an exclamation mark (!) is added to the front of the password field's data. This keeps the account from logging into the system but preserves the original password. The usermod -U command removes the exclamation mark, unlocks the account, and restores the original password.

When a password has not been set for an account, there will be two exclamation marks (!!) in the password field. This particular setting means either the account's password has not yet been set or the account does not accept logins. This setting is common for non-login accounts used by the system itself.

Last Password Change   The next field (15505 in this example) is the date of the last password change. This date is stored as the number of days since January 1, 1970.

Days until a Change Is Allowed   The next field (0 in this example) is the number of days before a password change is allowed.

Days before a Change Is Required   This field is the number of days after the last password change before another password change is required.

Days of Warning before Password Expiration If your system is configured to expire passwords, you may set it to warn the user when an expiration date is approaching. A value of 7, as in the preceding example, is typical.

Days between Expiration and Deactivation Linux allows for a gap between the expiration of an account and its complete deactivation. An *expired account* either can't be used or requires that the user change the password immediately after logging in. In either case, its password remains intact. A *deactivated account*'s password is erased, and the account can't be used until the system administrator reactivates it.

Expiration Date This field shows the date on which the account will expire. As with the last password change date, the date is expressed as the number of days since January 1, 1970. This option is helpful in the case of students, interns, auditors, contract staff, seasonal workers, and similar temporary users.

Special Flag This field is reserved for future use and normally isn't used or contains a meaningless value. This field is empty in the preceding example.

For fields relating to day counts, a value of -1 or 99999 indicates that the relevant feature has been disabled. The /etc/shadow values are generally best left to modification through the usermod and chage commands because they can be tricky to set manually—for instance, it's easy to forget a leap year or the like when computing a date as the number of days since January 1, 1970.

Similarly, because of its hashed nature, the password field can't be edited effectively except through passwd or similar utilities. You can cut and paste a value from a compatible file or use crypt, but it's generally easier to use passwd. Copying hashed passwords from other systems is also somewhat risky because it means that the users will have the same passwords on both systems, and this fact will be obvious to anybody who's acquired both hashed password lists.

 Real World Scenario

Network Account Databases

Many networks employ network account databases, such as the Lightweight Directory Access Protocol (LDAP), Kerberos realms, and Active Directory (AD) domains. These systems move account database management onto a single centralized computer (often with one or more backup systems). This approach's advantage is that users and administrators need not deal with maintaining accounts independently on multiple computers. A single account database can handle accounts on dozens (or even hundreds or thousands) of different computers, greatly simplifying day-to-day administrative tasks and users' lives.

Linux can participate in these systems. In fact, some distributions provide options to enable such support at OS installation time. Typically, you must know the name or IP address of the server that hosts the network account database, and you must know what protocol that server uses. You may also need a password or some other protocol-specific

(continued)

information, and the server may need to be configured to accept accesses from the Linux
system you're configuring.

Using such a system with Linux means that most user accounts won't appear in /etc/
passwd and /etc/shadow. Groups may not appear in /etc/group. However, these files
will still hold information on local system accounts and groups.

Activating use of such network account databases after installing Linux is a complex
topic. It involves installing appropriate software and modifying various configuration
files. Such systems often alter the behavior of tools such as passwd and usermod in subtle
or not-so-subtle ways. If you want to use such a system, you'll have to consult documentation specific to the service you intend to use.

Deleting Accounts

On the surface, deleting user accounts is easy. You may use the userdel command to do
the job of removing a user's entries from /etc/passwd and, if the system uses shadow passwords, /etc/shadow. The userdel command takes just three parameters:

Remove User Files   The -r or --remove parameter causes the system to remove the user's
mail spool, all files in the user's home directory, and the user's home directory itself.

Force Deletion   You can force deletion of the account while a user is logged in by using the
-f or --force option in conjunction with -r. This option also forces removal of the mail
spool even if it's owned by another user and forces the removal of the home directory even
if another user uses the same home directory.

Get Help   The -h or --help option summarizes userdel options.

As an example, removing the sally account is easily accomplished with the following
command:

```
# userdel -r sally
```

You may omit the -r parameter if you want to preserve the user's files. Be aware of one
potential complication: Users may create files *outside* of their home directories. For instance,
many programs use the /tmp directory as "scratch space," so user files often wind up there.
These files are deleted automatically after a certain period, but you may have other directories in which users may store files. To locate all such files, you can use the find command
with its -uid parameter (or -user, if you use find before deleting the account). For instance,
if sally was UID 1029, you can use the following command to locate all of her files:

```
# find / -uid 1029
```

The result is a list of files owned by UID 1029 (formerly sally). You can then go
through this list and decide what to do with the files—change their ownership to someone
else, delete them, back them up, and so on.

WARNING   It's wise to do *something* with a deleted user's files. If you leave them on the system without changing the file's ownership, they may be assigned ownership to a new user if the deleted user account's UID is reused. If these files contain information that the new user should not have, the new user and you may be accused of violating company policy or even crimes.

A few servers—most notably Samba—keep their own list of users. If you run such a server, it's best to remove the user's entry from that server's user list when you remove the user's main account. In the case of Samba, this is normally done by using the smbpasswd command and its -x option, as in **smbpasswd -x sally** to delete the sally account from Samba's database.

Configuring Groups

Linux provides group configuration tools that parallel those for user accounts in many ways. Groups are not accounts so many features of these tools vary. Their layout is similar to that for account control files, but the details differ.

Adding Groups

Linux provides the groupadd command to add a new group. This utility is similar to useradd but has fewer options. The groupadd syntax is as follows:

groupadd [-g *GID* [-o]] [-r] [-f] *groupname*

The parameters for this command let you adjust its operation:

Specify a GID   You can provide a specific GID with the -g *GID* parameter. If you omit this parameter, groupadd uses the next available GID.

Create a System Group   The -r parameter instructs groupadd to create a group with a GID of less than SYS_GID_MIN, as defined in /etc/login.defs. Groups with GIDs in this range are considered *system groups*, which are similar to system accounts. System groups are normally used by system tools or to help control access to system resources, such as hardware device files. Not all distributions support this option.

Force Creation   Normally, if you try to create a group that already exists, groupadd returns an error message. The -f parameter suppresses that error message. Not all versions of groupadd support this parameter.

In most cases, you'll create groups without specifying any parameters except for the group name itself:

groupadd Production

This command creates the Production group, giving it whatever GID the system finds convenient—usually the highest existing GID plus 1. Once you've done this, you can add users to the group, as described in the next section. When you add new users, you can add them directly to the new group using the useradd command described earlier.

 Remember, to add current users to a new group, the usermod command is used. This utility was discussed earlier in the section "Using usermod."

Modifying Group Information

Group information, like user account information, may be modified either by using utility programs or by directly editing the underlying configuration file, /etc/group. There are fewer options for modifying groups than for modifying accounts, and the utilities and configuration files are similar.

Using *groupmod*

The groupmod command modifies an existing group's settings. Its syntax is as follows:

groupmod [-g *GID* [-o]] [-n *newgroupname*] *oldgroupname*

The options to this command modify its operation:

Specify a GID   Specify the new group ID using the -g *GID* option. The groupmod returns an error if you specify a new group ID that's already in use.

Specify a Group Name   Specify a new group name with the -n *newgroupname* option.

Using *gpasswd*

The gpasswd command is the group equivalent to passwd. The gpasswd command also enables you to modify other group features and to assign *group administrators*—users who may perform some group-related administrative functions for their groups. The basic syntax for this command is as follows:

gpasswd [-a *user*] [-d *user*] [-R] [-r] [-A *user*[,...]] [-M *user*[,...]] *group*

The options for this command modify its actions:

Add a User   The -a *user* option adds the specified user to the specified group.

Delete a User   The -d *user* option deletes the specified user from the specified group.

Disallow newgrp **Additions**   The -R option configures the group not to allow anybody to become a member through newgrp.

Remove Password   The -r option removes the password from a group.

Add Group Administrators   The root user may use the -A *user*[,...] parameter to specify group administrators. Group administrators may add members to and remove members from a group and change the group password. Using this parameter completely overwrites the list of administrators, so if you want to add an administrator to an existing set of group administrators, you must specify *all* of their usernames.

Add Users   The -M *user*[,...] option works like -A, but it also adds the specified user(s) to the list of group members.

If entered without any parameters except a group name, gpasswd changes the password for the group.

Group passwords are rarely used anymore and are considered a security risk. The primary purpose behind group passwords was to allow a user to change their primary group temporarily to a group to which they did not belong.

For example, a user may need group access for a particular project. If the user is *not* a group member, the user can still type the **newgrp** *group* command. The user is prompted for a password. If the user knows the password, the newgrp command allows the indicated group to be set as the user's current group. This is termed "logging into the group" because the newgrp command requests a password in this case. This password is the group password. If the correct password is not entered, the switch to the new current group is denied.

Proper system security demands that passwords are never shared among users. A group password violates this security principle. It is better for the system administrator to add users to needed groups. See Chapter 10 for more information on system security.

Understanding the Group Configuration Files

Group information is stored primarily in the /etc/group file. Like account configuration files, the /etc/group file is organized as a set of lines, one line per group. A typical line in this file resembles the following:

```
project1:x:504:sally,sam,ellen,george
```

Each field is separated from the others by a colon. The meanings of the four fields are as follows:

Group Name   The first field (project1 in the preceding example) is the name of the group.

Password   The second field (x in the preceding example) is the group password. Distributions that use shadow passwords typically place an x in this field; others place the hashed password directly in this field.

GID   The group ID number (in this example, 504) goes in this field.

User List   The final field is a comma-delimited list of group members.

Users may also be members of a group based on their own /etc/passwd file primary group specification. For instance, if user george has project1 listed as his primary group, he need not be listed in the project1 line in /etc/group. If user george uses newgrp to change to another group, though, he won't be able to change back to project1 unless he's listed in the project1 line in /etc/group.

Systems with shadow passwords also use another file, /etc/gshadow, to store shadow password information about groups. This file stores the shadow password and information for group administrators, as described earlier in "Using gpasswd."

If you configure Linux to use a network account database, the /etc/group file is present and may define groups important for the system's basic operation. As with /etc/passwd and /etc/shadow, though, important user groups are likely to be defined only on the network account server, not in /etc/group.

Deleting Groups

Deleting groups is done via the groupdel command, which takes a single parameter: a group name. For instance, **groupdel project3** removes the project3 group. You can also delete a group by editing the /etc/group file (and /etc/gshadow, if present) and removing the relevant line for the group. It's better to use groupdel, because groupdel checks to see whether the group is any user's primary group. If it is, groupdel refuses to remove the group; you must change the user's primary group or delete the user account first.

As with deleting users, deleting groups can leave files that no longer belong to a group. They only have a GID. You can locate these files with the find command, which is described in more detail in Chapter 4. For instance, if a deleted group used a GID of 1003, you can find all of the files on the computer with that GID by using the following command:

```
# find / -gid 1003
```

Once you've found any files with the deleted group's ownership, you must decide what to do with them. If the GID is ever reused, it can lead to confusion and even security breaches. Therefore, it's usually best to delete the files or assign them other group ownership using the chown or chgrp command.

Viewing Individual Account Records

When you're managing user accounts, groups, and passwords, individual account information often needs to be reviewed. However, it can be tedious to locate particular records in the various account management files.

Often, system administrators will use the grep command to search through these files for particular records:

```
$ grep Christine /etc/passwd
Christine:x:501:501::/home/Christine:/bin/bash
$
```

Another method for record retrieval uses the get entry command, getent. The getent command allows you to access records stored in one of the system databases. Only databases configured in the Name Service Switch (NSS) file, /etc/nsswitch.conf, can be accessed.

The general syntax for this command is as follows:

getent *database key*

The *database* parameter can be any of the NSS configured system databases. For our purposes here, *database* can be one of the following files:

passwd   (the /etc/passwd file)

shadow   (the /etc/shadow file)

group   (the /etc/group file)

The *key* parameter is the item whose database record you wish to view. For our purposes here, it is a user account name. For example, suppose you want to search the /etc/passwd file for the Christine user account:

```
$ getent passwd Christine
Christine:x:501:501::/home/Christine:/bin/bash
$
```

You may search only one database at a time, and only those with superuser privileges can successfully search the /etc/shadow file with the getent command. Everyone else will receive no response from such a query:

```
$ getent shadow Christine
$
```

The getent command is useful for viewing which users have membership in a particular group. In this case, the *key* parameter in the getent group command is the group's name:

```
$ getent group Production
Production:x:504:sally,Christine
$
```

Be aware that in the /etc/group file, an individual user's record does not contain all of a user's group memberships. Thus, when you use the user account name for *key* in the getent group command, only the user's primary group and GID is displayed:

```
$ getent group sally
sally:x:503:
$
```

To search for all a user's group memberships, use the groups command instead:

```
$ groups sally
sally : sally users Production project1
$
```

The get entry, getent, command is a handy utility that can search many more databases than those shown here. For further information, enter **man getent** to read the utility's man pages.

If the *key* parameter is left off of the getent command, the entire designated database is displayed:

```
$ getent passwd
root:x:0:0:root:/root:/bin/bash
bin:x:1:1:bin:/bin:/sbin/nologin
daemon:x:2:2:daemon:/sbin:/sbin/nologin
[…]
$
```

Tuning User and System Environments

Text-mode user environments are controlled through shell configuration files. For bash, these may include the following files:

/etc/profile

Files in the /etc/profile.d directory

/etc/bash.bashrc

/etc/bashrc

~/.bashrc

~/.bash_profile

~/.bash_login

~/.profile

The files in /etc are global configuration files, which affect all users. The configuration files located in users' home directories affect individual users' accounts and can be customized by individual users.

All of these files control the various bash options, including environment variables—named variables that hold data for the benefit of many programs. For instance, you might set the $EDITOR environment variable to the name of your favorite text editor. Some (but not all) programs that launch editors pay attention to this environment variable and launch the editor you specify.

As a system administrator, you can change the global bash configuration files to add, remove, or change the environment variables that all users receive. Generally speaking, you should do so because the documentation for a specific program indicates that it uses particular environment variables. You can also see all of your current environment variables by using the env, printenv, or set command. The list is rather long, so you may want to pipe it through less, as in **env | less**.

A user environment can also be tuned by adjusting the default set of files created by useradd. As described earlier in "Adding Users," useradd copies files from the *skeleton directory* (/etc/skel by default) into a newly created home directory.

Typically, the skeleton directory contains a handful of user configuration files, such as .bashrc. You can add files (and even directories) to this directory, including user configuration files, a starting directory tree, a README file for new users, and anything else you like.

Because skeleton directory files are copied into users' home directories and users are given ownership of them, the users can read, change, and even delete their file copies. Thus, you shouldn't place any options in the files that are sensitive from a security point of view or that users should not be able to change. Keep in mind that entries you place into global bash configuration files can easily be overridden by individual users via manual bash commands or other configuration files too.

Changes you make to the skeleton directory files won't automatically be moved into existing users' directories. The file changes will affect *only* new users. This fact makes the global files (such as /etc/profile) preferable to /etc/skel files for any changes to system defaults that you want to implement system-wide. This is particularly true if you expect that you'll ever want to modify your changes.

Various programs set environment variables themselves, and some are maintained automatically by bash. For instance, bash maintains the PWD environment variable, so you shouldn't try to set it in a configuration script. Also, be aware that adjusting the bash configuration files affects only bash. If a user's default shell is something else or if a user doesn't use a text-mode shell (say, if the user logs into a graphical environment and launches programs from a GUI menu), setting environment variables in the bash configuration files will do no good.

Using Log and Journal Files

Linux maintains log files that record various key details about system operation. These log files are typically stored in the /var/log directory. The /var directory is part of the File Hierarchy Standard (FHS) covered in Chapter 4. You can begin reviewing /var/log files immediately. However, it is important to know how to change the log file configuration. You do this by configuring the syslogd daemon.

There are several issues to consider when configuring and reviewing log files. Some servers and other programs perform their own logging and must be configured independently of syslogd. You may want to configure one computer to send its log files to another system as a security measure. You should be aware of issues surrounding log file rotation. If your computer doesn't properly manage existing log files, they can grow to consume all of your available disk space, at least on the partition on which they're stored.

Many distributions are switching to the systemd utilities, including using the journal file. Journal files present a very different way of recording and reporting on a system's operation details. The daemon for journaling is systemd-journald, and understanding how to configure it is important for proper journal file management.

Understanding *syslogd*

Most Linux systems employ a special daemon to handle log maintenance in a unified way. The traditional Linux daemon log manager is syslogd, which is often installed from a package called sysklogd. The syslogd daemon handles messages from servers and other user-mode programs. It's usually paired with a daemon called klogd, which is generally installed from the same software package as syslogd. The klogd daemon manages logging of kernel messages.

 Other choices for system loggers exist. For instance, syslog-ng is a replacement that supports advanced options. Many distributions use rsyslogd, which provides improved filtering capabilities and higher performance. It is nicknamed the "rocket-fast system for log processing." The focus here is on the traditional syslogd logger. Others are similar in principle, and even in some specific features, but differ in many details.

The basic idea behind a system logger is to provide a unified means of handling log files. The daemon runs in the background and accepts data delivered from servers and other programs that are configured to use the log daemon. The daemon can then use information provided by the server to classify the messages and direct them to an appropriate log file. This configuration enables you to consolidate messages from various servers into a handful of standard log files. The arrangement can be much easier to use and manage than potentially dozens of log files from the various servers running on the system.

In order to work, of course, the log daemon must be configured. In the case of syslogd, this is done through the /etc/syslog.conf file. (The rsyslogd configuration file is /etc/rsyslog.conf, and it is similar to syslog.conf.) The next section describes the syslog.conf file's format in more detail.

Setting Logging Options

The format of the /etc/syslog.conf file is conceptually simple, but it provides a great deal of power. Comment lines, as in many Linux configuration files, are denoted by a hash mark (#). Non-comment lines take the following form:

```
facility.priority    action
```

In this line, the *facility* parameter is the type of program or tool that generated the message to be logged. The *priority* is the parameter for the importance of this message. The *action* is a file, remote computer, or other location that's to accept the message. The *facility* and *priority* are often referred to collectively as the *selector*.

Valid parameters for the *facility* are as follows:

authpriv Security and authorization messages

cron cron daemon messages

daemon Various system daemon messages

kern Kernel messages

lpr Printing system messages

mail Mail system messages

news News daemon messages

syslog Internally generated syslog messages

user User-level messages

uucp Unix-to-Unix copy program (uucp) daemon messages

local0 through **local7** Locally defined application messages

Many of these names refer to specific servers or program classes. For instance, mail servers and other mail-processing tools typically log messages using the mail facility. Most servers that aren't covered by more specific parameters use the daemon facility.

In older Linux distributions, you may find additional facility names. The facilities security, auth, and mark should no longer be used. The security facility was identical to the auth facility parameter. Both have been replaced by the authpriv facility name.

The mark facility name is now used internally only. It originally was a facility for adding messages (--MARK--) to log files to indicate syslogd was still working.

For the *facility* parameter in the /etc/syslog.conf file, an asterisk (*) refers to all facilities. You can specify multiple facilities in one selector by separating the facility names with commas (,).

Valid parameters for *priority* are as follows:

debug Debugging level messages for application development (least important)

info Normal operation messages

notice Abnormal messages that are not a concern

warning Messages that indicate an error will occur if action is not taken

err Non-urgent failure and error messages

crit Urgent failure and error messages concerning secondary systems

alert Urgent failure and error messages concerning primary systems

emerg Panic messages indicating system is unusable (most important)

These priorities represent ascending levels of importance. The debug level logs, as the name implies, messages for debugging programs that are misbehaving. The crit, alert, and emerg priorities log the most important messages, which indicate very serious problems.

 In older Linux distributions, you may find additional priority names. The error, warn, and panic priority names should no longer be used. Instead, replace warn with the warning priority, replace error with err, and replace panic with the emerg priority.

When a program sends a message to the system logger, it includes a priority parameter; the logger logs the message to a file if you've configured it to log messages of that level *or higher*. Thus, if you specify a *priority* code of alert, the system will log messages that are classified as alert or emerg but not messages of crit or below.

An exception to this rule is if you precede the priority parameter by an equal sign (=), as in =crit, which describes what to do with messages of crit priority *only*. An exclamation mark (!) reverses the meaning of a match. For instance, !crit causes messages *below* crit priority to be logged. A *priority* of * refers to all priorities.

You can specify multiple selectors for a single action by separating the selectors with a semicolon (;). Note that commas are used to separate multiple facilities within a single selector, whereas semicolons are used to separate multiple selectors as a whole. Examples of complete selectors appear shortly.

Most commonly, the *action* parameter is a filename, typically in the /var/log directory tree. The messages, syslog, and secure files in this directory are three common and important log files, although not all distributions use all of these files. Another possible logging location includes a remote machine name preceded by an at sign (@) to log data to the specified system. You can also have a username list of individuals who should see the message, if they're logged in. For this last option, an asterisk (*) means all logged-in users.

Some examples should help clarify these rules. The first is a fairly ordinary and simple entry:

```
mail.*        /var/log/mail
```

This line sends all log entries identified by the originating program as related to mail to the /var/log/mail file. Most of the entries in a default /etc/syslog.conf file resemble this one. Together, they typically cover all of the facilities mentioned earlier.

Some messages may be handled by multiple rules. For instance, another rule might look like this one:

```
*.emerg          *
```

This line sends all emerg-level messages to all users who are logged into the computer using text-mode tools. If this line and the earlier mail.* selector are both present, emerg-level messages related to mail will be logged to /var/log/mail *and* displayed on users' terminals.

A more complex example logs kernel messages in various ways, depending on their priorities:

```
kern.*                  /var/log/kernel
kern.crit               @logger.pangaea.edu
kern.info;kern.!err     /var/log/kernel-info
```

The first of these rules logs all kernel messages to /var/log/kernel. The second line sends critical kernel messages to logger.pangaea.edu. (This computer must be configured to accept remote logs, which is a topic not covered in this book.)

Finally, the last line sends kernel messages that are between info and err in priority to /var/log/kernel-info. Because err is the priority immediately above crit, and because info is the lowest priority, these four lines cause *all* kernel messages to be logged two or three times: once to /var/log/kernel as well as either to the remote system and the console *or* to /var/log/kernel-info.

Most distributions ship with reasonable system logger settings, but you may want to examine these settings and perhaps adjust them. If you change them, be aware that you may need to change some other tools. For instance, all major distributions ship with tools that help rotate log files.

In addition to the system logger's options, you may be able to set logging options in individual programs. For instance, you may tell programs to log routine information differently at varying priorities. Some programs also provide the means to log via the system log daemon or via their own mechanisms. Details vary greatly from one program to another, so you should consult the program's documentation for details.

Manually Logging Data

For the most part, the system logger accepts log entries from system tools, such as servers. Occasionally, though, you may want to create a log entry manually or have a script do so. The tool for this job is known as logger, and it has the following syntax:

```
logger [-isd] [-f file] [-p pri] [-t tag] [-u socket] [message ...]
```

Options to logger permit changing its default function:

Record logger **PID**   The -i option records the process ID (PID) of the logger process along with other data.

Output to Standard Error   You can echo data to standard error as well as to the log file by using the -s option. An interactive script might use this feature to alert users to problems.

Log Using Datagrams   The -d option causes logger to use datagrams rather than a stream connection to the system logger socket. This is an advanced feature that you should use only if you're instructed to do so in documentation or if you understand the networking issues involved.

Log a File   You can log the contents of a file by using the -f *file* option. Be cautious with this option; if *file* is big, your system log file can grow to a ridiculous size!

Identify a Priority   The -p *priority* option specifies a priority, as described earlier.

Log Tags   You can add a tag with the -t *tag* option. This is useful if you want to identify a script or other program that created the log entry.

Specify a Socket   Ordinarily, logger calls the default system log tools to do its job. You can log directly to a network socket using the -u *socket* option if you prefer.

Specify a Message   If you don't specify a file using -f *file*, logger will log whatever you type after other options as the message to be logged. If you don't provide a message on the command line, logger accepts the input you type on subsequent lines as information to be logged. You should terminate such input by pressing Ctrl+D.

As an example, suppose you want to log the message "shutting down for system maintenance" to the system log. You can do so by typing the following command:

```
$ logger shutting down for system maintenance
```

The result will be an entry like the following, probably in /var/log/messages:

```
Jul 29 14:09:50 localhost root: shutting down for system maintenance
```

Adding parameters changes the details of what's logged as just described. You can place a call to logger in a script as a way of documenting the script's activities. For instance, a system backup script might use logger to record details such as its start and stop times and the number and size of the files that it has backed up.

Rotating Log Files

Log files are intended to retain information about system activities for a reasonable period of time, but system logging daemons provide no means to control the size of log files. Left unchecked, log files can therefore grow to consume all of the available partition space on which they reside. To avoid this problem, Linux employs *log file rotation tools*. These tools rename and optionally compress the current log files, delete old log files, and force the logging system to begin using new log files.

The most common log rotation tool is a package called logrotate. This program is typically called on a regular basis via a cron job. (The upcoming section "Running Jobs in the Future" describes cron jobs in more detail.) The logrotate program consults a configuration file called /etc/logrotate.conf, which includes several default settings and typically refers to files in /etc/logrotate.d to handle specific log files. A typical /etc/logrotate. conf file includes several comment lines, denoted by hash marks (#), as well as lines to set various options, as illustrated by Listing 7.1.

Listing 7.1: Sample */etc/logrotate.conf* file

```
# Rotate logs weekly
weekly
# Keep 4 weeks of old logs
rotate 4
# Create new log files after rotation
create
# Compress old log files
compress
# Refer to files for individual packages
include /etc/logrotate.d
# Set miscellaneous options
notifempty
nomail
noolddir
# Rotate wtmp, which isn't handled by a specific program
/var/log/wtmp {
    monthly
    create 0664 root utmp
    rotate 1
}
```

Most of the lines in Listing 7.1 set options that are fairly self-explanatory, or that are well explained by the comments that immediately precede them. For instance, the weekly line sets the default log rotation interval to once a week. If you see an option in your file that you don't understand, consult the man page for logrotate.

The last few lines of Listing 7.1 demonstrate the format for the definition of a specific log file. These definitions begin with the filename for the file (multiple filenames may be listed, separated by spaces), followed by an open curly brace ({). They end in a close curly brace (}). Intervening lines set options that may *override* the defaults. For instance, the /var/log/wtmp definition in Listing 7.1 sets the monthly option, which tells logrotate to rotate this log file once a month, overriding the default weekly option. Such individual file definitions are common.

The following are examples of features that are often set in these /etc/logrotate.d definitions:

Rotated File Naming   Ordinarily, rotated log files acquire numbers in their names, such as messages.1 for the first rotation of the messages log file. Using the dateext option causes the rotated log file to obtain a date code instead, as in `messages-20130210` for the rotation performed on February 10, 2013.

Compression Options   As already noted, `compress` causes `logrotate` to compress log files to save space. This is done using `gzip` by default, but you can specify another program with the `compresscmd` keyword, as in `compresscmd bzip2` to use `bzip2`. The `compress options` keyword enables you to pass options to the compression command (say, to improve the compression ratio).

Creation of New Log Files   The `create` option causes `logrotate` to create a new log file for use by the system logger or program. This option takes a file mode, an owner, and a group as additional options. Some programs don't work well with this option, though. Most of them use the `copytruncate` option instead, which tells `logrotate` to copy the old log file to a new name and then clear all of the data out of the original file.

Time Options   The `daily`, `weekly`, and `monthly` options tell the system to rotate the log files at the specified intervals. These options aren't always used. Some configurations use a size threshold rather than a time threshold for when to rotate log files.

Size Options   The `size` keyword sets a maximum size for a log file. It takes a size in bytes as an argument (adding `k`, `M`, or `G` to the size changes it to kilobytes, megabytes, or gigabytes, respectively). For instance, `size 100k` causes `logrotate` to rotate the file when it reaches 100kB in size.

Rotation Options   The `rotate` *x* option causes *x* copies of old log files to be maintained. For instance, if you set `rotate 2` for the `/var/log/messages` file, `logrotate` will maintain `/var/log/messages.1` and `/var/log/messages.2` in addition to the active `/var/log/messages` file. When that file is rotated, the following occurs in the `/var/log/` directory:

   `messages.2` is deleted

   `messages.1` is renamed to `messages.2`

   `messages` is renamed to `messages.1`

   A new `messages` file is created

Mail Options   If you use `mail` *address*, `logrotate` will email a log file to the specified address when it's rotated out of existence. Using `nomail` causes the system not to send any email; the log is quietly deleted.

Scripts   The `prerotate` and `postrotate` keywords both begin a series of lines that are treated as scripts to be run immediately before or after log file rotation, respectively. In both cases, these scripts end with the `endscript` keyword. These commands are frequently used to force `syslogd` or a server to begin using a new log file.

Typically, servers and other programs that log data either do so via the system logging daemon *or* ship with a configuration file that goes in `/etc/logrotate.d` to handle the server's log files. These files do a reasonable job, but you may want to double-check them. For instance, you might discover that your system is configured to keep too many or too few old log files for your taste, in which case adjusting the `rotate` option is in order.

You should check the /var/log directory and its subdirectories. If you see huge numbers of files accumulating or if files are growing to an unacceptable size, you may want to check the corresponding logrotate configuration files. If an appropriate file record doesn't exist in /etc/logrotate.d, create one. Use a working file's record as a template, modifying it for the new file. Pay particular attention to the prerotate and postrotate scripts. You may need to consult the documentation for the program that's creating the log file to learn how to force that program to begin using a new log file.

Reviewing Log File Contents

Log files do no good if they simply accumulate on the system. They are to be used as a means of identifying problems or documenting normal activity. For example, when a server isn't responding as you expect, you should check your log files as part of your troubleshooting procedures.

Log files can be useful in less troublesome situations as well, such as helping you to identify a server's load so as to plan upgrades. Several procedures, many of which involve tools described elsewhere in this book, can help you access your log files:

Paging through Whole Log Files   You can use a pager program, such as less (see Chapter 1), to view the entire contents of a log file. A text editor can fill the same role.

Searching for Keywords   You can use grep (see Chapter 1) to pull lines out of log files that contain keywords. This can be particularly handy when you don't know which log file is likely to hold an entry. For instance, typing **grep eth0 /var/log/*** locates all lines in all files in the /var/log directory that contain the string eth0.

Examining the Start or End of a File   You can use the head or tail command (see Chapter 1) to examine the first or last lines of a log file. The tail command is particularly handy; you can use it to look at the last few records right after you take some action that you would expect to produce some diagnostic log file entries.

Monitoring Log Files   In addition to checking the last few lines of a log file, tail can monitor a file on an ongoing basis, echoing lines to the screen as they're added to the file. You do this with the -f option to tail, as in **tail -f /var/log/messages**.

Overall, you should probably examine your log files from time to time to become familiar with their contents. This will help you spot abnormalities when the system begins misbehaving or when you want to use log files to help track down an unwelcome visitor.

Log file entries can be noticeable by their absence as well as by any suspicious content within them. Intruders often try to cover their tracks by editing syslogd log files to remove the entries that betray their unauthorized accesses. Sometimes, though, they're sloppy about this and just delete all of the log entries from the time in question. If you notice unusual gaps in your log files, such as a space of an hour with no entries on a system that normally logs a couple dozen entries in that period, you may want to investigate further.

Exploring the *systemd* Journal System

Many distributions are embracing systemd system services, including system initialization (see Chapter 5). Another systemd service is the journal utility. The systemd journal service provides backward compatibility for most syslogd functionality. However, with systemd journal implementation there are changes to the way system message logging is handled. Special configuration files, different log file search utilities, and a vastly more secure logging function are just a few of the modifications.

The three primary systemd journal service components are described here:

1. daemon: The systemd journaling service is handled by the systemd-journald daemon.

2. Configuration file: The journal service's configuration is set in the /etc/systemd/ journald.conf file.

3. Search utility: The program used to search through the journal log files is journalctl.

Each of these systemd journal service pieces is covered in the following sections.

Understanding *systemd-journald*

The systemd-journald daemon is a system service that brings together and stores logging data. What differentiates it from the rsyslogd and syslogd daemons is that it provides structure and indexed log files (called *journals*) in a secure manner. Therefore, not only are the journal files easier to search, it is harder for system intruders to cover their tracks.

> Many distributions that have switched to systemd no longer install the rsyslogd or syslogd services by default. However, backward compatibility is maintained, should you decide to install those services.

Journal entries may come from several sources. The journal entries are created from server messages, user-mode program messages, and kernel messages just like the messages the syslogd daemon collects. In addition, however, journal entries are created from *all* system service messages, such as generated error messages and boot time communications. The systemd journal service can store journal entries regardless of their size, metadata, or format.

Another advantage of using the systemd-journald service over traditional logging daemons is that journal files are automatically rotated if they grow above certain limits. This reduces log file maintenance issues and complexity.

There are two types of journal message data files: system and user. System journal message data files are owned by a special group, systemd-journal. The systemd-journal members can read the journal message data files but not write to them. Only the systemd-journald daemon can write message data to the journals.

By default, each user who logs into the system has journal message data collected and stored. Users do not own their journal message data files, nor can they manually write data to them. They can, however, read their files.

As with other daemons, the system initialization files should start the systemd-journald daemon at system boot time. Once up and running, the service stores persistent journal data in the /var/log/journal/ directory, if configured to do so.

Configuring *systemd-journald*

The systemd-journald service is configured using the /etc/systemd/journald.conf file. Most options in this file are commented out by a hash (#) mark. Often, you do not need to make any changes to this file, because the systemd-journald defaults are sufficient. However, if you want your system to use the nicer features of journald, you need to make setting modifications.

Many settings already have values set and just need the hash mark removed. However, there may be a few entries that either have no value set or need their value modified. The following settings are in the journald.conf file:

Setting the Journal Data Location   The Storage option setting determines where to store the journal data. The primary values for this option are auto, persistent, volatile, and none.

Most systems have the Storage option set to auto. The auto value will configure journald to store journal log data in the /var/log/journal/ directory. However, the directory must already exist and have the proper permissions set. If it does not exist, then journal data is stored in the volatile /run/log/journal/ directory, and the data is erased when the system shuts down.

> If you are using the default journald settings or have set Storage=auto in your configuration, your journal files will not be persistent. To make your journal files persistent, you will need to create the journal file directory. Using superuser privileges, type **mkdir -p /var/log/journal/** and reboot your system.

The persistent value is similar to auto; however, it automatically creates the /var/log/journal/ directory if needed. The volatile value keeps the journal data only in the /run/log/journal/ directory. The none value sets no data to be kept, and any data received by the systemd-journald daemon is discarded.

Compressing the Journal Data   You can reduce journal file space consumption via compression. The Compress option set to yes will compress journal log data using xz compression (see Chapter 4 for more details on xz compression).

Controlling Journal Data Filesystem Space Usage   There are six /etc/systemd/journald .conf options that control filesystem space usage. Three options have the System prefix in their name and are used only for /var/log/journal/ data. The other three options have the Runtime prefix and are used only for /run/log/journal/ data.

The SystemMaxUse and RuntimeMaxUse options determine the maximum filesystem space amount that the journal data may consume. It is stated as a percentage and defaults to 10%.

The SystemKeepFree and RuntimeKeepFree options determine the minimum amount of filesystem space that must be available for other applications or uses. It is stated as a percentage and defaults to 15%. This setting may be modified by the systemd-journald daemon at system boot time if the current free filesystem space is below the configured setting.

Rotating Journal Data Files   The journald daemon rotates journal data files if you simply set an option in the /etc/systemd/journald.conf configuration file. One option is SystemMaxFileSize. Data file rotation is then triggered by journal data file *size*. By default, the size of the SystemMaxFileSize is set to 1/8 of the SystemMaxUse size setting. You can specify the size value in bytes or use size unit suffixes such as K, M, G, T, and so on.

The other option, MaxFileSec, determines the rotation schedule via a *time increment*. The MaxFileSec value is often set to 1month, indicating that file rotation will occur after the data is one month old. The various time settings are suffixed by time units, such as year, month, week, and so on.

Sharing Journal Data   For backward compatibility purposes, you can set the journald daemon to share data with the syslogd, rsyslogd , or klogd daemons. This is accomplished via the ForwardToSyslog and ForwardToKMsg options.

When the ForwardToSyslog option is set to yes, messages received by the journald daemon are forwarded to the syslogd or rsyslogd. When the ForwardToKMsg option is set to yes, data received by journald is forwarded to the kernel log buffer.

For a full list of the various systemd-journald settings stored in the /etc/systemd/journald.conf file, along with a description, type **man journald.conf** at the command prompt.

Viewing Journal Data

To view all of the systemd-journal collected data, the journalctl utility is used. This command provides several means of filtering the data, and it is an extremely powerful utility.

To view the collected *system* journal data using journalctl, you can operate as a superuser. An even better technique is to add users who need access to system journal data to the systemd-journal group (see the section "Configuring Groups" earlier in this chapter). Remember, users do not need to belong to the special group to view their own journal data.

If you just want to view all of the journal data entries starting with the oldest first, simply use journalctl with no options as shown in Figure 7.1.

You can see from Figure 7.1 that there is a great deal of journal data that is collected. The first line displayed by the journalctl command denotes when this particular journal file was started and when the message data was last collected.

Notice in Figure 7.1 that each journal entry is time-stamped. These time stamps use real time adjusted for the system's time zone. The system's hostname (localhost.localdomain in the previous example) is also included. The facility or client passing the message data to journald is listed next. You may observe that kernel has issued a great deal of messages in Figure 7.1. This is due to the journal data file being started at system boot time. The journal entry record's last field item is the message itself.

FIGURE 7.1   Output from the `journalctl` command with no options set

```
-- Logs begin at Fri 2014-10-10 17:40:13 EDT, end at Thu 2014-10-16 16:10:04 EDT
Oct 10 17:40:13 localhost.localdomain systemd-journal[50]: Runtime journal is us
Oct 10 17:40:13 localhost.localdomain systemd-journal[50]: Runtime journal is us
Oct 10 17:40:13 localhost.localdomain kernel: Initializing cgroup subsys cpuset
Oct 10 17:40:13 localhost.localdomain kernel: Initializing cgroup subsys cpu
Oct 10 17:40:13 localhost.localdomain kernel: Initializing cgroup subsys cpuacct
Oct 10 17:40:13 localhost.localdomain kernel: Linux version 3.11.10-301.fc20.x86
Oct 10 17:40:13 localhost.localdomain kernel: Command line: BOOT_IMAGE=/vmlinuz-
Oct 10 17:40:13 localhost.localdomain kernel: e820: BIOS-provided physical RAM m
Oct 10 17:40:13 localhost.localdomain kernel: BIOS-e820: [mem 0x0000000000000000
Oct 10 17:40:13 localhost.localdomain kernel: BIOS-e820: [mem 0x000000000009fc00
Oct 10 17:40:13 localhost.localdomain kernel: BIOS-e820: [mem 0x00000000000f0000
Oct 10 17:40:13 localhost.localdomain kernel: BIOS-e820: [mem 0x0000000000100000
Oct 10 17:40:13 localhost.localdomain kernel: BIOS-e820: [mem 0x000000005fff0000
Oct 10 17:40:13 localhost.localdomain kernel: BIOS-e820: [mem 0x00000000fffc0000
Oct 10 17:40:13 localhost.localdomain kernel: NX (Execute Disable) protection: a
Oct 10 17:40:13 localhost.localdomain kernel: SMBIOS 2.5 present.
Oct 10 17:40:13 localhost.localdomain kernel: DMI: innotek GmbH VirtualBox/Virtu
Oct 10 17:40:13 localhost.localdomain kernel: e820: update [mem 0x00000000-0x000
Oct 10 17:40:13 localhost.localdomain kernel: e820: remove [mem 0x000a0000-0x000
Oct 10 17:40:13 localhost.localdomain kernel: No AGP bridge found
Oct 10 17:40:13 localhost.localdomain kernel: e820: last_pfn = 0x5fff0 max_arch_
Oct 10 17:40:13 localhost.localdomain kernel: MTRR default type: uncachable
Oct 10 17:40:13 localhost.localdomain kernel: MTRR variable ranges disabled:
lines 1-24
```

The `journalctl` utility displays the collected journal data through a pager. By default, it uses the pager set by the environment variable $SYSTEMD_PAGER and *not* the $PAGER variable. You can display the collected journal data without using a pager by typing **journalctl --nopager** at the command prompt.

The `journalctl` command's power lies in its ability to parse out data without much effort. The basic `journalctl` command syntax is as follows:

journalctl [*options...*] [*matches...*]

The options specified by *options* are as you would expect, pass parameters that modify the `journalctl` command's behavior. For example, if you need some help on using the command, you can type **journalctl --h** at the command line. Here are a few helpful options:

-a   Display all data fields, including long fields and unprintable characters.

-e   Jump to the data file's end inside the pager utility.

-l   Display all printable data fields fully.

-n *number*   Show the most recent journal data and limit it to *number* of lines. If *number* is not specified, it shows 10 recent data lines.

-r   Reverse the output of the journal data so that the newest data shows first.

Instead of wading through all of the journal data, the `journalctl` command uses *matches* that allow you to filter out what you don't need to view. This snipped example shows the command to use if you only want to see kernel messages:

```
$ journalctl _TRANSPORT=kernel

-- Logs begin at Fri 2014-10-10 17:48:13 EDT, end at Thu 20[...]
Oct 10 17:48:13 localhost.localdomain kernel: Initializing [...]
Oct 10 17:48:13 localhost.localdomain kernel: Initializing [...]
Oct 10 17:48:13 localhost.localdomain kernel: Initializing [...]
[...]
Oct 16 14:50:32 localhost.localdomain kernel: NET: Register[...]
lines 2173-2195/2195 (END)
```

The *matches* option can specify any special journal fields or fields that are application defined. All of the special journal fields can be found in the `systemd.journal-fields` man pages and fall into four main categories:

User   Fields passed directly from a client application and stored in the journal data.

Trusted   Trusted fields added only by the `systemd-journald` daemon.

Kernel   Kernel messages stored in the journal data.

Fields logged on a different program's behalf   Its category name says it all.

The following useful fields can be used as `matches` options that fall within these categories:

PRIORITY=*value*   Compatible with the `syslogd` priority settings, the *value* parameter is set between 0 for emerg and 7 for debug to find journal data for these priority messages types.

_UID=*user_id*   *user_id* is set to a particular user's UID to find journal data concerning a particular user.

_HOSTNAME=*hostname*   Journal data messages are found that concern a particular originating host.

_TRANSPORT=*transport*   Journal data received from the *transport* parameter is displayed. The *transport* parameter is set to `driver`, `syslog`, `journal`, `stdout`, or `kernel`.

_UDEV_SYSNAME=*device_name*   Displays journal data kernel messages for *device_name*. Valid *device_name* settings show in the `/sys/` directory.

OBJECT_PID=*process_ID*   Journal message data related to a program with the PID of *process_ID*.

You may notice that some *matches* options are prefixed with an underscore. These fields are called *trusted journal fields* and they indicate that the data was added by the `systemd-journald` daemon itself and was not altered by malicious users or programs.

Combining various `journalctl` *options* parameters, along with the *matches* options, allows you to parse out the journal message data you need. The following code snippet looks only at the system journal file's last six lines by using the -n 6 option. It also filters out all message data except for that which is associated with the root user, who has a UID of zero (0):

```
$ journalctl -n 6 _UID=0
-- Logs begin at Fri 2014-10-10 17:48:13 EDT, end at Thu 20[...]
Oct 16 15:57:16 localhost.localdomain login[1582]: FAILED L[...]
Oct 16 15:57:16 localhost.localdomain login[1582]: PAM 2 mo[...]
Oct 16 15:57:22 localhost.localdomain systemd[1]: getty@tty[...]
Oct 16 15:57:22 localhost.localdomain systemd[1]: Stopping [...]
Oct 16 15:57:22 localhost.localdomain systemd[1]: Starting [...]
Oct 16 15:57:22 localhost.localdomain systemd[1]: Started G[...]
$
```

There are more powerful filtering `journalctl` selections. To learn more about the various filter choices available, type **man journalctl** at the command prompt.

The `systemd-journald` journal message data entries are all time-stamped using real time adjusted for the system's time zone. Thus, an important reason for maintaining system time is to maintain accurate journals.

Maintaining the System Time

Linux depends on its system clock. Tools such as `cron` and `at` (described later in the section "Running Jobs in the Future") run programs at specified times, the make development tool uses files' time stamps to determine which ones need attention, and so on. Therefore, you should be familiar with how Linux deals with time, how to change the time zone, how to set the time, and how to keep the clock accurate.

Understanding Linux Time Concepts

The *x*86 and *x*86-64 computers that most often run Linux, as well as most other computers of this general class, have two built-in clocks. The first of these clocks, sometimes called the *hardware clock*, maintains the time while the computer is turned off. When you boot Linux, it reads the hardware clock and sets the *software clock* to the value it retrieves. The software clock is what Linux uses for most purposes while it's running.

Some OSs set their clocks to the local time. This approach is simple and convenient for people who are used to dealing mainly with local time, but for purposes of networking, it's inadequate. When it's 4:00 a.m. in New York, it's 1:00 a.m. in Los Angeles, so network protocols that rely even partly on time can become confused (or at the very least, create confusing log entries) when they operate across time zones. Linux sets its clock to

Coordinated Universal Time (UTC). For most purposes, UTC is identical to *Greenwich mean time (GMT)*. GMT is the time in Greenwich, England, unadjusted for daylight savings time, and is maintained by a series of atomic clocks stationed around the world. This approach means that Linux systems in New York and Los Angeles (and London and Moscow and Tokyo) should have identical UTC times, assuming all are set correctly.

For communicating with users, though, these systems need to know their time zones. For instance, when you type `ls -l` to see a file listing complete with time stamps, Linux reads the time stamp in UTC. It then adds or subtracts the appropriate amount of time so that the time stamp displays using your local time. Local time is occasionally called "wall clock" time.

All of this means that you must be able to set the computer's time zone. On most systems, this is done at system installation. The distribution's installer asks you for your time zone and sets things up correctly. If you erred during installation, or if you need to change the time zone for any reason, refer to Chapter 6, which describes how to set your local time zone.

The certification exam's objective 108.1 includes the files /usr/share/ zoneinfo, /etc/timezone, and /etc/localtime. These files are also included under objective 107.3 and are described in Chapter 6, which covers that objective.

Both the hardware clock and the software clock are notoriously unreliable on standard *x*86 and *x*86-64 hardware. The hardware clock depends on battery power and tends to drift. The software clock, after being updated to the hardware clock's time at boot, is maintained in software. Thus, your clock can easily end up being several minutes off the correct time within a month or two of being set. To deal with this problem, Linux supports various network protocols for setting the time. The most popular of these is the *Network Time Protocol (NTP)*, which is described in the upcoming section "Using Network Time Protocol."

Manually Setting the Time

You can manually set your system's clocks. As stated earlier, Linux maintains two clocks: the hardware clock and the software clock. The main tool to set the software clock is date, which has the following syntax when setting the clock:

```
date [-u|--utc|--universal] [MMDDhhmm[[CC]YY][.ss]]
```

Used without any options, this command displays the current date and time. If you pass a time to the date command, it sets the *software* clock to that time. This format contains a month, a day, an hour, and a minute at a minimum, all in two-digit codes (*MMDDhhmm*). You can optionally add a two- or four-digit year and the seconds within a minute if you like. You should specify the time in a 24-hour format. For instance, to set the time to 3:02 p.m. on October 27, 2016, you'd type the following command:

```
# date 102715022016
```

By default, date assumes that you're specifying the time in local time. If you want to set the clock in UTC, include the -u, --utc, or --universal option.

Because *x86* and *x86-64* hardware maintains both software and hardware clocks, Linux provides tools to synchronize the two. Specifically, the hwclock utility lets you set the hardware clock from the software clock, or vice versa, as well as to do a few other things. Its syntax is fairly straightforward:

```
hwclock [options]
```

You can specify options to accomplish several goals:

Show the Hardware Clock   To view the hardware clock, pass the -r or --show option. The time is displayed in local time, even if the hardware clock is set to UTC.

Set the Hardware Clock Manually   To set the hardware clock to a date you specify, you need two options: --set and --date=*newdate*. The *newdate* option is in the date format that the date program accepts.

Set the Hardware Clock Based on the Software Clock   If you've set the software clock, you can synchronize the hardware clock to the same value with the --systohc option.

Set the Software Clock Based on the Hardware Clock   If your hardware clock is accurate but your software clock is not, you can use the --hctosys option to set the software clock to the hardware clock's value. This option is often used in a SysV startup script to set the system clock when the computer first boots.

Specify UTC or Local Time   You can tell Linux to treat the hardware clock as storing UTC by using the --utc option or to treat it as holding local time by using the --localtime option. The default is whichever was last used when the hardware clock was set.

Ordinarily, you won't use hwclock directly very often. You may need to use it after a daylight savings time shift if you maintain your hardware clock in local time, but most distributions include scripts that manage this task automatically. You may also want to use it once in a while to keep the hardware clock from drifting too far from an accurate time; but again, many distributions do this automatically as part of the system shutdown procedure.

Using Network Time Protocol

Sometimes maintaining truly accurate system time is important. This is true for a few scientific, business, and industrial applications (such as astronomical measurements or determining the start and stop times for television broadcasts). In a networked environment, maintaining the correct time can be more important. Time stamps on files may become confused if a file server and its clients have different times, for instance.

For these reasons, several protocols exist to synchronize the clocks of multiple systems. Of these, Network Time Protocol (NTP) is the most popular and flexible. You should first understand the basic principles of NTP operation. You can then go on to configuring an NTP server for your network and setting up other systems as NTP clients.

Understanding NTP Basics

One of the most popular, flexible, and accurate network time tools is NTP. This protocol creates a tiered hierarchy of time sources, as illustrated in Figure 7.2. At the top of the structure are one or more highly accurate time sources. These time sources include atomic clocks or radio receivers that pull their times from broadcast time signals based on atomic clocks. These are referred to as *stratum 0* time servers, but they aren't directly accessible to any but the *stratum 1* time servers to which they're connected. These stratum 1 computers run NTP servers that deliver the time to *stratum 2* servers, which deliver the time to *stratum 3* servers, and so on, for an arbitrary number of strata.

FIGURE 7.2 NTP enables an expanding pyramid of computers to set their clocks to a highly accurate source signal.

The key to NTP is the fact that each server can deliver time to an expanding number of clients. For instance, a stratum 1 server may have 1,000 clients, each of which may also have 1,000 clients, and so on. Each increase in the stratum number slightly decreases the accuracy of the time signal, but not by much. A stratum 4 system's clock should be accurate to well under a second, which is accurate enough for almost all purposes. More important, if you run a network, you can set aside one computer to act as an NTP server. Your other computers' clocks (NTP clients) can obtain time from that one server.

NTP works by measuring the round-trip time for network packets between the server and the client. The two systems exchange packets with embedded time stamps. The client then adjusts its time so that it is synchronized with the server. This time adjustment is based upon *both* the source's time stamp *and* the packet's estimated travel time. For this reason, when you select an NTP source (as described next, in "Locating a Time Source"), you should pick one with the *shortest* possible network time delay, all other things being equal.

The main Linux NTP server program functions as both a server and a client. It sets its clock based on the server time to which it's pointed, and it enables other systems to set their clocks based on its own clock. Even the end points in the NTP hierarchy (the stratum 4 and some stratum 3 servers in Figure 7.2) often run the full NTP server package.

The NTP daemon, ntpd, monitors for and adjusts the clock drift that's common in computers' clocks. These actions result in more accurate timekeeping than is possible with a program that simply sets the clock and then ignores it until the next time the program is run. In part, this is done through the `ntp.drift` file, which is usually buried in `/var/lib/ntp` but is sometimes stored in `/etc`. This file holds information about the software clock's inaccuracies, and so it can be used to correct for them. A full NTP server periodically operates as an NTP client by checking with its source time systems to keep the system time set correctly and to update the `ntp.drift` file.

Locating a Time Source

You may think that just picking an NTP server with a low stratum number (such as stratum 1) to use is ideal. Most likely you will be blocked from using a low stratum–numbered time server. Blocking direct access to low stratum servers helps to lighten the load on those servers. This improves the NTP network's overall performance.

To locate an NTP server, you should consult one or more of several sources:

Your ISP   Many Internet service providers (ISPs), including business networks and universities, operate NTP servers for the benefit of their users. These servers are usually very close to your own in a network sense, making them good choices for NTP. You should consult your ISP or the networking department at your organization to learn if such a system is available.

Your Distribution's NTP Server   Some Linux distributions operate NTP servers for their users. If you happen to be close to these servers in a network sense, they can be good choices.

Public NTP Server Lists   Lists of public NTP servers are maintained at `http://support.ntp.org/bin/view/Servers/WebHome`. These servers can be good choices, but you'll need to locate the one closest to you in a network sense and perhaps contact the site you choose to obtain permission to use it.

The closest server in a network sense may not be the closest computer in a geographic sense. For instance, a national ISP may route all traffic through just one or two hub sites. The result can be that traffic from, say, Atlanta, Georgia, to Tampa, Florida, may go through Chicago, Illinois. Such a detour is likely to increase round-trip time and decrease the accuracy of NTP. In such a situation, a user in Atlanta may be better off using a Chicago NTP server than one in Tampa, even though Tampa is much closer geographically.

Public NTP Server Pool   The pool.ntp.org subdomain is dedicated to servers that have volunteered to function as public NTP servers. These servers are accessed in a round-robin fashion by hostname, so you can end up using different servers each time you launch NTP. Thus, using the public NTP server pool can be a bit of a gamble, but the results are usually good enough for casual users or if you don't want to spend time checking and maintaining your NTP configuration.

To use the pool, you can configure your NTP server to use either the pool.ntp.org subdomain name or a numbered host within that domain, such as 0.pool.ntp.org. You can narrow the list geographically by adding a geographic name to the domain name, as in north-america.pool.ntp.org for servers located in North America. For details, consult http://support.ntp.org/bin/view/Servers/NTPPoolServers.

Once you've located a few possible time servers, try using ping to determine the round-trip time for packets to this system. If any systems have very high ping times, you may want to remove them from consideration. This example shows the times associated with using the ping command on a set of North America NTP pool servers:

```
$ ping -c 3 0.north-america.pool.ntp.org
PING 0.north-america.pool.ntp.org (50.22.155.163) 56(84) bytes of data.
[...]
--- 0.north-america.pool.ntp.org ping statistics ---
3 packets transmitted, 3 received, 0% packet loss, time 2068ms
rtt min/avg/max/mdev = 61.110/62.387/64.111/1.265 ms
$
```

Here, when a smaller NTP pool subset is used with the ping command, you can see that the average round trip time (rtt) is slightly lower. Thus, this might be a better time source to use for this system:

```
$ ping -c 3 0.us.pool.ntp.org
[...]
--- 0.us.pool.ntp.org ping statistics ---
3 packets transmitted, 3 received, 0% packet loss, time 2047ms
rtt min/avg/max/mdev = 39.159/40.180/40.701/0.740 ms
```

Configuring NTP Servers

When you're setting up a network to use NTP, select one system (or perhaps two for a network with several dozen or more computers) to function as the primary NTP server. This computer needn't be very powerful, but it must have high availability and access to the Internet. You can then install the NTP server and configure it.

Most Linux distributions ship the NTP software in a package called ntp or ntpd. Look for this package (see Chapter 2) and, if it's not already installed, install it. If you can't find this package, check www.ntp.org/downloads.html. This site hosts NTP source code, which you can compile and install. If you don't install your distribution's own NTP package, you'll need to create your own system initialization startup script or start the NTP daemon in some other way.

Once NTP is installed, look for its configuration file, /etc/ntp.conf. This file contains various NTP options, but the most important are the server lines:

```
server 0.us.pool.ntp.org
server 1.us.pool.ntp.org
server 0.north-america.pool.ntp.org
```

Each of these lines points to an NTP server pool. When your local NTP daemon starts up, it contacts all of the servers specified in /etc/ntp.conf, measures their accuracy against each other, and settles on *one* as its primary time source. Typically, you list about three NTP servers in your primary NTP server system's /etc/ntp.conf file. This practice enables your time server to weed out any source servers that deliver a bad time signal. It also gives automatic fallback in case a source server becomes temporarily or permanently unavailable.

Before you can start up your NTP primary server, there is one more step. You must eliminate insane time. If any NTP client has a system time that varies 17 minutes or more from the NTP server's time, all NTP requests will be *ignored*. This is called *insane time*. When it requests NTP services from the primary time source, the NTP primary server that you are setting up is considered an NTP client. Therefore, you must eliminate the chances of insane time before you start.

To eliminate the chances of insane time, you can do a manual time synchronization. Some distributions have the ntpdate command for this function, while others use the netdate utility. Unfortunately, the ntpdate utility is deprecated, and thus it could disappear from the NTP package at any time.

The recommended method for manual time synchronization is to use the ntpd -gq command. The NTP daemon will let you perform manual time synchronization in an insane time situation if you use the -g option. Also needed is the -q option, which allows this one-time operation to occur and returns you to the command prompt. Therefore, in the example here, the ntpd -gq command is used:

```
# date
Sat Oct 11 13:16:02 EDT 2015
#
```

```
# sudo ntpd -gq
ntpd: time set -3593.675537s
#
# date
Sat Oct 11 12:16:23 EDT 2015
#
```

Using the date command along with ntpd in the previous example, it shows that the original system time was off by more than 17 minutes. (Actually it was an hour off!) Thus, insane time was occurring in this situation. Using the ntpd -gq command to manually time sync allowed insane time to be eliminated. The time was synchronized using a server listed in the /etc/ntp.conf file shown earlier. Now automated NTP time synchronization using the NTP daemon will work.

 The NTP daemon *cannot* be running when you issue the ntpd -gq command. If it is, you will get no warning message or error message, just a prompt back with no time synchronization completed. If you are having additional odd issues trying to synchronize time manually, add the -d option for debugging to the command. Type **ntpd -dgq** to attempt manual synchronization in debugging mode.

If you have an older distribution, though not recommended, you can still manually synchronize the system's time using the ntpdate utility or netdate utility. For both commands, you must append a timer server's URL to the command. In the ntpdate example here, the server URL is taken from a previous /etc/ntp.conf file example:

```
# date
Sat Oct 11 13:39:02 EDT 2015
#
# ntpdate 0.us.pool.ntp.org
11 Oct 12:39:39 ntpdate[2915]:
step time server 204.9.54.119 offset -3583.019385 sec
#
# date
Sat Oct 11 12:39:43 EDT 2015
#
```

Once you set your NTP configuration file and eliminate insane time, you can start your NTP daemon, ntpd. Typically, this is done via a system startup script or manually using the appropriate system initialization command (see Chapter 5). Here the NTP daemon is started using a SysV service command:

```
# service ntpd start
```

WARNING Not only do system initializations and their commands vary among distributions, but so do the service names. To start the NTP daemon on some distributions, you use the service name ntpd, as shown in the previous example. With other distributions, the NTP service is started using the service name ntp.

To help verify that NTP is working, you can use the ntpq command utility. This utility either operates in an interactive mode or accepts command-line arguments. To operate it in interactive mode, simply type **ntpq**, as shown in the example here:

```
$ ntpq
ntpq>
```

Once you are in interactive mode, you can type **help** to see all of the available commands. To check on your NTP server, type the **peers** command at the prompt. When you wish to leave the interactive mode, type **exit** and you are returned to the command line.

It is simpler to use ntpq from the command line, without entering into interactive mode. For example, to check on your NTP server, type **ntpq -p** and immediately the statistics are shown. The -p option for ntpq is equivalent to the --peers option. Figure 7.3 shows the results of using this command.

FIGURE 7.3 The ntpq program enables you to verify that an NTP server is functioning correctly.

```
$
$
$ ntpq -p
     remote           refid      st t when poll reach   delay   offset  jitter
==============================================================================
+xen1.rack911.co 66.228.59.187    3 u   62   64  377   70.860  50.792  64.989
+services.quadra 216.229.0.50     3 u   62   64  377   73.656  54.360  81.708
*pbx.denvercolo. 64.250.229.100   2 u   58   64  377   69.612  49.216  43.059
+clock.trit.net  43.77.130.254    2 u   17   64  377   80.813  60.543  80.360
$
$ _
```

The ntpq -p command displays the servers to which your NTP server is connected. In Figure 7.3, four external servers are listed. The refid column shows the server to which each system is synchronized, the st column shows the stratum of the server, and additional columns show more technical information. The server to which your system is synchronized is denoted by an asterisk (*). Other servers with good times are indicated by plus signs (+), and most other symbols (such as x and -) denote servers that have been discarded from consideration for various reasons.

Be aware that if your NTP daemon is not running, you will get an odd error message from the ntpq command:

```
$ ntpq -p
ntpq: read: Connection refused
$
```

 You won't see a server selected as the source until a few minutes after you restart the NTP daemon. The reason is that your local NTP process takes a while to determine which of the sources is providing the best signal.

Configuring NTP Clients

Once you've configured one or more NTP primary servers, you can configure the rest of your computers to point to them. Their configuration is done just like the NTP server configuration, with a couple of exceptions:

- You set your NTP clients to refer to the NTP server (or servers) you've just configured rather than to an outside NTP source. This way, your local systems won't put an unnecessary burden on the outside NTP server you've selected.

- You may want to ensure that your NTP clients can't be accessed as servers. This is a security measure. You can do this by using the restrict default ignore line in the ntp.conf file. This line tells the computer to ignore all incoming NTP requests.

Once you've configured a client, restart its NTP daemon. You can then use ntpq to check its status. You should see that it refers only to your network's *own* NTP server or servers. These systems should be listed as belonging to a stratum with a number that is one higher than the servers to which they refer.

 Real World Scenario

Tracking Employee Time

Keeping accurate time on a Linux system is important for network applications and various system utilities. However, it may also be an important task for business management purposes. Many companies need to maintain accurate system time in order to run time clock applications.

Time clock applications allow employers to track and record employee time. These time records are used to produce payroll or project tracking reports accordingly. To record their start time, employees may physically punch into a time clock, virtually punch in, log into the system, and so on. The application uses the Linux system's accurate time to track correctly how much time an employee spent at work or spent on a particular project or even on a particular task.

You can locate Free and Open Source Software (FOSS) time applications on such sites as http://sourceforge.net. Search for *time punch clock software* on the site for applications that may meet your company's needs. You can also search for these applications using your favorite Internet search engine. Use search terms such as *Linux punch clock application*, *Linux time clock application*, or *Linux time tracking application*.

Running Jobs in the Future

Some system maintenance tasks should be performed at regular intervals and are highly automated. For instance, creating backups (archives) is often an automated task, which is repeated at least daily. Linux provides a means of scheduling tasks to run at specified times. This tool is the cron program, which runs what are known as *cron jobs*. A related tool is at, which enables you to run a command on a one-time basis at a specified point in the future, as opposed to doing so on a regular basis as cron does.

Understanding the Role of *cron*

The cron program is a daemon, so it runs continuously, looking for events that cause it to spring into action. Unlike most daemons, which are network servers, cron responds to temporal events. Specifically, it "wakes up" once a minute, examines configuration files in the /var/spool/cron/ and /etc/cron.d/ directories and the /etc/crontab file, and executes commands specified by these configuration files if the time matches the time listed in the files.

There are two types of cron jobs: *system cron jobs* and *user cron jobs*. System cron jobs are run as root and perform system-wide maintenance tasks. By default, most Linux distributions include system cron jobs that clean out old files from /tmp, perform log rotation (as described earlier, in "Rotating Log Files"), and so on.

Ordinary users can create user cron jobs, which might run some user programs on a regular basis. You can also create a user cron job as root. This might be handy if you need to perform some task at a different time than is supported by the system cron jobs, which are rigidly scheduled.

One critical point to remember about cron jobs is that they run unsupervised. Therefore, you shouldn't call any program in a cron job if that program requires user input. For instance, you wouldn't run a text editor in a cron job.

Creating System *cron* Jobs

The /etc/crontab file controls system cron jobs. This file normally begins with several lines that set environment variables, such as $PATH (sets the path) and $MAILTO (sets the address to which programs' output is mailed). The file then contains several lines that resemble the following:

```
02 4 * * * root run-parts /etc/cron.daily
```

This system crontab record begins with five fields that specify the time to run the indicated job:

The minute of the hour (0–59)

The hour of the day (0–23)

The day of the month (1–31)

The month of the year (1–12)

The day of the week (0–7)

For the day of the week, both 0 and 7 correspond to Sunday. For both the month of the year and the day of the week values, you can use the first three letters of the name rather than a number if you prefer. The hour of the day is listed in military time. For example, to indicate that a job is to run at 1:00 p.m., you would list 13 for that field.

In all cases, you can specify multiple field values in several ways:

▪ An asterisk (*) matches all possible values.

▪ A list separated by commas (such as 0,6,12,18) matches any of the specified values.

▪ Two values separated by a dash (-) indicate a range, inclusive of the end points. For instance, 9-17 in the hour field specifies a time of from 9:00 a.m. to 5:00 p.m.

▪ A slash, when used in conjunction with some other multi-value option, specifies stepped values. A *stepped value* is a range in which some members are skipped. For instance, */10 in the minute field indicates a job that's run every 10 minutes.

After the first five fields, /etc/crontab entries continue with the account name to be used when executing the program (root in the preceding example) in the sixth field. In the record's seventh field, the command to be run, and any included options or parameters, is listed (run-parts /etc/cron.daily in this example).

The run-parts command runs all executable programs, with certain restrictions, contained in a designated directory. Thus, in the preceding example, all of the executable programs in the /etc/cron.daily/ directory would be run. Type **man run-parts** to learn more about this command.

The default /etc/crontab entries generally use run-parts, cronloop, or a similar utility that runs any executable scripts within a directory. The preceding example runs all of the scripts in /etc/cron.daily/ at 4:02 a.m. every day.

Most distributions include monthly, daily, weekly, and hourly system cron jobs. These cron jobs each correspond to a script in a directory called /etc/cron.*interval*/, where *interval* is a word associated with the run frequency. Other distributions place these scripts in a location named slightly differently, the /etc/cron.d/*interval*/ directories.

 The exact times chosen for system cron jobs to execute vary from one distribution to another. Normally, though, daily and longer-interval cron jobs run early in the morning—between midnight and 6:00 a.m. Check your /etc/crontab file to determine when your system cron jobs run.

To create a new system cron job, you may create a script to perform the task that you want performed (as described in Chapter 9, "Writing Scripts, Configuring Email, and Using Databases"). Copy that script to the appropriate /etc/cron.*interval* or /etc/cron.d/*interval* directory. When the runtime next rolls around, cron will run the new script.

 Before submitting a script as a cron job, test it thoroughly. This is particularly important if the cron job will run when you're not around. You don't want a bug in your cron job script to cause problems by filling the hard disk with useless files or producing thousands of email messages when you're not present to correct the problem quickly.

If you need to run a cron job at a time or interval that's not supported by the standard /etc/crontab, you can either modify that file to change or add the cron job runtime or create a user cron job, as described shortly. If you choose to modify the system cron job facility, model your changes after an existing entry, changing the times and script storage directory as required.

 System cron job storage directories should be owned by root, and only root should be able to write to them. If ordinary users can write to a system cron directory, unscrupulous users can write scripts to give themselves superuser privileges and place them in the system cron directory. The next time cron runs those scripts, the users will gain full administrative access to the system.

Creating User *cron* Jobs

To create a user cron job, you use the crontab utility, not to be confused with the /etc/crontab configuration file. The syntax for crontab is as follows:

```
crontab [-u user] [-l | -e | -r] [file]
```

If given without the -u *user* parameter, crontab modifies the cron job file (sometimes called the *user crontab*) associated with the current user.

 The crontab utility can become confused by the use of su to change the current user identity, so if you use this command, it's safest to also use -u *user*, even when you're modifying your own user crontab file.

If you want to work directly on a user crontab file, use the following crontab utility options:

-l causes the crontab utility to display the current user crontab file.

-r removes the current user crontab file.

-e opens an editor so that you can edit the current user crontab file.

 The vi editor is the default editor when you use the crontab -e command. However, you can change this by setting the VISUAL or EDITOR environment variable.

Alternatively, you can create a cron job configuration file and pass the filename to crontab using the *file* parameter. For instance, **crontab -u tbaker my-cron** causes the crontab program to use my-cron for tbaker's cron jobs. In other words, it copies tbaker's my-cron file into the directory in which it stores user cron jobs, making a few minor changes along the way.

Whether you create a user crontab file and submit it via the *file* parameter or edit it via -e, the format of the user crontab file is similar to that described earlier. You can set environment variables by using the form *VARIABLE=value*. You also can specify a command preceded by five numbers or wildcards to indicate when the job is to run. In a user crontab, you do *not* specify the username used to execute the job, as you do with system cron jobs. That information is derived from the crontab file's owner.

 The word *crontab* has three related but distinct meanings: It can refer to the crontab program, to the /etc/crontab file, or to the file that holds user cron jobs.

Listing 7.2 shows a sample user crontab file. This file runs two programs at different intervals. The fetchmail program runs every 30 minutes (on the hour and half hour), and clean-adouble runs on Mondays at 2:00 a.m. Both programs are specified via complete paths, but you can include a PATH environment variable and omit the complete path specifications.

Listing 7.2: A sample user *crontab* file

```
SHELL=/bin/bash
MAILTO=tbaker
HOME=/home/tbaker
```

```
0,30 * * * * /usr/bin/fetchmail -s
0 2 * * mon /usr/local/bin/clean-adouble $HOME
```

Ultimately, user crontab files are stored in one of the following directories:

```
/var/spool/cron/
/var/spool/cron/tabs/
/var/spool/cron/crontabs/
```

Each file in this directory is named after the user under whose name it runs. For example, tbaker's crontab file might be called /var/spool/cron/tabs/tbaker. You shouldn't directly edit the files in this directory; instead, use the crontab utility to make changes.

Access to the cron facility may be restricted in several ways:

Executable Permissions   The permissions on the cron and crontab programs may be restricted using standard Linux permissions mechanisms, as described in Chapter 4. Not all distributions configure themselves in this way. For those that do, users who need to schedule jobs using cron should be added to the appropriate group. This group is often called cron. However, you should check the group owner and permissions on the /usr/sbin/cron and /usr/bin/crontab program files to be sure.

Allowed Users List   The /etc/cron.allow file contains a list of users who should be permitted access to cron. If this file is present, *only* users whose names appear in the file may use cron. All other users are denied access. If this file isn't present, *anybody* may use cron, assuming access isn't restricted by executable permissions or a disallowed-users list.

Disallowed-Users List   The /etc/cron.deny file contains a list of users who should be denied access to cron. If this file is present, *any* user whose name appears in the file is denied access to cron. Users not listed may use cron, assuming executable permissions and the allowed-users list don't restrict access.

Exercise 7.2 guides you through the process of creating user cron jobs.

EXERCISE 7.2

Creating User cron Jobs

Implementing cron jobs can be a useful way to run programs at regular times. In this exercise, you'll create a simple user cron job that will mail you the output of an ip -s link command on a daily basis. This exercise assumes that you're authorized to use cron as an ordinary user. To configure your cron job, follow these steps:

1.   Log into the Linux system as a normal user.

2.   Launch a terminal emulator from the desktop environment's menu system if you used a GUI login method.

3. Create and edit a file called cronjob in your home directory. Use your favorite text editor for this purpose. The file should contain the following lines:

```
SHELL=/bin/bash
MAILTO=yourusername
00 12 * * * /sbin/ip -s link
```

Substitute your email address on the Linux system or elsewhere for *yourusername*. The cron facility uses the MAILTO environment variable to determine to whom to email the output of cron jobs.

4. Type **crontab cronjob** to install the cronjob file as a cron job. Note that this command replaces any user crontab files that may exist. If you've already defined a user crontab file for your account, you should edit your existing user cronjob file to add the line calling ip -s link rather than create a new file.

5. Wait for noon (00 12 in the cron time format). When this time rolls around, you should have a new email waiting for you with the contents of the ip -s link output.

Instead of waiting for noon, you can substitute a time that's a couple of minutes in the future. Remember that cron specifies minutes first, followed by the hour in a 24-hour format. For instance, if you create the file at 3:52 p.m., you might enter 54 15 as the first two numbers on the final line of the file. This will cause the cron job to execute at 15:54 on a 24-hour clock, or 3:54 p.m.

Using *anacron*

The cron utility is a great tool for performing certain tasks (such as rotating log files) on systems that are up most or all of the time. It's a much less useful tool on systems that are regularly shut down, such as laptop or tablet computers. Frequently, late-night cron jobs are never executed on such systems, which can lead to bloated log files, cluttered /tmp directories, and other problems.

WARNING   If your system is down the exact time that a cron job is scheduled to run, the job will *not* be run when the system boots back up. In fact, the cron job will not run until its next scheduled time. This is due to the fact that the cron daemon will *not* check for jobs that should have run during a system downtime. This means a script that should run every day could be skipped for one whole day!

One solution to such problems is the *anacron* utility. This program is designed as a supplement to cron to ensure that regular maintenance jobs are executed at reasonable intervals. The anacron utility works by keeping a record of programs that it should execute and how frequently it should do so. The frequency is set by number of days. Whenever anacron runs, it checks to see when it last executed each program that it's configured to manage. If a period greater than the program's execution interval has passed, anacron runs the program.

Typically, anacron itself is run from a system startup script, and perhaps from a cron job. You can then reconfigure your regular system cron jobs as anacron jobs and be *sure* they'll execute even on systems that are regularly shut down for long stretches of time.

 No matter how you run anacron, you should be sure to disable any cron jobs that anacron now handles. If you don't do so, those tasks will be performed twice, which may needlessly burden your system.

Like cron, the anacron utility is controlled through a configuration file named after itself: /etc/anacrontab. This file consists of three main line types:

1. Comment lines denoted by a leading hash mark (#)

2. Environment variable assignments

3. Job definition records

The job definition record contains four fields:

period   delay   identifier   command

The first field, *period*, is how frequently, in days, the command should be run. For example, a 1 (one) in this field means run it every day. A 30 in the period field means run the command every 30 days.

The second field, *delay*, is a delay period, in minutes, between the time anacron starts and the time the command is run, if it should be run. The delay feature is intended to help keep the system from being overloaded if anacron determines it needs to run several commands when it starts up. You can specify different *delay* times to stagger the running of the jobs.

The third field, *identifier*, is a string that identifies the command. Its purpose is to identify the job in messages, log files, and for special execution. For example, you can pass the identifier to the anacron utility on the command line to have anacron check and, if necessary, run only that one command.

Finally, the fourth field, *command*, is the command to be run. This is a single command or script name, optionally followed by any parameters that it may take.

Listing 7.3 shows a sample /etc/anacrontab file. This file sets a couple of environment variables. The PATH environment variable is particularly important if any scripts call programs without specifying their complete paths.

Listing 7.3: Sample */etc/anacrontab* file

```
SHELL=/bin/bash
PATH=/usr/local/sbin:/usr/local/bin:/sbin:/bin:/usr/sbin:/usr/bin
# format: period delay job-identifier command
1       5       cron.daily      run-parts /etc/cron.daily
```

```
7        10       cron.weekly     run-parts /etc/cron.weekly
30       15       cron.monthly    run-parts /etc/cron.monthly
```

The three job definition records in Listing 7.3 tell anacron to run the run-parts command, passing it the name of a different directory for each line. This command is used on some distributions to run cron jobs, so the effect of calling it from anacron is to take over cron's duties. The first line, run once a day, causes anacron to run (via run-parts) the scripts in /etc/cron.daily; the second line causes the scripts in /etc/cron.weekly to be run once a week; and the third, run once every 30 days, runs the scripts in /etc/cron.monthly.

Of course, to do any good, the anacron utility must be called itself. This is typically done in one of two ways:

Via a Startup Script   You can create a startup script to run anacron. For example, a simple SysV startup script (see Chapter 5) that takes no options but runs anacron should do the job.

Via a cron Job   You can create a cron job to run anacron. Typically, this call will replace your regular system cron job entries (in /etc/crontab), and you'll probably want to call anacron on a daily basis or more frequently.

The startup script approach is best employed on systems that are shut down and started up frequently, such as laptops or desktop systems that are regularly shut down at the end of the day. One drawback to this approach is that it can cause sluggish performance when the system is booted if anacron needs to run a time-consuming task.

Because anacron measures its run intervals in days, it's not a useful utility for running hourly cron jobs. Thus, you shouldn't eliminate any hourly system cron jobs when you edit your cron configuration for anacron.

Calling anacron via a cron job can shift the burden to off-hours. This ensures that anacron and the jobs it handles are run fairly frequently, if not on a completely regular basis. Alternatively, you can call anacron more frequently than once a day. For instance, if it's called once every six hours, it will almost certainly be called during a typical eight-hour workday. ·

If important jobs need to be run daily, be sure to call anacron **several times a day**. This way, any unexpected system downtime will not allow daily critical jobs, which must run every day, to skip an entire day.

Using *at*

Sometimes cron and anacron are overkill. You may simply want to run a single command only once at a specific future time. For this task, Linux provides another command: at. In ordinary use, this command only needs a single option: a time to run. This time can take any of several forms:

Time of Day   You can specify the time of day as *HH:MM*, optionally followed by AM or PM if you use a 12-hour format. If the specified time has already passed, the operation is scheduled for the next occurrence of that time—that is, for the next day.

Time Keywords   The keywords noon, midnight, or teatime stand for what you'd expect (teatime is 4:00 p.m.).

Day Specification   To schedule an at job more than 24 hours in advance, you must add a date specification after the time-of-day specification. This can be done in numeric form, using the format *MMDDYY*, *MM/DD/YY*, or *DD.MM.YY*. Alternatively, you can specify the date as *month-name day* or *month-name day year*.

A Specified Period in the Future   You can specify a time using the keyword now, a plus sign (+), and a time period, as in now + 2 hours to run a job in two hours.

The at utility is not installed on all distributions. If your Linux system doesn't have it, install it using information from Chapter 2. Also, the at command relies on a daemon, atd, to be running. If your system has the at utility but doesn't start atd automatically, you may need to configure a startup script (see Chapter 5) to do so.

When you run at and give it a time specification, the program responds with its own prompt, at>, which you can treat much like your normal bash or other command shell prompt. When you're done typing commands, press Ctrl+D to terminate input. Here is an example of entering a single command interactively into the at utility:

```
$ at now +1 hour
at> ip -s link
at> <EOT>
job 1 at 2015-10-14 11:28
$
```

In the preceding example, the at command is issued along with a time, now +1 hour, which will cause any entered commands to start running in one hour. The command, ip -s link, is entered at the at> prompt, and then the utility is exited by pressing Ctrl+D, which shows as <EOT> at the command line. Notice that a job number and the exact time that the command will run is displayed when the at utility is exited.

Instead of interactively entering commands, you can pass a file with commands by using the -f parameter to at. For example, typing **at -f commands.sh noon** will use the commands.sh file's contents as the commands to run at noon.

The at utility's support programs include atq, which lists pending at jobs. To use atq, simply type its name. The program supports a couple of options, but chances are you won't need them. If you do, consult atq's man page for details. An example of using atq when there is a pending job is as follows:

```
$ atq
1        2015-10-14 11:28 a Christine
$
```

The atrm command removes an at job from the queue. To use atrm, type the program name or the at job number, as returned by atq. For instance, to remove a job using its job number:

```
$ atq
1        2015-10-14 11:28 a Christine
$
$ atrm 1
$ atq
$
```

Once the job is removed, it's a good idea to double-check that it is really gone by using the atq command again.

> The batch command was another utility that worked much like the at utility. It was unique because you could schedule a script to run when the system load was at a lower usage level. It is often no longer included on distributions but is sometimes maintained as a script, /usr/bin/batch. This script simply calls the at utility and submits your job with a higher nice level (see Chapter 2).

The at facility supports access restrictions similar to those of cron. Specifically, the /etc/at.allow and /etc/at.deny files are used. However, there are a few different rules with at access:

- If neither at.allow nor at.deny exists, *only* root may use the at command.
- If at.allow exists, the users it lists may use the at command.
- If at.deny exists, everybody *except* those mentioned in this file may use the at command.

These access rules differ from those for cron, in which everybody is granted access if neither access-control file is present. This tighter default security on at means that the program is seldom installed with restrictive execute permissions. Of course, you can use program file permissions to deny ordinary users the ability to run at if you want an extra layer of security.

Summary

Routine system administration involves a variety of tasks, many of which center around user management. Adding, deleting, and modifying user accounts and groups are critical tasks that all system administrators must master. Because they are also related to users, you should know where to go to modify the default user environment.

System log and journal files are critical troubleshooting tools that are maintained by the system. You should be able to configure what data is logged to what files and know how to use these log and journal files.

Time management is important in Linux. Setting the Linux clocks (both hardware and software) and configuring NTP to keep the software clock accurate are important tasks. Tools that rely on the time include cron, anacron, and at, which enable the system to run programs in the future. These tools are used for many common system tasks, including rotating log files.

Exam Essentials

Summarize methods of creating and modifying user accounts.   Accounts can be created or modified with the help of tools designed for the purpose, such as useradd and usermod. Alternatively, you can directly edit the /etc/passwd and /etc/shadow files, which hold the account information.

Describe the function of groups in Linux.   Linux groups enable security features to be applied to arbitrary groups of users. Each group holds an arbitrary collection of users, and group permissions can be set on files, giving all group members the same access rights to the files.

Explain the purpose of the skeleton files.   Skeleton files provide a core set of configuration files that should be present in users' home directories when those directories are created. They provide a starting point for users to modify their important shell and other configuration files.

Summarize how to configure system logging.   System logging is controlled via the /etc/syslog.conf file. Lines in this file describe what types of log data, generated by programs, are sent to log files and to which log files the log messages should go.

Describe how log rotation is managed.   Log rotation is controlled via the /etc/logrotate.conf file (which typically refers to files in /etc/logrotate.d/). Entries in these files tell the system whether to rotate logs at fixed intervals or when they reach particular sizes. When a log rotates, it's renamed (and possibly compressed), a new log file is created, and the oldest archived log file may be deleted.

Summarize how to review journal data.   The systemd-journald service is responsible for journal message data. The daemon is controlled via the /etc/systemd/journal.conf configuration file. This journal message data can only be viewed using the journalctl utility. To view system journal data, you must either use superuser privileges or be a member of the systemd-journal group. Users can view their own user journal data files. To view the entire current journal data file, simply use the journalctl command with no parameters. To parse out journal data, use the various filters available with the journalctl utility via parameters.

Explain the two types of clocks in *x*86 and *x*86-64 hardware.   The hardware clock keeps time when the computer is powered down, but most programs don't use it while the computer is running. Such programs refer to the software clock, which is set from the hardware clock when the computer boots.

Summarize the function of NTP.   The Network Time Protocol (NTP) enables a computer to set its clock based on the time maintained by an NTP server system. NTP can function as a tiered protocol, enabling one system to function as a client to an NTP server and as a server to additional NTP clients. This structure enables a single highly accurate time source to be used by anywhere from a few to (theoretically) billions of computers via a tiered system of links.

Explain the difference between system and user cron jobs.   System cron jobs are controlled from /etc/crontab, are created by root, and may be run as any user (but most commonly as root). System cron jobs are typically run at certain fixed times on an hourly, daily, weekly, or monthly basis. User cron jobs may be created by any user (various security measures permitting), are run under the authority of the account with which they're associated, and may be run at just about any repeating interval desired.

Describe how to configure anacron jobs.   The anacron jobs are controlled from the /etc/anacrontab file. The file is checked to see when each listed job was last executed, and it ensures that the designated time period between executions is followed. Time periods are listed in number of days. No time period can be less than one day, and therefore jobs needing to be run more than one time per day should not use anacron. Often, anacron itself is run from a system startup script or from a cron job.

Review Questions

1. When a user account has been locked using the usermod -L command, you will see what in the /etc/shadow file's record for that user?

   A. An x in the password field

   B. An !! in the password field

   C. A blank password field

   D. A zero (0) at the front of the password field

   E. An ! at the front of the password field

2. What commands can be used to add user accounts to a Linux system?

   A. useradd *username*

   B. adduser *username*

   C. useradd -c "*full name*" *username*

   D. usradd *username*

   E. passwd *username*

3. An administrator types **chage -M 7 *time***. What is the effect of this command?

   A. The *time* account's password must be changed at least once every seven days.

   B. All users must change their passwords at least once every seven days.

   C. All users are permitted to change their passwords at most seven times.

   D. The *time* account's age is set to seven months.

   E. The account database's time stamp is set to seven months ago.

4. What is wrong with the following /etc/passwd file entry?
   sally:x:1029:Sally Jones:/home/myhome:/bin/passwd

   A. The default shell is set to /bin/passwd, which is an invalid shell.

   B. The username is invalid. Linux usernames can't be all lowercase letters.

   C. The home directory doesn't match the username.

   D. Either the UID or the GID field is missing.

   E. The hashed password is missing.

5. You want sally, who is already a member of the Production group, also to be a member of the Development group. What is the best way to accomplish this?

   A. Use the groupadd Development sally command.

   B. Use the groupadd Production sally command.

   C. Manually edit the /etc/group file, and change the Development group's record to Development:501:sally.

   D. Use the usermod -G Development sally command.

   E. Use the usermod -a -G Development sally command.

6. What types of files might you expect to find in /etc/skel? (Select three.)

    A. A copy of the /etc/shadow file

    B. An empty set of directories to encourage good file management practices

    C. A README or similar welcome file for new users

    D. A starting .bashrc file

    E. The RPM or Debian package management database

7. What would a Linux system administrator type to remove the nemo account and its home directory?

    A. `userdel nemo`

    B. `userdel -f nemo`

    C. `userdel -r nemo`

    D. `rm -r /home/nemo`

    E. `usermod -D nemo`

8. Which of the following system logging codes represents the *highest* priority?

    A. `info`

    B. `warning`

    C. `crit`

    D. `debug`

    E. `emerg`

9. Which of the following configuration files does the `logrotate` program consult for its settings?

    A. `/etc/logrotate.conf`

    B. `/usr/sbin/logrotate/logrotate.conf`

    C. `/usr/src/logrotate/logrotate.conf`

    D. `/etc/logrotate/.conf`

    E. `~/.logrotate`

10. You want to create a log file entry noting that you're manually shutting down the system to add a new network card. How might you create this log entry, just prior to using shutdown?

    A. `dmesg -l "shutting down to add network card"`

    B. `syslog shutting down to add network card`

    C. `rsyslogd "shutting down to add network card"`

    D. `logger shutting down to add network card`

    E. `wall "shutting down to add network card"`

11. Your manager has asked that you configure `logrotate` to run on a regular, unattended basis. What utility/feature should you configure to make this possible?

   A. at

   B. logrotate.d

   C. cron

   D. inittab

   E. ntpd

12. You've set your system (software) clock on a Linux computer to the correct time, and now you want to set the hardware clock to match. What command might you type to accomplish this goal?

   A. `date --sethwclock`

   B. `ntpdate`

   C. `sysclock --tohc`

   D. `time --set -hw`

   E. `hwclock --systohc`

13. As root, you type **date 12110710**. What will be the effect?

   A. The software clock will be set to 7:10 a.m. on December 11 of the current year.

   B. The software clock will be set to 12:11 p.m. on October 7 of the current year.

   C. The software clock will be set to 7:10 a.m. on November 12 of the current year.

   D. The software clock will be set to 12:11 p.m. on July 10 of the current year.

   E. The software clock will be set to July 10 in the year 1211.

14. What will be the effect of a computer having the following two lines in /etc/ntp.conf?

```
server pool.ntp.org
server tardis.example.org
```

   A. The local computer's NTP server will poll a server in the public NTP server pool; the first `server` option overrides subsequent `server` options.

   B. The local computer's NTP server will poll the `tardis.example.org` time server; the last `server` option overrides earlier server options.

   C. The local computer's NTP server will poll both a server in the public NTP server pool and the server at `tardis.example.org` and use whichever site provides the cleanest time data.

   D. The local computer's NTP server will refuse to run because of a malformed `server` specification in `/etc/ntp.conf`.

   E. The local computer's NTP server will poll a computer in the public NTP server pool but will fall back on `tardis.example.org` if and only if the public pool server is down.

15. You've configured one computer (`gateway.pangaea.edu`) on your five-computer network as an NTP server that obtains its time signal from `ntp.example.com`. What computer(s) should your network's other computers use as their time source(s)?

    A. You should consult a public NTP server list to locate the best server for you.

    B. Both `gateway.pangaea.edu` and `ntp.example.com`

    C. Only `ntp.example.com`

    D. Only `gateway.pangaea.edu`

    E. None. NTP should be used on the Internet, not on small local networks.

16. Which of the following tasks are most likely to be handled by a `cron` job? (Select two.)

    A. Starting an important server when the computer boots

    B. Finding and deleting old temporary files

    C. Scripting supervised account creation

    D. Monitoring disk partition space status and emailing a report

    E. Sending files to a printer in an orderly manner

17. Which of the following lines, if used in a user `cron` job, will run `/usr/local/bin/cleanup` twice a day?

    A. `15 7,19 * * * tbaker /usr/local/bin/cleanup`

    B. `15 7,19 * * * /usr/local/bin/cleanup`

    C. `15 */2 * * * tbaker /usr/local/bin/cleanup`

    D. `15 */2 * * * /usr/local/bin/cleanup`

    E. `2 * * * * /usr/local/bin/cleanup`

18. You're installing Linux on a critical business system. Which of the following programs might you want to add to ensure that a daily backup job is handled correctly?

    A. `tempus`

    B. `anacron`

    C. `crontab`

    D. `ntpd`

    E. `syslog-ng`

19. What do the following commands accomplish? (The administrator presses Ctrl+D after typing the second command.)

    ```
    # at teatime
    at> /usr/local/bin/system-maintenance
    ```

    A. Nothing; these commands aren't valid.

    B. Nothing; `teatime` isn't a valid option to `at`.

    C. Nothing; you may only type valid bash built-in commands at the `at>` prompt.

    D. Nothing; `at` requires you to pass it the name of a script, which `teatime` is not.

    E. The `/usr/local/bin/system-maintenance` program or script is run at 4:00 p.m.

20. How might you schedule a script to run once a day on a Linux computer? (Select two.)

    A. Place the script, or a link to it, in `/etc/cron.daily`.

    B. Use the at command to schedule the specified script to run on a daily basis at a time of your choosing.

    C. Create a user `cron` job that calls the specified script once a day at a time of your choosing, and install that `cron` job using `crontab`.

    D. Use run-parts to schedule the specified script to run on a daily basis.

    E. Type **crontab -d *scriptname***, where *scriptname* is the name of your script.

Chapter

8

Configuring Basic Networking

THE FOLLOWING EXAM OBJECTIVES ARE COVERED IN THIS CHAPTER:

✓ 109.1 Fundamentals of Internet protocols

✓ 109.2 Basic network configuration

✓ 109.3 Basic network troubleshooting

✓ 109.4 Configure client-side DNS

Most Linux systems are connected to a network, either as clients or as servers (and often as both). Even home computers and dedicated appliances such as smartphones usually connect to the Internet. For this reason, setting up Linux's basic networking tools is necessary for configuring Linux completely. To begin this task, you must first understand the basics of modern networking, such as the nature of network addresses and the types of tools that are commonly used on networks. From there, you can move on to Linux network configuration, including tasks such as setting a computer's address, routing, and name resolution. Unfortunately, network configuration sometimes goes wrong; understanding the tools and techniques used to diagnose and fix network problems is a necessary part of network configuration. Thus, this chapter covers the basics of network troubleshooting.

Understanding TCP/IP Networking

Networking involves quite a few components that are built atop one another. These include network hardware, data packets, and protocols for data exchange. Together, these components make up a *network stack*. The most common network stack today is the *Transmission Control Protocol/Internet Protocol (TCP/IP)* stack, but this isn't the only stack available. Nonetheless, understanding the basics of TCP/IP theory will help you configure and manage networks.

Knowing the Basic Functions of Network Hardware

Network hardware is designed to enable two or more computers to communicate with one another. Modern computers have network interfaces built into their motherboards, but internal (PCI, PCIe, or similar) network cards and external (USB, PC Card, and similar) network interfaces are also available. Many networks rely on wires or cables to transmit data between machines as electrical impulses, but network protocols that use radio waves or even light to do the job are growing rapidly in popularity.

Sometimes the line between network hardware and peripheral interface ports can be blurry. For instance, a parallel port normally isn't considered a network port, but when it's used with the *Parallel Line Interface Protocol (PLIP)*, http://tldp.org/HOWTO/PLIP .html, the parallel port becomes a network device. In the past, a USB or RS-232 serial port frequently became a network interface when used with the *Point-to-Point Protocol (PPP)*, typically in conjunction with a telephone modem. Such connections are rare today, but they're still possible. If you need to know how to configure a PPP connection, consult your distribution's documentation or the PPP HOWTO at http://tldp.org/HOWTO/PPP-HOWTO/.

At its core, network hardware facilitates the transfer of data between computers. The hardware that's most often used for networking includes features that help this transfer in various ways. For instance, such hardware may include ways to address data intended for specific remote computers, as described later in the section "Addressing Hardware." When basically non-network hardware is pressed into service as a network medium, the lack of such features may limit the utility of the hardware or extra software may be required to make up for the lack. If extra software is required, you're unlikely to notice the deficiencies as a user or system administrator because the protocol drivers handle the work, but this makes the hardware more difficult to configure and more prone to sluggishness or other problems than dedicated network hardware.

Investigating Types of Network Hardware

Linux supports several types of common network hardware. The most common is Ethernet, which comes in several varieties. Most Linux servers use *twisted-pair cabling*, which consists of pairs of wires twisted around each other to minimize interference. Such varieties of Ethernet are identified by a *T* suffix to the Ethernet variety name, as in 10BaseT or 100BaseT. The numbers denote the speed of the protocol in megabits per second (Mbps). In the late 1990s, 100BaseT took over from 10BaseT as the standard in office and even home networks. More recently, 1000BaseT and Ethernet variants that use either wired or optical cabling and that are capable of 1000Mbps speeds (that is, Gigabit Ethernet) have become the standard, with 10 Gigabit Ethernet now available in many server environments.

Other types of network hardware exist, but most are less common than Ethernet. These include Token Ring, LocalTalk, Fiber Distributed Data Interface (FDDI), High-Performance Parallel Interface (HIPPI), and Fiber Channel. Token Ring was common on some IBM-dominated networks in the 1990s, but it has steadily been losing ground to Ethernet for years. Likewise, LocalTalk was the favored medium for early Macintosh computers, but modern Macs ship with Ethernet instead of LocalTalk. FDDI, HIPPI, and Fibre Channel are all high-speed interfaces that are used in high-performance applications. Some of these protocols support significantly greater maximum cable lengths than does Ethernet, which makes them suitable for linking buildings that are many yards, or even miles, apart.

In the Linux workstation world, wireless networking (aka Wi-Fi) is an exception to Ethernet's dominance. Common wireless protocols include 802.11a, 802.11b, 802.11g, and 802.11n. These protocols support maximum speeds of 11Mbps (for 802.11b), 54Mbps (for 802.11a and 802.11g), or 300 Mbps (for 802.11n). With the exception of the rarely used 802.11a, Wi-Fi protocols are compatible with one another, albeit at the speed of the slowest protocol in use. Wireless networking is particularly useful for laptop computers, but it's even handy for desktop computers in homes and small offices that don't have adequate wired network infrastructures in place.

> If you use a wireless protocol, your data is transmitted via radio waves, which are easily intercepted. Wireless protocols include optional encryption, but this feature is sometimes disabled by default, and some varieties of wireless encryption are notoriously poor. If you use wireless network products, be sure to enable Wi-Fi Protected Access (WPA) or, better, WPA2 encryption. The weaker Wired Equivalent Privacy (WEP) encryption is easily broken. For added protection, use a strong encryption protocol, such as the Secure Shell (SSH) login tool or Secure Sockets Layer (SSL) encryption, when transferring any data that's even remotely sensitive, and be extra cautious about security on networks that support wireless access. In a typical configuration, an intruder who can break into your wireless access point appears to the rest of your network the same as any other local user, so protecting that access point is extremely important.

In addition to the network hardware in your computers, you need network hardware outside the computers. With the exception of wireless networks, you need some form of network cabling that's unique to your hardware type. (For 100BaseT Ethernet, get cabling that meets at least Category 5, or Cat-5, specifications. Gigabit Ethernet works best with Cat-5e or optical cables.) Many network types, including twisted-pair Ethernet, require the use of a central device known as a hub or switch. You plug every computer on a local network into this central device, as shown in Figure 8.1. The hub or switch then passes data between the computers.

FIGURE 8.1   Many networks link computers together via a central device known as a hub or switch.

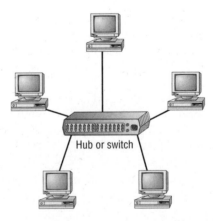

As a general rule, switches are superior to hubs. *Hubs* mirror all traffic to all computers, whereas switches are smart enough to send packets only to the intended destination.

Switches also allow *full-duplex transmission*, in which both parties can send data at the same time (like two people talking on a telephone). Hubs permit only *half-duplex transmission*, in which the two computers must take turns (like two people using walkie-talkies). The result is that switches let two computers engage in full-speed data transfers with each other; with a hub, these two transfers would interfere with each other.

Computers with Wi-Fi adapters can be configured to communicate directly with one another, but it's more common to employ a wireless access point, which links together both wireless and Ethernet devices. Most home network wireless access points also include a router to help connect your home network to a broadband provider, such as cable or DSL, for Internet access.

Understanding Network Packets

Modern networks operate on discrete chunks of data known as *packets*. Suppose you want to send a 100KiB file from one computer to another. Rather than send the file in one burst of data, your computer breaks it down into smaller chunks. The system might send 100 packets of 1KiB each, for instance. This way, if there's an error sending one packet, the computer can resend just that one packet rather than the entire file. (Many network protocols include error-detection procedures.)

When the recipient system receives packets, it must hold onto them and reassemble them in the correct order to re-create the complete data stream. It's not uncommon for packets to be delayed or even lost in transmission, so error-recovery procedures are critical for protocols that handle large transfers. Some types of error recovery are handled transparently by the networking hardware.

There are several types of packets, and they can be stored within each other. For instance, Ethernet includes its own packet type (known as a *frame*), and the packets generated by networking protocols that run atop Ethernet, such as those described in the next section, are stored within Ethernet frames. All told, a data transfer can involve several layers of wrapping and unwrapping data. With each layer, packets from the adjacent layer may be merged or split up.

Understanding Network Protocol Stacks

It's possible to think of network data at various levels of abstractness. For instance, at one level, a network carries data packets for a specific network type (such as Ethernet); the data packets are addressed to specific computers on a local network. Such a description, while useful for understanding a local network, isn't very useful for understanding higher-level network protocols, such as those that handle email transfers. These high-level protocols are typically described in terms of commands sent back and forth between computers, frequently without reference to packets. The addresses used at different levels also vary, as explained in the upcoming section "Using Network Addresses."

A *protocol stack* is a set of software that converts and encapsulates data between layers of abstraction. For instance, the stack can take the commands of email transfer protocols, and the email messages that are transferred, and package them into packets. Another layer of the stack can take these packets and repackage them into Ethernet frames. There are several layers to any protocol stack, and they interact in highly specified ways. It's often possible to swap out one component for another at any given layer. For instance, at the top of each stack is a program that uses the stack, such as an email client. You can switch from one email client to another without too much difficulty; both rest atop the same stack. Likewise, if you change a network card, you have to change the driver for that card, which constitutes a layer very low in the stack. Applications above that driver can remain the same.

Each computer in a transaction requires a compatible protocol stack. When they communicate, the computers pass data down their respective stacks and then send data to the partner system, which passes the data up its stack. Each layer on the receiving system sees the data as packaged by its counterpart on the sending computer.

Protocol stacks are frequently represented graphically in diagrams like Figure 8.2, which shows the configuration of the TCP/IP protocol stack that dominates the Internet today. As shown in Figure 8.2, client programs at the application layer initiate data transfers. These requests pass through the transport, Internet, and link layers on the client computer, whereupon they leave the client system and pass to the server system. (This transfer can involve a lot of complexity not depicted in Figure 8.2.) On the server, the process reverses itself, with the server program running at the application layer replying to the client program. This reply reverses the journey, traveling down the server computer's stack, across the network, and up the stack on the client. A full-fledged network connection can involve many back-and-forth data transfers.

FIGURE 8.2 Information travels "down" and "up" protocol stacks, being checked and repacked at each step of the way.

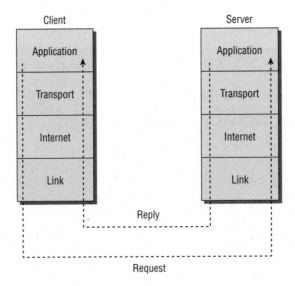

Each component layer of the sending system is equivalent to a layer on the receiving system, but these layers need not be absolutely identical. For instance, you can have different models of network cards at the link layer, or you can even use entirely different network hardware types, such as Ethernet and Token Ring, if some intervening system translates between them. The computers may run different OSs and hence use different—but logically equivalent—protocol stacks. What's important is that the stacks operate in compatible ways.

Linux was designed with TCP/IP in mind, and the Internet is built atop TCP/IP. Other protocol stacks are available, though, and you may occasionally run into them. In particular, NetBEUI was the original Microsoft and IBM protocol stack for Windows, AppleTalk was Apple's initial protocol stack, and Internet Packet Exchange/Sequenced Packet Exchange (IPX/SPX) was Novell's favored protocol stack. All three are now fading in importance, but you may still need to use them in some environments. Linux supports AppleTalk and IPX/SPX but not NetBEUI.

Knowing TCP/IP Protocol Types

Within TCP/IP, several different protocols exist. Each of these protocols can be classified as falling on one of the four layers of the TCP/IP stack, as shown in Figure 8.2. The most important of the Internet- and transport-layer protocols are the building blocks for the application-layer protocols with which you interact more directly. These important Internet- and transport-layer protocols include the following:

IP   The *Internet Protocol (IP)* is the core protocol in TCP/IP networking. Referring to Figure 8.2, IP is an Internet-layer (aka a network-layer or layer 2) protocol. IP provides a "best effort" method for transferring packets between computers—that is, the packets aren't guaranteed to reach their destination. Packets may also arrive out of order or corrupted. Other components of the TCP/IP stack must deal with these issues and have their own ways of doing so. IP is also the portion of TCP/IP with which IP addresses are associated.

IPv6   IP version 6, called *IPv6*, is the update to the original IP stack (often called IPv4). It provides expanded features that help move IP into the next century. For example, IPv4 uses 32-bit addresses, but IPv6 uses 128-bit addresses, providing addresses for up to 3.4 × 10^{38} devices! IPv6 includes a new feature known as *stateless address auto-configuration (SLAAC)*, which simplifies initial network setup. This feature is similar in some ways to the Dynamic Host Configuration Protocol (DHCP) that's commonly used on IPv4. A workstation can determine the network address structure and assign itself a unique address automatically.

ICMP   The *Internet Control Message Protocol (ICMP)* is a simple protocol for communicating data. ICMP is most often used to send error messages between computers—for instance, to signal that a requested service isn't available. This is often done by modifying an IP packet and returning it to its sender, which means that ICMP is technically an Internet-layer protocol, although it relies upon IP. In most cases, you won't use programs that generate ICMP packets on demand; they're created behind the scenes as you use other protocols. One exception is the ping program, which is described in more detail in "Testing Basic Connectivity."

UDP   The *User Datagram Protocol (UDP)* is the simplest of the common transport-layer (aka layer 3) TCP/IP protocols. It doesn't provide sophisticated procedures to correct for out-of-order packets, guarantee delivery, or otherwise improve the limitations of IP. This fact can be a problem, but it also means that UDP can be faster than more sophisticated tools that provide such improvements to IP. Common application-layer protocols that are built atop UDP include the Domain Name System (DNS), the Network File System (NFS), and many streaming-media protocols.

TCP   The *Transmission Control Protocol (TCP)* may be the most widely used transport-layer protocol in the TCP/IP stack. Unlike UDP, TCP creates full connections with error checking and correction as well as other features. These features simplify the creation of network protocols that must exchange large amounts of data, but the features come at a cost: TCP imposes a small performance penalty. Most of the application-layer protocols with which you may already be familiar, including the Simple Mail Transfer Protocol (SMTP), the Hypertext Transfer Protocol (HTTP), and the File Transfer Protocol (FTP), are built atop TCP.

You may notice that the name of the TCP/IP stack is built up of two of the stack's protocol names: TCP and IP. This is because these two protocols are so important for TCP/IP networking generally. TCP/IP, though, is much more than just these two protocols; it includes additional protocols, most of which (below the application layer) are rather obscure. On the other hand, a TCP/IP exchange need not use both TCP and IP—it could be a UDP or ICMP exchange, for instance.

Understanding Network Addressing

In order for one computer to communicate with another over a network, the computers need to have some way to refer to each other. The basic mechanism for doing this is provided by a network address, which can take several different forms, depending on the type of network hardware, protocol stack, and so on. Large and routed networks pose additional challenges to network addressing, and TCP/IP provides answers to these challenges. Finally, to address a specific program on a remote computer, TCP/IP uses a port number, which identifies a specific running program, something like the way a telephone extension number identifies an individual in a large company. The following sections describe all of these methods of addressing.

Using Network Addresses

Consider an Ethernet network. When an Ethernet frame leaves one computer, it's normally addressed to another Ethernet card. This addressing is done using low-level Ethernet features, independent of the protocol stack in question. Recall, however, that the Internet is composed of many different networks that use many different low-level hardware components. A user may have a dial-up telephone connection (through a serial port) but connect to one server that uses Ethernet and another that uses Token Ring. Each of these devices uses a different type of low-level network address. TCP/IP requires something more to integrate across different types of network hardware. In total, three types of addresses are important when you're trying to understand network addressing: network hardware addresses, numeric IP addresses, and text-based hostnames.

Addressing Hardware

One of the characteristics of dedicated network hardware, such as Ethernet or Token Ring cards, is that they have unique hardware addresses, also known as *Media Access Control (MAC) addresses*, programmed into them. In the case of Ethernet, these addresses are 6 bytes in length, and they're generally expressed as hexadecimal (base 16) numbers separated by colons. You can discover the hardware address for an Ethernet card by using the ifconfig command. Type **ifconfig eth*n***, where *n* is the number of the interface (0 for the first card, 1 for the second, and so on). You'll see several lines of output, including one like the following:

```
eth0      Link encap:Ethernet   HWaddr 00:A0:CC:24:BA:02
```

This line tells you that the device is an Ethernet card and that its hardware address is 00:A0:CC:24:BA:02. What use is this, though? Certain low-level network utilities and hardware use the hardware address. For instance, network switches use it to direct data packets. The switch detects that a particular address is connected to a particular wire, and so it sends data directed at that address only over the associated wire. The *Dynamic Host Configuration Protocol (DHCP)*, which is described in the upcoming section "Configuring with DHCP," is a means of automating the configuration of specific computers. It has an option that uses the hardware address to assign the same IP address consistently to a given computer. In addition, advanced network diagnostic tools are available that let you examine packets that come from or are directed to specific hardware addresses.

For the most part, though, you don't need to be aware of a computer's hardware address. You don't enter it in most utilities or programs. It's important for what it does in general.

 Linux identifies network hardware devices with type-specific codes. With most distributions, Ethernet hardware is eth*n*, where *n* is a number from 0 up. The first Ethernet device is eth0, the second is eth1, and so on. (Fedora uses a more complex Ethernet naming system, though.) Wireless devices have names of the form wlan*n*. Unlike most Linux hardware devices, network devices don't have entries in /dev; instead, low-level network utilities take the device names and work with them directly.

Managing IP Addresses

Earlier, we said that TCP/IP, at least in its IPv4 incarnation, supports about 4 billion addresses. This figure is based on the size of the IP address used in TCP/IP: 4 bytes

(32 bits). Specifically, $2^{32} = 4,294,967,296$. For IPv6, 16-byte (128-bit) addresses are used. Not all of these addresses are usable; some are overhead associated with network definitions, and some are reserved.

The 4-byte IPv4 address and 6-byte Ethernet address are mathematically unrelated. This can be the case for IPv6, too, although the IPv6 standard allows the IPv6 address to be built, in part, from the computer's MAC address. In any event, the TCP/IP stack converts between the MAC address and the IP address using the Address Resolution Protocol (ARP) for IPv4 or the Neighbor Discovery Protocol (NDP) for IPv6. These protocols enable a computer to send a *broadcast query*—a message that goes out to all the computers on the local network. This query asks the computer with a given IP address to identify itself. When a reply comes in, it includes the hardware address, so the TCP/IP stack can direct traffic for a given IP address to the target computer's hardware address.

> The procedure for computers that aren't on the local network is more complex. For such computers, a router must be involved. Local computers send packets destined for distant addresses to routers, which send the packets on to other routers or to their destination systems.

IPv4 addresses are usually expressed as four base-10 numbers (0–255) separated by periods, as in 172.30.9.102. If your Linux system's protocol stack is already up and running, you can discover its IP address by using ifconfig, as described earlier. The output includes a line like the following, which identifies the IP address (inet addr):

```
inet addr:172.30.9.102  Bcast:172.30.255.255   Mask:255.255.0.0
```

Although it isn't obvious from the IP address alone, this address is broken into two components: a network address and a computer address. The network address identifies a block of IP addresses that are used by one physical network, and the computer address identifies one computer within that network. The reason for this breakdown is to make the job of routers easier—rather than record how to direct packets destined for each of the 4 billion IP addresses, routers can be programmed to direct traffic based on the packets' network addresses, which is a much simpler job.

IPv6 addresses work in a similar way, except that they're larger. Specifically, IPv6 addresses consist of eight groups of four-digit hexadecimal numbers separated by colons, as in fed1:0db8:85a3:08d3:1319:8a2e:0370:7334. If one or more groups of four digits is 0000, that group or those groups may be omitted, leaving two colons. Only one such group of zeros can be compressed in this way, because if you removed two groups, there would be no way of telling how many sets of zeros would have to be replaced in each group. You can see the IPv6 address assigned to an interface with the inet6 entry in the ifconfig output:

```
inet6 addr: fe80::a00:27ff:fe23:4594/64 Scope:Link
```

IPv6 uses two types of network addresses—*link-local* and *global*. Most Linux distributions automatically assign a link-local IPv6 address to all network interfaces to communicate on the local networks. The fe80:0000:0000:0000: link-local address has become the de facto standard for IPv6 network interfaces.

The Linux system creates a link-local IPv6 network address using this network address along with a combination of the MAC address of the network interface. This ensures that the system will have a unique IPv6 address on the local system, and it can instantly communicate with other IPv6 devices on the local network without any configuration.

Link-local addresses are nonroutable; they can only be used for local network connectivity. An IPv6 global address utilizes a network address advertised by a router on the local network so that systems can communicate across network boundaries and out onto the Internet. Either you can statically assign an IPv6 global address or you can use a DHCPv6 server to assign IPv6 global addresses automatically on a network.

Using Networks

The *network mask* (also known as the *subnet mask* or *netmask*) is a number that identifies the portion of the IP address that's a network address and the part that's a computer address. It's helpful to think of this in binary (base 2) because the netmask uses binary 1 values to represent the network portion of an address and binary 0 values to represent the computer address. The network portion ordinarily leads the computer portion. Expressed in base 10, these addresses usually consist of 255 or 0 values, 255 being a network byte and 0 being a computer byte. If a byte is part network and part computer address, it will have some other value. Figure 8.3 illustrates this relationship, using the IP address 172.30.9.102 and the netmask 255.255.0.0.

FIGURE 8.3   TCP/IP addresses are combined with a netmask to isolate the network address.

IP Address	172.30.9.102	10101100 00011110 00001001 01100110

Netmask	255.255.0.0	11111111 11111111	00000000 00000000

Network Address	172.30.0.0	10101100 00011110 00000000 00000000

Another way of expressing a netmask is as a single number representing the number of network bits in the address. This number usually follows the IP address and a slash. For instance, 172.30.9.102/16 is equivalent to 172.30.9.102 with a netmask of 255.255.0.0—the last number shows the network portion to be two solid 8-bit bytes and hence it's 16 bits. This format is called the *Classless Inter-Domain Routing (CIDR)* form. The longer notation showing all 4 bytes of the netmask is referred to as *dotted quad* notation. IPv6 netmasks work just like IPv4 netmasks, except that larger numbers are involved and IPv6 favors hexadecimal over decimal notation.

On modern IPv4 networks, netmasks are often described in CIDR form. Such network masks can be broken at any bit boundary for any address. For instance, 192.168.1.7 could have a netmask of 255.255.0.0, 255.255.255.0, 255.255.255.128, or various other values. (Keeping each byte at 0 or 255 reduces the odds of human error causing problems, but it sometimes isn't practical, depending on the required or desired sizes of subnets.) Traditionally, though, IPv4 networks have been broken into one of several classes, as summarized in Table 8.1. Classes A, B, and C are for general networking use. Class D addresses are reserved for *multicasting*—sending data to multiple computers simultaneously. Class E addresses are reserved for future use. There are a few special cases within most of these ranges. For instance, the 127.*x.y.z* addresses are reserved for use as *loopback* (aka *localhost*) devices—these addresses refer to the computer on which the address is entered. Addresses in which all of the machine bits are set to 1 refer to the network block itself—they're used for broadcasts. The ultimate broadcast address is 255.255.255.255, which sends data to all computers on a network segment. (Routers normally block packets directed to this address. If they didn't, the Internet could easily be brought to its knees by a few people flooding the network with broadcast packets.)

TABLE 8.1   IPv4 network classes and private network ranges

Class	Address range	Reserved private addresses
A	1.0.0.0–127.255.255.255	10.0.0.0–10.255.255.255
B	128.0.0.0–191.255.255.255	172.16.0.0–172.31.255.255
C	192.0.0.0–223.255.255.255	192.168.0.0–192.168.255.255
D	224.0.0.0–239.255.255.255	none
E	240.0.0.0–255.255.255.255	none

Within each of the three general-use network classes is a range of addresses reserved for private use. Most IP addresses must be assigned to individual computers by a suitable authority, lest two systems on the Internet both try to use a single address. Anybody can use the reserved private address spaces, though. (These address blocks are sometimes referred to as RFC 1918 addresses, after the standards document—RFC 1918—in which they're defined.) The caveat is that routers normally drop packets sent to these addresses, effectively isolating them from the Internet as a whole. The idea is that these addresses may be safely used by small private networks. Today, they're often used behind Network Address Translation (NAT) routers, which enable arbitrary numbers of computers to "hide" behind a single system. The NAT router substitutes its own IP address on outgoing packets and then directs the reply to the correct system. This is very handy if you want to connect more computers to the Internet than you have IP addresses.

> We generally use reserved private addresses for examples in this book. Unless otherwise specified, these examples work equally well on conventional assigned (non-private) IP addresses.

IPv6 has its equivalent to private addresses. Besides link-local address, IPv6 also uses *site-local addresses*, which may be routed within a site but not off site. They begin with the hexadecimal number fec, fed, fee, or fef.

IPv4 address classes were designed to simplify routing, but as the Internet evolved, they became restrictive. Thus, today they serve mainly as a way to set default netmasks, such as 255.0.0.0 for Class A addresses or 255.255.255.0 for Class C addresses. Most configuration tools set these netmasks automatically, but you can override the settings if necessary.

IP addresses and netmasks are extremely important for network configuration. If your network doesn't use DHCP or a similar protocol to assign IP addresses automatically, you must configure your system's IP address manually. A mistake in this configuration can cause a complete failure of networking or more subtle errors, such as an inability to communicate with just some computers.

> Non-TCP/IP stacks have their own addressing methods. NetBEUI uses machine names; it has no separate numeric addressing method. AppleTalk uses two 16-bit numbers. These addressing schemes are independent from IP addresses.

Broadcasting Data

We mentioned broadcasts earlier. A *broadcast* is a type of network transmission that's sent to all the computers on a local network, or occasionally all of the computers on a remote network. Under TCP/IP, a broadcast is done by specifying binary 1 values in all of the machine bits of the IP address. The network portion of the IP address may be set to the network's regular value, and this is required for directed broadcasts, that is, those that are sent to a remote network. (Many routers drop directed broadcasts, though.) In many cases, broadcasts are specified by the use of 255.255.255.255 as an IP address. Packets directed at this address are sent to all of the machines on a local network.

Because the broadcast address for a network is determined by the IP address and netmask, you can convert between the broadcast address and netmask, given one of these and a computer's IP address. If the netmask happens to consist of whole-byte values (expressed as 0 or 255 in dotted quad notation), the conversion is easy: Replace the IP address components that have 0 values in the dotted quad netmask with 255 values to get the broadcast address. For instance, consider a computer with an IP address of 172.30.9.102 and a netmask of 255.255.0.0. The final two elements of the netmask have 0 values, so you swap in 255 values for these final two elements in the IP address to obtain a broadcast address of 172.30.255.255.

In the case of a CIDR address that has non-255 and non-0 values in the netmask, the situation is more complex because you must resort to binary (base 2) numbers. For instance, consider a computer with an IP address of 172.30.9.102 and a netmask of 255.255.128.0 (that is, 172.30.0.0/17). Expressed in binary, these numbers are

```
10101100 00011110 00001001 01100110
11111111 11111111 10000000 00000000
```

To create the broadcast address, you must set the top (network address) values to 1 when the bottom (netmask) value is 0. In this case, the result is

```
10101100 00011110 01111111 11111111
```

Converted back into base 10 notation, the resulting broadcast address is 172.30.127.255. Fortunately, you seldom need to perform such computations. When configuring a computer, you can enter the IP address and netmask and let the computer do the binary computations.

Understanding Hostnames

Computers work with numbers, so it's not surprising that TCP/IP uses numbers as computer addresses. People, though, work better with names. For this reason, TCP/IP includes a way to link names for computers (known as *hostnames*) to IP addresses. In fact, there are several ways to do this, some of which are described in the next section, "Resolving Hostnames."

As with IP addresses, hostnames are composed of two parts: *machine names* and *domain names*. The former refers to a specific computer and the latter to a collection of computers. Domain names are not equivalent to the network portion of an IP address, though; they're completely independent concepts. Domain names are registered for use by an individual or organization, which may assign machine names within the domain and link those machine names to any arbitrary IP address desired. Nonetheless, there is frequently some correspondence between domains and network addresses because an individual or organization that controls a domain is also likely to want a block of IP addresses for the computers in that domain.

Internet domains are structured hierarchically. At the top of the hierarchy are the top-level domains (TLDs), such as .com, .edu, and .uk. These TLD names appear at the *end* of an Internet address. Some correspond to nations (such as .uk and .us, for the United Kingdom and the United States, respectively), but others correspond to particular types of entities (such as .com and .edu, which stand for commercial and educational organizations, respectively). Within each TLD are various domains that identify specific organizations, such as sybex.com for Sybex or loc.gov for the Library of Congress. These organizations may optionally break their domains into *subdomains*, such as `cis.upenn.edu` for the Computer and Information Science department at the University of Pennsylvania. Even subdomains may be further subdivided into their own subdomains; this structure can continue for many levels but usually doesn't. Domains and subdomains include specific computers, such as `www.sybex.com`, Sybex's web server.

When you configure your Linux computer, you may need to know its hostname. This will be assigned by your network administrator and will be a machine name within your organization's domain. If your computer isn't part of an organizational network (say, if it's a system that doesn't connect to the Internet at all or if it connects only via a dial-up account), you'll have to make up a hostname. Alternatively, you can register a domain name, even if you don't use it for running your own servers. Check

`www.icann.org/registrar-reports/accredited-list.html`

for pointers to accredited domain registrars. Most registrars charge between $10 and $15 per year for domain registration. If your network uses DHCP, it may or may not assign your system a hostname automatically.

If you make up a hostname, choose an invalid domain name. This will guarantee that you don't accidentally give your computer a name that legitimately belongs to somebody else. Such a name conflict might prevent you from contacting hosts that have the real domain name, and it could cause other problems as well, such as misdirected email. Four TLDs—`.example`, `.invalid`, `.localhost`, and `.test`—are reserved for fictitious domain names. Three second-level domains—`.example.com`, `.example.net`, and `.example.org`— are also reserved, and so they may be safely used.

Resolving Hostnames

The *Domain Name System (DNS)* is a distributed database of computers that converts between IP addresses and hostnames. Every domain must maintain at least two DNS servers that can either provide the names for every computer within the domain or redirect a DNS query to another DNS server that can better handle the request. Therefore, looking up a hostname involves querying a series of DNS servers, each of which redirects the search until the server that's responsible for the hostname is found. In practice, this process is hidden from you because most organizations maintain DNS servers that do all of the tedious work of chatting with other DNS servers. You need only point your computer to your organization's DNS servers. This detail may be handled through DHCP, or it may be information that you need to configure manually, as described later in the section "Configuring Linux for a Local Network."

Sometimes, you need to look up DNS information manually. You might do this if you know the IP address of a server through non-DNS means and suspect your DNS configuration is delivering the wrong address or to check whether a DNS server is working. Several programs can be helpful in performing such checks:

nslookup   This program performs DNS lookups (on individual computers by default) and returns the results. It also sports an interactive mode in which you can perform a series of queries. This program is officially deprecated, meaning that it's no longer being maintained and will eventually be dropped from its parent package (bind-utils or bind-tools on most distributions). Thus, you should get in the habit of using host or dig instead of nslookup.

host   This program serves as a replacement for the simpler uses of nslookup, but it lacks an interactive mode, and of course many details of its operation differ. In the simplest case, you can type **host** *target.name*, where *target.name* is the hostname or IP address you want to look up. You can add various options that tweak the program's basic operation; consult host's man page for details.

dig   This program performs more complex DNS lookups than host. Although you can use it to find the IP address for a single hostname (or a hostname for a single IP address), it's more flexible than host.

whois   You can look up information on a domain as a whole with this command. For instance, typing **whois sybex.com** reveals who owns the sybex.com domain, who to contact in case of problems, and so on. You may want to use this command with -H, which omits the lengthy legal disclaimers that many domain registries insist on delivering along with whois information. Check the man page for whois for information on additional options.

Exercise 8.1 illustrates the use of the nslookup, host, and dig tools.

EXERCISE 8.1

Practice Resolving Hostnames

The differences between nslookup, host, and dig are best illustrated by example. In this exercise, you'll practice using these three tools to perform both forward and reverse DNS lookups. To do so, follow these steps:

1. Log into a Linux text-mode session or launch a terminal window in a GUI session.

2. Type **nslookup www.google.com**. You may substitute another hostname; however, one key point of this hostname is that it resolves to multiple IP addresses, which nslookup shows on multiple Name: and Address: lines. This practice is common on extremely popular sites because the load can be balanced across multiple computers. Note also that nslookup reports the IP address of the DNS server it uses, on the Server: and Address: lines. (The latter includes the port number, as described later in the section "Network Ports.")

3. Type **host www.google.com**. The output of this command is likely to be somewhat briefer than that of the nslookup command, but it should report the same IP

addresses for the server. Although host doesn't report the DNS server's address, it is IPv6 enabled, so it reports an IPv6 address as well as the site's IPv4 addresses.

4. Type **dig www.google.com**. This output is significantly longer than that of either nslookup or host. In fact, it closely resembles the format of the configuration files used to define a domain in a DNS server. In the case of www.google.com, that hostname is defined as a CNAME record that points to www.l.google.com, which in turn has several A-record entries that point to specific IP addresses. (This structure could change by the time you read this, though, and of course it's likely to be different if you examine other hostnames.) You'll also see several NS records that point to the domain's name servers, and you'll see additional A records that point to the name servers' IP addresses.

5. Perform nslookup, host, and dig queries on IP addresses, such as one of those returned by your lookups on www.google.com. (This is known as a *reverse lookup*.) In each case, the tool should return a hostname. Note, however, that the hostname might not match the one you used originally. This is because multiple hostnames can point to the same IP address and the owner of that IP address decides which hostname to link to the IP address for reverse lookup purposes. In some cases, the tool will return an NXDOMAIN error, which means that the IP address's owner hasn't configured reverse lookups.

6. Perform similar queries on other computers, such as ones associated with your school, employer, or ISP. Most hostnames have just one IP address associated with them, and you may see other differences too.

Sometimes DNS is overkill. For instance, you might just need to resolve a handful of hostnames. This may be because you're configuring a small private network that's not connected to the Internet at large or because you want to set up a few names for local (or even remote) computers that aren't in the global DNS database. For such situations, /etc/hosts may be just what you need. This file holds mappings of IP addresses to hostnames on a one-line-per-mapping basis. Each mapping includes at least one name, and sometimes more:

```
127.0.0.1     localhost
192.168.7.23  apollo.luna.edu  apollo
```

In this example, the name localhost is associated with the 127.0.0.1 address, and the names apollo.luna.edu and apollo are tied to 192.168.7.23. The first of these linkages is standard; it should exist in any /etc/hosts file. The second linkage is an example that you can modify as you see fit. The first name is a full hostname, including the domain portion; subsequent names on the line are aliases—typically the hostname without its full domain specification.

Once you've set up an /etc/hosts file, you can refer to computers listed in the file by name, whether or not those names are recognized by the DNS servers that the computer uses. One major drawback to /etc/hosts is that it's a purely local file; setting a mapping in one computer's /etc/hosts file affects name lookups performed by that computer alone. Thus, to work on an entire network, you must modify the /etc/hosts files on all of the computers on the network.

Linux normally performs lookups in /etc/hosts before it uses DNS. You can modify this behavior by editing the /etc/nsswitch.conf file, which configures the Name Service Switch (NSS) service. More specifically, you must adjust the hosts line. This line lists the order of the files and dns options, which stand for /etc/hosts and DNS, respectively:

```
hosts:      files dns
```

Reverse the order of the files and dns options to have the system consult DNS before it consults /etc/hosts.

> The /etc/nsswitch.conf file supports many more options. For instance, you can perform name resolution using Windows NetBIOS calls or a Lightweight Directory Access Protocol (LDAP) server by adding appropriate options to the hosts line, along with the necessary support software. The passwd, shadow, and group lines control how Linux authenticates users and manages groups. You should not attempt to change these configurations unless you understand the systems involved, but you should be aware of the importance of /etc/nsswitch.conf generally.

In addition to /etc/hosts, Linux supports a file called /etc/networks. It works much like /etc/hosts, but it applies to network addresses and it reverses the order of the names and the IP address on each line:

```
loopback 127.0.0.0
mynet 192.168.7.0
```

This example sets up two linkages: the loopback name to the 127.0.0.0/8 network and mynet for the 192.168.7.0/24 network. It's seldom necessary to edit this file.

Network Ports

Contacting a specific computer is important, but one additional type of addressing is left: The sender must have an address for a specific program on the remote system. For instance, suppose you're using a web browser. The web server computer may be running more servers than just a web server—it may also be running an email server or an FTP server, to name just two of many possibilities. Another number beyond the IP address enables you to direct traffic to a specific program. This number is a network port number, and programs that access a TCP/IP network typically do so through one or more ports.

> Port numbers are features of the UDP and TCP protocols. Some protocols, such as ICMP, don't use port numbers.

When they start up, servers tie themselves to specific ports, which by convention are associated with specific server programs. For instance, port 25 is associated with email servers, and port 80 is used by web servers. Table 8.2 summarizes the purposes of several important ports. A client can direct its request to a specific port and expect to contact an appropriate server. The client's own port number isn't fixed; it's assigned by the OS. Because the client initiates a transfer, it can include its own port number in the connection request, so clients don't need fixed port numbers. Assigning client port numbers dynamically also enables one computer to run several instances of a single client easily because they won't compete for access to a single port.

TABLE 8.2   Port numbers, their purposes, and typical Linux servers

Port number	TCP or UDP	Purpose	Example Linux servers
20	TCP	File Transfer Protocol (FTP) data	ProFTPd, `vsftpd`
21	TCP	FTP	ProFTPd, `vsftpd`
22	TCP	Secure Shell (SSH)	OpenSSH, Dropbear
23	TCP	Telnet	`in.telnetd`
25	TCP	Simple Mail Transfer Protocol (SMTP)	Sendmail, Postfix, Exim, qmail
53	TCP and UDP	Domain Name System (DNS)	Berkeley Internet Name Domain (BIND; aka named), dnsmasq, djbdns
67	UDP	Dynamic Host Configuration Protocol (DHCP)	Internet Software Consortium (ISC) DHCP (dhcpd), dnsmasq
80	TCP	Hypertext Transfer Protocol (HTTP)	Apache, Roxen, `thttpd`
110	TCP	Post Office Protocol version 3 (POP3)	Dovecot, Qpopper, popa3d
111	TCP and UDP	Portmapper	NFS, NIS, other RPC-based services
113	TCP	auth/ident	`identd`
119	TCP	Network News Transfer Protocol (NNTP)	InterNetNews (INN), Diablo, Leafnode

TABLE 8.2   Port numbers, their purposes, and typical Linux servers *(continued)*

Port number	TCP or UDP	Purpose	Example Linux servers
123	UDP	Network Time Protocol (NTP)	ntpd
139	TCP	NetBIOS Session (Windows file sharing)	Samba
143	TCP	Interactive Mail Access Protocol (IMAP)[1]	Dovecot, Cyrus IMAP, UW-IMAP
161	UDP	Simple Network Management Protocol (SNMP)	Net-SNMP
162	UDP	SNMP trap messages	Net-SNMP
177	UDP	XDMCP	XDM, KDM, GDM
389	TCP	LDAP	OpenLDAP
443	TCP	HTTP over SSL (HTTPS)	Apache, Roxen
445	TCP	Microsoft Directory Services (DS)	Samba
465	TCP	SMTP over SSL; or URL Rendez-vous Directory (URD)[2]	Sendmail, Postfix, Exim, qmail; or network routers
514	UDP	Remote system logging	rsyslogd
631	TCP	Internet Printing Protocol (IPP)	Common Unix Printing System (CUPS)
636	TCP	Lightweight Directory Access Protocol (LDAP) over SSL	OpenLDAP
993	TCP	IMAP over SSL	Dovecot, Cyrus IMAP, UW-IMAP
995	TCP	POP3 over SSL	Dovecot, Qpopper, popa3d
5900+	TCP	Remote Framebuffer (RFB)	Virtual Network Computing (VNC): OpenVNC, TightVNC, TigerVNC
6000–6007	TCP	The X Window System (X)	X.org-X11, XFree86

[1]Some sources expand *IMAP* as *Internet Message Access Protocol* or *Internet Mail Access Protocol.*

[2]Port 465 is officially registered for URD; however, it's also commonly used as a secure email delivery port, although this isn't the officially designated purpose of this port.

One key distinction in TCP/IP ports is that between *privileged ports* and *unprivileged ports*. The former have numbers less than 1024. Unix and Linux systems restrict access to privileged ports to root. The idea is that a client can connect to a privileged port and be confident that the server running on that port was configured by the system administrator and can therefore be trusted. Unfortunately, on today's Internet, this trust would be unjustified based solely on the port number, so this distinction isn't very useful. Port numbers greater than 1024 may be accessed by ordinary users.

Clients and Servers

An important distinction is the one between clients and servers. A *client* is a program that initiates a network connection to exchange data. A *server* listens for such connections and responds to them. For instance, a web browser, such as Firefox or Opera, is a client program. You launch the program and direct it to a web page, which means that the web browser sends a request to the web (HTTP) server at the specified address. The web server sends back data in reply to the request. Clients can also send data, like when you enter information in a web form and click a Submit or Send button.

The terms *client* and *server* can also be applied to entire computers that operate mostly in one or the other role. Thus, a phrase such as *web server* is somewhat ambiguous—it can refer either to the web server program or to the computer that runs that program. When this distinction is important and unclear from context, we clarify it (for instance, by referring to "the web server program").

Fortunately, for basic functioning, you need to do nothing to configure ports on a Linux system. You may have to deal with this issue if you run unusual servers, though, because you may need to configure the system to link the servers to the correct ports. This can sometimes involve editing the /etc/services file, which maps port numbers to names, enabling you to use names in server configurations and elsewhere. This file consists of lines that begin with a name and end with a port number, including the type of protocol it uses (TCP or UDP):

```
ssh      22/tcp      # SSH Remote Login Protocol
ssh      22/udp      # SSH Remote Login Protocol
telnet   23/tcp
smtp     25/tcp
```

Configuring Linux for a Local Network

Now that you know something about how networking functions, the question arises, how do you implement networking in Linux? Most Linux distributions provide you with the means to configure a network connection during system installation. Therefore, chances are good that networking already functions on your system. In case it doesn't, though, the following sections summarize what you must do to get the job done. Actual configuration can be done using either the automatic DHCP tool or static IP addresses. Linux's underlying network configuration mechanisms rely on startup scripts and their configuration files, but you may be able to use GUI tools to do the job instead.

Network Hardware Configuration

The most fundamental part of network configuration is getting the network hardware up and running. In most cases, this task is fairly automatic—most distributions ship with system startup scripts that auto-detect the network card and load the correct driver module. If you recompile your kernel, building the correct driver into the main kernel file will also ensure that it's loaded at system startup.

If your network hardware isn't correctly detected, though, subsequent configuration (as described in the upcoming sections "Configuring with DHCP" and "Configuring with a Static IP Address") won't work. To correct this problem, you must load your network hardware driver. You can do this with the modprobe command:

```
# modprobe tulip
```

You must know the name of your network hardware's kernel module (tulip in this example). Chapter 3, "Configuring Hardware," describes the task of hardware configuration and activation in more detail.

Configuring with DHCP

One of the easiest ways to configure a computer to use a TCP/IP network is to use DHCP, which enables one computer on a network to manage the settings for many other computers. It works like this: When a computer running a DHCP client boots up, it sends a broadcast in search of a DHCP server. The server replies (using nothing but the client's hardware address) with the configuration information the client needs to enable it to communicate with other computers on the network—most important, the client's IP address and netmask and the network's gateway and DNS server addresses. The DHCP server may also give the client a hostname and provide various other details about the network. The client then configures itself with these parameters. The IP address isn't assigned permanently; it's referred to as a *DHCP lease*, and if it's not renewed, the DHCP server may give the lease to another computer. Therefore, from time to time the client checks back with the DHCP server to renew its lease.

Three DHCP clients are in common use on Linux: pump, dhclient, and dhcpd (not to be confused with the DHCP server, dhcpd). Some Linux distributions ship with just one of these, but others ship with two or even all three. All distributions have a default DHCP client—the one that's installed when you tell the system you want to use DHCP at system installation time. Those that ship with multiple DHCP clients typically enable you to swap out one for another simply by removing the old package and installing the new one.

Ideally, the DHCP client runs at system bootup. This is usually handled either by its own startup script, as described in Chapter 5, "Booting Linux and Editing Files," or as part of the main network configuration startup file (typically a startup script called `network` or `networking`). The system often uses a line in a configuration file to determine whether to run a DHCP client. For instance, Red Hat and Fedora set this option in a file called `/etc/sysconfig/network-scripts/ifcfg-name`, where *name* is the name of the network interface, such as p2p1. The line in question looks like this:

```
BOOTPROTO="dhcp"
```

> Recall that most distributions use eth0 to refer to the computer's first Ethernet port, eth1 for the second (if present), and so on. Fedora names its interfaces differently, though, and does so in a way that's inconsistent from one computer to another.

If the `BOOTPROTO` variable is set to something else, changing it as shown here will configure the system to use DHCP. It's usually easier to use a GUI configuration tool to set this option, though.

Ubuntu uses the `/etc/network/interfaces` file for a similar purpose, but the details differ. On a system that uses DHCP, a line like the following appears:

```
iface eth0 inet dhcp
```

Details may vary, of course; for instance, the interface name (eth0) may be something else. You may prefer to use the GUI system configuration tools to adjust these options.

Once a DHCP client is configured to run when the computer boots, the configuration task is done—at least, if everything works as it should. On very rare occasions, you may need to tweak DHCP settings to work around client-server incompatibilities or to have the DHCP client do something unusual. Consult the man page for your DHCP client if you need to make changes. You'll then have to modify its startup script or a file to which it refers in order to change its operation.

If you need to run a DHCP client manually, you can usually do so by typing its name (as root), optionally followed by a network identifier, as in **dhclient eth0**, to have the DHCP client attempt to configure eth0 with the help of any DHCP server it finds on that network.

Configuring with a Static IP Address

If a network lacks a DHCP server, you must provide basic network configuration options manually. You can set these options using interactive commands, as described shortly, but to set them in the long term, you adjust a configuration file such as `/etc/sysconfig/network-scripts/ifcfg-name` or `/etc/network/interfaces`. Listing 8.1 shows a typical `ifcfg-name` file, configured to use a static IP address. (Note that this file's exact location and name may vary from one distribution to another.)

Listing 8.1: A sample network configuration file

```
DEVICE="p2p1"
BOOTPROTO="static"
IPADDR="192.168.29.39"
NETMASK="255.255.255.0"
NETWORK="192.168.29.0"
BROADCAST="192.168.29.255"
GATEWAY="192.168.29.1"
ONBOOT="yes"
```

Several specific items are required, or at least helpful, for static IP address configuration:

IP Address   You can set the IP address manually via the ifconfig command (described in more detail shortly) or via the IPADDR item in the configuration file.

Network Mask   The netmask can be set manually via the ifconfig command or via the NETMASK item in a configuration file.

Gateway Address   You can manually set the gateway via the route command. To set it permanently, you need to adjust a configuration file, which may be the same configuration file that holds other options or another file, such as /etc/sysconfig/network/routes. In either case, the option is likely to be called GATEWAY. The gateway isn't necessary on a computer that isn't connected to a wider network—that is, if the computer works *only* on a local network that contains no routers.

DNS Settings   In order for Linux to use DNS to translate between IP addresses and hostnames, you must specify at least one DNS server in the /etc/resolv.conf file. Precede the IP address of the DNS server by the keyword nameserver, as in nameserver 192.168.29.1. You can include up to three nameserver lines in this file. Adjusting this file is all you need to do to set the name server addresses; you don't have to do anything else to make the setting permanent. You can also set your computer's local domain name in this file using the domain option, as in domain luna.edu, to set the domain to luna.edu.

The network configuration script may hold additional options, but most of these are related to others. For instance, Listing 8.1 has an option specifying the interface name (DEVICE="p2p1"), another that tells the computer to assign a static IP address (BOOTPROTO="static"), and a third to bring up the interface when the computer boots (ONBOOT="yes"). The NETWORK and BROADCAST items in Listing 8.1 are derived from the IPADDR and NETMASK items, but you can change them if you understand the consequences.

Unfortunately, these configuration details vary from one distribution to another. For instance, if you use Ubuntu, you would edit /etc/network/interfaces rather than /etc/sysconfig/network-scripts/ifcfg-eth0. The precise layout and formatting of information in the two files differ, but the same basic information is present in both of them. You may need to consult distribution-specific documentation to learn about these details. Alternatively, GUI tools are usually fairly easy to figure out, so you can look for them.

If you aren't sure what to enter for the basic networking values (the IP address, network mask, gateway address, and DNS server addresses), you should consult your network administrator. Do not enter random values or values that you make up that are similar to those used by other systems on your network. Doing so is unlikely to work at all, and it could conceivably cause a great deal of trouble—say, if you mistakenly use an IP address that's reserved for another computer.

As just mentioned, the ifconfig program is critically important for setting both the IP address and netmask. This program can also display current settings. Basic use of ifconfig to bring up a network interface resembles the following syntax:

```
ifconfig interface up addr netmask mask
```

For instance, the following command brings up eth0 (the first Ethernet device on most distributions) using the address 192.168.29.39 and the netmask 255.255.255.0:

```
# ifconfig eth0 up 192.168.29.39 netmask 255.255.255.0
```

This command links the specified IP address to the device so that the computer responds to the address and claims to be that address when sending data. To link an IPv6 address to the device, use the inet6 and add options:

```
# ifconfig eth0 up inet6 add 4201:00e4::23db:1fda:002a/10
```

The ifconfig command doesn't set up a route for traffic beyond your current network. For that, you need to use the route command:

```
# route add default gw 192.168.29.1
```

Substitute your own gateway address for 192.168.29.1. (Routing and the route command are described in more detail shortly, in "Configuring Routing.") Both ifconfig and route can display information on the current network configuration. For ifconfig, omit up and everything that follows; for route, omit add and everything that follows. For instance, to view interface configuration, you might issue the following command:

```
# ifconfig eth0
eth0:   flags=4163<UP,BROADCAST,RUNNING,MULTICAST>  mtu 1500
        inet 192.168.1.85  netmask 255.255.255.0  broadcast 192.168.1.255
        inet6 fe80::a00:27ff:fed6:d741  prefixlen 64  scopeid 0x20<link>
        ether 08:00:27:d6:d7:41  txqueuelen 1000  (Ethernet)
        RX packets 17075  bytes 25152002 (23.9 MiB)
        RX errors 0  dropped 0  overruns 0  frame 0
        TX packets 6863  bytes 480192 (468.9 KiB)
        TX errors 0  dropped 0 overruns 0  carrier 0  collisions 0
```

When configured properly, ifconfig should show a hardware address (ether), an IP address (inet), an IPv6 address if assigned (inet6), and additional statistics. There should be few or no errors, dropped packets, or overruns for both received (RX) and transmitted (TX) packets. Ideally, few (if any) collisions should occur, but some are unavoidable if your network uses a hub rather than a switch. If collisions total more than a few percent of the total transmitted and received packets, you may want to consider replacing a hub with a switch. To use route for diagnostic purposes, you might try the following:

```
# route -n
Kernel IP routing table
Destination Gateway       Genmask        Flags Metric Ref  Use Iface
0.0.0.0     192.168.1.254 0.0.0.0        UG    1024   0    0   eth0
192.168.1.0 0.0.0.0       255.255.255.0  U     0      0    0   eth0
```

 The -n option to route causes it to not attempt to find the hostnames associated with IP addresses. Although hostnames are often useful, this lookup can be slow or fail altogether if your DNS configuration is broken, so using -n with route is sometimes necessary.

This shows that data destined for 192.168.1.0 (that is, any computer with an IP address between 192.168.1.1 and 192.168.1.254) goes directly over eth0. The first line shows the *default route*, which describes what to do with everything that doesn't match any other entry in the routing table. This line specifies the default route's gateway system as 192.168.1.254. If it's missing or misconfigured, some or all traffic destined for external networks, such as the Internet, won't make it beyond your local network segment.

As with DHCP configuration, it's almost always easier to use a GUI configuration tool to set up static IP addresses, at least for new administrators. The exact locations of the configuration files differ from one distribution to another, so the examples listed earlier may not apply to your system.

Configuring Routing

As explained earlier, routers pass traffic from one network to another. You configure your Linux system to contact systems on the local network directly. You also give the computer a router's address, which your system uses as a gateway to the Internet at large. Any traffic that's not destined for the local network is directed at this router, which passes it on to its destination. In practice, there are likely to be a dozen or more routers between you and most Internet sites. Each router has at least two network interfaces and keeps a table of rules concerning where to send data based on the destination IP address. Your own Linux computer has such a table, but it's probably very simple compared to those on major Internet routers.

Linux can function as a router, which means it can link two or more networks together, directing traffic between them on the basis of its routing table. This task is handled, in part, by the route command. This command can be used to do much more than specify a single gateway system, though, as described earlier. A simplified version of the route syntax is as follows:

```
route {add | del} [-net | -host] target [netmask nm] [gw gw]
 [reject] [[dev] interface]
```

You specify add or del along with a *target* parameter (a computer or network address) and optionally other parameters. The -net and -host options force route to interpret the target as a network or computer address, respectively. The netmask option lets you set a netmask as you desire, and gw lets you specify a router through which packets to the specified *target* parameter should go. (Some versions of route use gateway rather than gw.) The reject keyword installs a blocking route, which refuses all traffic destined for the specified network. (This is *not* a firewall, though.) Finally, although route can usually figure out the interface device (for instance, eth0) on its own, you can force the issue with the dev option.

As an example, consider a network in which packets destined for the 172.20.0.0/16 subnet should be passed through the 172.21.1.1 router, which isn't the default gateway system. You can set up this route with the following command:

```
# route add -net 172.20.0.0 netmask 255.255.0.0 gw 172.21.1.1
```

Incorrect routing tables can cause serious problems because some or all computers won't respond. You can examine your routing table by typing **route** alone and compare the results to what your routing table should be. (Consult a network administrator if you're not sure what your routing table should contain.) You can then delete incorrect routes and add new ones to replace them, if necessary. Ultimately, of course, changing your configuration files is the best solution, but typing a couple of route commands will do the trick in the short term.

One more thing you may need to do if you're setting up a router is to enable routing. Ordinarily, a Linux system won't forward packets it receives from one system that are directed to another system. If Linux is to act as a router, though, it must accept these packets and send them on to the destination network (or at least to an appropriate gateway). To enable this feature, you must modify a key file in the /proc filesystem:

```
# echo "1" > /proc/sys/net/ipv4/ip_forward
```

This command enables IP forwarding. Permanently setting this option requires modifying a configuration file. Some distributions set it in /etc/sysctl.conf:

```
net.ipv4.ip_forward = 1
```

Other distributions use other configuration files and options, such as /etc/sysconfig/sysctl and its IP_FORWARD line. If you can't find it, try using grep to search for ip_forward or IP_FORWARD, or modify a local startup script to add the command to perform the change.

Using GUI Configuration Tools

Most distributions include their own GUI configuration tools for network interfaces. For instance, Fedora and Red Hat ship with a custom GUI tool called Network Configuration (system-config-network), and SUSE has a text-mode and GUI tool called YaST. The details of operating these programs differ, but the GUI configuration tool provides a means to enter the information described earlier.

Although the exam doesn't cover GUI network configuration tools, they're generally easier to locate and use than the configuration files in which settings are stored. Thus you may want to look for your distribution's tool and learn to use it. Once you understand the principles of network configuration (IP addresses, DHCP, and so on), you shouldn't have any trouble entering the necessary information in the GUI fields. Figure 8.4 shows the Fedora Network Configuration tool.

FIGURE 8.4 Using the Fedora Network Configuration tool to configure the IP address information.

The precise details of how to configure a Linux system using GUI tools differ from one distribution to another. For instance, SUSE's YaST doesn't lay out its options in precisely the same way as Fedora's Network Configuration tool. The basic principles are the same, though; you must choose whether to use static IP address assignment or an automatic system such as DHCP and enter a number of key options, depending on what configuration method you choose.

Using the *ifup* and *ifdown* Commands

Most Linux distributions today ship with two commands, ifup and ifdown, that combine the functions of several other network commands, most notably ifconfig and route.

In their simplest forms, they bring interfaces up or shut them down based on information in whatever files your distribution uses to store network configuration data:

```
# ifup eth0
Determining IP information for eth0... done.
```

After you issue this command, eth0 will be fully configured, including all routing information, assuming you've properly configured it by using your distribution's network configuration tools or by manually editing configuration files such as /etc/network/interfaces and /etc/sysconfig/network-scripts/ifcfg-*name*. You can bring the interface down with equal ease by typing **ifdown eth0**.

The ifup and ifdown commands are useful for verifying that the network settings are configured properly for the next time the computer boots. They're also useful if you want to take down the network or bring it back up again quickly, because you can type fewer commands and you don't need to remember all of the details of IP addresses, routes, and so on. If you need to experiment or debug a problem, though, using ifconfig and route individually is preferable, because they give you finer control over the process.

The ifup and ifdown commands are implemented as scripts that consult the configuration files and run the relevant low-level commands behind the scenes.

Configuring Hostnames

The hostnames described earlier (in the section "Resolving Hostnames") are configured in a couple of ways:

On DNS   Your network administrator should be able to add an entry for your system to your network's DNS server. This entry should make your computer addressable by name from other computers on your local network, and perhaps from the Internet at large. Alternatively, remote systems' /etc/hosts files can be modified to include your system.

On Your Local Computer   Various local programs should know your computer's name. For instance, you may want to have your hostname displayed as part of a command prompt or entered automatically in email messages. For this task, you must set your hostname locally. Note that this is entirely independent of your DNS hostname. In theory, you can set the two to very different values, but this practice is likely to lead to confusion and perhaps even failure of some programs to operate properly.

The most basic tool for setting your hostname locally is called, appropriately enough, hostname. Type the command alone to see what your hostname is, or type it with a new name to set the system's hostname to that name:

```
# hostname nessus.example.com
```

Similar commands, domainname and dnsdomainname, display or set the computer's domain name (such as example.com). The domainname command sets the domain name as used by Network Information System (NIS), whereas dnsdomainname sets the domain name as used by DNS. These commands don't affect remote servers—just the name given to programs that use calls designed for these servers.

Many Linux distributions look in the /etc/hostname or /etc/HOSTNAME file for a hostname to set at boot time. Thus, if you want to set your hostname permanently, you should look for these files, and if one is present, you should edit it. Fedora uses /etc/sysconfig/network for this purpose, among others. If you can't find one of these files, consult your distribution's documentation; it's conceivable that your distribution stores its hostname in some unusual location.

In Exercise 8.2, you'll familiarize yourself with some of the tools used to configure basic network settings. You'll use these tools both to study and to change your network configuration.

EXERCISE 8.2

Configuring a Network Connection

In this exercise, the assumption is that the computer is correctly configured to use an IPv4 Ethernet network, including both the local network and a larger network (probably the Internet) via a router.

Some of the procedures in this exercise can easily break your network connectivity if something goes wrong. If this happens, typing **ifdown** followed by **ifup** is one way to recover. If this fails, rebooting the computer is almost certain to work, although it's a radical solution.

To study and modify your system's network configuration, follow these steps:

1. Log into the Linux system as a normal user.

2. Launch an xterm from the desktop environment's menu system, if you used a GUI login method.

3. Acquire root privileges. You can do this by typing **su** in an xterm or by using sudo (if it's configured) to run the commands in the following steps.

4. Type **ifconfig**. This command displays information about your local network settings for all of your network interfaces. Most systems have both a loopback interface (lo) and an Ethernet interface (eth0). Look for a line in the Ethernet section that includes the string inet addr:. The following 4-byte number is your IP address. Write it down, as well as the value of your netmask (Mask:). Study the other information in this output too, such as the number of received (RX) and transmitted (TX) packets, the number of errors, the number of collisions, and the Ethernet adapter's hardware address.

5. Type **route -n**. The output is your computer's routing table information. This normally includes information about the loopback network address (127.0.0.0/24), the local network address, and a default route (identified as the route for 0.0.0.0). Some systems may display fewer or additional lines, depending on local configuration. The default route includes an IP address under the Gateway column. Write down that address.

6. Use ping to test connectivity to both local and remote computers. (This command is described in more detail in the section "Testing Basic Connectivity.") You need the name or IP address of at least one local computer and at least one distant computer (beyond your local router). Type **ping** *address*, where *address* is the name or IP address of each test machine. Perform this test for localhost or 127.0.0.1, your own machine (use the IP address you noted in step 4), your local router (use the IP address you noted in step 5), and a distant computer (if you're connected to the Internet, you can use an Internet-accessible site, such as www.linux.org). All of these ping tests should be successful. Note, however, that some computers are configured to ignore packets sent by ping. Thus some of these tests may fail if you run into such systems. You can learn the configuration of local computers from their administrators, but for Internet sites, you may want simply to try another site if the first one you test fails.

7. Bring down the local Ethernet connection by typing **ifconfig eth0 down**.

8. Repeat steps 4–6. Note that the eth0 interface is no longer shown when you type ifconfig, all routes associated with it have been removed from the routing table, and pinging systems accessible from the interface no longer work. (Linux retains some information about its former Ethernet link, so you may still be able to ping the computer itself via its former eth0 address.)

9. Bring the local Ethernet connection back up by typing **ifconfig eth0 up** *address* **netmask** *mask*, where *address* is the original IP address and *mask* is the original netmask, both as identified in step 4.

10. Repeat steps 4–6. Note that the ifconfig command automatically added back your local network to the routing table but that the default route is still missing. As a result, you can't contact any systems that are located off the local network. If your DNS server is such a system, this means that your ability to contact even local machines by name may be impaired as well.

11. Restore the default route by typing **route add default gw** *gateway*, where *gateway* is the router address you identified in step 5.

12. Repeat steps 4–6. If your network configuration is typical, all connectivity should be restored. (Some more exotic systems may still be lacking certain routes, or you may have a network status icon on your desktop that may get confused and you'll need to restart your desktop.)

Real World Scenario

Using PPP with DSL

Broadband users, and particularly those with Digital Subscriber Line (DSL) connections, sometimes have to use a variant of PPP to make their connections. PPP is a login-based way to access the Internet—you use a PPP utility to initiate a connection to a remote computer, which includes an exchange of a username and a password. A decade ago, PPP was used in dial-up Internet access (and it's still used in this capacity), but some DSL providers have adapted PPP for their own purposes. In the case of DSL, this configuration method is called PPP over Ethernet (PPPoE).

In many cases, the simplest way to use a PPPoE configuration is to purchase a broadband router. This device attaches to the DSL modem and makes the PPPoE connection. The broadband router then works just like an ordinary Ethernet or Wi-Fi router, as far as your local computers are concerned, so you can configure Linux as you would on any other local network.

If you must connect a Linux system directly to a DSL network that uses PPPoE, you must use a Linux PPPoE client. Most Linux distributions ship with such clients, but configuration details vary from one distribution to another. Your best bet is to look for your distribution's GUI network configuration tool; chances are that you'll be able to find a set of options that are clearly labeled as applying to DSL or PPPoE.

Diagnosing Network Connections

Network configuration is a complex task, and unfortunately, things don't always work as planned. Happily, there are a few commands that you can use to help diagnose a problem. Five of these are ping, traceroute, tracepath, netstat, and tcpdump. Each of these commands exercises the network in a particular way and provides information that can help you track down the source of a problem. You can also use some common network programs that aren't primarily debugging tools in your debugging efforts.

Testing Basic Connectivity

The most basic network test is the ping command, which sends a simple ICMP packet to the system you name (via IP address or hostname) and waits for a reply. In Linux, ping continues sending packets once every second or so until you interrupt it with a Ctrl+C keystroke. (You can instead specify a limited number of tests via the -c *num* option.) Here's an example of its output:

```
$ ping -c 4 speaker
PING speaker (192.168.1.1) 56(84) bytes of data.
```

```
64 bytes from speaker.example.com (192.168.1.1): icmp_seq=1 ttl=64 time=0.194ms
64 bytes from speaker.example.com (192.168.1.1): icmp_seq=2 ttl=64 time=0.203ms
64 bytes from speaker.example.com (192.168.1.1): icmp_seq=3 ttl=64 time=0.229ms
64 bytes from speaker.example.com (192.168.1.1): icmp_seq=4 ttl=64 time=0.217ms
--- speaker ping statistics ---
4 packets transmitted, 4 received, 0% packet loss, time 3002ms
rtt min/avg/max/mdev = 0.194/0.210/0.229/0.022 ms
```

This command sent four packets and waited for their return, which occurred quite quickly (in an average of 0.210ms) because the target system was on the local network.

For IPv6 addresses, you'll need to use the ping6 command. However, if you have multiple interfaces on your Linux system, you must be careful if using a link-local IPv6 address:

```
$ ping6 -c 4 fe80::c418:2ed0:aead:cbce
connect: Invalid argument
```

The problem is that the system doesn't know which interface to use to access the link-local address. To solve this, you can add the interface name after the link-local address, separated by a percent sign:

```
$ ping6 -c 4 fe80::c418:2ed0:aead:cbce%eth0
PING fe80::c418:2ed0:aead:cbce%eth0(fe80::c418:2ed0:aead:cbce) 56 data
bytes
64 bytes from fe80::c418:2ed0:aead:cbce: icmp_seq=1 ttl=128 time=1.47 ms
64 bytes from fe80::c418:2ed0:aead:cbce: icmp_seq=2 ttl=128 time=0.478 ms
64 bytes from fe80::c418:2ed0:aead:cbce: icmp_seq=3 ttl=128 time=0.777 ms
64 bytes from fe80::c418:2ed0:aead:cbce: icmp_seq=4 ttl=128 time=0.659 ms

--- fe80::c418:2ed0:aead:cbce%eth0 ping statistics ---
4 packets transmitted, 4 received, 0% packet loss, time 3003ms
rtt min/avg/max/mdev = 0.478/0.847/1.475/0.378 ms
$
```

By pinging systems on both local and remote networks, you can isolate where a network problem occurs. For instance, if you can ping local computers but not remote systems, the problem is most probably in your router configuration. If you can ping by IP address but not by name, the problem is with your DNS configuration.

Tracing a Route

A step up from ping is the traceroute command, which sends a series of three test packets to each computer between your system and a specified target system. The result looks something like this:

```
$ traceroute -n 10.1.0.43
traceroute to 10.1.0.43 (10.1.0.43), 30 hops max, 52 byte packets
```

```
1  192.168.1.1  1.021 ms   36.519 ms  0.971 ms
2  10.10.88.1   17.250 ms  9.959 ms   9.637 ms
3  10.9.8.173   8.799 ms   19.501 ms  10.884 ms
4  10.9.8.133   21.059 ms  9.231 ms   103.068 ms
5  10.9.14.9    8.554 ms   12.982 ms  10.029 ms
6  10.1.0.44    10.273 ms  9.987 ms   11.215 ms
7  10.1.0.43    16.360 ms  *          8.102 ms
```

The -n option to this command tells it to display target computers' IP addresses rather than their hostnames. This can speed up the process a bit, particularly if you're having DNS problems, and it can sometimes make the output easier to read—but you may want to know the hostnames of problem systems because that can help you pinpoint who's responsible for a problem.

This sample output shows a great deal of variability in response times. The first hop, to 192.168.1.1, is purely local; this router responded in 1.021, 36.519, and 0.971 milliseconds (ms) to its three probes. (Presumably, the second probe caught the system while it was busy with something else.) Probes of most subsequent systems are in the 8 to 20ms range, although one is at 103.068ms. The final system has only two times; the middle probe never returned, as the asterisk (*) on this line indicates.

For IPv6 addresses, use the traceroute6 command. It's important to remember, though, that you can only trace global addresses; link-local addresses are nonroutable.

Using traceroute and traceroute6, you can localize problems in network connectivity. Highly variable times and missing times can indicate a router that's overloaded or that has an unreliable link to the previous system on the list. If you see a dramatic jump in times, it typically means that the physical distance between two routers is great. This is common in intercontinental links. Such jumps don't necessarily signify a problem unless the two systems are close enough that a huge jump isn't expected.

What can you do with the traceroute output? Most immediately, traceroute is helpful in determining whether a problem in network connectivity exists in a network for which you're responsible. For instance, the variability in the first hop of the preceding example could indicate a problem on the local network, but the lost packet associated with the final destination most likely is not a local problem. If the trouble link is within your jurisdiction, you can check the status of the problem system, nearby systems, and the network segment in general.

 Some routers are configured in such a way that traceroute isn't a useful tool; these routers block all traceroute data, either to themselves only or for all packets that pass through them. If your traceroute output contains one or two lines of all asterisks but everything else seems OK, chances are that you've run into such a system. If you see nothing but asterisks after a certain router but diagnostic tools such as ping still work, a router is probably blocking all traceroute operations.

The tracepath program (and the IPv6 tracepath6 program) is an alternative to traceroute. In basic operation, it's similar, although it produces one line of output for each test packet and so yields longer outputs than traceroute. There are also fewer tracepath options than there are traceroute options.

Checking Network Status

Another useful diagnostic tool is netstat. This is something of a Swiss Army knife of network tools because it can be used in place of several others, depending on the parameters it's passed. It can also return information that's not easily obtained in other ways. Here are some examples:

Interface Information   Pass netstat the --interface or -i parameter to obtain information about your network interfaces similar to what ifconfig returns. (Some versions of netstat return information in the same format, but others display the information differently.)

Routing Information   You can use the --route or -r parameter to obtain a routing table listing similar to what the route command displays.

Masquerade Information   Pass netstat the --masquerade or -M parameter to obtain information about connections mediated by Linux's NAT features, which often go by the name *IP masquerading*. NAT enables a Linux router to "hide" a network behind a single IP address. This can be a good way to stretch limited IPv4 addresses.

Program Use   Some versions of netstat support the --program (or -p) parameter, which attempts to provide information about the programs that are using network connections. This attempt isn't always successful, but it often is, so you can see what programs are making outside connections.

Open Ports   When used with various other parameters, or without any parameters at all, netstat returns information about open ports and the systems to which they connect.

All Connections   The --all or -a option is used in conjunction with others. It causes netstat to display information about the ports that server programs open to listen for network connections, in addition to already-open connections. This use of netstat is described in more detail in Chapter 10, "Securing Your System."

Keep in mind that netstat is a very powerful tool and its options and output aren't entirely consistent from one distribution to another. You may want to peruse its man page and experiment with it to learn what it can do.

Examining Raw Network Traffic

One advanced network troubleshooting tool is tcpdump. This utility is a *packet sniffer*, which is a program that can intercept network packets and log them or display them on the screen. Packet sniffers can be useful diagnostic tools because they enable you to verify that a computer is actually receiving data from other computers. They also enable you to examine the data in its raw form, which can be useful if you understand enough of the protocol's implementation details to spot problems.

> Although packet sniffers are useful diagnostic tools, they can also be abused. For instance, unscrupulous individuals can run packet sniffers to capture passwords that others send over the network. Depending on your network configuration, this trick can work even if the packet sniffer isn't running on either the sending or the receiving computer. For this reason, many organizations have policies forbidding the use of packet sniffers except under limited circumstances. Thus, before running a packet sniffer, you should obtain written permission to use it from an individual who is authorized to grant such permission. Failure to do so can lead you into serious trouble, possibly losing your job or even being sued.

In its most basic form, you can use tcpdump by typing its name:

```
# tcpdump
tcpdump: verbose output suppressed, use -v or -vv for full protocol decode
listening on eth0, link-type EN10MB (Ethernet), capture size 96 bytes
19:31:55.503759 IP speaker.example.com.631 > 192.168.1.255.631: UDP,
 length: 139
19:31:55.505400 IP nessus.example.com.33513 > speaker.example.com.domain:
 46276+ PTR? 255.1.168.192.in-addr.arpa. (44)
19:31:55.506086 IP speaker.example.com.domain > nessus.example.com.33513:
 46276 NXDomain* 0/1/0 (110)
```

The first thing to note about this command is that you must run it as root; ordinary users aren't allowed to monitor network traffic in this way. Once it's run, tcpdump summarizes what it's doing and then begins printing lines, one for each packet that it monitors. (Some of these lines can be quite long and so may take more than one line on your display.) These lines include a time stamp, a stack identifier (IP in all of these examples), the origin system name or IP address and port, the destination system name or IP address and port, and packet-specific information. Ordinarily, tcpdump keeps displaying packets indefinitely, so you must terminate it by pressing Ctrl+C. Alternatively, you can pass it the -c *num* option to have it display *num* packets and then quit.

Even this basic output can be very helpful. For instance, consider the preceding example of three packets, which was captured on nessus.example.com. This computer successfully received one broadcast packet (addressed to 192.168.1.255) from speaker.example.com's UDP port 631, sent a packet to speaker.example.com, and received a packet from that system directed at nessus.example.com rather than sent as a broadcast. This sequence verifies that at least minimal communication exists between these two computers. If you were having problems establishing a connection, you could rule out a whole range of possibilities based on this evidence, such as faulty cables or a firewall that was blocking traffic.

If you need more information, tcpdump provides several options that enhance or modify its output. These include -A to display packet contents in ASCII, -D to display a list of interfaces to which tcpdump can listen, -n to display all addresses numerically, -v (and additional -v options, up to -vvv) to display additional packet information, and -w *file* to write the captured packets to the specified file. Consult tcpdump's man page for more details on these options and for additional options.

Using Additional Tools

In addition to specialized network diagnostic programs, you can use some common user programs as debugging tools. One of the most useful of these may be Telnet. This program and protocol is mainly a remote login tool; type the program name followed by the name of a remote system to receive a login prompt on that system:

```
$ telnet speaker
Trying 192.168.1.1...
Connected to speaker.
Escape character is '^]'.
speaker login: harry
Password:
Last login: Mon Apr 25 21:48:44 from nessus.example.com
Have a lot of fun...
harry@speaker:~>
```

WARNING   Telnet is a poor choice as a remote login protocol because it's entirely unencrypted. As a general rule, you should remove the Telnet server from your system and never use the telnet client program. It can be a useful lowest-common-denominator protocol on sufficiently protected private networks, though, and the telnet client can also be a handy tool for debugging, as described next. Chapter 10 describes SSH, which is a much safer alternative to Telnet.

You can use Telnet to debug network protocols; if you give it a port number after the remote hostname, the telnet program connects to that port, enabling you to interact with the server:

```
$ telnet speaker 25
Trying 192.168.1.1...
Connected to speaker.
Escape character is '^]'.
```

```
220 speaker.example.com ESMTP Postfix
```
HELO nessus.example.com
```
250 speaker.example.com
```

This example connects to port 25, which is used by email servers. After connecting, enter a HELO command, which is used by SMTP to identify a client; the remote system responded with a 250 code, which indicates an accepted command.

Of course, to use Telnet in this way, you must know a great deal about the protocol. Even without this knowledge, though, you can use Telnet to test whether a server is running: If you try to connect but get a Connection refused error message, you know that a remote server isn't running or is inaccessible for some reason (say, because it's being blocked by a firewall). If you get in (to the Escape character message shown in the earlier example or beyond), the server is running, although it may not be working correctly. This test works only for protocols that use TCP. Some tools use UDP instead, and Telnet won't connect with them.

Sometimes the File Transfer Protocol (FTP) can be a useful diagnostic tool as well. This program, as its name suggests, enables you to transfer files between systems. To use it, type the program name followed by the FTP server's name. You'll then see a login prompt and be able to issue FTP commands:

```
$ ftp speaker
Connected to speaker.
220 (vsFTPd 1.2.1)
Name (speaker:harry): harry
530 Please login with USER and PASS.
SSL not available
331 Please specify the password.
Password:
230 Login successful.
Remote system type is UNIX.
Using binary mode to transfer files.
ftp> get zathras.wav
local: zathras.wav remote: zathras.wav
200 PORT command successful. Consider using PASV.
150 Opening BINARY mode data connection for zathras.wav (109986 bytes).
226 File send OK.
109986 bytes received in 0.104 secs (1e+03 Kbytes/sec)
ftp> quit
221 Goodbye.
```

This example retrieves a single file, zathras.wav, from the remote computer. The basic ftp client displays a file size, transfer time, and transfer rate (1e+03 Kbytes/sec—in other words, 1 × 103KiB/s, or 1,000KiB/s). This can be a useful way to test your network transfer speed, although you'll get more reliable results with files that are several hundred kilobytes or larger in size. In addition to get, which retrieves files, you can issue commands such as put to upload a file, ls or dir to display the remote system's directory contents, cd to change directories on the remote system, delete to remove a file, and quit or exit to exit from the program. You can use the help or ? command to see a list of available ftp commands.

Like Telnet, FTP is a poor choice of protocol for security reasons. The same SSH protocol that can substitute for Telnet can also handle most FTP duties. One important exception exists to the rule to not use FTP, though: using anonymous FTP sites is a common method of distributing public files on the Internet. You can download Linux itself from anonymous FTP sites. These sites typically take a username of anonymous and any password (your email address is the conventional reply) and give you read access to their contents. In most cases, you can't upload files to anonymous FTP sites, and you can access only a limited number of files.

You can access public FTP sites using a web browser. Enter a URL that begins with ftp://, such as ftp://downloads.example.org, and the web browser connects to the site using FTP rather than HTTP.

Summary

Linux is a network-enabled OS, and it relies on its networking features more than do most OSs. This networking is built around TCP/IP, so you should understand the basics of this protocol stack, including IP addresses, hostnames, and routing. Most Linux distributions provide tools to configure networking during system installation, but if you want to change your settings temporarily or permanently, you can do so. Tools such as ifconfig and route can temporarily change your network configuration, and editing critical files or running distribution-specific utilities enables you to make your changes permanent.

Exam Essentials

Describe the information needed to configure a computer on a static IP network. Four pieces of information are important: the IP address, the netmask (aka the network mask or subnet mask), the network's gateway address, and the address of at least one DNS server. The first two are required, but if you omit either or both of the latter two, basic networking will function, but you won't be able to connect to the Internet or use most DNS hostnames.

Determine when using /etc/hosts rather than DNS makes the most sense.   The /etc/ hosts file provides a static mapping of hostnames to IP addresses on a single computer. Therefore, maintaining this file on a handful of computers for a small local network is fairly straightforward, but when the number of computers rises beyond a few or when IP addresses change frequently, running a DNS server to handle local name resolution makes more sense.

Summarize tools you can use to translate between hostnames and IP addresses.   The nslookup program can perform these translations in both directions using either command-line or interactive modes, but this program has been deprecated. You're better off using host for simple lookups and dig for more complex tasks.

Describe the function of network ports.   Network ports enable packets to be directed to specific programs; each network-enabled program attaches itself to one or more ports, sending data from that port and receiving data directed to the port. Certain ports are assigned to be used by specific servers, enabling client programs to contact servers by directing requests at specific port numbers on the server computers.

Explain when you should use static IP addresses or DHCP.   Static IP address configuration involves manually entering the IP address and other information and is used when a network lacks a Dynamic Host Configuration Protocol (DHCP) server or when a computer shouldn't be configured by that server (say, because the computer *is* the DHCP server). DHCP configuration is easier to set up on the client but works only if the network has a DHCP server system.

Explain what the route command accomplishes.   The route command displays or modifies the routing table, which tells Linux how to direct packets based on their destination IP addresses.

Describe some basic network diagnostic tools.   The ping program tests basic network connectivity, and traceroute and tracepath perform similar but more complex tests that can help you localize where on a route between two systems a problem exists. The netstat utility is a general-purpose network status tool that can report a wide variety of information about your network configuration. Packet sniffers such as tcpdump provide detailed information about the network packets "seen" by a computer, which can be a useful way to verify that certain packet types are actually being sent or received.

Review Questions

1. Which types of network hardware does Linux support? (Select three.)
    A. Token Ring
    B. Ethernet
    C. DHCP
    D. NetBEUI
    E. Fibre Channel

2. Which of the following is a valid IPv4 address for a single computer on a TCP/IP network?
    A. 202.9.257.33
    B. 63.63.63.63
    C. 107.29.5.3.2
    D. 98.7.104.0/24
    E. 255.255.255.255

3. You want to set up a computer on a local network via a static TCP/IP configuration, but you lack a gateway address. Which of the following is true?
    A. Because the gateway address is necessary, no TCP/IP networking functions will work.
    B. TCP/IP networking will function, but you'll be unable to convert hostnames to IP addresses or vice versa.
    C. You'll be able to communicate with machines on your local network segment but not with other systems.
    D. Since a gateway is needed only for IPv6, you'll be able to use IPv4 but not IPv6 protocols.
    E. Without a gateway address available, you'll be unable to use DHCP to simplify configuration.

4. Using a packet sniffer, you notice a lot of traffic directed at TCP port 22 on a local computer. What protocol does this traffic use, assuming it's using the standard port?
    A. HTTP
    B. SMTP
    C. Telnet
    D. SSH
    E. NNTP

5. What network port would an IMAP server normally use for IMAP exchanges?
    A. 21
    B. 25
    C. 110

    D. 143

    E. 443

6. Which of the following are *not* Linux DHCP clients? (Select two.)

    A. pump

    B. dhcpcd

    C. dhcpd

    D. dhclient

    E. ifconfig

7. Which of the following types of information are returned by typing `ifconfig eth0`? (Select two.)

    A. The names of programs that are using eth0

    B. The IP address assigned to eth0

    C. The hardware address of eth0

    D. The hostname associated with eth0

    E. The kernel driver used by eth0

8. Which of the following programs is conventionally used to perform a DNS lookup?

    A. host

    B. dnslookup

    C. pump

    D. ifconfig

    E. netstat

9. Which of the following commands should you type to add to host 192.168.0.10 a default gateway of 192.168.0.1?

    A. `route add default gw 192.168.0.10 192.168.0.1`

    B. `route add default gw 192.168.0.1`

    C. `route add 192.168.0.10 default 192.168.0.1`

    D. `route 192.168.0.10 gw 192.168.0.1`

    E. `route host gw 192.168.0.1`

10. Which of the following commands might bring up an interface on eth1? (Select two.)

    A. `dhclient eth1`

    B. `ifup eth1`

    C. `ifconfig eth1`

    D. `network eth1`

    E. `netstat -up eth1`

11. What is the purpose of /etc/hostname, if it's present on the system?

    A. It holds the hostname of a package repository server.

    B. It holds a list of servers that resolve hostnames.

    C. It holds a list of IP addresses and associated hostnames.

    D. It holds the hostname of the local gateway computer.

    E. It holds the computer's default hostname.

12. Network accesses to parts of the Internet work fine, but several common sites have stopped responding (even when addressed via raw IP addresses). Which of the following tools will be most helpful in diagnosing the source of this problem?

    A. netstat

    B. ping

    C. traceroute

    D. ifconfig

    E. dig

13. What value identifies an IPv6 address as a link-local address?

    A. The address uses the MAC address of the system.

    B. The address starts with fe80.

    C. The address starts with fee.

    D. The address starts with 2001.

14. How can you learn what programs are currently accessing the network on a Linux system?

    A. Type **ifconfig -p eth0**.

    B. Examine /proc/network/programs.

    C. Type **netstat -p**.

    D. Examine /etc/xinetd.conf.

    E. Type **dmesg | less**.

15. To diagnose a problem with an IMAP server (imap.example.com), you type **telnet imap.example.com 143** from a remote client. How can this procedure help you? (Select two.)

    A. You can verify basic connectivity between the client computer and the server program.

    B. By examining the output, you can locate intermediate routers that are misbehaving.

    C. By using an encrypted protocol, you ensure that a packet-sniffing intruder doesn't cause problems.

    D. Once connected, you can type IMAP commands to test the server's response to them.

    E. Once you've logged into the remote system, you can examine its IMAP log files.

16. You're configuring a new system, and your network administrator scribbles its IP address (172.25.78.89), netmask (255.255.255.0), gateway address (172.25.79.1), and DNS server address (10.24.89.201) on a piece of paper. You enter this information into your configuration files and type **ifup eth0**, but you find that you can't access the Internet with this computer. Which of the following is definitely true?

A. Because the DNS server is on a completely different network, it won't function properly for your system. You should ask for the local network's DNS server's IP address.

B. The netmask identifies the gateway as being on a different network segment than the computer you're configuring, so the two can't communicate directly. You most likely misread one address.

C. Because the IP addresses involved are private IP addresses, there's no way for them to access the Internet. You must ask for public IP addresses for this system or use only your local private network.

D. The computer's IP address is a Class B address, but the netmask is for a Class C address. This combination can't work together, so you must obtain a new IP address or netmask.

E. The ifup utility works only for computers that use DHCP, so using a static IP address as specified in the question won't work correctly.

17. What is the purpose of the -n option to route?

A. It causes no operation to be performed; route reports what it would do if -n were omitted.

B. It precedes the specification of a netmask when setting the route.

C. It limits route's output to descriptions of non-Internet routes.

D. It forces interpretation of a provided address as a network address rather than a host address.

E. It causes machines to be identified by IP address rather than hostname in output.

18. What is the purpose of /etc/resolv.conf?

A. It holds the names of network protocols and the port numbers with which they're associated.

B. It controls whether the computer's network options are configured statically or via a DHCP server.

C. It specifies the IP address of a DHCP server from which the computer attempts to obtain an IP address.

D. It holds the routing table for the computer, determining the route that network packets take to other computers.

E. It sets the computer's default search domain and identifies (by IP address) the name servers that the computer may use.

19. Which of the following entries are found in the /etc/hosts file?

A. A list of hosts allowed to access this one remotely

B. Mappings of IP addresses to hostnames

C. A list of users allowed to access this host remotely

D. Passwords for remote web administration

E. A list of port numbers and their associated protocols

20. How can you reconfigure Linux to use DNS queries prior to consulting /etc/hosts?

A. Edit the /etc/resolv.conf file, and be sure the nameserver dns line comes before the nameserver files line.

B. As root, type **nslookup dns**.

C. Edit the /etc/named.conf file, and change the preferred-resolution option from files to dns.

D. Edit /etc/nsswitch.conf, and change the order of the files and dns options on the hosts: line.

E. As root, type **dig local dns**.

Chapter

9

Writing Scripts, Configuring Email, and Using Databases

THE FOLLOWING EXAM OBJECTIVES ARE COVERED IN THIS CHAPTER:

✓ 105.1 Customize and use the shell environment

✓ 105.2 Customize or write simple scripts

✓ 105.3 SQL data management

✓ 108.3 Mail Transfer Agent (MTA) basics

This chapter covers a number of topics. The first of these relates to shell management. Linux shells (introduced in Chapter 1, "Exploring Linux Command-Line Tools") can be customized in various ways. Knowing how to do this will help you to be productive when using Linux. You may need to set various options to use particular programs. In addition, similar changes may need to be made on a global level so that all of your users can work effectively.

Shell scripting is another topic covered by this chapter. You can write scripts to help automate tedious repetitive tasks or to perform new and complex tasks. Scripts perform many of Linux's startup functions (described in Chapter 5, "Booting Linux and Editing Files"), so mastering scripting will also help you to manage the startup process.

The next major chapter topic is Structured Query Language (SQL) data management. Many Linux installations rely on a SQL database to store information, and so you may need at least a minimal grounding in how to interact with SQL databases.

Finally, this chapter describes the basics of email management under Linux. Several Linux email packages exist, and you're not expected to understand their configuration details for the exam. However, you should know a few basics, such as how to configure email forwarding, examine mail queues, and otherwise interact with a Linux mail server that's already working.

Managing the Shell Environment

Chapter 1 introduced Linux shell use, including topics such as command completion, history, redirection, and the basics of environment variables. Now it's time to go further with more details about environment variables, aliases, and configuration files. Using this information, you'll be able to customize your shell environment to suit your personal tastes or change the default environment for all of the users on your system.

Reviewing Environment Variables

As described in Chapter 1, environment variables provide the means to pass named data (variables) to programs launched from a shell or a subshell. A *subshell* is a child process that is created by either the shell or a shell script when a program is initiated.

Shells themselves also rely on environment variables. For instance, $HOSTNAME conventionally holds the computer's name, such as carson.example.com. A program that needs to know the computer's name can refer to $HOSTNAME to obtain this information.

You set an environment variable manually via an equal-sign assignment operator. To make the variable available to subshells, you then use the `export` command:

```
$ HOSTNAME=carson.example.com
$ export HOSTNAME
```

Using the semicolon (;) list operator, you can combine these two commands into one line as follows:

```
$ HOSTNAME=carson.example.com ; export HOSTNAME
```

You can further combine these two commands into one command for even more brevity:

```
$ export HOSTNAME=carson.example.com
```

On a bash command line, you can refer to an environment variable by using the echo command to examine a single variable (as in **echo $HOSTNAME**). To see *all* of the environment variables, use one of these commands: env, set, or printenv.

The output variation of the commands env, set, and printenv are rather subtle. The set command displays both environment variables and user-defined variables in an alphabetically sorted list. The env and printenv commands do not sort their output and do not show user-defined variables. In addition, the env command has additional functionality that the printenv command does not have.

Setting an environment variable as just described sets it for the shell or (when used with export) for subshells you create. Keep in mind that these variable settings disappear when you log out because they are not *persistent*. A variable (or other configuration setting) is persistent, if it keeps its definition—even if the process that set it is no longer around. If you set an environment variable manually at the command line and then log out of the system or shut down the computer, that variable loses the definition you gave it. How to make these environment variable settings persistent is covered in the section "Modifying Shell Configuration Files" later in this chapter.

Understanding Common Environment Variables

You may encounter many common environment variables on your system. You can find out how environment variables are configured by typing **env**, **set**, or **printenv** without any options. When typed without options, env returns all of the environment variables that are currently set in a format similar to that of bash environment variable assignments:

```
$ env | grep HOSTNAME
HOSTNAME=carson.example.com
```

Of course, the variables you see and their values will be unique to your system and even your account—that's the whole point of environment variables. Table 9.1 summarizes common variables that you may see in this output.

TABLE 9.1   Common environment variables and their meanings

Variable name	Explanation
DISPLAY	This variable identifies the display used by the X windows server. It's usually set to :0.0, which indicates the first display on the current computer. You can run multiple X sessions on one computer, in which case each one gets a different DISPLAY number—for instance, :0.0 for the first session and :1.0 for the second session. When you use X in a networked environment, this value may be preceded by the name of the computer at which you're sitting, as in machine4.luna.edu:0.0. This value is set automatically when you log in, but you may change it if necessary.
EDITOR	Some programs launch the program pointed to by this environment variable when they need to call a text editor for you to use. Thus, changing this variable to your favorite editor can help you work in Linux. It's best to set this variable to a text-mode editor because GUI editors may cause problems if they're called from a program that was launched from a text-mode login.
HISTSIZE	This variable determines the number of commands that will be saved in your history file.
HOME	This variable points to your home directory. Some programs use it to help them look for configuration files or as a default location in which to store files.
HOSTNAME	This is the current TCP/IP hostname of the computer.
LANG	The system holds your current language, specified as a locale, using this variable. Locales are described further in Chapter 6, "Configuring the X Window System, Localization, and Printing."
LD_LIBRARY_PATH	A few programs use this environment variable to indicate directories in which library files may be found. It works much like PATH.
LOGNAME	This variable holds your username when you are logged into the system.
MAIL	This variable holds the location of the user's mail spool. It's usually /var/spool/mail/*username*.
PAGER	If set, this variable determines the pager to use for output by programs, such as man.

Variable name	Explanation
PATH	This is an unusually important environment variable. It sets the *path* for a session, which is a colon-delimited list of directories in which Linux searches for executable programs when you type a program name. For instance, if PATH is /bin:/usr/bin and you type **ls**, Linux looks for an executable program called ls in /bin and then in /usr/bin. If the command you type isn't on the path, Linux responds with a command not found error. The PATH variable is typically built up in several configuration files, such as /etc/profile and the .bashrc file in the user's home directory.
PS1	This is the default prompt in bash. It generally includes variables of its own, such as \u (for the username), \h (for the hostname), and \W (for the current working directory). This value is frequently set in /etc/profile, but users often override it.
PWD	This is the present working directory. This environment variable is maintained by the system. Programs may use it to search for files when you don't provide a complete pathname.
SHELL	This variable holds the path to the current command shell.
TERM	This variable is the name of the current terminal type. To move a text-mode cursor and display text effects for programs like text-mode editors, Linux has to know what commands the terminal supports. The TERM environment variable specifies the terminal in use. This information is combined with data from additional files to provide terminal-specific code information. TERM is normally set automatically at login, but in some cases you may need to change it.
TZ	You can set this environment variable to your own time zone, which is most useful if that's different than the computer's time zone—for instance, if you're using a computer remotely. Chapter 6 describes the formats you can use when setting the time zone in this way.
USER or USERNAME	This is your current username. It's a variable that's maintained by the system.

WARNING

The PATH variable sometimes includes the current directory indicator (.) so that you can easily run programs in the current directory. This practice poses a security risk, though, because a troublemaker can create a program with the same name as some other program (such as ls) and trick another user into running it by simply leaving it in a directory the victim frequents. Even the root user may be victimized this way. For this reason, it's best to omit the current directory from the PATH variable, especially for the superuser. If it's really needed for ordinary users, put it at the end of the path.

Any given system is likely to have several other environment variables set, but these are fairly obscure or relate to specific programs. If a program's documentation says that it needs certain environment variables set, you can set them in the appropriate shell configuration file. How to make these settings is covered in the section "Modifying Shell Configuration Files."

 Environment variable names are usually preceded by a dollar sign ($) in scripts and on shell command lines, *except* when they're assigned. Getting this detail wrong can produce results that you weren't expecting; for instance, typing **echo HOSTNAME** produces the output HOSTNAME rather than the computer's hostname.

If you want to know the value of one variable, you can use the echo command, which echoes what you type to the screen. If you pass to it a variable name preceded by a dollar sign ($), echo returns the value of the variable. Here's an example:

```
[christine@server01 etc]$ echo $PS1
[\u@\h \W]\$
```

This command reveals that the PS1 environment variable is set to [\u@\h \W]\$, which in turn produces a bash prompt like [christine@server01 etc]$. Exercise 9.1 illustrates how you can change your bash prompt.

EXERCISE 9.1

Changing Your bash Prompt

This exercise describes how to change your bash prompt to show the current time and number of jobs managed by the shell. To accomplish this task, follow these steps:

1. Press Ctrl+Alt+F2, and log into the Linux system as a normal user.

2. Type **export PS1="\T; \j jobs> "**. The backslash (\) is an escape character that denotes special data to be inserted into the prompt when used in the PS1 environment variable. \T is expanded into the current time in 12-hour format, and \j is expanded into the number of jobs the shell manages. The man page for bash has a complete list of expansions the PS1 variable accepts. The result of typing this command should be an immediate change in your prompt to resemble something like 04:42; 0 jobs>.

3. Wait for a minute, and then run a program in the background by typing its name and appending an ampersand (&). For instance, you can type **sleep 10 &** to run the sleep program in the background for 10 seconds. You should see the number of jobs increase, and the time should change.

4. To make this change permanent, edit the .bashrc file in your home directory. Load this file into your favorite editor, and add a line to its end that reads export PS1="\T; \j jobs> ". Save the file, and exit the editor. (Shell configuration files are described in more detail in the section "Modifying Shell Configuration Files.")

5. To test your change to .bashrc, log out and then log back in again. Instead of your distribution's default prompt, you should see the new one.

6. If you don't like the new prompt, edit .bashrc again and delete the line you added in step 5.

Using Aliases

Most Linux shells, including bash, support command *aliases*, which are new names that you can give to regular commands. Typically, you'll use aliases as follows:

- To assign easier-to-remember names to obscure commands
- To implement desirable command options as a command's default
- To create a shortened version of a command to minimize typing

You can define aliases at any bash prompt, but that won't make them persistent. To make aliases persistent, you need to include them in your bash startup scripts, as described in the section "Modifying Shell Configuration Files."

To implement an alias, you use the following syntax:

```
alias alias_name='command'
```

The alias_name parameter is what you want to type at the command prompt, and the shell substitutes *command* for whatever you type. As an example, consider the ls command, which lists the contents of a directory. A popular option combination for this command is -alF, which shows a long listing display of a directory's contents along with hidden files and file types. If you want to use this option as the default, you can use the alias command:

```
$ alias ls='ls -alF'
```

In this example, ls becomes an alias for an extended version of itself. After you type this alias command, typing **ls** will work as if you'd typed **ls -alF**.

If you want to see if a particular command has an alias set, you can also use the alias command as follows:

```
$ alias ls
alias ls='ls -alF'
$
```

To remove an alias setting, use the `unalias` command:

```
$ unalias ls
$ alias ls
-bash: alias: ls: not found
$
```

Notice in the previous example that the alias was checked to ensure that the `unalias` command worked properly. Once an alias is removed, the shell will let you know that a command alias is not found. Note that this does not remove the `ls` command, only its alias.

You can use an alias name that's unrelated to the original command name. For instance, suppose you want to type **bye** instead of **logout** to terminate a text-mode login session. You can do so with `alias`:

```
$ alias bye='logout'
```

In practice, this particular alias isn't likely to be useful if you type it manually at a command prompt. That is because you'll log out of a session and the alias will no longer be set. Remember, an alias set at the command prompt is not persistent. If you want to keep this alias for every login session, include it in a bash startup script and it will be created automatically whenever you log in.

Modifying Shell Configuration Files

Configuring shells requires editing shell configuration files. These files can be classified in a couple of ways. First, files may be global files that affect all users of a shell or local files that affect just one user. Second, files may be login files that are launched only by a login process (such as a text-mode console login) or non-login files that are launched by other processes (such as when starting a terminal emulator window in the GUI). The result is a 2 × 2 matrix of configuration files, as shown in Table 9.2. (This table shows only bash configuration files; consult your shell's documentation if you're using another shell.)

TABLE 9.2   Common bash configuration files

Type of file	Login file location	Non-login file location
Global	`/etc/profile` and files in `/etc/profile.d`	`/etc/bashrc` or `/etc/bash.bashrc`
User	`~/.bash_login`, `~/.profile`, or `~/.bash_profile`	`~/.bashrc`

Precisely which of these files are used differs from one distribution to another. No matter the name, though, these files are shell scripts. Shell scripting is described in more detail in the section "Writing Scripts," but most bash startup scripts contain a series of commands. These commands may include both built-in bash commands and external commands.

In a user directory, you may find all three user login bash configuration files listed in Table 9.2, depending on your distribution. If you have two or more user bash configuration files, the first file found in the following ordered list is run and the rest are ignored:

~/.bash_profile

~/.bash_login

~/.profile

Global configuration files affect all users of a system. However, their settings may be overridden by individual users, either in user configuration files or in commands the users type themselves. Thus, you shouldn't rely on global configuration files to set options that shouldn't be changed by users. For that, you should look to global security features, such as permissions on executable files.

The /etc/skel directory holds files that are copied to individual users' home directories when their accounts are created. These files are sometimes called *skeleton files*. Typically, this set of files includes local bash startup files. You can examine these files and, if necessary, alter them to suit your local needs. Changes to these files affect only *new* accounts—not existing accounts. If you want to make a change that affects both existing and new users, you should edit a global configuration file instead.

Just as shells have startup scripts, they may also have logout scripts—scripts that run when the user logs out. For bash, this script is ~/.bash_logout. Most distributions don't create this script as part of users' default home directories, but individual users can do so. The logout script might execute programs to clean up temporary directories, remove security keys from memory, clear the screen, or perform other tasks that are appropriate when a user logs out.

WARNING   One problem with logout scripts is that they may not work well when users log in multiple times. If you regularly have multiple sessions open, such as multiple Linux virtual terminal logins, be careful about what you do in a logout script. You could wipe out important temporary files when you log out of just one session.

Another global bash configuration file is the /etc/inputrc file for keyboard customization and setting terminal behavior. Users can create or modify their own keyboard configuration file, which is the ~/.inputrc file or the value of $INPUTRC if set.

When the system starts up or a user logs into the system, the configuration files are read, terminal behavior is configured, and the keyboard's key bindings are set. A *key binding* is a connection between a set of keys being pressed and a command being launched or an action being taken. For example, when you press the Up arrow key at the command prompt, the last command entered is displayed.

You can see your current key bindings by typing **bind -p** at a virtual console terminal prompt. This may not work in some distributions' GUI terminal emulators.

The files consist of lines that look like this:

```
M-Control-u: universal-argument
```

This line maps the Meta-Ctrl+U keystroke to the universal-argument action. The Meta key is usually the Esc key on *x86* or *x86-64* systems, and the universal-argument action is one of many possible actions defined by the readline software library. The readline library is one of the basic text-mode input libraries used by Linux.

In most cases, there's no need to adjust the /etc/inputrc and ~/.inputrc files because the default readline key mappings work well for *x86* systems with standard keyboards. If you find that certain keystrokes don't work the way they should in text mode, though, you may want to research these configuration files further. You can find out more by typing in **info rluserman** at the command prompt.

The GUI uses its own keyboard input routines, so the /etc/inputrc and ~/.inputrc files don't affect programs run in the GUI, This is true even if text-mode programs run inside a terminal emulator window.

Writing Scripts

You'll do much of your work on a Linux system by typing commands at a shell prompt. As you use Linux, though, you're likely to find some of these tasks to be repetitive. If you need to add 100 new users to the system, for instance, typing **useradd** 100 times can be tedious. Fortunately, Linux includes a way to cut through the tedium: *shell scripts*. These are simple programs written in an interpreted computer language that's embedded in the Linux shell you use to type commands.

Many Linux system startup scripts are in fact shell scripts. Therefore, understanding shell scripting is necessary if you want to modify a Linux startup script.

Most Linux systems use bash by default, so shell scripts are often written in the bash shell scripting language, but dash and other shell scripting languages are similar. You're *not* restricted to running shell scripts written in your default shell. A shell script's first line identifies the shell that should be used to run the script.

Like any programming task, shell scripting can be quite complex. Consequently, this chapter barely scratches the surface of what can be accomplished through shell scripting. Consider reviewing online tutorials, such as the *Advanced Bash-Scripting Guide* at `http://tldp.org/LDP/ abs/html/`. You can also consult a book on the topic, such as Blum and Bresnahan's *Linux Command Line and Shell Scripting Bible, 3rd Edition* (Wiley, 2015), for more information.

To create a shell script, you must first know how to begin editing one. Once you do so, you'll find that one of the easiest tasks to do is to call external commands. More advanced tasks include using variables and conditional expressions.

Beginning a Shell Script

Shell scripts are plain-text files, so you can create them in text editors. A shell script begins with a line that identifies the shell that's used to run it, such as the following:

```
#!/bin/bash
```

The first two characters are a special code that tells the Linux kernel that this is a script. The rest of the first line indicates the program that's to interpret the script. Notice that the program's absolute pathname is included. The /bin/bash shell will be interpreting the script's contents because it is listed in the first line. This line is sometimes called the *shebang*, *hashbang*, *hashpling*, or *pound bang* line.

 On most systems, /bin/sh is a symbolic link that points to the /bin/bash shell. However, it can point to some other shell, such as the /bin/dash shell. It's dangerous to use the /bin/sh in your shell scripts as part of the first line. This is especially true if you run the scripts on various Linux distributions and the scripts use a particular shell's specific features. You should specify the actual shell instead of the /bin/sh link.

After the first line, shell scripting languages consider a hash mark (#) as a comment character. This allows you to embed comments within your scripts because the script utility ignores characters on a script line after the hash mark.

Using Commands in Shell Scripts

One of the most basic features of shell scripts is the ability to run commands to perform various tasks for you. You may use both the shell's internal and external commands by including their names in the script. You can also specify command parameters in a script. For example, suppose that you like to view the date and time in a format different than the default format displayed by the date command. However, you have a difficult time remembering all of the syntax required and don't want to use an alias. A simple shell script can remember the syntax for you as shown here:

```
$ date +%A', '%B' '%e' '%I':'%M%p
Thursday, October 23 01:50PM
$
$ cat mydate.sh
#!/bin/bash
#
# Show the Day & Time
####################
#
date +%A', '%B' '%e' '%I':'%M%p
#
$
```

Notice the date command's complicated syntax used on the command line to produce a specially formatted display. The same command is listed in the mydate.sh script. There is no need to commit this date command syntax to memory because the shell script will produce the desired results for you!

The first script line identifies it as a script. After the first line, any hash (#) marks denote comments. The rest of the script looks just like the commands you might type to accomplish the task manually.

Some script writers will include a command's complete path. For example, instead of just typing date in the script, they type /bin/date. Listing the absolute path name ensures that the script will find the programs—even if the PATH environment variable changes. However, if the command's files move for any reason, such as the result of a package upgrade, scripts that use absolute path names will break.

A comprehensive script command list is impossible because you can run any installed program as a command in a script. A few commands that are commonly used in scripts are included in the following list:

- File manipulation commands, such as ls, mv, cp, and rm. You can use these commands to help automate repetitive file maintenance tasks.

- The grep command locates files that contain specific strings. It is described in Chapter 1.

- The find command searches for file and directory names based on filenames, ownership, and similar characteristics. It is described in Chapter 4.

- The cut command extracts text from fields in a file. It is described in Chapter 1.

- The sed program is also described in Chapter 1. It provides many of the capabilities of a conventional text editor but via commands that can be typed at a command prompt or entered in a script.

- The echo command provides the ability to send a message to the script's user. You can pass various options to echo or just a string to be shown to the user. For instance, echo "Done with Script" causes a script to display the specified string.

Many of these commands are extremely complex. You can consult the descriptions located elsewhere in the book or their man pages for more information.

Running a Shell Script

When you're done writing the shell script, you can modify it so that it's executable. You do this with the chmod command, as described in Chapter 4, "Managing Files." Specifically, you use the +x option to add execute permissions, along with the indicator for who needs access. For instance, to make a file called my-script.sh executable for your use only, you issue the following command:

```
$ chmod u+x my-script.sh
```

It's possible to set a script's SUID or SGID bits. (See Chapter 4 for information about the SUID and SGID bits.) Doing so is potentially dangerous, particularly if the script is owned by root, for reasons described in Chapter 4. You should therefore be very cautious about applying the SUID and SGID bits to scripts.

You can run shell scripts by using several different methods. Some methods create subshells, while others do not. Some methods require execute permission, while others do not require it.

To demonstrate the differences between these techniques, the following script will be run using the various methods:

```
$ cat my-script.sh
#!/bin/bash
#
### Show process "forest"
ps -o pid -o ppid -o cmd --forest
#
### Give status
```

```
echo Done with Script
#
$
$ ls -l my-script.sh
-rw-rw-r--. 1 Christine User 116 Oct 23 11:28 my-script.sh
$
```

The my-script.sh uses the ps command (see Chapter 2) with some special options. The -o options will display the process ID (PID) number and the parent process ID (PPID) number, along with the commands (CMD) being executed. The --forest option shows parent processes graphically. Notice that the my-script.sh file has *no* execute permissions set on it.

The following list describes the various script execution methods:

bash *script-name*   Typing the script's name, preceded by bash, tells Linux to run the script in the current directory rather than searching the current path:

```
$ bash my-script.sh
  PID  PPID CMD
 2821  2820 -bash
 2867  2821  \_ bash my-script.sh
 2868  2867     \_ ps -o pid -o ppid -o cmd --forest
Done with Script
$
```

This method does not require execution permission to run the script. However, it does create a subshell to run the script as indicated by the bash my-script.sh line in the output's third line.

./ *script-name*   Typing the script's name, preceded by ./, tells Linux to run the script in the current directory rather than searching the current path:

```
$ ./my-script.sh
-bash: ./my-script.sh: Permission denied
$
$ chmod u+x my-script.sh
$
$ ./my-script.sh
  PID  PPID CMD
 2821  2820 -bash
 2883  2821  \_ /bin/bash ./my-script.sh
 2884  2883     \_ ps -o pid -o ppid -o cmd --forest
Done with Script
$
```

This method does require execution permission. As you can see in the preceding example, the chmod u+x command is needed in order to use this execution method. It also creates a subshell to run the script as indicated by the /to/bash ./my-script.sh example line.

/directory-location/script-name   Just typing in the script's full path and name is needed when the script is not located in your current working directory:

```
$ chmod u-x my-script.sh
$
$ mv my-script.sh /home/Christine/NewDir/
$
$ /home/Christine/NewDir/my-script.sh
-bash: /home/Christine/NewDir/my-script.sh: Permission denied
$
$ chmod u+x /home/Christine/NewDir/my-script.sh
$
$ /home/Christine/NewDir/my-script.sh
  PID  PPID CMD
 2821  2820 -bash
 2905  2821  \_ /bin/bash /home/Christine/NewDir/my-script.sh
 2906  2905      \_ ps -o pid -o ppid -o cmd --forest
Done with Script
$
```

This method also requires the execution permission to be set on the script. It creates a subshell to run the script as well.

script-name   Just typing in the script's name requires the shell script to be moved to a directory on your path, such as /usr/local/bin. This is the preferred method for scripts that will be used by others:

```
$ cd /home/Christine/NewDir
$
$ sudo mv my-script.sh /usr/local/bin/
[sudo] password for Christine:
$
$ chmod a+x /usr/local/bin/my-script.sh
$
$ echo $PATH
/usr/lib64/qt-3.3/bin:/usr/local/bin:/bin:/usr/bin:
/usr/local/sbin:/usr/sbin:/sbin:/home/Christine/bin
$
$ my-script.sh
```

```
 PID  PPID CMD
2821  2820 -bash
2928  2821 \_ /bin/bash /usr/local/bin/my-script.sh
2929  2928     \_ ps -o pid -o ppid -o cmd --forest
Done with Script
$
```

This method requires the appropriate execution permission to be set. Since it will be used by all system users, the chmod a+x command is used to grant execute permission to everyone. Note that the $PATH environment variable contains the directory /usr/local/bin, where the my-script.sh file was moved. Also note that this method creates a subshell when the script is run.

sh *script-name* Typing the script's name, preceded by sh, is nearly identical to preceding it with the bash command. It tells Linux to run the script in the current directory rather than searching the current path:

```
$ sudo mv /usr/local/bin/my-script.sh /home/Christine/
[sudo] password for Christine:
$
$ cd /home/Christine
$
$ chmod a-x my-script.sh
$
$ sh my-script.sh
  PID  PPID CMD
 2821  2820 -bash
 2973  2821 \_ sh my-script.sh
 2974  2973     \_ ps -o pid -o ppid -o cmd --forest
Done with Script
$
```

This method does not require execution permission to run the script, and it creates a sub-shell to run the script as indicated by the sh my-script.sh line in the output.

source *script-name* Typing the keyword source before the script name tells the bash shell to use a method type called *sourcing*. When you source a script, a subshell is not created to run the script.

```
$ source my-script.sh
  PID  PPID CMD
 2821  2820 -bash
 3095  2821 \_ ps -o pid -o ppid -o cmd --forest
Done with Script
$
```

Notice that no new process (subshell) was created to run the my-script.sh script. It ran in the current bash shell (PID 2821). This method also does not require execute permission.

. *script-name* Typing a dot (.) and then a space before the script name also tells the bash shell to use the sourcing method type. Be careful; don't forget to include the space between the dot and the script name:

```
$ . my-script.sh
  PID  PPID CMD
 2821  2820 -bash
 3157  2821 \_ ps -o pid -o ppid -o cmd --forest
Done with Script
$
```

This method also does not create a subshell. The script ran in the current bash shell (PID 2821). In addition, this method does not need execute permission set on the file.

exec ./*script-name* The last method for executing script uses the exec command. This method *does* need execute permission set on the file. Be aware, if you are following along with the book and executing scripts, you will need to add a pause to the bottom of your script. Here the sleep 10 command was added to the my-script .sh script so the script will pause for 10 seconds before completing. This is needed because the exec command will *exit* the current bash shell when it is done running the script:

```
$ cat my-script.sh
#!/bin/bash
[...]
sleep 10
echo Done with Script
#
$
$ chmod a+x my-script.sh
$
$ exec ./my-script.sh
  PID  PPID CMD
 2821  2820 /bin/bash /home/Christine/my-script.sh
 3197  2821 \_ ps -o pid -o ppid -o cmd --forest
```

Notice that the ./ execution method had to be placed before the script's name. This is because exec is not truly a script execution method. It does not create a subshell but instead replaces the current shell with an executable image environment to run the script. A script execution method must be included in the exec command line in order to run a script. You cannot source a script using exec, however. Only execution methods that create a *subshell* will work with the exec command:

```
$ exec source my-script.sh
-bash: exec: source: not found
$
$ exec . my-script.sh
-bash: exec: .: not found
$
$ exec bash my-script.sh
  PID  PPID CMD
 3257  3256 bash my-script.sh
 3301  3257  \_ ps -o pid -o ppid -o cmd --forest
$
```

The exec program's primary value is not in running scripts. Instead, it is often used to run a program from within a script.

There are only two methods listed previously that are considered sourcing methods: the source command and the dot (.). Using a sourcing method that causes a script to run *in the current shell*, as opposed to launching a new instance of the shell (subshell), has some important implications:

- When you source a script, it will have access to environment variables set in the calling shell. This is true even if you haven't exported them. Without sourcing, only environment variables that you explicitly export become available to scripts you run.

- If you source a script and if that script sets an environment variable, that variable will become available (or will be changed) in the calling shell's environment. If you run the script without using a sourcing method, any environment variables it sets will remain local to it and to the programs that it calls. This is true even if the script exports the variables.

- Running a script without sourcing imposes overhead costs associated with launching the new shell instance (subshell). These costs are normally negligible, but if a script calls itself recursively or calls many other scripts, sourcing those scripts within the first script may improve performance.

- Sourcing a script causes it to execute in the calling shell's language, whereas running a script normally causes it to use the shell language specified on the shebang line.

Many administrative tasks conducted via shell scripts require you to process data and provide a means for temporary storage. For this reason, scripting languages include additional features to help you make your scripts useful.

Using Variables in Shell Scripts

Variables can help you expand the utility of scripts. A variable is a placeholder in a script for a value that will be determined when the script runs. Variables' values can be passed as parameters to scripts, generated internally to the scripts, or extracted from the script's environment.

Understanding Positional Parameter Variables

Variables that are passed to the script are frequently called *positional parameters*. The individual parameters are represented by a dollar sign ($) followed by a number from 0 to 9—$0 stands for the name of the script, $1 is the first parameter to the script, $2 is the second parameter, and so on.

To show parameter variables in action, a simple script for creating user accounts has been written (see Chapter 7, "Administering the System," for more information on creating user accounts). Keep in mind that this script will not work for all distributions because it uses the useradd command, whereas some distributions use the adduser command. If you want to use it on your Linux system, some modifications may be required:

```
$ cat mkuser.sh
#!/bin/bash
#
# Create user accounts & their passwords
#########################################
#
# Create user account ###
echo Account for $1 is being created...
#
useradd $1
#
# Set user account password ###
#
echo Password for $1 is being set...
#
passwd $1
#
echo Account is ready for use.
#
#########################################
$
```

Notice in the mkuser.sh script that the positional parameter, $1, is used in both the useradd and the passwd commands as well as in a couple of echo commands. Also notice that in the previous example, the script's first line, the shebang, shows that /bin/bash acts as the script's program interpreter. After that first line, you see both hash marks (#) denoting comments or actual bash shell commands.

Notice that some of the mkuser.sh script's hash marks are on lines by themselves. This provides spacing in the script, which adds to its readability. Shell scripts should be easy to read. This helps when script modifications are needed.

The mkuser.sh script creates an account and changes the account's password based upon the account name being passed as positional parameter $1. Because the script needs superuser privileges to accomplish its task, the sudo command is used when executing the script, as shown here:

```
$ chmod u+x mkuser.sh
$
$ sudo ./mkuser.sh River
Account for River is being created...
Password for River is being set...
Changing password for user River.
New password:
Retype new password:
passwd: all authentication tokens updated successfully.
Account is ready for use.
$
$ tail -1 /etc/passwd
River:x:506:510::/home/River:/bin/bash
$
```

Notice that the position parameter variable passed to the mkuser.sh script has the value of River. Therefore, in every spot where the $1 variable was in the script, River is now used instead. This script, though very simple, can be used effectively, for instance for creating multiple user accounts at one time.

With a little modification to the mkuser.sh script, you can grab more positional parameters from the command line and create more than one account at a time! Here's a snipped example:

```
$ cat mkuser.sh
#!/bin/bash
#
[...]
#
passwd $1
#
echo Account is ready for use.
#
# Create user account ###
echo Account for $2 is being created...
#
useradd $2
#
```

```
# Set user account password ###
#
echo Password for $2 is being set...
#
passwd $2
#
echo Account is ready for use.
#
#########################################
$
```

The script now has additional code to handle creating a second user account using the name passed as the second positional parameter, $2. Here is the modified script in action:

```
$ sudo ./mkuser.sh Malcolm Inara
[sudo] password for Christine:
Account for Malcolm is being created...
Password for Malcolm is being set...
Changing password for user Malcolm.
New password:
Retype new password:
passwd: all authentication tokens updated successfully.
Account is ready for use.
Account for Inara is being created...
Password for Inara is being set...
Changing password for user Inara.
New password:
Retype new password:
passwd: all authentication tokens updated successfully.
Account is ready for use.
$
$ tail -2 /etc/passwd
Malcolm:x:507:507::/home/Malcolm:/bin/bash
Inara:x:508:511::/home/Inara:/bin/bash
$
```

Two parameters are now passed to the script, Malcolm and Inara. The mkuser.sh script handles them both via positional parameters. The script uses $1 as a variable to handle the Malcolm parameter and $2 as a variable to handle the Inara parameter.

You may want to be able to send any number of user accounts to be created to the mkuser.sh script. However, you'll need either test constructs or a loop to handle this requirement. These topics are covered shortly in this chapter.

Understanding User-Defined Variables

A *user-defined variable* is a variable defined by a user for various purposes, such as temporarily storing data. It can be used within a script or at the command line. The following example demonstrates defining a user-defined variable, called My_Var, at the command line:

```
$ My_Var="Hello World"
$
$ echo $My_Var
Hello World
$
```

Once the variable has been set, various programs or other commands can use it, such as the echo command. Notice that when setting the My_Var variable's value, there is no dollar sign ($) in the variable's name. However, when used with the echo command, the dollar sign must be included.

> It is difficult to remember when to use and when not to use the dollar sign ($) with an environment or user-defined variable. Just remember that if you are doing anything *with* the variable, use the dollar sign. If you are doing anything *to* the variable, such as assigning a value to it, don't use the dollar sign.

You can remove both environment and user-defined variables. The unset command accomplishes this task, as shown in the example here:

```
$ echo $My_Var
Hello World
$
$ unset My_Var
$
$ echo $My_Var

$
```

Notice that in the preceding example, once the variable was unset, the echo $My_Var command just displays a blank line. This indicates that the variable has been removed. Using the unset command can be very useful in scripts as well as the command line.

Variables are often assigned *within* scripts. They may hold data pertinent for a script's execution. Script variables can also be set from a command's output, which is useful! You can then use these variables' values in conjunction with normal commands as if they were command parameters.

Be careful when creating new variable names. It is best to use either all lowercase names or mixed-case names. Remember that most environment variable names are all uppercase letters. If you use all uppercase variable names in your scripts, you may accidently reset an environment variable! This could have serious consequences.

To demonstrate setting variables in a script, the mkuser.sh shell script shown earlier has been modified. The first modification was to remove the account creation commands for the $2 positional parameter, since they are not needed here. A few additional echo commands were added to make the displayed output easier to read. Another modification was to create a user-defined variable, Username, and set it to the $1 parameter's value. Here is the mkuser.sh after it was modified:

```
$ cat mkuser.sh
#!/bin/bash
#
# Create user accounts & their passwords
#########################################
#
# Set variables ###
#
Username=$1
#
# Create user account ###
echo
echo Account for $Username is being created...
echo
#
useradd $Username
#
# Set user account password ###
#
echo Password for $Username is being set...
echo
#
passwd $Username
#
# Display account record ###
#
User_Record=$(grep $Username /etc/passwd)
#
```

```
echo
echo Here is $Username\'s record\:
echo $User_Record
echo
#
echo Account is ready for use.
#
#######################################
$
```

There is another modification that you may have noticed in the mkuser.sh script. This modification is rather interesting. A variable, User_Record, was set to the *results* of a grep command. You can capture a command's results by placing the command between two parentheses and preceding it with a dollar sign. Thus when the grep $Username /etc /password command executes, instead of its output going to the display (STDOUT), it is redirected to the User_Record variable! This method of storing a command's results in a variable is sometimes called "command substitution."

There is an older method for storing a command's results in a variable using back-tick (`) characters. Back-tick characters are not single quotes ('). The back-tick key is typically shared with the tilde (~) character on your keyboard. To use them for storing a command's results, you replace the parentheses with back-ticks and remove the dollar sign. Therefore, the line in the mkdir.sh script would look like this instead:

```
User_Record=`grep $Username /etc/passwd`
```

Using back-ticks has fallen out of favor. They are hard to see and often confused with single quotes. It's preferable to use the $(*command*) for storing command results in a variable.

To show you how these variables perform within the modified mkuser.sh script, the script is run here:

```
$ sudo ./mkuser.sh Jayne

Account for Jayne is being created...

Password for Jayne is being set...

Changing password for user Jayne.
New password:
Retype new password:
```

```
passwd: all authentication tokens updated successfully.

Here is Jayne's record:
Jayne:x:509:512::/home/Jayne:/bin/bash


Account is ready for use.
$
```

That works great! The script successfully used two methods of defining variables.

In addition to assigning variables with the assignment operator (=), you can read variables from standard input using the read command, as in read *response_variable*, to read input. The script user's response is stored in the *response_variable* for later access as $*response_variable*. This method of variable assignment is useful for scripts that must interact with users. For instance, instead of reading the username from the command line, the mkuser.sh script may be modified to prompt the user for the username.

Here are the first few lines of the modified mkuser.sh script:

```
$ cat mkuser.sh
#!/bin/bash
## Create user accounts & their passwords
#######################################
#
# Obtain variable value ###
#
echo
echo -e "Please enter username for account: \c"
read Username
#
# Create user account ###
[...]
```

Instead of using Username=$1, the script employs the use of an echo statement to ask the user for the username. The read command accepts the user's input and stores it in the variable Username. The rest of the script is unchanged.

 Notice that the echo command uses a few special options. The -e option enables the interpretation of backslash escapes. In other words, it allows the use of the \c option at the output's end. The \c option will stop output from echo. These two options allow the script user to type a response on the same line as the question.

Here is the modified `mkuser.sh` script in action. The only difference is that the script asks for the username instead of having to pass the username as a parameter. Therefore, the output has been snipped:

```
$ sudo ./mkuser.sh
[sudo] password for Christine:

Please enter username for account: Kaylee

Account for Kaylee is being created...
[...]
Here is Kaylee's record:
Kaylee:x:510:513::/home/Kaylee:/bin/bash

Account is ready for use.
$
```

This `mkuser.sh` script version works equally as well as the others. By using the various user-defined variable options, you can create scripts to meet any requirements.

Using Environment Variables in Scripts

One special type of variable, the environment variable, was mentioned in the section "Managing the Shell Environment," earlier in this chapter. Environment variables are assigned and accessed just like other shell script variables. The difference is that the script or command that sets an environment variable uses the `export` command (in bash). This makes the variable's value accessible to subshells. For example, suppose you set an environment variable in `Script_A` and `Script_A` starts `Script_B` in a manner that creates a subshell. `Script_B` can use the environment variable too!

Environment variables are often set in shell startup scripts, but the scripts you use can access them. For instance, your script may call a program that checks for the `$DISPLAY` environment variable and abort if it finds that this variable isn't set. Remember, most environment variable names are all uppercase, whereas non-environment shell script variables should all be lowercase or mixed case.

Using variables in shell scripts is handy. However, if a script user forgets to enter data for the variable, there can be serious consequences. Thankfully, shell-scripting languages support several constructs that help to avoid these problems, as covered in the upcoming chapter sections.

Using Conditional Expressions

Scripting languages support several types of *conditional expressions*. These expressions enable a script to perform one of several actions contingent upon some condition—typically the value of a variable.

One common command that uses conditional expressions is the `if-then` statement. The simplest form of this statement tests only the success or failure of a command, and its syntax is as follows:

```
if command
then
      commands
fi
```

Notice that the syntax keywords consist of `if` to designate the command (*command*) to issue, `then` to appoint what happens if the command is successful, and `fi` to designate the end of the statement. To test this statement out, the `testit.sh` script was created:

```
$ cat testit.sh
#!/bin/bash
#
# Testing if statements
#######################
#
if date
then
    echo "It worked"
fi
#
$
```

In the `testit.sh` script, the `date` command is issued. If it works correctly, the code in the `then` section is run. Here is this script in action:

```
$ chmod u+x testit.sh
$
$ ./testit.sh
Sat Oct 25 16:36:43 EDT 2015
It worked
$
```

You can also add an `else` section to your `if-then` statement. This will allow commands to be executed, if the command is *not* successful. The `testit.sh` script has been modified to include an `else` section as well as an incorrect date command:

```
$ cat testit.sh
#!/bin/bash
#
# Testing if statements
#######################
#
```

```
if dte
then
    echo "It worked"
else
    echo "It did not work"
fi
#
$
$
$ ./testit.sh
./testit.sh: line 6: dte: command not found
It did not work
$
```

When this version of testit.sh ran, the else section was triggered because there is no dte command. If there were a dte command, the then section of the if-then-else statement would have been triggered.

This very basic if-then-else statement syntax has limited use. Where it really becomes valuable is when you can test a variable's value. Before looking at testing a variable in an if-then-else statement, you need to learn about the test command. The syntax for this command is fairly simple:

test *condition*

If the condition (*condition*) listed in the test command evaluates to true, the test command exits with a zero status code. If the condition evaluates to false, the test command exits with a nonzero status code. Here is the testit.sh script again, this time modified to try out the test command:

```
$ cat testit.sh
#!/bin/bash
#
# Testing if statements
#######################
#
# Set variable's value
#
My_Variable="Hello World"
#
# Test variable's value
#
if test "$My_Variable"
then
    echo $My_Variable
else
```

```
        echo "Nothing to show"
fi
#
$ ./testit.sh
Hello World
$
```

In the preceding script example, the test command determines if the variable My_Variable has any content. Since it does, when the script is executed, the echo command in the then section is executed.

Now if the My_Variable is set to null in the script, as you would expect, the test command results trigger the else section:

```
$ cat testit.sh
#!/bin/bash
#
# Testing if statements
#######################
#
# Set variable's value
#
My_Variable=""
[...]
$
$ ./testit.sh
Nothing to show
$
```

There is an alternative way to define the test condition without using the test command. The syntax in an if-then-else statement is as follows:

```
if [ condition ]
then
      commands
else
      other commands
fi
```

The condition represented by [condition] is more commonly known as the test condition, and it replaces the test command in comparison syntax. Both the test condition and the test command can evaluate three condition types:

- Numeric comparisons
- String comparisons and tests
- File comparisons and tests

Each comparison uses its own comparison syntax. For example, to test if two numbers are equal, the number comparison uses the -eq comparison syntax. To test if two strings are equivalent, the string comparison uses the = comparison syntax.

 WARNING For variables that will be used to store integers, you should use the declare command as follows: declare -i *variable*. If you do not include a declaration in your shell script, when you do integer test comparisons, the results may not be what you intended!

You can also test a variable's contents without a comparison. For example, to test if a string has a length of zero, use the -z syntax. To test if a file exits, use the -f syntax. To see a complete listing of the various available comparisons, tests, and their syntaxes, type **man test** at the command line.

By modifying the mkuser.sh script, you can test the user's input. The useradd command would throw an error if used without giving it a username. To avoid this error, the variable Username is tested to ensure that it is not zero length. The if statement uses a test condition -z, which tests for a variable of zero length. This ensures that the variable Username contains a value before attempting the useradd command.

Here is a segment of the modified script:

```
$ cat mkuser.sh
#!/bin/bash
#
[...]
# Test variable for content ###
#
if [ -z $Username ]
then
    echo
    echo You did not provide a username
    echo Leaving script...
    exit
fi
#
# Create user account ###
[...]
$
```

Now the modified script can be tested. Instead of a username being entered at the prompt, only the Enter key is pressed:

```
$ sudo ./mkuser.sh
[sudo] password for Christine:
```

```
Please enter username for account:
```

```
You did not provide a username
Leaving script...
$
```

In the script's execution, a username was not entered and this meant that the Username variable was zero length. Thus, the if-then test condition triggered the then section's commands, and the script was exited. Zero-length variables can cause many problems in your scripts! It is a good idea to check for them always.

WARNING   The test condition syntax [*condition*] must have a space after the first bracket ([) and before the closing bracket (]). If you leave out the space, your if statements will generate an error.

Test conditions may be combined with the logical "and" (&&) or logical "or" (||) operators. When conditionals are combined with &&, *both* sides of the operator must be true for the condition as a whole to be true. When || is used, if *either* side of the operator is true, the condition as a whole is true. You will see an example of using these combined test conditions in the next section, "Using Loops."

If a variable can have two or more values, you can use nested if statements to test for these conditions. The general syntax is as follows:

```
if [ condition1 ]
then
     commands
elif [ condition2 ]
then
     more commands
fi
```

Notice that instead of an else keyword, the elif keyword is used. This syntax is useful should you need to check for a couple of values. However, this can get awkward very quickly if you need to check for more than just a couple of values. A cleaner approach is to use the case statement:

```
case word in
   pattern1)
     command(s)
   ;;
   pattern2)
     command(s)
   ;;
```

```
  pattern3)
    command(s)
  ;;
    ...
esac
```

For a case statement, *word* is likely to be a variable and each instance of *pattern* is a possible value of that variable. The patterns can be expanded much like filenames, using the same wildcards and expansion rules (* to stand for any string, for instance). You can match an arbitrary number of patterns in this way. Each set of commands must end with a double semicolon (;;), and the case statement as a whole ends in the string esac (case backward).

NOTE The case statement can be made more compact if needed. For example, the pattern, commands, and ending double semicolon can all be on the same line, as follows:

pattern1) command(s) ;;

This reduces the script's readability. However, this compacted syntax is there if you need it.

The mkuser.sh can be modified to include a simple case statement. Here are the mkuser.sh script's modified sections:

```
$ cat mkuser.sh
#!/bin/bash
[...]
echo -e "Please enter username for account or type Exit: \c"
read Username
#
# Test variable for content ###
#
if [ -z $Username ]
[...]
#
case $Username in
   Exit)
      echo Leaving script...
      exit
   ;;
   *)
      echo
      echo Account for $Username is being created...
```

```
    ;;
esac
#
# Create user account ###
[...]
$
```

In this modification, the user can enter either a username to be created or **Exit** to leave the script. The case statement checks for Exit, and if it's found, the commands in the Exit section are executed. Anything else entered is assumed to be a username, and the script continues.

Upon execution, bash executes the commands associated with the first pattern to match the variable's contents. Execution then jumps to the line following the esac statement; any intervening commands don't execute. If no patterns match the word, no code within the case statement executes.

To see how this works, the modified mkuser.sh script is run. The script user enters **Exit** instead of a username:

```
$ sudo ./mkuser.sh
[sudo] password for Christine:

Please enter username for account or type Exit: Exit
Leaving script...
$
```

This works as expected. A case statement is very handy for handling multiple variable values—for example, if all of your system's usernames needed to have mixed case and numbers at their end. In the mkuser.sh script, you could test for proper usernames and then run the results through a case statement, letting the script user know what username problems (if any) exist.

Using Loops

Conditional expressions are sometimes used in loops. *Loops* are structures that tell the script to perform the same task repeatedly until some condition is met (or until some condition is no longer met). The performed task is typically a command or series of commands.

There are three primary loop types that you can use in a shell script. Two of the loop types are based on a test condition, while the other loop type executes its task(s) for a certain number of list items. The loop types and their conditions are as follows:

- while condition tests true
- until condition tests true
- for items in list

Each loop type is useful for various purposes. When designing a script that requires a loop, you need to spend time thinking through which loop type will serve your requirements best.

Looking at *while* loops

The `while` loop's commands execute *while* its test condition returns a true. The basic form of this loop type goes like this:

```
while [ condition ]
do
    commands
done
```

To show an example of the while loop, the `mkuser.sh` script has been modified. The loop allows for the removal of several previously needed tests. Here is a snipped listing of the modified script:

```
$ cat mkuser.sh
#!/bin/bash
#
# Create user accounts & their passwords
#######################################
#
# Obtain variable value ###
#
echo
echo -e "Please enter username for account or type Exit: \c"
read Username
#
while [ $Username != "Exit" ]
do
    # Create user account ###
    #
    useradd $Username
    #
    # Set user account password ###
[...]
    #
    echo Account is ready for use.
done
#
echo Leaving script...
```

```
exit
#
##########################################
$
```

The commands within the while loop, listed between the do and done construct, will execute as long as the Username variable is *not* set to Exit. This will allow multiple users to be added while running the script. First the exit feature is tested:

```
$ sudo ./mkuser.sh
[sudo] password for Christine:

Please enter username for account or type Exit: Exit
Leaving script...
$
```

The script's exit feature works perfectly. Once the Username variable was set to Exit, the while loop returned a false. This test condition result caused none of the commands between do and done to run. Remember that the while loop's commands will execute *only* if its test condition returns a true.

Now the modified script is tested for when no username is entered:

```
$ sudo ./mkuser.sh
[sudo] password for Christine:

Please enter username for account or type Exit:
./mkuser.sh: line 12: [: !=: unary operator expected
Leaving script...
$
```

There's a problem! This test condition threw an error: unary operator expected. This is due to the Username variable now being set to nothing (null). When the shell interprets this test condition, instead of seeing the "" != "Exit" condition, it sees the != "Exit" test condition. It appears to the shell that the variable is missing.

There is an easy fix for this problem. Just encase the variable name in double quotation marks as follows:

```
while [ "$Username" != "Exit" ]
```

Now the shell will see "" != "Exit" if the variable Username is set to null. This fix will keep the test condition from generating an error.

There is another solution to the problem, if you know this script will run in the bash shell. You can use double brackets to enclose a test condition [[*condition*]] that might test an empty variable.

One issue still exists—your script should exit if it encounters a Username variable set to null. This can be handled a couple of different ways. One way is use an if-then statement as discussed earlier in the chapter. However, since while loops are now being discussed, here is a solution using a modified while loop test condition:

```
while [ "$Username" != "Exit" ] && [ "$Username" != "" ]
```

Using a compound test condition allows the shell to test *both* for the Username variable not being equal to Exit *and* for the Username variable not being equal to null. If both test conditions are true, then the commands in the while loop's do and done sections will execute.

Looking at *until* loops

An until loop takes a slightly different approach. An until loop's commands execute *until* its test condition returns a true. The basic form of this loop type is as follows:

```
until [ condition ]
do
    commands
done
```

It looks almost identical to the while loop. It takes only a few modifications to a single script line to make the mkuser.sh script use an until loop instead of a while loop. The while loop test condition currently looks like this:

```
while [ "$Username" != "Exit" ] && [ "$Username" != "" ]
```

To change this to an until loop, the script line is modified to appear as follows:

```
until [ "$Username" = "Exit" ] || [ "$Username" = "" ]
```

Now the statement says to execute the commands in the do and done construct *until* the variable Username equals Exit *or* the variable Username equals null.

As you can see, there are fairly subtle differences between a while loop and an until loop. However, those differences can significantly impact your script if test conditions are not written correctly.

A handy tool to use with until or while loops is the shift command. Positional parameters in shell scripts were covered earlier in the chapter. One of the great ways to use these parameters is by incorporating the use of the shift command.

With the shift command, you do not need to know the total number of positional parameters passed to the script. The shift command removes the value of the $1 parameter, moves the $2 parameter's value into $1, moves the $3 parameter's value into $2, and so on.

When shift has passed the last parameter, the $1 variable becomes null. Using a loop to test for $1 being set to null and incorporating the shift command into the loop's do/done construct allows for clean handling of passed parameters.

The `mkuser.sh` script has been modified to use `shift` within its `until` loop. Here is the snipped script with the changes highlighted:

```
$ cat mkuser.sh
#!/bin/bash
#
# Create user accounts & their passwords
######################################
#
# Obtain variable value ###
#
Username=$1
#
until [ "$Username" = "" ]
do
[...]
    # Grab next Username
    #
    shift
    Username=$1
    #
done
#
echo Leaving script...
exit
#
######################################
$
```

The Username variable is initially set to the positional $1 parameter's value before the `until` loop. The `until` loop's test condition checks to see if Username's variable value is null. If the test returns a false, the commands between do and done are run. Close to the end of the do/done commands is the `shift` command. The `shift` command removes the value of the $1 parameter and shifts the positional parameters' values as described earlier. Notice that the Username variable must be set again to $1's value, after the `shift` command, because the $1 variable's value has changed. The loop will continue until a null value is shifted into the $1 parameter.

To help you understand a little better how this works, the modified `mkuser.sh` script is shown in action here. Notice that four parameters are passed to the script:

```
$ sudo ./mkuser.sh Wash Zoe Simon Shepherd
[sudo] password for Christine:
```

```
[...]
Here is Wash's record:
Wash:x:511:514::/home/Wash:/bin/bash

[...]
Here is Zoe's record:
Zoe:x:512:515::/home/Zoe:/bin/bash

[...]
Here is Simon's record:
Simon:x:513:516::/home/Simon:/bin/bash

[...]
Here is Shepherd's record:
Shepherd:x:514:517::/home/Shepherd:/bin/bash

Account is ready for use.
Leaving script...
$
```

That works great! Now you can simply pass the usernames who need accounts to the script, which will greatly speed up the account creation process.

Looking at *for* loops

A for loop is rather different in its operation compared to `while` and `until` loops. The for loop does not test any conditions, but instead executes its commands *for* a certain number of list items. The basic syntax of the for loop is as follows:

```
for variable in list
do
    commands
done
```

When the for loop starts, variable (*variable*) is assigned the first item in the list's (*list*) value. The commands in the do/done construct are executed one time. The variable is then assigned the second list item's value, and the commands in the do/done construct are executed one time again. This continues until each list item's value has been assigned to the variable.

A simple example of a for loop is shown in the `showforloop.sh` script here:

```
$ cat showforloop.sh
#!/bin/bash
#
# Demonstrate a for loop
```

```
########################
#
for Number in 1 2 3
do
    echo $Number
done
#
$
```

This script's for loop will process the commands in the do/done construct section for each list item. In this case, the list items are the numbers 1, 2, and 3. Here is the script in action:

```
$ chmod u+x showforloop.sh
$
$ ./showforloop.sh
1
2
3
$
```

You can see that the script assigns each item in the list to the variable Number. It then executes the command in the do/done construct. Because the command is echo $Number, the script's output shows the variable's value upon each iteration of the for loop.

NOTE   Notice that *all three* loop types use the do/done construct to surround the commands that are executed within the loop.

What is handy about the for loop is that you do not have to use numbers in your list. You can also use words, as shown here:

```
$ cat showforloop.sh
#!/bin/bash
#
# Demonstrate a for loop
########################
#
for Pet in Cat Dog Bird
do
    echo $Pet
done
#
$
```

```
$ ./showforloop.sh
Cat
Dog
Bird
$
```

The seq command is another handy command to use with the for loop. It's great if you need a large amount of numbers in your list. Instead of typing in all the numbers, you can use the seq command. Its basic syntax is as follows:

```
seq BeginningNumber IncrementAmount EndingNumber
```

You don't have to include all of the parameters in the command. By default, BeginningNumber is assumed to be one (1), and the IncrementAmmount defaults to one (1). For instance, if you type **seq 10**, a list of numbers 1 through 10 is generated. Here are a few seq examples:

```
$ seq 3
1
2
3
$ seq 2 4
2
3
4
$ seq 2 2 4
2
4
$
```

Using the showforloop.sh script, the for loop is modified to use a seq command as shown here:

```
$ cat showforloop.sh
#!/bin/bash
#
# Demonstrate a for loop
#######################
#
for Number in $(seq 2 2 100)
do
    echo $Number
done
#
$
```

The seq command's results must be used in the for loop's list. Therefore, the seq command is encased in $(). Once the seq command's results are captured in the list, the for loop will iterate starting with the Number variable at 2. The Number variable will be incremented by 2 each time the loop iterates. The for loop will stop after the Number variable has been assigned 100, as a snipped output shows here:

```
$ ./showforloop.sh
2
4
6
[...]
98
100
$
```

Using loops and commands like seq allow a script's size to be reduced. Another construct that can reduce the number of shell script lines is a command list, which happens to be covered in the next section.

Using Lists

You can chain together commands using various list operators. This is called a *list* or a list of commands. You can use the following operators:

- Semicolon (;)
- Ampersand (&)
- Double ampersand (&&)
- Double vertical line or pipe (||)

You have already seen a few command list examples, such as this one used near the chapter's beginning:

```
$ HOSTNAME=carson.example.com ; export HOSTNAME
```

In the previous example, both the HOSTNAME variable setting and the export command are executed, but sequentially. In other words, when the HOSTNAME variable setting completes, then the export command executes. Another example that has output better demonstrates this order:

```
$ date ; pwd
Tue Oct 28 14:09:38 EDT 2015
/home/Christine
$
```

You can see that the date command executes first and displays its STDOUT. When the date command is complete, then the pwd command executes, also displaying its STDOUT.

Thus, the semicolon (;) operator allows you to list two or more commands on the same command line.

You can have your commands run almost simultaneously by using the ampersand (&) operator. As mentioned in Chapter 2, any command with an ampersand listed after it is sent to the background to execute. Commands without ampersands are run in the foreground. Using the previous example, here is what occurs when the ampersand operator is used, sending the date command to the background to execute while pwd executes in the foreground:

```
$ date & pwd
[1] 3276
/home/Christine
$ Tue Oct 28 14:20:28 EDT 2014

[1]+  Done                    date
$
```

Even more powerful is the use of the double ampersand (&&) and double pipe (||) symbols. With the double ampersand (&&), the second command is executed *only* if the first command completes successfully:

```
$ dte && pwd
-bash: dte: command not found
$
$ date && pwd
Tue Oct 28 14:23:00 EDT 2015
/home/Christine
$
```

In the first command list shown in the previous example, an incorrect date command was mistyped as dte. Thus, it failed and therefore the second command, pwd, was not executed. However, in the second attempt, the correct command name, date, was entered. It ran successfully and allowed pwd to execute.

With the double pipe (||) operator, the second command will be executed only if the first command *does not* execute successfully. Using the date and pwd command example again, but with a double pipe operator, this time you can see that the pwd command executes only when the first command does not work properly:

```
$ dte || pwd
-bash: dte: command not found
/home/Christine
$
$ date || pwd
Tue Oct 28 14:28:00 EDT 2014
$
```

The value of lists within a script is that you can streamline functionality. Going back to the mkuser.sh script, if a user did not have appropriate privileges to run the script, several errors would display. This is sloppy, as shown here:

```
$ ./mkuser.sh Saffron
./mkuser.sh: line 14: /usr/sbin/useradd: Permission denied

Password for Saffron is being set...

passwd: Only root can specify a user name.

Here is Saffron's record:


Account is ready for use.
Leaving script...
$
```

You can fix this by using a list with the useradd command. The required modification appears as follows:

```
useradd $Username  || break
```

Besides useradd, there is an additional command added to the command list, break. If the useradd command does not work successfully, then the double pipe operator will trigger the break command, causing the while loop to terminate. This makes for a much cleaner-looking script execution when problems occur, as shown here:

```
$ ./mkuser.sh Saffron
./mkuser.sh: line 14: /usr/sbin/useradd: Permission denied
Leaving script...
$
```

That's much better! Now if an error occurs, the script displays the error message and exits immediately.

Using Functions

A *function* is a part of a script that performs a specific subtask and can be called by name from other parts of the script. Functions are defined by placing a set of parentheses () after the function name and enclosing the lines that make up the function within curly braces {}:

```
function_name() {
   commands
}
```

The keyword function may optionally precede the function name. In either event, the function is called by name as if it were an ordinary internal or external command.

Functions are very useful in helping to create modular scripts. Going back to the mkuser.sh script, we can put together a function that can be used throughout the script:

```
# Function Declarations ###
#
err_function() {
    echo "An error has occurred!"
    echo "Exiting script immediately..."
    exit
}
```

This new function will help with the useradd command list. The original list looked like this:

```
useradd $Username  || break
```

With the declared err_function function, the command list can look like the following:

```
useradd $Username  || err_function
```

If the useradd command does not complete successfully, the err_function will be called. This allows for a great deal more flexibility in a shell script.

NOTE Functions aren't run directly and in the order in which they appear in the script. They're run only when called in the main body of the script.

To show the function in action, the mkuser.sh script will be run without enough privileges, as shown here:

```
$ ./mkuser.sh Saffron
./mkuser.sh: line 21: /usr/sbin/useradd: Permission denied
An error has occurred!
Exiting script immediately...
$
```

That works great. You can now add all kinds of additional features, such as sending an email to the system administrator about this attempt and/or logging the attempt in the journal or a log file.

Shell scripts are useful tools, and creating them requires practice. Exercise 9.2 begins your exploration of shell scripts, but in the long run you'll need to learn to design your own shell scripts by doing more than copying examples from this book!

EXERCISE 9.2

Creating a Simple Script

This exercise presents a shell script that gives you the option of using less to read every text file (with a name ending in .txt) in the current directory. To begin with this script, follow these steps:

1. Log into the Linux system as a normal user.

2. Launch a terminal emulator from the desktop environment's menu system if you used a GUI login method.

3. Start an editor, and tell it to edit a file called testscript.sh.

4. Type the following lines into the editor:

```
#!/bin/bash
for file in $(ls *.txt)
do
   echo -n "Display $file? "
   read answer
   if [ $answer == 'y' ]
      then
          less $file
   fi
done
```

Make sure you've typed every character correctly—any mistake may cause the script to misbehave.

5. Save the file, and exit the editor.

6. Type **chmod u+x testscript.sh** to add the executable bit to the file's permissions.

7. Type **./testscript.sh** to run the script. If there are no text (*.txt) files in your current directory, the script displays a no such file or directory error message, but if any text files are present, the script gives you the option of viewing each one in turn via less.

This simple example script illustrates several important script features, such as variable assignment and use, for loops, and if-then conditional expressions.

Managing Email

Email is an important network service. Linux relies on email even in a completely non-networked environment. Certain Linux subsystems, such as cron (described in Chapter 7), may use email to notify you of activities. For this reason, most Linux distributions ship with email server software installed and configured for basic activities. You should understand the basics of email and be able to identify the specific email server package your system is running.

Understanding Email

Several protocols exist to manage email. The most common of these is the *Simple Mail Transfer Protocol (SMTP)*, which is designed as a *push* mail protocol, meaning that the sending system initiates the transfer. This design is good for sending data, so SMTP is used through most of a mail delivery system. The final stage, though, often employs a *pull* mail protocol, such as the Post Office Protocol (POP) or the Internet Message Access Protocol (IMAP). With these protocols, the receiving system initiates the transfer. This is useful when the receiving system is an end user's workstation, which may not be powered on at all times or able to receive incoming connections.

SMTP was designed to enable a message to be relayed through an arbitrary number of computers. For instance, an end user may compose a message, which is sent to the local SMTP server. SMTP servers are also known as *Mail Transfer Agents (MTAs)*. The MTA looks up a recipient system and sends the message to that computer. This system may use its own internal routing table to redirect the message to another local computer from which the message may be read, either directly or via a POP or IMAP server. These servers are also known as Mail User Agents (MUAs).

The basic steps for the creation, transfer, and delivery of email are as follows:

1. A user creates an email message using an email client, called a Mail User Agent (MUA).
2. The MUA gives the email to a Mail Submission Agent (MSA).
3. The MSA then hands off the email to a Mail Transfer Agent (MTA).
4. The MTA is responsible for transferring the email to the Mail Delivery Agent (MDA).
5. The Mail Delivery Agent handles delivering the email to the Mail User Agent (MUA).
6. The recipient user then reads the email message via the MUA.

This arrangement is illustrated in Figure 9.1. Bear in mind that the number of links in this chain is variable and depends on how each system is configured. In the simplest case, local email stays on just one system. In theory, an arbitrarily large number of computers can be involved in an email exchange.

MTA can function as both a server (receiving mail from other systems) and a client (sending mail to other systems). Therefore, you must deal with both sides of the configuration equation. The primary focus in this chapter will be on email's MTA.

Choosing Email Software

Linux supports quite a few email MTA servers. Most likely, one of the major servers will be installed on your system by default. If not, and if you want to install one, you'll have to pick one. You may also want to change your email server if you need a more advanced configuration. Four email MTA servers are popular on Linux:

Sendmail   The sendmail program (www.sendmail.org) was for many years the dominant email server package on the Internet. It has lost some of its dominance to other servers.

Nonetheless, sendmail remains a popular server. It's very powerful, but it can be hard to configure because its configuration file formats are rather difficult.

FIGURE 9.1   Basic email transfer

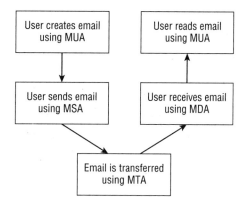

Postfix   Postfix (www.postfix.org) was designed as a modular replacement for sendmail. While sendmail uses a single program that does everything, Postfix uses multiple programs, each of which handles its own specific small task. This design improves security—at least in theory. Postfix tends to be easier to configure than sendmail, and it's become the default email server on many Linux distributions.

Exim   Although Exim (www.exim.org) is a huge server like sendmail, it has a much simpler configuration file format and so is easier to configure. A few Linux distributions use Exim as the default email server.

Qmail   The fourth major Linux email server, qmail (www.qmail.org), is a modular server with security as a major design goal. Like Postfix and Exim, qmail is easier to configure than sendmail. It's not often the standard email server in Linux distributions because its license is a bit strange and complicates qmail distribution with Linux. However, many system administrators like qmail enough that they replace their distributions' standard email servers with qmail.

 These email service packages may also provide additional services besides MTA. For example, they may also provide MSA services.

You have several ways to learn which email MTA server your Linux distribution runs. The two most reliable are to use ps (described in Chapter 2, "Managing Software") to look for running processes or to use your package management tools (also described in Chapter 2) to see which package is installed. In either case, you may need to check for each of the programs in turn. For example, you might see results like these:

```
$ ps ax | grep sendmail
31129 pts/2    R+      0:00 grep sendmail
```

```
$ ps ax | grep postfix
 7778 ?         Ss     0:45 /usr/lib/postfix/master
31132 pts/2     S+     0:00 grep post
```

The search for a process containing the string sendmail failed, but the search for postfix returned a process called /usr/lib/postfix/master. Thus, it appears that Postfix is running on this system.

> Keep in mind that your distribution may *not* have an email MTA server installed by default. In that case, if you desire to work with one, you will need to choose a server from the list presented earlier and install it using your Linux distribution's package management tools (see Chapter 2).

You can also look for executable files for each email MTA server in /usr/bin or /usr/sbin. Be aware that many Linux email servers include a program called *sendmail*. This program is not the sendmail program discussed earlier, but instead an interface to other email servers. This is done for compatibility reasons, because the original sendmail program was in many distributions. Also, it provided a compatible interface for scripts and administrators' helps for other email servers. This program is one of the sendmail emulation layer commands.

Working with Email

Along with understanding which email MTA server your system has or which one you desire to install, you also need to know how to complete a few common administrative tasks. These tasks involve sending and receiving mail using the mail utility, email queue management, configuring aliases, and forwarding email.

Sending and Receiving Email

Linux supports a wide variety of email clients, some of which were mentioned earlier in "Choosing Email Software." Chances are that you'll use a full-fledged email client for your personal email. However, you should also know how to use the command-line—based mail program. This tool is a very basic command-line email utility. It has the advantage of being usable from a script. Therefore, you can write a script to handle some email tasks automatically, and perhaps even run that script automatically.

The mail program is intended to be used on the command-line to send or receive messages. The basic syntax for mail, including its most useful options for *sending* email, is as follows:

```
mail [-v] [-s subject] [-c cc-address] [-b bcc-address] to-address
```

The basic syntax for *receiving* email is as follows:

```
mail [-v] [-f [name] | -u user]
```

Unlike most email readers, the `mail` command supports reading only the local email queue, not email stored on remote servers and read via the POP or IMAP protocols.

You can achieve various goals with the options to `mail`:

Use Verbose Operation   As with many commands, the -v option produces more verbose output. This may be helpful if you need to debug problems.

Specify a Subject Line   The -s *subject* option enables you to specify a subject line.

Set a Carbon Copy Address   You can send a message to multiple people by using the -c *cc-address* and -b *bcc-address* options. These options vary in that the -b option produces a "blind" copy, meaning the recipient's address doesn't appear in the address list. This is useful if you want to send a copy of an email discreetly to somebody, but some spam filters may delete such emails.

Set the Recipient's Address   The main recipient's email address is required and terminates the `mail` command's line for an outgoing email.

Read Email   To read your email, optionally pass the -f option to the program followed by the name of the mail spool file. Alternatively, you can use the -u *user* option to read the mail of the specified user.

This list of options is incomplete, but it includes the most important features. You should consult the man page for `mail` to learn about more unusual options.

If you want to try out these `mail` commands but your Linux system does not have a working email MTA server and you do not want to (or cannot because you are not the administrator) set up an email server, try an older distribution. Old Fedora distributions, such as Fedora 13, often have sendmail already configured. If you have an old computer lying around, you can install the older distribution there, or install it within free virtualization software, such as VMPlayer or VirtualBox.

As an example of `mail` in action, consider the task of sending a quick email message. Here's an example of a test email:

```
$ mail -s "Test email" Christine
This is a test email.
EOT
$
```

After you type the `mail` command, the program waits for input via standard input, but there's no prompt. You signal the end of the message by pressing Ctrl+D. This example shows a simple one-line message. After you press Ctrl+D, the program displays EOT, which stands for End of Transmission, and the message is on its way.

To use `mail` in a script, you can use input redirection to pass it the contents of a file to be mailed:

```
mail -s "Automated alert!" < /tmp/alert.txt john
```

This line, if included in a script, sends the contents of the `/tmp/alert.txt` file to the user `john` with the `"Automated alert!"` subject line.

You can use `mail` to read incoming email too, but only if it's stored on a local Linux mail spool. In this case, you'll normally use `mail` interactively. Type **mail**, and you'll see the contents of your mail spool. Each message has a summary line that lists the sender, date, and subject, among other things:

```
0046 sally@luna.edu  Sun Jan 13 18:27 116/4262  Priorities
```

This is message number 46, it's from `sally@luna.edu`, it arrived on January 13 at 18:27 (6:27 p.m.), it has 116 lines and 4262 bytes (including headers), and its subject is `Priorities`.

To read a message, type its number. You can then delete the message by typing **d** or reply to it by typing **r**.

As a practical matter, most people prefer to use more sophisticated email readers for their day-to-day mail reading. You'll probably find `mail` more useful for the scripted sending of email than for reading email or sending personal email.

On Linux, email is tied intricately to user accounts. The mail server holds incoming messages for each user, typically in a file in the `/var/spool/mail/` directory. For instance, the file that holds the mail for the user `john` is the `/var/spool/mail/john` file. Some email servers store incoming mail in users' home directories, such as `~/Maildir`. This incoming mail file or directory is referred to as the user's mail spool.

WARNING   You may recall that the `userdel` command, described in Chapter 7, includes options related to handling users' mail spools. If you delete a user account but leave the user's mail spool intact, the mail can still be accessed. If the mail server software stores mail in `/var/spool/mail`, leftover mail spools can cause problems if you eventually reuse an old username.

Checking the Email Queue

An email server manages a queue of email messages that it must deliver. The email server sends email messages to another computer or stores them in local users' mail spools. Various problems can lead to a temporary or permanent inability to deliver messages. When a problem seems to be temporary, such as a network routing failure, the email server must store the message and try to deliver it again later. Thus, a Linux server's email queue may contain undelivered messages. Knowing how to identify these messages and manage the queue can help you keep your email subsystem working smoothly.

The `mailq` program is the main tool to help in email queue management. This program was originally part of the sendmail package, but Postfix, Exim, qmail, and other Linux

MTA servers have all implemented compatible commands. Unfortunately, command options differ between implementations. The basic command, without any options, shows the contents of the email queue on all systems:

```
$ mailq
-Queue ID- --Size-- ----Arrival Time---- -Sender/Recipient-------
5B42F963F*      440 Fri Jan 18 13:58:19  sally@example.com
                                         benf@luna.edu
-- 0 Kbytes in 1 Request.
```

This example, taken from a system running Postfix, shows one message in the queue along with relevant identifying information. The exact display format varies from one MTA server to another. In most cases, typing **mailq** is equivalent to typing **sendmail -bp**.

> If your system uses a different MTA than sendmail, often the sendmail -bp command will still work. This command is often implemented as a sendmail emulation layer command. You can see all the various sendmail emulation layer commands available on your system by typing **man sendmail** at the command-line.

If a network connection or upstream email server goes down temporarily, email messages can pile up in the queue. Your MTA server will ordinarily attempt redelivery at a later date. However, if you want to clear the queue, you can do so. Typing **sendmail -q** will do the job with most MTA servers. Some have other equivalent commands, such as postqueue in Postfix or runq in Exim.

All email servers offer a wide variety of advanced options to prioritize email delivery, accept messages on the command line, debug email connections, and so on. Unfortunately, commands and procedures to use these features vary from one email server to another. You should therefore consult your server's documentation to learn how to use these features.

Redirecting Email

Email aliases enable one address to stand in for another one. For instance, all email servers are supposed to maintain an account called postmaster. Somebody who's responsible for maintaining the system should read email to this account. One way to do this is to set up an alias linking the postmaster name to the name of a real account. You can do this by editing the aliases file, which usually resides in /etc or sometimes in /etc/mail.

The aliases file format is fairly straightforward. Comment lines begin with hash marks (#), and other lines take the following form:

name: *address1*[,*address2*[,...]]

The *name* parameter that leads the line is a local name, such as postmaster. Each address (*address1*, *address2*, and so on) can be one of the following:

- A local account name to which the messages are forwarded
- A local file name in which messages are stored (denoted by a leading slash)

- A command through which messages are piped (denoted by a leading vertical bar character)
- A file name whose contents are treated as a series of addresses (denoted by a leading `:include:` string) or a full email address (such as `fred@example.com`)

A typical default configuration includes a few useful aliases for accounts such as postmaster. Most such configurations map nearly all of these aliases to root. However, reading mail as root is inadvisable because doing so increases the odds of a security breach or other problems due to mail reader bugs. Thus, you may want to set up an alias line as follows:

```
root: username
```

This redirects all of root's mail, including mail directed to root via another alias, *username*. The *username* value is most likely to be a local username or a valid remote email address. However, it can take any of the forms described earlier.

Some mail servers, including sendmail, Postfix, and qmail, require you to compile /etc/aliases into a binary file before an alias will take effect. To do so, use the newaliases command:

```
# newaliases
```

Exim has a newaliases command for compatibility with sendmail. By default, however, it doesn't do anything.

> You should always test out an alias after you make modifications to the
> alias configuration file. If it doesn't work, you may have forgotten to run
> the newaliases command!

Another approach to redirecting mail is to do so at the user level. In particular, you can edit the ~/.forward file in a user's home directory to have mail for that user sent to another address. Specifically, the ~/.forward file should contain only the new address. This address can be either a username on the current computer or an entire email address on another computer.

Forwarding email has the advantage that individual users can employ it. It's also handy in situations such as when a user scheduled to be away for several weeks asks another employee to fill in for them.

A drawback of forwarding email is that it can't be used to set up aliases for nonexistent accounts or for accounts that lack home directories. The ~/.forward file can also be changed or deleted by the account owner, which might not be desirable if you want to enforce a forwarding rule, which the user shouldn't be able to override.

Managing Data with SQL

The *Structured Query Language (SQL)*, as its expanded name suggests, is a language used for retrieving data from a database. In practice, SQL is implemented in several different database products. Thus, you should know a little about the SQL products that are available for Linux. With a SQL package installed, you can begin learning about the principles of using SQL and move on to actual data storage and retrieval.

Picking a SQL Package

SQL is a language for accessing data, and specific SQL packages implement that language. This distinction is similar to the one between a network protocol (such as SMTP) and the servers that implement it (such as sendmail, Postfix, and Exim). In principle, you can use any SQL package to satisfy your SQL database needs. In practice, specific products that store data using SQL may work better with (or even require) particular packages. The following products are among the common choices in Linux:

MySQL   Oracle owns this SQL implementation, which has been released under the GPL. Most major Linux distributions include MySQL in their package databases. For a complete installation, you'll probably need to install multiple packages, such as a client, a server, and perhaps development tools. You can learn more at www.mysql.com.

PostgreSQL   This SQL implementation evolved from the earlier Ingres software (the name *PostgreSQL* is a compressed form of *post-Ingres SQL*). It's available under the BSD license and is available as multiple packages in most Linux distributions. As with MySQL, you'll most likely have to install a client, a server, and perhaps additional support packages. PostgreSQL is headquartered at www.postgresql.org.

SQLite   This package, based at www.sqlite.org, is a library that implements SQL. As such, it's not a stand-alone database; instead, it's intended to provide programs with a way to store data using a SQL interface within the program. If you install a program that uses SQLite, your distribution's package manager should install the relevant libraries for you. If you want to write a program that requires database access and you don't want to install a complete client-server SQL package such as MySQL, SQLite may be just what you need.

There are dozens more SQL database products for Linux. For the purpose of learning SQL, MySQL or PostgreSQL should do fine. If you have a specific purpose in mind for using SQL, though, you should research SQL packages in more detail. You may need a particular product for compatibility with other software, or you may need a SQL package that provides specific features.

As just noted, some SQL packages, including MySQL and PostgreSQL, operate on a client-server model: One program (the server) manages the database, while another (the client) provides users and programs with access to the database. Such implementations can work over a network, enabling users at multiple client systems to access a centralized database server.

Understanding SQL Basics

SQL is a tool for accessing databases, and more specifically, relational databases. Figure 9.2 illustrates data in a relational database. Each *row* (sometimes known as a tuple) represents a single object or other item, and each *column* (sometimes referred to as an attribute or field) represents a specific feature. The combination of rows and columns is referred to as a *table*. Each database may contain multiple tables, and SQL supports multiple databases. Thus, to access data, you must first select a database and a table, as described in more detail shortly.

The table data is unordered, at least conceptually. You can impose an order on query results, as described shortly. For example, you may retrieve data from the database represented by Figure 9.2 and order the results according to cost (the final column).

A database enables retrieval of information that matches specific criteria. You can search for all of the green objects in Figure 9.2, for instance. You can also insert, delete, and update information in a table. SQL supports multiple tables, so you can have, for example, different tables for office property and for employees who work in your office.

FIGURE 9.2   A relational database stores data in a table, with each row representing one object or item and each column representing specific attributes.

attributes (columns)

lizard	green	5 inches	soft	$10
tree	green	10 feet	medium	$200
pillow	white	18 inches	soft	$5
brick	red	8 inches	hard	$1
banana	yellow	8 inches	soft	$0.10

tuples (rows)

Columns (attributes) in a database hold specific types of data, and swapping them around makes little sense. For instance, it's clear that the second column in Figure 9.2 is a color, whereas the final column is a price or value, expressed in dollars. It wouldn't make sense to enter green as a price or $1.00 as a color. The restrictions placed on what may appear in a column are known as a *domain* or a *data type*. The domain for the second column is a set of color names, whereas the domain for the final column is a numeric value expressed in dollars. Table 9.3 summarizes some common SQL data types.

Additional data types exist. Table 9.3 is intended to give you a feel for what's available and to list some of the data types you're likely to encounter. Some implementations also support unique data types. Each of these data types has its own features. For instance, mathematic operators can manipulate the numeric data types (INTEGER, DECIMAL, and so on).

Using MySQL

To learn about SQL, you should have access to a SQL database. For purposes of demonstration, the MySQL package is used as a reference in this discussion. Other SQL implementations are similar to what is described here, but some details differ. One of these details is how to start the database. In the case of MySQL, your distribution should include a SysV or other startup script for the SQL server. This server may also need to be configured with its own root password. Debian and related distributions will prompt for this when you install the package, but you may need to set this manually with other distributions.

TABLE 9.3 Common SQL data type

Data Type Name	Purpose
INTEGER (aka INT)	4-byte integer value
SMALLINT	2-byte integer value
DECIMAL	Precision storage of decimal values
NUMERIC	Precision storage of decimal values
FLOAT	Floating-point number
DOUBLE PRECISION	Floating-point number stored with twice the precision of FLOAT
DATETIME	A date and time
DATE	A date
TIME	A time, in *HH*:*MM*:*SS* format; may be a time of day or a period of time
CHAR	One or more characters
VARCHAR	A variable number of characters
ENUM	An enumerated list, such as small, medium, or large
SET	Data that may have zero or more values, as in any of the set of nuts, sprinkles, fudge, and cherry for ice cream toppings

Starting to Use MySQL

To begin a SQL session, you should first ensure that the server is running, as just described. You can then start the SQL client. In the case of MySQL, this program is called mysql:

```
$ mysql
```

If you've just installed MySQL for learning purposes, it may have no databases defined. To learn what's defined, you can use the SHOW DATABASES command:

```
mysql> SHOW DATABASES;
+--------------------+
| Database           |
+--------------------+
| information_schema |
+--------------------+
1 row in set (0.00 sec)
```

This example illustrates an important feature of SQL: Commands are terminated by semicolons (;). There are a few exceptions to this rule, but if you forget the semicolon, you're likely to see a new prompt that reads -> rather than mysql>, at least in MySQL. You can use this fact to split your commands across multiple lines, if you like. If you forget the semicolon that terminates a command, you can enter it by itself on the -> prompt line.

In this example, one database is already defined: information_schema. Some installations define a database called test. If you see such a database, you can probably use it for your own tests. However, other users may be able to see and modify the test database, so don't store important data in it.

 SQL commands are conventionally shown in uppercase. However, SQL commands are case insensitive, so you can type your commands in uppercase, lowercase, or any mixture of case you like.

Creating Databases and Tables

If no database for testing purposes exists, you can create one with the CREATE DATABASE command, which takes a database name as an option:

```
mysql> CREATE DATABASE test;
Query OK, 1 row affected (0.00 sec)
```

 Although SQL commands are case insensitive, database names are not. Thus, be sure to create the database name using whatever case you intend to use to refer to it in the future.

If you type **SHOW DATABASES**, you'll see the test database in addition to any that already existed. Regardless of whether test existed when you first started MySQL or it had to be created, you can begin using it with the USE command:

```
mysql> USE test;
```

Within each database, tables must be created and selected for use. The commands to do so are similar to the commands used to create and select databases. In a newly created database, no tables exist:

```
mysql> SHOW TABLES;
Empty set (0.00 sec)
```

The response Empty set denotes an empty database. To fill the database with data, you must first decide on a table structure—what sort of data you want to record. For instance,

Figure 9.2 shows various attributes of common objects: their names, colors, sizes, hardness levels, and values in dollars. To create a table that includes columns for these five attributes, you use a CREATE TABLE command, passing it various details:

```
mysql> CREATE TABLE objects (name VARCHAR(30), color VARCHAR(20),
    -> size FLOAT, hardness ENUM('soft','medium','hard'),
    -> value DECIMAL(10,2));
Query OK, 0 rows affected (0.01 sec)
```

This example creates a table with five columns: name, color, size, hardness, and value. Each column has an associated data type, as described in Table 9.3. A few points worth noting about this table definition are as follows:

- The name and color columns are both VARCHAR data type (see Table 9.3) examples, but with different sizes. The name field may be up to 30 characters, whereas color may be up to 20 characters. If these were defined as CHARs, each name would have to be precisely 30 characters in size, with each color precisely 20 characters. A limited set of colors can be specified using an ENUM data type rather than a VARCHAR data type. Presumably you wouldn't want to limit object names this way.

- The size column is a FLOAT data type, which is less precise than an integer data type, but it can hold real (non-integer) numbers. Figure 9.2 includes sizes in inches and feet, but in practice you'll need to convert everything to one unit—probably inches in this case.

- Note the syntax for defining the ENUM data type: the list of values as a whole is enclosed in parentheses (()), and each enumerated value is enclosed in single quotes (') and separated from other values by a comma (,).

- The DECIMAL value includes a specification of the number of digits (10 in this example) and the number of digits after the decimal point (2 in this example), separated by a comma. Some implementations support a MONEY data type that can be used in this case, but MySQL lacks this data type, so DECIMAL is the best choice for the job. A DECIMAL type is better for currency than FLOAT because a FLOAT type is likely to introduce rounding errors because of the way numbers are encoded in a FLOAT value. Such errors are typically unacceptable in currency, although they may be tolerable in some applications.

If you need to create a table with other types of values, you should consult the documentation for your specific SQL implementation to see what data types it supports.

With the table created, you may want to verify that it's been created correctly. You can do so by typing the **DESCRIBE objects;** command. The result should be a summary of the fields that you've just created for the objects table.

Storing Data

You can now begin to store data in your database. To do so, use the INSERT INTO command:

```
mysql> INSERT INTO objects
    -> VALUES('lizard','green',6,'soft',10.00);
```

This example creates an entry for the first row of Figure 9.2 (but with one piece of incorrect data, which is deliberate). You can verify that the database now holds this information by typing the **SELECT * FROM objects;** command. The result is a listing of all of the data in the objects table, which in this case should be just the one entry. (The next section, "Retrieving Data," covers data retrieval in more detail.)

This example entered incorrect data for one field: The lizard is entered in the table as being 6 inches in size rather than 5. You can correct this error by using UPDATE:

```
mysql> UPDATE objects SET size=5 WHERE name='lizard';
Query OK, 1 row affected (0.00 sec)
Rows matched: 1  Changed: 1  Warnings: 0
```

This example begins with the keyword UPDATE and the table name (objects). The example then tells MySQL what to update: SET size=5. In other words, set the size field to 5. The WHERE keyword begins a specification of which rows to change. In this case, with only one row present, you can use any data or even omit WHERE, along with the rest of the line up to the semicolon. In most cases, though, you must provide enough criteria to identify the column *uniquely* that you want to change. In this example, the name of the object is used—hence name='lizard', which tells MySQL to change the data for all rows for which the name field is lizard.

Before you continue with data retrieval activities, you should complete a database. Exercise 9.3 will guide you through this process.

EXERCISE 9.3

Creating a SQL Database

In this exercise, you'll continue creating a small database. This exercise assumes that you've performed the steps described in "Creating Databases and Tables" and "Storing Data" and that you therefore have a SQL database called test that contains a table called objects, which contains one entry based on the first line in the matrix in Figure 9.2.

To complete this database, follow these steps:

1. If you're not currently running MySQL, do so by typing **mysql** or whatever command you use to access your MySQL databases.

2. If you're not already using the test database, type **USE test;** to begin using the test database.

3. Type **INSERT INTO objects VALUES('tree', 'green', 120, 'medium', 200);**. (You may split this command across lines if you like.) This entry is based on the second row of Figure 9.2, but note that the size value has been expressed in inches.

4. Verify that you entered the data correctly by typing **SELECT * FROM objects;** and verifying that the new entry is present.

5. Repeat step 3 (and step 4, if you like) for the remaining rows in Figure 9.2.

If you like, you can continue and enter more data; however, if you do so, some subsequent examples may not work as described.

Retrieving Data

The whole point of having a database is to be able to retrieve data from it. The main command for doing so has already been described: SELECT. This command's power lies in its ability to accept specifications of *what* to select. You can use a variety of keywords to select data that match various criteria. These include exact matches or matches to a range of values. The overall form of SELECT can be described in this way:

SELECT *field(s)* FROM *table* [WHERE *conditions*] [ORDER BY *field*]

Previous examples of SELECT have used an asterisk (*) as field(s), meaning that the command returns all of the columns that match the remaining criteria. You can instead specify columns by name. For instance, suppose you're interested only in the colors and values of objects. You can view this restricted set of data using SELECT:

mysql> **SELECT value,color FROM objects;**

```
+--------+--------+
| value  | color  |
+--------+--------+
|  10.00 | green  |
| 200.00 | green  |
|   5.00 | white  |
|   1.00 | red    |
|   0.10 | yellow |
+--------+--------+
5 rows in set (0.00 sec)
```

The *field(s)* criteria appear as a comma-separated list of columns. In this example, the criteria were listed in the reverse order from their database order, and so they appear in the reverse order in the output.

A more interesting way to retrieve data is to use WHERE *conditions*. This tool has already been mentioned in reference to updating data. You can use *conditions* to retrieve specific data in several ways:

Exact Matches Using a column name, an equal sign, and a value to match returns only for those rows that match the specified value. For instance, typing **SELECT * FROM objects WHERE color='green';** returns the two entries for green objects (lizard and tree).

Numeric Tests You can retrieve data that match certain numeric criteria. For instance, to retrieve data on all objects that are greater than 10 inches in size, you can type **SELECT * FROM objects WHERE size>10;**.

Alphabetic Tests   The greater-than (>) and less-than (<) operators work on letters as well as numbers. This fact can be used to retrieve data based on the first letter of a string. For example, type **SELECT * FROM objects WHERE name>'b';** to retrieve records where the name begins with b or later letters in the alphabet. (Although this example uses a greater-than operator, it does in fact match the letter b.)

Multiple Tests   You can combine multiple criteria using the AND and OR operators. For instance, to retrieve data on soft objects valued at more than $7.50, you can type **SELECT * FROM objects WHERE hardness='soft' AND value>7.50;**.

You can have MySQL return the data as an ordered list by specifying a field name after the ORDER BY keyword:

```
mysql> SELECT * FROM objects WHERE hardness='soft' ORDER BY value;
+--------+--------+------+----------+-------+
| name   | color  | size | hardness | value |
+--------+--------+------+----------+-------+
| banana | yellow |    8 | soft     |  0.10 |
| pillow | white  |   18 | soft     |  5.00 |
| lizard | green  |    5 | soft     | 10.00 |
+--------+--------+------+----------+-------+
3 rows in set (0.00 sec)
```

Combining Data from Multiple Tables

As noted earlier, a database may contain multiple tables. This feature of SQL enables you to create tables for different functions. For instance, Figure 9.2 might represent a database of object characteristics that are of interest to you. You might also have a database containing objects' locations and conditions (on a 10-point scale), as shown in Table 9.4. Occasionally, you may need to combine these two tables to create a master table on which you can perform queries. For you to do so, the two tables must have one *matching* field. This matching field is used to bind the two tables together. In addition, each table must have one field whose value uniquely identifies each row. This uniquely identifying field is known as a *primary key*. In the case of Figure 9.2, the first column (called name) can serve as a primary key. In the case of Table 9.4, the Object ID column will do the job.

You can create this table much as you created the first one:

```
mysql> CREATE TABLE locations (id INTEGER, name VARCHAR(30),
    -> location VARCHAR(30), cond INTEGER);
mysql> INSERT INTO locations VALUES(1, 'banana', 'kitchen', 9);
```

Additional INSERT operations will fill out the table. At this point, you can use the SELECT operator to select data based on fields from both tables. For instance, suppose you want to know where all of the green objects are located. The first table (objects) contains color data but not locations, whereas the second table (locations) holds locations but not color data. You can accomplish the goal by using a few tricks:

```
mysql> SELECT objects.name, objects.color, locations.location
    -> FROM objects, locations
    -> WHERE objects.name=locations.name AND objects.color='green';
+--------+-------+-------------+
| name   | color | location    |
+--------+-------+-------------+
| tree   | green | backyard    |
| lizard | green | living room |
+--------+-------+-------------+
2 rows in set (0.00 sec)
```

TABLE 9.4   Data on object locations and conditions

Object ID	Object name	Location	Condition
1	banana	kitchen	9
2	banana	kitchen	8
3	tree	backyard	2
4	brick	garage	10
5	brick	garage	9
6	brick	backyard	9
7	lizard	living room	8

MySQL automatically combines the two tables and produces output based on the criteria you specify. The final output in this example includes the name, color, and location of the objects, even though each table has just two of those three values.

A second way to combine data from multiple tables is to use JOIN. This approach is very similar to the preceding one, but you specify one table using FROM and the other using JOIN:

```
mysql> SELECT objects.name, objects.color, locations.location
    -> FROM objects
    -> JOIN locations
    -> WHERE objects.name=locations.name AND objects.color='green';
```

Combining data lets you simplify the structure of your database in certain situations. The examples used here illustrate this fact. The data in the objects table describes objects generically, whereas the data in the locations table describes objects specifically. This design enables each table to be relatively small. If all of the data were stored in a single table, that table would require multiple entries for each item, duplicating a lot of data. By splitting the data across tables, each table can be much smaller, thus reducing storage space.

A retrieval command that requires special mention is GROUP BY. This command is used in conjunction with mathematical operators, such as SUM(), to *restrict* the selection to specified columns. For instance, suppose you want to know the total value of all of the objects in the database, grouped by object type. You can do as follows, combining data from both tables:

```
mysql> SELECT objects.name, objects.value, SUM(value)
    -> FROM objects, locations
    -> WHERE locations.name=objects.name
    -> GROUP BY value;
```

The result is a summary of the values of all of the objects by type. Omitting the GROUP BY clause produces an error message in MySQL.

Deleting Data

Sometimes your data need to be deleted. Table 9.4 suggests that the tree in the backyard is ill—its condition rating is just 2 on a 10-point scale. Perhaps you'll decide to cut it down and therefore remove it from the locations database. To do so, you'll use the DELETE command, which takes the following form:

```
DELETE FROM table WHERE conditions
```

For instance, to delete that now-removed tree, you can type the following command:

```
mysql> DELETE FROM locations
    -> WHERE name='tree' AND location='backyard' ;
Query OK, 1 row affected (0.05 sec)
```

In this specific case, the WHERE condition is more detailed than it needs to be. This is because the backyard tree is the only one in the table. As usual, when deleting any sort of data on a computer, though, it's better to be overly cautious than sloppy.

Before deleting data, try using SELECT to see what data your WHERE conditions match. Doing this will help you to avoid accidentally deleting too much data.

You can delete all of the data from a table by using a variant of the DELETE command: **DELETE * from locations;**. This command deletes all of the table's data without deleting the table itself. This may be useful if the table is hopelessly messed up from experimentation. An even more drastic deletion operation is DROP: **DROP TABLE locations;**. This example completely eliminates the locations table. Naturally, this is an extremely dangerous command, but you may want to use it when cleaning up your own SQL practice session.

Learning More about SQL

SQL is a very complex topic, and this chapter can only scratch the surface. For more information, you should read more from various sources. Your own SQL package's documentation can be a good starting point, particularly if you need to use features that are unique to your implementation. Books on SQL, such as Alan Beaulieu's *Learning SQL, 2nd Edition* (O'Reilly, 2009) and Larry Rockoff's *The Language of SQL* (Cengage Learning, 2010), are also worth reading if you need to do more than trivial SQL work.

Summary

Linux administrators must have at least a basic understanding of shell scripts. Many configuration and startup files are in fact shell scripts. Being able to read them, and perhaps to modify them, will help you administer your system. Being able to create new shell scripts is also important because doing so will help you simplify tedious tasks and create site-specific tools by putting together multiple programs to accomplish your goals.

Email server administration is another task with which you must have at least a passing familiarity. Although most Linux systems don't operate as full-blown email servers, most Linux installations do include email servers for processing locally generated email. You can configure email forwarding and perform a few other tweaks without delving too heavily into email server configuration.

The final topic of this chapter, SQL use, will help you manage simple databases stored using the Structured Query Language (SQL). Many programs rely on SQL for their operation, so being able to perform simple SQL queries will help you work with these programs. You may even decide to set up databases to help manage your own tasks, such as tracking computer equipment.

Exam Essentials

Explain the function of environment variables.   Environment variables are used to store information on the system for the benefit of running programs. Examples include the PATH environment variable, which holds the locations of executable programs, and HOSTNAME, which holds the system's hostname.

Describe various shell script components.   A shell script combines several commands, possibly including conditional expressions, variables, and other programming features. A shell script must start with a shebang line to let the kernel know it is a script and indicate the shell interpreter to use. Each script component has a specific syntax needed for proper shell execution and logic flow. A shell script is run using various methods. Each method may or may not create a subshell and may or may not require the execution bit to be set.

Describe the purpose of shell aliases.   Aliases enable you to create a command "shortcut"—a simple command that can stand in for a different or longer command. Aliases are typically defined in shell startup scripts as a way to create a shortened version of a command. Aliases also allow useful command options to be used as the new default or they create an easier-to-remember version of a command.

Summarize the major SMTP servers for Linux.   Sendmail was the most common SMTP server a decade ago, and it is still very popular today. Postfix and Exim are often supplied as the default mail servers on modern distributions, whereas administrators sometimes install qmail. Postfix and qmail use modular designs, whereas sendmail and Exim do not.

Explain the difference between an email alias and email forwarding.   An email alias is configured system-wide, typically in /etc/aliases. It can set up forwarding for any local address, even if that address doesn't correspond to a real account, and if the system is properly configured, only root may edit /etc/aliases and therefore modify aliases. Email forwarding, on the other hand, is handled by the ~/.forward file in a user's home directory; it is intended as a means for users to control their own email forwarding without bothering the system administrator.

Summarize the structure of a SQL database.   Each SQL installation consists of a number of named databases, each of which in turn may contain multiple tables. Each table can be thought of as a two-dimensional array of data. Each row in a table describes some object or concept (inventory items, employees, movies in a personal DVD collection, and so on), and each column in a table holds data about these objects or concepts (model number, salary, or director, for example).

Describe the commands used to enter data in a SQL database.   The INSERT command inserts a single entry into a database. It requires a table name and a set of values, as in INSERT INTO movies VALUES('Brazil', 'Terry Gilliam', 1985);. The UPDATE command can be used in a similar way to update an existing entry, but you must use SET to specify the column to set and WHERE to identify the row or rows to be modified.

Explain the commands used to extract data from a SQL database.   The SELECT command retrieves data from a SQL database. It can be used with a variety of additional options, such as FROM, JOIN, and WHERE, to identify the table or tables from which data should be retrieved and to locate specific values of interest.

Review Questions

1. Which environment variable stores the format for the command prompt?

   A. PROMPT

   B. PSI

   C. PAGER

   D. PS1

   E. None of these variables store the format for the command prompt.

2. You want to create a shortcut command for the command cd ~/papers/trade. Which of the following lines, if entered in a bash startup script, will accomplish this goal?

   A. `alias cdpt='cd ~/papers/trade'`

   B. `export cdpt='cd ~/papers/trade'`

   C. `alias cdpt 'cd ~/papers/trade'`

   D. `alias cd 'cdpt ~/papers/trade'`

   E. `env cdpt `cd ~/papers/trade``

3. What is the purpose of the EDITOR environment variable?

   A. If it's set to Y (the default), the shell environment permits editing of commands; if it's set to N, such editing is disallowed.

   B. It specifies the filename of the text editor that bash uses by default while you're entering commands at its prompt.

   C. If you type **edit *filename*** at a command prompt, the program specified by EDITOR will be launched.

   D. If it's set to GUI, programs call a GUI editor; if it's set to TEXT, programs call a text-based editor.

   E. Some programs refer to EDITOR to determine what external editor to launch when they need to launch one.

4. In what environment variable is the current working directory stored?

   A. PATH

   B. CWD

   C. PWD

   D. PRESENT

   E. WORKING

5. If typed in a bash shell, which of the following commands will create an environment variable called MYVAR with the contents mystuff that will be accessible to any created subshells? (Choose all that apply.)

   A. `export MYVAR='mystuff'`

   B. `MYVAR='mystuff'`

    C. `MYVAR='mystuff'; export MYVAR`

    D. `echo $MYVAR mystuff`

    E. `setenv MYVAR mystuff`

6. What file might a user modify to alter their own bash environment?

    A. `/etc/inputrc`

    B. `/etc/bashrc`

    C. `$HOME/bashrc`

    D. `$HOME/.profile_bash`

    E. `~/.bashrc`

7. What commands might you use (along with appropriate options) to learn the value of a specific environment variable? (Select two.)

    A. `env`

    B. `DISPLAY`

    C. `export`

    D. `echo`

    E. `cat`

8. Immediately after creating a shell script called `a_script.sh` in a text editor, which method will not work to run the script?

    A. Typing **`bash a_script.sh`** at the command line.

    B. Typing **`./a_script.sh`** at the command line.

    C. Typing **`. a_script.sh`** at the command line.

    D. Typing **`source a_script.sh`** at the command line.

    E. Any of the above will work.

9. Describe the effect of the following short script, `cp1.sh`, if it's called as `cp1.sh big.c big.cc`:

```
#!/bin/bash
cp $2 $1
```

    A. It has the same effect as the `cp` command—copying the contents of `big.c` to `big.cc`.

    B. It compiles the C program `big.c` and calls the result `big.cc`.

    C. It copies the contents of `big.cc` to `big.c`, eliminating the old `big.c`.

    D. It converts the C program `big.c` into a C++ program called `big.cc`.

    E. It interprets the `big.c` and `big.cc` files as bash scripts.

10. Where are the commands iterated by the loop located within the loop?

    A. Within the then statement section

    B. Between the double semicolons (;;)

    C. Within the case and esac constructs

  D. Within the test statement

  E. Between do and done constructs

11. Which of the following lines identify valid shell scripts on a normally configured system? (Select two.)

  A. `#!/bin/script`

  B. `#!/bin/bash`

  C. `#!/bin/tcsh`

  D. `!#/bin/sh`

  E. `!#/bin/zsh`

12. Which of the following are valid looping statements in bash shell scripting? (Select all that apply.)

  A. `for`

  B. `while`

  C. `if-then`

  D. `until`

  E. `case`

13. Your SMTP email server receives a message addressed to `postmaster`. The `postmaster` username has an alias of `john` on this computer. Assuming that the system is properly configured, who will receive the email message?

  A. `postmaster`

  B. `john`

  C. The account listed in `~/.forward`

  D. `root`

  E. No user, because an alias was set

14. Which of the following is *not* a popular SMTP server for Linux?

  A. Postfix

  B. Sendmail

  C. Fetchmail

  D. Exim

  E. qmail

15. You see the following line in a script:

```
mail -s "Error" -c abort < /tmp/msg root
```

What is the effect of this line, if and when it executes?

  A. An email is sent to the user `Error`, the script is aborted using `root` privileges, and error messages are written to `/tmp/msg`.

  B. An email with the subject of `Error` and the contents from `/tmp/msg` is sent to the local users `root` and `abort`.

    C. An email with the subject of Error and the contents of /tmp/msg is sent to the local user root, and then the script is aborted.

    D. An email is sent with Error priority to the local user root, and the email system is then shut down with error messages being stored in /tmp/msg.

    E. An email with the subject of Error and contents of /tmp/msg is sent to root, and information on this is logged with priority abort.

16. Your Internet connection has gone down for several hours. What command can you use to check if there is a long list of jobs in the email queue?

    A. service sendmail status

    B. lp -d queue ~/Maildir

    C. sendmail -bq

    D. mailq

    E. ls /var/spool

17. You examine your /etc/aliases file and find that it contains the following line:

root: jody

What can you conclude from this?

    A. Email addressed to jody on this system will be sent to the local user root.

    B. Email addressed to root on this system will be sent to the local user jody.

    C. The local user jody has broken into the system and has acquired root privileges.

    D. The local user jody has permission to read email directly from root's mail queue.

    E. The administrator may log in using either username: root or jody.

18. You've just installed MySQL and run it by typing **mysql**. How would you create a database called fish to store data on different varieties of fish?

    A. Type **NEW DATABASE fish;** at the mysql> prompt.

    B. Type **CREATE DATABASE fish;** at the mysql> prompt.

    C. Type **NEW DATABASE FISH;** at the mysql> prompt.

    D. Type **DATABASE CREATE fish;** at the mysql> prompt.

    E. Type **DB CREATE fish;** at the mysql> prompt.

19. Which of the following are true statements about SQL tables? (Select two.)

    A. Multiple tables may exist in a single SQL database.

    B. Tables may be combined for cross-table searches using the DROP command.

    C. Tables consist of rows, each of which holds attributes, and columns, each of which defines a specific database item.

    D. Careful table design can reduce the amount of data entry and database storage size.

    E. Tables are stored on disk using a lossy compression algorithm.

20. What is the effect of the following SQL command, assuming the various names and data exist?

```
mysql> UPDATE stars SET magnitude=2.25 WHERE starname='Mintaka';
```

A. It returns database entries from the stars table for all stars with magnitude of 2.25 and starname of Mintaka.

B. It sets the value of the stars field in the magnitude set to Mintaka, using a precision of 2.25.

C. It sets the value of the magnitude field to 2.25 for any item in the stars table with the starname value of Mintaka.

D. It combines the stars and magnitude=2.25 tables, returning all items for which the starname is Mintaka.

E. It updates the stars database, creating a new entry with a starname value of Mintaka and a magnitude of 2.25.

Chapter

10

Securing Your System

THE FOLLOWING EXAM OBJECTIVES ARE COVERED IN THIS CHAPTER:

- ✓ 1.110.1 Perform security administration tasks
- ✓ 1.110.2 Set up host security
- ✓ 1.110.3 Securing data with encryption

Chances are that you take basic security measures in your daily life, such as locking the door to your house or apartment, not advertising an upcoming vacation on social media, not setting your smartphone down in a store, and so on. Such measures can minimize the risk of theft or even personal injury. Similar measures on a computer can help protect the computer from compromise.

This chapter covers several security issues: restricting access to the computer by port number, managing the security of individual programs, managing passwords, setting miscellaneous account security options, and using encryption to secure data. Understanding these basics will help you begin to secure your computer.

There is no such thing as a 100 percent secure computer. You can take steps to improve security, but there is absolutely no guarantee that you will not have security problems. You must decide (or the organization for which you work must decide) just how much effort to put into securing your systems, and live with the threat level that remains. This chapter's security information can help you start securing your computer. If you need more security information, you can start your research at websites such as the SANS Institute, www.sans.org, and Gibson Research Corporation, www.grc.com.

Administering Network Security

Linux systems are often used as server computers. On such systems, network security is particularly important because incorrectly configured servers can provide troublemakers with a way into your computer. There are several methods for protecting networked computers from unwanted outside access. Some of the simplest methods involve blocking or restricting access to network servers via their network ports. (Network ports are described in Chapter 8, "Configuring Basic Networking.") You can check for existing network connections, check for open ports (that is, ports that are in use by a server program), use super daemon restrictions to limit access, and disable servers that you're not using.

The popular media uses the term *hacker* to refer to computer criminals. This word has an older meaning. It also refers to individuals who are skilled with computers and who have *no* malicious intent. Many Linux programmers consider themselves hackers in this positive sense. Therefore, terms such as *troublemaker* and *attacker* are used in this chapter to refer to computer criminals.

Using Super Server Restrictions

Many network server programs directly open network ports and listen for connections. Some distributions have network server programs that work through an intermediary: a *super server* or *super daemon*. This is a program that listens for network connections on behalf of another program. When a connection is initiated, the super server hands off control of that connection to the intended server.

You can employ security checks in the super daemon to protect the servers it manages. Linux has two primary super daemons:

    inetd

    xinetd

In the following pages, configuring super server basics are described with particular emphasis on their security features. In the case of inetd, security is handled by a package called TCP wrappers. By contrast, xinetd's security features are built into xinetd itself.

Whenever possible, apply redundant access controls. For instance, use *both* a server's own security features and the super daemon's security features to block unwanted access. This helps protect against bugs and incorrect configurations. For example, if a problem emerges in the super server configuration, the secondary block will probably halt the attacker. If you configure the system correctly, such an attack will also leave a log file message to alert you that the super server didn't do its job.

Configuring *inetd*

The inetd package is a legacy super daemon in Linux. Most likely you will never run into it. However, it is listed in the certification exam objectives.

The inetd package is deprecated, and it is typically no longer installed on Linux distributions. However, because it is a legacy super server that deserves some review, it is still covered in the certification exam objectives.

Setting Up *inetd*

Services that launched via inetd were controlled through the /etc/inetd.conf file or files in /etc/inetd.d/. The /etc/inetd.conf file consisted of a series of lines, one for each server. A typical line was similar to the following:

```
ftp stream tcp nowait root /usr/sbin/tcpd /usr/sbin/in.ftpd -l
```

Instead of using a single monolithic /etc/inetd.conf file, later versions of inetd enabled you to split the configuration into several files in the /etc/inetd.d/ directory. Doing so allowed easier addition or deletion of server configurations by adding or deleting their configuration files. For brevity, the following paragraphs refer only to /etc/inetd .conf, but the description applies to files that were in /etc/inetd.d/ as well.

Each line in /etc/inetd.conf consisted of several fields separated by one or more spaces. The meanings of these fields were as follows:

Service Name   The first field (ftp in the preceding example) was the name of the service as it appeared in the /etc/services file.

Socket Type   The socket type entry told the system what type of connection to expect—a reliable two-way connection (stream), a less reliable connection with less overhead (dgram), a low-level connection to the network (raw), or various others.

Protocol   This was the TCP/IP Transport layer protocol used, usually tcp or udp.

Wait/No Wait   For dgram socket types, this entry specified whether the server connected to its client and freed the socket (nowait) or processed all of its packets and then timed out (wait). Servers that used other socket types would specify nowait in this field.

User   This was the username used to run the server. The root and nobody users were common choices, but others were possible as well. As a general rule, servers were run with a low-privilege user whenever possible as a security precaution. Some servers required root access, though.

Server Name   This was the server's filename. In the preceding example, the server is specified as /usr/sbin/tcpd, which is the TCP wrappers binary. As described shortly in "Controlling Access via TCP wrappers," this program was an important security tool and was usually included as the means of launching programs via inetd.

Parameters   Everything after the server name consisted of parameters that were passed to the server. If you used TCP wrappers, you would pass the name of the true target server (such as /usr/sbin/in.ftpd) in this field, along with its parameters.

The hash mark (#) was a comment symbol for /etc/inetd.conf. Therefore, if a server was running via inetd and you wanted to disable it, you would place a hash mark at the start of the line. If you wanted to add a server to inetd.conf, you needed to create an entry for it.

After modifying inetd.conf, you had to restart the inetd super daemon. It was generally restarted using a SysV startup script as described in Chapter 5, "Booting Linux and Editing Files." On most computers, typing something similar to the following would have worked:

```
# /etc/init.d/inetd restart
```

Controlling Access via TCP Wrappers

The TCP wrappers package provides a library known as libwrap. Older TCP wrappers packages used with inetd provided a program known as tcpd. The inetd did not call a server directly; instead, inetd called tcpd, which did two things: It checked whether a client was authorized to access the server, and if the client had this authorization, tcpd called the server program.

 Even though inetd has gone the way of the dinosaurs, TCP wrappers is still available for use on Linux systems. For example, the FTP server, vsftpd, uses TCP wrappers. If a network service uses TCP wrappers, then it uses the libwrap library. You can determine if a network service uses TCP wrappers or not by typing **ldd *NetworkServiceDaemon* | grep libwrap** at the command line. If you get output, then the network service uses TCP wrappers.

TCP wrappers is configured through two files: /etc/hosts.allow and /etc/hosts.deny. The first of these specifies computers that are allowed access to the service. Systems not listed in hosts.allow are not permitted access. By contrast, hosts.deny lists computers that are not allowed access; all other systems are granted access to the service. If a computer is listed in both files, hosts.allow takes precedence.

Both files use the same basic format. The files consist of lines in the following form:

```
daemon-list : client-list
```

The *daemon-list* variable is a list of servers using the names for the servers that appear in /etc/services. Wildcards are also available, such as ALL for all servers.

The *client-list* variable is a list of computers to be granted or denied access to the specified daemons. You can specify computers by name or by IP address. Also, you can specify a network by using a leading or trailing dot (.) when identifying networks by name or IP address block, respectively. For instance, .ivytech.edu refers to all computers in the ivytech.edu domain, and 192.168.7. refers to all computers in the 192.168.7.0/24 network. You can also use various wildcard options in the *client-list* variable, such as ALL (all computers).

The EXCEPT operator creates an exception. For example, the following *client-list* setting is placed in the hosts.deny file:

```
[...]: 192.168.7. EXCEPT 192.168.7.105
```

The preceding *client-list* setting would block all computers in the 192.168.7.0/24 network. However, an exception would be made for 192.168.7.105.

The man pages for hosts.allow and hosts.deny (they're actually the same document) provide additional information about more advanced features. You should consult them if you build TCP wrappers rules.

Configuring *xinetd*

The xinetd program is an *extended* super daemon. It provides the functionality of the legacy inetd, plus security options that are similar to those of TCP wrappers.

Setting Up *xinetd*

The /etc/xinetd.conf file controls the xinetd super daemon. On distributions that use xinetd, this configuration file contains only global default options. At the file's bottom is a directive to include files stored in the /etc/xinetd.d/ directory:

```
includedir /etc/xinetd.d
```

Each server that should run via xinetd installs a file in /etc/xinetd.d/ with its own configuration options. Those file options are then included in the main xinetd configuration file.

 If you cannot find the /etc/xinetd.conf file on your system, most likely the xinetd package is not installed. See Chapter 2, "Managing Software," for information on how to install this package on your system if desired.

Whether the server entry goes in /etc/xinetd.conf or in a file in /etc/xinetd.d/, the configuration information is similar to that in the inetd.conf file. However, the xinetd configuration information is spread across multiple lines and labeled more explicitly. The following shows an xinetd configuration example:

```
$ cat /etc/xinetd.d/rsync
# default: off
[...]
service rsync
{
        disable = yes
        flags            = IPv6
        socket_type      = stream
        wait             = no
        user             = root
        server           = /usr/bin/rsync
        server_args      = --daemon
        log_on_failure  += USERID
}
$
```

One xinetd configuration parameter that is commonly present is disable. If you include the line disable = yes in a service definition, xinetd ignores this server. Some server packages install startup files in /etc/xinetd.d/ and have this option set by default. You must edit the file and change the entry to read disable = no to enable the server. You can also temporarily disable a set of servers by listing their names in the defaults section of the main xinetd.conf file on a line called disabled.

It's generally wise to make sure that as many servers as possible are disabled in the xinetd configuration files. As a general rule, if you don't understand what a server does, leave it disabled. This will improve the security of your system by eliminating potentially buggy or incorrectly configured servers.

After you make changes to xinetd's configuration, you must either reload the configuration file or restart the super server. For example, on a system using SysV startup scripts, you do this by running the appropriate script located in either /etc/init.d/ or /etc/rc.d/init.d/ and passing either the reload or restart parameter:

```
# /etc/init.d/xinetd restart
```

Controlling Access via *xinetd*

Security is handled on a server-by-server basis through the use of configuration parameters in either /etc/xinetd.conf or the server-specific configuration files. Some of these options are similar to the function of hosts.allow and hosts.deny:

Network Interface   The bind option tells xinetd to listen on only one network interface for the service. For instance, you can specify bind = 192.168.23.7 on a router to have it listen only on the Ethernet card associated with that address. This feature is extremely useful in routers, but it isn't as useful in computers with just one network interface. You can, however, use this option to bind a server only to the loopback interface, 127.0.0.1, if a server should be available only locally. You might do this with a configuration tool like the Samba Web Administration Tool (SWAT). A synonym for this option is interface.

Allowed IP or Network Addresses   You can use the only_from option to specify IP addresses, networks (as in 192.168.78.0/24), or computer names on this line, separated by spaces. The result is that xinetd will accept connections only from these addresses, similar to TCP wrappers' hosts.allow entries.

Disallowed IP or Network Addresses   The no_access option is the opposite of only_from; you list computers or networks here that you want to blacklist. This is similar to the hosts.deny file of TCP wrappers.

Access Times   The access_times option sets times during which users may access the server. The time range is specified in the form *hour*:*min*-*hour*:*min*, using a 24-hour clock. Note that this option affects only the times during which the server will *respond*. If the xinetd access_times option is set to 8:00-17:00 and somebody logs in at 4:59 p.m. (one minute before the end time), that user may continue using the system well beyond the 5:00 p.m. cutoff time.

You should enter these options into the configuration files in /etc/xinetd.d/ that correspond to the servers you want to protect. Place the lines between the opening brace ({) and closing brace (}) for the service. If you want to restrict *all* of your xinetd-controlled servers, you can place the entries in the defaults section in /etc/xinetd.conf.

NOTE   Some servers provide access control mechanisms similar to those of TCP wrappers or xinetd. For instance, Samba provides hosts allow and hosts deny options that work much like the TCP wrappers file entries. These options are most common on servers that are awkward or impossible to run via xinetd.

 Real World Scenario

Configuring a Firewall

Although the exam objectives don't mention firewalls, you should be familiar with the concept. A *firewall* is a filter that restricts access to and/or from computers or services. Broadly speaking, two types of firewalls exist: *packet-filter firewalls*, which work by blocking or permitting access based on low-level information in individual data packets (such as source and destination IP addresses and ports), and *proxy filters*, which partially process a transaction (such as a web page retrieval) and block or permit access based on high-level features in this transaction (such as the filename of an image in the web page).

In Linux, the kernel includes packet-filter firewall capabilities, which can be programmed via the iptables program. You can set up rules by typing **iptables** followed by various options that define specific restrictions, such as limits on the IP addresses that may access a specific network port. Creating an effective firewall requires learning iptables in detail and writing a script that calls this program repeatedly to set up specific rules. The nftables program is slated to replace the iptables program. See netfilter.org/projects/nftables for the current status of this program.

Many distributions make things easier by providing a generic firewall script that you can configure using a GUI tool or text-based command. For example, Ubuntu offers the Uncomplicated Firewall utility, ufx, to help set up iptables rules. These tools are generally designed for protecting a single computer against unwanted outside access. Check your distribution's GUI system administration options and man pages for a firewall configuration tool. You may be able to set security based on a few levels (high, medium, and low security, for instance) or in a somewhat more refined manner.

Linux can also function as a firewall computer that protects an entire network; however, such a configuration is likely to require in-depth knowledge of iptables, as well as topics which include configuring Linux as a router.

Disabling Unused Servers

Quite a few server programs ship with most Linux distributions. This can be a great advantage because you don't need to install additional software to get a server package up and running. On the other hand, this very advantage can be a drawback. If you're not careful, you can end up running a network service and not even realize it's installed!

For security reasons, you should periodically audit your servers' network services and disable any service that you find isn't necessary. For example, if your Linux system functions only as a print server, it should not be running the Apache web server daemon, httpd. Limiting the network service programs running on a system equates to fewer attack points for a troublemaker.

Several audit tools exist, such as netstat, lsof, and remote network scanners. You can also search your local configuration files for clues about what may be running. Unused servers can be disabled by uninstalling the package or by reconfiguring the server.

Using *netstat*

One way to begin auditing network security is to look for network activity or open ports on a computer. One older tool that can help in this respect is netstat. This useful program provides many different options and output formats to deliver information about routing tables, interface statistics, and so on.

The netstat program is considered obsolete, though you may still find it on some Linux distributions. It is also listed in the certification exam's objectives and therefore needs to be covered here. However, the current utility to use for network auditing and displaying network information is the ip program. See the man pages for more information on the ip utility.

For spotting unnecessary servers, you can use netstat with its -a and -p options. The -a option shows all network sockets. The -p option shows the PID and program name that owns a shown socket.

The output displayed by netstat is so wide that it has to be split into two separate snipped displays for the book, as shown here. This first netstat output display shows the three left-hand columns of information:

```
# netstat -ap
Active Internet connections (servers and established)
Proto Recv-Q Send-Q [...]
tcp       0      0 [...]
tcp       0      0 [...]
tcp       0      0 [...]
tcp       0      0 [...]
tcp       0      0 [...]
tcp       0      0 [...]
tcp       0      0 [...]
tcp       0      0 [...]
[...]
#
```

This second netstat output display shows the four right-hand columns of information:

```
# netstat -ap
Active Internet connections (servers and established)
[...]Local Address          Foreign Address    State   PID/Program name
[...]*:sunrpc               *:*                LISTEN     1096/rpcbind
[...]*:ssh                  *:*                LISTEN     1401/sshd
[...]0 localhost:ipp        *:*                LISTEN     1276/cupsd
[...]*:40952                *:*                LISTEN     1239/rpc.statd
[...]localhost:smtp         *:*                LISTEN     1503/master
[...]0 192.168.56.101:ssh   192.168.56.1:49159 ESTABLISHED 2421/sshd
[...]0 *:sunrpc             *:*                LISTEN     1096/rpcbind
[...]*:ssh                  *:*                LISTEN     1401/sshd
[...]
#
```

There is so much information when you issue this command on your system(s) that it would be wise to pipe it into the less command like so: **netstat -ap | less**. Also, you may need to adjust your screen's resolution to prevent columns from wrapping in the netstat output to your screen.

 The netstat command can be run as an ordinary user, but it may not return as much information. Specifically, only root and a process's owner see the PID/Program name column information.

The netstat command with the -ap options shows active network sockets that can reveal the presence of servers that are running on your computer. The Local Address and Foreign Address columns specify the local and remote addresses, including both the hostname or IP address and the port number or associated name from /etc/services. Entries that are not actively connected will show the local address and the foreign address as asterisks (*).

The State column specifies that the server is listening (LISTEN) for a connection or that a connection is currently active (ESTABLISHED). There are several additional states as well, besides the two shown in the preceding example. Type **man netstat** to learn about more potential State statuses.

The final column in this output, under the PID/Program name heading, indicates the process ID (PID) and program name of the service using this port. Notice that several services are currently listening for connection requests. However, there is only one established connection whose PID is 2421, and its program is the Secure Shell daemon (sshd).

It may take some time to peruse the output of netstat, but doing so will leave you with a much-improved understanding of your computer's network connections. If you spot servers listening for connections that you didn't realize were active, you should investigate the matter further. Some servers may be innocent or even necessary. Others may be pointless security risks.

> To spot servers listening for connections quickly, type **netstat -lp** rather than **netstat -ap**. The result will show all servers that are *listening* for connections, omitting client connections and specific server instances that are already connected to clients.

Exercise 10.1 demonstrates the use of netstat to monitor network port use.

EXERCISE 10.1

Monitor Network Port Use

To get started with netstat, follow these steps:

1. Log into the Linux system as a normal user. (Acquiring root privileges will produce more complete output, as described earlier, but it isn't strictly necessary for this exercise.)

2. Launch a terminal from the desktop environment's menu system if you used a GUI login method.

3. Type **netstat -ap | less**, and page through the output. Chances are you'll see quite a few entries for servers, which are listening for new connections and for established connections to local servers or from local clients to remote servers. Pay particular attention to servers that are listening for new connections. You can identify those servers by the keyword LISTEN displayed in the State column of the output.

4. Type **netstat -ap | grep ssh** to find connections involving SSH. Depending on your configuration and the servers you have running, you may see no output or many lines of output.

5. Determine your system's IP address by typing the **ifconfig** command.

6. In another terminal login session, initiate an SSH connection to your computer. (The Secure Shell is discussed later in the section "Configuring SSH.") For instance, type **ssh 192.168.78.5** if the IP address you obtained in step 5 is 192.168.78.5.

7. Type **netstat -ap | grep ssh** in your *original* session (not in your SSH connection). Compare the output to that which you obtained in step 4. The output should have an additional line reflecting the session you initiated in step 6.

8. Log out of the SSH session you initiated.

9. Type **netstat -ap | grep ssh** again. The output should be missing the line for the session you've now closed.

If you're using a multiuser system, additional SSH sessions may come and go during the course of this exercise, reflecting the activities of other users.

Using *lsof*

The lsof program nominally lists open files. It can be used to identify what files are open in a directory, find who's accessing them, and so on. The definition of a *file* used by lsof is broad because it includes network connections. Thus, you can use lsof to audit your network ports. With the -i parameter, the lsof command will show you not only various services listening for connections, but also any current network connections to those services. Here is an example:

```
# lsof -i
COMMAND    PID    USER    FD    TYPE DEVICE SIZE/OFF NODE NAME
rpcbind   1096     rpc    6u    IPv4  11127      0t0  UDP *:sunrpc
[...]
cupsd     1276    root    9u    IPv4  11828      0t0  UDP *:ipp
sshd      1401    root    3u    IPv4  12397      0t0  TCP *:ssh (LISTEN)
sshd      1401    root    4u    IPv6  12401      0t0  TCP *:ssh (LISTEN)
[...]
sshd      3014    root    3r    IPv4  23963      0t0  TCP⏎
192.168.56.101:ssh->192.168.56.1:49165 (ESTABLISHED)
dhclient  3016    root    7u    IPv4  24029      0t0  UDP *:bootpc
#
```

As in the output of netstat shown earlier, this output is snipped for brevity's sake. Notice that there are three lines that begin with sshd. The first two sshd lines show servers that are listening for connections on the ssh ports. These lines are identified by the fact that the NAME column takes the form *:*service* (LISTEN), where *service* is the service name or port number. Other columns in the output reveal additional information, such as the PID and username associated with the port access.

The third line beginning with sshd shows an outgoing connection from 192.168.56.101 (the system on which the lsof -i command was typed) to the ssh port on 192.168.56.101. Such connections are identified by the existence of two IP addresses (or hostnames) in the NAME column and by the keyword ESTABLISHED in the same column.

> If you type **lsof -i** as an ordinary user, you'll see only your own network connections. Thus, in order for this command to be a useful diagnostic for system security, you must run it using superuser privileges or as root.

You can restrict the output of lsof by including an address after the -i option. The address takes the following form:

[46][*protocol*][@*hostname*|*hostaddr*][:*service*|*port*]

The lsof -i address syntax is as follows:

The digit 4 or 6 that represents an IPv4 or IPv6 connection

protocol, which is a protocol type (TCP or UDP)

hostname or *hostaddr,* which is the computer hostname or IP address associated with a remote system *service*, which is a service name (from /etc/services)

port, which is a port number

For instance, suppose you want to verify that no FTP server is running on a computer. You can search for any connections associated with the FTP port:

lsof -i :ftp

Alternatively, you can replace ftp with 21, because 21 is the port number associated with the FTP port. (See Chapter 8 for common network port numbers.) In either case, this command returns a list of all processes associated with FTP connections, both incoming and outgoing. If no such connections exist, the command returns no output. Be sure to note which output lines are linked with the *server,* as opposed to *client* processes. Even if you're not running an FTP server locally, the preceding command may produce dozens of lines of output if users on the computer are accessing remote FTP clients.

> Another use of lsof is in identifying who is accessing files. This might be handy if you need to unmount a filesystem (including a network filesystem) but can't because of in-use files. This command is also useful if you suspect inappropriate activities involving file access.

To perform a general audit of the network services your system is offering, you can pipe the output into the less command. This will allow you to review the network services methodically and determine if there is any need to disable them.

Using Remote Network Scanners

Network scanners, such as Nmap, can scan for open ports on the local computer or on other computers. Nmap is a very easy to use utility for conducting security audits on your systems.

> Besides being used by network administrators for legitimate purposes, network scanners are often used by troublemakers to locate systems to attack. Many organizations have policies *forbidding* the use of network scanners except under specific conditions. Therefore, you should check these policies and obtain explicit permission to perform a network scan. Failure to do so could cost you your job or even result in criminal charges, even if your intentions are honorable.

Nmap is capable of performing basic checks for open ports. To conduct this simple audit using the nmap utility, add the -sT parameters. Your first scan should be done using the loopback address (127.0.0.1). This allows you to see what network services are being offered by your system without any firewall settings interfering with the results:

```
$ nmap -sT 127.0.0.1

Starting Nmap 5.51 ( http://nmap.org ) at 2015-03-07 13:16 EST
Nmap scan report for localhost (127.0.0.1)
Host is up (0.0011s latency).
Not shown: 996 closed ports
PORT     STATE SERVICE
22/tcp   open  ssh
25/tcp   open  smtp
111/tcp open  rpcbind
631/tcp open  ipp

Nmap done: 1 IP address (1 host up) scanned in 0.24 seconds
$
```

In the preceding example's Nmap results, you can see that four network services
(ssh, smtp, rpcbind, and ipp) are currently listening for services requests at designated
ports (22, 25, 111, 631). However, to see what services can be reached outside the firewall,
you need to conduct another scan.

 Most Linux distributions do not come with the nmap utility installed by
default. See Chapter 2, "Managing Software," to learn how to install
software packages, such as nmap.

This scan is almost exactly like the preceding example. It uses the same nmap options,
-sT. However, this time, the machine's IP address is used instead of the loopback address.
This will allow you to see what services are not being blocked by a firewall:

```
$ nmap -sT 192.168.56.101

Starting Nmap 5.51 ( http://nmap.org ) at 2015-03-07 13:20 EST
Nmap scan report for 192.168.56.101
Host is up (0.00049s latency).
Not shown: 998 closed ports
PORT     STATE SERVICE
22/tcp   open  ssh
111/tcp open  rpcbind

Nmap done: 1 IP address (1 host up) scanned in 13.18 seconds
$
```

Notice that this time, only two services are displayed. Keep in mind that even though the
outside world may not see all of the services, you still should disable unneeded
network services.

The -sT option allows you to scan for services using TCP. Some network services use
UDP. To scan for these with nmap, use the -sU option as shown here:

```
$ sudo nmap -sU 127.0.0.1
[sudo] password for Christine:
```

```
Starting Nmap 5.51 ( http://nmap.org ) at 2015-03-07 13:27 EST
Nmap scan report for localhost (127.0.0.1)
Host is up (0.000022s latency).
Not shown: 997 closed ports
PORT     STATE           SERVICE
68/udp   open|filtered  dhcpc
111/udp  open            rpcbind
631/udp  open|filtered  ipp

Nmap done: 1 IP address (1 host up) scanned in 1.29 seconds
$
```

Notice that superuser privileges are required to run a UDP scan, whereas they were not required for running a TCP scan. In the previous example, there are three network services being offered: dhcpc listening at port 68, rpcbind listening at port 111, and ipp listening at port 631.

Nmap is capable of more sophisticated scans, including "stealth" scans that aren't likely to be noticed by most types of firewalls, ping scans to detect which hosts are active, and more. The Nmap man page provides details. You can also find out more about Nmap at www.nessus.org.

Another scanning tool called Nessus, which is built atop Nmap, provides a graphical user interface. It also offers a means of performing automated and sophisticated tests. Nessus is a more sophisticated scanner in that it checks for known vulnerabilities.

Nessus comes as separate client and server components; the client enables you to control the server, which does the actual work. You can find out more about Nessus at www.nessus.org.

You can use a stand-alone Linux boot CD-ROM to perform security checks on a network. Special Linux distributions intended for this purpose, such as Kali Linux (http://www.kali.org), provide easy access to Nmap and other network security tools. These special distributions enable quick checks of a network's security even if no computer on that network regularly runs Linux.

Using *fuser*

Another handy network port auditing tool is the fuser command. You can use this tool to determine the processes currently using a particular network port. For example, to see what process is currently using network port 22, use fuser and pass the port number and network protocol in the following manner:

```
$ sudo fuser 22/tcp
[sudo] password for Christine:
22/tcp:               1415  1881  1885
$
```

```
$ ps 1415
  PID TTY      STAT   TIME COMMAND
 1415 ?        Ss     0:00 /usr/sbin/sshd
$
$ ps 1881
  PID TTY      STAT   TIME COMMAND
 1881 ?        Ss     0:00 sshd: Christine [priv]
$
$ ps 1885
  PID TTY      STAT   TIME COMMAND
 1885 ?        S      0:00 sshd: Christine@pts/0
$
```

In the preceding display, the fuser command produces three process IDs (PIDs). Each of these processes is using port 22 with TCP. Using the ps command, you can investigate each process further. However, there is an easier way. Simply add the -v option on the fuser command to see all of the processes' information in one straightforward command:

```
$ sudo fuser -v 22/tcp
                      USER        PID ACCESS COMMAND
22/tcp:               root       1415 F.... sshd
                      root       1881 f.... sshd
                      Christine  1885 F.... sshd
$
```

This method provides a quick analysis of who is using port 22. Notice that each time you use fuser, superuser privileges are required.

The ACCESS column in the preceding display indicates whether or not the process has a file open (f) or a file open for writing (F). The fuser utility is similar to the lsof utility in that it can also view processes accessing files.

> Notice that the fuser command uses the syntax of *Port/Protocol* to denote which port and protocol to inspect. This option matches the output of the syntax used by Nmap's scan output. Therefore, in security scripts, you could use various filter commands (see Chapter 1, "Exploring Linux Command-Line Tools") to pull information from nmap output and feed it into fuser commands to produce audit or security incident reports.

There is also another format of the fuser command to view network processes using a particular port. In the following example, the -n option is used. Notice that the -v option is still included; however, the formatting of the port number and network protocol have changed:

```
$ sudo fuser -nv tcp 22
[sudo] password for Christine:
                      USER        PID ACCESS COMMAND
22/tcp:               root       1415 F.... sshd
                      root       1881 f.... sshd
                      Christine  1885 F.... sshd
$
```

This displays the exact same output as previously. Since they both display the same thing, use the syntax that is easier for you to remember.

To obtain information for other ports and protocols, just modify the options passed to the fuser command. For example, to check what processes are accessing port 631 using the UDP protocol, issue the following fuser command:

```
$ sudo fuser -nv udp 631
                    USER        PID ACCESS COMMAND
631/udp:            root       1276 F.... cupsd
$
```

Each of the various auditing tools covered so far provide different types of information that can be useful for different security tasks. One task, however, doesn't come with a helpful auditing tool. You must sit down and review server configuration files, as covered in the next section.

Examining Configuration Files

Most Linux server packages include configuration files. Thus, you may be able to spot installed but unwanted servers by looking for their configuration files.

Startup scripts are described in Chapter 5, "Booting Linux and Editing Files," so review that chapter for details of how they're managed. If you find such a script for a server that you know you don't want to run, you should disable it as described in Chapter 5. Keep in mind that server startup scripts and management tools are different depending upon whether your distribution uses SysV, Upstart, or systemd for managing system services.

Be aware that many startup scripts start entire subsystems that aren't directly network-related. Thus, you'll probably see startup scripts that you don't recognize. You should not automatically disable these scripts because they may be necessary even if you don't recognize the name. If in doubt, leave them in place until you can research the matter further.

 Try doing a Web search on the name of the startup script, possibly in conjunction with "Linux" or "startup script." Chances are that you'll find a helpful reference.

If your system uses xinetd, you should examine your xinetd configuration files for unwanted servers. Unlike system startup scripts, super servers launch network servers only, not non-network services. Therefore, you should take a more aggressive approach to disabling entries that you don't recognize from your super server configuration than you do with system startup scripts.

On older distributions using the SysV startup system, /etc/inittab deserves examination. This file is used to control some of the earliest stages of the startup process. Older /etc/inittab installations would start processes that accepted text-mode logins. They also started additional similar processes used to accept logins via dial-up modems and RS-232 serial ports. This can be an issue from a security viewpoint. While it's unlikely, you may be surprised to find a long-forgotten old dial-up modem still connected to a computer server. You want to check to ensure that an older system isn't listening for dial-up modem connections! Files called /etc/init/tty# (where # is a number) control local login access, whereas /etc/init/ttyS# files control RS-232 serial or modem access.

Modern systems lack /etc/inittab or have only very basic /etc/inittab files. Typically, the original /etc/inittab functions have been moved into other files, such as startup scripts or files in /etc/init. You won't ordinarily need to modify such configurations.

Uninstalling or Reconfiguring Servers

Once you've identified an unnecessary server, your task becomes one of shutting it down. Broadly speaking, two options exist.

First, you can disable the server by changing its startup script configuration or, if it uses the system's super daemon, disabling it in the daemon's configuration files. Consult Chapter 5 for details on how to change a server's startup script and/or the preceding sections on xinetd for details on how to disable xinetd via its configuration files. Disabling the server in this way has the advantage that you can easily reactivate it in the future if you decide to do so. It has the disadvantage that the server's files will continue to consume disk space, and the server might be accidentally reactivated in the future.

Second, you can completely uninstall the server using your distribution's package management tools or by otherwise deleting its files. Chapter 2, "Managing Software," describes this task. Completely uninstalling software has the advantage of reducing the risk of accidental reactivation. However, it has the drawback that it will take more effort to reactivate the server should you decide to do so in the future.

Overall, completely removing the server is generally preferable unless you merely want to disable a server temporarily. If you decide to reactivate the server in the future, you can always reinstall it.

Administering Local Security

Security isn't limited to networking—local security issues can be as much of a threat as remote intruders. Thus, you should attend to some local security matters: securing passwords, limiting root access to the computer, auditing user access, setting user limits, and tracking down SUID/SGID files.

Securing Passwords

A default Linux configuration relies heavily on passwords. Users' passwords are their keys into the system. Careless password handling is much like the careless handling of physical keys. In either case, security breaches can result. Understanding these risks is critical to maintaining system security, but this is one task for which you *must* enlist the help of your users. You should also be aware of some of the tools that Linux provides to help keep passwords secure. (Most of the details concerning password-related commands are described in Chapter 7, "Administering the System.")

Looking at Password Risks

Passwords can end up in attackers' hands in various ways, and you must take steps to minimize the risk. You can take the following steps to improve your system's security:

Use Strong Passwords   Users should employ good passwords, as described shortly in "Choosing a Good Password." Educate your system's users on how to build strong passwords and use policies and tools to enforce them.

Change Passwords Frequently   You can minimize the chance of damage due to a compromised password by changing passwords frequently. Some Linux tools can help to enforce such changes, as described briefly in the section "Using Tools for Password Management," and in more detail in Chapter 7.

Use Shadow Passwords   If an attacker has gained access to your system or a regular user is a troublemaker, be aware that either of them can read data stored in the password file /etc/passwd. This is because the /etc/passwd file is world-readable. If for some reason your Linux distribution stores its passwords in there, your system is *vulnerable*! Even though passwords are hashed, there are several hashed password–cracking programs available. For this reason, you should store passwords in /etc/shadow. This file is only readable by the superuser.

All major Linux distributions use shadow passwords by default. If yours doesn't, you can type **pwconv** to move all password information from the /etc/passwd file to the locked-down /etc/shadow file. It's a good idea to run the pwck utility after the conversion to ensure that the files are in sync.

Keep Passwords Secret   You should remind your users not to reveal their passwords to others. Such trust is sometimes misplaced, and sometimes even a well-intentioned password recipient may slip up and let the password fall into the wrong hands. This can happen by writing the password down, storing it in electronic form, or sending it by email or other electronic means. Users shouldn't email their own passwords to themselves because email can be intercepted.

Use Secure Remote Login Protocols   Certain remote login protocols are inherently insecure because they allow data to traverse the network in an unencrypted form. Intervening computers can be configured to snatch passwords from such sessions. Because of this, it's best to disable Telnet, FTP, and other protocols that use cleartext passwords in favor of protocols that encrypt passwords, such as SSH and SFTP.

Be Alert to Shoulder Surfing   If your users log in using public terminals, as is common on college campuses and other open areas, it's possible that others will be able to watch them type their passwords, a practice sometimes called *shoulder surfing*. Users should be alert to this possibility and minimize such logins if possible.

Use Each Password on Just One System If one computer's password database is compromised and if users of that system reuse their passwords on other systems, those other systems can also be compromised. For this reason, it's best to use each password just once.

Unfortunately, the proliferation of websites that require passwords for access makes this rule almost impossible to enforce, at least without violating the rule of not writing the password down. (Web browsers can remember passwords for you, by storing them in a file—essentially, writing them down.) A reasonable compromise might be to use one password for the least-sensitive websites (such as online newspapers) and unique passwords for sensitive websites (such as banking sites) and login accounts.

Be Alert to Social Engineering Attackers often use *social engineering* to obtain passwords. This practice involves tricking individuals into giving up their passwords by pretending to be a system administrator or by otherwise misleading victims. Amazingly, a large percentage of people fall for this ploy.

A related practice is *phishing*, in which an attacker puts up a fake website or sends an email that seems to be from somebody else. The victim is then lured into revealing sensitive data (such as credit card numbers).

Some of these steps are things you can do, such as replacing insecure remote login protocols with encrypted ones. Others are things your users must do. This illustrates the importance of user education, particularly on systems with many users.

Choosing a Good Password

As a general rule, users tend to pick passwords that are too easy to guess, and they change those passwords infrequently. Fortunately, Linux includes tools to help make your users select good passwords and change them regularly.

Poor but common passwords include those based on the following:

- Any simple keyboard or alphanumeric combination, such as abcd or 123456
- The word password
- The names of family members, friends, and pets
- Favorite books, movies, television shows, or the characters in any of these
- Telephone numbers, street addresses, or Social Security numbers
- Any other meaningful personal information
- Any single word that's found in a dictionary (in *any* language)

The best possible passwords are random collections of letters, digits, and punctuation. Unfortunately, such passwords are difficult to remember. A reasonable compromise is to build a password in two steps:

1. Choose a base that's easy to remember but difficult to guess.
2. Modify that base in ways that increase the difficulty of guessing the password.

One approach to building a base is to use two *unrelated* words, such as *bun* and *pen*. You can then merge these two words (bunpen). Another approach, and one that's arguably better than the first, is to use the first letters of a phrase that's meaningful to the user. For instance, the first letters of "yesterday I went to the dentist" become yiwttd. In both cases, the base should not be a word in any language.

As a general rule, the longer the password, the better. Older versions of Linux could handle passwords of no more than eight characters, but those limits have been lifted by the use of the MD5 and SHA password hashes, which are the standard on modern Linux distributions. Many Linux systems require passwords to be at least four to six characters in length; the passwd utility won't accept anything shorter than the distribution's minimum.

With the base in hand, it's time to modify it to create a password. The user should apply at least a couple of several possible modifications:

Adding Numbers or Punctuation   One important modification is to insert random numbers or punctuation in the base. This step might yield, for instance, bu3npe&n or y#i9wttd. As a general rule, add at least two symbols or numbers.

Mixing Case   Linux uses case-sensitive passwords, so jumbling the case of letters can improve security. Applying this rule might produce Bu3nPE&n and y#i9WttD, for instance.

Growing the Haystack   A would-be intruder's task of discovering a password has been likened to finding a needle in a haystack. One way to make this task harder is to increase the size of the haystack. In password terms, this means making a password longer. You can do this by using longer words or phrases, of course, but this can make a password harder to remember and type. Even a size increase that simply repeats a single character can be helpful. Thus, you might turn the passwords into Bu3nn&EPiiiiiiiiiii or Dtt::::::::::::W9i#y.

Your best tool for getting users to pick good passwords is to educate them. Tell them that malicious individuals who know them or even who target them can guess their passwords. Inform users that their personal information can be looked up on social media, on company websites, on online professional networking sites, and so on. Educating your users on proper password creation and management will help them understand the potential threats and help to motivate at least some of them to pick good passwords.

Password cracking tools are not just available to attackers and trouble-makers. You can use them as well. Use password cracking tools against passwords in your system's /etc/shadow file. Work with your company's management first to determine how to handle users who habitually pick easily cracked passwords properly.

Another password security issue is password changes. Frequently changing passwords minimizes the window of opportunity for troublemakers to do damage. If an attacker obtains a password but it changes before that password is used, disaster is averted.

Some system administrators set up a honeypot account. A *honeypot account* is a system account with a fairly easy-to-crack password. The account is locked down from accessing anything on the system, and it's also monitored. If a login occurs, you know that the /etc/shadow file has been compromised and you can take appropriate actions, such as having all of your users change their passwords.

As described shortly, you can configure accounts to require periodic password changes. When so configured, an account will stop accepting logins after a time if the password isn't changed periodically. You can configure the system to warn users when this time is approaching. This is a very good option to enable on sensitive systems or those with many users.

Using Tools for Password Management

Most Linux distributions use shadow passwords by default, and for the most part, this chapter is written with the assumption that this feature is active. In addition to providing extra security by moving hashed passwords out of the world-readable /etc/passwd file and into the more secure /etc/shadow file, shadow passwords add extra account information.

One of the advantages of shadow passwords is that they support password aging and account expiration features. These features enable you to enforce password changes at regular intervals or to disable an account automatically after a specified period of time. You can enable these features and set the times using the chage command, which is described in more detail in Chapter 7.

The usermod utility, also described in Chapter 7, can be used to adjust some shadow password features, such as account expiration dates. The chage command is more thorough with respect to account security features, but usermod can adjust more nonsecurity account features.

Limiting *root* Access

Because root can do anything on a Linux computer, access to that account must of course be limited. On a system with a single administrator, this can be accomplished by having the administrator set a unique root password that nobody else knows. This user can then log in directly as root if needed.

Using *su*

The single system administrator just described can also use the su command to acquire root privileges. The su command's name stands for *switch user*, and it's used to switch to another user's account.

Typing **su** alone results in a prompt for the root password. If the user types that password correctly, the session effectively becomes a root session.

WARNING   If you just type **su** to access the root account, be aware that not everything may be set up correctly to perform tasks that require superuser privileges. It's better to type the command **su -** to switch to the root account. The dash (-) after the su command starts a new shell environment and executes the root's profile.

You can also type a username after su to acquire that user's privileges. When root does so, no password is required. This is sometimes handy for investigating problems reported by a single user.

To run a single program with root privileges, use -c to specify the program name. For example, type **su -c "lsof -i"** to run the lsof -i command as root.

Logging in directly as root is generally discouraged for several reasons: No record of who typed the password appears in log files; the root password can be intercepted in various ways; and if the user leaves the terminal, a passerby can hijack the computer. Using su is somewhat better than a direct login from a security point of view, because use of su generally leaves a trace in system logs of who became root.

Using *sudo*

A method of acquiring root access that is more secure than either direct logins or su is sudo. This program runs a single command as root; for instance, to run lsof -i as root, you type:

```
$ sudo lsof -i
[sudo] password for georgia:
```

In this example, the computer prompts for the *user's* (georgia's) password, not for the root password. The idea behind sudo is that you first configure the computer to accept certain users as sudo users. Those users may then use *their own* passwords to perform superuser tasks, even if those users don't have the root password.

All use of the sudo command is tracked. Pertinent data, such as who did what and when, is stored in the /var/log/secure file.

NOTE   Logging in as the root user can set up what is called a *repudiation environment*. A repudiation environment means that a person can deny actions. Therefore, if a system administrator uses the root account to perform some illegal or troublemaking activity, they can legally deny being responsible for that activity. Systems where every user has an account and password and no one can log into the root user's account sets up a *non-repudiation environment*. This means that actions are logged and responsibility for them cannot be easily denied. A non-repudiation environment can be created using sudo.

You can fine-tune what tasks users may perform using sudo. This is done via the /etc/sudoers configuration file. You must edit this configuration file via visudo, which is a variant of the vi editor (described in Chapter 5) that's used only to edit /etc/sudoers.

The /etc/sudoers file consists of two types of entries:

Aliases

User specifications

Aliases are basically variables. You can use them to define groups of commands, groups of users, and so on. User specifications link users to machines and commands (possibly using aliases for some or all options). Thus, you can configure sudoers such that georgia can run network programs with root privileges but not account maintenance tools, whereas henry can run account maintenance tools but not network programs.

Your default /etc/sudoers file probably includes several examples. Consider the following lines:

```
$ sudo cat /etc/sudoers
[sudo] password for Christine:

[...]
## Storage
Cmnd_Alias STORAGE = /sbin/fdisk, /sbin/sfdisk, /sbin/parted,[...]
#
## Processes
Cmnd_Alias PROCESSES = /bin/nice, /bin/kill, /usr/bin/kill,[...]
#
[...]
#
%sys ALL = STORAGE, PROCESSES
#
%disk ALL = STORAGE
#
%wheel ALL=(ALL) ALL
[...]
$
```

This example defines two command aliases, STORAGE and PROCESSES, each of which stands in for a set of commands. Users who are members of the sys group may use both sets of commands. Users who are members of the disk group may use the STORAGE commands but not the PROCESSES commands. Users who are members of the wheel group may use all commands, whether or not they're explicitly mentioned in /etc/sudoers.

WARNING   If you desire to set up a non-repudiation environment, be aware that some commands will need to be blocked within the /etc/sudoers file. For example, a user who is a member of the wheel group in the preceding /etc/sudoers file could type **sudo su -** at the command line. To prevent this from occurring, add the command you wish to block preceded by an exclamation point (!). However, once you add this blocked command, you must include all of the allowed commands. For example, the wheel group's record may now look like this:

%wheel ALL=(ALL) !/bin/su, /bin/, /sbin/, /usr/bin/, /usr/sbin/

Some distributions, such as Ubuntu, make heavy use of sudo. These distributions are designed to be administered exclusively via sudo, and they set up an /etc/sudoers file that provides at least one user with easy access to all system utilities. Other distributions don't rely on sudo this way, although you can tweak your sudo configuration to enable administration via sudo if appropriate.

Auditing User Access

There are various times you may need to view system user access. It could be that you are looking into a potential security break, performing an investigation for your company's HR department, determining if anyone is still logged on prior to a system shutdown, and so on. There are several tools available at the command line to conduct such audits.

Determining Who Is Logged On

For determining who is currently logged onto a system, there are two primary commands to use:

    who

    w

The who command simply shows you who is currently logged onto a system. It displays the username, their current terminal, and the time they logged into the system as follows:

```
$ who
Christine tty2          2015-11-10 11:53
Timothy    tty3         2015-11-10 12:33
Rich       tty4         2015-11-10 12:36
[...]
$
```

You can determine a great deal of additional information with the who command by using the -a option:

```
$ who -a
           system boot  2015-11-11 08:17
           run-level 5  2015-11-11 08:17
Christine + tty2         2015-11-11 11:53 00:38         1569
Timothy   + tty3         2015-11-11 12:33 00:41         1571
Rich      + tty4         2015-11-11 12:36 00:39         3086
LOGIN       tty5         2015-11-11 08:17               1576 id=5
LOGIN       tty6         2015-11-11 08:17               1578 id=6
[...]
$
```

The first line displayed shows when the system was booted. The second line shows the current system runlevel, which is 5. (See Chapter 5 for more information on runlevels.) The next several lines show what users are currently logged in, when they logged in, and their process ID (PID) numbers.

Finally, in the previous example, you can see the virtual console terminals that are not currently in use, such as tty5, and the PID for the program connected to that terminal. You can find out more about a particular program or logged-in user by using the ps command along with the listed PID. For example, you can see that the /sbin/mingetty program is handling the login screen at the tty5 virtual console terminal:

```
$ ps 1576
  PID TTY      STAT   TIME COMMAND
 1576 tty5     Ss+    0:00 /sbin/mingetty /dev/tty5
$
```

> The who command pulls its data from the /var/run/utmp or /run/utmp file, depending upon your distribution. To determine which file is used on your distribution by who, using superuser privileges, type **locate utmp** at the command line.

Though a much shorter command, by default, the w command shows a significant amount of information concerning logged-in users:

```
$ w
 13:24:25 up  5:07,  4 users,  load average: 0.00, 0.00, 0.00
USER      TTY      FROM            LOGIN@   IDLE   JCPU   PCPU   WHAT
Christin  tty2     -               11:53    48:00  1.83s  1.83s  -bash
Timothy   tty3     -               12:33    50:32  0.31s  0.31s  -bash
Rich      tty4     -               12:36    48:20  0.11s  0.11s  -bash
[...]
$
```

The w command shows not only who is logged into the system but also what they are doing as well as statistics concerning CPU usage. The JCPU column shows all of the CPU time used by any processes currently attached to a particular virtual console terminal. This time includes any currently running background jobs, but not previously run background jobs. The PCPU column shows all of the current CPU time consumed by the program listed in the WHAT column.

The w command uses the utmp file data for its display. Information stored in the /proc/ directory is used by the w command as well.

You can find out more about the w and who commands by looking through their man pages. While both the w and who commands are useful, they display only current information. If you need historical data on a particular user, there is a different command to use, as described in the next section.

Determining Last Access to the System

The last command can provide current and historical data concerning users logging into and out of your system. To display the information, simply type **last** at the command line. However, because there is potentially a great deal of information to display, it's a good idea to pipe the output into a pager, like less. Such a case is shown in Figure 10-1.

FIGURE 10.1   The last command output

```
Christin  tty2                          Wed Nov 12 08:10   still logged in
reboot    system boot  2.6.32-431.5.1.e Wed Nov 12 08:05 - 08:27  (00:21)
Christin  pts/0        192.168.56.1     Tue Nov 11 12:36 - 13:33  (00:57)
Rich      tty4                          Tue Nov 11 12:36 - down   (00:57)
Timothy   tty3                          Tue Nov 11 12:33 - down   (01:00)
Christin  tty2                          Tue Nov 11 11:53 - down   (01:40)
reboot    system boot  2.6.32-431.5.1.e Tue Nov 11 08:17 - 13:33  (05:16)
Christin  tty2                          Sat Nov  8 15:39 - down   (00:33)
Christin  pts/0        192.168.56.1     Sat Nov  8 15:12 - 16:12  (01:00)
reboot    system boot  2.6.32-431.5.1.e Sat Nov  8 14:38 - 16:12  (01:34)
Christin  pts/0        192.168.56.1     Fri Nov  7 13:16 - 13:38  (00:22)
```

The data displayed comes from the /var/log/wtmp file. The last command displays the newest data first. Therefore, you should see any users currently logged into the system, denoted by the still logged in tag. The date and time shown in each user record indicates when a user logged into the system and when they logged out. In some cases, a user was logged into the system when the system shut down, as indicated by the down keyword.

> Be aware that the /var/log/wtmp file may be rotated by the logrotate utility (see Chapter 7 for more information on logrotate). If you need to view older /var/log/wtmp file versions, you can use the -f option on the last command. For instance, if you rotate your wtmp file and an older version you want to view is named /var/log/wtmp.1, you should type **last -f /var/log/wtmp.1** at the command prompt.

If you want to view just a particular user's log in and out activities, you can pass the username as a parameter. For example, to see if anyone has been directly accessing the root account, enter the following:

```
$ last root
root     tty3                   Wed Nov 12 09:32 - 09:35  (00:02)
root     pts/0  192.168.56.1    Fri Nov  7 10:38 - 13:04  (02:25)
root     tty2                   Wed Oct 29 11:37 - down   (02:36)
root     tty3                   Fri Oct 10 08:03 - down   (02:20)
root     tty2                   Tue Sep 30 09:44 - down   (02:29)

wtmp begins Tue Mar 18 15:25:03 2015
$
```

Notice in the previous example that remote accesses are also logged, along with their source address (192.168.56.1). Also, you can see when the /var/log/wtmp file was started.

> Any attempts to use su - to log in as root are not recorded in these files. This is another reason the use of sudo should be employed to maintain a non-repudiation environment on your system.

Failed login attempts are stored in the /var/log/btmp file. To see any failed login attempts, you can also use the last command. Just add the -f option, as shown in this snipped example here:

```
$ sudo last -f /var/log/btmp
[sudo] password for Christine:
root     tty3              Wed Nov 12 09:35     gone - no logout
root     tty3              Wed Nov 12 09:35 - 09:35  (00:00)
[...]
btmp begins Sat Nov  8 15:11:24 2015
$
```

An easier way to display this information is to use the lastb command. The lastb command shows all of the failed login attempts and uses all of the same options as the last command. Here is a snipped example using lastb to display failed login attempts:

```
$ sudo lastb
[sudo] password for Christine:
root     tty3              Wed Nov 12 09:35 - 09:35  (00:00)
root     tty3              Wed Nov 12 09:35 - 09:35  (00:00)
[...]
btmp begins Sat Nov  8 15:11:24 2015
$
```

Notice that when using both the last command and the lastb command to display failed login attempts, you must have superuser privileges. This is due to the /var/log/btmp file being secured via permissions to keep attackers from changing failed login information as shown here:

```
$ ls -l /var/log/btmp
-rw-------. 1 root utmp 3840 Nov 12 09:35 /var/log/btmp
$
```

 Some distributions have the dump-utmp utility. If yours does, you can dump out any of the files covered in this last section in a human-readable format. This includes the utmp files, /var/log/wtmp files, and /var/log/btmp files. This tool is helpful in producing audit reports with shell scripts. To find out more about this utility, type **man dump-utmp** at the command prompt.

Another useful command in your auditing toolkit is the lastlog command. The last-log utility pulls data from the /var/log/lastlog file. You can determine when a particular user last logged into the system by adding the -u *username* option as shown here:

```
$ lastlog -u Christine
Username    Port    From       Latest
Christine   tty3               Wed Nov 12 10:20:36 -0500 2015
$
```

Be aware that if a particular user is logged into the system multiple times, lastlog will not display multiple login entries. It only shows the *last* time a user logged into the system.

It is helpful to view every account's /var/log/lastlog entry. You can use this as an auditing tool to determine if accounts that should not be logged into have been accessed. Here is a snipped example of this audit tool's display:

```
$ lastlog
Username        Port    From    Latest
root            tty3            Wed Nov 12 09:32:51 -0500 2015
[...]
sshd                            **Never logged in**
tcpdump                         **Never logged in**
Christine       tty3            Wed Nov 12 10:20:36 -0500 2015
sally                           **Never logged in**
Rich            tty4            Tue Nov 11 12:36:01 -0500 2015
Timothy         tty3            Tue Nov 11 12:33:08 -0500 2015
[...]
$
```

As you can see from the preceding example, the sshd account has never been logged into, and that is a good thing! All of the auditing tools covered in this section can help you keep an eye on your system to discover any potential security breaches. However, while seeing what happened in the past is helpful, it's even better to put limits in place to prevent bad things from happening in the future.

Setting Login, Process, and Memory Limits

Sometimes you may want to impose limits on how many times users may log in, how much CPU time they can consume, how much memory they can use, and so on. Imposing such limits is best done through a Pluggable Authentication Modules (PAM) module called pam_limits.

Most major Linux distributions use this module as part of their standard PAM configuration, so chances are you won't need to add it. However, you will still need to configure pam_limits. You do so by editing its configuration file, /etc/security/limits.conf. This file contains comments (denoted by a hash mark, #) and limit lines that consist of four fields:

domain type item value

Each of these fields specifies a particular type of information:

The Domain   The *domain* field describes the entity to which the limit applies. It can be a username; a group name, which takes the form @*groupname*; or an asterisk (*) wildcard, which matches everybody.

Hard or Soft Limits   The *type* field specifies the limit as hard or soft. A hard limit is imposed by the system administrator and cannot be exceeded under any circumstances, whereas a user may temporarily exceed a soft limit. You can also use a dash (-) to signify that a limit is both hard and soft.

The Limited Item   The *item* field specifies what type of item is being limited. Examples include core (the size of core files), data (the size of a program's data area), fsize (the size of files created by the user), nofile (the number of open data files), rss (the resident set size), stack (the stack size), cpu (the CPU time of a single process in minutes), nproc (the number of concurrent processes), maxlogins (the number of simultaneous logins), and priority (the process priority). The data, rss, and stack items all relate to memory consumed by a program. These and other measures of data capacity are measured in kilobytes.

The Value   The final field specifies the value that's to be applied to the limit.

As an example, consider a system on which certain users should be able to log in and perform a limited number of actions but not stay logged in indefinitely and consume vast amounts of CPU time. You can use a configuration like this one:

```
@limited  hard  cpu  2
```

This configuration applies a hard CPU limit of 2 minutes to the limited group. Members of this group can log in and run programs; however, if one of those programs consumes more than two minutes of CPU time, it will be terminated.

 CPU time and total system access time are two entirely different things. CPU time is calculated based on the amount of time the CPU is actively processing a user's data. Idle time (for instance, when a user's shell is active but no CPU-intensive tasks are running) doesn't count. Thus, a user can log in and remain logged in for hours even with a very low hard CPU time limit. This limit is intended to prevent problems caused by users who run very CPU-intensive programs on systems that shouldn't be used for such purposes.

Another way to set limits on system resource use is via the ulimit command. This command is a bash built-in command, so it affects only bash and programs launched from it. The ulimit syntax is as follows:

```
ulimit [options [limit]]
```

The options (*options*) define what is being limited:

Core File Limits   The -c option limits the size of *core dumps*, which are files created for debugging purposes in certain types of program crashes.

File Limits   The -f option limits the size of files that may be created by the shell, and -n limits the number of open file descriptors. (Most systems don't honor the -n limits, though.)

Process Limits   The -u option limits the number of processes a user may run, and -t limits the total CPU time in seconds.

Memory Limits   The -v option sets the total amount of virtual memory available to the shell, -s sets the maximum stack size, -m sets the maximum resident set size, -d limits programs' data set size, and -l sets the maximum size that may be locked into memory.

Hard and Soft Limits   The -H and -S options modify other options, causing them to be set as *hard* or *soft* limits, respectively. Hard limits may not be subsequently increased, but soft limits may be. If neither option is provided, ulimit sets both the hard and soft limits for the feature specified.

Current Settings   Passing -a causes ulimit to report its current settings.

The *limit* variable is typically a numeric value associated with the limit. The ulimit command is often found in system or user bash startup scripts, typically as ulimit -c 0, in order to prevent creation of core files, which can sometimes clutter a filesystem. If your users perform software development, you may want to ensure that you do *not* set this limit, or at least set it as a soft limit (as in ulimit -Sc 0) so that users may override it when necessary.

Because ulimit is a bash built-in command, its utility as a system security tool is limited. If users have access to GUI login tools or can log into the system in any way that bypasses bash (such as via SSH, depending on how it's configured), restrictions imposed by ulimit become meaningless. Thus you should treat ulimit as a way to prevent problems because of *accidental*, rather than intentional, abuse of the system.

One particular interesting limit involves the use of the /etc/nologin file. If this file is present, only root may log into the computer. Other users are shown the contents of this file when they attempt to log in.

In many respects, using /etc/nologin is like setting critical system limits to 0 for all other users. This file can be useful on dedicated server systems that have no regular console or remote shell users.

Locating SUID/SGID Files

Chapter 4, "Managing Files," describes the SUID and SGID bits. In brief, these are special flags that may be applied to executable program files. These flags cause Linux to treat the program as if it were run by the program file's owner (for SUID) or by the file's group (for SGID) rather than by the individual actually running the program. For instance, if a program's SUID bit is set and the program file is owned by bruce, the program, when run by anybody, will be able to access all of the files owned by bruce and otherwise behave as if bruce is running it.

The SUID and SGID bits are frequently associated with the root account in order to enable them to perform tasks that require special privilege. For instance, the passwd program (described in Chapter 7) is SUID root because only root may modify the Linux password database. Thus, for an ordinary user to change a password, some mechanism must exist to run a process as root. That mechanism, in the case of passwd, is the SUID bit.

The problem is that the SUID and SGID bits can be security risks. For instance, suppose the rm program's SUID bit was set. This program is normally owned by root, so setting the SUID bit on rm would mean that any user could delete *any* file on the computer! Although no Linux distribution sets the SUID bit on rm by default, the SUID bit can be set inappropriately or set by an attacker. For these reasons, you should periodically audit your system to find all of the SUID and SGID programs and, if appropriate, change their permission settings.

To do this, you can use the find command (see Chapter 4). In particular, you can use the -perm *mode* option, which searches for files with the specified permission mode. To search for SUID and SGID files, you should pass a *mode* value of +6000. The symbolic representation for both the SUID and SGID bits is 6000, and the plus sign (+) tells find to locate any file with any of the specified bits set. You may also want to pass the -type f option, which restricts the search to regular files. (Directories use the SUID and SGID bits differently, as described in Chapter 4.) Thus, to search the entire computer for SUID and SGID programs, you type this:

```
$ sudo find / -perm +6000 -type f
[sudo] password for Christine:
/lib64/dbus-1/dbus-daemon-launch-helper
/home/Christine/bigprogram.sh
/sbin/pam_timestamp_check
/sbin/netreport
/sbin/unix_chkpwd
[...]
$
```

You can search for SUID files alone by passing +4000 or -u=s. Also, you can search for SGID alone by passing +2000 or -g=s.

The result is a list of files, one per line, that have either the SUID or the SGID bits set. Programs that are likely to be present in this list include su, ping, mount, passwd, umount, and sudo. These programs all have a legitimate need to be so configured.

Most systems have additional SUID and SGID programs, some of which may seem trivial. If you have doubts about whether the program really needs SUID or SGID status, you should investigate further. Try verifying the package integrity using your package management tools and perform a Web search on the program name and *SUID* or *SGID*, as appropriate. You can also try changing the SUID status of the program using chmod, as described in Chapter 4, and see if it still works as it should when run by a normal user.

Programs that are SUID or SGID root, but shouldn't be, can be a sign of compromised system. Attackers might reconfigure programs this way in order to cause trouble more easily. Thus, if you find such programs, investigate the overall integrity of the system.

Configuring SSH

In the past, Telnet was the remote text-mode login protocol of choice on Linux and Unix systems. Unfortunately, Telnet is severely lacking in security features. Thus, in recent years SSH has grown in popularity, and it is now the preferred remote login tool. SSH can also handle file transfer tasks similar to those of FTP. For these reasons, knowing how to configure SSH can be very helpful. This task requires knowing a bit about SSH generally and about the SSH configuration files within Linux.

SSH is complex enough that only its basics are covered in this chapter. For more details, consult OpenSSH's documentation or a book on the topic, such as *SSH, The Secure Shell: The Definitive Guide, Second Edition*, by Daniel J. Barrett, Richard Silverman, and Robert G. Byrnes (O'Reilly, 2005) or *SSH Mastery: OpenSSH, PuTTY, Tunnels and Keys* (CreateSpace, 2012) by Michael W. Lucas.

Understanding SSH Basics

Linux supports remote login access through several different servers, including Telnet, Virtual Network Computing (VNC), and even X. Unfortunately most of these methods suffer from a major drawback: they transfer data over the network in an *unencrypted* form. This fact means that anybody who can monitor network traffic can easily snatch sensitive data, often including passwords. (VNC and a few other protocols encrypt passwords but not other data.)

This security limitation keeps these remote login tools from being highly useful. If using a remote access tool means that you'll be giving away sensitive data or compromising your entire computer, it's not a very useful tool.

Use these nonencrypting remote access tools at your own risk. It is better to not use them.

SSH was designed to close this potential major security hole by employing strong encryption techniques for all parts of the network connection. SSH encrypts the password exchange and all subsequent data transfers, making it a much safer protocol for remote access.

In addition to encryption, SSH provides file transfer features and the ability to *tunnel* other network protocols. This feature enables nonencrypted protocols to piggyback their data over an SSH connection, thus delivering SSH's encryption advantages to other protocols.

The main drawback of SSH is that the encryption and decryption consumes CPU time. This fact slows down SSH connections compared to those of direct connections and can degrade overall system performance. If you tunnel a protocol that transfers much more data, you may see a greater performance drop when using SSH. However, the improved security is generally worth the slight speed cost.

Several SSH servers are available for Linux, but the most popular by far is the OpenSSH server (www.openssh.org). This program was one of the first open source implementations of the SSH protocol. OpenSSH ships with most Linux distributions.

OpenSSH may be launched either via the xinetd super daemon or via a startup script. Most distributions deliver suitable startup scripts with their SSH packages.

If you make changes to your SSH configuration, you may need to pass the reload or restart option to the startup script, as in /etc/init.d/sshd reload. (Chapter 5 covers startup scripts in more detail.) However it's launched, the OpenSSH server binary name is sshd.

Setting SSH Options

For the most part, SSH works reasonably well when it's first installed, so you may not need to make any changes to its configuration. If you do need to make changes, though, these are mostly handled through the main SSH configuration file, /etc/ssh/sshd_config. You can also edit some additional files to limit access to the SSH server or to change how SSH manages the login process.

Configuring Basic SSH Features

The /etc/ssh/sshd_config file consists mainly of option lines that take the following form:

    option value

 Don't confuse the sshd_config file with the ssh_config file. The former controls the OpenSSH server, whereas the latter controls the SSH client program, ssh.

In addition to configuration lines, the sshd_config file holds comments, which are denoted by hash marks (#). Most sample configuration files include a large number of SSH options that are commented out. These lines specify the default values, so removing a line's hash mark without otherwise changing the value will have no effect.

Most options' default values are suitable for most systems. The following list includes some that you may want to check and, perhaps, change:

Protocol This option specifies the protocol levels OpenSSH understands. Possible values are 1 and 2. You can configure OpenSSH to support both protocols by separating them by a comma, as in 1,2 or 2,1, which are equivalent. OpenSSH protocol level 1 is no longer considered secure. Therefore, the safest configuration is to set Protocol 2. This limits the server's ability to communicate with older clients, though.

PermitRootLogin By default, this option is set to yes, which enables OpenSSH to accept direct logins by root. This is safer than a similar configuration under Telnet, but for a bit of added security, set this value to no. The result will be that anybody wanting to perform remote work using superuser privileges will need first to log in as an ordinary user.

X11Forwarding This option specifies whether OpenSSH's X tunneling features should be active. If you want to enable remote users to run GUI programs via SSH, you must set this option to yes. Doing so can slightly degrade security of the client's X display, though, depending on certain other options, hence the conservative default value of no.

For information about additional options, consult the man page for sshd_config. If you make changes to the SSH configuration, remember to restart it using the server's startup script.

Managing SSH Keys

Part of SSH's security involves *encryption keys*. Each server system and each user has a unique number, or key, for identification purposes. In fact, SSH uses a security system that involves two keys: a *public key* and a *private key*. These two keys are mathematically linked in such a way that data encrypted with a particular *public* key may be decrypted only with the matching *private* key.

When establishing an SSH connection, each side sends its public key to the other. Thereafter, each side encrypts data with the other side's public key, ensuring that only the intended recipient can decrypt the data. In practice, this is just the first step of the process, but it's critical. What's more, SSH clients typically retain the public keys of servers they've contacted. This enables them to spot changes to a public key. Such changes can be signs of tampering, so if a client detects such a change, it will warn its user of this fact.

Most OpenSSH server startup scripts include code that looks for stored public and private keys and, if they're not present, generates them. In total, four to six keys are needed: public and private keys for two or three encryption tools that SSH supports. These keys are normally stored in /etc/ssh and are called ssh_host_rsa_key and ssh_host_dsa_key for private keys, depending on the encryption algorithm used. For public keys, the same filenames are used, except a .pub filename extension is added to the file's name. Some systems also add ssh_host_rsa1_key and its associated public key.

If your system doesn't have these keys and you can't get the SSH server to start up, you can try generating the keys with the following ssh-keygen commands:

```
# ssh-keygen -q -t rsa1 -f /etc/ssh/ssh_host_key -C '' -N ''
# ssh-keygen -q -t rsa -f /etc/ssh/ssh_host_rsa_key -C '' -N ''
# ssh-keygen -q -t dsa -f /etc/ssh/ssh_host_dsa_key -C '' -N ''
```

Each of these commands generates both a private key (named in the -f parameter) and a public key (with the same name but with .pub appended).

Don't run these ssh-keygen commands if the SSH key files already exist! Replacing the working files will cause clients who've already connected to the SSH server to complain about the changed keys and possibly refuse to establish a connection.

> Be sure the *private* keys are suitably protected; if an intruder obtains one of these keys, the intruder can impersonate your system. Typically, these files should have 0600 (-rw------) permissions and be owned by root. The *public* key files (with .pub filename extensions) should be readable by all users, though.

When you configure a client system, you may want to consider creating a global cache of host keys. As already noted, the ssh program records host keys for each individual user. (It stores these in the ~/.ssh/known_hosts file.) When you set up the client, you can populate the global ssh_known_hosts file, which is normally stored in /etc or /etc/ssh. Doing so ensures that the public key list is as accurate as the sources you use to populate the global file. It also eliminates confirmation messages when users first connect to the hosts whose keys you've selected to include in the global file.

How do you create this file? One simple way is to copy the file from a user account that's been used to connect to the servers you want to include, as shown here:

```
$ sudo cp /home/Rich/.ssh/known_hosts  /etc/ssh/ssh_known_hosts
[sudo] password for Christine:
$
```

> In the past, you could review SSH's known hosts file in a text editor since it's a text-mode file. Now OpenSSH v4.0 and newer versions support hashing this file's data. When this feature is enabled, the information is *hashed* and stored. The idea is that you'll still be able to authenticate SSH servers to which you connect because a hash of the typed hostname will match a hash of the stored hostname. However, if an attacker steals your known hosts file, the attacker will be unable to determine the identities of the computers to which you've been connecting. An unfortunate side effect of this hashing is that you can't tell what servers it describes yourself.

Controlling SSH Access

You can limit who may access an SSH server in various ways. The most obvious and basic method is via password authentication. The usual SSH authentication method is to employ a username and password, much as Telnet does. The ssh client program sends the username automatically or as part of the command line. Therefore, you won't see a username prompt when logging in via ssh, as shown in the example here:

```
$ ssh Christine@192.168.56.101
Christine@192.168.56.101's password:
Last login: Wed Nov 12 10:20:36 2015
$
```

The ssh command syntax requires the username to be placed before the @ symbol, as shown in the previous example. After the @ symbol, the remote host's IP address or name is required. Once the connection is established, the username's password must be entered before access to the remote system is allowed.

Beyond password authentication, SSH supports several other types of limitations:

TCP Wrappers   If you run SSH from a super server or if the server was compiled with TCP wrappers support, you can use the /etc/hosts.allow and /etc/hosts.deny files to limit access by IP address. Note that if you launch SSH via a system startup script, this approach works only if the server was compiled to support it. This support may or may not be present in your distribution's standard SSH package.

Firewalls   As with all servers, you can restrict access by using a firewall. SSH uses TCP port 22. Technically, this isn't an SSH feature, but it's certainly useful for protecting an SSH server.

/etc/nologin   If this file is present, SSH honors it. As described earlier, this file's presence means that only root may log in. When a non-root user tries to log in locally, the file's contents are displayed as an error message. However, OpenSSH doesn't do this.

Copying Files via SSH

Besides remote login access, SSH includes a file-copying command too: scp. This command works much like the cp command for copying files locally. However, you must specify the target computer, and optionally the username, just before the target filename. For instance, to copy the file masterpiece.c to the lisa account on leonardo.example.com, you would type this:

```
$ scp masterpiece.c lisa@leonardo.example.com:
$
```

The colon (:) that terminates this command is extremely important! If you omit it, you'll find that scp works like cp, and you'll end up with a file called lisa@leonardo.example .com on the original system.

If you want to rename the file, you can do so by including the new name following the colon. Likewise, you can place the file in a particular directory in the same way, as follows:

```
$ scp masterpiece.c lisa@leonardo.example.com:~/art/mona.c
$
```

This example copies masterpiece.c to the ~/art directory on the target computer and renames it mona.c. If the specified directory doesn't exist, an error results and the file is not transferred. If you specify a directory *without* a trailing slash or filename and you mistype the directory name, scp will copy the file and rename it to your mistyped directory name. (scp works just like cp in this respect.)

Configuring Logins without Passwords

If you use SSH a lot or if you use it in automated tools, you'll no doubt become annoyed by the need to type a password with every connection. There is a way around this requirement: You can set up the SSH client with keys and give the client's public key to the server computer. With this configuration, the SSH client computer can identify itself, possibly obviating the need for you to type a password.

WARNING   Configuring SSH to operate without the use of passwords is convenient, but it does increase security risks. If somebody you don't trust ever gains access to your account on the SSH client system, that person will be able to log into the SSH server system as you without the benefit of your password. Thus, you should create a password-less login only from a client that's very well protected, if at all. Configuring access to the root account in this way is particularly risky!

To configure SSH not to require a password, follow these steps:

1. Log into the SSH client system as the user who will be performing remote access.

2. Type the following command to generate a version 2 SSH key:

```
$ ssh-keygen -q -t rsa -f ~/.ssh/id_rsa -C '' -N ''
$
```

NOTE   Step 2 generates a version 2 key. You can instead generate a version 1 key by typing **ssh-keygen -q -t dsa -f ~/.ssh/id_dsa -C '' -N ''**. This generates id_dsa and id_dsa.pub files. This procedure is *not* recommended because SSH version 1 is not as secure as version 2. However, these key files are listed in the certification objectives.

3. Step 2 generates two files: id_rsa and id_rsa.pub. Transfer the second of these files to the SSH server computer in any way that's convenient—via a USB flash drive, by using scp, or by any other means. Copy the file under a temporary name, such as temp.rsa.

4. Log into the SSH server system. If you use SSH, you'll need to type your password.

5. Add the contents of the file that you've just transferred to the end of the ~/.ssh/authorized_keys file. (This file is sometimes called ~/.ssh/authorized_keys2, so you should check to see which is present. If neither is present, you may need to experiment.) Typing **cat ~/temp.rsa >> ~/.ssh/authorized_keys** should do this job, if you stored the original file as ~/temp.rsa.

6. On some systems, you may need to modify permissions on the ~/.ssh/authorized_keys file and on the directories leading to it. The authorized_keys file may require 0600 permissions, and you may need to remove write permissions for any but the account's owner on your home directory and on the ~/.ssh directory.

If you now log out of the SSH server system and try to log in again via SSH from the client, you shouldn't be prompted for a password; the two computers handle the authentication automatically.

If this doesn't work, chances are the ~/.ssh/authorized_keys file needs another name, as described earlier. You may also want to check that the file includes a line matching the contents of the original public-key file on the client. Some older clients may require you to specify that you use version 2 of the SSH protocol by including the -2 option:

```
$ ssh -2 server
```

Using *ssh-agent*

Another SSH authentication option is to use the ssh-agent program. This program requires a password to initiate connections, so it's more secure than configuring logins without passwords; however, ssh-agent remembers your password, so you need to type it only once per local session. To use ssh-agent, follow these steps:

1. Follow the procedure for enabling no-password logins described in "Configuring Logins without Passwords," but with one change: Omit the -N '' option from the ssh-keygen command in step 2. You'll be asked for a passphrase at this step. This passphrase will be your key for all SSH logins managed via ssh-agent.

2. On the SSH client system, type **ssh-agent /bin/bash**. This launches ssh-agent, which in turn launches bash. You'll use this bash session for subsequent SSH logins.

3. In your new shell, type **ssh-add ~/.ssh/id_rsa**. This adds your RSA key to the set that's managed by ssh-agent. You'll be asked to type your SSH passphrase at this time.

From this point on, whenever you use SSH to connect to a remote system to which you've given your public key, you won't need to type a password. You *will*, however, have to repeat steps 2 and 3 whenever you log out, and the benefits will accrue only to the shell launched in step 2 or any shells that you launch from that one.

If you make heavy use of this facility, you can insert ssh-agent into your normal login procedure. For instance, you can edit /etc/passwd so that ssh-agent /bin/bash is your login shell. For a GUI login, you can rename your normal GUI login script (for instance, change ~/.xsession to ~/.xsession-nossh) and create a new GUI login script that calls ssh-agent with the renamed script as its parameter. Either action inserts ssh-agent at the root of your user process tree so that any call to SSH uses ssh-agent.

Using SSH Login Scripts

Ordinarily, an SSH text-mode login session runs the user's configured shell, which runs the shell's defined login scripts. The OpenSSH server also supports its own login script, sshrc (normally stored in /etc or /etc/ssh). The OpenSSH server runs this script using /bin/sh, which is normally a symbolic link to bash, so you can treat it as an ordinary bash script.

Setting Up SSH Port Tunnels

SSH has the ability to extend its encryption capabilities to other protocols, but doing so requires extra configuration. The way this is done is known as *tunneling*. Chapter 6 described a special type of SSH tunneling involving X, but the process can work for other protocols.

Figure 10.2 illustrates the basic idea behind an SSH tunnel. The server computer runs two server programs: a server for the tunneled protocol (Figure 10.2 uses the Internet Mail Access Protocol, IMAP, as an example) and an SSH server. The client computer also runs two clients: one for the tunneled protocol and one for SSH. The SSH client also listens for connections for the tunneled protocol; it's effectively both a client and a server. When the SSH client receives a connection from the tunneled protocol's client, the result is that the tunneled protocol's connection is encrypted using SSH, tunneled to the SSH server, and then directed to the target server. Thus, data passes over the network in encrypted form, even if the target protocol doesn't support encryption!

FIGURE 10.2   An SSH tunnel extends SSH's encryption benefits to other protocols.

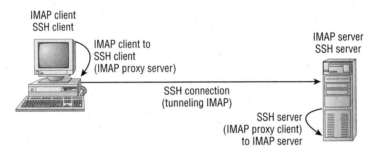

Of course, all of this requires special configuration. The default configuration on the server enables tunneling, but to be sure, check the /etc/ssh/sshd_config file on the server for the following option:

```
AllowTcpForwarding no
```

If this line is present, change no to yes. If it's not present or if it's already set to yes, you shouldn't need to change your SSH server configuration.

On the client side, you must establish a special SSH connection to the server computer. You do this with the normal ssh client program, but you must pass it several parameters. An example will help illustrate this use of ssh:

```
$ sudo ssh -N -f -L 142:mail.luna.edu:143 benf@mail.luna.edu
$
```

The -N and -f options tell ssh not to execute a remote command and to execute in the background *after* asking for a password, respectively. These options are necessary to create a tunnel.

The -L option specifies the local port on which to listen, the remote computer to which to connect, and the port on the remote computer to which to connect. This example listens on the local port 142 and connects to port 143 on mail.luna.edu.

The final parameter (benf@mail.luna.edu in this example) is the remote username and computer to which the tunnel goes. Note that this computer need not be the same as the target system specified via -L.

> If you want SSH on the client system to listen to a privileged port (that is, one numbered below 1024), you must execute the ssh program as root, as shown in the preceding example. If listening to a nonprivileged port is acceptable, the ssh client can be run as a normal user.

With the tunnel established, you can use the client program to connect to the local port specified by the first number in the -L parameter (port 142 in the preceding example). For instance, this example is intended to forward IMAP traffic, so you'd configure a mail reader on the client to retrieve IMAP email from port 142 on localhost. When the email reader does this, SSH kicks in and forwards traffic to the SSH server, which then passes the data on to the SSH server computer's local port 143, which is presumably running the real IMAP server.

All of this is hidden from the email reader program. As far as the reader program is concerned, it is retrieving email from a local IMAP server.

Preventing SSH Security Problems

SSH is intended to solve security problems rather than create them. Indeed, on the whole, using SSH is superior to using Telnet for remote logins, and SSH can also take over FTP-like functions and tunnel other protocols. Thus, SSH is a big security plus compared to using less-secure tools.

Like all servers, though, SSH can be a security liability if it's run unnecessarily or inappropriately. Ideally, you should configure SSH to accept *only* protocol level 2 connections and to refuse direct root logins. If X forwarding is unnecessary, you should disable this feature. If possible, use TCP wrappers or a firewall to limit the machines that can contact an SSH server. As with all servers, you should keep SSH up to date; there's always the possibility of a bug causing problems.

You should consider whether you really need a remote text-mode login server. Such a server can be a great convenience—often enough to justify the modest risk involved. For extremely high-security systems, though, using the computer exclusively from the console may be an appropriate approach to security.

One unusual security issue with SSH is its keys. As noted earlier, the private-key files are extremely sensitive and should be protected from prying eyes. Remember to protect the backups of these files as well. Protect system backup files as securely as you would the originals.

Using GPG

SSH is designed to encrypt interactive login sessions and file transfers. Sometimes, though, another type of encryption is desirable: You may want to encrypt messages sent via email or files sent to another person via some other means. Email was never designed as a secure data transfer tool, and most email messages pass through several email servers and network routers. A compromise at any one of these points enables an attacker to look at email traffic and extract sensitive data. Encrypting your email keeps such details private.

The usual tool for encrypting email is the GNU Privacy Guard package (GPG or GnuPG, www.gnupg.org). This package is an open-source reimplementation of the proprietary Pretty Good Privacy (PGP). In addition to encrypting entire messages, GPG enables you to "sign" messages digitally.

Generating Keys

To begin using GPG, if your distribution does not install the GPG software package by default, you will need to install the software (see Chapter 2). Chances are that if it's not installed by default, your distribution does include it in its repositories.

The next step is to generate keys. GPG keys are conceptually similar to SSH keys: You need a private key (aka a secret key) and a public key. As the names imply, the private key is kept private, but the public key is publicly available. You can sign your messages with your private key, and readers can verify it with your public key. Also, you can encrypt a message with another user's public key, and it can be decrypted only with that user's private key.

To generate keys, you use the gpg program with its --gen-key option:

```
$ gpg --gen-key
```

The program will ask you a series of questions. In most cases, answering with the defaults should work well, although you may have to type in your full name and email address. The keys are stored in a *keyring* (a file that holds keys) in the ~/.gnupg directory.

One question that you are asked when generating keys for gpg is the key size. Generally, the larger the key size, the more secure the encryption. Pick a key size that is at least 2,048 bits or larger.

Once you've generated your keys, you can *export* your public key:

```
$ gpg --export name > gpg.pub
```

This command saves the public key associated with *name* in the file gpg.pub. You can use your email address as *name*. If you create additional public keys or add others' public keys to your keyring, you specify those keys' names to export those keys.

After exporting your public key to a file, you can then make your public key available to others so that they may encrypt files to be sent to you or verify your signed messages. Adding the --armor option to the gpg --export command produces ASCII output, which may be preferable if you intend to email the key file. You can make the file accessible on your website, transfer it as an email attachment, or distribute it in various other ways.

Some distributions use gpg2 instead of the command gpg. If you have gpg2, you can use the same options as gpg. However, be sure to read through the gpg2 man pages. You may find that you want to install gpg alongside the gpg2 package.

One important method of distributing your public key is via a *keyserver*. This is a network server that functions much like a keyring. To send your public key to a keyserver, you can use the `--keyserver` *hostname* and `--send-keys` *keyname* options to gpg, as follows:

```
$ gpg --keyserver pgp.mit.edu --send-keys jennie@luna.edu
```

This example sends the public key for jennie@luna.edu from your public keyring to the server at pgp.mit.edu. Thereafter, anybody who wants to can retrieve the key from that server. The pgp.mit.edu server is a popular site for hosting PGP public keys.

Importing Keys

To encrypt a file you send to others, you must obtain their public keys. Ask your correspondents how to obtain them. Once you've done so, you can add their keys to your keyring (that is, the set of keys GPG maintains):

```
$ gpg --import filename
```

This command adds *filename* to your set of public keys belonging to other people.

WARNING   Although public keys are, by definition, public, there are security concerns relating to them. Specifically, you should be sure to use a *legitimate* public key. Hypothetically, a troublemaker could publish a fake public key in order to obtain sensitive communications or fake a signed email. For instance, George might distribute a fake GPG public key that claimed to be from Harold. George could then either sign messages claiming to be from Harold or intercept email sent to Harold that was encrypted using the fake key. Thus, you should use a communication method that is as secure as possible to distribute your public key and to receive public keys from others.

Once you've created your own key and, perhaps, imported keys from others, you can see what keys are available by using the `--list-keys` option to gpg:

```
$ gpg --list-keys
/home/gjones/.gnupg/pubring.gpg
--------------------------------
pub   1024D/190EDB2E 2015-09-05
uid                  George A. Jones <gjones@example.com>
sub   2048g/0D657AC8 2015-09-05
pub   1024D/A8B2061A 2015-09-05
uid                  Jennie Martin <jennie@luna.edu>
sub   2048g/4F33EF6B 2015-09-05
```

The uid lines contain identifiers that you'll use when encrypting or decrypting data, so you should pay particular attention to that information.

Cryptoparties are a popular way to exchange public keys. A group of friends gather together for an evening, each bringing a flash drive containing their own public key. One friend also brings a computer. The friends use the computer to swap public keys. At the end of the evening, the friends have had a good time socializing and get to take home their flash drives with everyone's public keys on it.

Revoking a Key

Sometimes, you might have cause to revoke a public key. For instance, suppose that you've stored a copy of your private key on a laptop computer and that laptop is stolen, or perhaps some employees have left your organization and you no longer want those individuals to be able to use the keys associated with their employee accounts. To revoke a key, you use the --gen-revoke *keyname* option to gpg:

```
$ gpg --gen-revoke jennie@luna.edu
```

The program asks you to answer a few questions, such as the reason for revoking the key. It then generates a key block, such as the following:

```
-----BEGIN PGP PUBLIC KEY BLOCK-----Version: GnuPG v2.0.19 (GNU/Linux)Comment:
A revocation certificate should follow
iEwEIBECAAwFAlBPvbkFHQBG28bACgkQbBimvBMO2y4uzwCeQiLkZx8jl2
jk+ hn0OKUl3EznmBQAn2WvtuQW+AP6wlvOvNU/qYi8a7t8=s0/s
-----END PGP PUBLIC KEY BLOCK-----
```

You should copy this text into a file (say, revocation.gpg) and import the file to your keyring:

```
$ gpg --import revocation.gpg
```

If you've distributed public keys associated with the revoked key, you should distribute this revocation too. If you've sent your public keys to a GPG keyserver, you can pass your revocation along in the same way that you sent your original public key:

```
$ gpg --keyserver pgp.mit.edu --send-keys jennie@luna.edu
```

Once this is done, you can generate and distribute a new set of keys, if desired.

Encrypting and Decrypting Data

To encrypt data, you use gpg with its --out and --encrypt options and, optionally, --recipient and --armor:

```
$ gpg --out encrypted-file --recipient uid --armor --encrypt original-file
```

You can use the UID from a gpg --list-keys output, or just the email address portion, as the *uid* in this command. If you haven't signed the recipient's key, you'll have to verify that you want to use that key. The result is a new file, *encrypted-file*, which holds an encrypted version of *original-file*.

If you omit the --armor option, the resulting file is a binary file. To send the binary file through email, you'll need to send it as an attachment. If you include the --armor option, the output is ASCII, so you can cut and paste the encrypted message into an email or send it as an attachment.

If you receive a message or file that was encrypted with your public key, you can reverse the encryption by using the --decrypt option:

```
$ gpg --out decrypted-file --decrypt encrypted-file
```

You'll be asked to enter your passphrase. The result should be a decrypted version of the original file.

In practice, GPG can be even easier to use than this description may make you think. GPG is primarily used to secure and verify email, so most Linux email clients provide GPG interfaces. These options call gpg with appropriate options to encrypt, sign, or decrypt messages. Details vary from one email client to another, so you should consult your email client's documentation for details.

Signing Messages and Verifying Signatures

As noted earlier, GPG can be used to sign messages so that recipients know that they come from you. To do so, use the --sign or --clearsign option to gpg:

```
$ gpg --clearsign original-file
```

The --sign option creates a new file with the same name as the original, but with .gpg appended to the filename. This file is encrypted using your private key so that it may be decrypted only with your public key. This means that anybody with your public key may read the message, and anybody who can read it knows that it's from you.

The --clearsign option works similarly, but it leaves the message text unencrypted and only adds an encrypted signature that can be verified by using your public key. The --clearsign option creates a file with a name that ends in .asc.

If you receive a signed message, you can verify the signature using the --verify option to gpg:

```
$ gpg --verify received-file
```

If any of the keys in your keyring can decode the message or verify the signature, gpg displays a Good signature message. To read a message that was encrypted via the --sign option, you must decrypt the message via the --decrypt option, as described earlier.

Summary

Maintaining system security is both important and time-consuming. A great deal of security emphasis is on network security. To achieve a high level of network security, properly configuring the server's super daemon and disabling unused servers goes a long way. Attending to passwords and performing miscellaneous tasks to keep your local accounts from becoming security risks are also important security tasks.

Encryption is a hot topic in security. SSH is a protocol and tool that can handle many network encryption tasks by encrypting two-way connections between computers. Typically used as a remote login protocol, SSH can also be used to transfer files or encrypt other protocols. When you want to encrypt data sent to another individual via a tool such as email, you can do so with the help of GPG. This package enables you to encrypt individual files, which can then be attached to or embedded in email messages and decrypted by the recipient.

Exam Essentials

Identify the purpose of a super server.   Super servers (also called super daemons), such as inetd and xinetd, manage incoming network connections for multiple servers. They can add security and convenience features, and they can help to minimize the memory load imposed by seldom-accessed servers.

Explain the function of super server port access controls.   Super servers or programs called by them (such as TCP wrappers) can restrict access to ports for the servers they manage. These restrictions occur at a higher level than a firewall's restrictions, and they apply only to the servers managed by the super server.

Summarize the tools that you can use to identify the servers running on a computer. The netstat and lsof programs both provide options to list all (or a subset of) the open network connections as well as programs that are listening for connections. Remote network scanners, such as Nmap, can probe another computer for open network ports. The fuser program can determine the processes currently using a particular network port. Perusal of local configuration files can also provide clues as to what's running on a computer.

Describe why SUID and SGID programs are potentially risky.   The set user ID (SUID) and set group ID (SGID) bits tell Linux to run the program as the user or group that owns the file. This is particularly risky when root owns the program file because it essentially elevates all users to root for the purposes of running the file, making bugs in the program more dangerous and raising the possibility of a clever user abusing the program to acquire full root privileges or otherwise wreaking havoc.

Explain why shadow passwords are important.   Shadow passwords store password hashes in a file that can't be read by ordinary users, thus making it harder for attackers on the local system to read the hashed passwords and use brute-force attacks to discover other users' passwords. Modern Linux distributions use shadow passwords by default.

Explain how to generate a good password.   Ideally, passwords should be random. Failing that, one good approach is to generate a base that's hard to guess and then modify it by adding digits and punctuation, changing the case of some characters, changing letter order, and significantly increasing the length of the password (even with repeated characters).

Explain why SSH is the preferred remote text-mode login tool.   The Secure Shell (SSH) protocol provides encryption for all traffic, including both the password exchange and all subsequent data exchanges, whereas older tools, such as Telnet, do not. This makes SSH much safer for the exchange of sensitive data, particularly over untrusted networks such as the Internet.

Identify the most important SSH configuration file.   The SSH server is controlled through the /etc/ssh/sshd_config file. The SSH client configuration file is /etc/ssh/ssh_config; don't confuse the two.

Describe the SSH public and private key files   These keys are normally stored in the /etc/ssh/ directory. Private key files are called ssh_host_rsa_key, ssh_host_rsa1_key, and ssh_host_dsa_key, depending on the encryption algorithm used. Public key files have the same filenames as their private keys, except a .pub filename extension is added.

Describe the function of GPG.   GPG enables public-key encryption of individual files or email messages. You can use GPG to encrypt sensitive data for transmission over email or other insecure means.

Review Questions

1. Typing **lsof -i | grep LISTEN** as root produces three lines of output, corresponding to the sendmail, sshd, and proftpd servers. What can you conclude about the security of this system?

    A. Everything is OK; the presence of sshd ensures that data are being encrypted via SSH.

    B. The sendmail and sshd servers are OK, but the FTP protocol used by proftpd is insecure and should never be used.

    C. The sendmail server should be replaced by Postfix or qmail for improved security, but sshd and proftpd are fine.

    D. Because sendmail and proftpd both use unencrypted text-mode data transfers, neither is appropriate on a network-connected computer.

    E. No conclusion can be drawn without further information; the listed servers may or may not be appropriate or authentic.

2. As part of a security audit, you plan to use Nmap to check all of the computers on your network for unnecessary servers. Which of the following tasks should you do prior to running your Nmap check?

    A. Back up /etc/passwd on the target systems to eliminate the possibility of it being damaged.

    B. Obtain the root passwords to the target systems so that you can properly configure them to accept the Nmap probes.

    C. Obtain written permission from your boss to perform the Nmap sweep.

    D. Configure /etc/sudoers on the computer you intend to use for the sweep, to give yourself the ability to run Nmap.

    E. Disable any firewall between the computer that's running Nmap and the servers you intend to scan.

3. Your login server is using PAM, and you want to limit users' access to system resources. Which configuration file will you need to edit?

    A. /etc/limits.conf

    B. /etc/pam/limits.conf

    C. /etc/security/limits.conf

    D. /etc/security/pam/limits.conf

    E. /usr/local/limits.conf

4. Which of the following tools might you use to check for open ports on a local computer? (Select three.)

    A. Nmap

    B. netstat

    C. lsof

    D. `portmap`

    E. `services`

5. Which of the following commands will locate all of the program files on a computer on which the SUID bit is set?

    A. `find / -type SUID`

    B. `find / -perm +4000 -type f`

    C. `find / -perm +SUID -type f`

    D. `find / -type +4000`

    E. `find / -suid`

6. The `/etc/sudoers` file on a computer includes the following line. What is its effect?

`%admin ALL=(ALL) ALL`

    A. Members of the `admin` group may run all programs with `root` privileges by using `sudo`.

    B. Users in the `admin` user alias, defined earlier in the file, may run all programs with `root` privileges by using `sudo`.

    C. The `admin` user alias is defined to include all users on the system.

    D. The `admin` command alias is defined to include all commands.

    E. The user `admin` may run all programs on the computer as `root` by using `sudo`.

7. Which command would you type, as `root`, to discover all the open network connections on a Linux computer?

    A. `lsof -c a`

    B. `netstat -ap`

    C. `ifconfig eth0`

    D. `nmap -sT localhost`

    E. `top -net`

8. A server/computer combination appears in both `hosts.allow` and `hosts.deny`. What's the result of this configuration when TCP wrappers runs?

    A. TCP wrappers refuses to run and logs an error in `/var/log/messages`.

    B. The system's administrator is paged to decide whether to allow access.

    C. `hosts.deny` takes precedence; the client is denied access to the server.

    D. `hosts.allow` takes precedence; the client is granted access to the server.

    E. The client is granted access to the server *if* no other client is currently accessing it.

9. When is the `bind` option of `xinetd` most useful?

    A. When you want to run two servers on one port

    B. When you want to specify computers by name rather than IP address

    C. When `xinetd` is running on a system with two network interfaces

D. When resolving conflicts between different servers

E. When xinetd manages a DNS server program

10. You've discovered that the Waiter program (a network server) is running inappropriately on your computer. You therefore locate its startup script and shut it down by removing that script. How can you further reduce the risk that outsiders will abuse the Waiter program? (Select two.)

A. By blocking the Waiter program's port using a firewall rule

B. By reading the Waiter program's documentation to learn how to run it in stealth mode

C. By tunneling the Waiter program's port through SSH

D. By uninstalling the Waiter package

E. By uninstalling any clients associated with Waiter from the server computer

11. You want to use xinetd access controls to limit who may access a server that's launched via xinetd. Specifically, only users on the 192.168.7.0/24 network block should be able to use that server. How may you do this?

A. Enter **hosts_allowed = 192.168.7.0/24** in the /etc/xinetd.conf configuration file for the server in question.

B. Enter **only_from = 192.168.7.0/24** in the /etc/xinetd.conf configuration file for the server in question.

C. Enter **server : 192.168.7.**, where *server* is the server's name, in the /etc/hosts.allow file.

D. Enter **server : 192.168.7.**, where *server* is the server's name, in the /etc/hosts.deny file.

E. Type **iptables -L 192.168.7.0** to enable only users of 192.168.7.0/24 to access the server.

12. Of the following, which is the best password?

A. Odysseus

B. iA710ci^My~~~~~~

C. pickettomato

D. Denver2Colorado

E. 123456

13. Which of the following types of attacks involves sending bogus email to lure unsuspecting individuals into divulging sensitive financial or other information?

A. Phishing

B. Script kiddies

C. Spoofing

D. Ensnaring

E. Hacking

14. Ordinary users report being unable to log onto a computer, but root has no problems doing so. What might you check to explain this situation?

    A. A misbehaving syslogd daemon

    B. A login process that's running as root

    C. The presence of an /etc/nologin file

    D. The presence of an SUID bit on /bin/login

    E. Inappropriate use of shadow passwords

15. Which servers might you consider retiring after activating an SSH server? (Select two.)

    A. SMTP

    B. Telnet

    C. FTP

    D. NTP

    E. Samba

16. You find that the ssh_host_dsa_key file in /etc/ssh has 0666 (-rw-rw-rw-) permissions. Your SSH server has been in operation for several months. Should you be concerned?

    A. Yes

    B. No

    C. Only if the ssh_host_dsa_key.pub file is also world-readable

    D. Only if you're launching SSH from a super server

    E. Only if you're using a laptop computer

17. For best SSH server security, how should you set the Protocol option in /etc/ssh/sshd_config?

    A. Protocol 1

    B. Protocol 2

    C. Protocol 1,2

    D. Protocol 2,1

    E. Protocol *

18. Why is it unwise to allow root to log on directly using SSH?

    A. Disallowing direct root access means that the SSH server may be run by a non-root user, improving security.

    B. The root password should never be sent over a network connection; allowing root logins in this way is inviting disaster.

    C. SSH stores all login information, including passwords, in a publicly readable file.

    D. When logged on using SSH, root's commands can be easily intercepted and duplicated by undesirable elements.

    E. Somebody with the root password but no other password can then break into the computer.

19. You've downloaded a GPG public key from a website into the file `fredkey.pub`. What must you do with this key to use it?

    A. Type `inspect-gpg fredkey.pub`.

    B. Type `gpg --readkey fredkey.pub`.

    C. Type `import-gpg fredkey.pub`.

    D. Type `gpg --import fredkey.pub`.

    E. Type `gpg-import fredkey.pub`.

20. You want to send an encrypted message to an email correspondent. You both have GPG. What do you need to exchange before you can send your encrypted message?

    A. Your correspondent must obtain your GPG public key.

    B. Your correspondent must obtain your GPG private key.

    C. You must exchange private keys with your correspondent.

    D. You must obtain your correspondent's GPG private key.

    E. You must obtain your correspondent's GPG public key.

Appendix

Answers

Chapter 1: Exploring Linux Command-Line Tools

1. D. Any of these approaches will work, or at least *might* work. (You might err when performing any of them.) Option B or C is likely to be the most efficient approach; with a long filename to type, option A is likely to be tedious.

2. E. The echo command is implemented internally to bash, although an external version is also available on most systems. The cat, less, tee, and sed commands are not implemented internally to bash, although they can be called from bash as external commands.

3. E. The echo command echoes what follows to standard output, and $PROC is an environment variable. Thus, echo $PROC displays the value of the $PROC environment variable, meaning that it must have been set to the specified value by you, one of your configuration files, or a program you've run. Although many environment variables are set to particular values to convey information, $PROC isn't a standard environment variable that might be associated with information described in options A, B, C, and D.

4. A. The pwd command prints (to standard output) the name of the current working directory. The remaining options are simply incorrect, although option B describes the cd command, and various tools can be used to reformat wide text for display or printing in fewer columns, as in option C.

5. A. The dot (.) character refers to the current working directory, and the slash (/) is a directory separator. Thus preceding a program name by ./ unambiguously identifies the intention to run the program that's stored in the current directory. Option B will run the first instance of the program that's found on the current path. Because paths often omit the current directory for security reasons, this option is likely to fail. The run command isn't a standard Linux command, so option C is unlikely to do anything, much less what the question specifies. Option D would be correct except that it reverses the order of the two characters. The effect is to attempt to run the .myprog file in the root (/) directory. This file probably doesn't exist, and even if it did, it's not the file the question specifies should be run. Option E runs the first instance of myprog found on the path, and additionally it runs the program in the background. (Chapter 2 covers background execution in more detail.)

6. E. By default, man uses the less pager to display information on most Linux systems, so option E is correct. Although an X-based version of man does exist (xman), the basic man doesn't use a custom X-based application (option A), nor does it use Firefox (option B) or the vi editor (option D). The info command and man are competing documentation systems, so option C is incorrect.

7. C. The > redirection operator stores a command's standard output in a file, overwriting the contents of any existing file by the specified name, so option C is correct.

Option A specifies the standard input redirection so that `ifconfig` will take the contents of `file.txt` as input. Option B is almost correct: the `>>` redirection operator redirects standard output, as requested, but it appends data to the specified file rather than overwriting it. Option D specifies a pipe; the output of `ifconfig` is sent through the `file.txt` program, if it exists. (Chances are it doesn't, so you'd get a command not found error message.) Option E redirects standard error, rather than standard output, to `file.txt` and so is incorrect.

8. C. The `&>` redirection operator sends both standard output and standard error to the specified file, as option C states. (The name of the file, `input.txt`, is intentionally deceptive, but the usage is still valid.) Option A mentions standard error but describes it as if it were an input stream, which it's not; it's an output stream. Option B mentions standard input, but the `&>` operator doesn't affect standard input. Because only option C is correct, neither option D nor E can be correct.

9. E. In principle, you can pipe together as many commands as you like. (In practice, of course, there will be limits based on input buffer size, memory, and so on, but these limits are far higher than the 2, 3, 4, or 16 commands specified in options A, B, C, and D.)

10. B. The `tee` command sends its output both to standard output and to a named file. Thus, placing the `tee` command (with an output filename) after another command and a pipe will achieve the desired effect. Options A and D redirect gabby's output to a file, which means you won't be able to see the output and interact with it. Option C sends the contents of `gabby-out.txt` to gabby as input, which isn't what's desired, either. Option E attempts to run `gabby-out.txt` as a program and use its output as command-line arguments to gabby, which is not what's desired.

11. C. The `2>` redirection operator redirects standard error only, leaving standard output unaffected. Sending standard error to `/dev/null` gets rid of it. Thus option C is correct. Option A pipes the standard output of `verbose` through the `quiet` program, which isn't a standard Linux program. Option B sends both standard output and standard error to `/dev/null`, so you won't be able to interact with the program as the question specifies you must be able to do. Option D redirects standard output only to the `junk.txt` file, so once again, interaction will be impossible—and you'll see the unwanted error messages on the screen. Option E's `quiet-mode` program is fictitious (or at least nonstandard), so this option is incorrect.

12. A. Option A correctly describes the difference between these two redirection operators. Option B is almost correct, but the `>>` operator will create a new file if one doesn't already exist. The `>>` operator does not redirect standard error (as stated in option C) or standard input (as stated in option D). Both operators will create a new file if one doesn't already exist, contrary to what option E states.

13. C. The `tail` command displays the final 10 lines of a file, so option C is correct. (You can change the number of lines displayed with the `-n` option.) The `uniq` command (option A) removes duplicate lines from a list. The `cut` command (option B) echoes the specified characters or fields from an input text file. The `wc` command (option D)

displays counts of the number of characters, words, and lines in a file. The fmt command (option E) is a plain-text formatter.

14. A. The pr program takes a text file as input and adds formatting features intended for printing, such as a header and blank lines, to separate pages. The command also pipes the output through lpr (which is a Linux printing command). Option A describes these effects and so is correct. Option B describes the effect of the cat program and so is incorrect. The conversion of tabs to spaces can be done by the expand program, so option C is incorrect. Although the specified command does print report.txt, error messages are not stored in the lpr file, so option D is incorrect. Because option A is correct, option E is incorrect.

15. B, C, D. The nl command numbers lines, so it does this task without any special options, and option B is correct. (Its options can fine-tune the way it numbers lines, though.) The cat command can also number lines via its -b and -n options; -b numbers non-blank lines, whereas -n numbers all lines (including blank lines). Thus options C and D are both correct. Neither the fmt command nor the od command will number the lines of the input file, so options A and E are both incorrect.

16. D. The expand command will remove tab stops at every eight characters. With newly formatted data stored in data1.txt via the > redirection symbol, option D is the correct choice.

    The od command will not remove tabs. Therefore, option A is incorrect. Option B does remove the tabs; however, the resulting data file, data.txt, will contain duplicate data records (due to the >> redirection option), some with tabs and some without. Therefore, option B is incorrect. There is not a --remove-tabs option on the fmt command, and thus option C is incorrect. The unexpand command does the opposite of the expand command, adding tab stops instead of removing them. Therefore, option E is incorrect.

17. C. The sed utility can be used to "stream" text and change one value to another. In this case, the s option is used to replace dog with mutt, making option C correct. The syntax in option A is incorrect, and choices B and D are incorrect because grep doesn't include the functionality needed to make the changes. Option E combines fmt, cut, and redirection in a way that simply won't work to achieve the desired goal.

18. B. The fmt command performs the desired task of shortening long lines by inserting carriage returns. It sends its results to standard output, so option B uses output redirection to save the results in a new file. The sed command of option A won't accomplish anything useful; it only replaces the string Ctrl-M with the string NL. Although these strings are both sometimes used as abbreviations for carriage returns or new lines, the replacement of these literal strings isn't what's required. Option C creates an exact copy of the original file, with the long single-line paragraphs intact. Although option D's pr command is a formatting tool, it won't reformat individual paragraphs. It will also add headers that you probably don't want. Option E's grep command searches for text within files; it won't reformat text files.

19. A. The grep utility is used to find matching text within a file and print those lines. It accepts regular expressions, which means you can place in brackets the two characters that differ in the words for which you're looking. Thus option A is correct. The syntax for sed, od, cat, and find wouldn't perform the specified task, so options B through E are all incorrect.

20. C. The bracket expression within the d[o-u]g regular expression in option C means that any three-character string beginning in d, ending in g, and with the middle character being between o and u will match. These results meet the question's criteria. Option A's dot matches any single character, so d.g matches all three words. The bracket expression [ou] in option B matches the characters o and u, but no other values. Since the question specifies that some other matches will be made, this option is incorrect. Option D's di*g matches dig, diig, diiig, or any other word that begins with d, ends with g, and contains any number of i letters in between. Thus option D matches dig but not dog or dug as required. Option E, like option A, uses a dot to match any character, so it will actually match certain four-letter words but not dog or dug.

Chapter 2: Managing Software

1. D. Because they must be compiled prior to installation, source packages require *more* time to install than binary packages, contrary to option D's assertion, thus making this option correct. The other options all describe advantages of source packages over binary packages.

2. A. The two systems use different databases, which makes coordinating between them difficult. Therefore, using them both simultaneously is inadvisable, making option A correct. Package management systems don't share information, but neither do their databases actively conflict, so option B is incorrect. Installing the same libraries using both systems would almost guarantee that the files served by both systems would conflict with one another, making option C incorrect. Actively using both RPM and Debian packages isn't common on any distribution, although it's possible with all of them, so option D is incorrect. The alien program converts between package formats. Although it requires that both systems be installed to convert between them, alien is not required to install both these systems, thus option E is incorrect.

3. E. RPMs are usually portable across distributions, but occasionally they contain incompatibilities, so option E is correct. The package format and software licensing have nothing to do with one another, so option A is incorrect. There is no --convert-distrib parameter to rpm, so option B is incorrect. Although recompiling a source package can help work around incompatibilities, this step is not always required, so option C is incorrect. Binary packages can't be rebuilt for another CPU architecture, so option D is incorrect; although source packages may be rebuilt for any supported architecture, provided the source code doesn't rely on any CPU-specific features.

4. B. The -i operation installs software, so option B is correct. (The -v and -h options cause a status display of the progress of the operation, which wasn't mentioned in the option.) Uninstallation is performed by the -e operation, and rebuilding source RPMs is done by the --rebuild operation (to either rpm or rpmbuild, depending on the RPM version), so options A and C are incorrect. Although the filename megaprog.rpm is missing several conventional RPM filename components, the rpm utility doesn't use the filename as a package validity check, so option D is incorrect. Option E describes a package upgrade, which is handled by the -U operation, not -i as in the question, so option E is incorrect.

5. A. The rpm2cpio program extracts data from an RPM file and converts it into a cpio archive that's sent to standard output. Piping the results through cpio and using the -i and --make-directories options, as in option A, will extract those files to the current directory. Option B creates a cpio file called make-directories that contains the files from the RPM package. Option C will uninstall the package called myfonts.rpm (but not the myfonts package). The alien utility has no --to-extract target, so option D is invalid. The rpmbuild utility builds a source RPM into a binary RPM, making option E incorrect.

6. E. An uppercase -P invokes the purge operation, which completely removes a package and its configuration files, so option E is correct. The -e parameter uninstalls a package for rpm, but not for dpkg, so option A is incorrect. The lowercase -p causes dpkg to print information about the package's contents, so option B is incorrect. The -r parameter removes a package but leaves configuration files behind, so options C and D are both incorrect. (Option D also specifies a complete filename, which isn't used for removing a package—you should specify only the shorter package name.)

7. C. You can specify Debian package archive sites in /etc/apt/sources.list, and then you can type apt-get update and apt-get upgrade to update a Debian system quickly to the latest packages, so option C is correct. GUI package management tools for Debian and related distributions exist, but they aren't apt-get, so option A is incorrect. The alien program can convert a tarball and install the converted package on a Debian system, but apt-get can't do this, so option B is incorrect. dpkg and apt-get both come with all Debian-based distributions, so option D is incorrect. The dpkg program can install only Debian packages on Debian-based systems, but apt-get can work with both package systems, so option E is backward.

8. E. The --get-selections action to dpkg displays the names of all installed packages, making option E correct. There is no showall option to apt-get, so option A is incorrect. The showpkg subcommand to apt-cache displays information about a named package when used without a package name, as in option B, but it displays no data. The dpkg -r action removes a package, so option C would remove the package called allpkgs if it were installed. The dpkg -i action installs a package, so option D is incorrect—and that option doesn't list a package name, which the -i action requires.

9. D. The update option to apt-get causes retrieval of new information, as described in option D. This option is perfectly valid, contrary to option A's assertion.

The apt-get program doesn't permit you to upload information to the Internet repositories, so option B is incorrect. Option C describes the effect of the upgrade or dist-upgrade options, not the update option. The upgrade or dist-upgrade options can upgrade APT itself, but update alone won't do the job, so option E is incorrect.

10. A, B. The Yum utility's update and upgrade options are nearly identical in effect, and either can be used to upgrade an individual package, such as unzip, so options A and B are both correct. The primary command options to yum don't use dashes, so options C and D are both incorrect. The check-update option to yum checks for the availability of updates, but it does *not* install them, so option E is incorrect.

11. B. Yum uses files in the /etc/yum.repos.d directory to locate its repositories, so you can add to the repository list by adding files to this subdirectory, as option B specifies, typically either by installing an RPM or by adding a file manually. Option A describes a method of adding a repository to a computer that uses APT, not Yum. Option C's add-repository subcommand is fictitious. Although the /etc/yum.conf file described in options D and E is real, it doesn't store repository data.

12. B. The /etc/ld.so.conf file holds the global library path, so editing it is the preferred approach. You must then type ldconfig to have the system update its library path cache. Thus, option B is correct. Although you can add a directory to the library path by altering the LD_LIBRARY_PATH environment variable globally, as in option A, this approach isn't the preferred one, so this option is incorrect. Option C simply won't work. Option D also won't work, although linking individual library files would work. This method isn't the preferred one for adding a whole directory, though. The ldd utility displays information on libraries used by executable files, so option E won't have the desired effect.

13. D. Programmers select libraries, not users nor system administrators. If you don't like the widgets provided by one library, you have few options, and option D is correct. (Many widget sets do provide a great deal of configurability, though, so you may be able to work around the problem in other ways.) Options A, B, and E describe fictitious options to ldconfig, rpm, dpkg, and the kernel. Option C wouldn't work; Qt-using programs would crash when they found GTK+ libraries in place of the Qt libraries they were expecting.

14. D. The kill program accepts various signals in numeric or named form (9 in this example) along with a process ID number (11287 in this example). Signal 9 corresponds to SIGKILL, which is an extreme way to kill processes that have run out of control, thus option D describes the effect of this command. Although you might use kill to kill network processes, you can't pass kill a TCP port number and expect it to work, so option A is incorrect. The program also won't display information about the number of processes that have been killed, making option B incorrect. To do as option C suggests, you'd need to tell kill to pass SIGHUP (signal 1), so the command would be kill -1 11287, and option C is incorrect. The kill program can't change the priority of a process, so option E is incorrect.

15. C, D. The top utility displays a dynamic list of processes ordered according to their CPU use along with additional system information, including load averages, so option C is correct. If you want only the load average at a specific moment, uptime (option D) may be better because it presents less extraneous information—it shows the current time, the time since the system was booted, the number of active users, and the load averages. Option A's ld command has nothing to do with displaying load averages. (It's a programming tool that links together program modules into an executable program.) There are no standard Linux programs called load (option B) or la (option E).

16. A. The --forest option to ps shows parent-child relationships by creating visual links between process names in the ps output, making option A correct. (Listing 2.4 shows this effect.) Options B and C are both valid ps commands, but neither creates the specified effect. Option D describes a fictitious ps option. Since options B, C, and D are incorrect, option E is also necessarily incorrect.

17. A. CPU-intensive programs routinely consume 90 percent or more of available CPU time, but not all systems run such programs. Furthermore, some types of program bugs can create such CPU loads. Thus, option A is correct, and you must investigate the matter more. What is dfcomp? Is it designed as a CPU-intensive program? Is it consuming this much CPU time consistently, or was this a brief burst of activity? Options B, C, D, and E all jump to conclusions or present fictitious reasons for the behavior being normal or abnormal.

18. E. The jobs command summarizes processes that were launched from your current shell. When no such processes are running, jobs returns nothing, so option E is correct. The jobs command doesn't check or summarize CPU load, so option A is incorrect. The jobs command also doesn't check for processes run from shells other than the current one, so option B is incorrect (processes running under your username could have been launched from another shell or from a GUI environment). There is no standard jobs shell in Linux, so option C is incorrect. Because the jobs output is limited to your own processes in the shell you're running, a blank output does *not* indicate a crashed system, making option D incorrect.

19. C, E. The nice command launches a program (crunch in this example) with increased or decreased priority. The default priority when none is specified is 10, and the nice -10 crunch command also sets the priority to 10, so options C and E are equivalent. Option A isn't a valid nice command because nice has no --value option. Option B is a valid nice command, but it sets the priority to –10 rather than 10. Despite the similarity in the form of options C and D, option D is not a valid nice command, and so it is incorrect. (When passing a numeric value to nice, you *must* use a preceding dash, -, or -n.)

20. D, E. Linux insulates users' actions from one another, and this rule applies to renice; only root may modify the priority of other users' processes, so option D is correct. Similarly, only root may increase the priority of a process in order to prevent users

from setting their processes to maximum priority, thus stealing CPU time from others, so option E is correct. Option A correctly describes nice, but not renice. The whole point of renice is to be able to change the priorities of existing processes. Contrary to option B, renice doesn't care about the shell from which renice or the target program was launched. Users may use renice to decrease their own processes' priorities, contrary to option C.

Chapter 3: Configuring Hardware

1. B, C. IRQs 3 and 4 are common defaults for RS-232 serial ports, so options B and C are both correct. IRQ 1 is reserved for the keyboard, so option A is incorrect. IRQ 8 is reserved for use by the real-time clock, so option D is incorrect. Although IRQ 16 exists on modern systems, it didn't exist on early *x*86 systems, and its purpose isn't standardized.

2. A. Modern firmware (BIOSs and EFIs) provides the means to disable many onboard devices, including sound hardware, in case you don't want to use them, so option A is correct. Although the alsactl utility mentioned in option B is real, it's used to load or store sound card mixer settings, not to disable the sound hardware. The lsmod command mentioned in option C displays information about loaded kernel modules, but it doesn't remove them or disable the hardware they use. Similarly, option D's lspci displays information on PCI devices, but it can't disable them. Contrary to option E, on-board sound hardware can usually be disabled.

3. E. The udev software creates and manages a dynamic /dev directory tree, adding entries to that directory for devices that exist on the target system, so option E is correct. The udev software has nothing to do with software development (option A). It doesn't unload drivers (option B) or load drivers (option C), although it does respond to the loading of drivers by creating appropriate entries in /dev. It also doesn't store BIOS configuration options in a file (option D).

4. E. SATA disks are *usually* handled by Linux's SCSI subsystem and so are referred to as /dev/sd*x*. However, some drivers handle these disks as if they were PATA disks and so refer to them as /dev/hd*x*. Thus, option E is correct, and both options A and C are incorrect. The /dev/mapper directory holds device files related to LVM and RAID configurations, not disk partition identifiers, so option B is incorrect. Option D (C:) is how Windows would likely refer to the first partition on the disk, but Linux doesn't use this style of disk identifier.

5. A, C, D. There are no files called /proc/ioaddresses or /proc/hardware, so options B and E are both incorrect. All the other files listed contain useful information; /proc/ioports holds information about I/O ports, /proc/dma holds information about DMA port usage, and /proc/interrupts holds information about IRQs.

6. B. Logical partitions are numbered 5 and up, and they reside in an extended partition with a number between 1 and 4. Therefore, one of the first two partitions must be an extended partition that houses partitions 5 and 6, making option B correct. Because one of the first two partitions is an extended partition, the other must be a primary partition, and there can be no more of either type of partition. This makes option A incorrect. Gaps in the range of partitions 1–4 are normal in MBR disks, contrary to option C. Because logical partitions are numbered starting at 5, their numbers won't change if /dev/sda3 is subsequently added, so option D is incorrect. On MBR disks, partitions 1–4 must be primary or extended partitions; logical partitions are numbered 5 and up. Thus option E is incorrect.

7. E. The /etc/fstab file contains the mapping of partitions to mount points, so /etc must be an ordinary directory on the root partition, not on a separate partition, making option E correct. Although option A's statement that the system won't boot is correct, the reason is not; /home holds user files, not critical system files. Options B and C describe restrictions that don't exist. Option D would be correct if /etc were not a separate partition.

8. D. The /home directory (option D) is frequently placed on its own partition in order to isolate it from the rest of the system and sometimes to enable use of a particular filesystem or filesystem mount options. The /bin and /sbin directories (options A and B) should *never* be split off from the root (/) filesystem because they contain critical executable files that must be accessible in order to do the most basic work, including mounting filesystems. The /mnt directory (option C) often contains subdirectories used for mounting removable media, or it may be used for this purpose itself. It's seldom used to access hard disk partitions directly, although it can be used for this purpose. The /dev directory (option E) usually corresponds to a virtual filesystem, which holds pseudo-files but is not stored on a disk partition.

9. A. The 0x0f partition type code is one of two common partition type codes for an extended partition. (The other is 0x05.) The 0x82 code refers to a Linux swap partition, and 0x83 denotes a Linux filesystem partition. Thus, it appears that this disk holds Linux partitions, making option A correct. Windows, FreeBSD, and Mac OS X all use other partition type codes for their partitions, so options B, C, and E are all incorrect. (Mac OS X is also rarely installed to MBR disks.) Partitions exist, in part, to enable different OSs to store their data side by side on the same disk, so mixing several partition types (even for different OSs) on one disk does not indicate disk corruption, making option D incorrect.

10. C. Linux's fdisk doesn't write changes to disk until you exit the program by typing **w**. Typing **q** exits without writing those changes, so typing **q** in this situation will avert disaster, making option C correct. Typing **w** (option B) would be precisely the wrong thing to do. Because fdisk doesn't write changes until you type **w**, the damage is not yet done, contrary to option A. Typing **u** (option D) or **t** (option E) would do nothing useful because those aren't undo commands.

11. E. The mkfs command creates a new filesystem, overwriting any existing data and therefore making existing files inaccessible, as stated in option E. This command

doesn't set the partition type code in the partition table, so option A is incorrect. The `mkfs` command is destructive, contrary to option B. The `-t ext2` option tells `mkfs` to create an ext2 filesystem; it's a perfectly valid option, so option C is incorrect. Although `mkfs` could (destructively) convert ext2fs to ext4fs, the `-t ext2` option clearly indicates that an ext2 filesystem is being created, so option D is incorrect.

12. B. Although they have similar names and purposes, Linux's `fdisk` isn't modeled after Windows's `FDISK`, so option B is correct and option A is not. Windows' `FDISK` does *not* have GUI controls, contrary to option C. Linux's `fdisk` does *not* format floppy disks, contrary to option D. Both programs manage MBR disks, contrary to option E.

13. E. Swap partitions aren't mounted in the same way as filesystems, so they have no associated mount points, making option E correct.

14. C. The `-t` option is used to tell `fsck` what filesystem to use, so option C is correct. (If this option isn't used, `fsck` determines the filesystem type automatically.) The `-A` option (option A) causes `fsck` to check all of the filesystems marked to be checked in `/etc/fstab`. The `-N` option (option B) tells `fsck` to take no action and to display what it would normally do without doing it. The `-C` option (option D) displays a text-mode progress indicator of the check process. The `-f` option (option E) is fictitious.

15. A. A default use of `df` reports the percentage of disk space used (option D) and the mount point for each filesystem (option E). The number of inodes (option B) and filesystem types (option C) can both be obtained by passing parameters to `df`. This utility does *not* report how long a filesystem has been mounted (option A), so that option is correct.

16. D. The journal of a journaling filesystem records pending operations, resulting in quicker disk checks after an uncontrolled shutdown, so option D is correct. Contrary to option A, journaling filesystems are, as a class, newer than non-journaling filesystems; in fact, the journaling ext3fs is built upon the non-journaling ext2fs. Although disk checks are quicker with journaling filesystems than with non-journaling filesystems, journaling filesystems do have `fsck` utilities, and these may still need to be run from time to time, so option B is incorrect. All Linux-native filesystems support Linux ownership and permissions; this isn't an advantage of journaling filesystems, contrary to option C. The journal of a journaling filesystem doesn't provide an unlimited "undo" feature, so option E is incorrect.

17. E. When typed without a filesystem type specification, `mount` attempts to auto-detect the filesystem type. If the media contains any of the specified filesystems, it should be detected and the disk mounted, so option E is correct.

18. B. The `/etc/fstab` file consists of lines that contain the device identifier, the mount point, the filesystem type code, filesystem mount options, the dump flag, and the filesystem check frequency, in that order. Option B provides this information in the correct order, and so it will work. Option A reverses the second and third fields, but is otherwise correct. Options C, D, and E all scramble the order of the first three fields and also specify the `noauto` mount option, which causes the filesystem not to mount automatically at boot time.

19. A, B, C. The user, users, and owner options in /etc/fstab all enable ordinary users to mount a filesystem, but with slightly different implications: user enables anybody to mount a filesystem—and only that user may unmount it; users enables anybody to mount a filesystem, and anybody may unmount it; and owner enables only the owner of the mount point to mount or unmount a filesystem. Thus, options A, B, and C are all correct. The owners parameter of option D doesn't exist. The uid=1000 parameter of option E tells Linux to set the ownership of files to UID 1000 on filesystems that lack Linux permissions features. Although this might be desirable for some disks, it doesn't enable the user with UID 1000 to mount the disk, so option E is incorrect.

20. A. Option A correctly describes the safe procedure for removing a removable medium that lacks a locking mechanism from a Linux computer. (Instead of typing **umount /media/usb**, you could type **umount /dev/sdb1**; in this context, the two commands are equivalent.) Option B reverses the order of operations; the umount command *must* be typed *before* you physically remove the flash drive. Option C also has it backward; the sync command would need to be issued *before* removing the drive. (The sync command can prevent damage when removing disks, but it isn't a complete substitute for umount.) There is no standard usbdrive-remove command in Linux, and if you were to write a script that calls umount and call it usbdrive-remove, pulling the flash drive quickly, as option D describes, would be exactly the wrong thing to do. The fsck command of option E checks a filesystem for errors. It's not necessary to do this before removing a disk, and it won't unmount the disk, so option E is incorrect.

Chapter 4: Managing Files

1. B. The touch utility updates a file's time stamps, as option B specifies. (If the specified file doesn't exist, touch creates an empty file.) You can't move files with touch; that's the job of the mv command, so option A is incorrect. Various tools can convert end-of-line formats, but touch is not one of them, so option C is incorrect. Testing the validity of disk structures, as in option D, is normally done on a whole-filesystem basis with fsck and related tools; touch can't do this job. You can write cached data to disk for a whole filesystem by unmounting it or by using sync, but touch can't do this, so option E is incorrect.

2. A, D. The –s and --symbolic options to ln are equivalent, and both create a symbolic (aka soft) link. Thus, options A and D are both correct. Options B, C, and E don't exist.

3. A. The –l parameter produces a long listing, including file sizes. The –a parameter produces a listing of all files in a directory, including the dot files. Combining the two produces the desired information (along with information about other files), so option A is correct. The –p, –R, –d, and –F options don't have the specified effects, so the remaining options are all incorrect.

4. D. When moving from one partition or disk to another, mv must necessarily read and copy the file and then delete the original if that copy was successful, as stated in option D. If both filesystems support ownership and permissions, they'll be preserved; mv doesn't need an explicit --preserve option to do this, and this preservation does not rely on having exactly the same filesystem types. Thus, option A is incorrect. Although mv doesn't physically rewrite data when moving within a single low-level filesystem, this approach can't work when you're copying to a separate low-level file-system (such as from a hard disk to a USB flash drive); if the data isn't written to the new location, it won't be accessible should the disk be inserted in another computer. Thus, option B is incorrect. Although not all filesystems support ownership and permissions, many do, and these attributes are preserved when moving files between them, so option C is incorrect. Although FAT is a common choice on removable media because of its excellent cross-platform support, other filesystems will work on such disks, so option E is incorrect.

5. A, B. If you try to create a directory inside a directory that doesn't exist, mkdir responds with a No such file or directory error. The --parents parameter tells mkdir to create all necessary parent directories automatically in such situations, so option A is correct. You can also manually do this by creating each necessary directory separately, so option B is also correct. (It's possible that mkdir one wouldn't be necessary in this example if the directory one already existed. No harm will come from trying to create a directory that already exists, although mkdir will return a File exists error.) Typing **touch /bin/mkdir**, as option C suggests, will likely result in an error message if typed as a normal user and won't help if typed as root, so this option is incorrect. Clearing away existing directories in the one/two/three tree won't help, so option D is incorrect. Option E's mktree command is fictitious.

6. D, E. The cpio and tar programs are common Linux archive-creation utilities, so options D and E are both correct. The restore command restores (but does not back up) data; its backup counterpart command is dump. Thus, option A is incorrect. The vi command launches a text editor; it's not used to create archives, so option B is incorrect. There is no standard tape command in Linux, so option C is incorrect.

7. E. With the tar utility, the --list (t) command is used to read the archive and display its contents. The --verbose (v) option creates a verbose file listing, and --file (f) specifies the filename—data79.tar in this case. Option E uses all of these features. Options A, B, C, and D all substitute other commands for --list, which is required by the question.

8. A. Symbolic links can point across filesystems, so creating a symbolic link from one filesystem (in which your home directory resides) to another (on the DVD) isn't a problem, making option A correct. Hard links, as in options B, C, and D, are restricted to a single filesystem and so won't work for the described purpose. Because symbolic links will work as described, option E is incorrect.

9. E. Option E is the correct command. Typing **chown ralph:tony somefile.txt**, as in option A, sets the owner of the file to ralph and the group to tony. The chmod

command used in options B and D is used to change file permissions, not ownership. Option C reverses the order of the filename and the owner.

10. C, E. The d character that leads the mode indicates that the file is actually a directory (option C), and the r symbol in the r-x triplet at the end of the symbolic mode indicates that all users of the system have read access to the directory (option E). Leading l characters, which this mode lacks, denote a symbolic link, so option A is incorrect. Although the x symbols usually denote executable program files, as specified in option B, in the case of directories this permission bit indicates that the directory's contents may be searched; executing a directory is meaningless. SUID bits are indicated by an s character in place of the owner's execute bit position in the symbolic mode. Since this position holds an x in this example, option D is incorrect.

11. C. The set user ID (SUID) bit enables programs to run as the program's owner rather than as the user who ran them. This makes SUID root programs risky, so setting the SUID bit on root-owned programs should be done only when it's required for the program's normal functioning, as stated in option C. This should certainly *not* be done for all programs because the SUID bit is *not* required of all executable programs, as option A asserts. Although the SUID root configuration does enable programs to access device files, the device files' permissions can be modified to give programs access to those files, if this is required, so option B is incorrect. Although SUID root programs are a security risk, as stated in option D, they're a necessary risk for a few programs, so option D goes too far. Many program files that should *not* be SUID root are owned by root, so option E is incorrect.

12. E. Using symbolic modes, the o+r option adds read (r) permissions to the world (o). Thus, option E is correct. Option A sets the mode to rwxr----x, which is a bit odd and doesn't provide world read access to the file, although it does provide world execute access. Option B sets the mode to rw-r-----, which gives the world no access whatsoever to the file. Option C adds read access to the file for the owner (u) if the owner doesn't already have this access; it doesn't affect the world permissions. Option D *removes* read access for *all* users, so it's incorrect.

13. D. Files start with a 666 permission bit octal number setting. Depending upon the umask setting, permission bits may be removed, but not added. Option D, 027, removes write permissions for the group and all world permissions. (Files normally don't have execute permissions set, but explicitly removing write permissions when removing read permissions ensures reasonable behavior for directories.) Therefore, Option D is correct. Option A, 640, is the octal equivalent of the desired rw-r----- permissions, but the umask sets the bits that are to be *removed* from permissions, not those that are to be set. Option B, 210, would remove write permission for the owner, but it wouldn't remove write permission for the group, which is incorrect. This would also leave all world permissions open. Option C, 022, wouldn't remove world read permission. Option E, 138, is an invalid umask because all the digits in the umask must be between 0 and 7.

14. E. Using quotas requires kernel support, the usrquota or grpquota (for user or group quotas) filesystem mount option, and activation via the quotaon command (which often appears in system startup scripts). Thus, option E is correct. Option A suggests that quotaon is not necessary, which is incorrect. Option B's statement that grpquota is invalid is incorrect. Option C's statement that these options *disable* quota support is backward. The usrquota and grpquota options are both valid, so option D is incorrect.

15. B. The repquota utility is used to summarize the quota information about the filesystem. When used with the -a option, it shows this information for all filesystems, so option B is correct. This command won't return useful information when typed alone, though, so option A is incorrect. The quotacheck utility checks quota information about a disk and writes corrections, so options C and D are both incorrect. The edquota utility enables you to edit quota information. It doesn't summarize quota information, and -a isn't a valid option to edquota. Thus, option E is incorrect.

16. D. The /opt directory tree exists to hold programs that aren't a standard part of a Linux distribution, such as commercial programs. These programs should install in their own directories under /opt; these directories usually have bin subdirectories of their own, although this isn't required. Thus, option D is correct (that is, it's a plausible possibility). The /usr/sbin directory holds programs that are normally run only by the system administrator, so it's not a likely location, making option A incorrect. The /etc/X11 directory holds X-related configuration files; so it's very unlikely that WonderCalc will be housed there, making option B incorrect. The /boot directory holds critical system boot files, so option C is incorrect. The /sbin directory, like /usr/sbin, is an unlikely location for user files, so option E is incorrect. (Furthermore, /sbin seldom contains subdirectories.)

17. A. The find utility (option A) operates by searching all files in a directory tree, and so it's likely to take a long time to search all of a computer's directories. The locate program uses a precompiled database, whereis searches a limited set of directories, and type searches the shell's path and built-in commands, so these commands will take less time. Thus, options B, C, D, and E are all incorrect.

18. C. The type command identifies a command, as executed by the shell, as being a built-in shell command, a shell alias, or an external command, whereas the whereis command helps find the location of external command files, thus option C is correct. Neither type nor whereis identifies the CPU architecture of a program file, can locate commands based on intended purpose, complete an incompletely typed command, or identify a command as a binary or a script; thus, the remaining options are all incorrect.

19. B. The find command includes the ability to search by username using the -user *name* option, where *name* is the username; thus option B is correct. The -uid option to find can also locate files owned by a user, but it takes a numeric user ID (UID) as an argument, so option A isn't quite correct. The locate command provides no ability

to search by user, so options C and D are incorrect. Although option E is a valid find command, it finds all of the files under /home with a *filename* of karen, not all files owned by the user karen, so this option is incorrect.

20. D. The which program searches the path just as bash does, but it prints the path to the first executable program it finds on the path. Thus option D is correct. The which program doesn't conduct an exhaustive search of the system, so there could be many more files called man on the system, contrary to option A. System package tools and which aren't closely related; option B is incorrect. Although /usr/bin/man would be run when the user whose which output matches that in the question types **man**, this may not be true of others because the path can vary from one user to another, thus option C is incorrect. The which program doesn't reveal file ownership information, so option E is incorrect.

Chapter 5: Booting Linux and Editing Files

1. C. The Master Boot Record (MBR) can contain a boot loader that is up to 446 bytes in size, so option C is correct. If more space is required, the boot loader must load a secondary boot loader. Although the boot loader is loaded into RAM (option A), it's not stored there permanently because RAM is volatile storage. Both /dev/boot and /dev/kmem (options B and D) are references to files on Linux filesystems; they're only available after the system starts and lots of other boot processes have occurred. The swap partition (option E) is used as an adjunct to RAM; the BIOS won't look there for a boot loader.

2. C. Runlevel 1 is single-user mode, and adding the digit 1 to the kernel's options line in a boot loader will launch the system in this runlevel, so option C is correct. Options A and B both present invalid kernel options and so are incorrect. Although the telinit command specified in options D and E will change the runlevel once the computer is running and runlevel 1 is a single-user mode, these commands are *not* passed to the kernel via a boot loader, so these options are both incorrect.

3. D. The kernel ring buffer, which can be viewed by typing **dmesg** (piping this through less is a good supplement), contains messages from the kernel, including those from hardware drivers. These messages may provide a clue about why the disk didn't appear, thus option D is correct. The /var/log/diskerror file (option A) is fictitious, as is /mnt/disks (option B). The /etc/inittab file (option C) doesn't directly control disk access, and so it is unlikely to provide useful information. The files specified in option E are GRUB Legacy and GRUB 2 configuration files, which don't contain information that could explain why a disk isn't responding.

4.   B. Ordinarily, Linux runs `init` (option B) as the first program; `init` then runs, via various scripts, other programs. The `dmesg` program (option A) is a user diagnostic and information tool used to access the kernel ring buffer; it's not part of the startup process. The `startup` program (option C) is fictitious. The `rc` program (option D) is a script that some versions of `init` call, typically indirectly, during the startup sequence, but it's not the first program that the kernel runs. LILO is an older boot loader for Linux on BIOS systems, and `lilo` (option E) is the command that installs this boot loader to the MBR. Since boot loaders run before the kernel loads, this option is incorrect.

5.   D. Option D is the correct GRUB 2 configuration file. Option A is a fictitious file; it doesn't exist. Although some of GRUB 2's boot loader code may be written to the MBR, as implied by option B, this isn't the location of the program's configuration file. Options C and D are both possible names for the GRUB Legacy configuration file, but that name is not shared by GRUB 2.

6.   A. The `initrd` keyword identifies an initial RAM disk file in the GRUB 2 configuration file, and a space separates this keyword from the filename. (Several variants on this syntax are possible.) Option B adds an equal sign (=), which renders the syntax incorrect. Options C, D, and E use the incorrect `initramfs` and `ramdisk` keywords instead of `initrd`.

7.   D. You use `grub-install` to install the GRUB Legacy boot loader code into an MBR or boot sector. When using `grub-install`, you specify the boot sector on the command line. The MBR is the first sector on a hard drive, so you give it the Linux device identifier for the entire hard disk, /dev/sda. Hence, option D is correct. Option A specifies using the grub utility, which is an interactive tool, and the device identifier shown in option A is a GRUB-style identifier for what would probably be the /dev/sda3 partition in Linux. Option B is almost correct, but it installs GRUB to the /dev/sda1 partition's boot sector rather than to the hard disk's MBR. Option C is the command to install LILO to the MBR rather than to install GRUB. Option E contains the same error as option B, and it also uses the fictitious `grub-legacy` command.

8.   B. The `root` keyword in a GRUB Legacy configuration file tells the boot loader where to look for files, including its own configuration files, kernel files, and so on. Because GRUB Legacy numbers both disks and partitions starting from 0, (hd1,5) refers to the sixth partition on the second disk, as option B specifies. Option A is incorrect because you pass the Linux root partition to the kernel on the kernel line, not via the GRUB root keyword. Options A, C, and E all misinterpret the GRUB numbering scheme. The GRUB installation location is specified on the `grub-install` command line, so options D and E are incorrect, and /dev/hd1,5 isn't a standard Linux device file, which also makes option D incorrect.

9.   B. The `initdefault` action specifies the default runlevel, so option B is correct. The remaining options are all taken from actual /etc/inittab files but don't have the specified meaning.

10. A, B, E. Runlevel 0 (option A) is the reserved runlevel for halting the system. Runlevel 1 (option B) is reserved for single-user mode. Runlevel 6 (option E) is reserved for rebooting. Runlevel 2 (option C) is the default runlevel on Debian and most distributions derived from it, but it does none of the things described in the question. Runlevel 5 (option D) is a regular, user-configurable runlevel, which isn't normally used for the things described in the question. (Many systems use it for a regular boot with a GUI login prompt.)

11. B, C. The first number in the runlevel output is the previous runlevel (the letter N is used to indicate that the system hasn't changed runlevels since booting). The second number is the current runlevel. Hence, options B and C are both correct, while options A and D are both incorrect. The runlevel changes very quickly, and the runlevel utility doesn't provide a code to indicate that the runlevel is in the process of being changed, so option E is incorrect.

12. A. The -c option to shutdown cancels a previously scheduled shutdown, as stated in option A. Options B and C describe the effects of the -r and -h options to shutdown, respectively. No shutdown option asks for confirmation before taking action, although you can delay a shutdown by specifying a shutdown time in the future, so option D is incorrect. No shutdown option closes open windows in X, except as a consequence of shutting down, so option E is incorrect.

13. B. The journalctl program displays the systemd log file, so option A is incorrect. Options C and D are commands used for the SysV initialization process, and Option E is the systemd process command. Option B, systemctl, is the correct answer.

14. B. The telinit command is used to change runlevels; when it's passed the 1 parameter, as in option B, telinit changes to runlevel 1, which is single-user mode. The runlevel command (option A) displays the current runlevel but doesn't change runlevels. Although telinit can be used to shut down or reboot the computer, the shutdown command (option C) can't be used to change runlevels except to runlevel 0 or 6. There is no standard single-user command (option D). The halt command (option E), like shutdown, can't be used to change to single-user mode.

15. A. The isolate command for the systemctl program allows you to change the target of the system. The rescue target specifies single-user mode. Option B changes the system to the default target, which may or may not be single-user mode. The journalctl program in Option C displays the systemd log files. The systemd program isn't used to change targets (Option D), and the start command only starts a single unit, not a target (Option E).

16. A. In vi, dd is the command-mode command that deletes lines. Preceding this command by a number deletes that number of lines. Thus option A is correct. Although yy works similarly, it copies (yanks) text rather than deleting it, so option B is incorrect. Option C works in many more-modern text editors, but not in vi. Option D works in Emacs and similar text editors, but not in vi. Option E works in many GUI text editors, but not in vi.

17. D. The :q! vi command does as option D states. Options A and E are both simply incorrect. Option B would be correct if this command was typed while in vi's insert

mode, but the question specifies that command mode is in use. To achieve option C, the command would be **:wq**, not **:q!**.

18. E. Vi is included on Linux emergency systems, embedded systems, and other systems where space is at a premium because its executable is tiny. Emacs is, in contrast, a behemoth. Thus option E is correct. Contrary to option A, vi isn't an X-based program (although X-based vi variants are available); Emacs can be used in text mode or with X. Extended Binary Coded Decimal Interchange Code (EBCDIC) is an obscure 8-bit character encoding system used on some very old mainframe OSs. When run on Linux, vi doesn't use EBCDIC; furthermore, EBCDIC offers few or no advantages over the American Standard Code for Information Interchange (ASCII). Thus option B is incorrect. Vi's modes, referred to in option C, have nothing to do with non-English language support. Option D is backward; it's Emacs that includes a web browser, email client, and other add-ons.

19. A, B, C. Typing **R** (option A) in command mode enters insert mode with the system configured to overwrite existing text. Typing **i** or **a** (options B and C, respectively) enters insert mode with the system configured to insert text. (The i and a commands differ in how they place the cursor; a advances one space.) Typing **:** (option D) in command mode enters ex mode (you typically type the ex-mode command on the same command line immediately after the colon). Pressing the Esc key (option E) returns vi to command mode from insert mode.

20. B. The Esc key exits vi's insert mode, as option B specifies. Typing a tilde (~) inserts that character into the file, so option A is incorrect. The Ctrl+X, Ctrl+C key combination exits from Emacs, but it's not a defined vi key sequence, so option C is incorrect. The F10 key and the Shift+Insert key combination also aren't defined in vi, so options D and E are both incorrect.

Chapter 6: Configuring the X Window System, Localization, and Printing

1. A. On most Linux systems, some runlevels don't run X by default, so using one of them along with the startx program (which starts X running) can be an effective way to test changes to an X configuration quickly, making option A correct. The telinit program changes runlevels, which is a lengthy process compared to using startx, so option B is incorrect. Unplugging the computer to avoid the shutdown process is self-defeating because you'll have to suffer through a long startup (if you use a non-journaling filesystem), and it can also result in data loss, thus option C is incorrect. The startx utility doesn't check the veracity of an X configuration file; it starts X running from a text-mode login, making option D incorrect. Reconfiguring an X server does not normally require network access; the X server runs on the computer at which you sit. Thus option E is incorrect.

2. D. The XF86Config and xorg.conf file design enables you to define variants or multiple components and easily combine or recombine them as necessary, using the structure

specified in option D. Options A, B, and C all describe fictitious structures. Option E is incorrect because the X.org-X11 and XFree86 configuration files use a text-mode structure, not a binary structure.

3. C. The vertical refresh rate range includes a maximum value, but that value may be reduced when the resolution and vertical refresh rate would demand a higher horizontal refresh rate than the monitor can handle. Thus, option C is correct. Since the resolution affects the maximum refresh rate, option A is incorrect. The color depth is irrelevant to resolution and refresh rate calculations, so option B is incorrect. The computations shown in options D and E are bogus, making these options incorrect.

4. E. Option E describes the correct location for this option. The ServerLayout section (referenced in option A) combines all of the other options together but doesn't set the resolution. The Modeline option in the Monitor section (as described in option B) defines *one* possible resolution, but there may be several Modeline entries defining many resolutions, and there's no guarantee that any of them will be used. The Modeline option doesn't exist in the Device section (as suggested by option C), nor is that section where the resolution is set. There is no DefaultResolution section (as referenced in option D).

5. B. By maintaining fonts on one font server and pointing other X servers to that font server, you can reduce the administrative cost of maintaining the fonts on all of the systems, so option B is correct. Font servers don't produce faster font displays than X's local font handling; if anything, the opposite is true. Thus, option A is incorrect. XFree86 4.*x* supports TrueType fonts directly, so option C is incorrect. Converting a bitmapped display into ASCII text is a function of optical character recognition (OCR) software, not a font server, so option D is incorrect. Neither X core fonts nor a font server handles font smoothing; for that, you need Xft. Thus, option E is incorrect.

6. C, E. XDMCP servers are typically launched either from a system startup script or by init (as specified in /etc/inittab), as described in options C and E. The XDMCP server then starts X. The Start folder mentioned in option A is a Windows construct, not a Linux construct. The ~/.xinitrc script mentioned in option B is an X login script used when starting X from the command line via startx; it's not used to start X automatically when the system boots. A boot manager, as described in option D, launches the kernel; it doesn't directly start X, so option D is incorrect.

7. E. The XDM greeting is a resource set in the /etc/X11/xdm/Xresources file, so option E is correct. XDM doesn't offer many options on its main screen and certainly not one to change its greeting, as described in option A. The kernel doesn't directly handle the login process, nor does it pass options directly to XDM, so option B is incorrect. Although the xorg.conf file mentioned in option C is real, this file provides no XDM configuration options because XDM is a separate program from the X server. There is no standard xdmconfig program, as mentioned in option D.

8. C. KDM and GDM add many features, one of which is a menu that enables users to select their desktop environment or window manager when they log in rather than specifying it in a configuration file, as option C states. Option A describes one of the

advantages of the Secure Shell (SSH) as a remote-access protocol. Option B describes a feature common to all three XDMCP servers. Option D describes the way both KDM and XDM function; GDM is the one that presents username and password fields in series rather than simultaneously. Although a failure of X to start usually results in a fallback to a text-mode login, this feature is not provided by the XDMCP server, so option E is incorrect.

9.   A. The xhost command controls various aspects of the local X server, including the remote computers from which it will accept connections, making option A correct. Option B sets the DISPLAY environment variable, which doesn't directly affect the X server (it does tell X clients which X server to use). Option C initiates a text-mode remote login session with penguin.example.com. Option D's xaccess is a fictitious program. Although logging into penguin.example.com via ssh may also initiate an X tunnel, this isn't guaranteed, and such a tunnel doesn't cause the local X server to accept *direct* connections from the remote computer, so option E is incorrect.

10.   A. As stated in option A, GNOME, KDE, and other user programs often override the keyboard repeat settings in the X configuration file. Option B has it almost backward; most Linux distributions have abandoned XFree86, and therefore its XF86Config file, in favor of X.org-X11 and its xorg.conf file. Option C is pure fiction; xorg.conf settings apply to all varieties of keyboards, and there is no standard usbkbrate program. Although some keyboards do have hardware switches, they don't affect X's ability to control the keyboard repeat rate, contrary to option D. Although you can set a keyboard's nationality in xorg.conf, this option is independent of the keyboard repeat rate settings, so option E is incorrect.

11.   C, E. The Orca and Emacspeak programs both provide text-to-speech conversion facilities, so options C and E are both correct. Braille is a form of writing that uses bumps or holes in a surface that can be felt by the reader. Although Linux supports Braille output devices, the question specifies computer-generated speech, which Braille is not, so option B is incorrect. SoX (option A) is an audio format converter, but it won't convert from text to speech. The talk program (option D) is an early Unix online text-mode "chat" program, but it has no built-in speech synthesis capabilities.

12.   B, E. Time zones are determined by the /etc/localtime file, so replacing that one with the correct file (a selection is stored in /usr/share/zoneinfo) will fix the problem, making option B correct. (You may also need to edit /etc/timezone or some other file to keep automatic utilities from becoming confused.) Utilities such as tzselect will make these changes for you after prompting you for your location, so option E is also correct. The hwclock program mentioned in option A reads and writes data from the system's hardware clock. Although it relies on time zone data, it can't adjust your system's time zone itself. There is no standard /etc/tzconfig file, although the tzconfig program, like tzselect, can help you set the time zone. Thus, option C is incorrect. The /etc/localtime file is a binary format; you shouldn't attempt to edit it in a text editor, making option D incorrect.

13. D. Linux, like Unix, maintains its time internally in Coordinated Universal Time (UTC), so setting the computer's hardware clock to UTC (option D) is the recommended procedure for computers that run only Linux. Although Linus Torvalds spent time at the University of Helsinki, Helsinki time (as in option A) has no special place in Linux. Local time (as in option B) is appropriate if the computer dual-boots to an OS, such as Windows, that requires the hardware clock to be set to local time, but this is the second-best option for a Linux-only system. Option C's US Pacific time, like Helsinki time, has no special significance in Linux. Internet time (option E) is an obscure way to measure time that divides each day into 1,000 "beats." It's not a time zone and is not an appropriate way to set your hardware clock.

14. C. When set, the LC_ALL environment variable (option C) adjusts all the locale (LC_*) variables, so setting this and then running the script will make the programs that your script uses work as if on a British computer. The BIOS has no location code data, so option A is incorrect. There is no standard /etc/locale.conf file, so option B is incorrect. There is no standard locale_set utility, so option D is incorrect. Although setting the TZ environment variable, as in option E, will set the time zone for your local shell to that for Great Britain, this won't affect the sort of text formatting options noted in the question.

15. A. The Unicode Transformation Format 8 (UTF-8) standard can encode characters for just about any language on Earth, while looking just like ordinary ASCII to programs that only understand ASCII. Thus UTF-8 (option A) is the preferred method for character encoding when a choice is possible. ASCII (option B) is an old standard that's adequate for English and a few other languages, but it lacks some or all characters needed by most languages. ISO-8859 (options C and D) is a standard that extends ASCII, but it requires separate encodings for different languages and so it is awkward when a computer must process data from multiple languages. ATASCII (option E) is a variant of ASCII used in the 1980s by Atari for its home computers; it's obsolete and inadequate today.

16. E. The smart filter makes a print queue "smart" in that it can accept different file types (plain text, PostScript, graphics, and so on) and print them all correctly, as in option E. Font smoothing is useful on low-resolution computer monitors, but not on most printers, and adding font smoothing is not a function of a smart filter, so option A is incorrect. A smart filter doesn't detect confidential information (option B) or prank print jobs (option D). The lpr program can be given a parameter to email a user when the job finishes (option C), but the smart filter doesn't do this.

17. B, D. The job ID (option B) and job owner (option D) are both displayed by lpq. Unless the application embeds its own name (option A) in the filename, that information won't be present. Most printers lack Linux utilities to query ink or toner status (option C); certainly lpq can't do this. Although knowing when your job will finish printing (option E) would be handy, providing this information is well beyond lpq's capabilities.

18. C. The lprm command (option C) deletes a job from the print queue. It can take the -Pqueue option to specify the queue and a print job number or various other

parameters to specify which jobs to delete. BSD LPD, LPRng, and CUPS all implement the `lprm` command, so you can use it with any of these systems, making option A
incorrect. Option B presents the correct syntax but the wrong command name; there
is no standard `lpdel` command. The `cupsdisable` command can be used to disable
the whole queue but not to delete a single print job, so option D is incorrect. Because
option C is correct, option E obviously is not.

19. B. PostScript is the de facto printing standard for Unix and Linux programs, as specified in option B. Linux programs generally *do not* send data directly to the printer port
(option A); on a multitasking, multiuser system, this would produce chaos because of
competing print jobs. Although a few programs include printer driver collections, most
forgo this in favor of generating PostScript, making option C incorrect. Printing utilities come standard with Linux; add-on commercial utilities aren't required, so option
D is incorrect. Verdana is one of several "web fonts" released by Microsoft. Although
many Linux programs *can* use Verdana for printing if the font is installed, most Linux
distributions don't install Verdana by default, and few Linux programs use it for printing by default even if it's installed, so option E is not correct.

20. B. The `mpage` utility (option B) prints multiple input pages on a single output page, so
it's ideally suited to the specified task. PAM (option A) is the Pluggable Authentication Modules, a tool for helping to authenticate users. 4Front (option C) is the name of
a company that produces commercial sound drivers for Linux. The `route` command
(option D) is used to display or configure a Linux routing table. The `411toppm` program
(option E) converts files from Sony's 411 image file format to the PPM image file format; it doesn't do the specified task.

Chapter 7: Administering the System

1. E. When the `usermod -L` *username* command is used, the *username* record in the
`/etc/shadow` file has its password field modified. An exclamation point (!) is placed in
front of the password, making the password inoperable and thus locking the account.
Therefore, option E is correct. An x exists in the `/etc/passwd` file's records' password
field, if the `/etc/shadow` file is used for passwords (which it should be) and does not
indicate a locked account. Therefore, option A is incorrect. Option B is only true when
an account has not yet had a password set. Therefore, option B is incorrect. Option C
is also incorrect. You would never have a blank password field for a user account's
`/etc/shadow` record, unless the file had been incorrectly manually modified. Manual
modifications of the `/etc/shadow` files are *never* recommended. A user record could
have a zero (0) as the first character in their password field, but this would be due to
the password being hashed, not locked. Therefore, option D is incorrect.

2. A, B, C. The `useradd` command is used to add user accounts to a Linux system, and
therefore option A is correct. The `adduser` command is available on some Linux

distributions, and it also allows you to add user accounts to the system. Thus, option B is correct as well. The useradd command has a valid -c option that allows you to enter comments, such as a user's full name. Therefore, option C is also correct. There is no usradd command, so option D is incorrect. The passwd command cannot add users to the system. Therefore, option E is incorrect.

3. A. The chage command changes various account expiration options. The -M parameter sets the maximum number of days for which a password is valid, and in the context of the given command, *time* is a username. Thus, option A is correct. Options B, C, D, and E are all made up.

4. D. The /etc/passwd entries have third and fourth fields of the UID and the GID, but this line has only one of those fields (which one is intended is impossible to determine); this example line's fourth field is clearly the fifth field of a valid entry. Thus, option D is the correct answer. Option A is incorrect because, although /bin/passwd is an unorthodox login shell, it's perfectly valid. This configuration might be used on, say, a Samba file server or a POP mail server to enable users to change their passwords via SSH without granting login shell access. The sally username is valid and thus, Option B is not a correct answer. You may have usernames that are all lowercase letters. Option C is a correct observation, but an incorrect answer; the username and the user's home directory name need not match. The hashed password is officially stored in the second field, but in practice, most Linux computers place the hashed passwords in the /etc/shadow file. An x value for the password is consistent with this use, so option E is incorrect.

5. E. Option E is the best way to accomplish the task, because it will add sally to the Development group without removing her from any other groups or potentially damaging the /etc/group file. Option A would attempt to add the groups Development and sally to the system, thus it is not even a valid choice. Option B, also not a valid choice, would attempt to add the groups Production and sally. Option C would work, but it is very dangerous to edit an account configuration file manually instead of using account tools. Therefore, option C is not the best choice. Option D would work, but it would remove sally from all of her other groups, including the Production group. Therefore, option D is not the best choice either.

6. B, C, D. Files in /etc/skel are copied from this directory to the new users' home directories by certain account-creation tools. Thus, files that you want in all new users' home directories should reside in /etc/skel. Options B, C, and D all describe reasonable possibilities, although none is absolutely required. Including a copy of /etc/shadow in /etc/skel (option A) would be a very bad idea because this would give all users access to all other users' hashed passwords, at least as of the moment of account creation. You wouldn't likely find package management databases (option E) in /etc/skel, since users don't need privileged access to this data, nor do they need individualized copies of it.

7. C. The userdel command deletes an account, and the -r option to userdel (option C) causes it to delete the user's home directory and mail spool, thus satisfying the terms of

the question. Option A deletes the account but leaves the user's home directory intact. Option B does the same; the -f option forces account deletion and file removal under some circumstances, but it's meaningful only when -r is also used. Option D's rm command deletes the user's home directory (assuming that it's located in the conventional place, given the username) but doesn't delete the user's account. Option E's usermod command can modify accounts, including locking them, but it can't delete accounts. Furthermore, the -D option to usermod is fictitious.

8. E. The emerg priority code (option E) is the highest code available and so is higher than all the other options. From highest to lowest priorities, the codes given as options are emerg, crit, warning, info, and debug.

9. A. The logrotate program consults a configuration file called /etc/logrotate.conf (option A), which includes several default settings and typically refers to files in /etc/logrotate.d to handle specific log files. The remaining options are all fictitious, at least as working log files for logrotate.

10. D. The logger utility can be used to create a one-time log file entry that you specify. In its simplest form, it takes no special arguments, just a message to be inserted in the log file, as in option D. The dmesg utility in option A is used to review the kernel ring buffer; it doesn't create log file entries. Option B's syslog command isn't a Linux user-mode command, although it is the name of the logging system generically as well as a programming language command name. Option C's rsyslogd is the name of one of several system logging daemons; it maintains the system log, but isn't used to manually insert log entries. Option E's wall command writes a message to all users logged into virtual console terminals. It won't create a log file entry as the question requires and is not installed on all distributions.

11. C. The logrotate program can be started automatically—and unattended—on a regular basis by adding an entry for it in cron, so option C is correct. The at utility (option A) would be used if you wanted the program to run only once. Option B, logrotate.d, is a file stored in the /etc directory, which defines how the program is to handle specific log files. The inittab file (option D) is used for services and startup and not for individual programs. The ntpd program (option E) is the Network Time Protocol daemon, which synchronizes the system's clock with outside time sources.

12. E. The hwclock utility is used to view or set the hardware clock. The --systohc sets the hardware clock based on the current value of the software clock, thus option E is correct. Option A's date utility can be used to set the software clock but not the hardware clock; it has no --sethwclock option. Option B's ntpdate is used to set the software clock to the time maintained by an NTP server; it doesn't directly set the hardware clock. Option C's sysclock utility is fictitious. Option D's time command is used to time how long a command takes to complete; it has no --set or --hw option and does not set the hardware clock.

13. A. The format of the date command's date code is [*MMDDhhmm*[[*CC*]*YY*][.*ss*]]. Given that the question specified an eight-digit code, this means that the ordering of the

items, in two-digit blocks, is month-day-hour-minute. Option A correctly parses this order, whereas options B, C, D, and E do not.

14. C. Multiple `server` entries in `/etc/ntp.conf` tell the system to poll all of the named servers and to use whichever one provides the best time data. Thus option C is correct. (The `pool.ntp.org` subdomain and numbered computers within that subdomain give round-robin access to a variety of public time servers.) Options A and B both incorrectly state that one `server` statement overrides another, when in fact this isn't the case. The `server` statements shown in the question are properly formed. These `server` entries are properly formed, so option D is incorrect. Although it is true that this configuration will result in use of `tardis.example.com` should the public-pool server be unavailable, as option E states, this is not the *only* reason the NTP server will use `tardis.example.com`; this could happen if the public-pool server provides an inferior time signal, for instance. Thus option E is incorrect.

15. D. Once you've configured one computer on your network to use an outside time source and run NTP, the rest of your computers should use the first computer as their time reference. This practice reduces the load on the external time servers as well as your own external network traffic. Thus option D is correct. (Very large networks might configure two or three internal time servers that refer to outside servers for redundancy, but this isn't necessary for the small network described in the question.) Option A describes the procedure to locate a time server for the first computer configured (`gateway.pangaea.edu`) but not for subsequent computers. Although configuring other computers to use `ntp.example.com` instead of or in addition to `gateway.pangaea.edu` is possible, doing so will needlessly increase your network traffic and the load on the `ntp.example.com` server. Thus options B and C are both incorrect. Contrary to option E, NTP is suitable for use on small local networks, and in fact it's very helpful if you use certain protocols, such as Kerberos.

16. B, D. The `cron` utility is a good tool for performing tasks that can be done in an unsupervised manner, such as deleting old temporary files (option B) or checking to see that disk space is not low (option D). Tasks that require interaction or do not occur on a scheduled basis, such as creating accounts (option C), aren't good candidates for `cron` jobs, which must execute unsupervised and on a schedule. Although a cron job could restart a crashed server, it's not normally used to start a server when the system boots (option A); that's done through system startup scripts or a super server. Sending files to a printer (option E) is generally handled by a print server such as the cupsd daemon.

17. B. User cron jobs don't include a username specification (tbaker in options A and C). The `*/2` specification for the hour in options C and D causes the job to execute every other hour; the `7,19` specification in options A and B causes it to execute twice a day, on the 7th and 19th hours (in conjunction with the 15 minute specification, that means at 7:15 a.m. and 7:15 p.m.). Thus, option B provides the correct syntax and runs the job twice a day, as the question specifies, whereas options A, C, and D all get something wrong. Option E causes the job to run once an hour, not twice a day.

18. B. The anacron program is a supplement to cron that helps ensure that log rotation, daily backups, and other traditional cron tasks are handled even when the computer is shut down (and, hence, when cron isn't running) for extended periods of time. This is the program to add to the system to achieve the stated goal, and option B is correct. There is no common Linux utility called tempus, so option A is incorrect. Option C's crontab is the name of a file or program for controlling cron, which is likely to be an unreliable means of log rotation on a laptop computer. The ntpd program (option D) is the NTP daemon, which helps keep the system clock in sync with an external source. Although running ntpd on a laptop computer is possible, it won't directly help with the task of scheduling log rotation. The syslog-ng package is an alternative system log daemon, but this program doesn't help solve the problem of missed daily backups when using standard cron utilities, so option E is incorrect.

19. E. The at command runs a specified program at the stated time in the future. This time may be specified in several ways, one of which is teatime, which stands for 4:00 p.m. Thus, option E is correct. The objections stated in options A, B, C, and D are all invalid. (You *may* pass a script to at with the -f parameter, but this isn't required, contrary to option D.)

20. A, C. The contents of /etc/cron.daily are automatically run on a daily basis in most Linux distributions, and the crontab utility can create user cron jobs that run programs at arbitrary time intervals, so both A and C are correct. The at command noted in option B can be used to run a program a single time, but not on a regular basis (such as daily). Option D's run-parts utility is used by some distributions as a tool to help run programs in the /etc/cron.* subdirectories, but it's not used to schedule jobs. Although the crontab program can maintain user crontabs, it's not used as shown in option E and it has no -d parameter at all.

Chapter 8: Configuring Basic Networking

1. A, B, E. Ethernet (option B) is currently the most common type of wired network hardware for local networks. Linux supports it very well, and Linux also includes support for Token Ring (option A) and Fibre Channel (option E) network hardware. DHCP (option C) is a protocol used to obtain a TCP/IP configuration over a TCP/IP network. It's not a type of network hardware, but it can be used over hardware that supports TCP/IP. NetBEUI (option D) is a network stack that can be used instead of or in addition to TCP/IP over various types of network hardware. Linux doesn't support NetBEUI directly.

2. B. IP addresses consist of four 1-byte numbers (0–255). They're normally expressed in base 10 and separated by periods. 63.63.63.63 meets these criteria, so option B is

correct. 202.9.257.33 includes one value (257) that's not a 1-byte number, so option A is incorrect. 107.29.5.3.2 includes five 1-byte numbers, so option C is incorrect. 98.7.104.0/24 (option D) is a network address—the trailing /24 indicates that the final byte is a machine identifier, and the first 3 bytes specify the network. Option E, 255.255.255.255, meets the basic form of an IP address, but it's a special case—this is a broadcast address that refers to *all* computers rather than to the *single* computer specified by the question.

3. C. The gateway computer is a router that transfers data between two or more network segments. As such, if a computer isn't configured to use a gateway, it won't be able to communicate beyond its local network segment, making option C correct. A gateway is not necessary for communicating with other systems on the local network segment, so option A is incorrect. If your DNS server is on a different network segment, name resolution via DNS won't work, as stated in option B; however, other types of name resolution, such as /etc/hosts file entries, will still work, and the DNS server might be on the local network segment, so option B is incorrect. Gateways perform the same function in both IPv4 and IPv6 networking, so option D is incorrect. DHCP functions fine without a gateway, provided that a DHCP server is on the same local network segment as its clients (as is normally the case), so option E is incorrect.

4. D. The Secure Shell (SSH) protocol uses port 22, so if the traffic to port 22 is using the correct protocol, it's SSH traffic and option D is correct. The Hypertext Transfer Protocol (HTTP; option A) is conventionally bound to port 80; the Simple Mail Transfer Protocol (SMTP; option B) uses port 25; Telnet (option C) uses port 23; and the Network News Transfer Protocol (NNTP; option E) uses port 119. None of these would normally be directed to port 22.

5. D. The Interactive Mail Access Protocol (IMAP) is assigned to TCP port 143. Ports 21, 25, 110, and 443 are assigned to the File Transfer Protocol (FTP), the Simple Mail Transfer Protocol (SMTP), the Post Office Protocol version 3 (POP3), and the Hypertext Transfer Protocol over SSL (HTTPS), respectively. Although some IMAP server programs also support POP3 and might therefore listen to both ports 110 and 143, the question specifies IMAP exchanges, so option D is the only correct answer.

6. C, E. Option C, dhcpd, is the Linux DHCP *server*. Option E, ifconfig, can be used for network configuration but is not itself a DHCP client. The others are all DHCP clients. Any given computer will use just one DHCP client (or none at all), but any one of A, B, or D will be available choices.

7. B, C. When used to display information on an interface, ifconfig shows the hardware and IP addresses (options B and C) of the interface, the protocols (such as TCP/IP) bound to the interface, and statistics on transmitted and received packets. This command does *not* return information about programs using the interface (option A), the hostname associated with the interface (option D), or the kernel driver used by the interface (option E).

8. A. The host program (option A) is a commonly used program to perform a DNS lookup. There is no standard dnslookup program (option B), although the nslookup

program is a deprecated program for performing DNS lookups. pump (option C) is a DHCP client. ifconfig (option D) is used for configuration of networking parameters and cards. netstat (option E) is a general-purpose network diagnostic tool.

9. B. To add a default gateway of 192.168.0.1, the command would be **route add default gw 192.168.0.1**, as in option B. Specifying the IP address of the host system (as in options A, C, and D) is not necessary and in fact will confuse the route command. Although route provides a -host option, using host (without a dash), as in option E, is incorrect. Furthermore, option E omits the critical add parameter.

10. A, B. The dhclient utility, if installed, attempts to configure and bring up the network(s) passed to it as options (or all networks if it's given no options) using a DHCP server for guidance. Thus option A may work, although it won't work if no DHCP server is available. Option B applies whatever network options are configured using distribution-specific tools and brings up the network. Thus options A and B both may work, although neither is guaranteed to work. Option C displays the network status of eth1, but it won't activate eth1 if it's not already active. There is no standard network utility in Linux, so option D won't work. The netstat utility is a network diagnostic tool; it won't bring up a network interface, so option E is incorrect.

11. E. Although not all systems use /etc/hostname, option E correctly describes it for those systems that use it. The file or files that hold information on package repository servers vary from one package system to another, so option A is incorrect. Option B describes the purpose of /etc/resolv.conf. Option C describes the purpose of /etc/hosts. Option D doesn't describe any standard Linux configuration file, although the gateway computer's IP address is likely to appear in a distribution-specific configuration file.

12. C. The traceroute command (option C) identifies the computers that lie between your own computer and a destination computer, along with some very basic information about network packet travel time and reliability. Thus, traceroute can help you track down the source of the described problem—perhaps a router that's critical to reaching all of the non-responsive systems has failed. The netstat and ifconfig utilities of options A and D both provide information about local network configuration options, but they most likely won't be of much help in diagnosing a problem that affects only some sites. The ping utility (option B) may help you quickly identify sites that have failed but won't be of much use beyond that. You can use dig (option E) to obtain information on the mapping of hostnames to IP addresses, but it won't help in resolving basic connectivity problems.

13. B. Both global and link-local IPv6 addresses can use the system MAC address as part of the IPv6 address, thus option A is incorrect. The fee network address identifies a site-local address but not a link-local address, so option C is also incorrect. An address that starts with 2001 would be a normal global address, making option D incorrect. IPv6 link-local addresses start with fe80, thus C is the correct answer.

14. C. The netstat program produces various network statistics, including the process IDs (PIDs) and names of programs currently accessing the network when it's passed the -p

parameter, thus option C is correct. The ifconfig program can't produce this information, and the -p option to this program is fictitious, so option A is incorrect. Option B's /proc/network/programs file is also fictitious. Option D's /etc/xinetd.conf file is real and may provide some information about some servers that are using the network (as described in Chapter 10), but this file won't provide information about all servers, much less about clients that are accessing the network. The dmesg command displays the kernel ring buffer, which doesn't contain information on programs that are currently accessing the network, so option E is incorrect.

15. A, D. If you get any response at all, you know that the basic network connection is working, including that the server is responding to the client. With basic knowledge of IMAP commands, telnet enables you to test the server's responses in more detail than most IMAP clients (mail readers) permit. Thus options A and D are both correct. Option B describes the functionality of traceroute or tracepath; telnet provides no information about intermediate routers' functionality, so option B is incorrect. Because neither telnet nor IMAP on port 143 uses encryption, option C is incorrect. Furthermore, a packet sniffer is likely to have no effect on the transfer of data; it just copies the data so that the packet sniffer's user can see it. Although telnet can be used for remote access in a way that could make option E correct, the question specifies using telnet to connect to port 143, which is the IMAP port, not the Telnet port. Thus, option E is incorrect. (Furthermore, using telnet for remote administration is very risky because telnet is an unencrypted protocol.)

16. B. The computer's IP address (172.25.78.89) and netmask (255.255.255.0) mean that the computer can directly address computers with IP addresses in the range of 172.25.78.1 to 172.25.78.254, but the gateway address (172.25.79.1) is outside of this range. Thus, either the IP address or the gateway address is wrong, and option B is correct. Nothing about the way DNS operates necessitates that the DNS server be on the same network segment as the DNS client, so option A is incorrect. Although private IP addresses are often isolated from the Internet, as option C specifies, Network Address Translation (NAT) can get around this limitation. Thus, although there could be some truth to option C, it's not certain to be true. The Class A/B/C distinctions are just guidelines that can be overridden by specific configurations. Thus option D is incorrect. Option E's assertion that ifup is used only on computers that use DHCP is incorrect; ifup can work on computers that use static IP addresses provided the relevant information is entered correctly.

17. E. The -n option is used when you want to use route to display the current routing table, and it does as option E specifies. There is no route parameter that behaves as options A or C specify. Option B describes the purpose of the netmask parameter to route. Option D describes the purpose of the -net parameter to route.

18. E. Option E correctly identifies the function of /etc/resolv.conf. Option A describes the purpose of /etc/services. Various distribution-specific configuration files perform the function described in option B, but /etc/resolv.conf is not one of these files. A DHCP client sends a broadcast to locate a DHCP server; there is no client

configuration file that holds the DHCP server's address, as option C describes. The routing table is maintained internally, although basic routing information may be stored in distribution-specific configuration files, so option D is also incorrect.

19. B. The /etc/hosts file holds mappings of IP addresses to hostnames, on a one-line-per-mapping basis. Thus option B is correct. The file does not list the users (option C) or other hosts (option A) allowed to access this one remotely, affect remote administration through a web browser (option D), or map port numbers to protocols (option E).

20. D. The /etc/nsswitch.conf file controls the order of name resolution, among other things. Option D correctly describes the procedure for changing the order in which Linux performs name resolution. The /etc/resolv.conf file mentioned in option A controls the DNS servers that Linux consults, but it doesn't control access to /etc/hosts. Option B's nslookup command resolves a hostname, so option B will return the IP address of the computer called dns, if Linux can find such a system. The /etc/named.conf file of option C is the configuration file for the standard name server. This server isn't likely to be installed on most Linux systems, and even if it is, the procedure described in option C is invalid. Like option B's nslookup, option E's dig looks up hostname-to-IP-address mappings, so option E will display such mappings for the computers called local and dns, if they exist.

Chapter 9: Writing Scripts, Configuring Email, and Using Databases

1. D. The PS1 environment variable contains various formatting codes preceded by a backslash (\) as well as text to be included in the primary command prompt. Therefore, option D is correct. There is no environment variable called PROMPT, nor is there an environment variable called PSI, so options A and B are incorrect. Programs that use a pager, such as less or more, use the PAGER environment variable. If the variable is set, the programs use the pager listed in the variable. Therefore, option C is incorrect. Option D is correct, so option E is incorrect.

2. A. The alias built-in command creates a duplicate name for a (potentially much longer) command. Option A shows the correct syntax for using this built-in command. It causes the new alias cdpt to work like the much longer cd ~/papers/trade. The export command in option B creates an environment variable called cdpt that holds the value cd ~/papers/trade. This will have no useful effect. Option C, if placed in a bash startup script, will cause an error because it uses incorrect alias command syntax, as does option D. Although env is a valid command, it's used incorrectly in option E, and so this option is incorrect.

3. E. Some programs use the EDITOR environment variable as described in option E. Contrary to option A, the EDITOR environment variable has nothing to do with

command-line editing. When you're typing at a bash command prompt, bash itself provides simple editing features, so option B is incorrect. (You can launch the editor specified by $EDITOR by typing Ctrl+X followed by Ctrl+E, though.) The edit command doesn't behave as option C suggests. (This command may be configured differently on different systems.) You can create links called GUI and TEXT to have the EDITOR environment variable behave as option D suggests, but this isn't a normal configuration.

4. C. The PWD environment variable holds the present working directory, so option C is correct. The PATH environment variable (option A) holds a colon-delimited list of directories in which executable programs are stored so that they may be run without specifying their complete pathnames. There are no standard CWD, PRESENT, or WORKING environment variables, so options B, D, and E are all incorrect.

5. A, C. Option A creates the desired environment variable. Option C also creates the desired environment variable. It combines the variable setting and the export of the MYVAR variable using a different method than option A uses. It combines the two commands on one line using a semicolon (;). Option B creates a local variable—but not an environment variable—called MYVAR, holding the value mystuff. After typing option B, you can also type **export MYVAR** to achieve the desired goal, but option B by itself is insufficient. Option D displays the contents of the MYVAR variable and also echoes mystuff to the screen, but it doesn't change the contents of any environment variable. Option E's setenv isn't a valid bash command, but it will set an environment variable in tcsh.

6. E. The ~/.bashrc file is a non-login bash startup script file. As such, it can be used to alter a user's bash environment, and option E is correct. The /etc/inputrc file is a global bash configuration file for keyboard customization and setting terminal behavior. The ~/.inputrc file is for users to create or modify their own keyboard configuration file. Therefore, option A is incorrect. The /etc/bashrc file is a global bash startup script. Editing it will modify users' bash environments, but an individual user should not be able to modify it, so option B is incorrect. There is no standard $HOME/bashrc file because the filename is missing its prefixed period (.). Thus, option C is incorrect. Likewise, option D's $HOME/.profile_bash doesn't refer to a user's configuration file and is incorrect. However, there is a $HOME/.bash_profile bash configuration file.

7. A, D. The env command displays all defined environment variables, so option A satisfies the question. (In practice, you might pipe the results through grep to find the value of a specific environment variable.) The echo command, when passed the name of a specific environment variable, displays its current value, so option D is also correct. DISPLAY is an environment variable, but it's not a command for displaying environment variables, so option B is incorrect. You can use the export command to create an environment variable but not to display the current settings for one, so option C is incorrect. Option E's cat command concatenates files or displays the contents of a file to the screen, but it doesn't display environment variables.

8. B. Before using the ./ execution method, the script must have at least one executable bit set. Therefore, an error will be generated since chmod was not used to modify the execute permissions on the a_script file. Thus Option B is the correct choice since it

would *not* work. Option A uses the bash command to execute a script, and this will work fine without any file permission changes. Likewise, when you source a file using either the source command or a dot (.) and a space, there is no need to modify a scripts permission bits before executing the file. Therefore, option C and option D are incorrect because they also work fine.

9. C. The cp command is the only one called in the script, and that command copies files. Because the script passes the arguments ($1 and $2) to cp in reverse order, their effect is reversed—where cp copies its first argument to the second name, the cp1.sh script copies the second argument to the first name. Thus, option C is correct. Because the order of arguments to cp is reversed, option A is incorrect. The cp command has nothing to do with compiling (option B) or converting (option D) C or C++ programs, so neither does the script. The reference to /bin/bash in the first line of the script identifies the script itself as being a bash script; it does not cause the arguments to the script to be run as bash scripts, so option E is incorrect.

10. E. The commands iterated by the for, while, and until loops are located between the do and done constructs. Therefore, option E is correct. Commands in the then statement section are for an if-then construct, not a loop, thus option A is incorrect. Double semicolons are used for case constructs, but not loops, and so option B is incorrect. The case and esac keywords begin and end a case construct, and thus option C is incorrect. A test statement can be used to determine whether or not a loop's commands should iterate or not. However, it does not contain the actual commands to be iterated, and therefore option D is incorrect.

11. B, C. Valid shell scripts begin with the characters #! and the complete path to a program that can run the script. Options B and C both meet this description, because /bin/bash is a shell program that's installed on virtually all Linux systems and /bin/tcsh is often also available. There is no standard /bin/script program, so option A is incorrect. Options D and E are both almost correct; /bin/sh is typically linked to a valid shell and /bin/zsh is a valid shell on many systems, but the order of the first two characters is reversed, so these options are incorrect.

12. A, B, D. The for, while, and until statements are all valid looping statements in bash, so options A, B, and D are all correct. The if-then statement in bash's scripting language tests a condition and, if it is true, executes its commands *one* time only. Therefore, option C is incorrect. The case statement is a conditional, not a looping statement in bash, so option E is incorrect.

13. B. When aliases are properly configured, any email addresses sent to the email with an alias is received by the alias account. Therefore, option B is correct. The postmaster username would not receive the email because the alias is set to john, and so option A is incorrect. The ~/.forward file is associated with email forwarding, not aliases. Therefore, option C is incorrect. There is no reason for root to receive this email, so option D is incorrect. An alias *does* allow email to be sent to the alias account, so the statement in Option E does not make sense and is incorrect.

14. C. The Fetchmail program is a tool for retrieving email from remote POP or IMAP servers and injecting it into a local (or remote) SMTP email queue. As such, it's not

an SMTP server, so option C is correct. Postfix (option A), sendmail (option B), Exim (option D), and qmail (option E) are all popular SMTP email servers for Linux.

15. B. The -s option to mail sets the message subject line, and -c sets carbon copy (cc:) recipients. Input redirection (via <) reads the contents of a line into mail as a message. A mail command line normally terminates with the primary recipient. Thus, option B correctly describes the effect of the specified line. Options A, C, D, and E are all confused in their interpretation of the effects of mail parameters. Options A, B, and D also confuse input and output redirection, and option A incorrectly suggests that a script (or the mail program) can elevate its run status to root privileges.

16. D. To view your mail queue, use the mailq command (option D). The service sendmail status command is a SysV service status command and does not show mail queues, so option A is incorrect. Option B is a printer command and is therefore incorrect. Option C is close, but the correct command is sendmail -bp not -bq. Option E will show you the various directories within /var/spool and is therefore not the correct command.

17. B. The /etc/aliases file configures system-wide email forwarding. The specified line does as option B describes. A configuration like this one is common. Option A has things reversed. Option C is not a valid conclusion from this evidence alone, although an intruder conceivably may be interested in redirecting root's email, so if jody shouldn't be receiving root's email, this should be investigated further. Although the effect of option D (jody reading root's email) is nearly identical to the correct answer's effect, they are different; jody cannot directly access the file or directory that is root's email queue. Instead, the described configuration redirects root's email into jody's email queue. Thus, option D is incorrect. Because /etc/aliases is an email configuration file, not an account configuration file, it can't have the effect described in option E.

18. B. The CREATE DATABASE command creates a new database with the specified name. Because SQL commands are case insensitive, this command may be typed in uppercase or lowercase, and option B is correct. Options A and C both use the incorrect command NEW rather than CREATE, and option C specifies the database name as FISH rather than fish. (Database names *are* case sensitive.) Option D reverses the order of the CREATE and DATABASE keywords. Option E uses the fictitious command DB.

19. A, D. A single database may hold multiple tables, as option A suggests. Option D is also correct; if data is split across tables (such as into tables describing objects generically and specifically), databases can be more space efficient. Option B is incorrect because the DROP command doesn't combine tables—it *deletes* a table! Option C is incorrect because it reverses the meaning of rows and columns in a SQL table. A lossy compression algorithm, as the name suggests, deliberately corrupts or loses some data—an unacceptable option for a text database, making option E incorrect. (Lossy compression is used for some audio and video file formats, though.)

20. C. The UPDATE command modifies existing database table entries, and in this case it does so as option C describes. Option B also describes an update operation, but in a

confused and incorrect way. Options A and D both describe database retrieval operations, but UPDATE doesn't retrieve data. Option E mistakenly identifies stars as a database name, but it's a table name, and it mistakenly identifies the operation as adding a new entry (INSERT in SQL) rather than as modifying an existing entry (UPDATE in SQL).

Chapter 10: Securing Your System

1. E. The server names alone are insufficient to determine whether they're legitimate. The computer in question may or may not need to run any of these servers, and their presence may or may not be intentional, accidental, or the sign of an intrusion. Thus, option E is correct. Contrary to option A, the mere presence of an SSH server does not ensure security. Although, as option B asserts, FTP is not a secure protocol, it's still useful in some situations, so the mere presence of an FTP server is not, by itself, grounds for suspicion. Similarly, in option C, although some administrators prefer Postfix or qmail to sendmail for security reasons, sendmail isn't necessarily bad, and the names alone don't guarantee that the sshd and proftpd servers are legitimate. As option D states, sendmail and proftpd both use unencrypted text-mode transfers, but this is appropriate in some situations, so option D is incorrect.

2. C. Although Nmap and other port scanners are useful security tools, troublemakers also use them, and many organizations have policies restricting their use. Thus, you should always obtain permission to use such tools prior to using them, as option C specifies. A port scanner can't cause damage to /etc/passwd, so there's no need to back it up, contrary to option A. A port scanner also doesn't need the root password on a target system to operate, so you don't need this information, making option B incorrect. (In fact, asking for the root password could be seen as extremely suspicious!) Although you could use sudo to run Nmap, there's no need to do so to perform a TCP scan, and you can perform a UDP scan by running Nmap as root in other ways (such as via a direct login or by using su). Thus, option D isn't strictly necessary, although you might want to tweak /etc/sudoers as a matter of system policy. Because a firewall is part of your network's security, you probably want it running when you perform a network scan, contrary to option E. Furthermore, it would be safer to leave the firewall running and scan from behind it if you want to test the security of the network in case of a firewall breach.

3. C. The /etc/security/limits.conf (option C) file holds the configuration settings that allow you to limit users' access. The other options listed don't give the correct path to this file.

4. A, B, C. Nmap (option A) is usually used to perform scans of remote computers, but it can scan the computer on which it's run as well. The netstat (option B) and lsof (option C) utilities can both identify programs that are listening for connections (that is, open ports) on the local computer. The Network File System (NFS) and some other

servers use the portmap program (option D), but it's not used to identify open ports. There is no standard Linux services program (option E), although the /etc/services file holds a mapping of port numbers to common service names.

5. B. The -perm option to find locates files with the specified permissions, and +4000 is a permission code that matches SUID files. The -type f option restricts matches to files in order to avoid false alarms on directories. Option B uses these features correctly. Options A, C, and D use these features incorrectly. Option E specifies a fictitious -suid parameter to find.

6. A. Option A correctly describes the meaning of the specified line. A percent sign (%) identifies a Linux group name, and the remainder of the line tells sudoers to enable users of that group to run all programs as root by using sudo. The remaining options all misinterpret one or more elements of this configuration file entry.

7. B. The netstat command can do what is described in the question. The -ap options to the command are good choices to discover all the open network connections, so option B is correct. Although lsof can also accomplish the job, the -c a option is incorrect; this option restricts output to processes whose names begin with a. Thus, option A is incorrect. Option C's ifconfig command doesn't display open network connections, so it's incorrect. Although option D's nmap command will locate ports that are open on the localhost interface, it doesn't locate all open *connections*, nor does it locate connections on anything but the localhost interface. Option E's top command displays a list of processes sorted by CPU use, not open network connections (-net is an invalid option to top as well).

8. D. Option D is correct. TCP wrappers uses this feature to allow you to override broad denials by adding more specific access permissions to hosts.allow, as when setting a default deny policy (ALL : ALL) in hosts.deny.

9. C. The bind option of xinetd lets you tie a server to just one network interface rather than link to them all, so option C is correct. It has nothing to do with running multiple servers on one port (option A), specifying computers by hostname (option B), resolving conflicts between servers (option D), or the Berkeley Internet Name Domain (BIND) or any other DNS server (option E).

10. A, D. Using a firewall rule to block Waiter's port, as in option A, can increase security by providing redundancy; if Waiter is accidentally run in the future, the firewall rule will block access to its port. Uninstalling the program, as in option D, improves security by reducing the risk that the program will be accidentally run in the future. Most programs don't have a "stealth" mode, so option B is incorrect. (Furthermore, *reading* the documentation isn't enough; to improve security, you must change some configuration.) Tunneling Waiter's connections might have some benefit in some situations, but this configuration requires setup on both client and server computers and by itself leaves the server's port open, so option C is incorrect. Clients associated with the server program, installed on the server computer, pose little or no risk of abuse of the associated server; the clients on *other* computers are most likely to be used to abuse a server program, and you can't control that. Thus option E is incorrect.

11. B. Option B correctly describes how to accomplish this goal. Option A is incorrect because the `hosts_allowed` option isn't a legal `xinetd` configuration file option. Option C correctly describes how to configure the described restriction using TCP wrappers, which is generally used with `inetd`, but it's not the way this is done using `xinetd`. Option D is also a TCP wrappers description, but it reverses the meaning. Option E's `iptables` utility configures a firewall. Although a firewall rule could be a useful redundant measure, the question specifies an `xinetd` configuration, and option E's use of `iptables` is incorrect.

12. B. Ideally, passwords should be completely random but still memorable. Option B's password was generated from a personally meaningful acronym and then modified to change the case of some letters, add random numbers and symbols, and extend its length using a repeated character. This creates a password that's close to random but still memorable. Option A uses a well-known mythological figure, who is likely to be in a dictionary. Option C uses two common words, which is arguably better than option A, but not by much. Option D uses two closely related words separated by a single number, which is also a poor choice for a password. Option E uses a sequential series of numbers, which is a poor (but sadly common) password choice.

13. A. Phishing (option A) involves sending bogus email or setting up fake websites that lure unsuspecting individuals into divulging sensitive financial information or other sensitive information. Script kiddies (option B) are intruders who use root kits. Spoofing (option C) involves pretending that data is coming from one computer when it's coming from another. Ensnaring (option D) isn't a type of attack. Hacking (option E) refers to either lawful use of a computer for programming or other advanced tasks or breaking into computers.

14. C. The /etc/nologin file, if present, prevents logins from ordinary users; only root may log in. You might set this file when performing maintenance and then forget to remove it, thus explaining the symptoms in the question. Thus, option C is correct. The syslogd daemon mentioned in option A records system messages, and it is unlikely to produce the specified symptoms. The login process ordinarily runs as root and is normally SUID root, so options B and D are also incorrect. Shadow passwords, as in option E, are used on almost all modern Linux systems and are not likely to cause these symptoms.

15. B, C. SSH is most directly a replacement for Telnet (option B), but SSH also includes file-transfer features that enable it to replace FTP (option C) in many situations. SSH is not a direct replacement for the Simple Mail Transfer Protocol (SMTP, option A), the Network Time Protocol (NTP, option D), or Samba (option E).

16. A . The ssh_host_dsa_key file holds one of three critical private keys for SSH. The fact that this key is readable (and writeable!) to the entire world is disturbing, so option A is correct. In principle, a troublemaker who has acquired this file might be able to redirect traffic and masquerade as your system, duping users into delivering passwords and other sensitive data. Because of this, option B (no) is an incorrect response, and

the conditions imposed by options C, D, and E are all irrelevant, making all of these options incorrect.

17. B. SSH protocol level 2 is more secure than protocol level 1; thus option B (specifying acceptance of level 2 only) is the safest approach. Option A is the *least* safe approach because it precludes the use of the safer level 2. Options C and D are exactly equivalent in practice; both support both protocol levels. Option E is invalid.

18. E. Allowing only normal users to log in via SSH effectively requires two passwords for any remote root maintenance, improving security, so option E is correct. Whether or not you permit root logins, the SSH server must normally run as root, since SSH uses port 22, a privileged port. Thus, option A is incorrect. SSH encrypts all connections, so it's unlikely that the password, or commands issued during an SSH session, will be intercepted, so option B isn't a major concern. (Nonetheless, some administrators prefer not to take even this small risk.) SSH doesn't store passwords in a file, so option C is incorrect. Because SSH employs encryption, option D is incorrect (this option better describes Telnet than SSH).

19. D. Option D provides the correct command to import `fredkey.pub` prior to use. The `inspect-gpg`, `import-gpg`, and `gpg-import` commands of options A, C, and E are fictitious, and there is no `--readkey` option to gpg, as option B suggests.

20. E. The usual method of sending encrypted messages with GPG entails the sender using the recipient's public key to encrypt the message. Thus, option E is correct. Option A would be correct if your correspondent needed to send you an encrypted message, but the question only specifies you sending the encrypted message. Options B, C, and D all entail delivery of private keys, which is inadvisable at best, because private keys in the wrong hands permit the holder to impersonate the person who owns the keys.

Index

Index

[ ] (brackets) in file naming, 180
` (backtick) character, 21
| (pipe) character, 19–20
~ (tilde) character in commands, 6
/ (root) directory, 218
* (asterisk) in file naming, 179, 180
\ (backward slash) in file naming, 179
- (dash) in file naming, 178
. (dot) in file naming, 178
/ (forward slash) in file naming, 179
? (question mark) in file naming, 179, 180
~ (tilde) in file naming, 178
_ (underscore) in file naming, 178
" (quotation mark) in file naming, 179

A

Accelerated-X, 281
accessibility, X
    display, 312–314
    keyboard, 310–312
    mouse, 310–312
AccessX utility, keyboard, 310–312
accounts
    chage, 354–355
    configuration files, 355–357
    deleting, 358–359
    groups, 345–346
    network account databases, 357–358
    records, viewing, 362–364
    usermod, 352–353
    usernames, 345
    users, 344–345
    adding, 348–350
    password setting, 350–351
ACL (access control list), 205
AD (Active Directory), 357–358
addresses, network, 414–415
    base-10 numbers, 416
    broadcasts, 419–420
    DHCP and, 415
    IPv4, 416
    IPv6, 416–417
    link-local, 417
    MAC, 415
    managing, 415–316, 415–417
    network mask, 417–419
aliases, 459–460
alien utility, 75–77
answers to questions, 576–612
apt-cache, 67
apt-get, 68–71
archiving files, 187
    cpio utility, 191–194
    dd utility, 194–195
    tar utility, 188–191
    zip files, 188
assistive technologies in X, 314
at, 396–398
attackers, 525
automated tasks
    at, 396–398
    cron, 389
        anacron, 394–396
    cron jobs, 389
        creating, 390–391
        user cron jobs, 391–393

B

background processes, 95–96
backtick (`) character, 21
base-10 numbers, 416
BaseT cabling, 409
bash, 4–5
  environment variables, 455
  history, 11–12
  prompt, 458–459
bin directory, 219
binary packages, 49
BIOS (Basic Input/Output System), 109, 117
  boot loaders, 235–237
  boot partition, 236
bitmap fonts, 296
boot directory, 218
boot disks, 117–119
boot loaders
  BIOS, 235–237
  damaged, 246
  EFI, 237–238
  GRUB (Grand Unified Boot Loader), 234, 236
  GRUB 2, 243–245
  GRUB legacy
    configuring, 238–241
    installation, 242
    interacting, 242–243
  gummiboot, 246
  installation, 234
  LILO, 245
  LILO (Linux Loader), 234, 236
  Linux Kernel, 245
  overview, 235
  rEFInd, 245–246
  rEFIt, 245
  Syslinux, 245

boot process
  kernel ring buffer, 247
  messages, 248
  steps, 248–249
boot sector, 117
booting
  answers to questions, 590–593
  without keyboard, 112
Bounce Keys, 311
Bourne Again Shell, 4
Bourne shell, 4
bracket expressions, 35
Braille displays, 314
broadcasts, 419–420
Btrfs (butter eff ess), 146
built-in commands, 6–7

C

cabling (network), 409, 410
caches, rebuilding, 86–87
cat command, 22–23
cd command, 6
chage, 354–355
characters, translating, 27
chattr command, 212–213
checksums, 49
chgrp command, 200
chmod command, 206–208
chown command, 200
CHS geometry, 118
CIDR (Classless Inter-Domain Routing), 417
clients
  servers and, 427
  X remote access, 306–307
client-server, X remote access, 306–307
coldplug devices, 119–120
command completion, 9–10

command line, 4
  answers to questions, 576–579
  built-in commands, 6
  case, 11
  command completion, 9–10
  deleting text, 11
  editors, invoking, 11
  external commands, 6–9
  generating command lines, 20–21
  internal commands, 6–9
  moving within, 10
  retrieving commands, 10
  searching for commands, 10
  transposing text, 11
commands
  ` (backtick) character, 21
  ~ (tilde) in, 6
  aliases, 459–460
  built-in, 6–7
  editing, exercise, 12–13
  file management, 180–186
  file-combining, 22–24
  file-formatting, 28–31
  file-summarizing, 33–35
  file-transforming, 24–28
  file-viewing, 31–33
  shell scripts, 463–465
  shortcut characters, 6
concatenation, 22–23
conditional expressions, 478–479
configuration
  account files, 355–357
  networking
    answers to questions, 601–605
    connections, 436–437
    GUI configuration tools, 434
    hardware, 428
    hostnames, 435–436
    ifdown, 434–435
      ifup, 434–435
      routing, 432–433
      static IP address, 429–432
    shells, 13
      files, modifying, 460–462
    X font server, 299–300
cp (copy) command, 183–185
cpio files, 56–57
cpio utility, 191–194
cron, 389
  anacron, 394–396
cron jobs, 389
  creating, 390–391
    user cron jobs, 391–393
csh (C shell), 5
CUPS (Common Unix Printing System),
    321–322, 324
  configuration, 324
    files, editing, 325–326
  CUPS DDK, 327
  Gutenprint drivers, 327
  printer definitions, 327
  Web-based utilities, 327–329
cut command, 33–34

D

DAC (discretionary access control)
    model, 205
daemons, 344–345
  syslogd, 365, 366
databases
  answers to questions, 605–609
  installed files, 49
  network account databases, 357–358
  SQL, 504
  whatis, 15–16
D-Bus (Desktop Bus), 120
dd utility, 194–195

DDC (Data Display Channel), 289
Debian
    apt-cache, 67
    apt-get, 68–71
    compared to other formats, 73–74
    conventions, 63–64
    distributions, 63–64
    dpkg command set, 64–67
    dselect, 72–73
    package reconfiguration, 73
    tools, configuring, 74–75
default interactive shells, 5
default system shells, 5
dependencies, 49
    packages, 77–78
        rebuilding, 79–80
        replacing, 79
        startup scripts and, 80–81
        upgrading, 79
        versions, 80
    shared libraries, 86
dev directory, 220–221
development libraries, 80
DHCP, network configuration, 428–429
directories
    / (root) directory, 218
    var, 220
    sbin, 219
    /boot directory, 218
    commmands
        mkdir, 198
        rmdir, 198
    disk use monitoring and, 160–161
    media, 220
    /etc directory, 218
    dev, 220–221
    font directory, 296–297
    lib, 219
    bin, 219

    tmp, 220
    mnt, 220
    home, 220
    root, 220
    permissions, 204
    opt, 219–220
    proc, 221
    skeleton, 365
    usr, 219
    usr/local, 219
    usr/share/man, 219
    usr/X11R6, 219
disk error, partitioning and, 133
disk quotas, 213–214
    edquota command, 215–216
    support, 214–215
disk space, partitioning and,
    133
disks. *See* hard disks
display
    Braille, 314
    X, 312–314
DMA (direct memory addressing), 116
dmesg command, 247
DNS (Domain Name System),
    421–424
documents, here documents, 19
domain names, 420–421
dpkg package, 64–67
drivers, USB, 127–128
dselect package, 72–73
DSL (Digital Subscriber Line), 438
duplicate lines, deleting, 28
dynamic libraries, 82

E

echo command, 7
editors, invoking, 11

edquota command, 215–216
EEPROM (electronically erasable programmable read-only memory), 109
EFI (Extensible Firmware Interface), 109, 117
    boot loaders, 237–238
email, 497–498
    answers to questions, 605–609
    IMAP (Internet Message Access Protocol), 498
    mail, 500–502
    mailq, 502–503
    MTAs (Mail Transfer Agents), 498
    MUAs (Mail User Agents), 498
    queue, 502–503
    receiving, 500–502
    redirecting, 503–504
    sending, 500–502
    sendmail, 500
    SMTP (Simple Mail Transfer Protocol), 498
    software, 498–500
env command, 14
environment variables, 4, 13–14, 454–455
    bash, 455
    common, 455–458
environments
    system environments, 364–365
    users, 364–365
ESP (EFI System Partition), 117
etc directory, 218
Ethernet, 409
exit command, 7
expand command, 25

expansion cards, 120
    PCI, configuring, 121–122
expressions
    conditional, 478–479
    regexp, 37–38
    regular expressions
        bracket expressions, 35
        escape, 36
        grep, 36–38
        parentheses, 36
        range expressions, 35–36
        repetition operators, 36
        sed command, 38–40
        single characters, 36
        start/end of line, 36
        strings, 36
ext2fs (Second Extended File System), 145
ext3fs (Third Extended File System), 146
ext4fs (Fourth Extended File System), 146
extended partitions, 134
external commands, 6–9
external hard disks, configuration, 132
extracting text, 33–34

F

FAT (File Allocation Table), 147
    filenames and, 179
FDDI (Fiber Distributed Data Interface), 409
fdisk, 140–142
Fedora, 50
FHS (Filesystem Hierarchy Standard)
    FSSTND comparison, 217–218
    shareable files, 217
    static files, 217–218

syslogd daemon, 365
unshareable files, 217
variable files, 217–218
Fiber Channel, 409
file descriptors, 17
    STDERR (standard error), 17
    STDIN (standard input), 17
    STDOUT (standard output), 17–19
file management
    access, 200–213
    answers to questions, 586–590
    archiving, 187
        cpio utility, 191–194
        dd utility, 194–195
        tar utility, 188–191
        zip files, 188
    attributes, 212–213
    commands
        cp (copy), 183–185
        ls (list), 180–182
        mv (move), 185–186
        rm (remove), 186
        touch, 186
    directories, 198
        permissions, 204
    disk quotas, 213–214
        edquota, 215–216
        setting, 215–216
        support, 214–215
    FHS
        / (root) directory, 218
        var directory, 220
        sbin directory, 219
        /boot directory, 218
        media directory, 220
        /etc directory, 218
        dev directory, 220–221
        FSSTND comparison, 217–218
        lib directory, 219

        bin directory, 219
        tmp directory, 220
        mnt directory, 220
        home directory, 220
        root directory, 220
        opt directory, 219–220
        proc directory, 221
        usr directory, 219
        usr/local directory, 219
        usr/share/man directory, 219
        usr/X11R6 directory, 219
    find command, 222–223
    groups, 200, 210–212
    links, 195–197
    locate command, 223–224
    modes
        changing, 206–208
        default, 210–212
    naming files, 178–179
        wildcards, 180
    ownership
        changing, 200
        ls command, 199
    permissions
        ACL, 205
        bits, 201–205
        DAC model, 205
        directories, 204
        file type codes, 201
        MAC, 205
        RBAC, 205
        SELinux, 205
        strings, 202
        user mask, 210
        uses, 203
    type command, 225
    whereis command, 224
    which command, 224
file-combining commands, 22–24

file-formatting commands, 28–31
files
  footers, 32
  headers, 31–32
  installed file database, 49
  joining, 23–24
  journal files, 365–366
  libraries, locating, 83–85
  log files, 344, 365–366
  merging, 24
  naming, 178–179
    wildcards, 180
  open, listing, 534–535
  paging, 32–33
  printing, 30–31
  sorting, 26
  splitting, 26–27
  static, 217–218
  variable, 217–218
file-summarizing commands, 33–35
filesystems
  Btrfs, 146
  checking, 157–158
  creating, 148–150
  debugging interactively, 154–155
  ext2fs, 145
  ext3fs, 146
  ext4fs, 146
  FAT (File Allocation Table), 147
  HFS (Hierarchical File System), 147
  ISO-9660, 147
  JFS, 146
  journaling filesystems, 156
  maintenance, 151–155
  mounting, 161
    permanently, 167–169
    temporarily, 162–166
  NTFS (New Technology File System), 147
  parameters, tunable, 153–154
  partitioning and, 133
  ReiserFS, 146
  types, 145–148
  UDF (Universal Disc Format), 147
  unmounting, 161
    temporarily, 162–166
  virtual, 114
    syfs, 119
  XFS, 146
file-transforming commands, 24–28
file-viewing commands, 31–33
filters, 4
  file-combining commands, 22–24
find command, 222–223
firewalls, 530
firmware, 108
  BIOS (Basic Input/Output System), 109
  boot disks, 117–119
  DMA (direct memory addressing), 116
  EEPROM (electronically erasable programmable read-only memory), 109
  EFI (Extensible Firmware Interface), 109
  I/O addresses, 115–116
  IRQs (interrupt requests), 112–115
  ISA (Industry Standard Architecture), 114
  OpenFirmware, 109
  PCI (Peripheral Component Interconnect), 114
  POST (power-on self-test), 109
  UEFI (Unified EFI), 109
fmt command, 28

fonts
    default, 312–313
    X, 295
        bitmap, 296
        core fonts, 296–299
        font directory, 296–297
        font path, 297–299
        font server configuration, 299–300
        outline, 296
        TrueType, 296
        Xft, 300–301
foreground processes, 95–96
formatting, paragraphs, reformatting, 28
FSSTND (Filesystem Standard), FHS
    comparison, 217–218
functions, scripts, 495–496
fuser, 537–539

G

gdisk, 142–143
GDM (GNOME Display Manager), 302
    configuration, 305
    remote access and, 309
Ghostscript, 322, 323–324
GIMP Tool Kit (GTK+), 81
glibc, 81
GMT (Greenwich mean time), 380
GNU Parted, 140–142
GOK (GNOME On-Screen Keyboard),
    312
gpasswd, 360–361
GPG
    keys
        decryption, 566–567
        encryption, 566–567
        generating, 564–565
        importing, 565
        revoking, 566
    signing messages, 567
    verifying signatures, 567

GPL (General Public License), 50
GPT partitions, 135–136
grep command, 36–38
groupmod, 360–361
groups, 344, 345–346
    adding, 359–360
    configuration files, 361–362
    deleting, 362
    gpasswd, 360–361
    groupmod, 360
    GUIDs and, 346–347
    UIDs and, 346–347
GRUB (Grand Unified Boot Loader),
    234, 236
GRUB 2, 243–245
GRUB legacy
    configuration, 238–341
    installation, 242
    interacting with, 242
GTK+ (GIMP Tool Kit), 81
GUI (graphical user interface). *See also*
    X Window
    shells, 6
    X GUI login system, 301–302
        XDMCP server, 302–306
GUIDs (group IDs), 346–347
gummiboot, 246

H

hackers, 525
HAL (Hardware Abstraction Layer)
    daemon, 120
hard disks
    configuration, 129–132
    external, 132
    layout, 132–138
    mount points, 136–137
    partitioning
        benefits, 133
        common partitions, 137–138

creating partitions, 139–145
fdisk, 140–142
gdisk, 142–143
GNU Parted, 143–145
GPT partitions, 135–136
LVM (logical volume
    management), 136
MBR partitions, 134–135
multiple partitions, 139
physical volumes, 136
systems, 133–134
PATA (Parallel Advanced Technology
    Attachment), 129–130
SATA (Serial Advanced Technology
    Attachment), 130
hard links, 195–196
hardware
answers to questions, 583–586
coldplug devices, 119–120
expansion cards, 120
hotplug devices, 119–120
kernel modules, 122–123
    loading, 124–125
    removing, 125–126
network, 408–409
    cabling, 409–410
    configuration, 428
    Ethernet, 409
    hubs, 410–411
    switches, 410–411
    types, 409–411
    wireless networks, 409–410
SCSI (Small Computer System
    Interface), 130–132
hardware clock, 379
hashbang, 463
hashpling, 463
head command, 31–32
help system, man utility, 14–16
here documents, 19
HFS (Hierarchical File System), 147

HIPPI (High-Performance Parallel
    Interface), 409
history, 10
bash, 11–12
history command, 11
hostnames, 420–421
DNS (Domain Name System),
    421–424
network configuration and, 435–436
hotplug devices, 119–120
hubs, 410–411

I

ICMP (Internet Control Message
    Protocol), 413–414
ifdown, 434–435
if-then statement, 479
ifup, 434–435
IMAP (Internet Message Access
    Protocol), 498
inetd, 525–527
initialization process, 249–250
systemd, 258–259
    systemctl, 262–263
    targets, 259–260
    default, 261
    unit configuration, 260–261
    units, 259–260
SysV
    runlevel changes, 255–258
    runlevel functions, 250–252
    runlevel services, 252–255
Upstart, 263–264
    native methods, 264
    SysV compatible methods, 264–
        265
input
redirecting, 17–19
standard input, 17
insmod, 124–125

installation, boot loaders, 234, 235
    BIOS, 235–237
    damaged, 246
    EFI, 237–238
    GRUB 2, 243–245
    GRUB legacy, 238–243
    gummiboot, 246
    LILO, 245
    Linux Kernel, 245
    rEFInd, 245–246
    rEFIt, 245
    Syslinux, 245
installed file database, 49
internal commands, 6–9
I/O addresses, 115–116
IP (Internet Protocol), 413
IP addresses, static, 429–432
IPP (Internet Printing Protocol), 325–326
IPv4, 416
    classes, 418
IPv6, 413, 416–417
IRQs (interrupt request), 112–115
ISA (Industry Standard Architecture), 114
ISO-9660, 147

J

JFS (Journaled FileSystem), 146
jobs command, 94
join command, 23–24
joining files, 23–24
journal files, 365–366
    systemd-journald, 374–376
    viewing data, 376–379

K

KDM (KDE Display Manager), 302
    configuration, 305
    remote access and, 309

Kerberos, 357–358
kernel, 88
    modules, 122–123
        loading, 124–125
        removing, 125–126
kernel ring buffer, 247
keyboard
    AccessX utility, 310–312
    booting without, 112
    GOK (GNOME On-Screen
        Keyboard), 312
    onscreen keyboards, 312
Keyboard Repeat Rate, 311
kill, 97–99
killing processes, 97–99
ksh (Korn shell), 5

L

LBA (logical block addressing), 118
LDAP (Lighweight Directory Access
    Protocol), 357–358
ldconfig, 85–86
less command, 32–33
lib directory, 219
libraries, 48
    cache rebuilding, 86–87
    development libraries, 80
    dynamic, 82
    files, locating, 83–85
    managing, 85–86
    paths, 83–85
    principles, 81–83
    shared, 81
        changes, 82
        dependencies, 86
    static, 82
    widget sets, 81
LightDM (Light Display Manager), 302
    configuration, 305–306

LILO (Linux Loader), 234, 236, 245
lines
    duplicate, deleting, 28
    numbering, 29–30
link-local addresses, 417
links
    hard, 195–196
        creating, 196
    ln command, 196–197
    symbolic, 195–196
        creating, 196
Linux Kernel, 245
lists
    commands, 493–495
    processes, 88
ln command, 196–197
load average, 94
local security
    login limits, 551–553
    memory limits, 551–553
    passwords, 540–541
        risks, 541–542
        strong, 542–543
        tools, 544
    process limits, 551–553
    root access, 544
        su, 544–545
        sudo, 545–547
    SGID files, 553–554
    SUID files, 553–554
    user access audits, 547–551
locales, 318–321
localization
    answers to questions, 593–597
    locales, 318–321
    time zones
        individuals', 317–318
        Linux, 315–317
LocalTalk, 409
locate command, 223–224

log files, 344, 365–366
    contents, 373
    logging options, 366–369
    manual logging, 369–370
    rotating, 370–373
logical partitions, 134
login shells, 7
logout command, 7
logrotate, 370–373
lpr, 321–322
ls (list) command, 180–182, 199
lsmod command, 123
lsof, 534–535
lspci command, 121–122
LVM (logical volume management), 136

M

MAC (mandatory access control), 205
MAC (Media Access Control), 415
machine names, 420–421
mail, 500–502
mailq, 502–503
man utility, 14–16
Mandriva, 50
MBR partitions, 134–135
media directory, 220
merging files, 24
mkdir command, 198
modprobe, 124–125
Module section (X server), 285–286
mount command, 162–166
mount points, 136–137
mounting filesystems, 161
    permanently, 167–169
    temporarily, 162–166
mouse
    Click Options, 311
    Mouse Gestures, 312
    Simulated Mouse Clicks, 312

Mouse Keys, 311
Mouse Tracking, 311
tmp directory, 220
MTAs (Mail Transfer Agents), 498
multicasting, 418
multithreaded programs, 94
mv (move) command, 185–186
MySQL, 505, 506
    combining data, 512–514
    data retrieval, 511–512
    data types, 507
    databases, 508–509
    deleting data, 514
    starting sessions, 507–508
    storage, 509–510
    tables, 508–509

N

naming files, 178–179
    wildcards, 180
netstat, 531–533
network account databases, 357–358
network mask, 417–419
network printers, 329–330
network scanners, 535–537
networking
    addresses, 414–415
        base-10 numbers, 416
        broadcasts, 419–420
        DHCP and, 415
        IPv4, 416
        IPv6, 416–417
        link-local, 417
        MAC, 415
        managing, 415–316, 415–417
        network mask, 417–419
    broadcasts, 419–420
    CIDR (Classless Inter-Domain
        Routing), 417

configuration
    answers to questions,
        601–605
    connections, 436–437
    DHCP and, 428–429
    GUI configuration tools, 434
    hardware, 428
    hostnames, 435–436
    ifdown, 434–435
    ifup, 434–435
    routing, 432–433
    static IP address, 429–432
connections
    network status, 441
    route tracing, 439–441
    testing, 438–439
DSL (Digital Subscriber Line),
    438
hardware, 408–409
    cabling, 409, 410
    Ethernet, 409
    hubs, 410–411
    switches, 410–411
    types, 409–411
    wireless networks, 409–410
hostnames, 420–421
    DNS (Domain Name System),
        421–424
IPv4 classses, 418
multicasting, 418
packets, 411
ports, 424–427
protocol stacks, 411–412
TCP/IP, hardware, 408–411
traffic, 441–443
nice, 96–97
nl command, 29–30
mnt directory, 220
NTFS (New Technology File System),
    147

NTP (network time protocol), 381–383
    clients, 388
    servers, 384–388
    time source, 383–384
numbering lines, 29–30

O

octal dump (od), 25
od command, 25
home directory, 220
root directory, 220
open files, listing, 534–535
OpenFirmware, 109
operators, redirection, 18
outline fonts, 296
output, redirecting, 17–19

P

package management, 48
    RPM, 59–61
packages, 48–49
    binary packages, 49
    checksums, 49
    converting between, 75–77
    Debian
        conventions, 63–64
        distributions, 63–64
    dependencies, 49, 77–78
        rebuilding, 79–80
        replacing packages, 79
        startup scripts and, 80–81
        upgrading packages, 79
        versions, 80
        workarounds, 78–79
    installed file database, 49
    RPM
        compatibility issues, 52
        naming convention, 51

RPM (RPM Package Manager), 48
    uninstallation, 49
    upgrades, 49
packets, 411
paging through files, 32–33
paragraphs, reformatting, 28
partitioning
    benefits, 133
    common partitions, 137–138
    extended partitions, 134
    GPT partitions, 135–136
    logical partitions, 134
    LVM (logical volume management), 136
    MBR partitions, 134–135
    physical volumes, 136
    primary partitions, 134
    systems, 133–134
partitions
    bootable, 141
    creating, 139–145
    deleting, 141
    disk use monitoring, 158–160
    fdisk, 140–142
    gdisk, 142–143
    GNU Parted, 143–145
    multiple, 139
    swap partitions, 150
    type, 141
passwords, 540
    risks, 541–542
    setting, 350–351
    strong, 542–543
    tools, 544
paste command, 24
PATA (Parallel Advanced Technology Attachment), 129–130
paths, libraries, 83–85
PCI (Peripheral Component Interconnect), 114
    card configuration, 121–122

PCL (Printer Control Language), 323
permissions
    ACL, 205
    bits, 201–205
    DAC model, 205
    directories, 204
    file type codes, 201
    MAC, 205
    RBAC, 205
    SELinux, 205
    strings, 202
    symbolic, 208
    user mask, 210
    uses, 203
pgrep command, 94–95
pgrps, 96–97
physical volumes, 136
pids, 96–97
pipe (|) character, 19–20
pipes, 16
piping, 19–20
pkill command, 99
PLIP (Parallel Line Interface Protocol), 408–409
ports
    numbers, 425–426
    privileged, 427
    unprivileged, 427
positional parameter variables, 474–478
POST (power-on self-test), 109
PostgreSQL, 505
PostScript, 322–323
    PPD (PostScript Printer Definition), 325
pound bang, 463
PPD (PostScript Printer Definition), 325
PPP (Point-to-Point Protocol), 438
pr command, 30–31
primary groups, 345

primary partitions, 134
printing
    answers to questions, 593–597
    CUPs, printer definitions, 327
    files, 30–31
    Ghostscript, 322, 323–324
    IPP (Internet Printing Protocol), 325–326
    Linux architecture, 321–322
    to network printers, 329–330
    PCL (Printer Control Language), 323
    PostScript, 322
    PPD (PostScript Printer Definition), 325
    print queue, 321
        displaying information, 332–333
        lpq, 332–333
        lpr, 330–332
        lprm, 333
        removing jobs, 333
    system, 324
privileged ports, 427
processes, 48, 87
    background, 95–96
    foreground, 95–96
    jobs, 94
    kernel, 88
    killing, 97–99
    lists, 88
    pgrep, 94–95
    priorities, 96–97
protocol stacks, 411–412
ps, 88
    options, 89–90
    output, 90–92
    top tool, 92–94
opt directory, 219–220
pwd command, 6

R

range expressions, 35–36
RBAC (role-based access control), 205
Red Hat, 50–51
redirection, 16
   | (pipe) character, 19–20
   here documents, 19
   input, 17–19
   operators, 18
   output, 17–19
rEFInd, 245–246
rEFIt, 245
regexp, 37–38
regular expressions
   bracket expressions, 35
   escape, 36
   grep, 36–38
   parentheses, 36
   range expressions, 35–36
   repetition operators, 36
   sed command, 38–40
   single characters, 36
   start/end of line, 36
   strings, 36
ReiserFS filesystem, 146
remote access, X
   clients, 306–307
   client-server principles, 306–307
   SSH and, 308
rm (remove) command, 20, 186
rmdir command, 198
proc directory, 221
root, 9
routing, network configuration, 432–433
RPM (RPM Package Manager), 48

comparisons to other package formats, 62–63
compatibility issues, 52
configuration files, 61–62
data extraction, 56–57
distributions, 50–52
naming convention, 51
package management, 59–61
query output, 55–56
rpm command set, 52–56
rpm command
   operations, 53–54
   syntax, 52

S

SATA (Serial Advanced Technology Attachment), 130
sbin directory, 219
scripts, 462–463
   answers to questions, 605–609
   commands in, 463–465
   conditional expressions, 478–479
   functions, 495–496
   loops, 485–486
      for, 490–493
      until, 488–490
      while, 486–488
   running, 465–470
   shell scripts, 463
      commands in, 463–465
      running, 465–470
      variables, 470–478
   variables
      positional parameter variables, 471–473
      user-defined variables, 474–478
SCSI (Small Computer System Interface), 130–132

searches, for commands, 10
security
  answers to questions, 609–612
  GPG, 563
    decryption, 566–567
    encryption, 566–567
    keys, 564–566
    signature verification, 567
    signed messages, 567
  local
    login limits, 551–553
    memory limits, 551–553
    passwords, 540–544
    process limits, 551–553
    root accss, 544–547
    SGID files, 553–554
    SUID files, 553–554
    user access audits, 547–551
  network
    configuration files, 539–540
    firewalls, 530
    lsof, 534–535
    netstat, 531–533
    network scanners, 535–537
    partitioning and, 133
    servers, 530–533, 540
    super daemon, 525
    super server, 525–530
    TCP Wrappers, 527
  SSH (Secure Shell), 555–557
    access control, 558–559
    file copy, 559
    keys, 557–558
    login configuration, 560–561
    port tunnels, 561–563
sed command, 38–40
SELinux, 205
sendmail, 500
servers, clients and, 427
set command, 7

SGID files, 553–554
sh (Bourne shell), 4
shared libraries, 81
  changes, 82
  dependencies, 86
shebang, 463
shell scripts. *See* scripts
shells, 4
  configuration, 13
    files, modifying, 460–462
  default interactive, 5
  environment variables, 4, 454–455
  GUI and, 6
  login shells, 7
  options, 4
  scripts, 462
  starting, 5–6
  subshells, 454
  system shells, 5
Simulated Mouse Clicks, 312
skeleton directory, 365
Slow Keys, 311
smart filter in printing, 323–324
SMB/CIFS (Server Message Block/
  Common Internet File System),
  329–330
SMTP (Simple Mail Transfer Protocol),
  498
soft links, 195–196
software
  answers to questions, 579–583
  email, 498–500
software clock, 379
sort command, 26
sorting, files, 26
spaces
  converting from tabs, 25
  converting to tabs, 27–28
speech synthesis, 314
split command, 26–27

splitting files, 26–27
SQL (Structured Query Language), 504
    columns, 505
    MySQL, 505, 506
        combining data, 512–514
        data retrieval, 511–512
        data types, 507
        databases, 508–509
        deleting data, 514
        starting sessions, 507–508
        storage, 509–510
        tables, 508–509
    packages, 505
    PostgreSQL, 505
    rows, 505
    SQLite, 505
    table data, 505–506
SQLite, 505
SSH, X connection encryption, 308
SSH (Secure Shell), 555–557
    access control, 558–559
    file copying, 559
    keys, encryption, 557–558
    login configuration, 560–561
    port tunnels, 561–563
standard input, 17
startup scripts, package dependencies,
    80–81
static files, 217–218
static IP address, network configuration,
    429–432
static libraries, 82
STDERR (standard error), 17
STDIN (standard input), 17
STDOUT (standard output), 17–19
Sticky Keys, 310
streams, 16
subshell, 454
SUID (set user ID), 204–205
    files, 553–554

SUSE, 50
swap files, 150
swap partitions, 150
switches (network), 410–411
syfs virtual filesystem, 119
symbolic links, 195–196
symbolic modes, 207
symbolic permissions, 208
Syslinux, 245
syslogd daemon, 365, 366
system environments, 364–365
system shells, 5
system time
    GMT (Greenwich mean time), 380
    hardware clock, 379
    NTP (network time protocol), 381–388
    setting, 380–381
    software clock, 379
    UTC (Coordinated Universal Time),
        380
systemctl, 262–263
systemd, 249–250
systemd initialization process, 258–259
    systemctl, 262–263
    targets, 259–261
    units, 259–261
systemd-journald, 374–376
SysV, 249–250
    runlevel functions, 250–252
    runlevel services, 252–253
        current, 255
        default, 255
        halt, 257
        init, 256
        managing, 253–254
        poweroff, 257
        reboot, 257
        shutdown, 256–257
        telinit, 256
    startup scripts, 253

T

tabs
  converting from spaces, 27–28
  converting to spaces, 25
tail command, 32
tail-merging, 213
tar utility, 188–191
tarballs, 49
TCP (Transmission Control Protocol),
    414
TCP Wrappers, 527
TCP/IP (Transmission Control Protocol/
    Internet Protocol), 408
  hardware, 408–411
  ICMP (Internet Control Message
      Protocol), 413–414
  IP (Internet Protocol), 413
  IPv6, 413
  ports, 427
  TCP (Transmission Control Protocol),
      414
  UDP (User Datagram Protocol),
      414
tcsh shell, 5
terminal, 6
terminal emulator, shells and, 6
text, extracting, 33–34
text editors, vi
  modes, 265–266
  procedures, 266–269
  saving changes, 269–270
time command, 7
Time Out, 311
time zones
  individuals', 317–318
  Linux computers, 315–317
Token Ring networks, 409
top tool, 92–94
touch command, 186

tr command, 27
translating characters, 27
troublemakers, 525
TrueType fonts, 296
type command, 7, 225

U

udev, 120
UDF (Universal Disc Format), 147
UDP (User Datagram Protocol), 414
UEFI (Unified EFI), 109
UIDs (user IDs), 346–347
umask command, 210–212
umount command, 166
uname command, 6, 88
unexpand command, 27–28
uninstallation, 49
uniq command, 28
unprivileged ports, 427
upgrades, 49
UpStart, 249–250, 263–264
  native methods, 264
  SysV compatible methods, 264–265
USB (Universal Serial Bus), 108
  data transfer speed, 126
  device configuration, 126–127
  drivers, 127–128
  hubs, 127
  manager applications, 128–129
  ports, 127
user space programs, 120
user-defined variables, 474–478
usermod, 352–353
usernames, 345
users, 344–345
  adding, 348–350
  cron jobs, 391–393
  environments, 364–365
  groups, 345–346

GUIDs and, 346–347
  passwords, setting, 350–351
  UIDs and, 346–347
users, 97
\usr directory, 219
\usr/local directory, 219
\usr/share/man directory, 219
\usr/X11R6 directory, 219
UTC (Coordinated Universal Time), 315
  system clock, 380
utilities
  alien, 75–77
  man, 14–16

V

var directory, 220
variables
  environment variables, 4, 13–14, 454–455
    common, 455–458
  files, 217–218
  shell scripts
    positional parameter variabls, 471–473
    user-defined variables, 474–478
vi text editor
  case, 269
  change text, 269
  colon commands, 266
  Command Mode, 265
  editing procedures, 266–269
  Ex Mode, 265
  go to a line, 269
  Insert Mode, 265
  open text, 269
  saving changes, 269–270
  search, 269
  undo, 269

video, X Window System, 281–282
virtual filesystems, 114
  syfs, 119

W

wc command, 34–35
Web-based CUPS utilities, 327–329
whatis database, 15–16
whereis command, 224
which command, 224
widget sets, 81
Wi-Fi, 409–410
wildcards, file naming, 180
wireless networks, 409–410
word count, 34–35
writing scripts, 462

X

X Window System, 280
  Accelerated-X, 281
  accessibility, 310–314
  answers to questions, 593–597
  assistive technologies, 314
  configuration
    color depth, 291–292
    configuration files, 283–284
    configure-and-test cycle, 284–285
    keyboard, 286–287
    loading modules, 285–286
    monitor, 288–289
    mouse, 287–288
    resolution, 291–292
    utilities, 282–283
    video card, 289–290
  display information, 293–295
  fonts, 295
    bitmap, 296
    core fonts, 296–299

font directory, 296–297
font path, 297–299
font server configuration, 299–300
outline, 296
TrueType, 296
Xft, 300–301
GUI login system, 301–302
XDMCP server, 302–306
keyboard, 310–312
mouse, 310–312
multi-head displays, 292
remote access
client-server principles, 306–307
remote clients, 307–309
SSH and, 308
server, 280–282
video drivers, 281–282
window manager, 294
XFree86, 281
X.org-X11, 281
xargs command, 20–21
XDM (X Display Manager), 302
configuration, 304
remote access and, 309
XDMCP (X Display Manager Control
Protocol), 301–302

server, 302–303
GDM configuration, 305
KDM configuration, 305
LightDM configuration, 305–306
XDM configuration, 304
XFree86, 281
configuration files, 283–284
XFS (Extents File System), 146
Xft fonts, 300–301
xinetd, 528–530
X.org-X11, 281
configuration file, 283
xterm, 6

Y

Yellow Dog, 50
Yum, 57–61
configuration files, 61–62
yum command, 57–59

Z

zip files, 188
zsh (Z shell), 5